Legal and Regulatory Environment of Business

Fourth Edition

Samuel D. Hodge, Jr.

Mc Graw Hill Education

ISBN-13: 978-1-260-64240-7
ISBN-10: 1-260-64240-2

Solutions Program Manager: Nikki Schmitt
Project Manager: Lynn Nagel
Cover Photo Credits:
BXP61397h.tif © Brand X Pictures/PunchStock
87706957.tif © Jupiterimages

DEDICATION

*"It is an exciting time where the only limits you have
are the size of your ideas and the degree of your dedication."*

—*author unknown*

This book is dedicated to the more than 25,000 students that I have taught over the years at Temple University.

—*Samuel D. Hodge, Jr.*

ACKNOWLEDGMENTS

*"Tell everyone what you want to do
and someone will want to help you do it."*

—*W. Clement Stone*

This book is the product of a number of unselfish people who helped take an idea for a new course and turn it into a reality. This acknowledgment is a small token of my appreciation for that assistance and guidance. Therefore, many thanks are extended for the contributions by S. Jay Sklar, Kevin Fendl, Barbara Schneller, Michael Valenza, Joseph Beller, Avi Cohen and Terry Halbert, as well as the editorial and research assistance provided by Rachel Rempel.

TABLE OF CONTENTS

CASES LISTED ALPHABETICALLY

Part One
Law as the Foundation for the Business Enterprise

"Law is nothing else but the best reason of wise men applied for ages to the transactions and business of mankind."

—Abraham Lincoln

Law is the fabric of society that allows for the orderly administration of the government. It is not always perfect and seems to slowly adjust to the changing values of society. However, the law is a dynamic force that is not etched in stone and provides the only viable solution to maintaining order in both a business and personal setting.

Law for the Business Enterprise is an attempt to explain the legal system in the United States and abroad during a time in which the entrepreneur must conduct business in the face of changing government regulations. There is a purpose, however, for this interference on the state, federal and international levels. The United States has seen multiple wars, a great depression and recession and various business scandals. Nevertheless, the world continues to progress with new technologies, inventions, and medical advances that allow people to live much longer and more productive lives. Corporate governance and government regulations are partially responsible for this phenomenon.

New terms have also been coined to deal with this changing world, such as globalization, white collar crime, class action lawsuits, e-commerce, RICO, and insider trading. It is true that these laws and regulations add layers of bureaucracy, but they are the only way to protect society against unethical and illegal business practices.

The first part of this book will introduce students to the building blocks of the law. **Chapter One** will explain the foundation for the legal system in the United States: common law, or judge made law, and statutory law. The reader will also see how the law developed in one specific area, liquor liability, though an examination of the key judicial and legislative pronouncements on the topic. The reasons that our legal system is built upon precedent will be explained while the reader learns about status and process. This concept helps the reader understand court cases, because many rulings are based on the idea of wanting to protect certain classes, such as children and the government. The Chapter will conclude with a discussion on how to perform legal research.

Chapter Two will explore ethics, the moral principles that govern society. The reader will learn about the different ethical theories and how there is a distinction between what is legal and what is ethical. Issues involving whistle blowing, drug testing in the work place and sexual harassment will be presented, in order to highlight these important but controversial issues in the workplace.

Chapter Three focuses on the judicial systems. Article Three of the Constitution created the courts, but it was the last branch of the government to be addressed by the founding fathers, showing their lack of respect for this institution. In fact, the Supreme Court was the only judicial body specifically created in the Constitution, which then gave Congress the power to create the other federal courts. The framers of the Constitution would certainly be surprised to see how the courts have grown in stature and power over the years. This Chapter will discuss both the federal and state court systems, how judicial philosophies shape the law, as well as the rules of court as to where lawsuits may be filed.

CHAPTER 1

AN INTRODUCTION TO THE LEGAL AND REGULATORY ENVIRONMENT OF BUSINESS

The law is reason, free from passion.
—Aristotle

SECTION 1.1
INTRODUCTION

Law began long before recorded history so no one knows when the first society recognized rules and regulations. The bible provides the earliest narrative of a law when God prohibited Adam and Eve from eating the fruit from one tree. This prohibition was an example of an edict whose punishment was the expulsion from the Garden of Eden. From that moment forward, the law has become an integral part of society and is responsible for changing civilization from loosely organized groups to nations of diverse people from all walks of life who abide by a set of principles. Whether imposed by a religious mandate, a dictator or a democracy, the law establishes social norms and acceptable conduct. The law, however, is a dynamic force not capable of a single or simple definition. For instance, the Greek philosopher *Aristotle* believed that "law is a pledge that citizens of a state will do justice to one another." *Black's Law Dictionary* defines the term as "that which must be obeyed and followed by citizens, subject to sanctions or legal consequences." Regardless of how the term is defined, the law affects all aspects of life and establishes the parameters of acceptable conduct within society. These rules can be created by the legislature, administrative regulations, or be imposed by court decree. While one may not always agree with the law, deviations from these mandates may result in both criminal and civil liabilities.

In the face of expanding government regulations and a litigation-oriented society, businesses must be cognizant of the legal implications of their actions. Seemingly minor violations of the law may have significant financial and emotional consequences. Million-dollar verdicts occur with some frequency in the United States, and the courts recognize new or expanded theories of liability on a frequent basis.

Educated citizens, no matter what career path they may choose, should be aware of the ways in which the law impacts their lives in both a personal and a business setting. This text will expose the reader to the essential aspects of the law with an emphasis on the legal environment of business and government regulations. The basic tenets of contract, tort, and administrative law will be discussed as well as international, corporate and criminal law. For instance, this text will include a discussion of the types of legal entities one can form to run a business, as well as the public policy mandates that influence the operation of that business. The political, social and economic forces that affect change are also discussed, thereby providing guidance as to the future direction of the law in both the United States and around the world.

As the semester unfolds, the reader will be exposed to the foundations of American jurisprudence in a business setting. The legal concepts will be reinforced by following the legal difficulties encountered by Tyler's Sports Bar and Grill as it struggles to operate in today's complex business world. The reader will learn of Tyler's legal controversies through a series of written problems that the reader will be requested to solve. This approach will allow students to master and apply what they have learned to real world situations.

This text is also broken down into several segments. Part One will examine some of the basic principles of the law in the United States such as the evolution of our legal system and the doctrine of precedent. Part Two will expose the reader to certain categories of law—contracts, torts, property and cyber law. The final portion of the book will look at those laws that specifically affect the entrepreneur including how to form a business enterprise, employee rights, and the legal implications of dealing with international business transactions.

A number of the disturbing moral and political questions that plague society are addressed as legal issues. An appreciation of the law, and being mindful of the more significant legal decisions that have been rendered in the last few decades, tells us more about ourselves than most other American institutions or practices. Discussions about liquor liability, white collar crime, drug testing in the work place, and sexual harassment are couched in terms of legal principles and acted upon by the courts.[1]

SECTION 1.2
THE STUDY OF
BUSINESS LAW

The study of business law can be daunting because the law is fluid and can vary depending upon the type of business enterprise involved, or if the transaction involves the sale of goods. A course in business law helps an entrepreneur appreciate the essential elements of a contract, how government regulations affect the operation of a business, and to recognize the difference between a commercial and consumer transaction.

The law is not perfect, but it does establish a system of order and justice. What would traffic be like if we didn't have a motor vehicle code to establish rules of the road? How could we be secure in our homes if we didn't have the threat of imprisonment for those who violate the sanctuary of those residences?

The law can be complicated because legal documents aren't easy to understand and seem to be filled with Latin phrases. Instead of simply saying a person has filed an appeal to the United States Supreme Court, this procedure is labeled a **Writ of Certiorari.** Precedent becomes **stare decisis** and legal papers are filled with complex terms and phrases.

Change is occurring, but reform takes time. More and more contracts are required to be written in easy-to-understand language. For instance, we now have "plain language" leases and authors of contracts are penalized by the courts who construe ambiguities in a document against the drafter.

This text will attempt to simplify the law by explaining how it affects business pursuits in both theory and practice. Legal terms will be translated into common English and a variety of contemporary legal issues will be explored. It is only through this type of learning process that one may gain a better appreciation of the American system of jurisprudence.

SECTION 1.3 THE PLAYERS

PARK, BROWN & SMITH, P.C. ATTORNEYS AT LAW MEMORANDUM

TO: All Law Clerks

FROM: Peter Smith, Esquire

RE: Biographical Sketches

My name is Peter Smith, and I am the managing partner of the law firm *Park, Brown & Smith, P.C.* We are a multi-faceted firm which provides representation and counsel in all types of cases. We have been retained by Joseph Roberts to represent him in several disputes that have arisen. I am providing you with brief biographical sketches of the people whose legal problems you will hear about during the next few months.

Joseph and Estelle Roberts

After working in the construction field for a number of years, Joe Roberts decided to switch careers. Because of his love for sports and flare for cooking, Joe opened a sports bar with his next door neighbor, Donald Jones, M.D. The new venture is named Tyler's Sports Bar and Grill. Dr. Jones invested all of the start up money while Joe will run the business on a daily basis. The parties did not sign a written agreement memorializing the business arrangements between them, but they did hire an advertising agency to promote the sports bar and to create the following logo, which will be seen whenever you are asked to solve a problem on behalf of Tyler's Sports Bar and Grill.

Joe and his wife Estelle Roberts have been married for twenty-five years and have four children: Tony, Kathy, Brad and Greg.

Anthony Roberts

Joe and Estelle's son, Tony, is 23 years old. Throughout high school, Tony excelled in athletics and was the goalie on the soccer team. During his junior year, Tony took up football. His soccer background enabled him to become an outstanding kicker, and his high school team went on to win a state championship.

Tony was offered a full-paid scholarship to play college football. During his last year at college, he set a number of school records for points and field goal accuracy. The various scouting combines rated him as one of the top kickers in collegiate football. He subsequently tried out for the Stallions, the latest professional football expansion team, and was signed to a three-year contract.

Kathleen Roberts

Kathy is a 16-year-old who spends hours surfing the internet and tweeting. One might assume that she is a normal teenager, but Kathy has a serious problem. She has become a victim of the opioid crisis and has experimented with various narcotics, pain pills and designer drugs. As a result, she has detached herself from the day-to-day life of her family. Whenever her parents try to communicate with her, Kathy reacts with great hostility. Since her parents increasingly avoid any sort of confrontation with her, Kathy's decline continues.

Peter Christopher

Peter Christopher is a retired Army officer and veteran of several military conflicts. Following his discharge from service, Christopher opened a private investigation service specializing in undercover surveillance and industrial espionage. He lives next to the Roberts family but intensively dislikes his neighbors. He believes that the Roberts are undisciplined and uncouth. Needless to say, he and his next-door neighbors are constantly fighting.

Donald Jones, M.D.

Donald Jones always wanted to be a physician, and studied diligently to achieve this lofty goal. Upon graduating from medical school, he became a surgical resident at a hospital in Chicago. Following several years in a clinical rotation, he relocated to Philadelphia and is now a successful surgeon. Dr. Jones is Joe's other neighbor and silent partner in Tyler's Sports Bar and Grill.

SECTION 1.4
CASE ANALYSIS

COMMON LAW AND STATUTORY LAW

Most nations follow one of two legal systems: **common law** or **civil law**. Common law is traced back to England during the Middle Ages and was used by the various British colonies. This system recognizes the role of judges in making the law based upon the customs and traditions of the people. On the other hand, the civil law system developed in continental Europe around the same time and was applied by imperial powers such as Spain and Portugal and their colonies. This system was also adopted during the past few hundred years by countries formerly possessing distinctive legal traditions, such as Russia and Japan, that wanted to change their systems of jurisprudence in order to gain economic and political power comparable to that of Western European states. Its distinguishing feature is that the laws are made by a legislative body and the courts play a secondary role in their justice system.[2]

While the United States is a common law country, its laws originate by **legislative enactment** or by **judicial decree.** The creation of **statutory law** is the primary function of the legislature, whether it is on the federal, state, or municipal levels. These laws are designed to address specific problems in our society and to set forth rules to regulate areas of concern. This process is so important to the governance of the country that this law-making function is found in Article One of the United States Constitution.

Article Three of the Constitution empowers the judiciary with the authority to interpret the laws and to establish standards of care. This process is known as **common law**, or judge-made law. The court is empowered to pass judgment on what type of conduct is proper and valued in our society. These pronouncements are based upon the judge's perception of what is in the best interest of the people given the political, sociological, and economic climate of the time. The court even has the power to review a law passed by the legislature to ensure its constitutionality or to ascertain whether certain conduct falls within the contemplation of the statute.

These judicial pronouncements are rendered in the form of written explanations called **opinions** so that the parties to the litigation and the general public may understand the basis for the court's resolution of the dispute.

The application of common law to a particular problem requires a person to research and ascertain whether there are prior cases on point. On the other hand, statutory laws are already written and merely require their application to a specific case.[3] Common law is developed on a daily basis with each court decision. Statutory laws, however, are only created by the legislative and these laws are organized and codified into **codes.**[4]

COMMON LAW VERSUS STATUTORY LAW

	Common Law	**Statutory Law**
Creation of New Laws	These laws involve decisions made by judges	New laws are issued by different levels of the government
Also known as	Case law or opinions	Written laws, statutes or ordinances
Origin	Precedent or stare decisis	Legislature[5]

The study of law requires a review of court decisions in order to gain an appreciation as to how legal determinations are made, learn the rules that govern our conduct, and understand the factors that a judge weighs in rendering a decision.

Reading and understanding court decisions, however, is an acquired skill that takes time to learn. This ability is extremely important to master, as judicial decisions affect every aspect of our lives.

Donald Trump has been the subject of litigation on a multitude of occasions. In fact, it is estimated that these disputes exceed 3,500 cases and range from breach of contract to antitrust violations. One of those disputes will provide an example of the application of common law, or judge made law, and whether a judge should dismiss a lawsuit filed by Mr. Trump for defamation as the result of an unflattering story over a proposed building project in New York.

TRUMP V. CHICAGO TRIBUNE COMPANY
616 F. SUPP. 1434 (S. D. NEW YORK 1985)

Donald Trump, a real estate developer, brings this libel action against the Chicago Tribune Company ("Tribune") and Paul Gapp, an employee of the Tribune whose byline describes him as the Tribune's "architecture critic." Plaintiff's complaint seeks damages based upon statements contained in an article in which Gapp discussed Trump's plan to construct the tallest building in the world, a 150-story tower, on a landfill site at the southeast end of Manhattan Island. Plaintiff's complaint alleges that Gapp's criticism of the proposed venture, which was accompanied by an artist's illustration depicting a building which plaintiff calls "an atrocious, ugly monstrosity," damaged plaintiff's reputation as a developer conscious of aesthetic values. Defendant moves for dismissal of the complaint.

The article published by the Tribune began with the sentence: "The only remotely appealing aspect of Donald Trump's proposed 150-story Manhattan skyscraper is that it would not be done in the Fence Post Style of the 1970s. The following paragraph declared that "the world's tallest tower would be one of the silliest things anyone could inflict on New York or any other city." The piece went on to describe Trump Tower, another development by plaintiff, as a "skyscraper offering condos, office space and a kitschy shopping atrium of blinding flamboyance." Gapp characterized as "eyewash" Trump's statement that the new building would architecturally "balance" the two World Trade Center towers on the west side of lower Manhattan.

Plaintiff maintains that these comments were false and defamatory. Defendants argue that the contents of the Gapp article are entitled to immunity under the First Amendment protection of expressions of opinion. Expressions of one's opinion of another, however unreasonable, cannot be held libelous, and are thus entitled to absolute immunity from liability under the First Amendment. Opinion may be expressed through "rhetorical hyperbole" and "vigorous epithets," even in the most pejorative terms, but when the criticism takes the form of accusations of criminal or unethical conduct, or derogation of professional integrity in terms subject to factual verification, the borderline between fact and opinion has been crossed.

After a careful review of the record, this court has no doubt that the statements contained in the Tribune article are expressions of opinion. The very presentation of the article, under the heading of the "Design" column informs the reader that the article embodies commentary by a Tribune columnist, and is not a news story reporting factual material. From the first sentence, which describes the "only remotely appealing aspect" of the Trump project, the prose is cast in subjective terms; the very words Trump objects to, which refer to the proposal as "one of the silliest things anyone could inflict on New York" and describe the asserted aesthetic balance between the proposed tower and the World Trade Center as "eyewash," convey to the reader the highly personal and subjective nature of the judgments expressed.

The Supreme Court has held that describing a real estate developer's negotiating position as "blackmail" was a statement of opinion, as was the charge that workers refusing to join a union had "rotten principles," and "lacked character." The New York courts have held that calling a Judge incompetent, accusing a former director of the State Lottery of "gypping" and "systematically cheating" the public, and describing a teacher who had received pay to which he was not entitled while on sick leave as a "no-show" are all expressions of opinion which cannot be the predicate for a defamation action. These cases present claims far more compelling than those advanced by plaintiff, and each has been found to involve expressions of opinion entitled to First Amendment protection.

Plaintiff, having sought publicity for his proposal, finds that defendants do not like his proposed structure. He, on the other hand, does not like their conception any better. The words of the Latin proverb are particularly appropriate here: *De gustibus non est disputandum*, there is no disputing about tastes. The complaint is dismissed.

The second case, **Wisconsin v. Torbeck,** offers an illustration of statutory law and the difficulties in applying the language of a statute to a problem.

Every state has a law prohibiting the operation of a vehicle while under the influence of alcohol. Commonly known as "drunk driving," the offense refers to operating a vehicle while the driver's blood/alcohol content is above the legal limits set by statute. While state laws differ as to what constitutes intoxication, it generally ranges from .08 to .10.[6]

While the problems of driving under the influence are well known, thousands of common household products are abused with little notice. Inhaling fumes from glue, lighter fluid or dust remover seems innocent but these vapors can be more dangerous than street drugs with life-altering consequences. This practice raises the question as to whether operating a vehicle while under the influence of these chemical vapors can constitute driving under the influence.[7] The answer will depend upon how a state's statute defines drunken driving and use of inhalants.

It is important to remember that when interpreting a statute, one must look to see how the words are crafted in the statute, a concept known as statutory construction. The intent of the legislature is ascertained primarily from the language used in the statute. The court is required to give words their plain meaning, and to read the law as a whole. The court, however, is bound by the actual wording of the law and the intent is determined from what the legislature said and not what the judge thinks the law should have said. Thus, when the language is unambiguous, there is no reason for interpretation, and the court's only function is to declare the meaning of the statute as clearly as it is expressed.[8]

Consider the following case from Wisconsin as the court decides whether the huffing of DFE, a propellant used in gas duster products, constitutes driving under the influence because of the altered state of consciousness that it provides.

WISCONSIN V. TORBECK
344 Wis.2d 299 (2012)

On the afternoon of March 18, 2011, Deputy Putzer responded to a report of a single vehicle crash. As Putzer approached the scene, he noticed a Saturn Ion in a ditch and a Dodge Grand Caravan parked outside of the intersection. The driver of the Grand Caravan told Putzer that she was almost hit by the Saturn Ion. The driver of the Saturn Ion, Torbeck, was taken to a hospital to treat her injuries.

At the hospital, the deputy discussed the accident with Torbeck. He reported that she had acted in a confused manner and did not have much memory of the crash. A preliminary breath test revealed that Torbeck did not have any alcohol in her system. An emergency room doctor told the deputy that Torbeck "may be in an impaired state due to 'huffing' and possibly other prescription medication." Two of Torbeck's friends who were visiting her both said that they believed that Torbeck crashed her car after "huffing." Based on this information, Putzer cited Torbeck for operating a vehicle while intoxicated (OWI), in violation of Wis. Stat. § 346.63(1)(a). Torbeck then submitted to a blood test which indicated that she had the drug DFE in her system.

Wisconsin Stat. § 346.63(1)(a) provides that no person may drive or operate a motor vehicle while under the influence of an intoxicant, a controlled substance, a controlled substance analog or any combination of an intoxicant, to a degree which renders him or her incapable of safely driving.

For the State to charge Torbeck under § 346.63(1)(a), DFE must be either an intoxicant, a controlled substance, a controlled substance analog, or a drug. DFE is not listed as a controlled substance under either Wisconsin or federal law. The State presented no evidence that DFE is "substantially similar" in chemical structure to a controlled substance. For purposes of the OWI law, a "drug" is defined as:

(a) Any substance recognized as a drug in the official U.S. pharmacopoeia and national formulary or official homeopathic pharmacopoeia of the United States;

(b) Any substance intended for use in the diagnosis, cure, mitigation, treatment or prevention of disease or other conditions in persons;

(c) Any substance other than a device or food intended to affect the structure or any function of the body of persons; or

(d) Any substance intended for use as a component of any paragraph specified above does not include gases or devices intended for use or consumption in or for mechanical, industrial, manufacturing or scientific applications. Wis. Stat. § 450.01(10).

DFE is thus not a "drug" under Wisconsin law. As DFE is not a controlled substance, controlled substance analog, or drug, the State may only charge Torbeck if DFE is an "intoxicant." "Intoxicant" is not defined within the OWI statute. The State urges that we adopt a plain meaning definition by relying on Merriam–Webster's dictionary, which defines "intoxicant" as "something that intoxicates," and "intoxicate" as "to excite or stupefy by alcohol or drug especially to the point where physical and mental control is markedly diminished." According to the State, DFE "is a substance that causes euphoria and diminished motor control" and should thus be considered an intoxicant. Torbeck responds that "intoxicate" means to "excite or stupefy by alcohol or drug," and as DFE is neither alcohol nor a drug, DFE cannot be an intoxicant.

We agree with Torbeck that the legislature has not included DFE as an "intoxicant" within the OWI statute and thus affirm the dismissal of the charge.

**SECTION 1.5
THE LEGISLATIVE
PROCESS**

The power to make laws on the federal level is vested in **Congress** which sits for two year sessions. For instances, as of 2018, Congress was in its 115th session. Its legislative power is contained in Article One of the United States Constitution which provides:

> "All legislative powers herein granted shall be vested in a Congress of the United States. which shall consist of a Senate and House of Representatives."

Previously known as the Congress of the Confederation, this bicameral branch of the federal government created in 1789 consists of two lawmaking units. The **Senate** has of 100 members; two senators are elected from each state and serve six-year terms. The **House of Representatives** consist of 435 legislators, elected every two years from each state based upon population. Together these chambers make up Congress.

The chief function of Congress is to make the laws through debate and compromise that govern the people of this country. In addition, the Senate has the responsibility of consenting to treaties and confirming certain nominations of the President such as any appointment to the federal courts. The House has the power to pass laws raising revenue.

The work of Congress is initiated by the introduction of a proposal in one of four forms: a bill, joint resolution, a concurrent resolution and the simple resolution. A **bill** is the initial form used to introduce most legislation. A bill may originate in either the House of Representatives or the Senate. A bill started in the House of Representatives is designated by the letters "H.R." followed by a number, A Senate bill is designated by the letter "S" followed by its sequential number.

Any member of the legislature may introduce a bill while Congress is in session by placing the proposed law in a basket next to Clerk's desk in the House Chamber called the **hopper**. The person who introduces the bill is called the **sponsor** and more than one person can co-sponsor a bill. The bill is read by the presiding officer of the appropriate chamber who assigns it to the proper committee that has jurisdiction over the subject matter of the proposed law. For instance, the House Committee on Armed Services deals with matters involving military installations, service personnel, and military readiness. The Select Committee on Intelligence analyzes issues involving terrorism, homeland security, counterintelligence, and espionage. Each chamber plays a role in the impeachment process. The House of Representatives initiates the impeachment process and the Senate decides the outcome.

One of the most important phases of the Congressional process is the action taken by the Committee. It is at the Committee level that the most intense consideration is given to the proposed measure and where citizens are given the opportunity to testify about the proposed legalization.

If a bill is of sufficient importance and particularly if it is controversial, the Committee will usual set a date for public hearings. Each Committee is required to announce the date, place, and subject matter of any hearing to be conducted by the Committee. Witnesses may testify either voluntarily or at the request of the Committee. A vote is also taken to determine whether it will issue a favorable report or **table** the bill. Committee reports are a valuable element of the legislative history of a law. They are used by the courts, executive departments, agencies and the public, as a source of information regarding the purpose and meaning of the legislation.

When the Committee acts favorable on the bill, the chamber in which the proposed law originated votes on the bill. If that chamber passes the bill, the other house then considers it for passage. A bill that is agreed to by both the House of Representative and Senate it then forward to the President. If the chief executive signs the bill, it becomes the law. A bill may also become law when the President fails to return it to Congress within ten days noting an objection to the legislation. However, a **pocket veto** happens if the President receives the legislation within ten days of adjournment by Congress and the Chief Executive takes no action. The President may also **veto** the bill in which case the proposal does not become law. However, two-thirds of the members of Congress can vote to override the veto. In that event, the bill became the law. Thousands of bills are introduced each year but less than seven hundred are usually passed.

There is not a large difference between a joint resolution and a bill. The **joint resolution** is not proposed simultaneously in Congress but originates in either House and generally goes through the same review process as a bill. Their use is usually restricted to advancing a proposed amendment to the Constitution or for emergency appropriations.

A **concurrent resolution** is an informal pronouncement by Congress that does not have the effect of a law and does not require the signature of the President. For instance, it can be used to extend congratulations to someone over a special event such as the Philadelphia Eagles winning the Super Bowl.

A **simple resolution** is only passed by one chamber of Congress and represents a non-binding resolution that is not given to the President for signature. They generally deal with the internal affairs of the House or Senate such as the establishment of a new committee.

State and Federal laws are called **statutes**. Local laws are known as **ordinances**. To learn more about the activities of Congress, visit the official web sites of the House of Representatives or Senate. Those addresses are www.house.gov and www.senate.gov.

Most people are aware of the risks of driving a motor vehicle while intoxicated and newspapers are filled with tragic stories of innocent victims of such gross violations of the law. The police are also very aggressive in enforcing the laws involving drunk driving. Sobriety check points are routinely established; stiffer penalties have been imposed for conviction including mandatory jail time for repeat offenders and the blood/alcohol level establishing legal intoxication has been lowered to .08 in most jurisdictions.

The Center for Disease Control estimates that about 18,000 people are killed each year as the result of alcohol–related motor vehicle crashes and almost 1.5 million drivers are arrested for driving under the influence of alcohol or narcotics. These violations, however, are not limited to the adult population. Underage drinking is a large problem and a number of alcohol related deaths have been reported on college campuses because of binge drinking or accidents following the consumption of liquor.

A variety of judicial and legislative pronouncements have been issued concerning these problems. This chapter will examine the development of the law in Pennsylvania concerning the liability of a social-host for providing alcoholic beverages to a guest. Cases will be presented on the issue of **social host** liability so that the reader can see how different rulings have emerged depending upon the fact patterns presented.

The first case deals social host liability to a third party who is injured by the negligence of an intoxicated guest involved in an automobile accident after leaving a party. Is it the guest's consumption of alcohol or the social host furnishing of the alcohol that is the proximate cause of a subsequent accident?

A. The Caption

The first case is **Klein v. Raysinger** and this name is known as the **caption** since it identifies the parties to the lawsuit. In other words, Klein sued Raysinger so the former is known as the **plaintiff.** Raysinger is the **defendant** since he is the party being sued. When a case is appealed to a higher court, the names of the parties change. The person who appeals the decision is the **"appellant"** and the party against whom an appeal is filed is the **"appellee."**

B. The Citation

The **citation** tells the reader how to locate the case. In this instance, the citation is 470 A.2d 507 (Pa. 1983). "A.2d" refers to the book that contains this decision, or in this case, the Atlantic Reporter. Court cases are published by West Publishing Company which entity has divided the country into regions for reporting purposes. The Atlantic Reporter contains the regional appellate decisions of those states on the Atlantic side of the United States and includes such jurisdictions as Pennsylvania, New Jersey, Delaware and Maryland, Connecticut, Maine, New Hampshire and Vermont. The first set of these books is contained in series one or A. and covers the years 1895 to 1938. A.2d refers to the second series of books and covers the time frame from 1939 until 2010. A.3d contains judicial decisions from 2011 to the present. By comparison, California decisions are published in the Pacific Reporter and court cases from Massachusetts and New York are found in the Northeast Reporter.

The first number in the citation is 470 which refers to the volume of the book that contains the decision, and 507 is the page number on which the case is published. The information in the parenthesis identifies the state and appellate court who heard the case. For instance, Pa. is the abbreviation for the Pennsylvania Supreme Court. A decision from the Pennsylvania Superior court would be Pa. Super. The last information in the citation is the year in which the case was decided or in this case 1983.

C. Types of Opinions

The next item that appears after the caption is the name of the judge who authored the **opinion.** On appeal, one judge writes the opinion or body of the case for the "majority" of the court. Because an appellate court consists of a panel of three or more judges, a decision reached by more than half of the judges constitutes the **"majority opinion."** A decision rendered by the majority is the law. A judge authors a **"dissenting opinion"** when he or she disagrees with the result reached by the majority—however, the dissent has no value as precedent. A judge may also write a **"concurring opinion"** when the jurist agrees with the outcome of the case but wants to note a difference in logic for reaching the decision.

SECTION 1.7
BRIEFING OF A CASE

Breaking a case down into its component parts simplifies a person's understanding of the opinion. An opinion has four main parts:

1. The Action;
2. The Facts;
3. The Issue; and
4. The Opinion of the Court.

The Action—What kind of case is it? What remedy is being sought? For instance, does the case involve a criminal prosecution or a civil lawsuit for money damages?

The Facts—What happened? The reader should be concerned with the three *W's*: specifically, *Who* did *What* to *Whom?* The facts of a case are discussed in a narrative form.

The Issue—What question is presented to the court for it to decide?

The Opinion of the Court—First, the reader must ascertain what the court decided. In other words, how did the court answer the question posed in the Issue section? Second, and more importantly, what justification does the court provide for coming up with its answer? For example, what sociological, economic or political policies does the court use to justify its decision? Any dissenting or concurring opinions should also be noted in this section, but their discussion may be less detailed than the majority opinion.

An appellate court can affirm, reverse or remand the decision of a lower court. When a decision is **affirmed,** the appellate court determines that the lower court reached the correct decision. The appellate court **reverses** a decision when it finds that the lower court's decision was incorrect. A case may also be **remanded** to the trial court. This occurs when the appellate court finds that the trial judge committed an error in deciding the case, additional evidence must be obtained, or the lower court's decision must be clarified.

KLEIN v. RAYSINGER
470 A.2D 507 (PA. 1983)

McDermott, Justice.

On or about May 8, 1978, Michael Klein and his family were driving on the Pennsylvania Turnpike when they were struck in the rear by a vehicle driven by Mark Raysinger. Prior to the collision, Raysinger had been served alcoholic beverages at the home of the Gilligans. It is alleged that Raysinger was visibly intoxicated at the time he was served by the Gilligans, and that it was known that Raysinger would be driving. As a consequence, appellants' claim that the Gilligans are liable for the injuries they sustained in the accident.

This case is one of first impression in this jurisdiction. The Kleins' are requesting this Court to recognize a new cause of action in negligence, against a social host who serves alcohol to a visibly intoxicated person, whom the host knows, or should know, intends to drive a motor vehicle.

No social host who furnishes alcoholic beverages to any person shall be held legally accountable for damages suffered by such person, or for injury to the person or property of, or death of, any third person, resulting from the consumption of such beverages.

Ordinarily, a host who makes available intoxicating liquors to an adult guest is not liable for injuries to third persons resulting from the guest's intoxication. There might be circumstances in which the host would have a duty to deny his guest further access to alcohol. This would be the case where the host "has reason to know that he is dealing with persons whose characteristics make it especially likely that they will do unreasonable things." Such persons could include those already severely intoxicated, or those whose behavior the host knows to be unusually affected by alcohol. Also included might be young people, if their ages were such that they could be expected, by virtue of their youth alone or in connection with other circumstances, to behave in a dangerous fashion under the influence of alcohol.

Thus, the great weight of authority supports the view that in the case of an ordinary able bodied man, it is the consumption of the alcohol, rather than the furnishing of the alcohol, which is the proximate cause of any subsequent occurrence. This is in accord with the recognized rule at common law. We agree with this common law view, and consequently hold that there can be no liability on the part of a social host who serves alcoholic beverages to his or her adult guests.

Dissenting Opinion by Mr. Justice Manderino

Liquor dispensers who act negligently and cause harm should not be given any special privilege of immunity from liability. We do not give such immunity to automobile drivers. We do not give such immunity to drug dispensers. We do not give such immunity to homeowners. The establishment of a new immunity makes bad history. The combination of an intoxicated person and an automobile causes death and serious harm to many each day. Such victims are entitled to their day in court.

Can we declare as a matter of law that it is reasonable conduct to serve intoxicating liquors to a person who is in a state of visible intoxication? I think the question answers itself. In acting, a person is assumed to know what the reasonable man in the society knows. The common knowledge of the reasonable man certainly includes information concerning the effects of alcoholic beverages and the consequences of intoxication on human behavior. From the alleged facts, reasonable men could infer negligent conduct by the appellees.

As the court noted, the holding is a common law ruling in which the judges had to decide what they believed was proper and right under the circumstances. Simply put, they determined that there is no liability under Pennsylvania law on the part of a social host who serves alcohol to an adult guest. Would the result be the same, however, if the legislature issued a pronouncement on the subject or established a policy against furnishing liquor to certain classes of individuals such as children?

In 1972, the Pennsylvania legislature spoke on the issue of underage consumption of alcohol when it made it illegal for persons under 21 years of age to purchase or possess liquor. 18 Pa. C.S.A. §6308 provides:

a. A person commits a summary offense if he, being less than 21 years of age, attempts to purchase, purchases, consumes, possesses or knowingly and intentionally transports any liquor or malt or brewed beverages.

The legislative purpose of this statute is clear so that the law punishes anyone under the age of 21 for the consumption of alcohol in any amount, regardless of the blood/alcohol level produced. In other words, the police are not required to show a specific blood/alcohol level in children to establish its case. Will this statute change the result of social host immunity if the liquor is furnished to a minor? That is the issue in **Congini v. Portersville Valve Co.** in which the court had to decide whether this statute applied to an employer who supplied liquor to an employee at an office party who was under 21 years of age.

CONGINI V. PORTERSVILLE VALVE CO.
470 A.2D 515 (PA. 1983)

McDermott, Justice.

This appeal arises from an action for personal injuries sustained by Mark Congini in an automobile accident. At the time of the accident, Congini was eighteen years of age and an employee of Portersville. On December 22, 1978, Portersville held a Christmas party for its employees at which alcoholic beverages were served. Mark attended the party and, as a result of consuming an undisclosed amount of alcohol, became intoxicated.

Mark's car was parked at Portersville plant, which was the scene of the party, and Portersville, through one of its agents, had possession of the car keys. Although Portersville's agent was aware of Mark's intoxicated condition, the keys were given to Mark upon his request so that he could drive from the plant to his home.

While Mark was operating the car on the highway, he drove it into the rear of another vehicle which was proceeding in the same direction. As a result, Mark suffered multiple fractures and brain damage which have left him permanently disabled.

Appellants have alleged that defendant was negligent in providing Mark with alcoholic beverages to the point that he became intoxicated. This issue is similar to that raised in **Klein v. Raysinger, 470 A.2d 507 (1983)**, i.e., the extent to which a social host can be held liable for injuries sustained by his guest to whom he has served intoxicating liquors. This case, however, differs in two respects: that the guest here was a minor; and that the plaintiff is the guest to whom the intoxicants were served, rather than a third person injured by a person who was served alcoholic beverages.

In **Klein v. Raysinger,** we held that there exists no liability on the part of a social host for the service of intoxicants to his adult guests. In arriving at this decision we relied upon the common law rule that in the case of an ordinary able bodied man, it is the consumption of alcohol rather than the furnishing thereof, that is the proximate cause of any subsequent damage.

However, our legislature has made a legislative judgment that persons under twenty-one years of age are incompetent to handle alcohol. Under 18 Pa.C.S.§ 6308, a person "less than 21 years of age" commits a summary offense if he "attempts to purchase, purchases, consumes, possesses or transports any alcohol, liquor or malt or brewed beverages." Furthermore, under 18 Pa.C.S.A.§ 306, an adult who furnishes liquor to a minor would be liable as an accomplice to the same extent as the offending minor.

This legislative judgment compels a different result than Klein, for here we are not dealing with ordinary able bodied men. Rather, we are confronted with persons who are, at least in the eyes of the law, incompetent to handle the affects of alcohol.

Section 6308 of the Crimes Code represents an obvious legislative decision to protect both minors and the public at large from the perceived deleterious effects of serving alcohol to persons under twenty-one years of age. Thus, we find that defendants were negligent in serving alcohol to the point of intoxication to a person less than twenty-one years of age, and that they can be held liable for injuries proximately resulting from the minor's intoxication.

Under our analysis, an actor's negligence exists in furnishing intoxicants to a class of persons legislatively determined to be incompetent to handle its effects. Thus, although we recognize that an 18-year-old minor may state a cause of action against an adult social host who has knowingly served him intoxicants, the social host in turn may assert as a defense the minor's "contributory" negligence. It will remain for the fact finder to resolve whether the defendant's negligence was such as to allow recovery.

Roberts, Chief Justice, concurring.

I join in the mandate of the majority allowing the complaint, which seeks recovery for injuries allegedly caused by the serving of liquor by a social host to a visibly intoxicated minor guest, to proceed to trial. The Liquor Code mandates that it is "unlawful . . . for any licensee, or any employee, servant or agent of such licensee, or any other person, to sell, furnish or give any liquor . . . or to permit any liquor . . . to be sold, or given, to any person visibly intoxicated. . . ." The use of the language "any person visibly intoxicated" clearly manifests the Legislature's intention to prohibit the furnishing of alcoholic beverages to all visibly intoxicated persons, without regard to whether those persons are adults or minors.

Zappala, Justice, dissenting.

In **Klein v. Raysinger,** we held that no duty exists under the common law which would impose liability upon a social host who serves alcohol to an adult guest for conduct of the guest which results in injury to himself or to a third party. We recognized that it is the consumption of alcohol, rather than the furnishing of alcohol to an individual, which is the proximate cause of any subsequent occurrence.

In the instant case, however, the majority opinion concludes that liability of a social host may arise from the act of furnishing alcohol to a minor and that such liability may extend to harm suffered by the minor. By adopting this legal premise, the majority today is effectively overruling Klein and for that reason I must dissent.

I cannot agree, therefore, that liability should be imposed on a social host serving alcohol to a person under 21 based upon the rationale that minors are incompetent to handle alcohol. If it is consumption by an adult guest, rather than the furnishing of alcohol by a host, which is the proximate cause of subsequent occurrences, then it is not less compelling to conclude that it is a minor's voluntary consumption of alcohol which is the proximate cause of harm which results.

QUESTIONS FOR DISCUSSION:

1. The judges in **Congini** were identical to the judges who decided the **Klein** case. Do you agree that the statute applicable to underage drinking cited in **Congini** warranted a different result?

2. Do you agree with the dissenting judge who said that the majority was effectively overruling **Klein** by its decision?

3. Do you think that the court merely wanted to protect children by its decision?

4. Under this holding would a social host be liable for an injury if the adult served alcohol to a child but the minor was not visibly intoxicated?

Twelve years following the **Klein** and **Congini** decisions, the court was asked to decide yet another variation of social host liability. Up to this point, the court had held that a social host is not liable to a third party who is injured by an intoxicated guest. However an adult who serves liquor to a minor will be responsible because the legislature has decided to protect both minors and the public at large from the ill effects of serving alcohol to persons under twenty-one years of age. What social policies and protections come into play when a minor is the social host who serves liquor to another minor? Who will the law protect in this situation when both parties are incapable of appreciating the consequences of alcohol because of their tender years? That is the issue in **Currie v. Phillips.**

CURRIE v. PHILLIPS
70 D. & C. 4TH 401 (PA. COM. PL. 2005)

This action was commenced by Craig Currie, administrator of the estate of Robert Skaf. Plaintiff's complaint alleges that Skaf died after attending a party where he had consumed alcoholic beverages. The defendant, Phillips, owned the apartment building at 415 Taylor Avenue, Scranton, Pennsylvania and leased the premises to the additional defendants. At the time of Skaf's death, he was 20 years of age and a minor for alcohol consumption purposes.

Skaf's estate commenced the within action against Phillips as the owner of 415 Taylor Avenue, Scranton, Pennsylvania, where Skaf was found dead on April 28, 2002. Apparently, Skaf had gone to those premises to stay for the night, and during the early morning hours, he attempted to walk up a flight of stairs in which there were no handrails and apparently fell causing fatal injuries.

After service of the complaint, Phillips filed a writ of summons joining the additional defendants presenting claims against them for social host liability. The Phillips' joinder complaint avers that Potts was a tenant of 415 Taylor Avenue and on April 27, 2002, he sponsored the "Second Annual Beer Pong Tournament" with the other tenants which was held upon said premises. The attendees of the party were required to pay $5 to gain entrance to the event. Throughout the evening, the additional defendants provided nine kegs of beer to all party participants, including those under the age of 21.

The issue that must be clarified is whether a minor may be held liable for injuries sustained as a result of furnishing alcohol to another minor under the social host doctrine. The prevailing view on social host liability is found in **Kapres v. Heller, 640 A.2d 888 (Pa. 1994).** There the Supreme Court was confronted with the identical issue involving social host liability. In **Kapres,** the plaintiff was a student at Clarion University and attended three separate alcohol-related parties all hosted by minors. The plaintiff, who was 19 years old, ingested alcohol at all three parties, and while walking home, was struck by a vehicle and sustained numerous injuries. At the time of the accident the plaintiff had a blood alcohol content of .19. The plaintiff brought causes of action against the minor hosts who served him alcohol under the social host doctrine. He asserted that his intoxication proximately caused him to be hit by an automobile driven by an additional defendant. The minor defendants filed motions for summary judgment on the basis that they owed no duty to the minor plaintiff for injuries sustained as a result of his intoxication. In the opinion of the Supreme Court, Justice Cappy wrote, "it is more logical and consistent with the prevailing view on social host liability to find that one minor does not owe a duty to another regarding the furnishing or consumption of alcohol."

In **Kapres,** the court ultimately found that a plaintiff and defendant, who were both minors, were incompetent as a matter of law in handling alcohol. A minor is responsible under the law for his/her own actions in either furnishing or consuming alcohol. This notion was coupled with the standard set forth in **Klein v. Raysinger, 470 A.2d 507 (Pa. 1983)** where it addressed the idea of social host liability. In **Klein,** the court found that where an able bodied individual consumes alcohol, "it is the consumption of alcohol rather than the furnishing of the alcohol which is the proximate cause of any subsequent occurrence." The view accepted by the **Klein** court follows the common-law view.

There is an exception to the rule established in **Klein** which involves furnishing alcohol to a minor by an adult. This exception was established in **Congini v. Portersville Valve Company, 470 A.2d 515 (Pa. 1983).** The Supreme Court held that the rule in **Klein** is inapplicable in those situations where an adult provides a minor with alcohol. The concept that a minor is incompetent to handle alcohol has necessitated the exception to the rule of **Klein.** The premise for the exception is grounded in insuring the safety of minors. Yet, the minor himself is not totally blameless because the **Congini** court further held that the minor's contribution to his/her injuries will also be taken into account. This holding brings us back to the assertions made in **Kapres** case where the court expands upon the theory in **Klein** whereby under the law minors are considered incompetent to handle alcohol. It is logic and consistency that led the Supreme Court to hold that one minor owes no duty to another minor under the guise of social host liability regarding the furnishing and consumption of alcohol. We too agree that a minor is not liable to another minor for injuries that might have been sustained as a result of the host minor's distribution of alcohol to another under the age of 21. Therefore, the pleadings establish that there are no material facts in dispute upon the issue of social host liability so it is proper to grant the additional defendant Potts' judgment on the pleadings.

SECTION 1.8
STATUS AND PROCESS

Status and process is a concept that makes judicial decisions a little easier to understand. The principle is quite simple. If one is able to ascertain who enjoys favored status with the law, it is often possible to predict the outcome of a case without knowing the law.

Status and process requires an examination of the parties to the litigation. The outcome of the case will depend on whom the courts want to protect and what goals society wants to achieve.

For example, consider the institution of marriage. Does the law favor or frown upon marriage? Historically, the laws supported marriage and the outcome of a case was frequently decided to uphold that institution.

To prove that the law historically favored the institution of marriage, one merely has to think of how easy it is to become married and how difficult it was to obtain a divorce. Everyone is aware that a marital union can be created through a religious or civil ceremony. The law, however, went out of its way to establish marital relationships and had created the fiction of a **common law marriage.**

A common law marriage was just as valid as a religious or civil ceremony and required a formal divorce decree to dissolve.

What other institutions enjoy favor with the law? These groups would include children, incompetents, the disabled, the government, and religious organizations to name a few. For instance, the government, its agencies, and high ranking officials enjoy immunity from suit in most cases because the law protects these types of entities. After all, the government and its agents represent the members of society and is funded by the taxpayers.

Status and process, however, requires that one analyze the institution as it exists at the time of the court decision. As times change, so do the institutions that the law protects. With regard to marriage, women were traditionally viewed as the weaker of the sexes. Therefore, women in the past were automatically awarded one-third to one-half of the husband's net income in a support proceeding. Following the Equal Rights movement, and the shifting of public opinion, the role of women in today's society has vastly changed. They are considered equal to men and have made significant inroads in the market place. It is now common to see a female doctor, lawyer, construction worker, police officer or soldier. This equality of the sexes has resulted in change in the support laws. The courts now examine the earning capacity of each person instead of making an automatic award to the wife. This has resulted in court decisions requiring wives to pay support to husbands and giving husbands custody of the children.

An example of status and process is provided by examining the law dealing with the use deadly force. For instance, can a person use serious or deadly force to protect his property or will the homeowner be responsible if a trespasser is injured? That is the issue in **Katko v. Briney** and the case can be understood by simply weighing the competing interests of life versus property in order to determining who the law protects.

KATKO V. BRINEY
183 N.W. 2D 657 (IOWA, 1971)

The primary issue presented here is whether an owner may protect personal property in an unoccupied boarded-up farm house against trespassers and thieves by a spring gun capable of inflicting death or serious injury.

At defendants' request plaintiff's action was tried to a jury consisting of residents of the community where defendants' property was located. The jury returned a verdict for plaintiff and against defendants for $20,000 actual and $10,000 punitive damages.

Most of the facts are not disputed. In 1957 defendant, Bertha L. Briney inherited her parents' farmland. Included was an 80-acre tract in southwest Mahaska County where her grandparents and parents had lived. No one occupied the house thereafter.

There occurred a series of trespassing and house-breaking events with loss of some household items, the breaking of windows and "messing up of the property in general."

Defendants boarded up the windows and doors in an attempt to stop the intrusions. They had posted "no trespass" signs on the land. The nearest one was 35 feet from the house. Defendants set a "shot-gun trap" in the north bedroom where they secured it to an iron bed with the barrel pointed at the bedroom door. It was rigged with wire from the doorknob to the gun's trigger so it would fire when the door was opened. Briney first pointed the gun's trigger so an intruder would be hit in the stomach but at Mrs. Briney's suggestion it was lowered to hit the legs. Tin was nailed over the bedroom window. The spring gun could not be seen from the outside. No warning of its presence was posted.

Plaintiff worked regularly as a gasoline station attendant seven miles from the old house and considered it as being abandoned. He knew it had long been uninhabited. Plaintiff and McDonough had been to the premises and found several old bottles and fruit jars which they took and added to their collection of antiques. About 9:30 p.m. they made a second trip to the Briney property. They entered the old house by removing a board from a porch window which was without glass. While McDonough was looking around the kitchen area plaintiff went to another part of the house. As he started to open the north bedroom door the shotgun went off striking him in the right leg above the ankle bone. Much of his leg, including part of the tibia, was blown away.

Plaintiff testified he knew he had no right to break and enter the house with intent to steal bottles and fruit jars therefrom. He further testified he had entered a plea of guilty to larceny in the night-time of property of less than $20 value from a private building. He stated he had been fined $50 and costs and paroled during good behavior from a 60-day jail sentence.

The main thrust of defendant's defense in the trial court and on this appeal is that "the law permits use of a spring gun in a dwelling or warehouse for the purpose of preventing the unlawful entry of a burglar or thief."

The overwhelming weight of authority, both textbook and case law, supports the trial court's statement of the applicable principles of law.

Prosser on Torts, Third Edition, pages 116–118, states:

> The law has always placed a higher value upon human safety than upon

mere rights in property, it is the accepted rule that there is no privilege to use any force calculated to cause death or serious bodily injury to repel the threat to land or chattels unless there is also such a threat to the defendant's personal safety as to justify a self-defense . . . Spring guns and other man-killing devices are not justifiable against a mere trespasser, or even a petty thief. They are privileged only against those upon whom the landowner, if he were present in person would be free to inflict injury of the same kind.

Restatement of Torts, section 85, page 180 states: "The value of human life and limb, not only to the individual concerned but also to society, so outweighs the interest of a possessor of land in excluding from it those whom he is not willing to admit thereto that a possessor of land has no privilege to use force intended or likely to cause death or serious harm against another whom the possessor sees is about to enter his premises or meddle with his chattel, unless the intrusion threatens death or serious bodily harm to the occupiers or users of the premises.

The facts in **Allison v. Fiscus, 156 Ohio 120, 100 N.E.2d 237, 44 A.L.R.2d 369,** decided in 1951, are very similar to the case at the bar. There, plaintiff's right to damages was recognized for injuries received when he feloniously broke a door latch and started to enter defendant's warehouse with intent to steal. As he entered a trap of two sticks of dynamite buried under the doorway by defendant owner was set off and plaintiff was seriously injured. The court held the question whether a particular trap was justified as a use of reasonable and necessary force against the trespasser engaged in the commission of a felony should have been submitted to the jury. The Ohio Supreme Court recognized plaintiff's right to punitive or exemplary damages in addition to compensation damages. The jury's findings of fact including a finding defendants acted with malice and with wanton and reckless disregard, as required for an allowance of punitive or exemplary damages, are supported by substantial evidence. We are bound thereby.

Affirmed.

Katko v. Briney clearly demonstrates that a person cannot use force that will inflict death or serious bodily injury in the protection of property. Human life is simply more important than property. In **Commonwealth v. Johnston, 263 A.2d 376 (Pa., 1970),** however, the court was confronted with the issue as to whether a person can use deadly force in order to protect human life. While killing another without justification is illegal, a killing is excusable if it is committed in self-defense. This will occur when (1) the slayer reasonably believes that he is in imminent danger of great bodily harm, (2) he has attempted to flee the harm, and (3) deadly force is the only way to protect human life.

While the use of a shotgun in the protection of property is clearly excessive, is the owner of a store liable for an attack by a vicious dog that is allowed to roam the store at night in order to stop trespassers? Based upon the reasoning in **Katko v. Briney,** the store owner will be liable for the attack. The dog has been kept on the premises for the sole purpose of protecting property by inflicting serious harm to the intruder. Will liability, however, be imposed on a homeowner whose pet dog attacks a burglar that enters a home when no one is present? The answer is no. The dog is not kept at the family dwelling for the sole purpose of attacking people. Dogs are territorial and they will protect their master's home against an intruder.

Will the owner of a dog be liable if the animal bites a guest or if a large playful dog, has a habit of jumping on people? The law is well settled that a dog's owner will be liable for the actions of the pet if the owner knows or has good reason to know of the dog's dangerous or vicious propensities and fails to take reasonable measures to protect the guest from the pet's actions. The saying that "every dog is entitled to one bite" is not true. If a dog has displayed a vicious propensity in the past, the owner will be liable to another for a dog bite even if the animal has not bitten anyone previously. Likewise, the law imposes a duty of restraint on the owner of a dog when the owner knows of the animal's playful but dangerous propensity of jumping on individuals.

SECTION 1.9 CHRISTOPHER V. ROBERTS

Throughout the semester, you will be asked to solve a variety of legal disputes. The following is a problem dealing with the concept of status and process along with a suggested answer. When completing an assignment, please make sure that you answer all questions posed and explain your answer by citing to the appropriate case law. A one or two sentence response will not suffice.

PARK, BROWN & SMITH, P.C.
ATTORNEYS AT LAW
MEMORANDUM

SAMPLE PROBLEM

TO: All Law Clerks

FROM: Peter Smith, Esquire

RE: Kathy Roberts and the Purchase of Her Car

Kathy Roberts, a 16-year-old, related the following story to me.

Immediately after passing her driving test, Kathy decided she needed to buy a car. Unfortunately, she and her father, Joe Roberts, disagreed as to whether she was ready for what her father considered an "unnecessary extravagance." Joe had called his insurance agent and learned that the annual premium for insuring the car was more than what the automobile was worth.

Despite her father's objections, Kathy decided to secretly purchase a vehicle on her own. While walking home from school, she noticed that her next-door neighbor, Peter Christopher, had a *For Sale* sign in the window of a car parked in his driveway. The vehicle seemed perfect for Kathy's needs. The Honda was in good mechanical condition and Kathy was certain that her father would be favorably impressed with her conservative choice of transportation. Kathy contacted the neighbor and purchased the vehicle for $5,000.

When Kathy's father learned of the purchase, he exploded. "How dare you buy a car after I told you not to." Kathy had never seen her father more outraged. Even her sweetest smile couldn't calm him down. Not only did he suspend her driving privileges, but he even attempted to return the car to Christopher. Despite this, the neighbor refused to take the car back, claiming that a "deal is a deal." Two days later, Kathy figured that her father had calmed down enough for her to start driving the vehicle. Unfortunately, Kathy was unable to negotiate a sharp turn a block from home and demolished the Honda. As she sat on the curb crying, the hubcap of the vehicle rolled by her. Since this was the only thing left of the car, she picked it up and walked home.

Kathy spent the rest of the day calling friends for advice. One girl-friend told Kathy that she could obtain the return of her money from Christopher since she was only sixteen. The girlfriend had her money refunded from a record club that she had joined when she was fifteen. Relying on this advice, Kathy approached her neighbor and demanded her money back. She even offered Christopher the return of the hubcap. After all, that was all that was left of the car. Christopher laughed and said that Kathy had entered into a valid contract and she had destroyed the car.

Please read **Star Chevrolet v. Green** and apply the case to Kathy's problem. You must decide the following:

1. Should Kathy be able to rescind the contract and get her money back from Christopher?

2. Does it matter that the only thing she can return to Christopher is the hubcap, or must she pay to have the car repaired before she can disaffirm the contract?

3. Did status and process play any part in the Star Chevrolet decision? Explain your answer.

STAR CHEVROLET V. GREEN
473 SO.2D 157 (MISS. 1985)

Kevin Green was 16 years old on August 14, 1981, when he purchased a Camaro from Star Chevrolet. Title to the Camaro was in Kevin's name, and the $4,642.50 purchase price was drawn from his savings. The question of Kevin's age was not raised by the dealership. Kevin brought the car back to Star Chevrolet to repair several problems. Some time prior to November 1981, Green's Camaro became inoperable due to a blown head gasket. The disabled car was parked in front of his home for some four or five months. On November 16, 1981, Green informed Star Chevrolet that as a minor, he was disaffirming the contract and demanding the return of the funds he paid for the automobile. Star Chevrolet would not accept the car unless it was restored to its original condition.

Finally, Kevin fixed the head gasket himself and began to drive the car again. In June, 1982, the Camaro was destroyed in an accident. The insurance company paid Kevin $5,100 under the policy and he signed title to the vehicle over to the insurance company for its salvage value.

At trial, Kevin admitted that after he wrecked the car, the insurance company paid him $5,100, $500 more than the original purchase price. He used this money to buy another car. The court applied the rule of law that he who contracts with a minor does so at his own peril. It was ruled that the minor had "wasted" the vehicle, and, as a result, there was nothing for him to surrender to Star Chevrolet. It has long been settled that the contracts of infants or minors impose no liability upon them except for contracts for necessities, and in some special cases of actual and active fraud.

The general rule is that upon disaffirmance of a minor's contract, he is required to return the consideration only if it is still in his possession. The minor who disaffirms a contract is not obliged to return the consideration received by him or its equivalent where during his minority he has wasted, squandered, destroyed, used, or otherwise disposed of the consideration.

Disaffirmance at this point would have required the appellant to refund the full purchase price and the appellee, in turn, to return the damaged Camaro, since the law does not condition a minor's right to disaffirm a contract upon placing the other party in status quo, but only requires he return whatever consideration remains in the minor's hands. In this case, we hold that the appellant is entitled to a setoff, for the salvage value of the consideration which Green intentionally conveyed away (to the insurance company).

Name   **Please Print Clearly**

1. **Should Kathy be able to rescind the contract and obtain her money back from Mr. Christopher? (Support your answer with case law.)**

   Yes. Kathy should be able to obtain the return of her money even though the car has been destroyed. According to **Star Chevrolet v. Green,** the Mississippi Supreme Court merely requires a minor, when rescinding a contract, to return only the money or property remaining within his or her control. The child does not have to restore the parties to the status quo. The Court indicated that the purpose of this statute is for the benefit and protection of the minor; hence, an adult, in dealing with a minor, assumes the risk of loss.

   Assuming that Kathy Roberts lives in a place with a law similar to that in Mississippi, Kathy will be able to rescind the contract and get her money back. Typically, the law protects minors in their ability to enter into contracts, and requires that the minor return what is left from the contract. Kathy attempted to return the hubcap; the only property left in her possession, so she has properly rescinded the contract.

2. **Does it matter that the only thing Kathy can return to Christopher is the hubcap, or must she pay to have the car repaired before she can disaffirm the contract?**

   No, she does not have to pay to have the car repaired. Kathy fulfilled her requirements as a minor. The statute given to us to read only requires a minor to return the money or property he or she has left, or in this case, the hubcap. Kathy is not required to have the car repaired.

3. **Do you think that the concept of status and process played any part in the "Star Chevrolet" decision? Explain your answer.**

   Status and process played an important role in the Star Chevrolet decision. Under the concept of status and process, minors enjoy favored status in the law, and when a class such as children enjoys this status, it becomes easy to predict the outcome of the case. All things being equal, when one party enjoys favored status, and the other does not, it becomes clear who will be the winning side.

SECTION 1.10
PRECEDENT

Precedent is the process whereby judges apply the decisions and rules of prior cases to those over which they are currently deciding. As Justice Cardoza stated in an essay entitled, *The Nature of the Judicial Process,* "We recognize that no judicial system could do society's work if it eyed each issue afresh in every case that raised it." The formal legal term for this concept is **stare decisis.** This doctrine forms the backbone of the American legal system and offers litigants certainty, predictability and uniformity in the application of the law. As noted in **In re Larry A. Deboer, 1999 WL 33486710** (Bankr. D. Idaho), stare decisis provides that when the court has once laid down a principle of law as applicable to a given state of facts, it will adhere to that principle and apply it in future cases where the facts are substantially the same. This principle has long been a cornerstone of common law.

Judges will generally follow precedent but are not bound to do so in every situation. A legal principle may be changed by the legislature, and the court has the discretion to change the law as the social, political, or economic conditions change. Changes are also observed as members of the court, especially the United States Supreme Court, are replaced by jurists with different judicial or political philosophies.

A change in precedent may occur for a number of reasons including: (1) when the court is convinced that prior decisions are irreconcilable; (2) the application of a rule or principle has created confusion; (3) a rule of law has been inconsistently applied; (4) to correct a misconception in a decision; or (5) where the court believes that the reason for the law no longer exists, justice requires a change, and no vested property interests will be injured by the change. **Niederman v. Brodsky, 261 A.2d 84 (Pa. 1970).**

A bicycle is considered a vehicle for the purpose of the drunk driving laws. This holding is supported by multiple cases around the country and is clear precedent in the area. New forms of transportation, however are routinely created, so a question arises as to whether those devices will be treated as a vehicle for purposes of intoxication.

Consider a Segway, which is a two wheeled electronically powered scooter. Computers and motors in the base of the unit keep it upright. An operator directs the Segway to go forward by shifting their weight forward on the base. Gyroscopic sensors and fluid-based leveling sensors perceive the weight shift.[9] Would the same precedent apply to a person arrested for operating a Segway while intoxicated as it does to a bicycle?

STATE V. GREENMAN
825 N.W.2D 387 (Minn. App., 2013)

Minnesota challenges the dismissal of driving-while-impaired charges against Mark Greenman, contending that the lower court erred in concluding that a Segway electric personal assistive mobility device is not included in the definition of "motor vehicle" in the DWI statute. Because Greenman's operation of a Segway did not make him a driver of a motor vehicle under Minn. Statutes, we affirm.

On February 4, 2012, Greenman attempted to travel to his home by using his Segway. After traveling along the walking path, Greenman entered the road, and twice drifted across the center line of the road before being stopped by a police officer. The officer noticed that Greenman showed signs of intoxication and asked him to perform field sobriety tests, which Greenman failed. A breath test revealed that he had an alcohol concentration of .19. The state charged Greenman with a violation of Minnesota law which places restrictions on when an electric personal assistive mobility device may operate on a roadway.

In dismissing the criminal charges, the lower court relied upon **State v. Brown.** In **Brown,** this court held that a mobility scooter is not a motor vehicle for purposes of a DWI prosecution. The **Brown** court noted that the definition of "motor vehicle" specifically *excluded* "an electric personal assistive mobility device." The **Brown** court next analyzed the language of one of the DWI provisions at issue making it a crime for "any person to drive, operate, or be in physical control of any motor vehicle, when the person's alcohol concentration is 0.08 or

more." The **Brown** court ultimately determined that Brown's mobility scooter was a wheelchair that did "not meet the definition of vehicle, because it is generally not a device in, upon, or by which any person or property is or may be transported upon a highway". Accordingly, because Brown's scooter was not a "vehicle," the court concluded that it was not a "motor vehicle," as that term is used in the DWI laws.

The **Brown** court's interpretation of the DWI statute applies equally to Segways. The DWI statutes do not define a "personal assistive mobility device." A Segway is a two-wheeled, self-balancing, battery-powered device designed for use in places a car or bicycle cannot go, including in buildings. Minn. Statute "does not include an electric personal assistive mobility device." In addition, the traffic regulations specifically provide that "a person operating an electric personal assistive mobility device has the rights and responsibilities of a pedestrian." While Segways can operate on bike paths, the statute restricts operation on roadways to very limited situations. Thus, Greenman's Segway does not meet the definition of "vehicle," because it is generally not a "device in, upon, or by which any person may be transported upon a highway." Accordingly, it is not a motor vehicle for purposes of a DWI criminal prosecution.

Because a Segway is not a motor vehicle within the meaning of the Code, the lower court properly dismissed the DWI charges.

SECTION 1.11
SULLIVAN V. ROBERTS

PROBLEM ONE—A

PARK, BROWN & SMITH, P.C.
ATTORNEYS AT LAW
MEMORANDUM

TO: All Law Clerks

FROM: Peter Smith, Esquire

RE: Kathy's Party

Joe and Estelle Roberts decided to celebrate their 25th wedding anniversary by spending the weekend at the New Jersey shore. After arriving at the Borgata Hotel and Casino and checking into their room, Joe called home to touch base with his 16-year-old daughter who was spending the evening at home studying for an exam. Much to his surprise, Kathy answered the phone in a jovial mood with music blaring in the background. She obviously did not expect her father to be calling. It turns out that Joe's daughter had invited some of her friends over to the house for a party.

Mr. Roberts had a fit when he learned that some of Kathy's guests included a young man in whom they did not have a high level of trust. After a brief argument, Joe told Kathy that she and her friends better behave and not get into any trouble. He then hung up in a foul mood, went to one of the casino's bars and ordered several stiff drinks to settle his nerves. Joe just hated these confrontations with his daughter.

At three o'clock in the morning, the phone in Joe and Estelle's hotel room rung and it was Kathy. She was crying and told her parents that they needed to come home immediately because something horrible had happened. It turns out that some additional high school friends, including Brian Sullivan, stopped over that night when they learned that Mr. and Mrs. Roberts were not home.

Joe has a rather large bar in the family room that was stocked with all sorts of exotic liquor from his restaurant. This bar is the focal point of the room and has a large number of neon signs that illuminate the area. It turns out that Brian raided the bar that night and became highly intoxicated. He then left around midnight in an impaired condition and was involved in a tragic accident a mere block from Joe's home that left the minor seriously injured. It turns out that Brian was speeding and smashed into a tree on the side of a road.

To make a long story short, Brian's parents have filed a lawsuit against Mr. and Mrs. Roberts and their daughter on behalf of their minor son, Brian.

Please read the following case and let me know if Kathy and her parents are liable for the injuries sustained by Brian Sullivan as the result of his consumption of liquor.

WOODWARD V. BREGMAN
788 A.2D 983 (SUPER. CT. PA. 2001)

Following Brian Winwood's consumption of alcoholic beverages at Appellees' home, Timothy Winwood died and Brian Winwood was injured in a single-car accident in which Brian was driving. The Winwoods, who were minors, were visiting Appellees' daughter along with several other minors. Appellees were not home at the time of the Winwoods' approximately 1½ hour visit, but had received notice that their daughter was entertaining her friends at the home, including one friend in whom Appellees did not have a high level of trust. Appellees kept liquor in an accessible area of their home. Brian consumed liquor from the Appellees' supply on the night in question. His driving was thus impaired, resulting in the tragic accident.

In **Congini v. Portersville Valve Co., 470 A.2d 515 (1983),** our Supreme Court established social host liability for an adult who "knowingly served" a minor intoxicants. In **Alumni Ass'n v. Sullivan, 572 A.2d 1209 (1990),** the Pennsylvania Supreme Court refused to extend the **Congini** standard to impute liability to an adult who "knew or should have known" alcohol was being served to a minor on the adult's property. Rather, the court found no social host liability where the defendant was not "involved in the planning of the event or the serving, supplying or the purchasing of the liquor.

The trial court determined Appellants failed to establish Appellees knowingly furnished alcohol to the minors in this case. We agree. Appellees' argument centers on the following assertion: "[Appellees], knowing that there was a substantial risk of consumption of alcohol, allowed a group of possibly untrustworthy minors to gather at their home without supervision and with unfettered access to alcohol." This argument, while purportedly based on the holding in **Alumni Ass'n,** is essentially an argument for the precise holding the Supreme Court rejected in that case. Appellants argue that Appellees should have known that unsupervised underage drinking would occur at their home. However, Appellants presented no evidence that Appellees agreed to an underage-drinking event at their home, much less planned one. Further, Appellants presented no evidence that Appellees purchased alcohol for the purpose of consumption by minors. There was evidence presented that Appellees purchased the alcohol, but no evidence it was purchased for this event, which is an implicit part of the **Alumni Ass'n** holding. Finally, Appellants presented no evidence that Appellees supplied alcohol to the minors, other than the perfectly mundane event of storing alcohol in their home in an unlocked area. For this activity, we will not attribute social host liability.

PROBLEM ONE—A
ANSWER SHEET

Name   **Please Print Clearly**

1. Are Mr. and Mrs. Roberts liable to Brian Sullivan under the theory of social host liability?

_____

_____

_____

_____

_____

_____

_____

2. Under the cases presented in Chapter One, is Kathy liable as a social host? After all, she is the one who had the party at her parent's home.

_____

_____

_____

_____

_____

_____

_____

_____

3. Should Mr. and Mrs. Roberts be held liable because they should have known that unsupervised children could or would drink the liquor in the game room?

_____

_____

_____

_____

_____

_____

_____

_____

_____

_____

_____

_____

_____

_____

_____

_____

_____

_____

There is one other Pennsylvania case worthy of examination in the development of liquor liability law in this state. The reader has learned that there is no liability for a social host who serves liquor to an adult guest who becomes intoxicated. That holding, however, changes and liability will be imposed if the social host knowingly serves liquor to a minor. This exception occurs because of the courts' desire to protect children since they are incompetent to handle its effects. What happens if a party is held at the house of a homeowner by a third party and that adult is present at the time that liquor is served to a minor? That is the issue in **Koller v. Rose.**

KOLLER V. ROSE
5 PA. D. & C. 5TH 464 (PA. COM. PL. 2008)

On the evening of October 14, 2005, a party was held at defendant Neely's house. While defendant Neely was present at the time, the party was hosted by her nephew, Roth Neely, to whom she leased the basement of her home. Among others in attendance at the party was the defendant, Damian Rose, a minor who consumed alcohol at the residence.

On his way home from the party, defendant Rose was involved in a car accident and struck the plaintiff, Terina Koller, a pedestrian. Plaintiff filed a complaint alleging, in part, that defendant Neely was negligent under the theory of social host liability.

Neely filed a motion for summary judgment alleging that there was no evidence that: (1) she knew a party was scheduled at her home; (2) she purchased, helped purchase, delivered, or distributed the beer which was consumed at the party; (3) she invited defendant Rose or any other individual to the party; or (4) she "knowingly furnished" alcoholic beverages to defendant Rose or any other individual at the party.

In **Congini v. Portersville Valve Company,** the Pennsylvania Supreme Court determined that a social host is negligent per se in serving alcohol to the point of intoxication to a person less than 21-years of age. In **Orner v. Mallick, 515 Pa. 132, 527 A.2d 521 (1987),** the court explained its decision in Congini:

> In arriving at this conclusion we emphasized that in Pennsylvania our legislature has made a legislative judgment that persons under 21 years of age are incompetent to handle alcohol; and we accepted that legislative judgment as defining a duty of care on the part of adults vis-à -vis their minor guests.

(Thus), the Supreme Court employed the standard of "knowingly" furnishing intoxicating beverages to minors.

The Third Circuit Court of Appeals elaborated upon the **Congini** standard in **Fassett v. Delta Kappa Epsilon, 807 F.2d 1150 (3d Cir. 1986).** The Third Circuit held that a defendant who "knowingly" allows his or her premises to be used for the purpose of serving alcohol to minors may be liable even if the alcohol was provided by another individual.

In the instant matter, a genuine question of fact exists as to defendant Neely's liability as a social host. Neither party disputes the fact that defendant Neely did not supply any alcohol for the underage party. However, she was admittedly present at the party. Numerous witnesses saw defendant Neely interact with the underage children while they were drinking alcohol. Witnesses testified that defendant Neely talked with the minors and watched as they poured beer from the kegs. Defendant Neely was even seen carrying a cup of beer at one point. Furthermore, while the party originated in the basement apartment, it spread to the back porch and surrounding yard, which is part of defendant Neely's property that is not solely inhabited by her nephew.

Therefore, sufficient evidence exists to support the jury's conclusion that defendant Neely actually knew of alcohol consumption by minors on her premises. On that basis, summary judgment is not appropriate in this case.

SECTION 1.12 CLASSIFICATIONS OF LAW

It is common knowledge that medicine has specialties such as radiology, gastroenterology and cardiology. The law is also broken down into subsets with the major classifications being public law and private law.

Public law involves the rights of society, and those rights are usually represented by a governmental agency. An example of public law is the crime of murder. This criminal offense affects the right of all members of society to be safe and secure, and the crime is prosecuted by the District Attorney or Federal Prosecutor. The primary categories of public law are criminal law, constitutional law and administrative law.

Private law, on the other hand, involves matters between individuals, such as the leasing of an apartment, a claim against a doctor for making a mistake during surgery, or purchasing a new car. These matters are personal between the parties to the transaction or incident. The major classifications of private law are contract law, tort law, property law, and family law and the remedy is usually money.

The following is a brief explanation of the categories of public and private law, many of which will be separate topics in this book:

- **Criminal law** deals with the violation of those duties that an individual owes to his or her community and the breach of which requires the offender to make satisfaction to the public. As a result, a crime is a violation of the rights of society and not the individual victim of the crime. This distinction is immediately apparent when the victim of a crime does not want to prosecute the suspect. A district attorney can force a victim to testify against the accused if there is a compelling societal interest, such as in cases of child or spousal abuse or rape. Since the government is responsible for taking action against a criminal defendant on behalf of society, the caption of the case contains the name of the governmental unit, such as the "United States," "The State," or "The People" versus the defendant.

- **Constitutional Law** obviously involves the United States Constitution, which is the most important legal document in American jurisprudence. It establishes the branches of the government, creates the fundamental rights of the people and protects them from unlawful governmental interference. The Constitution is purposely written in broad and often vague terms so that it can adapt to changing times. This concept is called **constitutional relativity** and insures that this legal document will maintain its vitality. How does this occur? The courts continually interpret and apply the Constitution to current issues. The body of the Constitution consists of seven **Articles** and twenty-seven **Amendments.** The framework of the document creates an intentional distribution of power. The first three Articles of the Constitution apportion the power to run the country among the legislative, executive, and judicial branches of the government. Article I empowers the legislature to make the laws which the executive branch enforces pursuant to the authority granted to the President in Article II. Article III designates the judiciary as the branch of the government that interprets the Constitution.

- **Administrative Law** governs those agencies created by the legislature to deal with specialized areas and has staffed the agencies with experts in the field. From a definition point of view an **administrative agency** is a "governmental body charged with administering and implementing particular legislation." Administrative agencies have greatly increased in number over the past several decades in order to effectuate general policy mandates of the legislative and executive branches of the government at the national, state, and local levels. These agencies are unique because they enjoy legislative, executive and judicial powers. As public agencies, they protect a public interest or sector instead of a private right or person.

- **Contract Law** deals with the exchange of promises voluntarily made by the parties, which agreement is enforceable in court. We enter into a variety of contracts every day. Because of their informal nature, we rarely think of these agreements as contracts. Buying gas, getting lunch, taking public transportation, or buying a newspaper are examples of agreements entered into by the parties that represent valid contracts.

- **Tort Law** involves those private or civil wrongs for which the court will award money damages. Torts are classified into the categories of negligence, intentional torts and products liability

- **Property law** deals with the rights and duties that arise out of the ownership or possession of real property and personal property. **Real property** includes land and the ground upon which the land is located

which are considered part of the realty. **Personal property** consists of all other property and would include a book, a car, money, or even a folding chair. In other words, personal property includes everything not attached to the land. Personal property is further subdivided into tangible and intangible property. **Tangible property** is a physical object, such as this textbook. **Intangible property,** on the other hand, is personal property that is not a physical object. The ownership of intangible property is usually evidenced by a legal document. Examples of such property include a patent, invention, a copyright for published material, or a trademark to identify a manufacturer or merchant's product.

- **Family law** encompasses the rights, duties, and obligations involving marriages, civil unions, **domestic partnerships,** divorce, custody, child support, paternity, and other family related issues. This category of private law is exclusively regulated by state law, whose rules and regulations vary from jurisdiction to jurisdiction.

- **Cyberlaw** describes the evolving area of law dealing with the tasks and transactions handled over the Internet and other digital networks.[10] In just a few decades, we have seen the Internet become a powerful platform that has changed the way society does business and the way people communicate. It has also provided a "globalized" dimension to the world and has become the main source of information for millions of people, at home, school, and work.[10] The problem is that the law has not had time to adapt to this changing world. Thus, the courts struggle to apply existing principles to the unique issues presented in this digital age, while Federal and state legislatures enact laws to deal with the difficulties involving the technology.

SECTION 1.13 CORPORATE GOVERNANCE

Corporate governance is a phrase that has received much discussion in recent years. It refers to the legal rules that deal with the structure and process for the control and management of companies. In other words, it concerns the relationships among the controlling and minority shareholders, other stakeholders, the Officers, and Board of Directors. Proper corporate governance fosters sustainable economic development by increasing the performance of companies and increasing their ability to generate outside capital.[11]

Corporate governance is premised on ideas such as managing the business with integrity and fairness, adhering to the laws, accountability towards the stakeholders, being transparent with regard to all transactions, making the necessary disclosures and decisions, and a commitment to transacting business in an ethical way. This concept also requires those in control of a business to separate personal and corporate funds while managing a company.[12]

Society enjoys a level of confidence with a business that is known to have good corporate governance. For example, an active and independent Board of Directors contributes a lot towards promoting confidence in the market. Corporate governance is known to be an important element that foreign institutional investors examine when deciding which firms are worthy of investment. It also has a positive influence on the value of stock in a company. Maintaining a positive image on the corporate governance front can also make it easier for business to secure capital at more reasonable costs. Unfortunately, corporate governance often becomes the focus of discussions only after the exposure of a scandal.[13]

SECTION 1.14 **THE DOG BITE CASE** **PROBLEM ONE-B**	**PARK, BROWN & SMITH, P.C** **ATTORNEYS AT LAW** **MEMORANDUM**

TO: All Law Clerks

FROM: Peter Smith, Esquire

RE: The Dog Attack

Joe Roberts saw a story in a magazine that catered to the sports bar trade about a breeder in St. Louis who trained dogs to play ball. This prompted Mr. Roberts to come up with a marketing idea for Tyler's Sports Bar and Grill. He would buy a puppy from the breeder who would then train the dog to play football. Joe's idea was to dress the dog in an Eagles uniform and allow the bar patrons to throw a football to the canine.

Joe bought the dog at a cost of $2,000 but had to wait months for delivery because the puppy had to be trained. The breeder worked diligently with the puppy and soon the dog was catching every football tossed his way. The dog was even taught to run with the ball to the end zone and toss the pigskin up in the air as a parody of a touchdown celebration. The dog became so proficient with this task that he could toss the ball about 20 feet into the air and catch it on the way down.

Joe took possession of the eighty pound animal which he named "Wentz" when it was 8 months old, and brought the dog to Tyler's each day dressed in Eagles green. Joe even constructed an end zone in one corner of the bar complete with a goal post and bleachers where patrons could sit and drink while watching sporting events on large screen televisions.

Wentz was an instant success. Joe sold replica NFL footballs at a tidy profit which purchases would entitle the patrons to toss the ball to the pooch who would then perform his end zone celebration. When Joe was finished, the pouch would even pick up the football and bring it back to the person who initially threw it.

Things were going smoothly until a Monday Night Football game involving the Eagles and Redskins. This was also the first time the dog was asked to perform late at night and the pouch seemed out of sorts from the commotion.

In any event, Wentz was busy from the moment the game started and fans lined up to toss balls to the dog. By half time, Wentz had retrieved more than 100 footballs and was exhausted. Unfortunately, the next toss did him in. Wentz retrieved the thrown ball in the end zone but was way off target when he tossed it into the air as part of his end zone celebration. The errant ball landed in the end zone bleachers so Wentz dutifully ran after the ball to retrieve it. He jumped over the bleacher wall and landed on the lap of Ira Roseman causing everything to go flying including a cup of hot coffee which scalded the patron. When the customer screamed from being burned, Wentz became frightened and bit the customer.

Tyler's Sports Bar and Grill has been sued by Mr. Roseman and we have been asked to defend the bar. I have located the attached case which is the closest thing I could find to fit our fact pattern. Please read the case and let me know if Tyler's is liable to Mr. Roseman.

SWANSON V. TACKLING
335 GA. APP. 810 (CT. APP. GA. 2016)

The evidence shows that on April 26, 2012, Julia Tackling traveled with her seven-year-old son, J.R., and her then-boyfriend, Matthew Day, to spend a weekend with the Swansons, who are Day's mother and stepfather. Day's mother greeted them upon their arrival and introduced them to the Swansons' great danes, Gussy and Willow, who were "gated off" in another room. While Gussy sniffed J.R. and "seemed to be fine," Willow put her head over the gate "pretty close" to J.R. and "barked directly in his face." Willow's conduct made Tackling uncomfortable, and when they went to their bedroom for the evening, she told Day that she "did not want Willow loose around J.R. at any given time."

The next morning, Julia and J.R. went to the store to buy doughnuts for breakfast. While at the store, Julia purchased stuffed bunnies for the dogs because Willow "loved stuffed animals." After breakfast, J.R. asked Julia if he could give Willow one of the bunnies, and Julia let Willow into the sunroom where J.R. was holding the bunny under his arm. As soon as Willow came into the sunroom, she approached J.R. and, in an attempt to retrieve the bunny, bit his arm. When J.R. began to scream and cry, Willow also bit him on the head. This entire incident happened in a matter of seconds. Julia rushed J.R. to the hospital, where he was treated for his injuries. Tackling asserts that J.R.'s "serious and permanently disfiguring injuries" resulted from the defendants "failure to maintain proper control over Willow as required by law, and that this failure occurred despite their knowledge of the dog's vicious propensities. The Swansons moved for summary judgment, arguing that they could not be held liable for J.R.'s injuries because it was undisputed that, prior to the incident with J.R., Willow had never displayed any vicious tendencies. We agree.

In a typical dog bite case, a plaintiff must produce evidence of the vicious propensity of the dog in order to show that the owner had superior knowledge of the danger. Further, to infer the requisite knowledge, there "must be at least one incident that would cause a prudent person to anticipate the actual incident that caused the injury." And although a dog owner "need not be aware of the dog's propensity to do the exact same act that caused the injury at issue," the prior incident must be the same type as the incident at issue. Lastly, it is well settled that "a dog's menacing behavior alone does not demonstrate its vicious propensity or place its owner on notice of such propensity."

In the case, there is no evidence of a prior incident in which Willow exhibited behavior even remotely similar to biting, attacking, or otherwise

injuring a person. In fact, the Swansons' testimony was that prior to biting J.R., Willow had never bitten, chased, jumped on, nipped at, or even growled at anyone. Additionally, Dave testified that before this incident, he would have allowed Willow to be around small children, and that he "never would have expected Willow to bite a kid." While Willow barked in J.R.'s face when he arrived at the Swanson's' home, such behavior is insufficient to put the Swansons on notice that the dog would later attack and bite him.

Tackling argues that the Swansons were on notice of Willow's propensity to attack a child merely because she was protective of her toys and would "go after" them. But as previously noted, the law requires Tackling to offer evidence of a prior incident that is of the same type as the incident at issue. This, she has not done. Moreover, the undisputed evidence was that Willow went after or fetched her toys in a playful manner only if someone threw them. Suffice it to say, playing fetch bears no similarity to the act of biting someone.

In sum, Tackling has identified no evidence that Willow had ever bitten or attempted to bite anyone before, that she had a tendency to attack humans, or that the Swanson's otherwise had previous knowledge about her temperament that would have placed them on notice that she could bite someone. Thus, while we have the greatest sympathy for the injuries suffered by J.R., the trial court erred in denying the Swanson's motion for summary judgment dismissing the case.

PROBLEM ONE—B
ANSWER SHEET

Name   **Please Print Clearly**

1. Is the bar liable for the dog's actions in jumping into the stands and injuring Mr. Roseman?

_____

_____

_____

_____

_____

_____

_____

2. Is it a defense that the dog was not vicious and never bit anyone before?

_____

_____

_____

_____

_____

_____

_____

3. Does it matter that this was the first time the dog went into the end zone stand to retrieve the ball? Please explain.

_____

_____

_____

_____

_____

_____

_____

_____

_____

_____

_____

_____

_____

_____

_____

_____

SECTION 1.15
LEGAL RESEARCH[15]

The ability to do legal research can be a very helpful skill. While this type of research may seem intimidating, it can also become an intellectually rewarding experience once a person gets the hang of it. However, like other complex skills, it requires a basic understanding of the key resources and strategies which will enable a student to find the answers with the least amount of time and frustration.

Courts follow precedent so a judge will usually resolve a dispute in the same manner that previous courts within that jurisdiction have decided similar cases. The basic aim in conducting legal research, therefore, is to find a recorded instance of a suit that is similar to the matter of interest. This type of case is referred to as being "on point" or "on all fours" with the issue of the research. But a case is only on point if it is similar in relevant facts. Therefore, it is crucial to fully understand which facts are relevant, and which legal issues need to be answered.

Legal issues are the questions that must be decided by a court to resolve a particular conflict. In identifying these issues, the best starting point is to ask: what are the plaintiff's specific problems that bring this litigant to court in the first place? What is the person trying to achieve?

Once a person understands the facts and legal issues, the reader is ready to begin the assignment. This may require a trip to the law library. These facilities can seem intimidating at first but they become much less so once the researcher understands that publications fall into two basic categories; 1) primary sources and 2) secondary sources.

A **primary source** is the written law itself. These consist of the cases, statutes and legal decisions which can govern the fact pattern that a person is researching. Primary sources then fall into two subcategories, binding authority and persuasive authority. **Binding authority** is the writings which collectively form the law in the jurisdiction on a given subject. This would occur when the researcher finds a case in Pennsylvania exactly on point with the fact pattern of the problem that occurred in the Commonwealth. Finding these sources is the ultimate goal of most legal research. **Persuasive authority** is the law from other jurisdictions. For instance, a person conducting research on an issue under Pennsylvania law may find a case on point in New Jersey. While the New Jersey case will not govern the issue that the person is researching, it can give a better understanding of that law and may be helpful in swaying a Pennsylvania court to rule a certain way when the authority in the jurisdiction being studied leaves an issue open to question.

Secondary sources basically consist of all other writings on the law, including such things as law review articles, **treaties,** restatements, digests, and encyclopedias. While these are not the law or binding precedent, they are extremely useful tools for finding and understanding the law, and are usually a good place to start legal research. The following are examples of secondary sources:

A. Legal Dictionaries

The law is filled with unusual words and phrases which have a unique meaning in the legal world. The reader may feel that he or she can understand these phrases, but a **legal dictionary** is often a good place to make sure the meaning is right. While the easiest way to define terms may be through on-line legal dictionaries, such as those found at sites like Law.com (http://dictionary.law.com), the legal dictionaries available in the law library or bookstore are usually considered more authoritative.

B. Encyclopedias

Legal Encyclopedias are a good starting point for gaining a broad understanding of a legal issue. Some of these books are heavily annotated, meaning they provide lists of other sources that the reader will want to further consult. These annotations may lead directly to key primary sources on a given topic, or may list the main cases which other sources are likely to reference.

Encyclopedias are usually available for each state. For instance, Pennsylvania maintains two such sources; the *Pennsylvania Legal Encyclopedia and Summary of Pennsylvania Jurisprudence 2d*. In addition, there are also two national level encyclopedias; *Corpus Juris Secundum* (C.J.S.) and *American Jurisprudence 2d* (Am.Jur.2d). These books are arranged alphabetically by topic, so the researcher should start by looking for the topic in the index, which will then list more specific sub-topics along with the sections in which they can be found. Keep in mind that index lists subjects by their "section number" (abbreviated as §) rather than their page number. The section number will be found at the top of a page after the symbol, §, while the page number is usually at the bottom.

C. Form Books

Courts can be picky about the format of legal documents that they will accept for filing. They often require a standardized form and specific information to help manage their dockets. In addition, drafting a contract or agreement can be a daunting task. In this regard, most states have at least one set of form manuals, which will provide a brief discussion of the issues involved in drafting the document along with one or more examples of the necessary form. For instance, Pennsylvania lawyers and paralegals use the multi-volume book, Pennsylvania Transaction Guide, to draft a variety of legal documents. The co-editor of this book is Joseph Bongiovanni, an instructor in the Department of Legal Studies at Temple University.

D. Legal Periodicals

Most **legal periodicals** are published by bar associations or legal magazines, and generally come out on a monthly or bi-monthly basis. Aside from the American Bar Association Journal, most state law associations have their own journals. These periodicals discuss cutting edge issues that are of broad concern to the legal community. Still, other periodicals deal with more specialized topics specific to different types of legal practice, such as tax or litigation. These journals can usually be found at the reference desk of the law library. An example of this type of publication is the Pennsylvania Bar Quarterly.

E. Law Review Articles

Law review articles are usually published by law schools and provide very in-depth discussion of specific legal issues or important cases and statutes. While they are often written by law students, judges and attorneys may also contribute articles and they can form important contributions to the development of legal theory. Law review articles can be very helpful if the researcher knows little about an issue.

It sometimes makes sense to just take the assertions of an article at face value and not bother to review the footnotes. However, this should not be done when reading a law review article because the researcher would miss out on what's often the most valuable part. Law review articles are only written after extensive research. The footnotes will generally not be restricted to cases within a specific jurisdiction so they can still be helpful in finding cases from any jurisdiction.

F. Treatises

A **treatise** is dedicated to a single topic or area of law and describes the law in basic succinct paragraphs, often referred to as "black letter law." For instance, Prosser on Torts discusses legal issues common to tort law, such as negligence and proximate cause, while *Ohlbaum* on Evidence explains the basic rules of evidence in Pennsylvania. Treatises can be a good starting point for a very general discussion of the law on a given topic.

G. Restatements

Restatements are considered a form of treatise. They distill the rules of the common law as they have developed through numerous cases. Restatements explain that law in relatively simple paragraphs which cite to a wide variety of cases of the issue. While Restatements are a secondary source, and are not considered the law, some of these publications, such as the *Second Restatement of Torts,* are so influential that sections of them have been widely adopted by the courts as accurate statements of the law within that jurisdiction.

H. Digests

Digests are compilations that list the primary sources of case law by topic. Topics are listed alphabetically. Digests are available by state, region and court. Often the most useful digests are published by case law reporters, such as the West Case Law Reporter. To use one of these books you look up the topic in the index and find its "key number," then look up that number in the digest. The digest itself provides a list of cases dealing with that topic or issue, which in turn will lead the reader to relevant cases under the same number within the Case Law Reporter itself.

As for the very important primary sources of the law, these can be divided into two categories; case law or judge made law and statutory law or law made by the legislature.

1. Case Law

Case law refers to the written decisions issued by judges. When courts decide a case, the judges will often record a written "opinion" which recites the facts of the dispute, states the legal outcome and explains the court's reasoning. When a court with authority to establish precedent, such the United States Supreme Court, applies a legal rule to the facts, then the case forms a "holding." Under the rules of stare decisis, that holding will dictate the result in future cases within that jurisdiction that contain similar facts.

Many cases will be similar to the facts you are researching in some respects and different in others. The degree to which the relevant facts are similar to the issue being researched determines how much the case is "on-point" and how much force it will have under stare decisis for resolving the legal question at issue. In order to tell how "on-point", or relevant the case being examined is, it is a good idea to make a list of the similarities and differences between the case and the facts of a person's research. Such a list might look like the following:

Facts	**Client's Case**	**Published Case**
Similarities		
Differences		
Unknown		

This chart will allow a person to easily compare the cases. If there are many similarities and few differences, then it is more likely that the case is on-point. Keep in mind, however, that even one major difference can easily result in a case being "distinguished" from the case that the reader is concerned with. So once you notice a difference between the published case and the issue being researched, make sure that you go back and carefully re-read the case to see how much weight the court gave to that different fact in reaching its conclusion. If the outcome of the case seemed to hinge on the one fact which is unlike your own case, then this case is most likely distinguishable and may be of little help.

Cases are collected in large volumes of books known as reporters. Most cases are reported in two reporters known as **Westlaw** and **LEXIS.** These are enormous computerized databases which offer the most efficient way to access a case, or allow a person to search for specific words, terms and phrases within the case itself. However, these databases can only be accessed with an account. For instance, some Universities make available to students LEXIS/NEXIS, whose databank contains a partial listing of court cases on a topic.

Cases are also published in written form by several different publishers and the same case may be found in multiple books. The larger states, such as Pennsylvania, New York, California, Florida and Texas publish their own state's appellate decisions in volumes known as the official reporters. Courts at each level within a state may also publish their decisions in simple, chronological order in an official case reporter for that specific court. Other states have arranged for private publishing companies, such as West, to publish their cases in the appropriate regional reporter.

In addition to the written case reporters, many websites compile their own unofficial reporters, which can be accessed for free on the internet. One of the most widely used of these is FindLaw.com (available at www.findlaw.com/casecode), but others can be retrieved by going to an internet browser and typing in terms like "case law."

Cases decided by federal courts are compiled in their own federal reporters. The decisions of the federal district court will be published in the Federal Supplement and federal appellate decisions can be found in the Federal Reporter. The Supreme Court of the United States has its own opinions published in several different resources, such as the official United States Reports, the Supreme Court Reporter, which is an unofficial publication but provides editorial comments, and the Supreme Court Lawyers Edition, which is another unofficial version that provides further editorial comments.

2. Statutory Law

Statutes, also referred to as Codes, are statements of the law passed by the legislative body of a given jurisdiction. After the federal and state constitutions, statutes are the highest expression of law within a jurisdiction. This means that if a statute directly contradicts a common law rule, then the statute trumps the case law unless deemed unconstitutional. Because statutes are often very complicated, legislators rely on the courts to interpret the statutes and flesh out their hidden meanings.

Federal statutes are passed by the United States Congress, while state statutes are passed by the state legislatures. Federal statutory law is found in the United States Code, while the statutory law of different states is found in individual state codes. Statutes are also grouped together by subject matter and organized into "Titles" or "Chapters" devoted to different subjects, which are then further subdivided into section numbers.

The following is an example of a simple Pennsylvania statute on theft.

Title 18:   Crimes and Offenses

Article C: Offenses Against Property

Chapter 39:   Theft and Related Offenses

Section 3921:   Theft by Unlawful Taking or Disposition

(a) MOVABLE PROPERTY—A person is guilty of theft if he unlawfully takes, or exercises unlawful control over movable property of another with intent to deprive him thereof.

The citation for this statute is written as 18 Pa.C.S. §3921(a) (2009), which indicates that the law is found in Title 18 of the Pennsylvania Consolidated Statutes, at Section 3921, paragraph (a), which is still in force as of 2009.

Statutes are often amended or updated by the legislature, so one cannot automatically assume that the statute in the book is the current law. To ascertain if the law is "current," the reader must check the "pocket part" for this volume of the code. The pocket part is a supplemental booklet which is inserted at the very end of the volume. Because they are removable, pocket parts can be replaced on a yearly or even quarterly basis so that the law in the volume is always kept up to date. Once the researcher finds the appropriate statute, he or she must examine the back of the volume and look up the same section in the pocket part for any changes in the law.

To decide whether the statute applies to the facts of a case, it's best to break the law down into its basic "elements" and write these out as a set of steps, which are necessary pre-conditions required for the statute to apply. The following is a break-down of the elements present in the above statute:

A person is guilty of theft if he or she:

1) unlawfully takes, or exercises unlawful control,

2) over movable property,

3) when that property belongs to another, and

4) the person who takes it intends to deprive the other of such property

Every one of these elements must be present in the facts in order for this statute to apply. Thus, if the person has taken the property of another on a temporary basis with the intent to return it, the criminal has not committed theft under this section of the code.

The most useful codes for legal research are those which are annotated. These annotations contain case references which interpret the section of the code the researcher is examining. Cases are important because they not only demonstrate the application of the statute to given fact patterns, but they will often explain the law's meaning in language that is much easier to understand. Under the doctrine of stare decisis, once the statute is interpreted in a particular way by an appellate court, the lower courts within the jurisdiction are bound to follow that interpretation.

3. Legal Research on the Internet

The Internet has become a major source of information, communication, and even entertainment for people all over the world. Materials on a variety of subjects can be accessed at the touch of a key, including law-related topics. Court decisions, law review articles, and legislation are now instantly accessible.

A good start for legal research on the Internet is to visit a law-oriented directory or search engine. These resources can help you find subjects from different types of law to specific cases, legal news, and even U.S. Government sites. Several specific legal research sites are:

- **www.lawcrawler.com**
  Lawcrawler is a legal search engine that is powered by Alta Vista and allows for a comprehensive legal search on the topic of your choice.

- **www.findlaw.com**
  Findlaw is a legal subject index.

- **www.hg.org**

  Hieros Games has information on legal organizations, including every government in the world. This is a good research tool for those interested in practicing law.

- **www.ilrg.com**

  Internet Legal Resource Guide is a categorized index of over 3,100 select websites in 238 nations, islands, and territories.

- **www.nolo.com**

  Legal Encyclopedia is a self-help center on the Internet.

- **www.lawguru.com**

  This useful tool contains answers to frequently asked legal questions and has many interesting links.

- **www.lectlaw.com**

  The *Lectric Law Library* contains practical links such as "Legal help for the poor" and "How to fight your traffic ticket."

- **www.legis.state.pa.us**

  This website allows access to information from the Pennsylvania legislature, including the text of bills and the history of the legislation.

- **www.fedworld.gov**

  This site provides access to the search engine of the federal government.

- **www.lawoffice.com**

  West Publications has created this link to allow the public to gain access to the profiles of law firms and attorneys around the country.

- **www.aclu.org**

  This is the official site for the American Civil Liberties Union and offers information on civil liberty controversies, such as LGBT and women's rights.

- **www.uslaw.com**

  This comprehensive site covers all aspects of the legal field, including articles, current events, and chat rooms where you can submit questions to be answered by attorneys.

- **www.megalaw.com**

  This site discusses recent legal developments in the news and provides access to information in different legal fields, as well as information on state and federal court decisions.

- **www.itslegal.com**
  This site provides links to different legal topics, including real estate law, personal injury, credit and debt issues, family law, and employment law.

- **www.law.indiana.edu/v-lib**
  Indiana University School of Law-Bloomington's virtual law library allows searches about the legal field and provides links relating to the search.

- **www.law.com**
  The law.com connection features law-related articles and stories; summaries from local, state, and federal court decisions; law links, and other legal information.

- **www.prairielaw.com**
  Through articles, columns, and online discussions, this site offers information about the law including consumer concerns, crime, immigration and work related issues.

Now it's time to try one of these legal research tools. The Steven Spielberg movie, *Amistad,* is based upon an actual United States Supreme Court decision that decided the fate of African slaves who staged a shipboard revolt off the cost of Cuba, in an attempt to gain their freedom. The slaves ended up in America, but Spain demanded their return in order to face criminal prosecution for the uprising. American abolitionists became involved in the frey and the matter ended up in the courts. In a landmark decision, our highest court established the principle that all people are "presumptively free" and entitled to the protections of American law. This holding granted the African slaves the freedom they desired in order to return to their homeland. The Amistad, 40 U.S. 518 (1841). If you wish to read the case or learn more about the story, you merely have to access the Internet. If you submit the term Amistad to a search engine, it will take you to a variety of stories and references on the topic. You can also access www.findlaw. com which will take you to the home page of Find Law, whose research engine scans court cases and other legal information on most legal topics. Go to the box marked Supreme Court and click on it. The Supreme Court decision in the Amistad case should be visible when the page opens. You may also gain access to the case by typing "40 U.S. 518" in the appropriate box.

More and more courts are placing their dockets and other court related information on the Internet. For instance, a person can access the records of the Philadelphia Court of Common Pleas by going to http://courts.phila.gov. Depending on the search, one may check the dockets of a specific case, conduct a judgment search involving a specific person, or conduct a litigation search involving a person's name.

FOR GENERAL INFORMATION ON THE INTERNET

- **http://info.isoc.org/guest/zakon/Internet/History/HIT.html**
  Hobbs' Internet Timeline provides information about the Internet, the people who use it, and online culture.

- **www.columbia.edu/~hauben/netbook**
  Netizens: On the history and Impact of Usenet and the Internet—this site contains a collection of essays about the history, nature, and impact of the Internet.

- **http://home.netscape.com/eng/mozilla/3.0/handbook**
  The *Navigator Handbook Online* provides detailed information on how to use netscape navigator.

SECTION 1.16
INTERNET RESEARCH

PARK, BROWN & SMITH, P.C.
ATTORNEYS AT LAW
MEMORANDUM

PROBLEM ONE—C

To: All Law Clerks

FROM: Peter Smith, Esquire

RE: Internet Research on Bite Mark Identification

Park, Brown and Smith, P.C. has been consulted about representing a defendant who was convicted of first degree murder on the basis of a bite mark identification. The government called a dentist at trial, who testified that the wound found on the victim's buttocks, was consistent with a human bite mark that was made by the defendant's teeth. I have a hard time believing that this conclusion is accurate so I need research done on bite mark identification and whether it is a valid science.

Please research the topic on the internet. I want to learn if there are any articles on the scientific validity of bite mark evidence at a criminal trial. Have any organizations or courts expressed an opinion on the topic? Let me know the results of your internet research and provide me with an explanation as to how you uncovered the information. Please print out two of your resources and attach the first page of each site to this assignment.

PROBLEM ONE—C
ANSWER SHEET

Name _____ **Please Print Clearly**

1. Does the Internet have any resources on the topic of bite mark identification? If so, please list and describe 6 of the resources.

_____

_____

_____

_____

_____

_____

_____

_____

2. Please explain how you found these resources. How many resources were there on the validity of bite mark identification?

_____

_____

_____

_____

_____

_____

_____

_____

3. Please print out two of these references and attach the first printed page of each site to this answer.

_____

_____

_____

_____

_____

_____

_____

_____

_____

_____

_____

_____

_____

_____

_____

_____

_____

SECTION 1.17
THE FELDMAN WILL
ALTERNATE PROBLEM

PROBLEM ONE—D

PARK, BROWN & SMITH, P.C.
ATTORNEYS AT LAW
MEMORANDUM

TO: All Law Clerks

FROM: Peter Smith, Esquire

RE: The Feldman Will

Park, Brown & Smith, P.C. has been consulted by Jessie Felman, whose mother died after a five year struggle with cancer. During this time, her mother was in good mental health and capable of making informed decisions about her every day activities. Nevertheless, Jessie cared for her mother over the years by feeding and housing her, providing baths, taking her to doctor's appointments, dispensing the appropriate medicines, and providing other care. The client sacrificed her full-time career as an accountant; instead working part-time as a store clerk so she could make time to manage her mother's doctor appointments and other needs. Jessie said her mother told her last year that she was happy to have Jessie for a daughter and planned to write a will so that the client inherited the mother's estate. In fact, Jessie has a typed email from her mother dated January 5, 2018 which states:

> *Dear Jessie,*
>
> *I love you so much, my darling daughter! I plan to leave you my entire estate and all my money when I die.*
>
> > *Love,*
> > *Mom*

However, in a will that Mrs. Feldman's lawyer prepared shortly before her death, the decedent left her entire estate to her next door neighbor, Elma, whom the mother had known for a year and only spent time with the neighbor on two or three occasions. The will specifically stated: "I lied to my daughter. She is weak and needs to stop doing so much for other people. I don't care that she has taken care of me – I leave all my estate and money to my new friend, Elma."

Please read **In re: Estate of Kuralt** and answer the following questions:

1. Should Jessie receive the property from the mother's estate instead of Elma?

2. Does it matter that Elma did not care for or help the mother in any way, or should Jessie receive the property despite the will written by the lawyer since she did so much to care for her mother?

3. Did status and process play any part in the **In re: Estate of Charles Kuralt** decision? Explain your answer.

IN RE: ESTATE OF KURALT
2000 MONT. 359 (S. CT. MONT. 2000)

Charles Kuralt and Elizabeth Shannon maintained a long term and intimate personal relationship. Kuralt and Patricia Shannon desired to keep their relationship secret, and were successful in doing so that even though Kuralt's wife, Petie, who knew that Kuralt owned property in Montana, was unaware prior to Kuralt's untimely death, of his relationship with Shannon.

Over the nearly 30-year course of their relationship, Kuralt and Shannon saw each other regularly and maintained contact by phone and mail. Kuralt was the primary source of financial support for Shannon and established close, personal relationships with Shannon's three children. Kuralt provided financial support for a joint business venture managed by Shannon and transferred a home in Ireland to Shannon as a gift.

In 1985, Kuralt purchased a 20-acre parcel of property along the Big Hole River in Madison County, Montana. Kuralt and Shannon constructed a cabin on this 20-acre parcel. In 1987, Kuralt purchased two additional parcels along the Big Hole River which adjoined the original 20-acre parcel. These two additional parcels, one upstream and one downstream of the cabin created a parcel of approximately 90 acres and are the primary subject of this appeal.

On May 3, 1989, Kuralt executed a handwritten will which stated:

> "In the event of my death, I bequeath to Patricia Elizabeth Shannon all my interest in land, buildings, furnishings and personal belongings in Big Hole River, Montana."
>
> Charles Kuralt

Although Kuralt mailed a copy of this handwritten will to Shannon, he subsequently executed a formal will on May 4, 1994, in New York City. This Last Will and Testament, prepared with the assistance of counsel, does not specifically mention any of the real property owned by Kuralt. The beneficiaries of Kuralt's Last Will and Testament were his wife, Petie, and the Kuralts' two children. Neither Shannon nor her children are named as beneficiaries in Kuralt's formal will. Shannon had no knowledge of the formal will until the commencement of these proceedings. On April 9, 1997, Kuralt deeded his interest in the original 20-acre parcel with the cabin to Shannon. The transaction was disguised as a sale. However, Kuralt supplied the "purchase" price for the 20-acre parcel to Shannon prior to the transfer. After the deed to the 20-acre parcel was filed, Shannon sent Kuralt, at his request, a blank buy-sell real estate form so that the remaining 90 acres along the Big Hole could be conveyed to Shannon in a similar manner. Apparently, it was again Kuralt's intention to provide the purchase price. The second transaction was to take place in September 1997 when Shannon, her son, and Kuralt agreed to meet at the Montana cabin.

Kuralt, however, became suddenly ill and entered a New York hospital on June 18, 1997. On that same date, Kuralt wrote the letter to Shannon which is now at the center of the current dispute:

> "Dear Pat-
>
> Something is terribly wrong with me and they can't figure out what. After cat-scans and a variety of cardiograms, they agree it's not lung cancer or heart trouble or blood clot. So they're putting me in the

hospital today to concentrate on infectious diseases. I am getting worse, barely able to get out of bed, but still have high hopes for recovery … if only I can get a diagnosis! I'll keep you informed. I'll have the lawyer visit the hospital to be sure you inherit the rest of the place in Montana if it comes to that.

I send love to you & your daughter, Shannon. Hope things are better there!

Love,
C."

Enclosed with this letter were two checks made payable to Shannon. Kuralt did not seek the assistance of an attorney to devise the remaining 90 acres of the Big Hole land to Shannon. Therefore, when Kuralt died unexpectedly, Shannon sought to probate the letter of June 18, 1997, as a valid handwritten codicil or amendment to Kuralt's formal 1994 will.

The Estate contends that the lower court made legal errors which led to a mistaken conclusion about Kuralt's intent concerning the disposition of his Montana property. The Estate argues that the lower court failed to recognize the legal effect of the 1994 will, and, therefore, erroneously found that Kuralt, after his May 3, 1989 holographic will, had an uninterrupted intent to transfer the Montana property to Shannon. The Estate further argued that Kuralt's 1994 formal will revoked all prior wills. This manifest change of intention, according to the Estate, should have led the lower court to the conclusion that Kuralt did not intend to transfer the Montana property to Shannon upon his death.

Montana courts are guided by the bedrock principle of honoring the intent of the testator. *See* **In re Estate of Irvine** (1943), 114 Mont. 577. The June 18, 1997 letter expressed Kuralt's intent to affect a posthumous transfer of his Montana property to Shannon. Kuralt and Shannon enjoyed a long, close personal relationship which continued up to the last letter Kuralt wrote Shannon on June 18, 1997, in which he enclosed the checks to her. Likewise, Kuralt and Shannon's children had a long, family-like relationship which included significant financial support.

The lower court focused on the last few months of Kuralt's life to find that the letter demonstrated his testamentary intent. The conveyance of the 20-acre parcel for no real consideration and extrinsic evidence that Kuralt intended to convey the remainder of the Montana property to Shannon in a similar fashion provides substantial factual support for the lower court's determination that Kuralt intended that Shannon have the rest of the Montana property.

The June 18, 1997 letter expressed Kuralt's desire that Shannon inherit the remainder of the Montana property. That Kuralt wrote the letter *in extremis* is supported by the fact that he died two weeks later. Although Kuralt intended to transfer the remaining land to Shannon, he was reluctant to consult a lawyer to formalize his intent because he wanted to keep their relationship secret. Finally, the use of the term "inherit" underlined by Kuralt reflected his intention to make a posthumous disposition of the property. Accordingly, we conclude that the letter dated June 18, 1997 expressed a present testamentary intent to transfer property in Madison County to Patricia Shannon.

PROBLEM ONE—D
ANSWER SHEET

Name   **Please Print Clearly**

1. Should Jessie receive the property from the mother's estate instead of Elma?

_____

_____

_____

_____

_____

_____

_____

2. Does it matter that Elma did not care for or help the decedent in any way, or should Jessie receive the property despite the will written by the lawyer since she did so much to care for her mother?

_____

_____

_____

_____

_____

_____

_____

3. Did status and process play any part in the **In re: Estate of Charles Kuralt** decision? Explain your answer.

_____

_____

_____

_____

_____

_____

_____

_____

_____

_____

_____

_____

_____

_____

_____

_____

_____

_____

1. A 16-year-old went to a local car dealer in order to purchase an automobile. When the salesman learned of the customer's age, he refused to sell the car unless the purchase was made by an adult. A few hours later, the minor returned with an adult that the child had just met. The salesman sold the car to the adult and then assisted the buyer in having the title transferred to the youth. A few days later, the 16-year-old returned with his father and attempted to rescind the contract. Will the car dealer be required to take the automobile back and return the money? **Quality Motors, Inc. v. Johnny Hayes, 225 S. W. 2d 326 (Ark. 1949).**

2. The mother of a mentally challenged female was concerned that her 15-year-old daughter would become pregnant without understanding the consequences. The mother filed a "Petition To Have A Tubaligation Performed On A Minor" with the court. Although there was no legal authority for the court to order the sterilization, the judge felt that the procedure would be in the best interest of the child in order "to prevent unfortunate circumstances…" The child was taken to the hospital under the pretext of having her appendix removed, and the tubaligation was performed. Several years later, the child married and attempted to become pregnant. At this time, she learned that she had been sterilized. As a result of her inability to have children, she sued the judge, claiming that he violated her constitutional rights. Under the concept of status and process, will the judge be immuned from suit for his actions? **Judge Harold Strump v. Linda Sparkman, 435 U.S. 349 (1978).**

3. The parties to a lawsuit attended a settlement conference before the trial judge. During a break, the judge confronted the plaintiff in the hallway, and in a loud, angry voice, yelled at the plaintiff that his settlement demand was "Bull- - - -", and if he thought that there was money in the case, the plaintiff had "s- - - for brains!" The judge then told counsel for the plaintiff that the client "had to deal with him and now he was their enemy." Sometime later, the judge was interviewed by a reporter about the incident and denied that he had acted improperly, despite the plaintiff's allegation. This made it appear as though the plaintiff was lying. Subsequently, the plaintiff filed suit against Judge Williams for his improper conduct. Will the judge enjoy immunity for his actions, or should he be held responsible for the outbursts? Do you see a difference between the statements that the judge made during the settlement conference as opposed to those he made to the reporter? **Robert Soliz v. Alexander Williams, III, 74 Cal. App. 4th 577 (1999).**

4. Charles Kuralt, the former "On The Road" correspondent with CBS, maintained a longtime and intimate relationship with Elizabeth Shannon. This relationship was kept secret because Kuralt was married; Kuralt was the primary source of financial support for Shannon at the time. In 1989, the television personality sent Ms. Shannon a letter indicating that in the event of his death, he wanted her to own the property in Montana which was used as their retreat. In 1994, Kuralt executed a will naming his wife and children as the beneficiaries of his Estate. The will said nothing about the Montana property. In 1997, Kuralt decided to transfer the property to Shannon. The transaction was disguised as a sale, but it was Kuralt's intention to give Shannon the money for the transfer. Prior to the completion of the sale, Kuralt become critically ill. While in the hospital, he wrote a letter to Shannon and enclosed a check to complete the transfer with a notation that it was his intent for her to inherit the Montana property. Before the transfer could take place, Kuralt died. Subsequently, conflicting claims were made against the Montana property by both Kuralt's family and Ms. Shannon. Who do you believe is entitled to the property? Does status and process play any part in your decision? **In re: The Estate of Charles Kuralt, 2000 Mont. LEXIS 375 (2000).**

Footnotes:

1. Philosophy of Law 2012, Http://People.Brandeis.Edu/~Teuber/Lawintro.Html#Intro1, (last visited October 10, 2013).

2. The Common Law and Civil Law Traditions, The Robbins Collection, School of Law, University of California at Berkley, http://www.law.berkeley.edu/library/robbins/CommonLawCivilLawTraditions.html (last visited September 20, 2013).

3. *Id.*

4. *Id.*

5. Common Law vs Statutory Law, Diffen, http://www.diffen.com/difference/Common_Law_vs_Statutory_Law (last visited September 20, 2013).

6. Driving Under the Influence, The Free Dictionary by Farlex.

7. Samuel D. Hodge, Jr. and Connor Lacey, *Inhalants: What to Know About the Science and the Legal Implications*, The Practical Lawyer, Vol. 62, No. 5, October 2016, page 46.

8. **State v. Boreaux, 710 N.W.2d 169 (S.D. 2006).**

9. Segway PT, Wikipedia, http://en.wikipedia.org/wiki/Segway_PT (last visited October 6, 2013).

10. What is FOIA?, FOIA.gov, http://www.foia.gov/about.html (last visited October 6, 2013).

11. Cyberlaw, BusinessDictionary.com, http://www.businessdictionary.com/definition/cyberlaw.html (last visited September 20, 2013).

12. Internet Growth Statistics, Internet World Stats, http://www.internetworldstats.com/emarketing.htm (last visited September 20, 2013).

13. Corporate Governance, International Finance Corporation, http://www.ifc.org/wps/wcm/connect/Topics_Ext_Content/IFC_External_Corporate_Site/Corporate+Governance (last visited September 20, 2013).

14. Lisa Mary Thomson, What is Corporate Governance?, The Economic Times, January 18, 2009, http://articles.economictimes.indiatimes.com/2009-01-18/news/28462497_1_corporate-governance-satyam-books-fraud-by-satyam-founder (last visited September 20, 2013).

15. *Id.*

16. This section on legal research was written by Avi Cohen, Esquire.

KEY TERMS

Action

Administrative Agency

Administrative Law

Affirmed

Amendments

Appellant

Appellee

Articles

Bill

Binding Authority

Briefing of a Case

Caption

Case Law

Citation

Classifications of Law

Codes

Common Law

Common Law Marriage

Congress

Concurring Opinion

Concurrent Resolution

Constitutional Law

Constitutional Relativity

Contract Law

Corporate Governance

Criminal Law

Cyberlaw

Defendant

Digests

Dissenting Opinion

Domestic Partnership

Family Law

Form Books

House of Representatives

Hopper

Intangible Property

Internet Research

Joint Resolution

Judicial Decree

Judicial Opinion

Jury

Law Review Articles

Legal Dictionaries

Legal Encyclopedias

Legal Periodicals

Legislative Enactment

Lexis

Majority Opinion

Opinions

Ordinance

Personal Property

Persuasive Authority

Plaintiff

Pocket Veto

Precedent

Primary Source

Private Law

Property Law

Public Law

Real Property

Remanded

Restatements

Reversed

Secondary Source

Senate

Simple Resolution

Social Host

Stare Decisis

Sponsor

Statute

Status and Process

Statutory Law

Tangible Property

Tort Law

Treaties

Westlaw

CHAPTER 2

BUSINESS ETHICS
BY: TERRY ANN HALBERT
AND SAMUEL D. HODGE, JR.

Ethics is knowing the difference between what you have a right to do and what is right to do.

—Potter Stewart

**SECTION 2.1
AN OVERVIEW
OF ETHICS**

Peter Christopher is walking through a park and is attracted to a pond where children are swimming. He notices that some of the children's cries sound more like desperation than enjoyment, and soon he realizes that a child is drowning. Christopher is a trained life-guard. Since he is on his way to a concert, and not in the mood to get his clothes wet, Christopher turns away from the pond. Would he be violating the law by failing to help?

Surprisingly, the answer is no. Our legal system, which was greatly influenced by the notions of individual freedom, will not force a person to help a stranger in an emergency unless that person has somehow caused the problem in the first place or there is a **special relationship** between the parties, such as a parent and child. If, as in this example, an individual just happens to discover a stranger in grave danger, that person is legally allowed to continue walking without stopping to help.

This principle is probably understandable in terms of the basic principles of our legal system, which generally finds a person liable for some wrong or careless action, not for inaction, not for something they failed to do. There are also practical reasons why the law backs away from demanding a rescue in these kinds of situations: Where is the line to be drawn? Is there anyone who hears the child screaming responsible for jumping into the pond to help? Suppose a person cannot swim, or suppose the pond is polluted?

But beyond the law is the concept of what is right, what is **ethical.** One might believe that there are ethical reasons for trying to help the drowning child, regardless of what the law expects. In fact, this is the major difference between law and ethics: the law is about what one must do to avoid liability, while ethics is about "doing the right thing."

**SECTION 2.2
SOURCES OF
BUSINESS ETHICS**

Business ethics involves what is proper behavior in the business world. This definition, however, takes on various meanings in different cultures, making it challenging to provide a universal definition in international

67

markets. Nevertheless, certain actions are generally considered ethics violations.[1] For example, financial accounting continues to be a primary source of ethical misconduct in a business setting, and no amount of industry or governmental intervention is capable of stopping dishonest individuals from reporting financial information in an unethical manner.[2] Owners of businesses and their workers can also commit ethics violations on an individual basis, rather than on behalf of a commercial entity. During the past few decades, a variety of Ponzi, or financial schemes have been exposed, in which unscrupulous individuals have tricked firms, their stockholders, and investors into believing gross exaggeration of the financial statements of a business enterprise.[3] Bernie Madoff and Enron are examples that come to mind.

Traditional notions of ethics are being reexamined as the result of the Trump presidency. When the director of the independent Office of Government Ethics resigned in 2017, he commented, "In working with the Trump Administration, it has become clear that we need to strengthen the ethics program."[4] The following are some examples that demonstrate this point. Disregarding clear precedent, President Trump refused to release his tax returns so no one can ascertain if any conflicts of interest exist. He refused to place his assets in a blind trust after being elected, and his sons introduced a new hotel chain premised on the appeal of the President's brand. Kellyanne Conway's promoted a line of clothes on television sold by the President's daughter. Mr. Trump promoted his golf courses by dropping in on weddings taking place at his resorts, after publicly noting that couples should choose to have their weddings at the clubhouse because the president might just drop by.[5]

Not all ethical questions generate as much publicity and people can run into ethical dilemmas at work on a regular basis and some problems don't have an easy solution. For instance, how would you handle the following situation?

> Walt is employed as a computer analyst for a casino and remains after work to finish a project. Unfortunately, he is missing critical data but remembers that he had e-mailed the information earlier in the day to a co-worker. The co-worker keeps the passcode for his computer in the desk drawer so Walt retrieves it and logs into his friend's email account. As soon as Walt accesses the e-mail, he discovers a series of messages regarding wagers that the co-worker has placed over the last several days with a betting agency. There were also threatening messages about the co-worker's failure to pay other gambling obligations. Employees of casinos are prohibited from engaging in any form of gambling activity under penalty of discharge and other sanctions in order to avoid any conflict of interest at work.

Walt knows that he should report this matter to the casino and that his co-worker may be in personal danger but the disclosure would require him to admit that he illegally accessed someone's e-mail account. If Walt tells the co-worker that he is aware of the illegal gambling activity and threatening messages, it would require him to disclose that he improperly accessed the co-worker's computer. What should he do?[6]

Ethics concern a person's moral compass about what is right and wrong. Choices made within a business may be made by individuals or groups, but whoever renders them will be influenced by the culture of the firm. The determination to behave ethically is a moral decision; workers must decide what they think is the proper course of action. This may involve rejecting the path that would lead to the largest short-term profit.[7]

A. Advantages of Ethical Behavior

Ethical behavior and corporate responsibility can bring meaningful advantages to an enterprise. For instance, it may:

- Attract clients to the business' products, thereby increasing sales and profits;

- Entice workers to remain with the company, reduce employee turnover and increase productivity;

- Interest more people to work for the enterprise, reduce recruitment expenses and enable the business to lure the most talented employees; and

- Keep the firm's stock price high, thereby protecting the business from takeover.[8]

Many ethical dilemmas arise in an employment situation. For instance, ethical issues present themselves in the hiring, management and dismissal of the employees who staff a business. An ethical approach to the recruitment of workers requires that management be upfront with those applying for a position. Advertisements for employment should clearly state the duties of the job and questions about wages, tasks, hours of work, and expectations should be answered honestly. This protects both the business and interested worker from developing unrealistic expectations about the specifics of the job.[9]

The ethical nature of a business can be placed into three groups: the legitimate enterprise, the criminal operation and those businesses that fall within the middle of the two. Those engaged in the last two categories, however, risk making deception and dishonesty a way of life. In fact, the last choice can ruin an enterprise as infrequent temptations slowly transform the entity into a criminal enterprise.[10]

B. Sources of Ethical Standards

What are the sources of good ethical practice in business? These values are primarily obtained from three sources: culture, religion and the laws of the state. As a result, there is not a uniform standard around the world. These three sources, however, exert influence in varying amounts on people which end up being reflected in the ethics of the organization.[11]

1. Ethical Culture

A major source of ethical culture in an enterprise is the business owner. These leaders set the ethical direction of the business since they are responsible for all parts of the organization. While others may not always agree with the owner on his or her set of values, the owner may choose to hire only those who agree with his or her point of view on ethical conduct. An owner may also create an ethical code based upon that person's personal or religious beliefs.[12]

Before he died in 2014, the founder of Chick-Fil-A ran the company based upon family values influenced by his Southern Baptist beliefs. For instance, he made the decision to close on Sundays in 1946 when he started his first restaurant. He believed that all Chick-Fil-A employees should be able to spend time with their families, and worship if they choose to do so. The business still considers it part of its recipe for success. This thought process, however, has caused Chick-Fil-A to occasionally encounter a backlash from the public. For instance, in 2012, the founder of the business took a very public position against gay marriages when he said:

> "We're inviting God's judgment on our nation when we shake our fist at him and say we know better than you as to what constitutes a marriage. And, I pray God's mercy on our generation that has such a prideful, arrogant attitude that thinks we have the audacity to redefine what marriage is all about."[13]

When the owner of a large business issues a public statement on such a controversial issue, that person risks losing the support of many of the entity's customers. It is one thing to be an organization that stays closed on Sundays but it is another to imply that those in favor of same-sex marriage, many of whom are loyal customers, have a "prideful, arrogant attitude."[14] Setting aside the merits and wisdom of making such a controversial statement, no one can doubt the ethical direction and moral compass of the leadership of this fast food chain.

2. Professional Codes of Ethics

Another source of direction is **professional codes of ethics.** These principles are designed to assist professionals with transacting business with honesty and integrity. A code of ethics may set forth the mission and values of the business or organization, how individuals in that profession are supposed to approach problems, the ethical standards premised upon the organization's core values and the standards to which the professional will be held.[15]

A recent survey on business ethics shows that firms are recognizing the role of creating an ethical culture in today's business environment. 80% of those surveyed reported that their firm had a code of ethics or similar document and 57% provided training on ethical standards at work.[16] For instance, Garnett Company, Inc., a media and marketing solutions company with a diverse portfolio of broadcast, digital, mobile and publishing companies provides:

> "Every Gannett employee is responsible for ensuring that the company's actions and associations maintain the highest professional standards. These standards guarantee the independence and integrity of our news, editorial, information, advertising and marketing services. As an employee, you are obliged to report any suspected violation of company policy (including violations of accounting or auditing policy) or any suspected violation of the laws governing the Company's business."[17]

Morris Communications Company affirmatively states that providing an environment that supports honesty, trust, responsibility and citizenship for every worker clears the path for excellence in the workplace. Therefore, they have enacted a Code of Business conduct in which employees are told to report any suspected illegal or unethical behavior of company policy, including issues regarding accounting and auditing matters.[18]

Despite these ethical pronouncements, respondents to the survey admitted that they are experiencing greater pressure to act unethically. For instance, 35% reported that they feel under pressure to compromise their organization's standards for ethical conduct and 23% note that they have personally observed acts that were not in compliance with their company's stated ethics polices.[19]

Sample professional organizations that have adopted Codes of Ethics include the American Medical Association, the American Bar Association and the American Institute for Certified Public Accountants.

Let us look at an example. The primary duty of a lawyer or physician is to the client or patient. An accountant, however, is paid by the client to prepare an opinion on behalf of the public. Therefore, the primary allegiance of the CPA is more difficult to ascertain.[20] The American Institute of Certified Public Accountants is a national accounting organization with more than 300,000 CPAs. Its job is to promote and maintain high professional standards and practices. It is an authoritative source of standards and procedures in the accounting field and one of its primary tasks is to administer ethical standards through the development, interpretation and enforcement of its Code of Professional Conduct.[21] In this regard, its code establishes the responsibilities for the profession, the public and its clients.[22]

The Code of Professional Conduct offers guidance and rules to its members—those in public practice, industry, government and education—in the performance of their professional responsibilities. Adherence to the Code of Professional Conduct depends primarily on the understanding and actions of its members, secondarily on reinforcement by peers and public opinion, and ultimately on disciplinary proceedings, when required, against those who fail to comply with the Rules.[23]

Section 52, Article 1 sets forth the responsibilities of an accountant and provides that:

> "As professionals, certified public accountants perform an essential role in society. Consistent with that role, members of the American Institute of Certified Public Accountants have responsibilities to all those who use their professional services. Members also have a continuing responsibility to cooperate with each other to improve the art of accounting, maintain the public's confidence, and carry out the profession's special responsibilities for self-governance. The collective efforts of all members are required to maintain and enhance the traditions of the profession."

This Code of Professional Conduct provides generally accepted standards of auditing and accounting principles, regardless whether an accountant is a member of the AICPA. When these pronouncements are written in terms of "should," an accountant must follow the pronouncements in every applicable instance as though they were written in mandatory language.[24]

The following case provides an example of a violation of an ethics rule that prohibits a lawyer from having a sexual relationship with a client.

Iowa Supreme Court Attorney Disciplinary Board v. Marzen
779 N.W.2d 757 (Iowa 2010)

Jesse Marzen is an Iowa lawyer. A complaint was filed against Marzen with the disciplinary board by a woman named "Jane Doe." She alleged Marzen engaged in a sexual relationship with her after representing her in a mental health commitment hearing.

The board brought disciplinary charges against Marzen, alleging that Marzen engaged in sexual relations with Doe when she was his client. The legal framework for considering a charge of sexual misconduct is well established. Under our ethical rules, an attorney is prohibited from having a sexual relationship with a client when the client is not the lawyer's spouse or when the sexual relationship did not predate the initiation of the attorney-client relationship. Iowa R. Prof'l Conduct 32:1.8(j). This court has recognized that the professional relationship renders it impossible for the vulnerable layperson to be considered consenting to the sexual relationship.

The relevant facts relating to the charge of sexual misconduct first surfaced when Doe was involuntarily hospitalized after she overdosed on prescription drugs and alcohol, and expressed suicidal thoughts. Marzen was court-appointed to represent her in the hospitalization commitment hearing. After the hearing, Doe indicated that she needed transportation, and Marzen agreed to give her a ride. The two left together in Marzen's car. Doe testified Marzen took her to his house where they eventually engaged in various sex acts in the living room. To support her testimony, Doe provided a description of the layout of Marzen's home and offered testimony about the presence of a quarter-sized mole on his back. Additionally, she said Marzen had "funny"-appearing buttocks due to a loose fold of skin hanging from the lower portion of his buttocks. Doe also testified that she

engaged in sexual intercourse with Marzen on four additional occasions-once more in Marzen's home, once in the home where she was residing, once in an automobile driven by Marzen, and once at Marzen's law office. She described each encounter in graphic detail.

The board called several witnesses at the hearing in support of the testimony of Doe. One witness testified Marzen admitted in his presence to a sexual relationship with Doe. Another testified she observed Marzen and Doe emerge from a bedroom in the house where Doe was living following her release from the hospitalization commitment.

Marzen denied the existence of any sexual relationship with Doe. He acknowledged he had been at the house where Doe was staying on multiple occasions, but only for business purposes. With respect to the physical description of his body, Marzen claimed he had more than ten moles on his back, which Doe failed to mention, as well as a mole on the lower portion of his abdomen that Doe should have mentioned, if her descriptions of their sex acts were truthful.

Marzen denied the presence of a flap of loose skin on his buttocks. He did, however, acknowledge he weighed 325 pounds when he graduated from high school and lost between 125 and 150 pounds since that time.

The critical factual issue presented in the sexual-misconduct charge is whether the evidence supports a prohibited sexual relationship by a convincing preponderance of the evidence. We can only find a violation of sexual misconduct by a preponderance of the evidence that Marzen and Doe engaged in sexual relations during the time Marzen represented Doe. Marzen flatly denied Doe's description of his buttocks. Yet, he failed to further counter the claim with equally sharp and decisive evidence to verify his denial. The claim involved an unusual but distinctive condition of a private part of a person's body, and Marzen had the ability to disprove the existence of the condition and discredit Doe (but he did not). We also find Doe's testimony regarding the location of a mole on Marzen's back, which was surgically removed after the alleged incidents, was significant. The mole was another piece of evidence to support her version of their relationship.

On the whole, we find Doe's testimony, coupled with the corroborating evidence, is sufficient for us to conclude by a preponderance of the evidence that Doe and Marzen engaged in a sexual relationship. We also conclude the sexual relationship occurred during the time Marzen represented Doe on several legal matters. We suspend Marzen's license to practice law with no possibility of reinstatement for a period of not less than six months from the date of the filing of this opinion.

The **Hippocratic Oath** is one of the oldest binding documents in history and is applicable to health care professionals. Written in the 5th Century B.C., its principles are revered by physicians to this day: to treat the ill to the best of one's ability, maintain patient privacy, and teach medicine to the next generation. The Oath of Hippocrates is incorporated into the American Medical Association's Code of Medical Ethics and most medical school graduates swear to some form of the oath.[25] Is this Oath still relevant in the face of the way medicine is currently practiced?

While the oath's use is widespread by physicians, the ancient tenets are not fully followed. According to a survey of U.S. and Canadian medical schools, only 14 percent of current oaths prohibit euthanasia, 8 percent foreswear abortion, and only 3 percent prohibit sexual contact with patients, which were values all held sacred in the ancient version. These statistics show an unwritten changing of values among physicians. What is more interesting, however, is that the original oath called for "the opposite" of pleasure and fame for those who violated the oath, but fewer than half of the oaths taken today require the health care professional to be held accountable for not keeping the pledge.[26]

Some critics maintain that the original Hippocratic Oath is indefensible as a basis for modern medical morality because of the principles it does not include. Nothing is said about the complex political and financial restrictions upon which physicians must now render medical care. The role of patient values and beliefs in medical decision making is also not recognized. Finally, the Oath, written for a world in which pharmaceuticals, insurance companies, and legislative regulation did not exist, fails to protect the "discretionary space" needed by doctors to protect their patients from undue influences.[27]

Critics further maintain that the Hippocratic Oath does not meet the challenges facing medicine in the 21st century. The increase in government regulation, the third-party payer systems, and the democratization of medical knowledge all place added pressures on physicians that are new and their ethical implications are not properly addressed by the Hippocratic Oath. Institutionalized and team medicine also have significant implications for the modern practice of medicine which are not discussed by the famous Oath.[28]

The Hippocratic Oath requires a physician to assist people who need aid but doctors are often, reluctant to help because of the fear of a malpractice claim if something goes wrong. While doctors have the duty to treat their patients in an office or hospital situation, would an off-duty physician who volunteers her services be responsible if something goes wrong? That is the issue in **Gordon v. Howard.**

GORDON V. HOWARD
180 MICH. APP. 488 (CT. APP. MICH. 1989)

Rozalia Gordon was admitted to the emergency center at Beaumont Hospital after sustaining injuries in an automobile accident. The emergency room physician examined Gordon and determined that the situation required the services of a surgeon. He thereafter directed the unit secretary to contact the surgeon who was "on-call" that day.

Dr. Mario Villalba was the on-call surgeon. He was apparently unavailable, as he was attending a wedding that morning. Upon being informed that Dr. Villalba was not available, Dr. Howard was called, as he was preparing for a family activity. It is undisputed that Dr. Howard was not on-call. He agreed to come to the hospital after being told that the on-call surgeon was unavailable.

When Dr. Howard arrived at the hospital, Gordon was being taken from the emergency room to have a CAT scan performed. He immediately conducted a complete examination. While Gordon was in the CAT scan room, the decision was made to operate. When she was brought into the operating room, her condition was very poor. She lost cardiac function, attempts to resuscitate her heart were unsuccessful and she was pronounced dead.

Plaintiff thereafter commenced this suit against Dr. Howard and the pertinent section of the Good Samaritan statute provides:

"In instances where the actual hospital duty of that person did not require a response to that emergency situation, a physician... who in good faith responds to a life threatening emergency or responds to a request for emergency assistance in a life threatening emergency within a hospital or other licensed medical care facility, shall not be liable for any civil damages as a result of an act or omission in the rendering of emergency care, except an act or omission amounting to gross negligence or willful and wanton misconduct. [M.C.L. § 691.1502(1); M.S.A. § 14.563(12)(1).]"

Plaintiff claims that the court read the statute too broadly and that it should only be applied in the "biblical" or "classic" Good Samaritan situation, i.e., where the person renders care outside their job description or training. Plaintiff asserts that the statute should not be applied "when a trained professional, such as a surgeon, is summoned to the hospital to perform the duties for which he has been trained and for which he will be paid."

In **Matts v. Homsi, 106 Mich. App. 563 (1981),** a staff physician, who was not on-call and had no direct responsibility to respond to requests for assistance, was summoned to treat a young man with internal injuries sustained during an automobile accident. The trial court directed a verdict in favor of the physician as to the plaintiff's medical malpractice claim on the basis of the Good Samaritan statute. This Court affirmed, ruling that the statute was intended to afford partial immunity in instances where the situs of the emergency was actually within a hospital or other medical care facility. It was also held that the statute does not exist for persons whose actual function is to respond to emergency situations.

Michigan, like many other states, have enacted a Good Samaritan statute because many doctors were reluctant to render voluntary emergency care out of fear of malpractice suits. It was hoped that the Good Samaritan statute would encourage prompt treatment by excusing civil liability for ordinary negligence to those who render medical care in emergency situations. In accordance with the legislative intent, we believe that off-duty physicians, who are not on-call and have no duty to respond, are entitled to immunity under the Good Samaritan statute. A contrary ruling would only discourage off-duty physicians from responding to emergency calls, thus defeating the entire purpose of the statute. Under the facts of this case, Dr. Howard fell within the protection of the statute and, therefore, was properly granted summary judgment.

QUESTIONS FOR DISCUSSION:

1. Should people who are trained to rescue or assist others in emergency situations be held to a higher standard of care?

2. The Hippocratic Oath, which outlines the ethical goals of doctors, contains the following promise: "According to my power and judgment to use the medical knowledge for the benefit of those who suffer, as judged by myself to be fair, and to avoid from doing any harm or injustice." Is a doctor who fails to stop and render emergency aid liable to the victim as the result of the Hippocratic Oath?

3. Do you agree with the discussion in **Gordon v. Howard?**

All states contain Good Samaritan statutes that protect people who are medically trained from being held liable in an emergency rescue should they decide to help. These laws, however, do not demand that the medically-trained offer assistance in these situations. Today, a doctor may decide to "walk on by," unless she or he is already treating the patient, or is on duty in a medical facility offering treatment.

Over the years, a few exceptions to the "No Duty to Rescue Rule" have developed. There is the "Special Relationship" exception: between members of a family, between employers and employees, between providers of public transportation and passengers, or between owners of business and their customers; for instance, the law insists on a reasonable attempt at assistance in an emergency. So, if the person in the park was a father who was hearing his own drowning daughter's screams, he would have a duty to take reasonable steps to help her.

SECTION 2.3
ETHICAL THEORIES

Businesses have been under increased pressure to improve their ethical practices ever since corporate scandals such as Enron, WorldCom and Bernie Madoff. The rise of consumer activism online through social media postings has also increased the scrutiny of business activities. Pressure groups provide a good example of this activity. For example, external stakeholders focus on the practice of multinationals or industries with ethical issues.[29]

A business enterprise can no longer assert that it is an ethical operation if it disregards the unethical practices of its suppliers who use child or forced labor, violate the basic rights of workers or ignore health, safety and environmental standards.[30]

One merely has to look at Enron to understand the repercussions of unethical conduct in a business setting. Enron was at the top of the world at the turn of the century. However, the enterprise quickly fell apart in 2001, after it announced an earnings restatement. Within six weeks, the once powerful company declared bankruptcy and many employees and investors saw their retirement funds disappear with the company.[31]

Enron's fraud included both complex financial maneuvering and fabrication of numbers. One commentator called it a bigger deal than 9/11—a statement that, while fatuous, helps demonstrate the impact caused by the company's fall. The scandal rocked the foundation of the population's trust in the economy and created a cynicism toward corporate America that pervades many aspects of our politics and culture.[32]

Ethical issues are hard to scrutinize by the very nature of the questions they foster. Individuals have varying opinions about what is right and wrong. These questions touch basic beliefs about how the world should work. A challenge to these principles is frequently met with resistance and emotion. Yet, we learn from experience, and it is much better to learn about the consequences of ethics violations through indirect experience rather than by direct involvement.

The cost of ignorance is to remain a possible target through failure to take precautions, or failure to help someone wrestling with such an issue because we neither appreciate nor understand the problem. This can often make the difference between proper prevention and damage control.[33]

If ethics is about choosing the right behavior, the moral way to live one's life, how does society achieve this goal? There are many different ethical beliefs individuals can hold. Same-sex marriage is just one example of an issue that separates people who have very strong but completely opposite ethical beliefs. And in a multicultural society, doesn't it become even more difficult to decide on one single ethically correct position? Who is to say which personal or cultural ethical standard is correct or is there a universal ethic?

For centuries, human beings have struggled to determine the answers to these types of questions. Within Western civilization, two major philosophical theories about ethics have evolved:

1. **Utilitarian Theory:** Focuses on the consequences—both short and long term—of any particular action for all individuals affected. In other words, this theory places the locus of right and wrong on the consequences of selecting one action or policy over another. The Utilitarian Theory moves past the choice of one's own interests and looks at the interests of others.[34] Benefits and harms are balanced against one another, to determine which action produces the most happiness for the greatest number of people.

2. **Rights Theory:** Concerned with the reasons for action, not just the results. People have certain basic rights—the right to life, freedom of expression, privacy, for instance—that are of value in themselves and must be protected. This theory also includes the notion of "Universality:" Whatever we choose to do must be behavior we would be willing to have done to everyone, including to ourselves—a version of the Golden Rule.

Sometimes these two theories serve the same purpose. For example, a student who sees another student cheating on an exam employs her freedom of expression to alert the professor. Not only has she acted for ethical reasons—the Rights Theory—but she has come to the aid of the rest of the class, who benefit by having their grades accurately measured. Thus, she has also acted in accordance with the Utilitarian Theory, the greatest good (better grades) for the greatest number (the rest of the class).

Occasionally, however, the two theories are diametrically opposed to each other. The classic example is slavery, where a minority of the population is enslaved, but the rest of society benefited economically. Before the Civil War, the economy of the southern states prospered, providing the greatest good to the greatest number and satisfying the Utilitarian Theory. But the Rights Theory suffered, since human beings were enslaved, preventing them from enjoying the same rights as the other members of society.

Can you think of other examples where the two philosophies go hand-in-hand? How about situations where they diverge? Consider these examples when you work on the following problem.

SECTION 2.4
KATHY ROBERTS AND
EASTCOAST AIRLINES

PROBLEM TWO—A

PARK, BROWN & SMITH, P.C.
ATTORNEYS AT LAW
MEMORANDUM

TO: All Law Clerks

FROM: Peter Smith, Esquire

RE: Kathy Roberts and Eastcoast Airlines

Kathy Roberts decided to obtain a job in order to prove that she has finally grown up. To her credit, she landed a position in the real estate department of Eastcoast Airlines.

Eastcoast has tried to diversify by acquiring a number of properties in Florida. Eastcoast Airlines, like so many of its competitors, has been suffering substantial losses in the years since airline deregulation, and has a negative cash flow. Unless the company can control its high labor costs and increase its popularity with the flying public, bankruptcy is a possibility. Kathy's boss, Robert Stingle sees selling off the Florida properties, as an important way of alleviating the company's financial crisis.

Kathy contacted Silvertooth, Inc., a developer of nursing homes, about the Florida properties and found an interested buyer. The corporation thought that one of the parcels would be perfect for a retirement villa and would feature elaborate walking trails and outdoor recreational facilities.

Eastcoast had conducted a full environmental audit of the property six months earlier, and no problems were revealed. A copy of the report was given to a Silvertooth representative, who also examined the property and discovered no problems.

As negotiations progressed with Silvertooth, Kathy was approached by one of her friends at Eastcoast, Steve Flame. He told Kathy that there is highly toxic waste on the property that she is attempting to transfer to Silvertooth, Inc. The person who told Steve about the situation was recently in Florida at the site, and had found several buried metal containers marked "Danger! Biohazard. Radioactive medical waste." The containers were cracked and liquid was seeping out onto the ground. Steve said he wanted Kathy to know about the dangerous condition because he was concerned that innocent people would be harmed if the sale went through.

Kathy contacted her boss, but before she could mention the containers, Stingle told her it was vital that the sale be closed quickly, and that their jobs depended on it. Kathy consulted with a lawyer who explained that Florida law does not require disclosure of hazardous substances on commercial property so long as there hasn't been a fraudulent misstatement about the condition of the property.

Kathy is very upset. She knows that Silvertooth is considering other similar properties, and if she mentions the toxic spill problem to the potential buyer, they will back out of the sale. Kathy also realizes that she will never deal with Silvertooth again since Eastcoast didn't own any other property that is suitable for a retirement community.

Although there appears to be no legal consequences if Kathy says nothing, and allows the sale to go through, from an ethical perspective the situation might be different. Write an advisory memo to Kathy on the ethics of the choice she must make, "To Disclose or Not To Disclose?"

1. First apply the Utilitarian Theory. Who are the people affected by Kathy's decision? What choice would result in "the greatest good for the greatest number?"

2. Now do the analysis from the Rights Theory perspective. What rights do the various affected individuals and groups have in this situation? How do they weigh against one another? What would be the result if Kathy thinks about the Golden Rule?

3. Finally, summarize your own ethical opinion: If you were in Kathy's shoes, what would you do, and why?

PROBLEM TWO—A
ANSWER SHEET

Name _____ **Please Print Clearly**

1. First apply the Utilitarian Theory. Who are the people affected by Kathy's decision? What choice would probably result in "the greatest good for the greatest number?"

_____
_____
_____
_____
_____
_____
_____

2. Now do the analysis from the Rights Theory perspective. What rights do the various affected individuals and groups have in this situation? How do they weigh against one another? What would be the result if Kathy thinks about the Golden Rule?

_____
_____
_____
_____
_____
_____
_____
_____

3. Finally, summarize your own ethical opinion: If you were in Kathy's shoes, what would you do, and why?

_____

_____

_____

_____

_____

_____

_____

_____

_____

_____

_____

_____

_____

_____

_____

_____

_____

_____

SECTION 2.5
THE WHISTLEBLOWER

Suppose Kathy decides to warn Silvertooth about the hazardous waste and the deal falls through. Kathy feels good about this outcome, but not so good when she discovers that she has been fired. Since all her other work for Eastcoast has been highly commended, Ms. Roberts believes she was fired in retaliation for letting the toxic cat out of the bag. (Under the federal "Superfund" law, Eastcoast as owner of the property will be responsible for paying for the clean up of the site.)

Kathy is a **whistleblower**, a person who feels compelled to get certain information into the hands of the people who can act to correct a problem, when it seems that the problem won't be corrected otherwise. When employees "blow the whistle," they might tell a superior, or they might go outside their company and tell government authorities, or even the media.

There is no one exact definition of a whistleblower. As the court noted in **Winters v. Houston Chronicle Pub. Co., 795 S.W.2d 723 (Tex. 1990)**, a whistleblower is the person who sounds the alarm "when wrongdoing occurs on his or her beat, which is usually within a large organization." Another definition is set forth in a report co-edited by Ralph Nader in which it was said that whistleblowing is "the act of a man or woman who, believing that the public interest overrides the interest of the organization he serves, publicly blows the whistle if the organization is involved in corrupt, illegal, fraudulent, or harmful activity." *Whistle Blowing: The Report of the Conference on Professional Responsibility*, R. Nader, P. Petkas & K. Blackwell, eds. 1972.

What are Kathy's legal rights in this situation? She may have none. Unless she has an employment contract with Eastcoast for a certain stated time period, she is an **employee at will.** Kathy might be protected if she was part of the 14 percent of American workers who belong to a union. She could then argue she was fired in violation of a collective bargaining agreement between her union and her employer. (A union contract generally provides that workers cannot be fired unless for "just cause.") Finally, some state and federal laws protect whistleblowers who report violations of those laws to the government. For instance, Congress passed the **Whistleblower Protection Act of 1989** in order to strengthen and improve the protections of federal employees who report fraud, waste, abuse and unnecessary expenditures within the government. The Act, however, does not allow an employee to file a lawsuit for retaliation by a supervisor. Instead, the worker must pursue an administrative remedy that is usually administered by the U. S. Department of Labor. A number of states have also passed laws protecting the whistleblower.

The **Occupational Safety and Health Administration (OSHA)** has a Whistleblower Protection Program that enforces the provisions of more than twenty whistleblower statutes protecting employees who report violations of workplace safety, airline, commercial motor carrier, financial reform, food safety, health insurance reform, consumer product, environmental, motor vehicle safety, nuclear, pipeline, public transportation agency, railroad, maritime, and security laws. The protections provided to whistleblower apply to such things as worker participation in safety and health activities, reporting a work related injury, illness or fatality, or reporting a violation of the statutes.[35]

Protection from discrimination because of whistleblowing activity includes:

- Firing or laying off
- Blacklisting
- Demoting
- Denying overtime or promotion
- Disciplining
- Denial of benefits
- Failure to hire or rehire
- Intimidation
- Reassignment affecting prospects for promotion
- Reducing pay or hours[36]

Pennsylvania has enacted the **Whistleblower's Law** which provides that no employer may discharge, or otherwise retaliate against an employee because the employee makes a **good faith report** or is about to report to the employer or appropriate authority, an instance of wrongdoing or waste. A person who alleges a violation of this Act may bring a civil action within 180 days after the occurrence of the alleged violation. 43 P. S. §1421. The Superfund law, for example, would protect Kathy if she had gone straight to the Environmental Protection Agency with news about the spill. Since she told Silvertooth, she may not be protected.

Because a whistleblower may be protected under multiple laws, the initial step in reviewing a claim is to ascertain which statutes or common law actions may provide a remedy. Depending upon whom one works and in which state one is employed, the types of whistleblower protections vary. Also, employees may be protected under traditional tort or contract principles for damages resulting from retaliation for whistleblowing.[37]

One major restriction in a lot of whistleblower protection laws is the short statute of limitations; the failure to comply with a statute of limitations is a primary defenses tool. The statute of limitations usually starts running from the time an employee discovers that he or she will be retaliated against and not the last day of employment. Each jurisdiction has its own statute of limitations as well as Federal law protecting whistleblowers with some as short as 30 days.[38]

The National Whistleblowers Center notes that the following elements are the basic components of most whistleblower protection claims:

- That the claimant is an person covered under the specific statutory or common law relied upon for action;

- That the defendant is an employer or person covered under the statutory or common law relied upon for the action;

- That the plaintiff was involved in protected whistleblower activity;

- That the defendant knew or had reason to know that the plaintiff engaged in such activity;

- That the retaliation was motivated, at least in part, by the employee's engaging in protected activity;

- That the claimant was fired or otherwise discriminated against with respect to his or her compensation, terms, conditions or privileges or employment; or suffered some other wrong actionable under state tort or contract theory;

- That the person can show that he or she would not have been subject to an adverse action in the absence of their protected whistleblower conduct.[39]

Why does the law give so much freedom to employers to hire and fire workers as they see fit? Is "employment at will" a fair rule? How should society strike a balance between an employer's right to control and an employee's right to bring ethical concerns forward without fear of retaliation?

New employees are frequently perplexed to learn—in a job application, employment contract, or employee handbook, that they are "at will" employees. The workers are even more perplexed when they find out what this language means: An at-will employee can be discharged at any time for any reason except for age, sex, race and religion. If the employer discharges an at-will employee, the worker has very limited legal rights to fight that termination. For instance, if a worker is employed at will, the employer does not need good cause to fire that person in most states. In fact, unless the company provides some clear indication that it will only fire employees for good cause, the law presumes that the worker is employed at will.[40] Nevertheless, the at-will-worker cannot be discharged for a reason that violates public policy.

Many employers make it abundantly clear, in written policies, applications, handbooks, job evaluations, or other employment-related documents that their workers serve at-will. If an employee has signed a document stating he or she is an at-will employee, that is probably the end of the story. If the person has not signed such an agreement, the person should review the employee manual or other written workplace policies. What is noted as to the conditions under which a person can be discharged? Even if the company fails to explicitly state that the term is "at will," statements that a person can be discharged without good cause or "for any reason" are indications that your employer adheres to an at-will policy. Some employers, however, have written policies that mandate good cause to fire, provide an exclusive list of reasons for which employees can be discharged, or otherwise provide employees some job protections. If an employer has adopted these types of policies, the worker may be allowed to rely upon them.[41]

Most employees work under open-ended contracts of employment or contracts-at-will. In other words, the employment continues until such time as the employer or worker ends the relationship. Some others, however, work under a fixed-term or specified-purpose contract which is an agreement that terminates on a specified date or when a specific task is completed. For instance, most part-time faculty are employed by contract to teach at a University for a specific semester with no vested right for future employment.[42] These are contracts for a fixed term. What does an employee have to show in order to be successful in a Whistleblower's lawsuit for being fired after reporting some improper or illegal conduct?

HUNGER V. GRAND CENTRAL SANITATION
447 PA. SUPER. 575 (1995)

Mark Hunger appeals from the grant of summary judgment to Grand Central Sanitation and Gary Perin. We affirm under current precedent of this court.

Mark Hunger instituted this action against his former employer, Grand Central Sanitation, and Mr. Perin, who terminated him. The action is based upon wrongful discharge.

Appellant was employed by Grand Central Sanitation ("Grand Central") on June 28, 1990 as the company's safety director. Mr. Perin is the vice-president and owner of Grand Central. On September 7, 1991, Appellant became aware that hazardous materials consisting of blasting caps were being deposited into garbage containers at Shu-Deb Inc. ("Shu-Deb"). The complaint contains no averments about how Appellant became aware of this information. Grand Central picked up garbage for Shu-Deb and dumped it at a dump

site. Appellant knew that Grand Central was not licensed to dispose of hazardous materials and believed that it would be a violation of law if the company transported or disposed of hazardous materials. Appellant also became concerned about the safety of company employees from the danger of transporting blasting caps.

On September 9, 1991, Appellant told Mr. Perin about the information he received that blasting caps were being dumped into the containers at Shu-Deb. The next day, he contacted state and local police, asking for a description of blasting caps, which he had never seen. He also arranged to search Shu-Deb's garbage container.

On September 12, 1991, Appellant, accompanied by Pennsylvania State Police and members of the Bureau of Alcohol, Tobacco, and Firearms, went to search the contents of the garbage container. When Appellant and police arrived at Shu-Deb, the garbage had been collected, so police located the garbage truck that had the garbage and searched it. No hazardous materials were found. On October 4, 1991, Appellant was discharged as a result of the incident.

Appellant alleges that his wrongful discharge claim was dismissed improperly due to the public policy exception to the doctrine of at-will employment. In Pennsylvania, as a general rule, no common law cause of action exists against an employer for termination of an at-will employment relationship. ("An at-will employee may be terminated for good reason, bad reason, or no reason at all"). Moreover, exceptions to this rule have been recognized in only the most limited of circumstances, where discharges of at-will employees would threaten the clear mandates of public policy.

The public policy exception to the at-will doctrine was recognized in **Geary v. United States Steel Corp.**, 319 A.2d 174 (Pa. 1974), a case remarkably similar to the one at bar. There, the plaintiff was a salesman for the defendant and criticized company officials about the quality of the steel being produced. He was discharged even though the product was later determined substandard, and was subsequently withdrawn from the market. Geary alleged that his termination fell within a public policy exception to the at-will doctrine, since he was acting in the interest of the safety of the general public.

To state a public policy exception to the At-Will Employment Doctrine, the employee must point to a clear public policy articulated in the Constitution, in legislation, an administrative regulation, or a judicial decision. Furthermore, the stated mandate of public policy must be applicable directly to the employee and the employee's actions. It is not sufficient that the employer's actions toward the employee are unfair.

We have recognized a public policy exception only in extremely limited circumstances. If an employee is fired for performing a function that he is required to perform by law, an action for wrongful discharge on public policy grounds will be allowed. See e.g.,

Field v. Philadelphia Electric Co., (565 A.2d 1170 (Pa. 1989) (employee fired for reporting a nuclear safety violation that he was required to report under federal law); **Reuther v. Fowler & Williams, Inc.**, 386 A.2d 119 (Pa. 1978) (employer fired an employee for serving on a jury; public policy was violated since people are required by law to serve on jury and since service on jury has constitutional implications).

Herein, Appellant notes that it is illegal to transport hazardous materials without a license. We agree. However, Appellant admitted in his complaint that no blasting caps were discovered. Thus, Appellees did not violate the law. If Appellant had observed a deliberate violation of the law, reported it to proper authorities, and was fired, then there may have been a cause of action.

In this case, Appellant provides no specifics about how he "became aware" that blasting caps were being dumped. He fails to indicate the capacity of the person who informed him of this, the nature of his investigation into substantiating the reliability of the information, and why it was necessary to inform state and federal law enforcement officials about the situation immediately.

Our disposition of this case may have been different if Appellant discovered that his employer was deliberately transporting hazardous materials after being told of the situation. That is not what occurred, regardless of Appellant's concern with the public safety. The source of Appellant's "awareness" of the alleged illegal activities is completely unsubstantiated. Furthermore, his employer's criminal intent is not established. At most, one of the employer's customers was allegedly dumping illegal explosives.

Appellant's overzealous decision to treat the information he received as para-military matter was grounds for termination. By immediately bringing in state and federal officials after "becoming aware" of a possible violation of the law, Appellant embarrassed his employer and his employer's customer. Order affirmed.

SECTION 2.6
ETHICS, LAW
AND PRIVACY

It may be granted that there are areas of an employee's life in which his employer has no legitimate interest. An intrusion into one of these areas by virtue of the employer's power of discharge might plausibly give rise to a cause of action, particularly where some recognized facet of public policy is threatened.

—Pennsylvania Supreme Court
Geary v. U.S. Steel

As the Court in **Geary** suggests, there are times when an employer's power to control its employees is in danger of stretching too far. For instance, should an employer have the right to insist that none of its employees smoke cigarettes? Smoking in the workplace is becoming a thing of the past. Concerns about the impact of secondhand smoke and the comfort of non-smokers have prompted many states to enact "clean indoor air laws" that severely restrict smoking in the workplace. Some jurisdictions even prohibit smoking in all workplaces while other states have a variety of laws that restrict smoking at work in one way or another, such as designated areas, at hospitals and restaurants.[43] This change in the workplace is not surprising when one considers the following statistics. The Centers for Disease Control and Prevention estimates that 44.5 million people in this country smoke cigarettes even though this habit will result in the death or disability of half of all continuing smokers. In fact, the economic burden of tobacco use is staggering with more than $75 billion per year being spent in medical care and another $92 billion per year resulting from lost productivity. As for secondhand smoke exposure, it causes heart disease and lung cancer in non-smoking adults and non-smokers who are exposed to smoke at work or at home increase their risk of heart disease by at least 25%. Research also shows that smokers have a 50 percent greater absentee rate and produce 50 percent higher medical costs.

But does this mean that an employer should be able to screen and refuse to hire smokers, or fire them if they refuse to stop? And if these practices are allowed, what is to stop employers from insisting that employees change other expensive, unhealthy personal habits? What if a worker has a high cholesterol count, or is obese? Assuming that people who get regular exercise and eat sensibly are healthy and will produce fewer medical expenses, should an employer be able to insist that its workers eat salads for lunch and use a gym three times a week?

These are some of the questions raised by the conflict between employee privacy rights and an employer's interest in controlling its operations. There is also the question of testing. Workers with AIDS will end up with horrendous medical and insurance expenses. Therefore should employers be allowed to test their workers for the AIDS virus? (This is illegal under the Americans with Disabilities Act of 1990.) These types of issues were put to the test when Weyco, Inc, a Michigan firm specializing in employee benefit plans, informed their workers that as of January 1, 2005 anyone testing positive on nicotine testing would be fired. Not only would an employee be discharged if he or she was caught smoking at work, but the no-smoking policy also applied to employees who smoked while off of the job. While it is true that an employer may pay higher insurance costs because of the adverse consequences of smoking, should an employer be allowed to regulate what a worker does while home? According to the American Civil Liberties Union of Michigan, this practice is lawful since the state has no law barring employers from regulating employee practices outside of the office. As reported by *The Detroit News*, state and federal civil rights laws prohibit job action based upon color, age, gender, national origin and religion. Smoking, however, does not fall within one of these protected classes so an employer can enforce what it considers to be desirable traits and skills in the work place.

Twenty-nine states have enacted smoker protection laws that prohibit employers from discriminating against workers for using tobacco products. While these statutes vary from state to state, employers are generally prohibited from either declining to hire or fire an employee for utilizing tobacco during non-working hours and off the employer's premises.[44]

Marijuana has started to become accepted in society and the number of states that have legalized or decriminalized its use has increased causing employers to wonder whether they have to hire or continue to employ those who have prescriptions for medical marijuana and test positive on a drug screening. The right to insist upon a zero-drug tolerance policy has been upheld in several jurisdictions. Nevertheless, the courts in Massachusetts, Connecticut and Rhode Island have barred employers from discriminating against workers who use medical marijuana. Whether these isolated rulings are the beginning of a trend among courts remains to be seen.[45] The rationale for this position is set forth in the following case.

CALLAGHAN V. DARLINGTON FABRICS CORPORATION
2017 WL 2321181 (R.I. SUPER. 2017)

Over fifty years ago, pop culture addressed the use of marijuana in our society. Within the past decade, the General Assembly legalized the use of medical marijuana, and it became lawful to sell Rocky Mountain High cannabis in Colorado. Today, the debate rages in Rhode Island political circles over legalizing the recreational use of "pot."

Christine Callaghan has brought this action against Defendants, alleging employment discrimination with respect to hiring for an internship position because she held a medical marijuana card.

In June 2014, Plaintiff, then a master's student at the University of Rhode Island sought an internship as a requirement of her program. Her professor referred her to Defendant and Plaintiff met with Darlington Human Resources Coordinator. At this meeting, Plaintiff signed Darlington's Fitness for Duty Statement, acknowledging she would have to take a drug test prior to being hired. During this meeting, Plaintiff disclosed that she held a medical marijuana card, authorized by the Hawkins-Slater Act.

Because Ms. Callaghan put the corporation on notice that she was currently using marijuana, would not stop using marijuana while employed by the company, and could not pass the required pre-employment drug test, and thus could not comply with the corporation's drug-free workplace policy, the corporation did not hire her.

The Hawkins-Slater Act provides that "No school, employer, or landlord may refuse to enroll, employ, or lease to, or otherwise penalize, a person solely for his or her status as a cardholder." Another portion of the Hawkins-Slater Act, states that "nothing in this chapter shall be construed to require... an employer to accommodate the medical use of marijuana in any workplace."

This court finds that the General Assembly contemplated that the statute would require employers to accommodate the medical use of marijuana outside the workplace. This provision undermines Defendants' contention that its actions did not violate the Hawkins-Slater Act because its refusal to hire Plaintiff was based not on her cardholder status, rather her use of marijuana outside the workplace that prevented her from passing a drug test.

The General Assembly explicitly instructed the courts to construe the Hawkins-Slater Act broadly. Section 21-28.6-4(a), provides that "[a] qualifying patient cardholder who has in his or her possession a registry identification card shall not be … denied any right or privilege … for the medical use of marijuana." Employment is neither a right nor a privilege in the legal sense. However, the protection provided is. Thus, the Hawkins-Slater Act provides that employers cannot refuse to employ a person for his or her status as a cardholder, and that right may not be denied for the medical use of marijuana. The recreational user could cease smoking long enough to pass the drug test and get hired, and subsequently not be subject to future drug tests, allowing him or her to smoke recreationally to his or her heart's content. The medical user, however, would not be able to cease for long enough to pass the drug test, even though his or her use is necessary to treat or alleviate pain, nausea, and other symptoms associated with certain debilitating medical conditions.

The facts in this case are relatively straightforward. Plaintiff was denied the opportunity to apply for a job with Defendants because she believed she could not pass the pre-employment drug test. Plaintiff did inform Defendants that she was a medical marijuana cardholder and that she would obey state law and not bring marijuana into the workplace. Defendants do not contest that they denied her employment based on the fact that she could not pass the drug screening. Therefore, Defendants have violated the Hawkins-Slater Act. As a result, the Court grants Plaintiff's motion for summary judgment.

SECTION 2.7
DRUG TESTING

Illegal drug use is tremendously expensive. It cost the U.S. economy more than $740 billion annually, according to the Department of Justice's National Drug Intelligence Center. Bloomberg News notes that the cost of illegal drug use is similar to that of diabetes, which a government study places at more than $174 billion annually. Drug abuse, or addiction among workers can be expensive for business and industry, ranging from lost productivity, absenteeism, injuries, fatalities, theft and low employee morale, to an increase in health care, legal liability and workers' compensation costs. Also, drug abuse can cause issues at work including:

- After-effects of substance use, such as withdrawal, affecting job performance;

- Preoccupation with gathering and using substances while at work thereby interfering with concentration;

- Illegal activities at work such as selling illegal drugs to other workers; and

- Psychological or stress-related effects due to drug use by a co-worker that affects another individual's job performance.[46]

According to the National Workrights Institute, drug testing of employees without cause has increased steadily since 1986. Based upon a survey of 1,000 firms performed by the American Management Association, 51.5% of those employers engaged in some type of drug testing, represented a net growth of 140% since 1987. This organization maintains that there are better and more constitutional methods to address substance abuse in the workplace, such as education and treatment of employees. In support of their position, the Institute notes that growing awareness of health concerns associated with drug use, and drug education and prevention programs have contributed to a decline in drug use. They claim that indiscriminate testing for drugs is unfair and unnecessary. For instance, they maintain that it is unfair to force employees who are not even suspected of drug use, and whose job performance is satisfactory, to "prove" their drug free use through an uncertain procedure that violates personal privacy rights. These tests are unnecessary because they cannot show impairment and, thus, do not enhance an employer's ability to evaluate work performance.[47] Yet does this mean employers should be allowed to force their workers to undergo testing for illegal drugs?

Drug testing in the workplace had its inception when President Regan initiated such a program among federal employees. The President stated that the Federal Government, as the largest employer in the nation, is concerned with the well-being of its employees, the successful accomplishment of agency missions, and the need to maintain employee productivity. The executive Order also required that federal employees refrain from the use of illegal drugs whether on or off duty and provided that the head of each executive agency shall establish a program to test for the use of illegal drugs by employees in sensitive positions. Since this initiative, drug testing has become firmly embedded in the work place both inside and outside of the government and three types of programs have emerged: pre-employment screening, random drug testing and post-incident drug testing.

Drug testing college athletes is a well-established NCAA practice, in order to discourage student athletes from using performance-enhancing drugs. Drug testing is also allowed if a student's course of study involves safety risks, such as using heavy equipment. Can a college, however, implement a random drug testing of all students? That is the issue in the following case.

BARRETT V. CLAYCOMB
976 F. SUPP.2D 1104 (W. DT. MO. 2013)

The President of Linn State Technical College ("Linn State") implemented a policy, requiring all new Linn State students to be drug tested using urinalysis. Plaintiffs, representing a class of current and future students of the college, immediately filed suit seeking a declaratory judgment that this mandatory, suspicion-less drug-testing violated their constitutional rights.

The Fourth Amendment protects the right of Americans to be free from unreasonable searches and seizures. It is well-established that a urine drug test constitutes a search under the Fourth Amendment. Ordinarily, a search is unreasonable if it is conducted without individualized suspicion. Of particular relevance here, a suspicion-less search may be reasonable if it serves special governmental needs beyond the normal need for law enforcement.

In **Doe ex rel. Doe v. Little Rock Sch. Dist.,** **380 F.3d 349 (8th Cir. 2004),** the Eighth Circuit held that a suspicion-less search was unreasonable where the defendant school district "failed to demonstrate the existence of a need sufficient to justify" the search. In reaching this conclusion, the court rejected the school district's "generalized concerns about the existence of weapons and drugs in its schools," because there was "nothing in the record regarding the magnitude of any problems with weapons or drugs that it has actually experienced."

Defendants thus bear the burden of producing evidence to show that their case falls within the limited circumstances in which suspicion-less searches are permissible based on a concrete safety concern.

The facts in this case are largely undisputed. Linn State is a public, two-year college located in Missouri. Linn State offers at least twenty-eight distinct academic programs for the roughly 1,100 to 1,200 students who attend the institution. The academic programs offered are divided into five general categories: mechanical, electrical, civil, computer, and general education. Each of these programs is further divided into more specialized areas. As a technical school, many of the programs offered at Linn State involve a significant amount of hands-on training and manual exercises.

Over the course of Linn State's fifty-year history, there has never been an accident on campus that resulted in death or substantial bodily injury. There have been accidents that have required some medical attention, but there is no evidence that drug use caused or contributed to any accident in Linn State's history.

To override the requirements of the Fourth Amendment, the safety risks at issue must be of a unique or unusual degree. Certainly, there are innumerable common, daily activities that, if performed under the influence of an illicit drug, could fairly be said to pose a significant safety risk to others, such as driving a car. If suspicion-less searches are to remain "particularized exceptions," the applicability of the safety exception must be limited to circumstances that present unique safety hazards.

The risk of using illusory safety concerns to mask unconstitutional purposes is apparent in this case, as the evidence shows that the adoption of Linn State's drug-testing policy was motivated predominantly by considerations other than the safety interest for the students. The six "Program Goals" adopted by the Board of Regents do not even mention preventing accidents or injuries caused or contributed to by drug use, and instead focus on goals like improving retention and graduation rates. Likewise, the minutes from an advisory committee meeting show no indication that there were concerns for reducing or preventing drug-related accidents.

It is well-settled that "the collection and testing of urine intrudes upon expectations of privacy that society has long recognized as reasonable." Nonetheless, in some circumstances, individuals may have a diminished expectation of privacy with respect to the content of their urine. Where the evidence shows that students in a particular program are seeking accreditation in a heavily regulated industry or industries in which drug testing is the norm, the Court will take into account the diminished privacy expectations of these students. However, Defendants have not presented any other recognized basis for finding that Linn State students have limited privacy expectations. Accordingly, where there is little or no evidence suggesting that students in a given program are entering such a heavily regulated field, these students will be considered to have the full privacy expectations common to all adults, which are substantial.

Defendants' drug-testing policy is unconstitutional.

**SECTION 2.8
THE DRUG TESTING
OF TONY ROBERTS**

PROBLEM TWO—B

**PARK, BROWN & SMITH, P.C.
ATTORNEYS AT LAW
MEMORANDUM**

TO: All Law Clerks

FROM: Peter Smith, Esquire

RE: Tony's Drug Testing Problem

In the middle of the season with the Stallions, Tony Roberts took a short vacation during the team's off week and returned to Philadelphia. He spent Saturday night with an old girlfriend. They had dinner and went dancing at the Aztec Club on the waterfront. One thing led to another, and he spent the night at her apartment. The next day, it all seemed like a dream. Tony had spent much of the previous night high on something that she had given him to smoke. But it was Sunday, and he had to return to the Stallions.

The player arrived at practice on Monday, and the coach greeted the team with a stack of small, plastic specimen cups. "I hate to surprise you guys," said the coach, "But life can be surprising." Tony realized that he and his teammates were expected to produce a urine sample while the assistant coaches looked on. Tony felt embarrassed—but he also felt scared.

Therefore, he refused the test and the team suspended him. Read **"Luedtke v. Nabors Alaska Drilling Company"** and the materials about drug testing and answer the following questions:

1. What are the chances that Tony will show "positive" results from the urinalysis test?

2. If Tony does test positive and is fired from the team, would he win a lawsuit for wrongful discharge?

3. What ethical issues are raised here and what do you think is fair in this situation?

LUEDTKE V. NABORS ALASKA DRILLING, INC.
834 P.2D 1220 (ALASKA 1992)

This case addresses one aspect of drug testing by employers. A private employer, Nabors Alaska Drilling, Inc. [Nabors], established a drug testing program for its employees. Paul Luedtke worked on drilling rigs on the North Slope [and] refused to submit to urinalysis screening for drug use as required by Nabors. As a result [he was] fired.

Luedtke began working for Nabors, which operates drilling rigs on Alaska's North Slope, in February 1978. [He] began as a "floorman" and was eventually promoted to "driller." A driller oversees the work of an entire drilling crew. Luedtke started work with Nabors as a union member, initially being hired from the union hall. During his tenure, however, Nabors "broke" the union. Luedtke continued to work without a union contract. He had no written contract with Nabors at the time of his discharge.

During his employment with Nabors, Luedtke was accused twice of violating the company's drug and alcohol policies. Once he was suspended for 90 days for taking alcohol to the North Slope.

The other incident involved a search of the rig on which Luedtke worked. Aided by dogs trained to sniff out marijuana, the searchers found traces of marijuana on Luedtke's suitcase. Luedtke was allowed to continue working on the rig only after assuring his supervisors he did not use marijuana.

In October 1982, Luedtke scheduled a two-week vacation. Because his normal work schedule was two weeks of work on the North Slope followed by a week off, a two-week vacation amounted to 28 consecutive days away from work. Just prior to his vacation, he was instructed to arrange for a physical examination in Anchorage. He arranged for it to take place on October 19, during his vacation. It was at this examination that Nabors first tested Paul's urine for signs of drug use. The purpose of the physical, as understood by Luedtke, was to enable him to work on offshore rigs should Nabors receive such contracts. Although Luedtke was told it would be a comprehensive physical he had no idea that a urinalysis screening test for drug use would be performed. He did voluntarily give a urine sample but assumed it would be tested only for "blood sugar, any kind of kidney failure [and] problems with bleeding." Nabors' policy of testing for drug use was not announced until November 1, 1982, almost two weeks after Luedtke's examination.

[On] November 16, Luedtke received a letter informing him that his urine had tested positive for cannabinoids. The letter informed him that he would be required to pass two subsequent urinalysis tests, one on November 30 and the other on December 30, before he would be allowed to return to work. In response Luedtke hand delivered a letter drafted by his attorney to the Manager of Employee Relations for Nabors, explaining why he felt the testing and suspension were unfair. Luedtke did not take the urinalysis test on November 30 as requested by Nabors. On December 14, Nabors sent Luedtke a letter informing him that he was discharged for refusing to take the test on November 30.

The right to privacy is a recent creation of American law. The inception of this right is generally credited to a law review article published in 1890 by Louis Brandeis and his law partner, Samuel Warren. They wrote:

> Recent inventions...call attention to the next step which must be taken for the protection of the person, and for securing to the individual . . . the right "to be let alone." Instantaneous photographs and newspaper enterprise have invaded the sacred precincts of private and domestic life; and numerous mechanical devices threaten to make good the prediction that "what is whispered in the closet shall be proclaimed from the housetops."

While the legal grounds of this right were somewhat tenuous in the 1890's, American jurists found the logic of Brandeis and Warren's arguments compelling. By 1960, Professor Prosser could write that "the right of privacy, in one form or another, is declared to exist by the overwhelming majority of the American courts." He cited cases in which private parties had been held liable in tort for eavesdropping on private conversations by means of wiretapping and microphones, or for

peering into the windows of homes. Eventually the right to privacy attained sufficient recognition to be incorporated in several state constitutions.

Interpreting the Constitution of the United States, the United States Supreme Court in 1965 held that a Connecticut statute banning the use of birth control devices by married couples was "repulsive to the notions of privacy surrounding the marriage relationship." **Griswold v. Connecticut, 381 U.S. 479, 486 (1965).** The Supreme Court wrote that "specific guarantees in the Bill of Rights have penumbras, formed by emanations from those guarantees that help give them life and substance. Various guarantees create zones of privacy..." Since Griswold the Supreme Court has found the federal constitutional right of privacy to apply a number of other situations. **Roe v. Wade, 410 U.S. 113 (1973)** (right of privacy broad enough to encompass a woman's decision whether or not to terminate her pregnancy); **Eisenstadt v. Baird, 405 U.S. 438 (1972)** (regulation which made contraceptives less available to unmarried than married couples invalidated). But see **Bowers v. Hardwick, 478 U.S. 186 (1986)** (due process clause of Fourteenth Amendment does not confer any fundamental right on homosexuals to engage in acts of consensual sodomy).

Thus, the concept of privacy has become pervasive in modern legal thought. But a clear definition of this right...has eluded both courts and legal scholars. It is the fundamental nature of the concept that leads to such great difficulty in application.

The next question we address is whether a public policy exists protecting an employee's right to withhold certain "private" information from his employer.

We believe such a policy does exist, and is evidenced in the common law, statutes and constitution of this state. Alaska law clearly evidences strong support for the public interest in employee privacy. First, state statutes support the policy that there are private sectors of employee's lives not subject to direct scrutiny by their employers. For example, employers may not require employees to take polygraph tests as a condition of employment. In addition, Alaska Statute 18.80.200(a) provides:

> It is determined and declared as a matter of legislative finding that discrimination against an inhabitant of the state because of race, religion, color, national origin, age, sex, marital status, changes in marital status, pregnancy, or parenthood is a matter of public concern and that this discrimination not only threatens the rights and privileges of the inhabitants of the state but also menaces the institutions of the state and threatens peace, order, health, safety and general welfare of the state and its inhabitants. [It is] unlawful for employers to inquire into such topics in connection with prospective employment. Second, as previously noted, Alaska's constitution contains a right to privacy clause. Third, there exists a common law right to privacy.

[T]here is a sphere of activity in every person's life that is closed to scrutiny by others. The boundaries of that sphere are determined by balancing a person's right to privacy against other public policies, such as "the health, safety, rights and privileges of others." Luedtke claim[s] that whether or not [he] use[s] marijuana is information within that protected sphere into which his employer, Nabors, may not intrude. We disagree. As we have previously observed, marijuana can impair a person's ability to function normally.

We also observe that work on an oil rig can be very dangerous. We have determined numerous cases involving serious injury or death resulting from accidents on oil drilling rigs. In addition, the trial court expressly considered the dangers of work on oil rigs.

Where the public policy supporting Luedtke's privacy in off-duty activities conflicts with the public policy supporting the protection of the health and safety of other workers, and even Luedtke himself, the health and safety concerns are paramount. As a result, Nabors is justified in determining whether Luedtke is possibly impaired on the job by drug usage off the job.

We observe, however, that the employer's prerogative does have limitations. First, the drug test must be conducted at a time reasonably contemporaneous with the employee's work time. The employer's interest is in monitoring drug use that may directly affect employee performance. The employer's interest is not in the broader police function of discovering and controlling the use of illicit drugs in general society. In the context of this case, Nabors could have tested Luedtke immediately prior to [his] departure for the North Slope, or immediately upon his return from the North Slope, when the test could be reasonably certain of detecting drugs consumed there. Further, given Nabors' need to control the oil rig community. Nabors could have tested him at any time he was on the North Slope.

Second, an employee must receive notice of the adoption of a drug testing program. By requiring a test, an employer introduces an additional term of employment. An employee should have notice of the additional term so that he may contest it, refuse to accept it and quit, seek to negotiate its conditions, or prepare for the test so that he will not fail it and thereby suffer sanctions.

These considerations do not apply with regard to the tests Luedtke refused to take. Luedtke was given notice of the future tests. He did not take the test on November 30. As a result, Nabors was justified in discharging him.

THE PROBLEM OF THE FALSE POSITIVE

Both employers and employees share at least one concern: whether or not urinalysis is a reliable means of uncovering drug use. Employees are concerned over the accuracy of drug testing since they may be hired or fired on the basis of results. Employers are interested because they don't want to waste time and money ferreting out innocent workers, only to spend more time and money replacing them.

There are many serious reliability problems. Certain over-the-counter drugs may register as illegal ones, Test results on people using the familiar cold remedies Contac or Sudafed have (wrongly) indicated that they were on amphetamines. The pain relievers Datril and Advil have shown up as marijuana, and cough syrups containing dextromethorphan may register as opiate traces. False positives can be produced in the oddest ways: A person with the disease lupus (in remission) might appear to be taking amphetamines. A person who had ingested poppy seeds just before urinalysis might seem to have opium in his system. Research indicates that "passive inhalation" can also cause positive results. In other words, a person could test as a marijuana user, not because of actually smoking the drug, but because of being at a concert, a party, or on a bus where it was smoked.

How often are these mistakes made? The testing laboratories assert that the most commonly used procedures are 95-99 percent accurate. At best, then, the industry itself claims an inaccuracy rate of 1 percent. But since 4 to 5 million people are tested annually, 40,000 to 50,000 people must be falsely accused each year.

Perhaps most telling are the results of a 1987 study performed by the National Institute on Drug Abuse, which found that 20 percent of the 50 laboratories tested reported the presence of drugs in urine specimens when no drugs were present. These mistakes were made even though each laboratory had been warned in advance that its competence was about to be evaluated by the federal government.[48]

TEST REVELATIONS

Urinalysis picks up traces of certain substances in the blood. Although drug testing cannot tell an employer whether an employee was "high" while at work (it measures the presence of a substance, not the time it was ingested), it can reveal that the employee had used marijuana sometime during the past few weeks. Some substances linger in the body longer than others; drug tests can reveal that the subject smoked one marijuana cigarette as many as 81 days earlier, while cocaine traces will be undetectable after 2-3 days, and evidence of alcohol will be flushed from the body within a half day.

Urine tests can also reveal extraneous information—whether a worker is pregnant, or is taking medication for a heart condition, asthma, epilepsy, diabetes, or manic depression, for example.

CONTROL OF PERSONAL INFORMATION

Privacy is not just a matter of minimizing the amount of information known about a person. It also involves control over that information. Employees worry that the confidentiality of test results is not guaranteed. Will they become part of a permanent, computerized file, accessible to any number of people? Will a worker be blacklisted because of a false positive, and never know why his or her career was stagnating?

PROBLEM TWO—B
ANSWER SHEET

Name _____ **Please Print Clearly**

1. What are the chances that Tony will show "positive" results from the urinalysis test?

_____

_____

_____

_____

_____

_____

_____

_____

2. If Tony does test positive and is fired from the team, would he win a lawsuit for wrongful discharge?

_____

_____

_____

_____

_____

_____

_____

_____

3. What ethical issues are raised here and what do you think is fair in this situation?

_____

_____

_____

_____

_____

_____

_____

_____

_____

_____

_____

_____

_____

_____

_____

_____

_____

SECTION 2.9
SEXUAL HARASSMENT

What do the names Roger Ailes, Harvey Weinstein, Kevin Spacey, Mario Batali, Dustin Huffman, and Matt Lauer have in common? They are men who have been accused of sexual harassment as part of the "Me Too" movement. Activist Tarana Burke coined the phrase in 2007 as a way to use social media to reach sexual assault victims in underprivileged areas.[50] Up to this point, sexual harassment was often overlooked or not taken seriously. The "Me Too" movement has changed that with powerful men being ousted from their jobs seemingly overnight. So, what exactly does **sexual harassment** mean?

The **Equal Employment Opportunity Commission (EEOC)** describes sexual harassment as a form of gender discrimination and the U.S. Supreme Court has made employers liable for sexual harassment of their employees. Statistically, the Society for Human Resource Management indicates that 62% of businesses offer sexual harassment prevention training programs, and 97% have a written sexual harassment policy. However, most sexual harassment situations go unreported and the number of grievances filed with the EEOC has gradually decreased. Most complaints come from women but the number of complaints filed by men is increasing, along with the increasing amount of men filing complaints against female supervisors.[51]

A recent study determined that 1 out of every 4 women and 1 in 10 men has been sexually harassed at work. The top professions with the highest number of claims are: 1) Business, Trade, Banking, and Finance; 2) Sales and Marketing; 3) Hospitality; 4) Civil Service; and 5) Education, Lecturing, and Teaching.[52]

This form of harassment causes repercussions, including monetary damages and it can have a negative impact on the employee's physical and emotional health. These effects include anxiety, depression, sleep disorders, weight loss or gain, loss of appetite, and other neurological and health disorders.[53]

The Federal Government has stepped in to try and prevent this improper conduct from happening.

In 1964 Congress passed comprehensive **Civil Rights** legislation including this excerpt, known as **Title VII**:

a. It shall be an unlawful employment practice for an employer:

    1. to fail or refuse to hire or to discharge any individual, or otherwise to discriminate against any individual with respect to his compensation, terms, conditions, or privileges of employment because of such individual's race, color, religion, sex, or national origin.

The statute itself outlaws discrimination in broad, general language. The job of clarifying the statute by providing detailed examples of illegal discrimination is left to an administrative agency. In the case of Title VII, that government agency is the **Equal Employment Opportunity Commission (EEOC),** created by Congress to interpret and enforce the employment provisions of the Civil Rights Law.

In 1980, the EEOC adopted the following guidelines:

a. Harassment on the basis of sex consists of unwelcome sexual advances, requests for sexual favors, and other verbal or physical conduct of a sexual nature and will constitute sexual harassment when:

   1. Submission to such conduct is made either explicitly or implicitly a term or condition of an individual's employment;

   2. Submission to or rejection of such conduct by an individual is used as the basis for employment decisions affecting such individual; or

   3. Such conduct has the purpose or effect of unreasonably interfering with an individual's work performance or creating an intimidating, hostile, or offensive working environment.

b. In determining whether alleged conduct constitutes sexual harassment, the Commission will look at the record as a whole and at the totality of the circumstances, such as the nature of the sexual advances and the context in which the alleged incidents occurred. The determination of the legality of a particular action will be made from the facts, on a case by case basis.

c. An employer is responsible for its acts and those of its agents and supervisory employees with respect to sexual harassment, regardless of whether the specific acts complained of were authorized, or even forbidden by the employer and regardless of whether the employer knew or should have known of their occurrence. (In its first sexual harassment case, the Supreme Court in 1986 made it clear that in cases of "hostile environment" sexual harassment an employer would only be held responsible if he knew or should have known about the harassment.)

d. With respect to conduct between fellow employees, an employer is responsible for acts of sexual harassment in the workplace where the employer (or its agents or supervisory employees) knows or should have known of the conduct, unless it can show that it took immediate and appropriate corrective action.

e. Prevention is the best tool for the elimination of sexual harassment. An employer should take all steps necessary to prevent sexual harassment from occurring, such as affirmatively raising the subject, expressing strong disapproval, developing appropriate sanctions informing employees of their right to raise and how to raise the issue of harassment under Title VII, and developing methods to sensitize all concerned.

Types Of Sexual Harassment

Courts have identified two kinds of sexual harassment. The first is called **quid pro quo** (or "tangible benefit loss") and it happens when an employee is expected to give into sexual demands or suffer the loss of some specific job benefit: a raise, a promotion, or even the job itself. Quid pro quo harassment would exist where a woman is fired for refusing to go on a date with her supervisor, for example.

The other kind of harassment, labelled **hostile work environment**, involves less specific consequences. It could occur when a woman is constantly subjected to sexual harangues and obscenities in her workplace, or when she must repeatedly refuse unwanted sexual advances from her supervisor. Although she suffers no economic loss, she is a victim of discrimination because she must put up with a down-graded work atmosphere, pervaded with unpleasantness.

This second type of harassment has proved to be complicated: How offensive must the environment be to justify a complaint of sexual harassment? What factors should a court take into account in considering whether or not a particular workplace is so hostile to women that it discriminates against them?

PUNG V. REGUS MANAGEMENT GROUP
2017 WL 6550673 (D. Ct. Minn. 2017)

This case involves a consensual workplace relationship that ended and subsequent claims of harassment and retaliation.

In 2011, Scott Ravenscroft became Plaintiff's supervisor. In 2012, Plaintiff and Ravenscroft began a consensual, sexual relationship. In March 2014, Plaintiff told Ravenscroft that she wanted to end the relationship. After Plaintiff ended the relationship, Plaintiff alleges that Ravenscroft's behavior toward her became "very controlling" and that he treated her worse than her co-workers.

On June 4, 2014, Ravenscroft met with Plaintiff and threatened to put her on a "coaching plan." Ravenscroft suggested that Plaintiff's "numbers were lacking." Plaintiff expressed concern because she understood that coaching plans had been used in the past as a premise to terminate

an employee. Plaintiff explained that she thought Ravenscroft was targeting her because she ended their sexual relationship.

On June 23, 2014, a supervisor concluded that Ravenscroft's behavior had created an appearance of improper conduct. Ravenscroft was given a warning and informed that he would be terminated if the behavior continued. Ravenscroft remained responsible for Plaintiff's day-to-day reporting. Plaintiff asserts that co-workers noticed Ravenscroft's demeanor toward her, such as making "harsh" and "demeaning" comments to Plaintiff in e-mails and calling her questions "stupid" during conference calls.

In December 2014, Plaintiff was planning a client holiday party and she e-mailed Ravenscroft to ask for the amount of money that she could spend on such a party. Ravenscroft told Plaintiff to keep it under $250. Plaintiff ended spending $560 on the party. Plaintiff told a supervisor that she did not think the budget was appropriate, as the party was for 100 clients), and that she did not think she needed to follow the budget. On January 23, 2015, the supervisor decided that Plaintiff should be placed on a Performance Improvement Plan (PIP). This decision was based on Plaintiff's overspending on the holiday party.

On February 2, 2015, Regus implemented a Reduction in Force and Plaintiff's employment was terminated. Plaintiff points to evidence that the only reason she was on the PIP was the single incident of insubordination related to going over the holiday-party budget.

Title VII makes it an "unlawful employment practice for an employer ... to discriminate against any individual ... because of such individual's ... sex." Plaintiff alleges quid-pro-quo sexual harassment. To establish a case of quid-pro-quo harassment, a plaintiff must show that: (1) she was a member of a protected class; (2) she was subjected to unwelcome sexual harassment in the form of sexual advances or requests for sexual favors; (3) the harassment was based on sex; and (4) her submission to the unwelcome advances was an express or implied condition for receiving job benefits or her refusal to submit resulted in a tangible job detriment. Defendant moves for summary judgment on this claim. Defendant asserts that Ravenscroft did not threaten Plaintiff's position, seek sexual favors, or intimate that a failure to engage in a sexual relationship with him would impact Plaintiff's employment.

Plaintiff argues that her termination was the direct result of Ravenscroft's imposition of a budget for the holiday party and his subsequent complaint about Plaintiff going over the budget. Plaintiff submits that Ravenscroft was motivated to complain about the expenditure, because he was upset that Plaintiff refused to continue their sexual relationship and that she complained to HR about

his behavior. Plaintiff cites the following evidence to support a showing of discriminatory intent: (1) Ravenscroft came up with the $250 holiday party without relying on any specific company policy; (2) Plaintiff was the only employee who was disciplined for exceeding a party budget, despite the fact that other employees threw parties without strict budget constraints and Plaintiff had thrown similar parties in years past without incident.

The Court finds that a reasonable juror could conclude that Ravenscroft's treatment, and in particular his role in the issue regarding Plaintiff's holiday party expenditure, ultimately factored into Plaintiff's termination.

Plaintiff also asserts claims for hostile work environment sexual harassment. Unlike *quid pro quo* sexual harassment hostile work environment harassment arises when sexual conduct has the purpose or effect of unreasonably interfering with an individual's work performance or creating an intimidating, hostile, or offensive working environment. To prevail, Plaintiff must show that (1) she belongs to a protected group, (2) she was subject to unwelcome sexual harassment, (3) the harassment was based on sex, (4) the harassment affected a condition of employment, and (5) the employer knew or should have known of the harassment in question and failed to take proper remedial action. While behavior creating the hostile working environment need not be overtly sexual in nature, it must be unwelcome in the sense that the employee did not solicit or invite it, and the employee regarded the conduct as undesirable or offensive. In addition, the harassment must be sufficiently severe or pervasive to alter the conditions of employment and create an abusive working environment.

In support of her hostile work environment claims, Plaintiff argues that after she ended the sexual relationship, Ravenscroft's behavior was sufficiently severe and pervasive so as to alter her conditions of employment and that Regus failed to remedy the situation.

The Court concludes that Plaintiff's workplace interactions with Ravenscroft after their consensual relationship ended did not constitute the type of sustained, severe harassment required to make a claim of hostile work environment. There is evidence that Ravenscroft criticized Plaintiff's work. This evidence, however, is insufficient to support a hostile work-environment claim.

There is no evidence that Ravenscroft made physical contact with Plaintiff, used inappropriate language, or made sexual or intimidating comments to Plaintiff. Instead, the evidence shows that Ravenscroft may have been abrupt, critical, and sarcastic at times, but this behavior was not sustained so as to rise to the level of an abusive work environment.

QUESTIONS FOR DISCUSSION:

1. Do you agree with the court's ruling that Pung failed to make out a case for sexual harrassment?

2. Remember the two ethical theories: Utilitarian, focusing on consequences for all concerned, and Rights-based, focusing on the competing rights of all concerned. How does each theory guide us in looking at sexual harassment?

3. What do you think should be done about sexual harassment?

SECTION 2.10
SHARON ROCK
V. JOSEPH ROBERTS

PROBLEM TWO—C

PARK, BROWN & SMITH, P.C.
ATTORNEYS AT LAW
MEMORANDUM

TO: All Law Clerks

FROM: Peter Smith, Esquire

RE: Sexual Harassment

Joe Roberts owned a construction company a few years ago. However, it seems like a distant memory now that Joe owns a bar, but a case from his past has come back to haunt him. Joe's construction firm was mostly male employees. Over the years, the only women in the company were those who worked in the office: the receptionist, secretaries, and the bookkeeper. But Joe decided to hire a woman, Theresa Rock, for one of his crews. She was a certified electrician. Joe also liked her looks, especially since she was shapely, even in work clothes.

Things seemed to be going well with Ms. Rock. After about a month though, Joe saw something that made him wonder. On one of the stalls in the bathroom, he noticed lewd comments about Theresa. On a job site about a week later, he overheard some of his men laughing together about something. As he walked over to listen, he noticed Theresa pushing through the knot of men. She seemed upset. Joe asked what was going on. "It's Mizz Sensitive," said the foreman. "What's that about?" asked Joe. "Nothing. It's about nothing, but she wants it to be something." Joe changed the subject, and began talking about the job at hand.

Several weeks later, Theresa told Joe she had to talk to him. He was busy, but she seemed upset. Theresa explained that she felt she was being picked on by her co-workers. "Maybe they're jealous of me because I am a really good electrician, but I think they just hate me because I'm a woman. They think it's their kingdom or something." When Joe asked who was doing what, she was unsure. "Someone's been taking my equipment. I'll be missing a tool, or my hard-hat, things like that. And when I don't have the hat, the foreman sends me home." Joe asked her if she'd talked to the foreman. "I went to Bill right away, but he just said I was paranoid."

Joe spoke to Bill after his interview with Theresa, and got nowhere. It seemed that she was imagining things, and she couldn't take a joke. "It's rough out here," said the foreman. "Maybe she can't take it."

The next time Joe saw Theresa they were both in the parking area. It was early in the morning and no one else was around. Joe thought Theresa seemed a little depressed. He said, "Theresa, what about having dinner tonight?"

She looked up at him, squinted, paused and said, "Okay." But there was no chance to find out why Theresa seemed depressed. Later that day, Joe's secretary told him that Theresa had quit and gone home. Supposedly, the crane operator had dropped a stack of pallets from a height of about two stories onto the ground in front of Theresa. She had left the site in tears, telling the foreman she would never be back.

Last week, Joe received papers for a sexual harassment lawsuit that Theresa brought against him and his former company. She alleged that the atmosphere at work had been filled with tension from the minute she arrived, that she was belittled by sexual jokes and graffiti, constant teasing, and other harassing behavior—all of which, she alleged was due to the fact that she was a woman. She even accused Joe of sexual harassment for asking her out. The implication was that Joe would use his power over her as the boss, if she refused to go out with him.

Joe was shocked, and nervous about the probable reaction to the news by his wife. Based upon the materials in this section on Sexual Harassment, and **Rabidue v. Osceola Refining Company,** answer the following questions:

1. What are the types of sexual harassment, and which one(s) might apply to whom in this situation?

2. What is the likely outcome if a judge follows the reasoning of the majority in the **Rabidue** case?

3. What is the likely outcome if a judge follows the reasoning of Judge Keith in **Rabidue**?

4. Assume Joe is not liable for merely asking Theresa out on a date. Is he still liable for the behavior of his former employees?

RABIDUE v. OSCEOLA REFINING CO.
805 F.2D 611 (6TH CIR. 1986)

The plaintiff was a capable, independent, ambitious, aggressive, intractable, and opinionated individual. The plaintiff's supervisors and co-employees with whom plaintiff interacted almost uniformly found her to be an abrasive, rude, antagonistic, extremely willful, uncooperative, and irascible personality. She consistently argued with co-workers and company customers in defiance of supervisory direction and jeopardized Osceola's business relationships with major oil companies. She disregarded supervisory instruction and company policy whenever such direction conflicted with her personal reasoning and conclusions. In sum, the plaintiff was a troublesome employee.

The plaintiff's charged sexual harassment arose primarily as a result of her unfortunate acrimonious working relationship with Douglas Henry. Henry was a supervisor of the company's key punch and computer section. Occasionally, the plaintiff's duties required coordination with Henry's department and personnel, although Henry exercised no supervisory authority over the plaintiff nor the plaintiff over him. Henry was an extremely vulgar and crude individual who customarily made obscene comments about women generally, and on occasion, directed such obscenities to the plaintiff. Management was aware of Henry's vulgarity but had been unsuccessful in curbing his offensive personality traits during the time encompassed by this controversy. The plaintiff and Henry, on the occasions when their duties exposed them to each other, were constantly in a confrontational posture. The plaintiff, as well as other female employees, were annoyed by Henry's vulgarity. In addition to Henry's obscenities, other male employees from time to time displayed pictures of nude or scantily clad women in their offices and/or work areas, to which the plaintiff and other women employees were exposed.

[T]o prove a claim of abusive work environment premised upon sexual harassment, a plaintiff must demonstrate that she would not have been the object of harassment but for her sex. It is of significance to note that instances of complained sexual conduct that prove equally offensive to male and female workers would not support a Title VII sexual harassment charge because both men and women were accorded like treatment.

[S]exually hostile or intimidating environments are characterized by multiple and varied combinations and frequencies of offensive exposures which require the plaintiff to demonstrate that injury resulted not from a single or isolated offensive incident, comment, or conduct, but from incidents, comments or conduct which occurred with some frequency. To accord appropriate protection to both plaintiffs and defendants in a hostile and/or abusive work environment sexual harassment case, the trier of fact, when judging the totality of the circumstances impacting upon the asserted abusive and hostile environment must adopt the perspective of a reasonable person's reaction to a similar environment under essentially like or similar circumstances. Thus, in the absence of conduct which would interfere with that hypothetical reasonable individual's work performance and affect seriously the psychological well-being of that reasonable person under like circumstances, a plaintiff may not prevail. The plaintiff must also demonstrate that she was actually offended by the defendant's conduct and that she suffered some degree of injury as a result of the abusive and hostile work environment.

The trier of fact should also consider such objective and subjective factors as the nature of the alleged harassment, the background and experience of the plaintiff, her co-workers and supervisors, the totality of the physical environment of the workplace both before and after the plaintiff's introduction into its environs, coupled with the reasonable expectation of the plaintiff upon voluntarily entering that environment. As Judge Newblatt aptly stated in his opinion in the district court:

> Indeed, it cannot seriously be disputed that in some work environments, humor and language are rough hewn and vulgar. Sexual jokes, sexual conversation and girlie magazines may abound. Title VII was not meant to—or can— change this. It must never be forgotten that Title VII is the federal court mainstay in the struggle for equal employment opportunity for the female workers of America. But it is quite different to claim that Title VII was designed to bring about a magical transformation in the social mores of American workers.

In the case at bar, Henry's obscenities, although annoying, were not so startling as to have affected seriously the psyches of the plaintiff or other female employees. The evidence did not demonstrate that this single employee's vulgarity substantially affected the totality of the workplace. The sexually oriented poster displays had a de minimis effect on the plaintiff's work environment when considered in the context of a society that condones and publicly features and commercially exploits open displays of written and pictorial erotica at the newsstands, on prime-time television, at the cinema, and in other public places. In sum, Henry's vulgar language, coupled with the sexually oriented posters, did not result in a working environment that could be considered intimidating, hostile or offensive. It necessarily follows that the plaintiff failed to sustain her burden of proof that she was the victim of a Title VII sexual harassment violation.

KEITH, Circuit Judge, dissenting in part:

For seven years plaintiff worked at Osceola as the sole woman in a salaried management position. In common work areas plaintiff and other female employees were exposed daily to displays of nude or partially clad women belonging to a number of male employees at Osceola. One poster, which remained on the wall for eight years, showed a prone woman who had a golf ball on her breasts with a man standing over her, golf club in hand, yelling "Fore." And one desk plaque declared, "Even male chauvinist pigs need love..."

In addition, Computer Division Supervisor Doug Henry regularly spewed anti-female obscenity. Of plaintiff, Henry specifically remarked "All that bitch needs is a good lay" and called her "fat ass." Plaintiff arranged at least one meeting of female employees to discuss Henry and repeatedly filed written complaints on behalf of her herself and other female employees who feared losing their jobs if they complained directly. Osceola Vice President Charles Muetzel stated he knew that employees were "greatly disturbed" by Henry's language. However, because Osceola needed Henry's computer expertise, Muetzel did not reprimand or fire Henry. In response to subsequent complaints about Henry, a later supervisor, Charles Shoemaker, testified that he gave Henry "a little fatherly advice" about Henry's prospects if he learned to become "an executive type person."

In my view, Title VII's precise purpose is to prevent such behavior and attitudes from poisoning the work environment of classes protected under the Act. To condone the majority's notion of the "prevailing workplace" I would also have to agree that if an employer maintains an anti-Sematic workforce and tolerates a workplace in which "kike" jokes, displays of Nazi literature and anti-Jewish conversation "may abound," a Jewish employee assumes the risk of working there, and a court must consider such a work environment as "prevailing." I cannot. As I see it, job relatedness is the only additional factor which legitimately bears on the inquiry of plaintiff's reasonableness in finding her work environment offensive. In other words, the only additional question I would find relevant is whether the behavior complained of is required to perform the work.

PROBLEM TWO—C
ANSWER SHEET

Name   **Please Print Clearly**

1. What are the two types of sexual harassment, and which one(s) might apply to whom in this situation?

_____

_____

_____

_____

_____

_____

_____

_____

_____

2. What is the likely outcome if a judge follows the reasoning of the majority in the **Rabidue** case?

_____

_____

_____

_____

_____

_____

_____

_____

_____

3. What is the likely outcome if a judge follows the reasoning of Judge Keith in **Rabidue**?

_____

_____

_____

_____

_____

_____

_____

_____

4. Assume Joe is not liable for merely asking Theresa out on a date. Is he still liable for the behavior of his former employees?

_____

_____

_____

_____

_____

_____

_____

_____

_____

_____

SECTION 2.11 INTERNATIONAL BUSINESS ETHICS

When an enterprise transacts business in the international arena, a range of important issues arise that do not have easy answers as compared to conducting business in only one country. This dilemma is increasingly plaguing the multinational entity, and international business ethics has arisen to help address these matters. **International business ethics** attempts to deal with the problems of what to do in circumstances where ethical morals and dilemmas exist as a result of varying cultural practices.[54]

Business leaders must adopt a global standard of ethical practices to create a truly great, global business. In the 1970s, the federal government intervened to impose a set of standards by enacting the **Foreign Corrupt Practices Act (FPCA).** This law sent a chill throughout American businesses by criminalizing the act of making payments outside the U.S. in pursuit of contracts. Nevertheless, the practice of bribes to foreign officials and businesses has persisted. A number of U.S. executives have even lobbied Congress to relax the FPCA's provisions, maintaining that they are at a competitive disadvantage in bidding against non-U.S. firms.[55]

Many businesses routinely engage in international trade, a fact which has deepened the ethics debate. Issuing bribes to obtain business is a customary practice in many developing markets in the Middle East, Asia, Africa, and Eastern Europe. In fact, some entrepreneurs feel that they must play the game to be competitive. Witness Germany's Siemens (SI), which has admitted to paying nearly $2 billion in bribes, leading to the resignations of both its board chairman and CEO in 2007.[56]

International business ethics, however, is broader than just making bribes in foreign countries. It also includes human rights violations, environmental issues and conservation, corruption, extortion, and fraud. No significant consensus has developed on an international level dealing world problems such as pollution, conservation of natural resources, and other environmental concerns. As the result, solutions dealing with controls are largely left up to the individual countries.[57]

The international business ethics areas with the largest importance for multinational corporations involve issues dealing with anti-bribery efforts, the Convention on Combating Bribery of Foreign Public Officials in International Business Transactions and Inter-American Convention against Corruption. Human rights issues involving workers' rights, child labor, sweatshops, and prisoner labor also loom large in overseas factories, especially for those engaged in global outsourcing.[58]

The following is a brief summary of some of these initiatives. The **Convention on Combating Bribery of Foreign Public Officials in International Business Transactions** establishes standards to make criminal bribery of public officials in international business transactions illegal and provides for a number of related measures that make this policy effective. The law became effective in 1999 and is the only international anti-corruption agreement focused on the "supply side" of the bribery transaction. Forty countries have adopted this Convention, which covers the conduct of the entity making the bribe. It does not however, cover bribes paid to private persons or bribes paid to public officials for reasons other than obtaining or retaining a business or gaining other improper advantages in international business transactions.[59]

The **Inter-American Convention against Corruption** was enacted in 1996 and establishes an international legal framework aimed at eliminating bribery and corruption of government officials thereby protecting fair competitiveness in international transactions. Under the Convention, 40 nations agreed to prohibit and punish the offering of a bribe by its residents, and businesses, to a government official of another country of anything of a monetary value or benefit in connection with commercial transaction in exchange for any act or omission in the performance of that official's public duties.[60]

SECTION 2.12
PROBLEM CASES

1. Butler was shopping at a supermarket when she walked towards her car in the parking lot. Suddenly, she was assaulted and her pocketbook was stolen. An investigation showed that over a period of one year, there had been seven attacks on the Acme market premises. Five of these attacks, occurred in the parking lot during the four month period immediately preceding the assault on Butler. The supermarket had hired off-duty police officers to act as security guards during the evening hours. However, there was only one security guard on duty at the time of the attack. Does the supermarket owe a duty of care to safeguard its patrons when they are in the parking lot of their store? **Helen Butler v. Acme Markets, Inc., 426 A.2d 522 (N.J. App. 1981).**

2. The car being driven by Wagner collided with a bicycle ridden by a ten year old boy. The child's father, thinking that his son was dying, ran from the house, jumped from the porch over the steps, and onto the ground thereby fracturing his leg. The father sued the driver of the automobile on the basis that the father owed a duty to rescue his son and his injury was a natural consequence of the car driver's negligence. Wagner argued that the father rashly and unnecessarily exposed himself to danger and should be barred from recovery. Should the driver of the automobile be responsible for the father's broken leg? **Mark v. Wagner, 307 N.E. 2d 480 (Oh. App. 1977).**

3. Saltsman went to an entertainment complex in order to use the batting cage. The manager noticed a patron carrying alcoholic beverages and asked that individual to leave. In response, the patron slammed the cup of beer into the manager's face. Saltsman followed the assailant

to the parking lot in order to obtain a license plate number from the assailant's vehicle. This led to a physical encounter in which Saltsman was attacked by the assailant with a golf club. Saltsman sued the entertainment complex for his injuries. An investigation showed that there had been no similar criminal activity on the premises in the past. Is the sporting complex responsible for the injuries to Saltsman? **Doug Saltsman v. Michael Corazo, 721 A.2d 1000 (N.J. Super. 1998).**

4. Estella brought a sexual harassment suit against her employer, Garage Management Corporation, for sexual harassment by a person of the same sex. The employer argued that same sex harassment does not rise to the level of a hostile work environment because the aggrieved party cannot prove that the harassment complained of was based upon her sex. Does sexual harassment of an individual by a person of the same sex, give rise to a viable cause of action? **Estella v. Garage Management Corporation, 2000 W.L. 1228968 (S.D. N.Y. 2000).**

5. A high school student was engaged in a sexual relationship with one of her teachers. She did not report that relationship to school officials. After the couple was discovered having sex, the teacher was arrested and terminated from his employment. The school district had not distributed any type of official grievance policy for lodging sexual harassment complaints as required by Federal Regulations. The high school student then filed suit against the school district, claiming a violation of Title IX which provides inpertinent part, "that a person cannot be subjected to discrimination under any educational program or activity which receives federal financial assistance." An investigation into the incident revealed that no one in a supervisory power over the high school teacher knew of the affair with the student. Can the student recover damages for teacher-student sexual harassment because they failed to have a sexual harassment policy in place even though the school district officials were unaware of the teacher's misconduct? **Alida Gebser v. Lago Vista, Independent School District, 524 U.S. 274 (1998).**

SECTION 2.13
INTERNET REFERENCES

For a discussion of some of the topics contained in this chapter, see the following Internet sites:

A. *Drug Testing*

- **www.mrinc.com/**
  A drug testing company maintains this site and provides news on drug testing, and provides answers to frequently asked questions about drug testing in the workplace.

B. *Sexual Harassment*

- **www.capstn.com/quiz.html**
  This site offers a quiz about sexual harassment.

- **www.EEOC.gov/facts/fs-sex.html**
  The Equal Employment Opportunity Commission may be found at this address and Internet users may obtain information about sexual harassment, as well as the text of Title VII of the Civil Rights Act of 1964.

- **www.feminist.org/911/harass.html**
  This site lists various national hotlines for sexual harassment, including information on what to do if you or someone you know is sexually harassed.

C. Ethics

- **www.legalethics.com/ethics.law**
  This site provides ethics information in each state involving, lawyer ethics, confidentiality, and advertising.

- **www.usoge.gov/**
  The United States Office of Government Ethics Home Page is maintained at this location.

Footnotes:

1. David Ingram, *Examples of Ethics Violations in Business*, Chron, http://smallbusiness.chron.com/examples-ethics-violations-business-25673.html (last visited January 14, 2018.)

2. *Id.*

3. *Id.*

4. Robert Prentice, *Ethics Is Not a Word Under Trump Administration. It Should Be,* UT News, July 28, 2017, https://news.utexas.edu/2017/07/28/ethics-is-not-a-word-under-trump-administration (last visited January 13, 2018.)

5. *Id.*

6. Ethical Dilemma Examples, Your Dictionary, http://examples.yourdictionary.com/ethical-dilemma-examples.html (last visited September 22, 2013).

7. The Importance of Ethics in Business, The Time One Hundred, http://businesscasestudies.co.uk/cadbury-schweppes/ethical-business-practices/the-importance-of-ethics-in-business.html#axzz2hZ2GMC7X (last visited October 12, 2013).

8. *Id.*

9. Business Ethics, Small Biz Content, http://toolkit.smallbiz.nsw.gov.au/part/17/85/370 (last visited October 12 2013, 2013).

10. Ethical Issues within a Business, Boundless, https://www.boundless.com/business/business-ethics-and-social-responsibility/business-ethics/ethical-issues-within-a-business/ (last visited September 22, 2013).

11. Sources of Business Ethics, Management Study Guide, http://www.management-studyguide.com/sources-of-business-ethics.htm (last visited October 12, 2013).

12. Osmond Vitez, What are the Sources of an Organization's Code of Ethics?, Chron, http://smallbusiness.chron.com/sources-organizations-code-ethics-749.html (last visited October 12, 2013).

13. Jena McGregor, Chick-Fil-A President Dan Cathy Bites Into Gay-Marriage Debate, The Washington Post, July 19, 2012, http://www.washingtonpost.com/blogs/post-leadership/post/chick-fil-a-president-dan-cathy-bites-into-gay-marriage-debate/2012/07/19/gJQACrvzvW_blog.html (last visited September 22, 2013).

14. *Id.*

15. Definition of 'Code Of Ethics', Business Ethics, Investopedia, http://www.investope dia.com/terms/c/code-of-ethics.asp (last visited October 12, 2013).

16. Terri Eyden, Global Survey on Business Ethics, Accounting Web, June 21, 2012, http://www.accountingweb.com/article/global-survey-business-ethics/219380 (last visited September 22, 2013).

17. Ethics Violations Reporting Policy, Gannett, http://www.gannett.com/article/99999999/INVESTORREL0304/100429015/Ethics-Violations-Reporting-Policy (last visited September 22, 2013).

18. Reporting Ethics Violations, Morris Communications Company, Inc., http://morris.com/reporting-ethics-violations (last visited September 22, 2013).

19. Terri Eyden, Global Survey on Business Ethics, Accounting Web, *supra.*

20. Collins and Schultz, A Critical Examination of the AICPA Code of Professional Conduct, Journal of Business Ethics, Vol. 14, No. 1, January 1995, pages 31 to 41.

21. Belfiore v. American Institute of Certified Public Accountants, Inc., Not Reported in A.2d, 1994 WL 146393 (Conn. Super.)

22. Composition, Applicability and Compliance, American Institute of Certified Public Accountants, http://www.aicpa.org/Research/Standards/CodeofConduct/Pages/comp.aspx (last visited September 22, 2013).

23. *Id.*

24. Kanani v. Frost, Ruttenberg & Rothblatt, P.C., Not Reported in F. Supp. 2d, 2005 WL 1661521 (E.D. Mo., 2005).

25. Peter Tyson, The Hippocratic Oath Today, NOVA, March 7, 2001, http://www.pbs.org/wgbh/nova/body/hippocratic-oath-today.html (last visited September 29, 2013).

26. *Id.*

27. Emily Woodbury, The Fall of the Hippocratic Oath: Why the Hippocratic Oath should be Discarded in Favor of a Modified Version of Pellegrino's Precepts, *GUJHS.* 2012 July; Vol. 6, No. 2: 9-17.

28. *Id.*

29. Jim Riley, Business Ethics – Issues, Keller Graduate School of Management, DeVry University, http://tutor2u.net/business/strategy/business-ethics-issues.html (last visited September 22, 2013).

30. *Id.*

31. Jonathan Karpoff, The Decade's Worst Financial Scandals, Foster, April 5, 2010, http://www.foster.washington.edu/centers/facultyresearch/Pages/karpoff-scandals.aspx (last visited September 22, 2013).

32. *Id.*

33. Mary Lu Harding, Ethics Violations: Truth & Consequences, Institute for Supply Management, http://www.ism.ws/pubs/proceedings/confproceedingsdetail.cfm?Item Number=5245 (last visited September 22, 2013).

34. Utilitarian Theories, Online Guide to Ethics and Moral Philosophy, http://www.phil.cmu.edu/cavalier/80130/index.html (last visited September 22, 2013).

35. The Whistleblower Protection Program, Department of Labor, http://www.whistleblowers.gov/ (last visited September 22, 2013).

36. *Id.*

37. Know Your Rights FAQ, National Whistleblower Center, http://www.whistleblowers.org/index.php?option=com_content&task=view&id=34&Itemid=63 (last visited September 22, 2013).

38. *Id.*

39. *Id.*

40. Employment At Will: What Does It Mean?, Nola.com, http://www.nolo.com/legal-encyclopedia/employment-at-will-definition-30022.html (last visited September 22, 2013).

41. *Id.*

42. Contract of Employment, Citizens Information, http://www.citizensinformation.ie/en/employment/employment_rights_and_conditions/contracts_of_employment/contract_of_employment.html (last visited October 10, 2013).

43. Smoking in the Workplace, Nolo.com, http://www.nolo.com/legal-encyclopedia/smoking-workplace-29755.html (last visited September 22, 2013).

44. *Smoker Protection Law*, Wikipedia, https://en.m.wikipedia.org/wiki/Smoker_protection_law (last visited January 25, 2017).

45. Ilanit Fischler, *Courts Recognizing Employment Discrimination Causes of Action for Medical Marijuana Patients,* DBR Business Review, October 24, 2017,

46. New Report Estimates Illicit Drug Use Costs U.S. Economy More Than $193 Billion Annually, Newsroom, The Partnership at Drugfree.org,, http://www.drugfree.org/join-together/drugs/new-report-estimates-illicit-drug-use-costs-u-s-economy-more-than-193-billion-annually (last visited September 22, 2013).

47. Drugs and the Workplace, National Council on Alcoholism and Drug Dependence, http://www.ncadd.org/index.php/learn-about-drugs/workplace/242-drugs-and-the-workplace (last visited September 22, 2013).

48. Drug Testing in the Workplace, National Workrights Institute, http://workrights.us/?products=drug-testing-in-the-workplace (last visited September 22, 2013).

49. Alanna Vagianos, *The 'Me Too' Campaign Was Created By A Black Woman 10 Years Ago,*" Women, October 17, 2017, https://www.huffingtonpost.com/entry/the-me-too-campaign-was-created-by-a-black-woman-10-years-ago_us_59e61a7fe4b02a215b336fee (last visited January 15, 2018.)

50. Brandon Gaille, *23 Statistics on Sexual Harassment in the Workplace,* May 20, 2017, https://brandongaille.com/23-statistics-on-sexual-harassment-the-workplace/ (last visited January 15, 2018.)

51. "Labs Err on Drug Test, Study Finds," The Philadelphia Inquirer, April 8, 1987, at A3, col. 1.

52. Sexual Harassment in the Workplace, Workharrsement.net, http://www.workharass-ment.net/index.php (last visited September 22, 2013).

53. *Id.*

54. International Business Ethics, http://www.crimeradius.com/International_Business_Ethics (last visited September 22, 2013).

55. Bill George, Ethics Must Be Global, Not Local, Bloomberg Business Week, February 12, 2008, http://www.businessweek.com/stories/2008-02-12 ethics-must-be-global-not-localbusinessweek-business-news-stock-market-and-financial-advice (last visited September 30, 2013).

56. *Id.*

57. Lillian V. Blageff, International Business Ethics, International HR Journal, Volume 16, Issue 2, Spring 2007.

58. *Id.*

59. OECD Convention on Combating Bribery of Foreign Public Officials in International Business Transactions, Unicorn., http://www.againstcorruption.org/BriefingsItem.asp?id=8545(last visited September 30, 2013).

60. Lucinda Low, et. al., The Inter-American Convention Against Corruption: A Comparison with the United States Foreign Corrupt Practices Act, 38 Va. J. Int'l L. 243, Spring 1998.

KEY TERMS

Business Ethics
Convention on Combating Bribery
Drug Testing
Employee at Will
Equal Employment Opportunity Commission (EEOC)
Ethical
Ethics
Foreign Corrupt Practices Act (FPCA)
Good Faith Report
Good Samaritan Law
Hippocratic Oath
Hostile Environment
Hostile Work Environment
Inter-American Convention Against Corruption

International Business Ethics
Occupational Safety and Health Administration (OSHA)
Professional Codes of Ethics
Quid Pro Quo
Rights Theory
Sexual Harassment
Special Relationship
Title VII
Utilitarian Theory
Waste
Whistleblower
Whistleblower Protection Act of 1989
Whistleblower's Law

CHAPTER 3

THE COURTS

A Court is only as sound as its jury, and a jury is only as sound as the men who make it up.

Harper Lee
To Kill a Mockingbird, 1960

**SECTION 3.1
THE FEDERAL
COURT SYSTEM**

Today's legal environment makes it a very real risk that a business will become involved in the litigation process during its existence. This chapter will present an overview of the court system in the United States so that the business entrepreneur or executive may gain a better understanding of the different types of courts, their rules and their specializations.

Traditionally, a court is the arm of the government that resolves disputes through a legal process. People access the court to resolve their disputes in a peaceful manner. In this regard, the litigants present their best arguments to the "fact finder" and stress the facts that support their position. Each party also emphasizes the flaws in the opponent's case. The judge or jury then decides the outcome. American judicial tradition maintains that the truth will be gleaned through this adversary process.[1]

When a judge presides over a case, there are over 1,000 years of tradition behind the judicial process. Historically, justice for Anglo-Saxons, and even after the Norman invasion of 1066, was a mixture of local and royal governments. Local courts were handled by a lord or one of his stewards. The King's Court was presided over by the King.[2]

The Charter of 1629 created the General Court in the American colonies and gave them the power to decide all matters affecting the people. The ruling elite, however, initially refused to allow freemen to take part in the lawmaking process on the basis that their numbers would render the judicial tribunal inefficient.[3]

The most well-known incident in colonial America that provided the impetus for the right to a jury trial happened in New York in 1734. At the time, New York was one of the thirteen original colonies administered by a governor selected by the King of England. Peter Zenger, a journalist, published an article criticizing this official so the British authorities charged him with libel. Zenger was represented by Andrew Hamilton, who argued that his client was not guilty because the content of the published article was true.

Hamilton maintained that the issue of whether the journalist had committed libel should be left to the jury to decide. The court agreed and the jury system eventually became entrenched in American jurisprudence.[4]

Since so few attorneys existed in those early days, juries were allowed to decide not only factual questions, but also issues as to how the law should be interpreted in relation to the facts of the case. In turn, judges were permitted to make comments about the evidence.[5]

Today, juries can only decide questions of fact, such as whether a doctor committed malpractice by leaving a sponge in a patient's stomach during surgery. They cannot concern themselves with questions of law, which is the province of the court. Judges are also no longer allowed to comment on the evidence, because this is seen as a way of unfairly influencing the jury.[6]

The constitutional power for the court system is found in **Article Three** that provides: "the judicial power of the United States shall be vested in one Supreme Court, and in such other inferior courts as Congress may from time to time establish."

The court is also the last branch of the government to be addressed by the Constitution and very little direction is provided by the framers in that historic document. Article III merely creates the **Supreme Court of the United States** and it glaringly fails to set forth the Court's powers, composition or jurisdiction. In what one may call a lack of respect, the framers also gave Congress the power to create the remaining courts thereby making the court system seem subservient to the legislature.

Congress has three tasks in determining how the courts on the federal level will operate. First, the legislators decide how many judges there will be and where they will be assigned to preside. Second, through the confirmation process, Congress decides which of the President's nominees become federal judges. Third, they approve the federal court's budget and appropriate money for the judiciary to operate. Surprisingly, the court's budget is a very small part—substantially less than one percent—of the overall federal budget.[7]

The **President** is the individual who selects the federal judges with the "advice and consent" of the Senate. This Chief Officer usually consults senators and other elected officials about nominations for vacancies on the federal courts. The power to appoint new judges, however, is not the judiciary's only interaction with the executive branch. The Department of Justice, who has the task of prosecuting federal crimes and for representing the government in civil lawsuits, is the most frequent litigator in the federal court system. A few other executive branch agencies also affect the way the courts work. For instance, the United States **Marshals Service** provides security for the federal courthouses and its employees, and the General Services Administration builds and maintains federal courthouses.[8]

During its first few years of operations, the Supreme Court of the United States heard very few cases and was viewed as the weakest branch of the government. This perception changed dramatically in 1801 when John Marshall became the Chief Justice and issued the landmark ruling in **Marbury v. Madison.** This case established the fundamental principle that the Supreme Court uniquely has the power to declare a law of Congress unconstitutional. It is also the final arbiter of the meaning of the Constitution. With these powers, the Supreme Court became an equal partner in the government, and it has enjoyed that status ever since.[9]

The **federal courts** are frequently described as the guardians of the United States Constitution because their decisions protect the rights and liberties guaranteed by this historic document. While Congress makes the laws that govern the nation as a whole, the federal courts interpret and apply those edicts to resolve disputes.[10]

Presently, **the court of original jurisdiction** or trial court in the federal system is the District Court, and appeals are entertained by the **Circuit Court of Appeals.** On rare occasion, the Supreme Court of the United States will review a lower court's decision if it presents a compelling national question that needs to be answered.

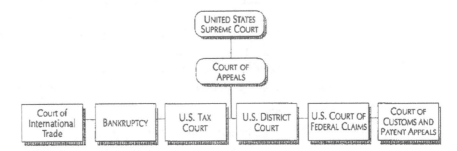

The **United States District Court,** or trial court, is in direct contact with the parties, hears the evidence, and applies the appropriate law to the facts of a case. There are ninety-four district courts in the United States and its territories. A state may have one or more district courts within its boundaries depending on its population. For example, the state of New York has four district courts within its boundaries, whereas Maine only has one.

Within the restrictions imposed by Congress, the federal courts may hear cases involving federal law, the United States Constitution, and disputes between citizens of different states where the amount in controversy exceeds $75,000. Congress has also created several specialized courts that hear cases involving very narrow issues, such as tax matters and customs or patent appeals.

The **Court of Appeals** is the intermediate **appellate court** within the federal court system. There are thirteen circuit courts throughout the United States. Eleven of the Circuits hear cases on appeal from the district courts within a particular circuit. For instance, the Third Circuit Court of Appeals, which is located in Philadelphia, was created in 1891 and hears cases appealed from the federal district courts in Pennsylvania, New Jersey, Delaware and the Virgin Islands. The twelfth circuit is devoted to hearing cases from the District of Columbia. Congress has also created one specialized court called the United States Court of Appeals for the Federal Circuit. This Federal Circuit hears appeals involving tort claims against the United States government, patent cases, and appeals from the United States **Court of Federal Claims** and the Court of International Trade. Parties may appeal to the Circuit Courts of Appeal as a matter of right.

Because the Supreme Court's decision to hear a case is discretionary, the Courts of Appeal are usually the last place that a party will appeal a federal case. When a Court of Appeals decides a case, that decision is binding over all of the district courts within that circuit.

The **Supreme Court of the United States** is the highest court of the land and is the final arbiter of all legal disputes. It handles a very limited number of cases each year and those disputes may start in federal or state courts, and they usually involve important issues about the Constitution or federal law.[11] As a result, it often decides very controversial issues that affect our daily lives. Supreme Court decisions establish precedent and bind all other courts. Commentators and constitutional scholars analyze each word of an opinion and predict how a particular holding will impact society.

The Court has undergone significant changes over the past fifty years and established legal doctrines have changed drastically. For example, the death penalty was unconstitutional but is now considered an appropriate punishment under certain circumstances.

What has caused this change? Shifting attitudes of the public certainly has an influence in court interpretation. The modification of the law, however, is more a reflection of the personalities of the Supreme Court members. There has been a dramatic turnover of Supreme Court justices during the past several decades, which has altered their judicial philosophy.

The court itself consists of a Chief Justice and eight Associate Justices who are appointed by the President of the United Sates subject to the confirmation of the Senate. Since its creation, there have been only seventeen Chief Justices; the first was John Jay and the current one is John G. Roberts.

There have been several changes to the composition of the court within the past few years. President Obama appointed two justices during his presidency. In 2009, he selected Sonya Sotomayor, the first Hispanic justice to the court. One year later, he appointed Elena Kagan. President Trump, soon after taking office, appointed Neal Gorsuch as the 113th justice. He filled the vacancy created by the death of Antonin Scalia. Gorsuch graduated from Harvard Law School and is known as a strict constructionist or conservative justice. The current composition of the court is as follows:

- John Roberts
- Samuel Alito, Jr.
- Ruth Bader Ginsburg
- Clarence Thomas
- Stephen Breyer
- Anthony Kennedy
- Sonia Sotomayor
- Elena Kagan
- Neil Gorsuch

At the current time, Justice Kennedy, a moderate, appears to wield the true power on the court. His vote tends to tip the scales in favor of the majority ruling.

It is not technically accurate to use the labels liberal and conservative when speaking about members of the Court. The proper terms for current judicial philosophies are activist v. judicial restraint oriented. An **activist** is one who views his or her role as bringing about social change. If there is something wrong with the system, a justice will take an active stance in imposing remedial measures to correct a problem. A justice that is **judicial restraint oriented** tends to believe that his or her role is merely to make sure that a rule is constitutional. If there is something wrong with the system, it is up to the legislature to bring about the necessary change.

In simplistic terms, a judicial restraint oriented or conservative judge has usually been appointed by a Republican president while an activist or liberal judge tends to have been appointed by a Democratic president. The tension between these two judicial philosophies has become pronounced in recent years as is demonstrated by the contentious confirmation hearings in the United States Senate. It seems that more time is spent on the candidate's political views than on the person's qualifications for the office.[12]

The operational aspects of the Supreme Court reveal that its term starts on the first Monday in October and ends when the list of scheduled cases is reached during the summer. Before World War II, the Supreme Court had 1,300 docketed cases. Today, about 10,000 cases are appealed each year and an additional 1,200 applications are filed that can be acted upon by a single Justice.[13] The Supreme Court is also a court of both original and appellate jurisdiction. Cases involving Ambassadors, Consuls, litigation between the Federal Government and a state as well as suits between states may be heard directly by the Supreme Court. There are no appeals of these decisions. Most cases, however, reach the Supreme Court on appeal of a lower court's decision. These appeals are originated by the filing of a **writ of certiorari** which is Latin for "we wish to be informed."[14]

History demonstrates that few appeals are actually heard by the court. In fact, the Justices decided between 100 to 150 cases a year even though it takes a mere four of nine jurists to agree to hear the appeal. This has become known as the "**Rule of Four.**" The Justices meet on Wednesdays and Fridays to review recent appeals and the junior most Justice acts as the "doorkeeper" when it is necessary to retrieve materials. Their deliberations are secret and what is said among the Justices is not available for public consumption.[15]

Supreme Court Rule 10 governs these petitions and provides that the acceptance of a case on a Writ of Certiorari is not a matter of right but within the sound discretion of the court and the appeal will only be entertained for compelling reasons. Some of the factors the court considers in determining whether to grant an appeal include:

A. A conflict in United States Court of Appeals decisions on the same issue;

B. A state's highest court has issued a ruling on an issue that conflicts with a decision of another state's highest court or with a United States Court of Appeal; or

C. A state court or a United States Court of Appeal has decided an important question of federal law that has not been, but should be, settled by the Supreme Court.

A Petition for a Writ of Certiorari is rarely granted when the alleged error merely consists of factual mistakes or the misapplication of a properly stated rule of law.

SECTION 3.2
THE STATE COURT
SYSTEM

We are a nation of states, each state maintaining its own independent court system. While the configuration of the court system will vary from jurisdiction to jurisdiction, each will have a trial court and at least one appellate court. The National Center for States Courts is an organization created to improve the administration of justice through leadership and service to state courts and courts around the world. They maintain a website that provides links to each state court in the country. The state court system in Pennsylvania however, is provided as an illustration. The court of original jurisdiction in Pennsylvania is the **Court of Common Pleas** and it was established as part of the Pennsylvania Constitution in 1776. It is subdivided into the following three divisions: the Trial Court, the Family Court, and Orphan's Court.

The Trial Division hears both civil and criminal cases. The Orphan's Court is concerned with matters involving estates, such as will contests, trusts, and incompetence hearings. Family Court decides juvenile cases and matters involving the family unit such as divorce, custody, support, paternity, and domestic violence.

To reduce the backlog of cases, a specialized court has been created to handle small disputes. In Philadelphia, this court is called the **Municipal Court** and is divided into civil and criminal divisions. It handles all landlord/tenant problems, civil disputes of $12,000 or less, criminal cases where the penalty involves five years or less imprisonment, and code violations. In the surrounding counties, magesterial district justices, who have offices in the various townships throughout the Commonwealth, handle these matters. Parties appearing in Municipal Court do not enjoy the right to a **jury** trial, so most cases can be appealed directly to the Court of Common Pleas at which time the person will receive a new trial equipped with a jury if so desired.

Because of the frequency and complexity of business related matters, an increasing number of state courts have established specialized forums to hear business related matters such as antitrust lawsuits, intellectual property issues, and complex mass torts. This type of system will allow judges to better understand the issues and to develop expertise in the area of business disputes. As the Ninth Judicial Circuit Court of Florida noted in establishing a business court, "The goal is to handle business litigation matters in an effective and efficient manner. Benefits of a business litigation section include the following: 1) implementation of standardized procedures; 2) higher degree of consistency of rulings on recurring issues; and 3) economic stimulus to the community."

PENNSYLVANIA STATE JUDICIAL SYSTEM

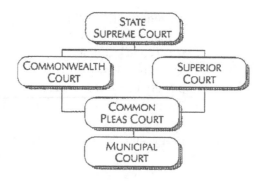

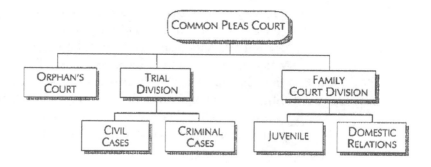

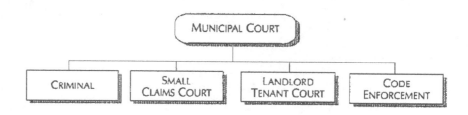

SECTION 3.3
THE JURY SYSTEM

The right to a trial by one's peers is a basic building block of American democracy guaranteed by the United States Constitution. In fact, it has been estimated that this country accounts for 95% of all jury trials in the world.[16] As the Supreme Court noted, "The guarantees of a jury trial reflect a profound judgment about the way in which the law should be enforced and justice administered. Providing an accused with the right to be tried by a jury of his peers gives him an inestimable safeguard against the corrupt or overzealous prosecutor and against the compliant, biased, or eccentric judge."[17]

While the right to a jury trial is firmly engrained in our system of jurisprudence, it was not conceived by the founders of this country. Jury trials have been in existence in England for centuries and some scholars contend that the concept originated in thirteenth-century England as an outgrowth of the *Magna Carta.*

During the founding days of this country, the right to a jury trial was brought to America by the English colonists. In fact, it was adopted by the First Congress of the American Colonists in 1765 with the declaration that "trial by jury is the inherent and invaluable right of every British subject in these colonies."

The founding fathers considered the concept to be so fundamental that it is contained in two different Amendments to the United States Constitution. The **Sixth Amendment** guarantees the defendant in a criminal case the right to a speedy and public trial by an impartial jury. The **Seventh Amendment** entitles citizens to a jury trial in civil cases involving a dispute of more than twenty dollars.

In application, a judge presides over the trial and decides **questions-of-law.** The jury, on the other hand, is the ultimate arbiter of the facts. They decide which party should win a controversy based upon the evidence presented at trial.

To better understand the distinction between a question of law and a question of fact, consider the following hypothetical situation:

> Joe Roberts is driving his car south on Broad Street and enters the intersection on what he maintains is a green light. Bill Smith is proceeding east on Montgomery Avenue and enters the same intersection on what he too alleges is a green light. The vehicles collide on Broad Street, and Roberts maintains that he is injured. Joe institutes suit against Smith for personal injuries.

The judge will inform the jury that a party who enters an intersection against a red light is negligent and responsible for the injuries caused by that negligence. This is a statement of law. On the other hand, it is up to the jury to decide which party entered the intersection after the light turned red. This is a determination of fact.

A jury in a criminal trial generally consists of twelve people whose decisions must be unanimous. The origin of this number is not clear. Some say it represents the number of apostles from the bible, Solomon's officers which numbered twelve, or twelve was a favorite number in medieval times. The Supreme Court, however, has noted that the number is a historical accident that became fixed in the fourteenth century. The essential feature of a jury rests in the collective judgment of a group of people, and in the community participation that results from that group's determination of innocence or guilt. The performance of this role is not dependent on a specific number of citizens that make up the jury.[18] Jury requirements, therefore, vary by state and type of proceeding. For instance, Pennsylvania requires that a defendant in a criminal trial be provided with twelve jurors and all must agree on the verdict. In a civil case, however, the verdict need not be unanimous, and the jury will consist of eight members unless a litigant specifically demands a trial by twelve.

More than 120,000 jury trials a year are conducted in the United States. In contrast, only about one-percent of trials in England are conducted with the help of a jury. France utilizes juries for only the most serious crimes, and Italy uses panels of three judges. Germany, Finland and Sweden have mixed tribunals of a professional judge and several laymen.[19] Russia has recently reinstituted the use of jury trials in serious criminal matters, and Japan started using six-person juries starting in 2009.

Mark Twain stated in a 1873 speech that: "We have a criminal jury system which is superior to any in the world; and its efficiency is only marred by the difficulty of finding twelve men every day who don't know anything and can't read."

Most legal experts agree that it is the best system available despite certain recognized short comings and occasional erroneous verdicts. After all, it is better to be tried by the collective judgment of one's peers than by the wisdom of a single individual. This is the backbone of a democracy.

The jury system does have inherent weaknesses. The law is very complicated, and a trial is an intimidating proceeding. Jurors are thrust into the role of deciding complex cases without the proper legal training or experience. As a generalization, they tend to be plaintiff oriented and are more apt to award money than to find for the defense. Verdicts also tend to be higher in metropolitan cities than those in rural counties.

An analysis of civil jury verdicts by the United States Department of Justice determined that in 53% of the cases, the jury found in favor of plaintiffs and awarded a total of 3.9 billion dollars in compensatory and punitive damages during the one-year period under review. The average finding was $37,000 and juries awarded punitive damages in 6% of the cases with a median punitive damage award of $50,000.[20]

On the other hand, some scholars have found the very weaknesses of the jury system to be its strength. In a speech given by Oliver Wendell Holmes on January 17, 1899, he stated:

"I confess that in my experience I have not found juries especially inspired for the discovery of truth . . . they will introduce into their verdict a . . . large amount . . . of popular prejudice, and thus keep the administration of the law in a court with the wishes and feelings of the community."[21]

SECTION 3.4 JURISDICTION

Jurisdiction refers to the power of a court to determine the merits of a dispute and to grant an aggrieved party relief. In order for a court to properly entertain an action, it must have jurisdiction over the subject matter in dispute and jurisdiction over the parties involved.

Subject matter jurisdiction is quite simple. The particular court where the dispute is heard must have the power to hear the kind of case that is in controversy. The courts are very specialized, and the plaintiff must institute suit before the proper court. For instance, a divorce proceeding may not be instituted in tax court. The court's power to hear these specific types of cases is usually granted by the legislature.

Jurisdiction over the person requires the court to have power to exercise its authority over the defendant. Traditionally, suit was instituted where the defendant could be found. This was either in the state where he resided or where he worked. Now, a court is considered to have jurisdiction over the parties when the defendant has "minimum contacts" with the state where the court is located (the **forum state**). **Minimum contacts** are generally deemed to exist when the defendant takes actions that are purposefully directed toward the forum state.

The rule of serving a defendant where the defendant can be found was expanded over time by the passage of long arm statutes that allow a jurisdiction to reach beyond the state boundaries to serve a defendant with the lawsuit. The most common **long arm statutes** deal with a non-resident who commits a tort within a state, a party who owns property in a state, and one doing business in a state.

In order to satisfy the requirements of due process, the Supreme Court has ruled that a state court may exercise personal jurisdiction over a non-resident defendant as long as there are *minimum contacts* between the defendant and the state in which the suit has been filed. The concept of minimum contacts protects defendants against the burdens of litigating in a distant or inconvenient court. Usually, a defendant will have some kind of presence in the forum. In the case of transacting business within a state, however, it is not necessary to have an office in that jurisdiction. Soliciting business through sales representatives or by placing an advertisement in a local newspaper have been held to constitute minimum contacts.

The Magic Kingdom is a Walt Disney property located in Florida but is incorporated in the state of Delaware. It has no offices in Pennsylvania and is not registered to do business in this jurisdiction. However, the corporation advertises in Pennsylvania newspapers on a regularly basis. Is this conduct sufficient to confer jurisdiction over Walt Disney in Pennsylvania over a Florida accident? That is the issue in the next case.

GAVIGAN V. WALT DISNEY WORLD, CO.
630 F. SUPP. 148 (E. D. PA. 1986)

Plaintiffs seek to recover for injuries allegedly sustained in a motor vehicle incident which occurred at the Walt Disney World Complex in Bay Lake, Florida. Plaintiffs are citizens Pennsylvania.

Defendant, Walt Disney World Co. ("Disney World"), is a Delaware corporation doing business in Florida; its principal business activity consists of the ownership and operation of an entertainment complex known as Walt Disney World. Defendant, Joseph Flanagan, an employee of Disney World, is a resident of Florida; he was involved in a Florida accident with the plaintiff.

When a defendant challenges the court's *in personam* jurisdiction, the plaintiff must assume the burden of proving that the defendant's activities in the forum state properly subjected the defendant to the court's jurisdiction. Defendant Walt Disney World contends that it is not subject to the jurisdiction of this court, because it is not qualified to do business in Pennsylvania, it has not incurred or paid taxes to the Commonwealth, it

has not appointed an agent for service of process, and it is not listed in any Pennsylvania telephone directories.

In response, Plaintiff contends that Disney World has engaged in extensive advertising activities within Pennsylvania to promote the entertainment complex operated by Disney World in Florida.

The question before the court is whether the contacts plaintiffs allege Disney World has had with the Commonwealth are sufficient to allow it to exercise jurisdiction over it. The extent of this court's *in personam* jurisdiction is governed by Pennsylvania's long-arm statute. Consistent with due process, the court may not exercise personal jurisdiction over a non-resident defendant, unless there are certain minimum contacts between the defendant and the forum state such that traditional notions of fair play and substantial justice are not offended. Two purposes underlie the requirement of minimum contacts: first, it protects the defendant against the burdens of litigating in a distant or inconvenient forum; second, it ensures that the states, through their courts, do not reach out beyond the limits imposed on them by their status as coequal sovereigns in a federal system.

Pennsylvania courts may exercise in *personam* jurisdiction over the defendant, but only if the defendant's business activities are so continuous and substantial as to make it reasonable for the state to exercise such jurisdiction. In **Garfield v. Homowack Lodge, Inc., 249 Pa. Super. 392, (1977),** the court held that Defendant's method of soliciting business in Pennsylvania consisted of such substantial and continuous activities as to render Defendant amenable to the court's jurisdiction. Garfield involved an accident at the ice rink of a resort hotel in New York. In that case, that defendant continuously advertised its resort through a Philadelphia newspaper, maintained a toll-free telephone number in Pennsylvania for lodge reservations, distributed brochures to travel agents and paid a fee to travel agents for bookingreservations at the lodge.

In this case, Plaintiff has produced documents which reflect the extensive advertising that has been conducted by Defendant in Pennsylvania. For instance, Plaintiff produced a copy of a four full-page advertisement, which ran in the *Philadelphia Inquirer* and promoted the entertainment complex operated by Defendant in Florida. At the top of each of the four pages appears the name "Walt Disney World" followed by the insignia which shows that the name is registered. In addition to promoting the many attractions at the Florida complex, the advertisement provides an 800 telephone number, which interested persons from Pennsylvania may use to make reservations. Furthermore, there are presently a number of advertisements for Defendant's Florida complex running on local Philadelphia television stations. These advertisements reflect an ongoing pattern of activity by defendant. Clearly, this was an activity by Disney World to promote its entertainment complex, and it preceded a major Disney promotional campaign at the John Wanamaker Department Store in Philadelphia.

Because I believe that the advertising and related promotional activities constitute continuous and substantial activities, I conclude that there is personal jurisdiction over Disney World.

With the advent of websites and their ability to convey information to people around the world, additional jurisdictional issues arise. For instance, is a business that places information about itself on the internet subject to lawsuits in any place where an individual can access the site even if the business has no presence in that state and has not solicited business in that state?

A series of cases have established the law concerning when jurisdiction in a particular location is proper based upon the type of Internet transaction and website involved. The courts use a sliding scale for ascertaining whether a nonresident has submitted to a state's jurisdiction by establishing the requisite contacts through Internet-based activity. At one end of the scale are cases where a defendant clearly does business over the Internet. If that person enters into contracts with citizens of another state that involve the repeated transmission of information over the Internet, jurisdiction is proper. At the opposite end of the spectrum are those cases where a defendant has simply posted information on a website which is accessible to users in another jurisdiction. This is called a passive website and does little more than to make information available to those who are interested in the information. This type of Internet transaction does not give rise to the exercise of personal jurisdiction. The middle ground is occupied by interactive websites where a person can exchange information with the host computer. In these situations, the exercise of jurisdiction is ascertained by looking at the level of interactivity and commercial nature of the exchange of information that occurs on the web site. See: **Zippo Mfg. v. Zippo Dot Com., 952 F. Supp. 1119 (W. D. Pa. 1997).**

It is now possible to buy large ticket items such as automobiles through the Internet and to participate in auctions conducted by organizations such as eBay. Suppose the product, which is the subject of the Internet transaction, is not what was promised? Where can the aggrieved party bring suit? That is the issue in the following case.

AERO TOY STORE, LLC V. GRIEVES
631 S. E.2D 734 (GA. APP. 2006)

Gordon Grieves, a Georgia resident, sued Aero Toy Store, a Florida company for breach of contract arising from Grieves' purchase of an automobile from Aero over the Internet. Aero moved to dismiss for lack of personal jurisdiction.

While conducting an Internet search of the eBay Motors auction website, Grieves identified a 2001 BMW car being offered for sale. The website contained a description of the BMW and its features. And it provided an "Ask seller a question" button that, when activated, identified Juan Almeida as the seller's agent. On or about April 13, 2004, Grieves began making e-mail inquiries to Almeida concerning the car. Almeida responded to Grieves with various e-mails.

Grieves asserts that, in reliance on Almeida's representations, he calculated his winning bid and that, after Almeida faxed copies of the purchase agreement to him, he signed the agreement, faxed it back to Almeida, and mailed a check to Aero in payment of the $31,926 purchase price.

In support of its motion to dismiss, Aero tendered an affidavit of its automotive manager, to show that it does not have any agents, representatives, officers, or employees in Georgia; that it is not licensed to do business in Georgia; that it does not own or rent property in Georgia; that it does not maintain an office in Georgia; and that it has no subsidiaries or business affiliates in Georgia. Aero maintained that, since its formation in 2002, it had made only two Internet sales to persons in Georgia totaling $193,199, amounting to less than one-half of one percent of its gross revenues.

Resolution requires us to review the traditional three-part test used in determining whether long arm jurisdiction exists based on the transaction of business, and then review a test developed in other jurisdictions for determining the existence of minimum contacts in cases involving the Internet.

In considering whether a Georgia court may exercise jurisdiction over a nonresident based on the transaction of business, we apply a three-part test:

Jurisdiction exists on the basis of transacting business in this state if (1) the nonresident defendant has purposefully done some act or consummated some transaction in this state, (2) if the cause of action arises from or is connected with such act or transaction, and (3) if the exercise of jurisdiction by the courts of this state does not offend traditional fairness and substantial justice.

Regularly doing or soliciting business in the state, deriving substantial revenue from goods or services in the state, having agents or representatives or officers or employees in the state, maintaining an office in the state, and having subsidiaries or business affiliates in the state are factors most directly relevant to the existence of general jurisdiction. Factors such as regularly doing or soliciting business, or deriving substantial revenue from goods or services, in this state may also be relevant in determining whether sufficient minimum contacts exist for the purpose of supporting specific jurisdiction, where such activities relate to the suit at hand.

In other jurisdictions, a line of decisions has developed recognizing the technological revolution ushered in by the Internet and utilizing a sliding scale for determining whether a nonresident has submitted to a state's long arm jurisdiction by establishing the requisite minimum contacts through Internet-based activity. This sliding scale was initially articulated in **Zippo Mfg. Co. v. Zippo Dot Com.** As recognized in that case, [a]t one end of the spectrum are situations where a defendant clearly does business over the Internet. If the defendant enters into contracts with residents of a foreign jurisdiction that involve the knowing and repeated transmission of computer files over the Internet, personal jurisdiction is proper. At the opposite end are situations where a defendant has simply posted information on an Internet website which is accessible to users in foreign jurisdictions. A passive website that does little more than make information available to those who are interested in it is not grounds for the exercise [of] personal jurisdiction. The middle ground is occupied by interactive websites where a user can exchange information with the host computer. In these cases, the exercise of jurisdiction is determined by examining the level of interactivity and commercial nature of the exchange of information that occurs on the website.

In **Butler v. Beer Across America,** a minor left alone at his Alabama home ordered 12 beers from corporate sellers in Illinois through the sellers' Internet website. Under the applicable provisions of the UCC, the beer was delivered to the carrier acting as the purchaser's agent in Illinois and then shipped by the carrier to the purchaser in Alabama. The purchaser's mother brought an action for damages against the sellers in federal district court in Alabama.

The court in **Butler** recognized that Alabama courts had found sufficient minimum contacts to support in personam jurisdiction over nonresident defendants in other actions related to out-of-state sale of goods to Alabama residents for use in Alabama, as in cases such as **Atlanta Auto Auction v. G & G Auto Sales.** The Butler court concluded, however, that the contacts in those cases differed in both kind and extent from the de minimis connections in the **Butler** case. Cases such as **Atlanta Auto Auction** involved sales of automobiles, with transactions presumably worth thousands of dollars each, as opposed to the less than $25 purchase in **Butler.** And applying **Zippo** principles, the **Butler** court found that **Beer Across America's** website did not anticipate the regular exchange of information across the Internet or provide for such interaction. The court concluded that, instead, it was more like an electronic bulletin board for the posting of information.

Similarly, in **Barton Southern Co. v. Manhole Barrier Systems,** the federal district court in Georgia found that the nonresident defendant's Internet website failed to furnish a Georgia contact adequate to support personal jurisdiction where there was nothing on the website showing an intent to reach out to persons living in Georgia and no evidence that any Georgia residents had done business with the defendant either through the Internet or otherwise.

In this case, unlike in **Barton Southern Co.,** the defendant operated an interactive website through which it has reached out to, and done business with, persons in Georgia. This case, like **Atlanta Auto Auction,** involves the sale of an automobile with the transaction worth thousands of dollars and involving shipment of an automobile to be operated in Georgia. The car was shipped into Georgia by the nonresident seller and not by a carrier acting as the resident buyer's agent. Although Aero does not have officers, employees, offices, or business affiliates in Georgia, and although the revenue it derives from goods sold here may not be substantial in relation to its overall revenue, it does regularly solicit business in Georgia through the Internet, and the revenue it has derived from shipping cars to Grieves and other persons in Georgia is substantial enough to establish sufficient minimum contacts with the state of Georgia in a case involving the exercise of specific jurisdiction. Applying the expansive interpretation of the "transacting any business" provision of our Long Arm Statute, the state court did not err in determining that Aero has established sufficient minimum contacts with this state to warrant exercise of personal jurisdiction over it in this case.

Judgment affirmed.

SECTION 3.5
VENUE

Venue is the place where a case should be heard. The plaintiff decides where to institute suit. This decision will rarely be disturbed unless the defendant can demonstrate a compelling reason to remove the matter to another jurisdiction. This will occur if the defendant cannot obtain a fair trial in the location where the lawsuit was filed because of prejudice or bias.

The following is an example of the Rules of Court pertaining to a change of venue:

(A) All motions for change of venue shall be made to the court in which the case is currently pending. Venue or venire may be changed by that court when it is determined after hearing that a fair and impartial trial cannot otherwise be had in the county where the case is currently pending.

(B) An order for change of venue shall be certified forthwith to the Supreme Court. The Supreme Court shall designate and notify the county of transfer or the county from which the jury is to be impaneled. Unless otherwise ordered by the Supreme Court, a judge from the county in which the complaint was filed shall preside over all proceedings in the trial court.

(C) Whenever a change of venire has been ordered, the jury shall be summoned, selected, and impaneled in the designated county of empanelment. The trial judge shall conduct the **voir dire,** unless otherwise ordered by the Supreme Court. The jury shall be transported to the county of the court where the case is currently pending.

The second reason for requesting a change of venue derives from the concept of **forum non-conveniens.** This Latin term means that the place of the trial is inconvenient for the parties and the witnesses involved in the litigation. A court may refuse to exercise jurisdiction over the parties if it would be more convenient for a court in another jurisdiction to hear the case.

The Boston Marathon Bombing is indelibly engrained into the nation's memory as the result of two bombings not far from the finish line. The bombing caused widespread terror and confusion with multiple fatalities and injuries. The episode was eventually linked to Dzhokhar Tsarnaev and his older brother who was killed by the police. Dzhokhar was arrested and charged with murder and other related offenses.

Tsarnaev pleaded not guilty and requested a change of venue, claiming that the he could not obtain a fair trial in Boston because of the extensive publicity that surrounded the case. The following is the disposition of that argument.

UNITED STATES V. TSARNAEV
157 F. SUPP. 3D 57 (D. MASS. 2016)

Dzhokhar Tsarnaev was tried on an indictment arising out of the bombings at the Boston Marathon. The jury returned a verdict, finding him guilty under all counts.

The defendant renews his venue argument, contending generally that local media coverage, local events, and postings on social networks during the course of the trial should raise a presumption of prejudice and require a conclusion that the District of Massachusetts was an improper venue for his trial. The defendant appears to be raising the claim under the Sixth Amendment to the Constitution.

In **Skilling v. United States**, the Supreme Court identified four factors relevant to a determination whether a presumption of prejudice should be indulged: (1) the size and characteristics of the community in which the crime occurred; (2) the nature of the publicity surrounding the case; (3) the time between the crime and the trial; and (4) whether the jury's decision indicated bias. 561 U.S. 358 (2010). The defendant does not expressly articulate

a legal framework for analyzing his claim, but it appears he seeks to advance an argument related primarily to the second and third factors.

Boston is located in a large, diverse metropolitan area. The geographic region from which the jury was drawn, the Eastern Division of the District of Massachusetts, includes about five million people living not just in Boston, but also in smaller cities and towns, encompassing urban, suburban, rural, and coastal communities. Residents in the area obtain their daily news from a variety of sources. In light of these facts, this factor weighs against a finding of presumed prejudice.

The main basis for the defendant's motion appears to be the extent and nature of the publicity concerning the case itself and the events at issue in it. He focuses largely on media coverage concerning observances of the anniversary of the bombings and the publicity of victims; coverage of foreign family witnesses; physical surroundings of the courthouse; and social media. It is certainly true that the local media gave substantial coverage to the anniversary of the bombings, its victims, and the 2015 marathon. What the defendant disregards, however, is the national—and international—interest in those same events and people. This was not a crime that was unknown outside of Boston. To the contrary, media coverage of the bombings when they occurred was broadcast live around the world, over the Internet and on television. The defendant's own pretrial poll, for instance, shows that even in his preferred venue, Washington, D.C., those polled overwhelmingly were familiar with the bombings. Nor did the crime affect an event about which only Bostonians are concerned. Although the Boston Marathon is an important event in the city and region, it is also an iconic event known worldwide.

The pretrial and trial proceedings were covered not only locally, but also nationally and internationally. National and international news outlets comprised approximately two-thirds of the media organizations that requested seats reserved for media in the trial courtroom and more than one-half of the media organizations that were ultimately assigned a seat or rotating seat there. Many others followed the proceedings from overflow rooms in the courthouse.

Newspapers around the world closely followed the trial as it unfolded, both in their print editions and on the Internet, focusing not just on the more significant trial events like opening statements and closing arguments, but even on the more particular aspects of the legal process. There is no reason to think—and certainly no specific evidence—that this extensive coverage would have been any different in kind or degree, if the trial had been conducted elsewhere.

In sum, the extensive coverage of the trial was not limited to this district. Consequently, moving the trial to another venue would not likely have eliminated or even substantially reduced the coverage. Furthermore, the media coverage of the trial as it unfolded was not demonstrably prejudicial to the defendant. And finally, the jurors gave repeated assurances that they were avoiding media reports about the case.

SECTION 3.6 STANDING

In accordance with the United States Constitution, courts are only permitted to hear actual cases or controversies. That is, courts cannot offer advisory opinions to people who are not actually involved in a dispute. The plaintiff in a lawsuit must have a direct and substantial interest in the outcome of the case that he or she intends to bring. This concept is referred to as **standing.** To meet this requirement, the plaintiff must show that he or she has actually been injured by the action that is the subject of the lawsuit. The injury can be physical, economic, environmental, or aesthetic, but must injure the plaintiff in fact. To have standing to have a case heard, it is also necessary that the relief sought by the plaintiff either correct or compensate for the harm alleged in the lawsuit.

Consider this example: Estelle was in the process of researching the environmentally fragile nature of the Nevada mountains when she discovered that someone planned to build an amusement park in that area. The park would have a detrimental effect on the environment in the mountain region. If Estelle makes no allegation of the way in which the building of the park would cause an actual injury to her personally, she will be denied standing to bring that case.

Soon after President Trump assumed office, he issued several Executive orders, temporarily banning citizens of predominantly Muslim countries from entering the United States. This ban set off a fire storm in the United States over the issue of immigration. The adverse reaction prompted a multitude of lawsuits, including one filed by Hawaii to stop the enforcement of the Executive order. The Trump Administration challenged the right of Hawaii to contest the order, claiming that the state did not have standing. That is the issue in **Hawaii v. Trump**.

HAWAII V. TRUMP
241 F. SUPP. 3D 1119 (D. HAWAII 2017)

On January 27, 2017, the President of the United States issued an Executive order entitled, "Protecting the Nation from Foreign Terrorist Entry into the United States." On March 6, 2017, the President issued another Executive order identically entitled, "Protecting the Nation from Foreign Terrorist Entry into the United States" ("Executive Order"). Like its predecessor, the Executive order restricts the entry of foreign nationals from specified countries and suspends entrants from the United States refugee program for specified periods of time.

Plaintiff, the State of Hawai'i, seeks a nationwide restraining order that would prohibit the Defendants from "enforcing or implementing the Executive order" before it takes effect. Article III, Section 2 of the Constitution permits federal courts to consider only "cases" and "controversies." Those two words confine the business of federal courts to questions presented in an adversary context and in a form historically viewed as capable of resolution through the judicial process. To satisfy Article III's standing requirements, a plaintiff must show (1) it has suffered an 'injury in fact' that is (a) concrete and particularized and (b) actual or imminent, not conjectural or hypothetical; (2) the injury is fairly traceable to the challenged action of the defendant; and (3) it is likely, as opposed to merely speculative, that the

injury will be redressed by a favorable decision. The gist of the question of standing is whether the petitioner has such a personal stake in the outcome of the controversy, as to assure concrete adverseness which sharpens the presentation of issues upon which the court so largely depends for illumination.

Hawai'i primarily asserts two proprietary injuries stemming from the Executive order. First, the state alleges the negative impacts that the Executive order will have on the University of Hawai'i system- both financial and intangible. The University is an arm of the state. The University recruits students, permanent faculty, and visiting faculty from the targeted countries. Students or faculty suspended from entry are deterred from studying or teaching at the University, now and in the future, irrevocably damaging their personal and professional lives and harming the educational institutions themselves.

The State of Hawai'i asserts that the Executive order also risks dissuading some of the University's current professors or scholars from continuing their scholarship in the United States and at the University. The State argues that the University will suffer non-monetary losses, including damage to the collaborative exchange of ideas among people of different religions and national backgrounds on which the state's educational institutions depend. This will impair the University's ability to recruit and accept the most qualified students and faculty, undermine its commitment to being one of the most diverse institutions of higher education in the world and grind to a halt certain academic programs.

Hawaii also contends that the Executive order will have the effect of depressing international travel to and tourism in Hawai'i, which directly harms Hawaii's businesses and, in turn, the state's revenue. The state points to data from the Hawaii Tourism Authority, which suggests that during the interval of time that the first Executive order was in place, the number of visitors to Hawai'i from the Middle East dropped. Because there is evidence that losses of current and future revenue are traceable to the Executive order, this injury to the state's proprietary interest also appears sufficient to confer standing.

For purposes of the instant motion, the state has demonstrated that: (1) its Universities will suffer monetary damages and intangible harms; (2) the state's economy is likely to suffer a loss of revenue, due to a decline in tourism; and (3) such harms can be sufficiently linked to the Executive order. Accordingly, at this stage of the litigation, the state has satisfied the requirements of Article III standing.

SECTION 3.7
FULL FAITH AND CREDIT

Full Faith and Credit is a constitutional mandate that requires each state to uphold the laws and decrees of every other state. As the Supreme Court noted in **Sherrer v. Sherrer,** 334 U.S. 343, the **Full Faith and Credit Clause** "is one of the provisions incorporated into the Constitution by its framers for the purpose of transforming an aggregation of independent sovereign states into a nation." This guarantee is contained in **Article Four** of the United States Constitution which provides that full faith and credit shall be given in each state to the public acts, records, and judicial proceedings of every other state. Essentially, this means that a judgment in one state will be enforced in another state as long as the first state has jurisdiction. Without this provision, the legal system would become uncertain and chaotic. People would never know if a different state would enforce a validly obtained judgment in another jurisdiction. How does this concept work in reality?

Assume that John Smith, a New Jersey resident and college student, goes to Florida for spring break. Upon his arrival in Florida, he rents a car, but unfortunately Smith runs over the clerk as he is pulling away from the rental agency. He is so distraught by the incident that he takes the next plane back to Newark International Airport in New Jersey. The clerk files suit in Florida for her injuries. John ignores the lawsuit since he has no plans of ever returning to Florida, and a judgment is rendered against him in the amount of $100,000. Is Smith correct in assuming that nothing can be done to him as long as he stays out of Florida? Pursuant to the "Full Faith and Credit Clause" of the Constitution, the Florida judgment can be transferred to New Jersey and be enforced in that jurisdiction. Florida had jurisdiction over the New Jersey resident, since he committed a tort in that state.

LEDOUX–NOTTINGHAM V. DOWNS
210 SO.3D 1217 (FLA. 2017)

In this case, we consider whether the Full Faith and Credit Clause of the United States Constitution requires enforcement of a sister state's judgment ordering grandparent visitation with minor children.

Ruth LeDoux–Nottingham, and the father of her minor children were divorced in Colorado in 2010. The father died in 2011 in Colorado. Immediately after the funeral, LeDoux–Nottingham and her minor children moved to Florida. Jennifer and William Downs (hereinafter "the Grandparents"), initiated a proceeding in Colorado seeking visitation with the children. LeDoux–Nottingham then filed a separate action in Florida to register the Colorado judgment dissolving her marriage and asking for a judicial determination that the Grandparents have no legal right to timesharing with her minor children. In October 2012, the Colorado court issued a final judgment awarding the Grandparents visitation with the minor children.

Since the Colorado order was a final judgment and emanated from a "child custody proceeding," it became enforceable in Florida pursuant to the Full Faith and Credit Clause. The Full Faith and Credit Clause of the United States Constitution provides that "Full Faith and Credit shall be given in each State to the public Acts, Records, and judicial Proceedings of every other State." Art. IV, § 1, U.S. Const. The Parental Kidnapping Prevention Act of 1980 (PKPA) requires "every State to enforce according to its terms ... any custody determination or visitation order. Congress' chief aim in enacting the PKPA was to extend the requirements of the Full Faith and Credit Clause to custody determinations and that the PKPA is a mandate directed to state courts to respect the custody decrees of sister States. Thus, there is no doubt that custody determinations of a sister state are entitled to full faith and credit.

Because the PKPA explicitly applies to "any custody determination or visitation determination," including those in which a grandparent claims a right to visitation of a child, the Colorado order is by the express terms of the PKPA subject to the commands of the Full Faith and Credit Clause.

We next consider whether a public policy exception to the Full Faith and Credit Clause exists that would prevent enforcement of the Colorado order in Florida. LeDoux–Nottingham asserts that enforcement of the Colorado order is not required in Florida because it would offend the right of privacy of the Florida Constitution and there is a public policy exception to the Full Faith and Credit Clause. While the Florida Constitution does protect the right of parents to raise their children free from unwarranted governmental interference, that state right is subordinate to the directives of the Federal Constitution, and the United States Supreme Court has made it clear that there is no public policy exception to the full faith and credit due final judgments of a sister state.

The Full Faith and Credit Clause "requires each State to recognize and give effect to valid judgments rendered by the courts of its sister States." It serves "to alter the status of the several states as independent foreign sovereignties, each free to ignore obligations created under the laws or by the judicial proceedings of the others, and to make them integral parts of a single nation." The Supreme Court thus continues to reject any notion that a state may elevate its own public policy over the policy behind a sister state's judgment and thereby disregard the command of the Full Faith and Credit Clause. The Colorado order is hereby upheld.

SECTION 3.8

COMITY

Comity is derived from the Latin word "comitas" which means courteous. In the arena of international law, this principle allows for the courteous recognition of the rules and laws of a foreign jurisdiction. States are simply not mandated to enforce the laws and judgments of another country. Rather, each determines on its own the extent to which it will provide courtesy and respect to a foreign sovereign taking into consideration the state's international obligations and rights of its own citizens.[22] Generally, as long as the laws of another country are not contrary to public policy or prejudicial to the interests of the forum jurisdiction, the law will be upheld.

Unlike the enforcement of judgments between states in the United States, there is no Constitutional mandate for a U.S. court to enforce a foreign judgment. Comity of nations is also not embodied in international law. Rather, a jurisdiction will use comity for public policy reasons.[23]

The following case provides an analysis of the considerations the court will examine when deciding to hear a matter that is pending in another country. The court looks at three factors: (1) international comity; (2) fairness to the litigants and (3) efficient use of scare judicial resources.

ITL INTERN., INC. v. WALTON & POST, INC.
741 F.SUPP.2D 1313 (S.D. FLA., 2010)

Plaintiffs, ITL International, Inc., doing business ("Master Foods"), and WM. Wrigley Jr. Company (collectively the "Plaintiffs") manufacture and sell various products in the United States and worldwide. Defendant Walton and Post is an international wholesale distributor located in Miami, Florida.

In December 1987, Master Foods and Walton & Post entered into an Importer Agreement, whereby Master Foods appointed Walton & Post as the sole Importer in the Dominican Republic of Plaintiffs' products. The Agreement contained, among others, the following provisions: This Agreement shall continue until either party gives at least three months written notice.

In March 23, 2007, Master Foods provided written notice to Walton & Post of its intent to terminate the agreement. As a result, Plaintiffs assert the termination became effective on June 24, 2007.

On March 8, 2007, Walton & Post filed a lawsuit under Dominican Law claiming that it qualified for the protection afforded under that law as the exclusive distributor of plaintiff's products in the Dominican Republic. The Dominican court found the Defendants in the Dominican action, liable to pay $14 million in termination damages. This decision is on appeal to the Supreme Court of the Dominican Republic.

After the unfavorable rulings in the Dominican Republic, Plaintiffs filed the instant action in Florida, asserting Walton & Post has breached the Agreement by seeking compensation upon termination and by causing things to be done that affect the importation, distribution and sale of products in the territory. Defendant moved to dismiss on international comity.

International comity is the recognition which one nation allows within its territory to the legislative, executive or judicial acts of another nation, having due regard both to international duty and convenience and to the rights of its own citizens or of other persons who are under the protection of its laws. Under the doctrine of international comity, even where a court has jurisdiction, it may abstain from exercising that jurisdiction where another sovereign's interest in the proceedings is greater than the United States' interests, or when a foreign sovereign has legislated on a matter of its own significant national concern.

Courts generally abstain under the doctrine of international comity where there are parallel proceedings, one in its jurisdiction and another in the foreign jurisdiction. Once a judgment on the merits is reached in one of the cases, failure to defer to the judgment would have serious implication for the concerns of international comity.

The Eleventh Circuit has identified three factors in determining whether a Court should exercise abstain from the exercise of jurisdiction: (1) international comity; (2) fairness to the litigants and (3) efficient use of scare judicial resources.

1. International Comity

Comity concerns include:(1) whether the judgment was rendered by a competent court utilizing proceedings consistent with civilized jurisprudence; and (2) whether the foreign judgment is prejudicial, in the sense of violating American public policy because it is repugnant to fundamental principles of what is decent and just.

Plaintiffs do not assert that the Dominican court was not competent or repugnant. Rather, Plaintiffs

attempt to argue that the current action is a separate action enjoining further breaches of contract. The Court disagrees. The parties' rights under the Agreement are at issue in both the Dominican actions and this action. Accordingly, the Court finds Plaintiffs' argument that this action is separate and distinct from the Dominican action without merit.

2. Fairness to the Litigants

To determine fairness to the litigants, the Court should consider (1) the order in which the suit was filed; (2) the more convenient forum and (3) the possibility of prejudice to parties resulting from abstention. Walton & Post filed the Dominican action over three years ago. Indeed, Plaintiffs actively litigated the Dominican action for several years. It was only after the Dominican Court of Appeals decision that Plaintiffs suddenly needed to proceed in the United States. Accordingly, the Court finds that this factor weighs in favor of abstention.

3. Efficient Use of Scarce Judicial Resources

In determining whether the action would be an efficient use of judicial resources the Court should consider (1) the inconvenience of the federal forum, (2) the desirability of avoiding piecemeal litigation, and (3) whether the alternative forum is likely to render a prompt disposition. The Southern District of Florida is a very busy district. The actions certainly have parties and issues in common. Indeed, the parties and the issues are virtually identical. Finally, the Dominican courts have already reached final judgment. Clearly, this factor weighs in favor of abstention.

Based on these factors, the Court shall abstain from exercising jurisdiction over this matter.

We live in a litigation oriented society whose members seem to institute suit over every conceivable problem. Cases range for class action lawsuits against the tobacco industry, former professional football players suing the NFL for traumatic brain injuries to a suit by Stella Liebeck against McDonalds as the result of severe burns she suffered after spilling hot coffee on her leg.

Rules have been established to govern the conduct of these lawsuits from the filing of the claim to verdict. These regulations are called the **Rules of Civil Procedure** and vary depending upon the type of proceeding and court. Matters before a Justice of the Peace or Municipal Court judge will be informal since they involve small amounts of money and litigants are encouraged to represent themselves. Jury trials are much more formal and the rules are complex. Failure to follow these court mandates may result in an adverse finding or dismissal of the lawsuit.

Civil litigation involves three distinctive but equally important parts: pleadings, discovery and the trial.

A. Pleadings

The **pleadings** consist of the initial documents filed with the court that set forth the theories of liability and damages requested by the plaintiff and the defenses by the party being sued. For instance, these documents in Pennsylvania state court include the complaint, answer, new matter, and affirmative defenses like comparative negligence and any counterclaim against the plaintiff or cross-claim against another defendant. The pleadings also establish the boundaries of the lawsuit since matters not asserted are generally waived. For instance, the defense of assumption of the risk or payment of a loan must be raised at this time or they will be lost as a defense.

B. Discovery

Discovery allows each party to find out more about the opponent's case. It is during this stage of the lawsuit that witnesses can be questioned under oath, a process called depositions; and counsel may also obtain copies of an opponent's documents and trial exhibits. In addition, a party's medical or psychological examinations may be ordered if relevant to the case.

C. Trial

Most civil lawsuits settle but some do proceed to trial. A **trial** is the final stage of the litigation process. It is at this judicial proceeding that evidence is presented, the witness is cross-examined, and factual disputes are resolved by the rendering of a verdict in favor of one of the parties.

In a civil case, the plaintiff has the burden of proof which is by the **preponderance of the evidence.** This means that in order for the plaintiff to win, the evidence of the parties is put on a scale and the plaintiff must tip the scales in his or her favor.

In a criminal case, the government will file a criminal complaint and the court will issue an arrest warrant or order the defendant to appear in court where the judge will inform the accused of the charges and make a decision regarding the amount of bail. There is no formal discovery process like in civil cases but the parties can engage in a limited discovery process.

Following the entering of a formal plea, such as guilty or not guilty, and the filing of any pre-trial motions, such as illegally seized evidence by the police the case proceeds to trial. At this proceeding, the District Attorney has the burden of proving the defendant guilty beyond a reasonable doubt. This means that the evidence is placed on a scale and in order to convict the defendant, the scale must totally tip out of balance in favor of the government.

SECTION 3.10 ALTERNATIVE DISPUTE RESOLUTION

Controversies may be resolved in ways other than by using the state and federal court systems, which may be too time-consuming or expensive. Parties may agree to submit to any of a number of alternative methods for resolving their disputes. In considering an **alternative dispute resolution** mechanism, the parties will focus on factors such as cost, who will represent them, who will arbitrate the dispute, and whether the alternative method will lead to a more helpful or fair resolution.

Arbitration is often used in a commercial setting where both parties agree to have a third party or arbitrator resolve the controversy. When the parties agree to abide by the arbitrator's decision, they are involved in a binding arbitration, and the court will automatically enforce the arbitrator's award. Both parties must agree on who the impartial arbitrator will be. Arbitration proceedings are usually informal, and the parties are not bound by the rules of evidence that control court cases.

Because of the binding nature of arbitration, courts will rarely overturn an arbitrator's decision unless there is clear evidence of fraud or gross misconduct.

Mediation is used primarily in disputes between labor and management, but is also suited for disputes between neighbors and family members. Mediation is different from arbitration because it is advisory in nature. A mediator makes recommendations to the parties in order to aid them in solving their differences. Successful mediation will keep the parties out of court. Mediation is gaining popularity in divorce cases by helping the parties work out their differences.

Private judging is used when both sides are constrained by time and can afford to hire a private judge. Private judging proceeds as a normal trial would be conducted.

Non-binding or **mini-trials** are another form of private dispute resolution in which the parties may or may not be represented by a lawyer. The parties usually submit their case to a panel of experts and a neutral advisor, who aids both sides. The panel and advisor suggest the likely outcome if the case were to go to court. This method is helpful for business disputes involving long processes of fact-finding.

Neighborhood Justice Centers derive from a program initiated in the 1970s. The centers receive their cases from local police or magistrates' offices. The cases usually involve neighborhood or family disputes, in which the two sides represent themselves before a panel of local residents. The aim is to avoid having the disputes escalate to the point where the criminal court system takes over.

SECTION 3.11
THE ARBITRATION
CLAUSE

PROBLEM THREE

PARK, BROWN & SMITH, P.C.
ATTORNEYS AT LAW
MEMORANDUM

To: All Law Clerks

FROM: Peter Smith, Esquire

RE: The Arbitration Clause

Joe Roberts needed a computer program for the ordering of food and drink by customers at Tyler's Sport's Bar and Grill by use of a touch screen at various stations throughout the business. Joe contacted his IT expert and told her what he needed. One week later, the computer person arrived at Tyler's to install the new software specially designed for restaurants.

The software program came in a sealed box and the IT person opened the plastic wrapper around the CD cover and installed the software onto the main computer in Joe's office. After the installation was completed, the computer expert showed Joe how to operate the various terminals in the restaurant in order to place an order. The installed program was designed and purchased from Point of Sales, Inc. and cost $1,000. The cost of installing the software and making sure that all of the terminals worked was another $250.

The IT person left the CD and box on Joe's desk along with the warranty materials. When Joe entered his office and saw the items on his desk, he threw everything away in the trash except for the CD.

It turns out that the CD was original sealed in a plastic wrapper with a notice that said "Important Warranty Information Inside. Please read the information since our liability for a product that does not work properly is limited to the return of the purchase price. By opening the CD cover and installing the software, you agree to be bound by the terms of the contract contained within the box." Joe never saw this warning since the IT person opened the CD and threw the wrapper away. Likewise, Joe never looked inside the box at the warranty since he threw the box into the trash. That warranty contained a notice in very large print that said: "**THE BUYER'S SOLE REMEDY FOR ANY DEFECT IN THE SOFTWARE OR BREACH OF WARRANTY IS LIMITED TO THE RETURN OF THE PURCHASE PRICE. ALL DISPUTES CONCERNING THIS PRODUCT MUST BE SUBMITTED TO BINDING ARBITRATION IN CALIFORNIA.**" The agreement also contained a clause that the buyer could opt out of the arbitration clause when he or she registers the product and checked off the box that stated the buyer rejected the arbitration clause. Since Joe threw the box away, he never registered the software on behalf of Tyler's Sports Bar and Grill.

After a few months of use, Joe was surprised that Tyler's cash receipts were so low. The business was constantly busy but the revenues were meager. Joe sat down with the invoices as well as the daily ledgers generated by the computer software. Much to his horror, Roberts discovered that the computer program did not work correctly and generating bills that were undercharging the customers by 50%. Joe estimated that the bar lost at least $50,000 in revenue. Joe called the software company to complain and was told that they would only refund the purchase price of the CD and explained that its policy was set forth on both the outside cover of the CD and on the printed warranty inside the box. They also refused to fix the glitch in the software. When Joe said that he was going to sue them, the software company merely said that Tyler's had to file for arbitration in California.

Roberts was furious by this caviler attitude and had to hire a software expert to immediately fix the problem which cost $2,500. I looked at the warranty information that the company sent me and it confirms the things that the Point of Sales, Inc. said to Joe during his conversation with them.

Joe wishes to file suit on behalf of the Tyler's in Philadelphia. I have done some preliminary research and have found the following case. Please read it and answer the questions following the decision.

NORCIA V. SAMSUNG
2015 WL 4967247 (N.D. CALIF. 2015)

On May 23, 2013, Norcia entered a Verizon store in San Francisco to purchase a Samsung Galaxy S4 phone. Norcia paid for the phone at the register, and a Verizon employee provided a receipt entitled "Customer Agreement" followed by the name and address of the Verizon store. The receipt stated the order location, Norcia's mobile number, the product identification number, and the contract end date.

A Verizon employee took the Galaxy S4 phone, still in its sealed Samsung box, to a table. The front of the product box stated "Samsung Galaxy S4." The back of the box stated: "Package Contains ... Product Safety & Warranty Brochure." The Verizon Wireless employee opened the box, unpacked the phone, and helped Norcia transfer his contacts from his old phone to the new phone. Norcia took the phone, the phone charger, and the headphones with him as he left the store, but he declined the offer by the Verizon Wireless employee to take the box and the rest of its contents.

The Samsung Galaxy S4 box contained, among other things, a "Product Safety & Warranty Information" brochure. The 101–page brochure consisted of two sections. Section 1 contained a wide range of health and safety information, while Section 2 contained Samsung's "Standard Limited Warranty" and "End User License Agreement for Software." The Standard Limited Warranty section explained the scope of Samsung's express warranty. In addition to explaining Samsung's obligations, the procedure for obtaining warranty service, and the limits of Samsung's liability, the warranty section included the following:

> "All disputes with Samsung arising in any way from this limited warranty or the sale, condition or performance of the products shall be

resolved exclusively through final and binding arbitration, and not by a court or jury."

Later in the section, a paragraph explained the procedures for arbitration and stated that purchasers could opt out of the arbitration agreement by providing notice to Samsung within 30 calendar days of purchase. It also stated that opting out "will not affect the coverage of the Limited Warranty in any way, and you will continue to enjoy the benefits of the Limited Warranty." Norcia did not take any steps to opt out.

In February 2014, Norcia filed a complaint against Samsung, alleging that Samsung misrepresented the Galaxy S4's storage capacity and rigged the phone to operate at a higher speed when it was being tested. The complaint alleged that these deceptive acts constituted fraud and violated the Consumers Legal Remedies Act.

Instead of filing an answer to the complaint, Samsung moved to compel arbitration by invoking the arbitration provision in the Product Safety & Warranty Information brochure.

Arbitration is a matter of contract and a party cannot be required to submit to arbitration any dispute which he has not agreed to submit. Therefore, we must determine whether a valid agreement to arbitrate exists. Samsung bears the burden of proving the existence of an agreement to arbitrate by a preponderance of the evidence.

Samsung claims that the inclusion of the arbitration provision in the Product Safety & Warranty Information brochure created a valid contract between Samsung and Norcia to arbitrate all claims related to the Galaxy S4 phone. Although the brochure is in the form of an express consumer warranty from Samsung to Norcia, the arbitration provision states that arbitration is required not only for "disputes with Samsung arising in any way from this limited warranty" but also for all disputes arising from "the sale, condition or performance of the products."

The essential elements for a contract are (1) parties capable of contracting; (2) their consent; (3) a lawful object; and (4) sufficient cause or consideration. A party who is bound by a contract is bound by all of its terms, whether or not the party was aware of them. A party cannot avoid the terms of a contract on the ground that he or she failed to read it before signing.

A contract for sale of goods may be made in any manner sufficient to show agreement, including conduct by both parties which recognizes the existence of such a contract. Courts must determine whether the outward manifestations of consent would lead a reasonable person to believe the offeree has assented to the agreement.

As a general rule, silence or inaction does not constitute acceptance of an offer. Courts have long held that an offer made to another, either orally or in writing, cannot be turned into an agreement because the person to whom it is made or sent makes no reply, even though the offer states that silence will be taken as consent, for the offerer cannot prescribe conditions of rejection so as to turn silence on the part of the offeree into acceptance.

There are exceptions to this rule, however. An offeree's silence may be deemed to be consent to a contract when the offeree has a duty to respond to an offer and fails to act in the face of this duty. An offeree's silence may also be treated as consent to a contract when the party retains the benefit offered.

Even if there is an applicable exception to the general rule that silence does not constitute acceptance, courts have rejected the argument that an offeree's silence constitutes consent to a contract when the offeree reasonably did not know that an offer had been made.

We now apply these principles of law to determine whether Norcia engaged in any conduct sufficient to show that he agreed to be bound by the arbitration agreement in the Product Safety & Warranty Information brochure. There is no dispute that Norcia did not expressly assent to any agreement in the brochure. Nor did Norcia sign the brochure or otherwise act in a manner that would show his intent to use his silence, or failure to opt out, as a means of accepting the arbitration agreement. Under the law, an offeree's inaction after receipt of an offer is generally insufficient to form a contract. Therefore, Samsung's offer to arbitrate all disputes with Norcia cannot be turned into an agreement because the person to whom it is made or sent makes no reply, even though the offer states that silence will be taken as consent, unless an exception to this general rule applies.

Samsung fails to demonstrate the applicability of any exception to the general rule that an offeree's silence does not constitute consent. Samsung has not pointed to any principle of law that imposed a duty on Norcia to act in response to receiving the Product Safety & Warranty Information brochure. Nor was there any previous course of dealing between the parties that might impose a duty on Norcia to act. Moreover, Samsung has not alleged that Norcia retained any benefit by failing to act. Indeed, the brochure states that Norcia was entitled to "the benefits of the Limited Warranty" regardless whether Norcia opted out of the arbitration agreement. In the absence of an applicable exception, the general rule for contract formation applies. Because Norcia did not give any outward manifestations of consent that would lead a reasonable person to believe the offeree has assented to the agreement, no contract was formed between Norcia and Samsung, and Norcia is not bound by the arbitration provision contained in the brochure.

To counter this conclusion, Samsung argues that Norcia was bound by the terms set forth in the brochure because the brochure is analogous to a shrink-wrap license, which we have held was enforceable, or is analogous to terms included in a box sent to the consumer referred to here as an "in-the-box" contract, which the court has held to be enforceable.

A "shrink-wrap license" is a form on the packing or on the outside of the CD–ROM containing the software which states that by opening the packaging or CD–ROM wrapper, the user agrees to the terms of the license. Where a notice on a package states that the user agrees to certain terms by opening the package, a court could reasonably conclude, consistent with contract law, that the user has a duty to act in order to negate the conclusion that the consumer had accepted the terms in the notice. This principle does not help Samsung, however. Even if a license to copy software could be analogized to a brochure that contains contractual terms, the outside of the Galaxy S4 box did not notify the consumer that opening the box would be considered agreement to the terms set forth in the brochure. Under these circumstances, the general rule that silence or inaction does not constitute acceptance is binding.

We also reject Samsung's argument that Norcia reasonably assented to the arbitration provision because he failed to opt out of the arbitration provision contained in the product box. Under the circumstances in this case, we conclude that Samsung's inclusion of a brochure in the Galaxy S4 box, and Norcia's failure to opt out, does not make the arbitration provision enforceable against Norcia.

Because Samsung failed to carry its burden of proving the existence of a contract with Norcia to arbitrate as a matter of law, Samsung's motion to compel arbitration is denied.

**PROBLEM THREE—A
ANSWER SHEET**

Name

Please Print Clearly

1. What is a "shrink-wrap license"?

_____

_____

_____

_____

_____

_____

_____

_____

_____

2. What are the elements of a valid contract as enumerated by the court?

_____

_____

_____

_____

_____

_____

_____

_____

_____

3. Please discuss the merits of Joe's claim and let me know, based upon the case, whether we will prevail. In other words, do we have to file for arbitration in California?

_____

_____

_____

_____

_____

_____

_____

_____

_____

_____

**SECTION 3.12
PROBLEM CASES**

1. Francis Thomas received an envelope at his New Jersey home with a return address from the Philadelphia Chamber of Commerce. Upon opening the letter, he discovered two tickets to a Philadelphia 76ers game. Mr. Thomas could not believe his good fortune and took his son to the contest at the First Union Center. During the second period, the Sheriff tapped Thomas on the shoulder and served him with a lawsuit concerning a motor vehicle accident that had happened one year earlier in New Jersey. Does the Philadelphia Court have jurisdiction over this New Jersey resident because Thomas was served with the lawsuit within its boundaries? See: **M. H. Eastburn v. Saul Turnoff, 147 A.2d 353 (Pa. 1959).**

2. Robert DeLuca had a long history of being involved in violent crimes. During his criminal trial for extortion, the trial judge empaneled an anonymous jury in order to safeguard the panel members' identities and to prevent jury tampering. Spectators were also screened and had to produce identification before being allowed into the courtroom. DeLuca claimed that his Sixth Amendment right to a public trial was violated by the judge's unusual actions. Do you agree? **United States v. Robert DeLuca, 96-1173, (1st Cir. Ct. 1998).**

3. A franchise agreement between Charles Jones and General Nutrition Companies, Inc., required that all disputes concerning the agreement be litigated in a Pennsylvania venue. Jones operated a GNC store in California. Following a dispute with General Nutrition, he sued GNC in California where his store was located, the contracts were entered into and the majority of witnesses resided. GNC requested a change of venue so that the case could be removed to Pennsylvania based upon the forum selection clause in the contract even though California does not favor this type of clause. Where should the case be heard? **Charles Jones v. GNC Franchising, Inc., CV-98-10611-DMT (9ᵗʰ Cir. Ct. 2000).**

4. Beer Across America sold beer to a minor via the Internet. The liquor was shipped from the store's location in Illinois to the child's home in Alabama. After the parents returned home from vacation, they discovered the beer in the refrigerator. This prompted the parents to file a suit in Alabama against the Illinois company for the unlawful sale of liquor to a minor. Beer Across America was not registered to do business in Alabama, and it owned no property within the state. Is a passive Internet site that can be accessed from anywhere in the world sufficient to confer jurisdiction over a non-resident defendant for doing business in Alabama? **Lynda Butler v. Beer Across America, 83 F. Supp. 2d 1261 (2000).**

SECTION 3.13
INTERNET REFERENCES

To learn more information about the court system and the jury selection process, see the following sites:

A. The Jury Process

- **www.fija.org**
  This is the official website for the Fully Informed Jury Association, a non-profit educational association devoted to providing information about jury duty, including a citizen's guide to this citizen function, and frequently asked questions.

- **www.edwright.com/voir_dire_intro.html**
  Tips on the voir dire process are offered on this site, which is maintained by an attorney.

- **www.geocities.com/heartland/7394/lysander.html**
  A historical justification for trial by jury is presented in this article.

B. The Court

- **www.law.emory.edu/caselaw**
  This site features federal court decisions from 1995 through the present.

- **http://law.about.com/newsissues/law/library/courts b1899_toc.htm**
  This site provides a general discussion on the federal court system.

- **www.uscourts.gov/faq.html**
  This Federal Judiciary homepage provides answers to frequently asked questions about the federal court system.

- **www.supremecourtus.gov**
  The Supreme Court's official site is contained at this address and contain copies of the Court's opinions, Court rules, and other general information.

- **http://vis.law.villanova.edu/locator/federalcourt.html**
  Villanova University School of Law maintains this website which provides access to federal court decisions from the district court to the United States Supreme Court. The law school's website also maintains a variety of links to legal magazines and search engines for law related subjects. You may access this site through: **http:// vls.law.villanova. edu/library/express/**

- **www.aopc.org/index/ujs/courtswork.htm**
  An overview of the Pennsylvania's court system can be found at this address.

- **http://oyez.nwu.edu**
  Northwestern University maintains this multimedia data base and virtual tour of the United States Supreme Court.

Footnotes:

1. *What is the Court*, Findlaw, http://litigation.findlaw.com/legal-system/what-is-a-court.html (January 15, 2018.)

2. *History of the Judiciary*, Courts and Tribunals Judiciary, https://www.judiciary.gov.uk/about-the-judiciary/history-of-the-judiciary/ (January 15, 2018.)

3. The New England Colonies, Encyclopedic Britannica, https://www.britannica.com/place/United-States/The-New-England-colonies#ref612323 (January 15, 2018.)

4. *Development in America from Colonial Times*, USLegal, https://courts.uslegal.com/jury-system/development-in-america-from-colonial-times/ (January 15, 2018.)

5. *Id.*

6. *Id.*

7. Federal Courts In American Government, Unites States Courts, http://www.uscourts.gov/FederalCourts/UnderstandingtheFederalCourts/FederalCourtsInAmericanGovernment.aspx (last visited September 22, 2013).

8. *Id.*

9. **Marbury v. Madison** http://usinfo.state.gov/usa/infousa/facts/democrac/9.htm.

10. "About U.S. Federal Courts," U.S. Courts, www.uscourts.gov/about.html.

11. "United States Supreme Court," U.S. Courts, www.uscourts.gov/supreme-court.html.

12. Reed, et. al., The Legal and Regulatory Environment of Business, The Court System, Chapter 6, McGraw Hill, Sixteenth Edition, 2013, at 78.

13. Supreme *Court of the United States,* Supreme Court Historical Society, http:// www.supremecourthistory.org/.

14. *How the Court Works,* The Supreme Court Historical Society, www.suprmecourthistory.org.

15. Id.

16. **Williams v. Florida, 399 U.S. 78 (1970).**

17. **Duncan v. Louisiana, 88 S. Ct. 1444 (1968).**

18. *American Bar Association Points: Trial by Jury,* www.abanet.org

19. See: *Criminal Justice across Europe,* www.crimeinfo.org.uk.

20. Civil Justice Statistics, U.S. Department of Justice Bureau of Justice Statistics, http://www.ojp.usdoj.gov/bjs/civil.htm.

21. Shrager and Frost, "The Quotable Lawyer," Facts on File, at 152.

22. New York Times, February 3, 1969 as cited in the "Quotable Lawyer" at 154.

23. Comity of Nations, Legal Information Institute, http://www.law.cornell.edu/wex/comity_of_nations(last visited September 22, 2013).

KEY TERMS

Activist
Alternative Dispute
    Resolution
Appellate Court
Arbitration
Article Four
Article Three
Circuit Court of Appeals
Comity
Copyright Act of 1976
Court of Appeals
Court of Common Pleas
Court of Federal Claims
Discovery
Federal Court
Forum Non-Conveniens
Forum State
Full Faith and Credit
Judicial Restraint Oriented
Jurisdiction
Jurisdiction over the Person
Jury
Long Arm Statute
Magna Carta
Mediation

Mini-Trials
Minimum Contacts
Municipal Court
Neighborhood Justice Centers
Non-Binding
Original Jurisdiction
Pleading
Private Judging
Questions-of-Law
Rule of Four
Rules of Civil Procedure
Service
Seventh Amendment
Sixth Amendment
Standing
State Court
Subject Matter Jurisdiction
Supreme Court of the United
    States
Supreme Court Rule 10
Trial
United States District Court
Venue
Voir Dire
Writ of Certiorari

Part Two
The Building Blocks of the Law for the Entrepreneur

Certain categories of law establish the building blocks for any discussion relating to the legal environment of business. These topics include contracts, torts, property and criminal law. Most enterprises, regardless of their size, will be affected by these mandates. Part Two of the book will therefore build this foundation one chapter at a time.

Chapter Four focuses on contract law. People and businesses enter into multiple contracts on a daily basis that give rise to legal implications. Buying supplies, paying wages to an employee or purchasing a building to run the enterprise all involve contracts. Regardless of the value of the agreement, every contract must have the same basic elements. These include an offer, acceptance, consideration, capacity and legality. The law of contracts has developed for the most part as the result of state law, either by statute or court pronouncement. This Chapter will discuss each element of a contract in detail and will show how the law changes if the transaction is covered by the Uniform Commercials Code.

Chapter Five discusses the law of torts. These private civil wrongs allow a party to recover monetary damages for the harm that has been suffered. Attention will be paid to the torts of negligence, those that are internationally committed, such as defamation, false imprisonment and battery, and will conclude with an explanation of products liability.

Chapter Six provides an overview of property law. This area deals with the rights and duties that arise out of the ownership or possession of real and personal property. This Chapter will examine the ways that property can be owned as well as how a person can obtain title to personal property and real estate.

Chapter Seven deals with white collar and other business related crimes. These offenses do not ordinarily involve crimes of violence, but cost the government and individuals billions of dollars annually. These offenses range from bribery to money laundering. On the other hand, businesses are also the victims of crimes such as burglary and shoplifting. This Chapter will discuss the more common crimes committed in a business setting, and will examine the rights that a business has if it is the subject of a criminal investigation.

Chapter Eight will explain the judicial remedies available to a person or business in the event that a party or business is aggrieved by the actions of another. These remedies will be divided into two parts: remedies at law and those in equity. The first category involves those remedies that result from a breach of contract or the commission of a tort and involve an award of money damages. Remedies in equity allow the court to fashion relief in order to do what is fair under the circumstances. Instead of money damages, this form of relief involves injunctions, recission of a contract and a Declaratory Judgment.

CHAPTER 4

LAW OF CONTRACTS

A verbal contract isn't worth the paper it is written on.

—**Samuel Goldwyn**

SECTION 4.1
INTRODUCTION

People and businesses routinely enter into contracts each day unaware of the legal ramifications of their bargains. Activities such as purchasing supplies, buying coffee or gasoline, paying an employee's salary, or offering health insurance to workers are contractual obligations. In fact, your taking this course and buying the book are contracts that have legal ramifications. If you think about it, the buyer of a product who demands the return of the purchase price because the item does not live up to one's expectations is really asserting a breach of contract claim.

A **contract** is the voluntary exchange of promises between two or more entities, creating a legal obligation that is enforceable in court. Most agreements are informal but people do occasionally enter into written contracts for things such as the purchase of a car or a home. Business transactions tend to be more formal because of the use of preprinted forms, or negotiated agreements that are drafted by attorneys, so more of these contracts are in writing. Regardless of the formality of the agreement or the purchase price, the following elements must be present in every contract:

1. Offer
2. Acceptance
3. Consideration
4. Capacity
5. Legality

The penalty for a breach of contract may range from nothing to substantial money damages. The contract may even dictate the consequences in the event of a breach of the agreement such as the forfeiture of the deposit or a set dollar amount. The contract may also specify how the dispute is to be resolved. For example, a contract may provide for binding arbitration or leave the parties to traditional court remedies, but specify the place where the lawsuit must be filed.

SECTION 4.2
KINDS OF CONTRACTS

The law of contract has developed for the most part as the result of state law; either by statute or judge made law. These legal tenets may be part of the common law of a particular jurisdiction or may arise through various state statutes such as the **Uniform Commercial Code.** This is a uniform act that regulates the sale of goods and certain other commercial transactions. A **good** is a movable item of personal property such as a car, television or book. On the other hand, the sale of land or a trademark would be excluded from this definition.

Contracts may be characterized in several different ways. The agreement may be classified as a bilateral or unilateral contract, depending on the number of promises involved. Contracts may be expressed or implied, depending on how the terms of the contract are set forth. Contracts may also be classified as valid, void, voidable, or unenforceable based on their validity and enforceability.

UNILATERAL AND BILATERAL CONTRACTS

Although contracts involve at least two parties, not all contracts involve two promises. When one party makes a promise in exchange for an act, a **unilateral contract** is formed. For example, the promise of a reward for the return of a lost ring forms the basis of a unilateral contract. Many people may search for the object, but only the person who returns the ring will receive the money from the owner. Also, once the party to whom a unilateral offer has been extended starts to perform the requested act, that person must be given a reasonable time to complete the job. For instance, if a homeowner tells the neighbors that he will give $1,000 to the first person who paints his house and a neighbor starts painting the walls of the dwelling later in the day, the homeowner cannot revoke the offer.

A **bilateral contract** is created when the parties exchange mutual promises to do some future act. For example, if Joe Roberts promises to sell his pet bear to a zoo for $5,000 and the zoo promises to buy the animal, a bilateral contract is formed at that moment in time. Both the buyer and seller are bound by their promises and are under a legal obligation to perform under the terms of their agreement. If Joe subsequently changes his mind, the zoo may sue him for the loss of the bargain. Most contracts are bilateral and not unilateral. In fact, in cases of doubt, the courts will favor a bilateral agreement.

Can a high school student sue her date if he stands her up for the prom? Is this agreement of the type that gives rise to an enforceable contract or is it merely a social engagement that only has moral significance? A student from Pennsylvania successfully sued her date when he was a "no-show" at her senior prom. The school district required all out-of-town prom dates to sign a written agreement to stay at the dance and see the student home after the prom.

The judge ruled that the date's failure to attend the prom was a breach of contract and the high school student was awarded $548 for her dress and court costs.

Customer loyalty is vital to the successful operation of a business. A buyer's willingness to purchases a particular brand over and over again is the result of a positive customer experience and the value of the item or service the customer receives from the transaction.[1] In turn, a **customer loyalty program** is an incentive offered by a business to its customers who regularly make purchases by giving free merchandise, gas rewards, or even an advanced release of products. Frequent flyer programs offered by airlines and restaurants that offer a free meal after so many purchases or buy one and get one free are examples.[2] What happens if a vendor decides to stop the program after people have purchased their products in reliance on the promotion? Is this a binding unilateral contract? That is the issue in the next case.

SATERIALE V. R. J. REYNOLDS TOBACCO COMPANY
697 F.3D 777 (CT. APP. 9TH CIR. 2012)

R. J. Reynolds Tobacco Company (RJR) operated a customer rewards program, called Camel Cash, from 1991 to 2007. Under the terms of the program, RJR urged consumers to purchase Camel cigarettes, to save Camel Cash certificates included in packages of Camel cigarettes, to enroll in the program and, ultimately, to redeem their certificates for merchandise featured in catalogs distributed by RJR. The number of Camel Cash certificates needed to obtain merchandise varied from as little as 100 to many thousands. This encouraged consumers to buy more packages of cigarettes together with Camel Cash and also to save or obtain Camel Cash certificates to redeem them for more valuable items.

RJR honored the program from 1991 to 2006, and during that time, Camel's share of the cigarette market nearly doubled from approximately 4 percent to more than 7 percent. In October 2006, however, RJR mailed a notice to program members announcing that the program would terminate as of March 31, 2007. The termination notice stated:

> "As a loyal Camel smoker, we [sic] wanted to tell you our Camel Cash program is expiring. C–Notes will no longer be included on packs, which means whatever Camel Cash you have is among the last of its kind.
>
> Now this isn't happening overnight—there'll be plenty of time to redeem your C–Notes before the program ends. In fact, you'll have from OCTOBER '06 through MARCH '07 to go to camelsmokes.com to redeem your C–Notes. Supplies will be limited, so it won't hurt to get there before the rush."

Beginning in October 2006, however, RJR allegedly stopped printing and issuing catalogs and told consumers that it did not have any merchandise available for redemption. Several of the plaintiffs attempted, without success, to redeem C–Notes or obtain a catalog during the final six months of the program. The plaintiffs had saved thousands of Camel Cash certificates that they were unable to redeem.

The plaintiffs do not dispute that RJR had the right to terminate the Camel Cash program effective March 31, 2007, but allege that RJR breached a contract by refusing to redeem C–Notes during the six months preceding program termination.

RJR made an offer to enter into a unilateral contract. In contrast to a bilateral contract, a unilateral contract involves the exchange of a promise for a performance. The offer is accepted by rendering a performance rather than providing a promise. Typical illustrations are found in offers of rewards or prizes.

RJR argues that its C–Notes were not offers, but invitations to make an offer. RJR relies on the general rule that advertisements of goods by display, sign, handbill, newspaper, radio or television are not ordinarily intended or understood as offers to sell.

It is very common, where one desires to induce many people to action, to offer a reward for such action by general publication in some form. If the statement calls for the performance or commencement of performance of specific acts, action in accordance with such an interpretation will make the offer irrevocable. There are many cases of an offer of a reward for the capture of a person charged with crime, for desired information, for the return of a lost article, for the winning of a contest, or for the redemption of coupons.

RJR's ostensible purpose in promoting the Camel Cash program was to induce as many consumers as possible to purchase. The operative question, therefore, is simply whether the advertiser, in clear and positive terms, promised to render performance in exchange for something requested by the advertiser, and whether the recipient of the advertisement reasonably might have concluded that by acting in accordance with the request a contract would be formed. We conclude that the plaintiffs have adequately alleged the existence of an offer to enter into a unilateral contract, whereby RJR promised to provide rewards to customers who purchased Camel cigarettes, saved Camel Cash certificates and redeemed their certificates in accordance with the catalogs' terms.

EXPRESS AND IMPLIED CONTRACTS

An **express contract** is one in which the parties spell out the specifics of their agreement in direct terms. The format of this type of contract may be written or oral. An apartment lease, bank loan or home purchase are examples of express contracts. These types of agreements are normally in writing and comprehensive in nature. Nevertheless, **express contracts** may be verbal, informal, and brief. For example, if you offer to sell this text to a classmate for $40 and the fellow student accepts your offer, an express contract has been formed.

Promises may also be inferred by the conduct of the parties in view of the surrounding circumstances. These contracts are **implied-in-fact** because it is reasonable to infer that the parties intend to create a contract by their conduct. In other words, it is formed by the actions of the parties. For example, it is reasonable to expect a person who picks up and eats a banana in a grocery store to pay for the fruit.

Another type of **implied contract** is one **implied-in-law** or a **quasi-contract.** This type of contract arises in order to prevent unjust enrichment. For example, an emergency room physician who renders aid to an unconscious patient in the hospital must be compensated for those services. The court will order reimbursement from the patient on the basis of a **contract implied-in-law,** even though the patient never consented to the emergency room treatment.

Read the following case in order to gain a better understanding on how implied contracts come into existence.

KAREN STAVINS ENTERPRISES, INC. V. CITY COLLEGE DISTRICT NO. 508 36 N.E.3D 1015 (ILL. APP. 2015)

The plaintiff alleges that City Colleges selected and hired nine actors to perform in a commercial to be broadcast on television and the internet, extolling the virtues of an education at City Colleges. According to the complaint, City Colleges hired each of the actors through the plaintiff as the talent agent for each of the actors. The actors performed their designated parts in the production, and the commercial was repeatedly broadcasted on television and the Internet. According to the complaint, the reasonable value of the actors' services along with the plaintiff's fees is $13,909.37, which City Colleges has refused to pay. The plaintiff specifically alleged that City Colleges did not have an expressed contract with it or the actors but asserts that City Colleges voluntarily accepted the services of the actors and the plaintiff without objection.

City Colleges acknowledges that it has the authority to award contracts involving expenditures from $5,000 to $25,000. City Colleges argued that the plaintiff cannot allege compliance with its policies

and procedures governing contracts and has failed to allege that an individual with the authority to enter into contracts on its behalf accepted the plaintiff's services or made any representations that its services would be accepted and paid for by City Colleges.

The plaintiff contends that it sought recovery based upon a contract implied-in-law and not based upon an express contract. A contract implied-in-law is not a contract at all. Rather, it is grounded in an implied promise by the recipient of services or goods to pay for something of value which it has received. A contract implied-in-law is one in which no actual agreement exists between the parties, but a duty to pay a reasonable value is imposed upon the recipient of services or goods to prevent an unjust enrichment. The essence of a cause of action based upon a contract implied-in-law is the defendant's failure to make equitable payment for a benefit that it voluntarily accepted from the plaintiff.

In order to state a claim based upon an implied contract, a plaintiff must allege specific facts in support of the conclusion that it conferred a benefit upon the defendant which the defendant has unjustly retained in violation of fundamental principles of equity and good conscience.

Stated otherwise, to be entitled to a remedy based upon a contract implied-in-law, a plaintiff must show that it has furnished valuable services or goods which the defendant received under circumstances that would make it unjust to retain without paying a reasonable value therefore.

The grounds for dismissal asserted by City Colleges is that it cannot be liable to the plaintiff absent compliance with its policies and procedures for awarding contracts which the plaintiff has failed to allege. However, when, as in this case, a plaintiff seeks recovery based upon a contract implied-in-law, recovery may be had despite the absence of compliance with its policies and procedures for awarding contracts.

In its complaint, the plaintiff alleged that: the actors who performed in City Colleges' commercial were hired and booked through the plaintiff; City Colleges hired those actors to perform in its commercial; the actors performed in the commercial; and City Colleges refused to pay the plaintiff for its services. We believe that these allegations sufficiently allege that the plaintiff provided a service to City Colleges; that City Colleges used those services under circumstances that would give a reasonable person notice that the plaintiff expected to be paid; and that, by refusing to pay the plaintiff for its services, City Colleges has unjustly retained a benefit in violation of fundamental principles of equity and good conscience. We conclude, therefore, that the complaint states a cause of action predicated upon a contract implied in law for the services rendered by the plaintiff.

Valid, Void, Voidable, and Unenforceable Contracts

Contracts may be classified according to their validity and enforceability. A **valid contract** satisfies all of the requirements of a binding and enforceable agreement, and either party may seek court intervention to uphold the terms of the bargain.

A contract is **voidable** if one of the parties has the legal right to withdraw from the arrangement without liability. Until this right is exercised, however, the contract remains valid and enforceable. For example, a contract with a child is voidable at the minor's election, since the minor lacks capacity to enter into the agreement. Nevertheless, the adult is bound by the terms of the contract and may not use the child's lack of capacity as a reason to disaffirm the bargain.

A **void contract** occurs when the agreement lacks one or more of the essential elements of a valid contract and can be attacked by either party to the agreement. Examples of a void contract include an agreement to perform an illegal act, or a contract which lacks consideration. An agreement to buy someone's vote in an election demonstrates a void contract, which has no force or effect.

An agreement is **unenforceable** when it satisfies the technical requirements of a valid contract but will not be enforced by the court. This type of contract leaves the aggrieved party without a remedy. For instance, a contract for the sale of land must be in writing to be enforceable. The courts, therefore, will not enforce an oral promise to transfer realty.

People enter into many contracts on a daily basis, and most of these agreements are informal, and oral in nature, but still constitute enforceable contracts. In ascertaining the intent of the parties to an oral contract, one must consider not only the language used in forming the oral agreement, but also the circumstances surrounding the making of the arrangements, the motives of the parties, and the purposes which the parties sought to accomplish. The major problem with an oral agreement is proving the existence of the arrangement. When a dispute arises over an oral contract, the courts are required to assess the credibility of the parties in trying to ascertain the thoughts of the litigants, since they are not set forth in writing.

With the growing number of lottery games offered by the states and gambling casinos, stories occasionally surface about family members, friends or co-workers pooling their money to buy lottery tickets or agreements made by people to share the winnings. Are these types of agreements enforceable or are they illegal betting contracts? That is the issue in **Sokaitis v. Bakaysa.**

SOKAITIS V. BAKAYSA
105 CONN. APP. 663 (CONN. APP. 2008)

On April 12, 1995, the plaintiff and the defendant, who are sisters, signed a written agreement. The agreement stated "this is a letter of agreement between the defendant and the plaintiff. This letter states that we are partners in any winning we shall receive, to be shared equally." On June 20, 2005, a winning Powerball lottery ticket, worth $500,000, was presented to the Connecticut lottery officials for payout. The winning ticket was presented by Joseph F. Troy, Sr., the brother of the parties, who indicated that he held the ticket jointly with the defendant. Lottery officials paid Troy and the defendant each $249,999. The defendant did not provide the plaintiff with any portion of the lottery winnings.

The plaintiff brought an action against the defendant for breach of contract. The plaintiff sought money damages equal to half of the defendant's Powerball winnings.

Section 52-553 (of the Connecticut Code) provides in relevant part: "All wagers, and all contracts of which the consideration is money or other valuable thing won, laid or bet, at any game, horse race, sport or pastime, and all contracts to repay any money knowingly lent at the time and place of such game, race, sport or pastime, to any person so gaming, betting or wagering, or to repay any money lent to any person who, at such time and place, so pays, bets or wagers, shall be void. . . ."

The plaintiff argues that "the parties' agreement is not a 'wagering contract' because it is a mutual exchange of promises to share profits from legal forms of gambling." Furthermore, the plaintiff argues that "money . . . won . . . at any game" was not the consideration for the agreement. In contrast, the plaintiff argued that the consideration was, in fact, the exchange of promises to share equally in the proceeds from the legal activity. We agree with the plaintiff.

We conclude that § 52-553 was not applicable to the agreement between the plaintiff and the

defendant. The statute makes void any wager or contract "of which the whole or any part of the consideration" is "money . . . won . . . at any game. . . ." In the present case, the plaintiff and the defendant promised to share equally in any winnings they received from various forms of legalized gambling, including the lottery. They did not make promises that were induced by the consideration of "money . . . won . . . at any game. . . ." Therefore, the consideration for the agreement was not the money that they won but rather their mutual promises to one another to share in any winnings they received. Consideration is "a benefit to the party promising, or a loss or detriment to the party to whom the promise is made . . ." Therefore, § 52-553 does not apply to the agreement between the plaintiff and the defendant because the consideration was not "money . . . won . . . at any game. . . ."

Therefore, the (lower) court improperly granted the defendant's motion for summary judgment and improperly rendered judgment in favor of the defendant.

SECTION 4.3
THE ELEMENTS OF
A CONTRACT

Intent is a primary factor in ascertaining whether there is an agreement between the parties to enter into a contract. This element is determined by words, conduct, and the surrounding circumstances. The courts apply an objective or reasonable person's standard in ascertaining the intentions of the parties based upon the totality of the circumstances. For example, an offer made by an intoxicated person should not be taken seriously. Likewise, an offer made in jest, in which no reasonable person would conclude that an offer was made, fails the objective person's standard.

Leonard v. Pepsi Co., Inc. is a famous case involving the soft drink promotion, *Pepsi Stuff,* and the request by a consumer to purchase a military jet from Pepsi based upon a television advertisement. The television commercial highlighted various items that a person could purchase by drinking Pepsi products. The advertisement was shown on television following the release of the movie "Top Gun," and featured a high-school student flying a fighter jet to class since he was late for school and the roads were congested. The commercial ended with the beverage company offering to sell the plane for seven million Pepsi points. The court was required to ascertain whether Pepsi objectively made an offer to sell the military jet as part of its promotion, or whether the proposal was merely a humorous presentation that no reasonable person should have taken seriously.

LEONARD V. PEPSICO, INC.
210 F.3ᴿᴰ 88 (S.D. N.Y. 2000)

This case arises out of a promotional campaign conducted by the distributor of Pepsi. The promotion entitled "Pepsi Stuff," encouraged consumers to collect "Pepsi Points" and redeem these points for merchandise featuring the Pepsi logo. Plaintiff saw the Pepsi Stuff commercial that he contends constituted an offer of a Harrier Jet.

Whether the television commercial constituted an offer is the central question in this case. The commercial opens with the appearance of a teenager preparing to leave for school, dressed in a shirt emblazoned with the Pepsi logo. While the teenager preens, the subtitle "T-SHIRT 75 PEPSI POINTS" scrolls across the screen. Bursting from his room, the teenager strides down the hallway wearing a leather jacket. The subtitle "LEATHER JACKET 1450 PEPSI POINTS" appears. The teenager opens the door of his house and puts on a pair of sunglasses. The drumroll then accompanies the subtitle "SHADES 175 PEPSI POINTS."

The scene then shifts to three young boys sitting in front of a high school building. The three boys gaze in awe as a Harrier Jet swings into view and lands by the side of the school building. Several students run for cover, and the velocity of the wind strips one hapless faculty member down to his underwear. While the faculty member is being deprived of his dignity, the voiceover announces: "Now the more Pepsi you drink, the more great stuff you're gonna get."

The teenager opens the cockpit of the fighter, holding a Pepsi. "[L]ooking very pleased with himself," the teenager exclaims, "Sure beats the bus," as the following words appear: "HARRIER FIGHTER 7,000,000 PEPSI POINTS."

Inspired by this commercial, Plaintiff set out to obtain a Harrier Jet. Plaintiff consulted the Pepsi Stuff Catalog. The Catalog specifies the number of Pepsi Points required to obtain promotional merchandise.

The Catalog notes that in the event that a consumer lacks enough Pepsi Points to obtain a desired item, additional Pepsi Points may be purchased for ten cents each; however, at least fifteen original Pepsi Points must accompany each order.

Although Plaintiff initially set out to collect 7,000,000 Pepsi Points by consuming Pepsi products, it soon became clear to him that buying Pepsi Points would be a more promising option. Through acquaintances, plaintiff ultimately raised about $700,000.

Plaintiff submitted an Order Form, fifteen original Pepsi Points, and a check for $700,008.50.

Defendant rejected Plaintiff's submission and returned the check, explaining that:

> The item that you have requested is not part of the Pepsi Stuff collection. The

Harrier jet in the Pepsi commercial is fanciful and is simply included to create a humorous and entertaining ad.

The general rule is that an advertisement does not constitute an offer. Advertisements and order forms are "mere notices and solicitations for offers which create no power of acceptance in the recipient." Under these principles, Plaintiff's letter constituted the offer. There would be no enforceable contract until Defendant accepted the Order Form and cashed the check.

Plaintiff's understanding of the commercial as an offer must also be rejected because the Court finds that no objective person could reasonably have concluded that the commercial actually offered consumers a Harrier Jet.

In evaluating the commercial, the Court must not consider what the commercial offered, but what an objective, reasonable person would have understood the commercial to convey.

Plaintiff's insistence that the commercial appears to be a serious offer requires the Court to explain why the commercial is funny.

First, the youth featured in the commercial is a highly improbable pilot, one who could barely be trusted with the keys to his parents' car, much less the prize aircraft of the United States.

Second, the notion of traveling to school in a Harrier Jet is an exaggerated adolescent fantasy.

Third, the number of Pepsi Points the commercial mentions as required to "purchase" the jet is 7,000,000. To amass that number of points, one would have to drink 7,000,000 Pepsi's (or roughly 190 Pepsis a day for the next hundred years—an unlikely possibility), or one would have to purchase approximately $700,000 worth of Pepsi Points. The cost of a Harrier Jet is roughly $23 million dollars, a fact of which plaintiff was aware when he set out to gather the amount he believed necessary to accept the alleged offer. Even if an objective, reasonable person were not aware of this fact, he would conclude that purchasing a fighter plane for $700,000 is a deal too good to be true.

In sum, there are two reasons why plaintiff's demand cannot prevail as a matter of law. First, the commercial was merely an advertisement, not an offer. Second, the tongue-in-cheek attitude of the commercial would not cause a reasonable person to conclude that a soft drink company would be giving away fighter planes as part of a promotion.

SECTION 4.4
OFFER

An **offer** is a proposal by one party (offeror) to the other (offeree) manifesting a willingness to enter into a valid contract. An offer has three requirements. It must be: (1) a definite proposal, (2) made with the intent to contract, and (3) be communicated to the party for whom the offer is intended.

For a proposal to be definite, the terms may not be vague or ambiguous. The offer should identify the subject matter of the transaction, the quantity, and the price of the object. If Joe Roberts informs a zoo that he is interested in selling his pet bear, and a zoo official replies, "We accept," a contract is not formed, since the parties failed to specify the price and other elements of the deal.

The second element of a valid offer requires the party who offers the proposal to intend to contract. Phases such as "Are you interested" or "Would you give me" are words of **preliminary negotiations.** Terms such as "I bid," "I will give you," or "My lowest price is," show a present intention to contract and constitute valid offers. An advertisement, however, is generally treated as a mere invitation to enter into discussions. It is not construed as an offer even though the ad contains a description of the item and the price. The justification for this rule is that the vendor never has an unlimited supply of the item for sale. This principle also applies to catalogs and circulars.

The final element of an offer requires it to be communicated to the offeree. In other words, the offeree must know of the proposal before it can be accepted. The mere fact that the offeree consents to identical terms of the offer does not create a contract if the person is unaware of the proposal. For example, an individual who returns a lost puppy to its owner unaware that a reward has been posted for the animal is not entitled to the reward. The good samaritan acted without knowledge of the offer so a binding contract is not formed.

Once a valid offer has been made, how long does that offer remain open? A rejection or counteroffer by the buyer terminates an offer. If in response to a $1,000 offer to sell a car, the buyer tenders $500, the original offer is terminated. An offer may also be revoked at any time before its acceptance, and an offer may terminate by its own terms. If a party is given five days to make a decision, the offer automatically terminates at the end of that five day period. An offer may also terminate if the subject matter of the bargain is destroyed before acceptance, if one of the parties dies, or if the proposal contract is deemed illegal.

SECTION 4.5 ACCEPTANCE

When you click the "Place Your Order" button on an internet site, tell the cab driver where to take you, or buy a ticket to a sporting event, you are accepting an offer to enter into a contract. These acts demonstrate an unqualified readiness to be bound by the other party's offer.[3] So, what is the definition of an acceptance?

An **acceptance** is the unconditional promise made by a party to be bound by the terms of the offer. Until this occurs, there has been no meeting of the minds. Also, a change in the proposal by the offeree constitutes a rejection of the offer and becomes a **counteroffer.**

The acceptance must follow the same format as the offer, and: (1) be made with the intent to contract, (2) be communicated to the offeror, and (3) be unconditional. An acceptance may occur by the return of a promise, the performance of an act, or by any other method of acceptance that is stated in the offer. In a bilateral contract, an offer to sell a car for $1,000 is accepted by the promise of the buyer to pay $1,000. In a unilateral contract, the offer is accepted by the performance of an act. For example, the individual who returns the lost item with knowledge of the reward has accepted the offer and is entitled to the money.

When a perspective insured submits an application to an insurance company for coverage, is that document an offer to contract in which the carrier has the decision to accept or reject or is it an acceptance of an offer that forms a binding contract? The answer depends on the nature of the negotiations and documentation. Generally, the customer makes the offer by submitting an application that the insurance company can accept or reject depending upon the risk. On the other hand, the insurance application can be phrased in such a manner that acceptance occurs automatically upon submission of the insurance form. In deciding the answer to this question, the courts will apply an objective analysis. Would an objective person looking at the transaction have reasonably believed that a contract was formed by submission of the documentation? That is the issue in the following case.

KIMREY V. AMERICAN BANKERS LIFE ASSURANCE COMPANY OF FLORIDA
2008 WL 746999 (W.D. VA. 2008)

Melanie Kimrey brought this suit against American Bankers Life Assurance Company ("ABA") to recover damages for ABA's refusal to pay a claim on an accidental death insurance policy following the death of her husband in a traffic accident. ABA argues that the Kimreys were not covered under the policy because an insurance contract was not formed between ABA and Kimrey before her husband's death.

ABA offered "Accidental Death Insurance" to Kimrey and her husband in connection with the mortgage on their house. ABA inserted a document in the mortgage closing papers which carried the heading "Enrollment Form." ABA's enrollment form listed three steps to enroll, to insure the Kimreys against accidental death for the remainder of their mortgage: 1) check single or joint coverage; 2) complete non-shaded areas, including your signature; and 3) mail back the enclosed envelope.

The form stated that by enrolling, the customer would get "6 months of complimentary coverage," and noted that once enrolled, the insured would receive a certificate of insurance that contained his or her effective date of coverage. Nothing in the form suggested that the effective date would not be the date on which the completed form was mailed or that it would be a future date. Throughout, ABA referred to the form as an "enrollment form" and never as an application.

Kimrey completed and mailed the form on or about April 5, 2006. On April 22, 2006, Mr. Kimrey was killed in an automobile accident, and ABA denied coverage.

ABA argues that Kimrey's completed enroll-ment form was an offer to contract for insurance by Kimrey that could be accepted only by ABA issuing a certificate of insurance containing an effective date of its choice. Kimrey argues that the ABA enrollment form constituted an offer to insure, which she accepted by completing and mailing the form, with coverage beginning from that date. The court finds that a reasonable person in Kimrey's position would have believed that the ABA enrollment form was an offer of insurance which could be accepted by completing and mail-ing the form.

Virginia courts apply the objective theory of con-tract to determine whether an offer was made and whether that offer was accepted, forming a contract. Under the objective theory of contract an offer has been made if a reasonable person in the offeree's position, in view of the offeror's acts and words and the surrounding circumstances, would believe that the offeror has invited the of-feree's acceptance. Where an offer has been made, Virginia courts apply the "mailbox rule" which provides that a contract is formed upon mailing the acceptance.

An insurance application is considered an offer to enter a contract which the insurer may accept or reject after determining whether the applicant is a desirable risk. This is so because, typically, an application is precisely that-an application that could be accepted or rejected. Under the objective theory of contract, a reasonable person would view an application as an offer subject to the insurer's acceptance, not the acceptance of an insurer's offer. But the paradigm can shift. The insurer could offer insurance that an offeree could accept. The insurer could market its insurance in such a way that a reasonable person in the offeree's position,

in view of the offeror's acts and words and the surrounding circumstances, would believe that the offeror has invited the offeree's acceptance.

With these precepts in mind, the court concludes that Kimrey's complaint alleges the formation of a contract of insurance. A reasonable person in Kimrey's position would have believed that the ABA enrollment form was an offer that she could accept by completing and mailing the form. The ABA enrollment form outlined the terms of the offered policy: the coverage, the exclusions, and the amount of the benefits. No statement in the documents expressed or implied that coverage would not begin immediately. The enrollment form, with headings like "Why Wait? Enroll Today . . .," left a reasonable person to under-stand that he had the power to accept this offer and that he would receive coverage by taking the prescribed steps, completing and mailing the form.

ABA argues that an applicant for life insurance is not covered until a policy is issued citing a line of Virginia cases. In each of these cases, how-ever, the application was clearly identified as an application and nothing positioned it as an offer of insurance that could be accepted by the pro-spective insured. In each case ABA cites, the insurance application expressly stated that it was not binding on the insurance company and that coverage would not commence until a policy was issued. Further, the applicant still had to submit to a medical examination after his application before the insurer issued the policy.

For the reasons stated, the court finds that a rea-sonable person in Kimrey's position would have believed that the ABA enrollment form was an offer which she could accept by completing and mailing the form.

A. Postal Reorganization Act

Suppose Joe Roberts receives an unsolicited package from a mail order company containing a DVD of his favorite movie. The video is accompanied by a letter, which states that if Joe does not want to purchase the movie, he merely has to return it in the envelope provided. Joe discards the letter but keeps the movie. Is he required to pay for the film?

The mail-order company will argue that by not returning the movie, Joe impliedly accepted the offer, even though he never ordered the product. Is the vendor correct?

Generally, silence or inaction alone is not an effective acceptance. The offeror has no power to unilaterally impose silence as to the manner of acceptance.

Businesses that send unsolicited products in the mail to potential customers now run afoul of the law. The **Postal Reorganization Act** and various state statutes make it an unfair trade practice to send unsolicited products to a customer in the mail. In fact, these products are to be considered gifts that may be kept by the consumer without having to pay for them. The following is part of the Act:

39 U.S.C. § 3009(a) *Mailing of unordered merchandise*

(a) Except for:

   (1) Free samples clearly and conspicuously marked as such, and

   (2) Merchandise mailed by a charitable organization soliciting contributions, the mailing of unordered merchandise constitutes an unfair method of competition and an unfair trade practice.

(b) Any merchandise mailed in violation of subsection (a), may be treated as a gift by the recipient, who shall have the right to retain, use, discard, or dispose of it in any manner he sees fit without any obligation whatsoever to the sender. All such merchandise shall have attached to it a clear and conspicuous statement informing the recipient that he may treat the merchandise as a gift to him and has the right to retain, use, discard, or dispose of it in any manner he sees fit without any obligation whatsoever to the sender.

B. Silence as Acceptance

Silence may constitute an acceptance if the offeree remains silent with the intent to accept the offer or where a prior course of dealings between the parties has treated silence as an acceptance. For example, a party who has contracted with a record club to accept a compact disc on approval every month may not sit back and keep the goods without paying for them.

C. Auctions

Auctions are gaining in popularity. Commercial establishments, like Sotheby's and Christie's, have been around for years. The internet, however, has introduced auctions as a way of buying to the average person. For example, eBay has become the world's online marketplace where millions of items are traded each day. If a person makes the highest bid at an auction, is that bid an offer or an acceptance?

There are two ways to offer something for sale at auction: with and without reserve. If the auction is **with reserve,** the auctioneer is merely inviting people to make offers and no contract is formed until the gavel is struck. As noted by eBay, a reserve price is a hidden minimum amount that the seller will accept for the item. The auctioneer may reject the highest bid and remove the item from sale if that reserve price is not met. The courts will treat this situation as though there has been no meeting of the minds. Auctions **without reserve** provide a different result with the highest bidder obtaining the product regardless of the bid. In fact, the seller may not withdraw the item once a legitimate bid is received.

D. Sealed Bids

Construction, municipal, and service contracts are frequently awarded on the basis of **sealed bids.** Is the highest bidder making an offer or making an acceptance requiring the awarding of the contract? The rules for sealed bids are very similar to an auction with reserve. The request for bids is merely an invitation to negotiate, and the bid constitutes an offer that can be accepted or rejected even if it is the highest one. No legal rights are formed until the bid is accepted.

An acceptance of an offer is valid only when it has been communicated to the offeror. Generally, the offer will dictate the medium, manner, and time by which the offer is to be accepted. For example, "you must call me by Friday if you wish to buy my car." The amount of time the offeree has to communicate the acceptance is generally as long as the offer remains open. If the offer does not specify the medium to be used, it is assumed that the acceptance is to be communicated by the same or similar medium as the offer was made.

E. Mailbox Rule

This can create a problem if the parties are using the mail because of the time delay between dispatch of the acceptance and its receipt by the offeror. The courts have resolved the problem by making the acceptance of the offer effective on dispatch. This is known as the **Mailbox Rule.** In other words, acceptance of the offer takes place as soon as it is mailed and not when it is received by the offeror. Revocation of an offer, however, is effective on receipt.

Look at the following case to see if a contract has been formed:

- On January 5, John sends Mike a letter offering to sell his car for $20,000.

- On January 7, Mike receives the offer.

- On January 8, John sends a letter to Mike revoking his offer.

- On January 9, Mike sends a letter to John accepting the offer.

- On January 10, Mike receives the letter of revocation.

- On January 11, John receives the letter of acceptance.

Under the mailbox rule, acceptance is effective on dispatch or when it is mailed and revocation is only effective when it is received. In this case, Mike accepted the offer on January 9 and did not receive the letter of revocation until two days letter. Therefore, there is a valid contract.

In the current age of technology, people are using traditional mail less and less. In fact, these types of communications are now known as "snail mail" because of its slow delivery. What happens to the mailbox rule with electronic communications that are instantaneous? Legislation has been proposed entitled the **Uniform Commercial Information Transaction Act (UCITA)** to deal with computer information transactions. Under this legislation, acceptance is only effective upon receipt. Because of the controversial nature of this law, only Virginia and Maryland have adopted its provisions.

What happens if the offer is not accepted by return mail but by a faster form of communication such as by a telephone call or faxed message is used? Has a contract been formed? That is the issue in **Trinity Homes, L.L.C. v. Fang.**

TRINITY HOMES, L.L.C. V. FANG
2003 WL 22699791 (VA. CIR. CT. 2003)

The primary issue is the effect of an alleged facsimile transmission by Damon Stewart (Stewart), the agent for Trinity Homes, L.L.C. to T. H. Nicholson, III (Nicholson), the agent for Ching Fang of the Agreement for Purchase & Sale of Real Estate (Agreement) dated June 17, 2002.

Stewart alleges that he placed the Agreement in his facsimile machine, dialed the number for Nicholson, pushed the button to start the facsimile and then went on an errand. There are no phone records relative to the alleged transmission of the facsimile transmission by Stewart. Shortly after Stewart alleged forwarded the facsimile to Nicholson, he received a phone call from Nicholson indicating that the Defendant did not wish to sell the property nor enter into a contract with Trinity Homes for that purpose.

Initially, it is necessary to consider whether facsimile (fax) transmissions are similar to or should be treated the same as the Mailbox Rule in regard to the acceptance of a contract. The Mailbox Rule states that once an offeree has dispatched his acceptance, it is too late for the offeror to revoke the offer. The Mailbox Rule has been accepted in most American jurisdictions The Restatement (of contracts also) addresses the issue of the application of the Mailbox Rule to electronic communication in §64, which states: "Acceptance given by telephone or other medium of substantially instantaneous two-way communication is governed by the principles applicable to acceptances where the parties are in the presence of each other." This is, therefore, a two-prong test: (1) the communication must be "substantially instantaneous"; and (2) the communication must be two-way. The rationale of the Restatement's position is that when parties are conversing using substantially instantaneous two-way communication, they are, in essence, in each other's presence.

To be substantially instantaneous, the transmission must occur within a few seconds, or, at most, within a minute or two. For a communication to be two-way, one party must be able to determine readily whether the other party is aware of the first party's communications, through immediate verbal response or, when the communication is face-to-face, through nonverbal cues. Further, if a communication is not two-way, the offeror will not know exactly when the offeree accepts and may attempt to revoke the offer after the offeree has already sent his instantaneous acceptance to the offeror. In such a situation, the Mailbox Rule should continue to apply and the contract should be considered accepted upon dispatch of the offeree's acceptance.

In **Osprey, LLC v. Kelly-Moore Paint Co., 984 P.2d 194 (Ok. 1999),** the plaintiff leased commercial property to the defendant. The lease required that the defendant provide notice of its intent to renew the lease at least six months prior to the expiration of the lease, and notice was to be given in writing and delivered personally or through registered first class mail. The defendant attempted to extend the lease by faxing a renewal letter on the last day of the notification period. The plaintiff denied receiving the fax, despite a fax record and telephone record confirming the transmission. Applying the Mailbox Rule, the court held that the faxed notice of the lease renewal was sufficient to timely exercise the lease renewal option because the notice was in writing, and the delivery of the notice by fax transmission served the same purpose of the authorized methods of delivery. The court stated specifically: "the fax log and telephone records show that the notice was property transmitted to Osprey. Transmitting the fax was like mailing an acceptance under the Mailbox Rule, where an offer is accepted when it is deposited in the mail." ("The telegraph is considered an instantaneous form of communication but is only a one-way form to which the Mailbox Rule does apply.").

This Court concludes that the Mailbox Rule is applicable in the instant cause and thus the issue is one of fact-whether or not the facsimile transmission was actually forwarded or transmitted by Stewart to Nicholson.

Stewart's fax machine was apparently one of early vintage and provided no verification of the transmission to Nicholson. Unlike in the Osprey case, there was no fax log and/or telephone records to show that the fax was properly transmitted to Nicholson. Stewart cannot say with certainty if the fax actually went through other than to say that he placed the fax in the fax machine, turned it on and then left before viewing and/or verifying its transmission. Further, Stewart did not recall looking at the fax machine by or through which the Agreement allegedly was transmitted, when he returned later in the afternoon from his errand.

The burden is on the plaintiff to prove by preponderance of the evidence that the fax transmission of the Agreement was actually made and accomplished. The Court in considering the totality of the evidence and the totality of the circumstances finds and concludes that the burden has not been met nor satisfied and finds for the Defendant.

SECTION 4.6
CONSIDERATION

Consideration is the answer to the query, "Why are you entering into this transaction?" or "What are you getting for being a party to this contract?" An agreement is only binding when there is consideration on the part of each entity to the contract.[4]

Consideration is what each party gives up in return for the act or promise of the other. This is called the **quid pro quo,** or "bargained for exchange." Two elements must be present to satisfy the requirement of consideration. It must appear that both parties intend to incur legal rights and liabilities, and the bargained for exchange must have legal value. For example, if a person purchases a slice of pizza from a vendor for $2.00, what is the consideration? The vendor is giving up a slice of pizza in exchange for $2.00. The consumer is giving up $2.00 and will receive a piece of pizza in return. This bargained for exchange is supported by consideration from both parties. If the merchant only has one slice of pizza left and the customer offers the vendor $20.00 in order to outbid three other customers, is the contract valid since the consideration is unequal? The value of the bargain does not have to be equal as long as fraud or undue influence is not present.

Several unique situations arise in which a contract appears to have been formed, but the agreement lacks consideration. Examples include an illusory promise, a pre-existing obligation, a moral obligation, and a contract supported by a past obligation.

A. Illusory Promise

An **illusory promise** is one in which the act of performance is left solely to the discretion of one party. The promisor has in effect agreed to do nothing but creates an illusion that mutual obligations were exchanged. For example, a person who agrees to purchase as many tickets to a concert as he wants, or a business which promises to sell as many books as it decides to release have agreed to do nothing.

B. Moral Obligation

A **moral obligation** is also insufficient consideration to support a contract. For instance, a parent's promise to give $1,000 to a child out of "love and affection" is not a valid contract.

C. Past Consideration

Past consideration will not support a future promise since no consideration exists. This may be illustrated by the promise of a person on his deathbed to transfer land to a neighbor for the assistance rendered two years earlier, as it is not a valid promise.

D. Pre-existing Obligation

A **pre-existing obligation** is one that lacks consideration because a party is already contractually bound to perform under a contract so there is no new consideration for the promise. For example, a person contracts with a builder for the purchase of a new house for $400,000. During construction, the builder tells the buyer that he needs $50,000 more to complete the project, since the cost of labor has increased. The buyer agrees but at settlement, she only offers the original $400,000 price. This is a pre-exiting obligation and there is no new consideration for the buyer's promise to pay the extra money. The builder was obligated to build the home and the company did nothing more for the promise of an additional $50,000. On the other hand, if the builder agrees to include metal doors and storm windows in the home for the additional $50,000, the promise is enforceable.

E. Guarantor

Not all individuals or businesses have sufficient credit to obtain a loan or merchandise on credit. Occasionally, a third person will be required to **guarantee** the obligation of the borrower in the event of a default. For instance, a college student may not have a sufficient credit history to finance the purchase of a new car, so the credit company will request a parent to co-sign the loan.

A **co-signer** may be considered either a surety or guarantor, depending upon the financial arrangement required by the lender. The primary difference between the two types of agreements is that a **surety** is primarily liable for the debt as though he or she borrowed the money. A **guarantor** is only secondarily liable. In other words, the creditor will look to the guarantor only after the debtor has defaulted and the creditor is unsuccessful in recovering the money from the borrower.

Is the promise of the third party to be responsible for the debts of another supported by consideration? These agreements are enforced on a variety of theories. Some jurisdictions find that the lender's extension of credit in reliance on the third party's promise to be responsible for the debt supplies the necessary consideration. Other courts rule that the consideration for the guaranty is supplied, if the primary debtor receives a benefit from the promise, such as the extension of credit. Some jurisdictions, such as New York, even hold that the mere signing of the agreement without more provides the necessary consideration and the court has to look no further.

F. Gift

Suppose a friend promises to give you \$500 in celebration of your 21st birthday but fails to deliver the gift as promised. Will the court enforce the promise? The promise of a **gift** is not supported by consideration and is unenforceable. The party promising the gift has not incurred any liability for the promise nor has the person with the birthday given up anything of legal value for the promise. This deficiency, however, may be overcome by showing that the recipient of the promise relied upon the gift to his detriment. For example, a graduate who pledges one million dollars to a university's building fund will be bound by that promise if the educational institution starts construction on the new structure based upon that gift.

WILLIAMS V. ORMSBY
131 OHIO 3D 427 (OHIO 2012)

We are asked to determine whether merely resuming a romantic relationship by moving into a home with another can serve as consideration for a contract. We hold that it cannot.

This case arises in the context of a non-marital relationship between Amber Williams and Frederick Ormsby. In May 2004, Frederick moved into Amber's house on Hardwood Hollow in Medina to which she had received title through her divorce settlement. Frederick began making the mortgage payments in August and paid the 2004 property taxes. He eventually paid the remaining mortgage balance of approximately \$310,000. In return, Amber gave Frederick title to the property in a deed dated December 15, 2004, that was recorded the same day.

Although the couple had planned to marry, they canceled their plans in January 2005 when Frederick's divorce did not occur. They did, however, continue to live together. After a disagreement in March 2005, Amber left the house. As a result of this separation, Amber and Frederick signed a document dated March 24, 2005, to immediately sell the Medina house and allocate the proceeds.

Two months later, the couple tried to reconcile. Amber refused to move back into the house with Frederick unless he granted her an undivided one-half interest in the property. On June 2, 2005, they signed a second document, making themselves "equal partners" in the Medina house and, among other things, providing for property disposition in the event that their relationship ended. Amber then returned to the house, and the couple resumed their relationship. But by April 2007, they were living in separate areas of the house, and although they tried counseling, Amber ended the relationship in September 2007.

Frederick contends that the only consideration offered for the June 2005 agreement was resuming a romantic relationship, which cannot serve as consideration for a contract. He argues that to enforce such a contract is the same as enforcing a contract to make a gift in consideration of love and affection. Amber counters that Frederick received a benefit that he bargained for. She maintains that the June 2005 agreement was supported by consideration.

A contract is as a promise, or a set of promises, actionable upon breach. Essential elements of a contract include an offer, acceptance, contractual capacity, consideration, a manifestation of mutual assent and legality of object and of consideration.

In this case, we are concerned with the legal enforceability of the June 2005 writing. Consideration may consist of either a detriment to the promisee or a benefit to the promisor. A benefit may consist of some right, interest, or profit accruing to the promisor, while a detriment may consist of some forbearance.

Flanders v. Blandy, 45 Ohio 108 (1887), is instructive on whether moving into the home with another while engaging in a romantic relationship is consideration for the formation of a contract. In Flanders, a father had intended to give his daughter certain bonds worth $2,000. But the daughter did not receive the bonds as a gift, because they were never delivered to her. Her father then delivered to her a written promise to pay her $2,000 in lieu of the bonds. Upon her father's death, the daughter sought to enforce the written promise, but we held that her father's promise to give her the value of the bonds was not enforceable as a contract, because that promise lacked consideration. Thus, for more than a century, love and affection alone have not been recognized as consideration for a contract.

Although the June document states that the agreement was made for valuable consideration, it does not specify what the consideration is. The document does not refer to fulfilling each other's needs, financial, emotional, physical, and social; the evidence demonstrates that the only consideration offered by Amber for the June 2005 agreement was her resumption of a romantic relationship with Frederick. There is no detriment to Amber in the June 2005 document, only benefit. Essentially, this agreement amounts to a gratuitous promise by Frederick to give Amber an interest in property based solely on the consideration of her love and affection. Therefore, the June 2005 document is not an enforceable contract, because it fails for want of consideration.

We hold that merely moving into a home with another while engaging in a romantic relationship is not consideration for the formation of a contract. To hold otherwise would open the door to palimony claims and invite a number of evidentiary problems.

**SECTION 4.7
TONY ROBERTS
AND THE
ENGAGEMENT RING
PROBLEM FOUR—A**

**PARK, BROWN & SMITH, P.C.
ATTORNEYS AT LAW
MEMORANDUM**

TO: All Law Clerks

FROM: Peter Smith, Esquire

RE: Tony Roberts v. Lillian Winter

During the off-season, Tony Roberts returned to his apartment in the Philadelphia area but he became restless and lonely. Being stuck in the city without his teammates and friends caused Tony to miss his favorite night spots in Chicago, Dallas, and New York. One evening, the football player decided to visit a new night spot featuring exotic dancers which had developed a reputation for serving gourmet food. While eating his meal, Tony struck up a conversation with Lil Winter, one of the exotic dancers, who was eating dinner before the start of her performance.

As the nightclub was closing, Tony invited Lil to his home for some late night entertainment. The couple hit it off instantly and found that they had much in common. Following a short romance, Tony asked Lil to marry him and Lil accepted. They spent the rest of the night talking and planning their future together. When the jewelry store opened the next morning, Tony and Lil were their first customers. After an hour of looking at rings, Tony purchased a 2-carat flawless diamond ring in an antique platinum setting for $18,000.

Tony also took Lil to a car dealer where he replaced her 10-year-old Ford with a new Mustang. The car would provide Ms. Winter with dependable transportation to visit him during the football season.

Unfortunately, the couple had a falling out two months later. Lil felt that things were moving too quickly and she wasn't ready to give up her dancing career. Once Tony recovered from the initial shock of their breakup, he realized that he had spent more than $50,000 on the car and ring. Tony requested the return of these items but Lil refused, claiming that they were unconditional gifts. Tony visited our office for advice. He maintains that the only reason he purchased the items was because Tony wanted his fiancée to be happy in their new relationship and future life together. Tony insists that the purchases were only given in anticipation of their pending marriage. Since Lil canceled their engagement, Tony believes that he is entitled to the return of the ring and car.

Please read the case of **Lindh v. Surman,** and answer these questions:

1. Does Lil get to keep the ring?

2. Who gets to keep the car?

3. What role does fault have in determining which items are to be returned?

Lindh v. Surman
702 A.2d 560 (Pa. Super. 1997)

This appeal requires resolution of whether the law should permit retention of an engagement ring by the donee, (the person receiving the gift) after the donor (the person giving the gift) of the ring breaks their engagement. The facts follow.

Rodger Lindh (Rodger) asked Janis Surman (Janis) to marry him on August 24, 1993. Janis accepted his proposal and Rodger gave Janis a diamond engagement ring worth approximately $21,000. Unfortunately, Rodger experienced misgivings about the impending marriage and requested the ring's return in October of 1993. Janis returned the ring. However, Janis and Rodger subsequently reconciled, and once again planned to marry. Rodger again gave the diamond ring to Janis and Janis wore it. Janis began to make wedding plans.

On March 20, 1994, Rodger unexpectedly informed Janis that he no longer loved her and broke their engagement. Rodger requested that Janis return the ring, but Janis refused. Litigation ensued. Rodger filed a civil action to recover the ring or its value.

Both Janis and Rodger agree that Pennsylvania follows the law of conditional gifts in engagement ring matters. They disagree over what condition renders the gift complete. Janis' position is that the conditional gift of an engagement ring is incident to the engagement itself. The condition attached to the gift is her agreement to marry Rodger. The condition of the gift thus satisfied, she should be entitled to retain the ring.

For his part, Rodger contends that his gift of the engagement ring to Janis was conditioned upon the marriage rather than her agreement to marry him. Because the condition, marriage, never took place, Rodger contends the trial court's award of the ring to him should be affirmed. We agree.

The law of conditional gifts is set forth in the Restatement of Restitution. With particular interest we note that engagement rings are treated differently from other *wedding* and/or *engagement gifts:*

GIFTS MADE IN RELIANCE ON A RELATION.

Gifts made in the hope that a marriage or contract of marriage will result are not recoverable, in the absence of fraud. Gifts made in anticipation of marriage are not ordinarily expressed to be conditional and, although there is an engagement to marry, if the marriage fails to occur without the fault of the donee, normally the gift cannot be recovered. If, however, the donee obtained the gift fraudulently or if the gift was made for a purpose which could be achieved only by the marriage, a donor who is not himself at fault is entitled to restitution if the

marriage does not take place, even if the gift was of money. If there is an engagement to marry and the donee, having received the gift without fraud, later wrongfully breaks the promise of marriage, the donor is entitled to restitution if the gift is an engagement ring, a family heirloom or other similar thing intimately connected with the marriage, but not if the gift is one of money intended to be used by the donee before the marriage.

We now turn to Pennsylvania cases, which apply the law of conditional gifts in antenuptial gift contests. We believe these cases make clear that in this Commonwealth, engagement rings are *conditional gifts.*

An early case, **Ruehling v. Hornung, 98 Pa. Super. 535 (1930),** reflects the Restatement's characterization of an engagement ring as a *conditional gift.* In Ruehling, the donor in contemplation of marriage presented his fiancée with a diamond ring, a diamond wristwatch, and a medallion. The question of who broke the engagement was in dispute and the donee refused to return the three items. In analyzing the status of the three gifts, this court set forth:

> [t]he contention of [the donor] appellant is that gifts to a person to whom the donor is engaged to be married, made in contemplation of marriage, are conditional; and that if the donee breaks the engagement the gifts or their value may be recovered by the donor.

We find no case in this State directly bearing on this question, but in (a law treaties) it is stated: 'A gift to a person to whom the donor is engaged to be married, made in contemplation of marriage, although absolute in form, is conditional; and upon breach of the marriage engagement by the donee the property may be recovered by the donor. But if the gift is made simply for the purpose of introducing the donor to the donee's acquaintance and to gain her favor, the property is not recoverable, although marriage does not ensue. So where a Christmas present is made by a man to his fiancée, it becomes her property and the subsequent breaking of the engagement does not entitle him to recover it back.'

Following a review of case law from other jurisdictions, the court stated:

It follows that in order to permit a recovery by plaintiff, it would be necessary to hold that the gifts were subject to the implied condition that they would be returned by the donee to the donor whenever the engagement was dissolved. Under such a rule the marriage would be a necessary prerequisite to the passing of an absolute title to a Christmas gift made in such circumstances. *We are unwilling to go that far, except as to the engagement ring.* Such a ring is given as a pledge or symbol of the contract to marry. We think that it is always given subject to the implied condition that if the marriage does not take place either because of the death, or a disability recognized by the law on the part of, either party, or by breach of the contract by the donee, or its dissolution by

mutual consent, the gift shall be returned. It only becomes the absolute property of the recipient if the marriage takes place.

Hence, as far back as 1929, this court has adhered to the law of *conditional gifts* with respect to engagement rings. The retention of the gift is subject to the implied condition that marriage takes place and absent that occurrence, for whatever reason, it is impossible for the gift to become complete.

Pennsylvania jurisprudence merely follows basic principles of restitution found in gift law in awarding antenuptial property. While Rodger, the donor in this case, proposed marriage, the marriage between Rodger and Janis did not occur. Thus, we find the gift of the ring to Janis at the time of their betrothal was subject to an *implied condition* requiring its return if the marriage did not take place.

After careful analysis, we affirm the order of the trial court which denied Janis post-trial relief and awarded judgment in Rodger's favor.

PROBLEM FOUR—A
ANSWER SHEET

Name

Please Print Clearly

1. Is Tony entitled to the return of the ring? Explain your answer.

2. Who is entitled to the car? Explain your answer.

_____

_____

_____

_____

_____

_____

_____

_____

_____

3. What role does fault have in deciding who is entitled to the items?

_____

_____

_____

_____

_____

_____

_____

_____

_____

_____

**SECTION 4.8
CAPACITY**

The courts will usually not disturb a contract freely entered into by parties of similar bargaining power. Nevertheless, when one of the individuals does not have the **capacity** to fully understand the ramifications of the contractual obligation, mutual assent to bargain is lacking. In this regard, the law provides protection to those deemed to lack the capacity to contract, such as children, the mentally challenged, and intoxicated individuals.

Contracts of a minor are voidable at the child's election. This means that the child may disaffirm the contract, but the adult is bound by the agreement. In order to disaffirm, the child does not have to return the adult to the status quo. The minor only has to return what is left of that purchased or received. In addition, a minor may ratify a contract upon reaching adult age. **Ratification** occurs when a child reaches maturity and expresses an intention to be bound by the agreement or fails to disaffirm the contract. For instance, a child who continues to drive a car that he purchased as a minor after reaching majority will be found to have ratified the contract.

Because of public policy considerations, a minor may not disaffirm certain types of contracts. These include **contracts for necessities** such as food and shelter, contracts with colleges or the armed forces, and agreements of minors involved in a business transaction. As noted in **Lein v. Centaur Motor Co. of Illinois,** a necessary is that thing that "supplies the personal needs of the infant, either those of his body, such as food, clothing, lodging, and the like, or those of his mind, as instruction suitable and requisite for the proper development of his mind." Also, something bought by the child is not transformed into a necessary just because the minor uses the item as part of a job. For instance, repairs to a truck used by the minor in his business would not constitute a necessary.

Insane individuals, like minors, lack the capacity to enter into binding contracts. Individuals are considered insane when they are unable to understand the nature and consequences of their acts at the time they entered into an agreement. Mere psychological or emotional problems are not enough. It is also irrelevant whether mental illness, senility, alcohol, or drug abuse causes the insanity. The only requirement is that the individual must be incompetent at the time of entering into the contract.

A contract entered into by one who has previously been adjudged incompetent by the court is void. An adjudication of incompetency is notice to the world that the person lacks the capacity to contract. Contracts entered into by persons claiming to be insane, but not adjudged insane by the court, are voidable. In the latter situation, it is the responsibility of the person claiming to be incompetent to prove that he or she was insane at the time of the agreement.

Unlike a child, an incompetent individual cannot disaffirm the contract unless he can return the parties to the status individual quo. The exception to this rule is if the other party knows of the disability but still enters into the contract. In that event, the incompetent person merely has to return what is left and does not have to return the parties to the status quo.

FLETCHER V. MARSHALL
260 ILL. APP.3D 673 (ILL. CT. APP. 1994)

Plaintiff alleges that Defendant is indebted to plaintiff in the sum of $2,500 for contribution towards rent. Plaintiff attached to the complaint a copy of a lease dated April 29, 1991 that was signed by Plaintiff and Defendant. The lease states that Plaintiff and Defendant agreed to rent an apartment for $525 per month. The lease term was July 1, 1991 to June 30, 1992.

At the trial, Plaintiff testified that, early in 1991, she and Defendant were in high school and were dating. Defendant's parent's ejected him from their home after Defendant completed high school and plaintiff and Defendant decided to rent an apartment and share the expenses.

Defendant took advantage of an opportunity to attend college and moved out of the apartment after "a couple of months." Plaintiff continued to live in the apartment and paid the entire rent amount for the remaining 10 months of the lease term.

Defendant testified that he signed the lease on April 29, 1991, and that he was 17 years old on that date. Plaintiff claimed that, although the apartment complex manager typed the lease on April 29, defendant did not sign the lease until June 30, 1991, after defendant's eighteenth birthday.

Defendant testified that he made rent payments. He moved out of the apartment because he and Plaintiff were not getting along and because he had an opportunity to attend college. Defendant's father testified that Defendant turned 18 on May 30, 1991.

Plaintiff's sole argument is that, although Defendant was a minor when he signed the lease, he ratified the lease after attaining majority by taking possession of the premises and paying rent. A contract of a minor is not void, but merely voidable at the election of the minor upon his attaining majority. After attaining majority, a person may either disaffirm or ratify a contract that he entered into while he was still a minor.

A contract of a minor is deemed ratified if the minor fails to disaffirm it within a reasonable time after attaining majority. Also, a minor ratifies a contract if, after becoming of age, he does any distinct and decisive act clearly showing an intention to affirm the contract. Once a person ratifies such a contract, he cannot thereafter avoid his obligations under it.

It is well established that whether a minor has disaffirmed a contract within a reasonable time after attaining majority is a question of fact dependent upon the circumstances of the case. In the context of ratification, the trier of fact will often have to infer from a person's actions that he intended to ratify a contract.

In the instant case, it is undisputed that, about two weeks after becoming 18 years of age, defendant moved into the apartment and paid rent. Here, there is no evidence on record that could give rise to a reasonable inference that Defendant's acts of moving into the apartment, living there for 1 ½ months, and making rent payments constituted anything other than an unequivocal ratification of the lease. Because he had already ratified the lease, his later attempt to disaffirm it by moving out of the apartment and refusing to make further payments was of no effect. Accordingly, we conclude that Defendant remained liable for the rent for the remainder of the lease term and is therefore liable to Plaintiff for the rent payments she made on Defendant's behalf.

SECTION 4.9
LEGALITY

The law requires that the purpose and subject matter of an agreement be legal in order for the contract to be valid. A contract is **illegal** if its performance is criminal, tortious, or against public policy. For instance, a contract to purchase illicit drugs or the agreement to reward a person for assaulting another are **illegal contract**s and are void as a matter of law.

Illegal contracts are void and neither party may seek court intervention to enforce the obligation even when one party has performed the act or promise specified in the agreement. Courts will simply leave the parties where it finds them. For example, the court will not enforce a gambling debt between two friends over a football game. The court takes the position that its enforcement of the illegal transaction makes the judiciary an indirect participant in the wrongful conduct.

The categories of illegal contracts are much broader than one might suspect. For example, an unlicensed entity that performs a service requiring a license, such as a plumber or electrician, may be precluded from recovering a fee on the basis that the contract is illegal. Likewise, an attorney is not allowed to share a fee with one who is not a lawyer. This type of fee sharing is illegal and the rationale is quite simple. A contrary ruling would permit a person to indirectly profit from an enterprise that he or she is directly not allowed to perform, unless properly licensed. That is the issue in the following case.

FARRELL V. WHITEMAN
200 P.3D 1153 (IDAHO 2009)

Damian Farrell sued Kent Whiteman to recover for architect services he rendered for Whiteman's condominium project in Ketchum. Whiteman asserted that Farrell was not entitled to be compensated because of his failure to comply with Idaho's architect licensing statutes. The district court awarded Farrell damages, and Whiteman appealed. We vacate the damage award.

Farrell, a Michigan-licensed architect, and Whiteman, a real estate developer, both Michigan residents, were friends for many years. Beginning in 2002, Farrell and Whiteman discussed the possibility of working together on a condominium project in Ketchum, Idaho. Farrell understood that he and Whiteman would be partners in the project and that in exchange for his work-which included designing the building, securing site plan approval, overseeing the development of the construction documents, and working as the project architect-he would receive twenty-five percent of the project's profits. Whiteman testified that they discussed a partnership and profit-sharing arrangement, but never reached an agreement regarding how Farrell would be compensated for his architectural services.

Farrell worked on the project until the end of July 2004. Some of Farrell's work was performed in Michigan, where he held an architect's license. However, Farrell also performed some work in Idaho before he received his license to practice architecture in Idaho in February 2004.

In July, 2004, Whiteman terminated Farrell from the project. Even after the project was completed, Whiteman refused to pay Farrell for his work. Farrell filed suit and Whiteman defended based on Idaho's architect licensing statutes, claiming that because Farrell had not complied with them, the entire contract was illegal and unenforceable.

Whiteman contends that the implied contract was illegal because Farrell did not have a license to practice architecture in Idaho until midway through his work on the project.

Idaho has long disallowed judicial aid to either party to an illegal contract. An illegal contract is one that rests on illegal consideration consisting of any act or forbearance which is contrary to law or public policy. Generally, when the consideration for a contract explicitly violates a statute, the contract is illegal and unenforceable. In most cases, the court will leave the parties to an illegal contract as it finds them.

Idaho Code § 54-301 reads: "In order to safeguard life, and property, and to promote the public welfare, any person practicing architecture, in Idaho, shall submit evidence of his qualifications so to practice and be licensed." The code defines the "practice of architecture" as: rendering or offering those services in connection with the design, construction, enlargement, or alteration of a building or a group of buildings.

Since the consequences of a court finding a contract to be illegal are harsh, only those contracts which involve consideration that is expressly prohibited by the relevant prohibitory statute are void. Such statutes must be narrowly construed, and only those contracts violating express provisions will be deemed illegal.

Farrell admittedly performed some architectural services in Idaho before he was licensed. Although courts should interpret statutes narrowly when applying the doctrine of illegality, the lower court went too far in interpreting the statute to merely require architects to be licensed at "critical times." This language does not appear anywhere in the statute, and no case law supporting this interpretation was offered. The statute reads "any person practicing or offering to practice architecture . . . in the state of Idaho, shall . . . be licensed." This unambiguously requires anyone who practices any architecture in Idaho to be licensed. Because Farrell was not licensed to practice architecture in Idaho until February 17, 2004, the architectural services he rendered before then were done pursuant to an illegal contract.

Although Farrell's work performed while unlicensed was illegal, his actions after receiving his license were certainly legal. "Where a transaction is composed of both benign and offensive components and the different portions are severable, the unobjectionable parts are generally enforceable." In other words, the implied contract in this case is chronologically separable. It was proper to award damages to Farrell for the services he rendered after he received his license. Where the services are severable, a person should not be penalized for the services he performed in compliance with the law.

We vacate the district court's award of damages and remand for further consideration consistent with this opinion.

SECTION 4.10
ESTELLE ROBERTS
V. TRI-COUNTY
GOLF CLUB

PROBLEM FOUR—B

PARK, BROWN & SMITH, P.C.
ATTORNEYS AT LAW
MEMORANDUM

TO: All Law Clerks

FROM: Peter Smith, Esquire

RE: Tri-County Golf Course

Estelle Roberts has a rather interesting problem. She agreed to play in a charity golf tournament at Tri-County Golf Club. To encourage golfers to join the event, a new and very expensive Mercedes was offered to anyone who hit a hole-in-one on the 8th hole. Estelle stepped up to the tee and hit her shot straight and true. The ball landed on the green and headed directly to the cup. When the golf ball was less than one inch away from the hole, the most amazing thing happened. A frog was hiding in the cup but became scared when he heard all of the noise. The frog jumped out of the hole just as the ball was about to drop in, brushing the ball aside. Because the golf course was in a wooded area surrounded by water, Tri-County had many animals on its property, but this was the first time that a frog had interfered with a golf shot. Estelle demanded her prize, and the golf club officials consulted with the tournament judge. This individual happened to be Dr. Leonard Mauro, who promptly denied Estelle's claim to the prize. Since the ball did not go into the hole, Mauro said the shot did not fulfill the terms of the offer. Mauro directed Estelle to shoot the ball over.

Joe Robert's wife wishes to sue the golf course in order to claim the prize. I have looked at the tournament's entry form that Estelle signed when she made her $500.00 donation to play in the event. That form notes: "Disputes concerning the winner of the tournament, the scoring of any round, or other issues involving a specific shot will be determined solely by the appointed judge whose decisions are final in all matters relating to the event." The signs promoting the tournament advertised that any person who shoots a hole-in-one on the designated hole will be awarded a new Mercedes.

Estelle claims that she is being denied the Mercedes since Dr. Mauro has a bias against the Roberts' family. This physician is currently engaged in litigation with Joe Roberts over a malpractice claim.

I have found one case that deals with the awarding of a disputed prize in a contest. Please read **Giunto v. Florida Panthers,** and let me know whether you think we will be successful in a claim against the golf course.

GIUNTO V. FLORIDA PANTHERS HOCKEY CLUB, LTD.
745 S.2D 1020 (FLA. APP. 1999)

Giunto completed a sweepstakes application for the "Coca-Cola/Blockbuster/Florida Panthers Sweepstakes." The application contained contest rules (the "Entry Form Rules"). Pursuant to the Entry Form Rules, ten persons would be chosen to receive free tickets to one of ten different Florida Panthers home games. At the game, the ticket winner would be given a chance to win $1,000,000 by shooting a hockey puck across the ice "into and through a special small goal." Mr. Giunto was selected as one of the persons to have a try at the $1,000,000 prize.

Giunto appeared at the Florida Panthers game for his attempt at the prize. Just prior to his attempt, Mr. Giunto signed a Spectator Agreement to Participate ("SAP"). Included on the SAP was the requirement that in order for the contestant to win, the puck had to "pass completely through" the goal.

The target in this case was a piece of plywood placed in front of the hockey goal. At the bottom of the plywood sheet, a small slot had been created, somewhat larger than the hockey puck.

From a position of 118 feet from the hockey goal, Giunto took the contest shot. A videotape shows that the puck hit the corner of the small slot and rebounded from side to side. It did not go completely through the opening, but came to rest just slightly within the slot. A contest judge declared that the shot was unsuccessful.

Giunto sued the Sponsors for breach of contract alleging that he had successfully made the goal. Giunto contended that the controlling contest requirement was that the puck pass "into and through" the goal; that the SAP requirement that the puck pass "completely through" the goal was a nullity; and that "into and through" was satisfied if any part of the puck entered the opening, even if the puck did not pass completely through the opening.

The Sponsors claimed that Mr. Giunto's claims were barred because the contest judge had made the determination that Mr. Giunto did not successfully make the shot. The Entry Form Rules provided, "By participating in this sweepstakes, entrants agree to abide by and be bound by these official rules and the decisions of the judges, which are final in all matters relating to this sweepstakes." By submitting the application containing the Entry Form Rules, Mr. Giunto agreed to abide by the decision of the judges.

Other jurisdictions have held that "when a contestant agrees to be bound by the decisions of a tournament director or an awards committee, such decisions are final and binding on contestants absent evidence of fraud, gross mistake, or lack of good faith." **National Amateur Bowlers, Inc. v. Tassos, 715 F. Supp. 323 (D. Kan. 1989)** (holding that decisions of the tournament committee would be final, unless there was "fraud, intentional or gross mistake, or lack of good faith").

The contest judge determined that Mr. Giunto had not successfully made the hockey shot. There was neither pleading nor proof of fraud, gross mistake, or lack of good faith. When the puck entered the plywood slot but did not pass completely through it, the contest judge was required to decide whether Mr. Giunto had won under the contest rules. The judge's decision was binding on Mr. Giunto.

As to the question of whether the puck had to pass "into and through," or "completely through" the opening, Mr. Giunto signed the SAP which stated, "I understand that the Official Rules are as follows: The puck must pass completely through the target template." This document clearly informed Mr. Giunto, before he took his contest shot, that the judges would interpret "into and through" to mean "completely through" in order to win. The contest judge's ruling was in accordance with that interpretation.

PROBLEM FOUR—B
ANSWER SHEET

Name _____ **Please Print Clearly**

1. What arguments can we advance on behalf of Estelle as to why she should be awarded the prize?

_____

_____

_____

_____

_____

_____

_____

_____

2. What arguments will be raised by the country club?

_____

_____

_____

_____

_____

_____

_____

_____

3. Based upon the Florida Panthers case, who should win? Please explain your answer so that I can inform Estelle of her legal rights.

SECTION 4.11
STATUTE OF FRAUDS

Most contracts are informal and need not be in writing to be enforceable. The **Statute of Frauds** provides an exception to this basic rule. Based upon a seventeenth-century English law, known as the Act for the Prevention of Frauds and Perjuries, certain types of contracts must be in writing and signed by the individual against whom enforcement is sought. The purpose of this rule is to prevent perjured testimony in claiming the existence of an oral contract when one never existed.

The Statute of Frauds vary by state, but the following types of agreements generally must be in writing:

1. Contracts that cannot be performed within one year;

2. Contracts involving the sale or lease of real estate;

3. Contracts to be liable for the debts of another; and

4. Contracts for the sale of goods over $500.00.

The writing itself need not follow a specific format or be a formal legal document. In fact, a binding contract may be pieced together through a series of letters or correspondence between the parties. Faxes, telegrams and Western Union Mailgrams also satisfy the requirements for a written contract.

As for the specific elements of the writing, the Statute of Frauds is satisfied if the documentation sets forth the basics of the agreement, such as the identity of the parties, the subject matter of the contract, and be signed.

In this age of electronic commerce, how is the Statute of Frauds satisfied in an Internet transaction? The **Electronic Signature in Global and National Commerce Act** was enacted by Congress in 2000 and provides that a signature, contract, or other record used in interstate or international commerce may not be denied legal effect because an electronic signature or electronic record was used in its formation. This means that a digital or electronic signature must be treated in the same manner as an inked signature on a piece of contract.

The Statute of Frauds is a flexible rule, and the courts recognize exceptions to the doctrine to prevent an injustice. For example, a party will be deemed estopped to deny the existence of an oral contract when the goods have been specially manufactured, the goods have been received by the buyer, or if the individual admits the existence of the agreement in a court document. An aggrieved party may also receive court help in the enforcement of an oral contract, in order to prevent unjust enrichment to the defendant and a disproportionately harsh penalty upon the plaintiff.

ARYA GROUP, INC. V. CHER
91 CAL. RPTR. 2D 815 (CT. APP. CAL. 2000)

Arya Group, Inc. appeals from the order dismissing its action against Cher and the Inshallah Trust. Arya contends the trial court's ruling constituted an abuse of discretion because the allegations in Arya's complaint show Arya is entitled to relief under theories of breach of contract and unjust enrichment.

The material allegations of Arya's complaint, which we assume to be true for purposes of this review, may be summarized as follows. Cher is the beneficiary and trustor of the Inshallah Trust, which is the record owner of property in Malibu. In June 1996, representatives of Cher and the Inshallah Trust negotiated an oral agreement with Arya, whereby Arya was to design and construct a house on the Malibu property. Cher consented to pay Arya for Arya's provision of design, construction, general contracting and supervision services. She further agreed that Arya would "be paid progress payments upon periodic percentages of project completion." The parties' oral agreement was subsequently memorialized in a written contract, which was delivered to Cher in early October 1997. Cher never signed the contract, despite her promise to do so.

Between June 1996 and November 1997, Cher assured Arya that the contract would be honored and that Arya would receive full compensation for the construction services it provided under the contract. In fact, Arya did receive payment from Cher for a number of services it discharged under the contract.

Commencing in August 1997 Cher requested that Arya meet with Bussell, a designer who had previously worked with Cher on speculative residential projects. In the course of meeting with Bussell, Arya showed Bussell the plans and designs for the Malibu property. Unbeknownst to Arya, the meetings with Bussell were part of a plan by Cher (who had never intended to sign the contract with Arya or honor its terms) to induce Arya to divulge information relating to the Malibu property so Cher could terminate her contract with Arya without paying Arya for the services it had provided, and replace Arya as the general contractor.

In November 1997, Cher terminated her agreement with Arya, without paying the balance then due Arya. In addition, Cher contacted several of Arya's subcontractors in an effort to induce them to breach their contracts with Arya and work directly with Cher. They also misappropriated for their own use the plans, designs and drawings Arya had prepared, and had the permits issued to Arya transferred to Cher's name.

We are called upon to decide whether Arya is precluded under Business and Professions Code section 7164 from pursuing a breach of contract claim as a result of its failure to secure a signed written contract for the construction of Cher's residence. Section 7164 reads: "Every contract, between an owner and a contractor, for the construction of a single-family dwelling to be retained by the owner for at least one year, shall be evidenced in a writing signed by both parties . . ."

Although the California Supreme Court acknowledged that, generally speaking, a contract made in violation of a regulatory statute is void, it stressed that the rule is not an inflexible one to be applied in its fullest rigor under all circumstances. The court noted that in compelling cases, illegal contracts will be enforced in order to avoid unjust enrichment to a defendant and a disproportionately harsh penalty upon the plaintiff. The court explained, "In each case, the extent of enforceability and the kind of remedy granted depend upon a variety of factors, including the policy of the transgressed law, the kind of illegality and the particular facts." **Asdourian v. Araze, 211 Cal. Rptr. 703 (Cal. 1985).**

It appears that Cher is a highly sophisticated homeowner with previous involvement in residential construction projects, that her legal representatives assisted her in negotiating the Malibu construction project agreement with Arya, that Arya had already completed a substantial amount of the work it contracted to perform when Cher terminated the parties' agreement, and that Cher would be unjustly enriched if she were not required to compensate Arya for the reasonable value of its work. Under these circumstances, we decline to hold that Arya's non-compliance with section 7164 absolutely forecloses it from seeking to enforce the oral agreement it purportedly made with Cher, which was allegedly memorialized in an unsigned written contract. On the other hand, should it become apparent in the course of a trial that the facts are otherwise than as alleged, and are such as to place the case outside the exception to the general rules regarding enforceability of illegal contracts, our holding would not preclude Cher from reasserting her position about unenforceability of any agreement between her and Arya in the absence of a signed written contract.

Consequently, we hold that Arya may seek to enforce its contract claim against Cher to the extent Cher would otherwise be unjustly enriched as a result of her failure to compensate Arya for the reasonable value of its work on the Malibu construction project.

SECTION 4.12
MOVIE CONTRACT

PROBLEM FOUR—C

PARK, BROWN & SMITH, P.C.
ATTORNEYS AT LAW
MEMORANDUM

TO: All Law Clerks

FROM: Peter Smith, Esquire

RE: Movie Contract

I need your assistance with the soon to be released film, *"The Real Tragedy of Rock and Roll."*

The late John De Simone of Seattle, Washington, gained notoriety a number of years ago when he attempted to kill a famous singer, who was considered one of the founders of rock and roll. The Seattle resident became psychotic as the result of medication he took for his health. During an acute episode, the decedent concluded that teenagers were being brainwashed by the singer's music, and that the recording star had to be killed to stop that process.

The singer was in Seattle for a concert when De Simone put his plan in action. He loaded his car with explosives and drove to the concert hall. The load, however, was unstable and detonated two blocks away from the intended target. De Simone was killed, and several historic buildings in the Seattle underground were damaged.

Due to the passage of time, this incident has been largely forgotten but that is about to change. The surviving child of De Simone is a Seattle physician who went to medical school with my daughter. He learned that True Films, Inc. had decided to make a movie about this incident. Because of my expertise in entertainment law, Dr. De Simone contacted me about the film project.

The doctor wanted me to stop the movie production about his father but that was not a viable legal option. My job, therefore, was to reduce the impact of the movie on the life of Dr. De Simone. With the threat of a lawsuit for invasion of privacy, I was able to achieve this goal by charging the decedent's name in the film, and in having the movie filmed in San Francisco, as though the events occurred in that city.

Parts of the signed movie contract are as follows:

THIS AGREEMENT is made by and between True Films, Inc. ("Film Company") and Brad De Simone ("Son").

1. Film Company wishes to film and license for distribution the motion picture, *The Real Tragedy of Rock and Roll* ("Picture").

2. The Picture is to depict certain events in the life of John De Simone.

3. Son is a physician in the Seattle area and is concerned that the Picture may have a negative impact on his life because of the disclosure of private, embarrassing facts about his family.

4. In exchange for the execution of this Agreement, the parties agree that:

    (a) No part of the Picture will be filmed in the Seattle area and the movie will depict all events as though they had happened in San Francisco.

    (b) All references to John De Simone in the movie and publicity about the film will be changed to "Tony Volpe."

    (c) The film will not mention or depict any member of John De Simone's family.

    (d) Son will be provided with a copy of the screenplay within ten days of the execution of this Agreement for review and editing.

5. Film Company further warrants that the Director of the Picture shall abide by the terms of this Agreement.

6. In consideration of the foregoing warranties, Son grants the Film Company the non-exclusive right to depict John De Simone in any manner consistent with the terms of this Agreement in the movie *The Real Tragedy of Rock and Roll.*

7. Son releases the Film Company from all liability, including any liability for libel, defamation, and invasion of privacy.

8. Son waives all equitable remedies that may be available to him for a breach of this Agreement including the issuance of an injunction, any action for specific performance of this contract, and he understands that his exclusive remedy shall be limited to the recovery of monetary damages.

Once this contract was signed, a discussion ensued about whether Dr. De Simone had any documents concerning his father. He searched the attic and found a suitcase filled with newspaper accounts and news clips of the incident. Dr. De Simone had mixed feelings about releasing the materials but was willing to consider the request. Because True Films was about to start production, the director asked if he could review the items while the doctor decided what he wanted to do about the request.

A number of letters were exchanged between the film company and our client about the matter. Because of time deadlines, the Director used the materials in the film, assuming that everything had been worked out. Our client initially granted permission to use the materials but then changed his mind. The master copy of the film is at the distributor and copies of the movie are ready for release to the theaters.

Dr. De Simone wants to block the showing of the film and hold True Films liable for the actions of the director. I have pieced together the following sequence of events.

On August 12, 2018 Dr. De Simone mailed an offer to True Films allowing for use of the items in exchange for a $25,000 donation to the Mental Health Association of Seattle. The film company was given 10 days to accept the offer, at which time the offer would automatically terminate.

On August 15, 2018 True Films received the letter from Dr. De Simone.

On August 16, 2018 Dr. De Simone changed his mind about granting permission to use the materials in the film. He thought the public would misconstrue his father's actions and not remember that the decedent had planned the events while in a psychotic state. Accordingly, Dr. De Simone mailed a second letter to the film company retracting the offer of August 12.

On August 18, 2018 True Films received the letter of revocation.

On August 19, 2018 the film company sent Dr. De Simone a letter accepting the offer, and immediately made a $25,000 donation to the Mental Health Association of Seattle.

On August 20, 2018 Dr. De Simone received the film company's letter of acceptance but ignored it because he had already sent the letter of revocation.

Dr. De Simone wants to know his rights. Is there a valid contract to use the materials in the film? Can he legally revoke his offer even though the doctor promised that the offer was to remain open for ten (10) days? What remedies does Dr. De Simone have against the film company and can he stop the release of the film by obtaining an injunction? Is the film company liable for the director's actions?

**PROBLEM FOUR—C
ANSWER SHEET**

Name   **Please Print Clearly**

1. Is there a valid contract to use the materials in the film?

_____

_____

_____

_____

_____

_____

_____

_____

2. Can the doctor properly revoke the offer even though he stated that the offer was to remain open for ten (10) days?

_____

_____

_____

_____

_____

_____

_____

_____

_____

3. What remedies does Dr. De Simone have against the film company and can he stop the release of the film by obtaining an injunction?

_____

_____

_____

_____

_____

_____

_____

_____

_____

4. Is the film company liable for the Director's actions in including the materials in the film?

_____

_____

_____

_____

_____

_____

_____

_____

_____

SECTION 4.13
UNIFORM
COMMERCIAL CODE

The **Uniform Commercial Code** is the most complete of all the uniform laws in the United States. The purpose of the Code is to make uniform the laws involving commercial transactions in each state such as the law of sales, banking, secured transactions and other business contracts. Over the years, the provisions have been modified but the same basic scheme exists. The Uniform Commercial Code is broken down into the following nine articles:

Article	Title
Article One	General Provisions
Article Two	Sales
Article Two-A	Leases
Article Three	Negotiable Instruments
Article Four	Bank Deposits
Article Four-A	Fund Transfers
Article Five	Letters of Credit
Article Six	Bulk Transfers and Sales
Article Seven	Documents of Title
Article Eight	Investments Securities
Article Nine	Secured Transactions

The Code is not involved with real estate transactions but with personal property such as merchandise. Because of the Code's requirement of good faith and reasonableness, a number of the provisions will be different than the general rules of contract law.

This section shall be limited to a review of some of the provisions in Article Two which deal with the sale of goods. Because this uniform law is a legislative mandate, it is important to see how certain terms are defined in the Code.

Most definitions involving the Uniform Commercial Code are contained in Article One and apply to all of the Articles. Let us look at some of the individual provisions of the Code to see how this bundle of laws works.

A **consumer** refers to an individual who enters into a transaction primarily for personal, family, or household purposes.

A **good** refers to an item that is movable at the time of identification to a contract for sale. The term includes future goods, specially manufactured goods, growing crops, and other identified things attached to realty.

A **seller** means a person that sells or contracts to sell goods.

A **sale** consists in the passing of title from the seller to the buyer for a price.

A **merchant** is a person that deals in goods of that kind or otherwise holds itself out by occupation as having knowledge or skill peculiar to the practices or goods involved in the transaction. The Uniform Commercial Code holds merchants to a higher standard of care than non-merchants.

A **buyer in the ordinary course of business** refers to a person that buys goods in good faith, without knowledge that the sale violates the rights of another person in the goods, and in the ordinary course from a person in the business of selling goods of that kind.

A **bill of lading** refers to a document evidencing the receipt of goods for shipment issued by an entity engaged in the business of transporting or forwarding goods.

A **lease** is the transfer of the right to possession and use of goods for a term in return for consideration.

A. Entrustment

Joe Roberts decided to surprise his wife for their 25th wedding anniversary by secretly taking her engagement ring to the jeweler to have it reset in a new wedding band. Joe picked out a platinum setting which complemented her original stone by surrounding it in alternating diamonds and emeralds. Because the ring had to be specially made, Joe left his wife's stone with the jeweler hoping that she would not miss the ring while it was being reset. The owner returned two days later as instructed but the merchant could not locate the gem anywhere in the store. It turns out that the jeweler mistakenly sold the diamond with the new setting to another customer. Because of the sentimental value of the ring and the horrible mistake made by the merchant, can Mr. Roberts obtain the return of the ring from the buyer?

The Uniform Commercial Code provides in Section 2-403 that any **entrustment** of the possession of goods to a merchant who deals in goods of that kind gives that entity the power to transfer all rights of the entruster to a buyer in the ordinary course of business.

Three reasons have been articulated in support of this Code provision: (1) it protects the innocent buyer who believes the merchant has legal title to the goods because the items are in the merchant's possession; (2) the clause is based on the idea that the entruster is in a better position than the innocent buyer to protect against the risk of the dishonesty or mistake of the dealer; and (3) the principle of entrustment facilitates the flow of commerce when buyers in the ordinary course of business are involved.

Would the same result occur if a person brings her car to the gas station to have a flat tire repaired only to have the mechanic sell the car to a different customer? The gas station is not in the business of selling automobiles so the original owner would be able to demand its return.

B. Risk of Loss

Ascertaining who bears the **risk of loss** is important when the goods are damaged or lost. Surprisingly, the answer does not depend upon who owns the goods. In the absence of an agreement, Section 2-509 of the UCC governs who has the risk of loss and the answer depends upon such factors as whether the seller is a merchant, how the goods are to be delivered, or if a warehouse is involved.

Where the contract requires the seller to ship the goods, the risk of loss will pass to the buyer when confirming goods are delivered to the carrier. This is known as a **shipment contract.** On the other hand, if the agreement requires the seller to deliver the items to a specified destination, the risk of loss does not pass until the items have been delivered to that destination. This is known as a **destination contract.** For instance, Tyler's Sports Bar and Grill orders 100 cases of imported beer from a vendor in Baltimore and the terms are "F.O.B. Shipment." The beer is picked up by an independent trucking company at the seller's place of business but the bottles are destroyed in transit when the vehicle is in an accident. Who has the risk of loss? Since this is a shipment contract, so long as the seller delivered confirming goods to the trucking company, the risk of loss passed to the buyer as soon as the items were given to the trucking company. On the other hand, if the contract called for the beer to be sent "F.O.B. Destination," then the risk of loss would remain with the seller until confirming goods are delivered to Tyler's place of business in Philadelphia.

A different set of rules apply if the merchandise is stored at a warehouse owned by a third party. This third person is known as a **bailee.** When goods held by a bailee are the subject of a **bill of lading,** the risk of loss passes to the buyer upon possession of these documents. If the items, however, are not covered by documents of title, the risk of loss passes to the purchaser only when the third person acknowledges the buyer's right to possession of the goods. In international trade, it is common for merchandise to be sold through bills of lading. The seller of a product will provide a bank with the documents of title which will then be given to the buyer upon payment for the goods. The paperwork will allow the buyer to go to the warehouse and obtain possession of the merchandise. This ensures that international transactions go smoothly. For instance, if the beer company ships its alcoholic drinks to a refrigerated warehouse owned by the city of Philadelphia for distribution throughout the tri-state area, when a bar places an order for the imported beer, it will receive the bill of lading from the bank after paying for the goods. So, when Tyler's orders 100 cases of beer, the owner of the bar must go to the bank, pay for the beer and obtain the bill of lading. After Tyler's performs these steps but before the beer can be picked up, the roof of the warehouse collapses and the beer is destroyed. Who has the risk of loss? Since the merchandise was stored in a warehouse and the buyer has taken possession of the documents of title, the risk of loss has passed to the buyer.

The last rule on risk of loss covers that situation where the goods are in possession of the seller and the buyer is to pick them up at the store. In this case, the risk of loss passes to the customer on receipt of the goods if the seller is a merchant; otherwise, the risk passes to the buyer on tender of delivery. Returning to the bar, Tyler's needs two large screen televisions so the manager goes to an electronics store and buys them. After paying for the items, he learns that the boxes will not fit into his small pickup truck. The merchant agrees to hold the television while the buyer secures a larger truck. In the interim, a fire occurs at the store and the goods are destroyed. Under Section 2-509 of the Uniform Commercial Code, the electronics store bears the risk of loss since the goods have not been delivered. On the other hand, if the seller is not a merchant, the risk of loss passes as soon as the goods are tendered to the buyer. This only requires the seller to make the goods available to the buyer and to give the buyer notification reasonably necessary to enable him to take delivery. For instance, if the manager of Tyler's buys his next door neighbor's large screen television and asks the seller to hold the item until the next week, the risk of loss passes to the buyer at the point of sale.

WILSON V. BRAWN OF CALIFORNIA, INC.
132 CAL. APP. 4TH 549 (CAL. APP. 2005)

Brawn markets clothing through its catalogs and over the Internet. When a customer places an order, Brawn packages it and holds it at its warehouse, where it is picked up by a common carrier and delivered to the customer, using an address provided by the customer. At all times, the terms of Brawn's mail order form required the customer to pay the listed price for the goods purchased, plus a delivery fee and a $1.48 "insurance fee."

Plaintiff purchased items from Brawn's catalogue, each time paying the insurance fee. On February 13, 2002, he brought suit against Brawn, contending that in charging the fee, Brawn violated the Unfair Competition Law. Plaintiff's suit was premised on the theory that by charging customers an insurance fee, Brawn suggested to them that they were receiving a special benefit-insurance against loss in transit-when in fact, customers did not need insurance against loss in transit because Brawn already was required to pay for that loss as a matter of law.

Uniform Commercial Code Section 2-509 sets forth the general rules for determining which party bears the risk of loss of goods in transit. Where the contract requires or authorizes the seller to ship the goods by carrier (a) If it does not require him to deliver them at a particular destination, the risk of loss passes to the buyer when the goods are delivered to the carrier; but (b) If it does require him to deliver them at a particular destination and the goods are then duly tendered while in the possession of the carrier, the risk of loss passes to the buyer when the goods are duly so tendered as to enable the buyer to take delivery.

Under this Article the "shipment" contract is regarded as the normal one and the "destination" contract as the variant type. The seller is not obligated to deliver at a named destination and bear the concurrent risk of loss until arrival, unless he has specifically agreed so to deliver, or the commercial understanding of the terms used by the parties contemplates such a delivery. It follows that a contract is not a destination contract simply because the seller places an address label on the package, or directs the carrier to "ship to" a particular destination. Thus a "ship to" term has no significance in determining whether a contract is a shipment or destination contract for risk of loss purposes."

It is not at all uncommon for a contract to shift the risk of loss to the buyer at the point at which the seller delivers the goods to a common carrier, while calling for the seller to pay for delivery and insurance. The Commercial Code recognizes this type of contract in its provisions pertaining to the term "C.I.F." The term C.I.F. means that the price includes in a lump sum the cost of the goods and the insurance and freight to the named destination. The C.I.F. contract is not a destination but a shipment contract with risk of subsequent loss or damage to the goods passing to the buyer upon shipment if the seller has properly performed all his obligations with respect to the goods. Delivery to the carrier is delivery to the buyer for purposes of risk and title. In a standard "C.I.F." contract, the buyer bears the risk of loss in transit even though the cost of insurance is rolled into the purchase price and is in fact paid by the seller. By breaking out the cost of insurance, and requiring the buyer to pay it, Brawn's mail order contracts even more clearly place the risk of loss in transit on the buyer.

Other evidence is consistent with the conclusion that Brawn intended the contracts to be shipment contracts. Brawn's own insurance covers goods lost while in Brawn's possession, but it does not cover goods destroyed or lost after the goods left Brawn's physical possession. Brawn pays California use tax, rather than sales tax, on the theory that the goods were "sold" when they left Brawn's place of business, located outside of California. Brawn records the revenue for the goods sold at the point of shipment, and removes the goods from its inventory at the time of shipment.

In sum, nothing in Brawn's conduct, and nothing in the delivery or insurance terms of Brawn's mail order forms, suggests that it was offering anything other than a standard, C.I.F.-type shipment contract, which the customers agreed to when they used Brawn's mail order form to purchase goods.

C. Requirement of Good Faith

The law of contracts provides that an agreement which lacks an important term, such as price or quantity, will not be enforceable because of indefiniteness. So, a contract between neighbors for the sale of a car that fails to specify the price is not enforceable. It is missing a key element of the contract.

That is not the result under the Uniform Commercial Code which requires that every contract impose an **obligation of good faith** in its performance or enforcement. For instance, Section 2-204 provides that even though one or more elements of a contract are missing, an agreement for the sale of goods is valid and will not fail for indefiniteness if the parties intended to make a contract. The courts will simply fill in the gaps by ascertaining what is commercially reasonable under the circumstances. This is demonstrated in the following example. If an appliance company contracts with a television manufacturer for the purchase of 100 large screen televisions that must be delivered two weeks before Super Bowl Sunday, but nothing is said about the cost, the Code mandates that the price will be what is reasonable at the time of delivery of the merchandise.

D. Consideration

Consideration is an essential element of every contract. If a party offers to sell his racing car for $25,000 and tells the buyer that he has one week to make up his mind, this offer can be revoked anytime before acceptance. The promise to keep the offer open for one week is not supported by consideration. This result changes under the Code if one of the parties to the contract is a merchant. Section 2-205 states that an offer by a merchant to buy or sell goods in a signed writing which gives assurances that it will be held open is not revocable, for lack of consideration, during the time stated or if no time is stated for a reasonable time not to exceed three months.

Another change dealing with consideration is the addition of new terms in the contract by one of the parties. Section 2-209(1) provides that "an agreement modifying a contract . . . needs no consideration to be binding." Therefore, no new consideration needs to be provided for the subsequent promise.

E. Firm Offer

Section 2-205 implements a new type of offer, the **firm offer,** or an irrevocable offer by the merchant that cannot be revoked. More specifically, a merchant who makes an offer in a signed writing to buy or sell goods, which gives assurances that the offer will be held open, cannot be revoked for lack of consideration during the time stated. If no time is listed in the offer, then it remains open for a reasonable time which period cannot exceed three months. This rule is much different than normal contract law which requires consideration to keep the offer open for a specified period of time. The firm offer provides an example of where the merchant is held to a higher standard under the Uniform Commercial Code.

Suppose Tyler's Sports Bar and Grill desires to buy imported beer from Germany. The manager of the bar contacts a beer distributor who sends the bar the following signed note: "We agree to sell you 100 cases of imported German beer for your Oktoberfest at $10 a case. This offer is valid for 30 days." One week later, there is a strike at the shipping dock in Philadelphia and the beer cannot be offloaded requiring the boat to be rerouted to Baltimore. The beer is then unloaded at that port of entry and shipped by truck to the distributor in Philadelphia at an added expense of $5 a case. Before the expiration of the thirty days, Tyler's contacts the distributor to buy 100 cases of beer at $10 a case but the seller now demands $15 a case for the alcoholic beverage. Must the distributor sell the beer at the original price or can it increase the charge to $15? The disturber is a merchant and made a firm offer which was accepted before the expiration of the stated term. Therefore, the offer cannot be revoked and the beer must be sold to the bar at $10 a case.

F. Statute of Frauds

As noted previously, most contracts do not have to be in writing to be enforceable. If the contract is orally made and a dispute arises, the issue becomes one of credibility and which party the court believes is telling the truth about the events. Under normal contract law, however, certain types of agreements must be in writing to be enforceable. The Uniform Commercial Code addresses the issue when dealing with a contract for the sale of goods. Section 2-201 provides that a contract for the sale of good for the price of $500 or more is not enforceable unless there is some writing sufficient to indicate that a contract for sale has been made between the parties and signed by the party against whom enforcement is sought. That writing will not be considered invalid merely because it omits or incorrectly states a term agreed upon but the contract is not enforceable beyond the quantity of the goods shown in such writing.

If both parties to an oral agreement are merchants, and if within a reasonable time, a written memo in confirmation of the contract is sent, the Statute of Frauds has been satisfied unless written objection to its contents by the receiving party is given within 10 days after receipt of the note.

There is an exception to the State of Frauds and its requirements of a writing. If the goods are to be specially manufactured for the buyer and are not suitable for resale to others in the seller's ordinary course of business, and the seller has started their manufacturing or made commitments for their procurement, the oral contract will be enforced. For example, if Tyler's calls a manufacturer of dishes and orders 1,000 plates that are to be specially made in the shape of a football and are to prominently contain the name of the bar across the front of the plate, the bar will be bound by this oral contract. This is a specially designed order and the plates cannot be resold in the ordinary course of the manufacturer's business.

G. Counteroffer

Traditional contract principles require the offeree to accept the terms of the offer as proposed. An acceptance with different terms or conditions rejects the original offer and presents a new proposal that can be accepted or rejected by the original offeror. For instance, if Tyler's Sports Bar and Grill accepts an offer to buy an adjacent property for $300,000 but adds to the acceptance that is contingent upon obtaining the proper zoning to use the lot for a bar, that new term rejects the original offer and there is no contract.

Section 2-207 provides that if the contract is for the sale of goods and the acceptance contains additional terms, those new requirements do not reject the original offer but merely serve as a proposal for addition to the contract. If the contract is between merchants, however, such terms shall become part of the contract, unless:

(a) the offer expressly limits acceptance to the terms of the offer;

(b) they materially alter it; or

(c) notification of objection to them has already been given or is given within a reasonable time after notice of them is received.

Under the Code, if a vendor offers to sell Tyler's Sports Bar and Grill 10 cases of premium Vodka at $25 a case and Tyler's accepts the offer but notes that the Vodka must be delivered to its place of business within 5 days, the new delivery term becomes part of the contract. Both Tyler's and the vendor are merchants with respect to liquor, so Section 2-207 applies to the transaction.

H. Specificity of Terms

Generally, a contract must spell out the terms of an offer, such as quantity, delivery terms and price of the items to be valid. Under Section 2-305, however, these omissions are not fatal. The Code provides that the parties can conclude a contract for sale of goods even if the price is not settled. In such a case, the price will be the reasonable price at the time for delivery; or, the price is left to be agreed upon by the parties and they fail to so agree. Suppose that Tyler's agrees to buy 10 cases of premium Vodka but nothing is said about the price. The law will find that a contract has been created and the price for the vodka will be the reasonable price for the product when it is delivered.

I. Acceptance

The mailbox rule demands that acceptance takes place on dispatch and revocation on receipt.

Also, the means of acceptance is generally in the same format in which the offer was made. In other words, if the offer is transmitted by mail, the acceptance must be done in the same manner. The UCC provides for much greater flexibility. If the offer does not dictate a particular method of acceptance, Section 2-206 provides that an offer shall be construed as inviting acceptance in any manner and by any medium reasonable under the circumstances.

J. Warranties

When individuals use the term "warranty," they are usually talking about a specific type of guarantee that the Code calls an "**express warranty.**" These are affirmative promises about the quality and features of the items being sold. Claiming that a camera is "waterproof to 50 feet," that a car gets "30 mpg on the highway," or that glue dries within 30 seconds are examples of express warranties.[5]

The Uniform Commercial Code, however, is more expansive in defining a warranty. Section 2-313 creates an express warranty under three situations:

(a) When there is an affirmation of fact or promise made by the seller to the buyer which relates to the goods and becomes part of the basis of the bargain.

(b) Any description of the goods which is made part of the bargain creates an express warranty that the goods shall conform to that description.

(c) Any sample which is made part of the bargain creates an express warranty that the whole of the goods shall conform to the sample or model.

It is not necessary that the seller use formal words such as "warrant" or "guarantee" or that she have a specific intention to make a warranty. If it is foreseeable that the buyer will rely on the statement made by the seller, then a warranty will be created. However, a statement as to the value of the goods or one that is merely a seller's opinion does not create a warranty. For instance, a seller's statement that this is "the best car money can buy" is merely an opinion and does not create an express warranty. On the other hand, a statement that "this car is rustproof" is a warranty.

The UCC has extended warranties to two other situations that will arise by implication. Section 2-316 provides that in the absence of an exclusion, a **warranty of merchantability** shall be implied with the sale of a good. This means that the product must be of merchantable quality and properly packaged as long as the seller is a merchant with respect to goods of that type. In other words, the item must be of average quality and pass without objection in the trade.

The second implied warranty deals with **fitness for a particular purpose.** Section 2-315 provides that where the seller has reason to know of the particular purpose for which the goods are to be used and the buyer has relied upon the seller's skill or judgment to select those goods, there is an implied warranty that the items shall be fit for that purpose. For instance, if a homeowner goes into a paint store and asks for a paint that will be suitable for the outside of a house down the shore and the seller recommends a particular brand of oil based paint for the job, an implied warranty is created that the paint is fit for that purpose.

SECTION 4.14
E-CONTRACTS

The Internet has forced businesses to ponder how they can form legally binding contracts in ecommerce transactions but the answer is simple. Traditional principles of contract law have equal application to Internet transactions. In other words, electronic or e-contracts and electronic signatures are just as valid as old-style paper agreements signed by a pen. Definitionally, an **electronic contract** is a transaction fashioned and "signed" in electronic form.[6] The only difference with an internet contract is the introduction of new terms, such as "click-wrap agreements" and "digital signatures."

For instance, the online purchase of a computer printer from Amazon.com is no different than buying a computer printer from the nearest Best Buy electronics store, as the same principles of contract law will apply to both transactions. The offer and acceptance constitute the agreement to buy the printer, whether it is accomplished by placing the item in an online shopping cart and checking out, or by carrying the printer to the cashier in the store. The consideration, or *quid pro quo,* is the exchange of the printer for the requested cash price. The contract is perfectly legal, and as long as the buyer is over 18, the parties have the capacity to contract.

Computer software may be obtained by downloading the program directly from the Internet or by installing the software from a CD. In each case, the software is accompanied with a license that limits the buyer's remedies, if the software does not work properly.

A **clickwrap license** will accompany the installation of a program from the web. The user is required to click through a series of screens before the program can be successfully installed. These screens contain non-negotiable terms and conditions imposed by the seller. Most people do not read these materials and merely click "I accept" to the questions, since it is the only way to advance the installation.

A **shrinkwrap license** receives its name from the fact that computer software is contained in a box and packaged in a cellophane shrinkwrap. When the box is opened, the CD is in an envelope that includes a printed license.

By opening the envelope or by using the software, the buyer agrees to be bound by the terms of the license.

These licenses are generally enforced by the courts even though they favor the software company, limit the buyer's rights in the event of a problem and are seen by the user for the first time after the software has been purchased.

The following case has to do with the enforceability of a clickwrap agreement and the terms and conditions contained in that agreement.

MALLH V. SHOWTIME NETWORKS, INC.
2017 WL 5157247 (S.D. N.Y. 2017)

This case involves a contract dispute between Victor Mallh ("Mallh") and Showtime Networks Inc. ("Showtime") arising out of Showtime's streaming of an August 26, 2017 boxing match between Floyd Mayweather, Jr. and Conor McGregor (the "Event"). Mallh purchased a live stream of the Event from Showtime but was unable to view substantial portions of it due to technical failures. Showtime has moved to compel arbitration. For the following reasons, Showtime's motion to compel arbitration is granted.

Showtime is an entertainment company that owns and operates a commercial-free premium television program service. Showtime also offers events to consumers live on a pay-per-view basis.

On August 26, 2017, Mallh paid $99.95 to view the Event as a live stream via www.showtimeppv.com (the "Website"). To purchase the live stream, all users of Showtime's website streaming service—had to agree to Showtime's terms of use ("TOU"). Specifically, every person who purchased the live stream had to take certain steps. First, users needed to access a webpage describing the Event. At that point, users were transferred to a purchase page.

The purchase page was dedicated to the steps required to transact the purchase which had boxes that purchasers were required to fill with their email address, credit card, and billing address information. Clicking on the hyperlinked words "Terms of Use" took users to a page containing the complete TOU. To complete the purchase, users were required to check both the box indicating that they had read and agreed to the TOU. The page also contained the following arbitration clause and class action waiver: "If you have any dispute with or claim against us or any of our affiliates arising out of or relating to the Services or these Terms, and the claim is not resolved by calling our customer service department, you and we each agree to resolve such disputes through an individual binding arbitration. Class actions are not permitted. You and we are each waiving the right to a trial by jury or to participate in a class action. Any such arbitration shall be administered by the American Arbitration Association and be conducted in accordance with its Commercial Arbitration Rules. Such hearing will take place in the U.S. county of your residence, or otherwise in Los Angeles, California. In addition, the TOU contains a choice of law provision selecting California law."

Mallh contends that he did not realize that by signing up to watch the Event he was being asked to submit claims against Showtime to arbitration on a non-class action basis. He asserts that he was unable to watch a substantial portion of the Event because Showtime's service continually logged him out.

During the periods in which he was able to watch the Event, the pictures were delayed, cut out, or otherwise incomplete. Mallh asserts further that he has tried to obtain a refund but has not succeeded.

Mallh filed this class action on August 28, 2017. A party to an arbitration agreement seeking to avoid arbitration generally bears the burden of showing the agreement to be inapplicable or invalid. Under California law, an agreement to arbitrate exists where there is a reasonably conspicuous notice of the existence of contract terms and unambiguous manifestation of assent to those terms. Courts around the country have recognized that an electronic click can suffice to signify the acceptance of a contract as long as the layout and language of the site give the user reasonable notice that a click will manifest assent to an agreement.

Clickwrap agreements require users to affirmatively click an "I agree" box after being presented with terms of use. Courts routinely uphold clickwrap agreements for the principal reason that the user has affirmatively assented to the terms of agreement by clicking "I agree."

It is undisputed that access to the Event was provided to the plaintiff through the defendant's website, and that his purchase of the live stream of the Event required him to click on a box indicating that he had read and agreed to the TOU. The TOU contained an arbitration provision and class action waiver requiring the plaintiff to arbitrate his disputes with the defendant on an individual basis. The agreement to arbitrate and class action waiver were reasonably conspicuous and the plaintiff's click gave his unambiguous consent to those agreements.

Clicking a hyperlinked phrase is the twenty-first century equivalent of turning over the cruise ticket. In both cases, the consumer is prompted to examine terms of sale that are located somewhere else. Moreover, the "I have read and agree to" language clearly prompts users to review the TOU, and a purchase may not be affected without clicking that acknowledgment.

Once a user accesses the TOU, the arbitration clause and class action waiver are reasonably conspicuous. Under these circumstances, a purchaser of the Event would be on reasonably conspicuous notice of the arbitration clause and class action waiver. Because notice of the arbitration clause and class action waiver was reasonably conspicuous and Mallh unambiguously manifested assent, Showtime's motion to compel arbitration is granted.

SECTION 4.15
AGENCY

Businesses act through their **agents** whether it is an employee or third party, and these agents have the power to enter into contracts on behalf of their **principals.** Agency law deals with these relationships and in what context an agent can bind a principal. Examples of agents include sports or music representatives, employees, realtors, public adjusters, buying agents, auctioneers, and attorneys.

The Restatement (Third) of Agency provides that an agency relationship is created "when one person (the "principal") manifests assent that another person (the "agent") shall, subject to the principal's right of control, have power to affect the principal's legal relations through the agent's acts and on the principal's behalf." These relationships are generally created by the mutual agreement between the principal and agent and can be expressed or implied. Examples of an expressed agency include when an attorney represents an injured party in a personal injury claim based upon the signing of a contingency fee agreement and when a realtor lists and sells a person's home upon the signing of a listing agreement. An agency relationship, however, can also be created by the actions of the parties without the necessity of a formal contract. This type of implied agency can occur in an employment situation, such as when a sales clerk has the power to bind the store on a customer purchase, even though there is no written contract that expressly provides that power.

An agent's duties and obligations to the principal are usually governed by the terms of a written agreement. Nevertheless, an agent acts in a position of trust which allows the principal to relax the care and vigilance ordinarily used. Therefore, an agent may not act in her own self-interests and she owes the principal a duty of loyalty and good faith. A sports agent, for instance, cannot make a deal with a team to sign one player at a lower salary so that another player the agent represents can obtain a higher salary or better deal.

An agent is clothed with authority to act on behalf of the principal and to enter into contracts to bind her master. This authority may be express, implied or apparent. **Express authority** is established by written or spoken words that signify the principal has delegated authority, and the agent has accepted that grant of power to act on behalf of he master. An attorney handling a personal injury claim pursuant to a contingent fee agreement would have the power to hire an investigator to interview witnesses, obtain the client's medical records and to take photographs of the accident scene. These tasks will be spelled out in the fee agreement.

The parties do not always spell out all of the details of the agencies and there will be situations when the agent must exercise discretion. Do those actions which are contained in the agency agreement or conversations between the principal and agent bind the principal? This concept is known as implied authority and consists of those actions which are reasonably necessary and proper for the agent to carry out the terms of the agency and which are not prohibited by the agreement. An attorney would be authorized to obtain the services of an accident reconstruction expert in the investigation of a claim, even though the agreement is silent on this issue, since that is a reasonable necessary and proper expense.

Apparent authority involves those situations where the master's conduct would lead a reasonable person to conclude that the agent is clothed with authority to act on the master's behalf. An agent with apparent authority can bind the principal to a contract, even though that contract may exceed the principal's grant of authority or express instructions to the contrary. The manager of a bar would have the apparent authority to bind her employer to the purchase of an exotic beer that costs $10 a bottle even though the employee was given specific instructions not to buy any beer that costs more than $1 a bottle, unless the seller was aware of this limitation.

Gaines v. Kelly raises the question as to whether a mortgage broker acts on behalf of a bank in order to bind that institution under the theory of apparent authority or whether the broker is merely a middleman.

GAINES V. KELLY
235 S.W.3D 179 (TEX. 2007)

In this appeal, we must determine whether representations, allegedly made by a mortgage broker that a loan would be funded, may be attributed to a lender for purposes of a borrower's claim against that lender.

In December 1998, Roger Kelly signed an Agreement with Robert Thompson, acting on behalf of Commercial Realty Advisors, Inc., to assist him in obtaining financing for a 31-acre tract in Texas. Although Kelly did not own the property, he held an option to purchase the property and needed financing.

Thompson approached Russell Gaines, an officer of Southwest Guaranty Mortgage Corp., about a loan for Kelly, providing Gaines with preliminary information about the proposed transaction. Gaines in turn provided Thompson with a loan application that Thompson delivered to Kelly. Kelly completed the application and returned it to Thompson, who delivered it to Gaines.

Kelly's attorneys pressed Gaines for a loan commitment because of the imminent expiration of Kelly's option on the property. On December 23, Southwest Guaranty issued a thirty-day loan commitment conditioned upon receipt of a title report.

When the subsequent title report indicated that Kelly did not have an ownership interest in the tract, Gaines asked for additional documentation concerning Kelly's ownership and the pre-sold lots. Kelly's attorneys, however, insisted that Southwest Guaranty fund the loan, and, when Gaines declined, Kelly promptly filed suit.

In his fraud claim, Kelly alleged that Thompson told him during the application process that the loan was a "done deal" and that he relied on this false statement to his financial detriment.

An agent's authority to act on behalf of a principal depends on some communication by the principal either to the agent or to the third party. The evidence clearly substantiates Thompson's authority to deliver the loan documents to Kelly. There is no evidence, however, that Thompson had actual authority to negotiate the loan, and thus the question is whether he had apparent or implied authority to do this.

Apparent authority is based on estoppel, arising "either from a principal knowingly permitting an agent to hold himself out as having authority or by a principal's actions which lack such ordinary care as to clothe an agent with the indicia of authority, thus leading a reasonably prudent person to believe that the Agent has the authority he purports to exercise." The principal's full knowledge of all material facts is essential to establish a claim of apparent authority based. Moreover, when making that determination, only the conduct of the principal is relevant. Thus, to determine an agent's apparent authority, we examine the conduct of the principal and the reasonableness of the third party's assumptions about authority.

Kelly submits that he reasonably believed that Thompson possessed apparent authority in this case similar to that of the agent in **Walker Insurance Services v. Bottle Rock Power Corp., 108 S.W.3d 538 (Tex. App. 2003).** Walker sued Bottle Rock, a California power company, for a fee that was to be paid if a bond was acquired under specific time constraints. At issue was whether the alleged agent, Arlie Beane, had apparent authority to negotiate or contract with Walker on behalf of the power company. The court of appeals concluded that he did have the authority, noting that most of the negotiations were conducted through Beane and that his efforts were "accepted and ratified" by Bottle Rock. Moreover, Wilson testified that "one of Bottle Rock's directors confirmed his understanding of Beane's authority to act and negotiate on its behalf." On this evidence, the court concluded that Beane was no mere middle-man but rather Bottle Rock's "point man" for obtaining the bond on its behalf. Kelly likewise suggests that Thompson was no mere middleman in his dealings with Gaines, but the evidence is otherwise.

Initially signing as Kelly's mortgage broker, Thompson located Southwest Guaranty as a possible lender, brought the parties together, and facilitated the paperwork for the loan. There is no evidence, however, that Thompson had any role in the negotiations. Instead, the evidence indicates that Thompson acted merely as a middleman.

In further contrast to **Walker Insurance Services,** the evidence in this case consists almost entirely of acts or statements attributed to the alleged agent, Thompson, rather than to the principal, Gaines. Declarations of the alleged agent, without more, are incompetent to establish either the existence of the alleged agency or the scope of the alleged agent's authority. Instead, apparent authority must be based on the acts of the principal and is limited to the scope of responsibility that is apparently authorized.

Gaines testified that he gave loan documents to Thompson for delivery to Kelly because Thompson said that he "would be the best bird dog to get it done." Gaines also testified that Thompson solicited the loan on behalf of Southwest Guaranty. There were also blank loan forms on Southwest Guaranty letterhead in Thompson's office.

Gaines' testimony clearly indicates that Gaines used Thompson as an intermediary to deliver loan documents and facilitate the transaction. But evidence that Thompson brought the parties together, delivered the paperwork, and assisted in its completion is not evidence that Gaines authorized or acquiesced in Thompson's representation that the loan was "a done deal." Nor is the existence of blank Southwest Guaranty loan forms in Thompson's office evidence that Thompson had authority to commit funds. The record does not show that Thompson was authorized to fill in the loan forms, there is no evidence he was authorized to sign them on Southwest Guaranty's behalf thus rendering them "a done deal."

Kelly complains that Thompson, acting for Gaines, fraudulently misled him into believing that the loan was "a done deal." Thus, the relevant issue is whether Thompson's agency included the authority to commit Gaines and Southwest Guaranty to the loan.

Because an agent's authority is presumed to be co-extensive with the business entrusted to his care, it includes only those contracts and acts incidental to the management of the particular business with which he is entrusted. The evidence here fails to raise a fact issue about whether Thompson's agency included the apparent authority to commit the funds or obligate Gaines to terms other than those agreed to in the parties' contract, and thus Thompson's alleged assurance that the loan would close cannot be imputed to Gaines or Southwest Guaranty. Accordingly, we render judgment that Kelly takes nothing.

SECTION 4.16 PROBLEM CASES

1. Story promised his nephew $5,000 if he would refrain from drinking liquor, using tobacco, swearing, or playing cards until he became 21 years of age. The nephew fulfilled the terms of this promise and requested the money upon becoming 21. This request was refused on the basis that the contract lacked consideration. Did the nephew provide legal consideration for the promise so that he may be awarded the money? **Hamer v. Sidway, 27 N.E. 25 (N.Y. 1891).**

2. Pemerton accepted an invitation to appear on "The Jerry Springer Show." In exchange, she received airfare from Tennessee, and her expenses were paid for two days in Chicago. Prior to the show's taping, she signed a document entitled "Jerry Springer Consent and Release" which provided that any dispute arising out of her appearance on the show would be resolved by binding arbitration with the American Arbitration Association. Pemerton sued Springer in state court for the injuries she received when her arch enemy burst from behind the scenes and beat Pemerton about the head and shoulders during the taping. Pemerton claims that Springer promised not to invite her assailant to the studio. Pemerton asserts that the Release does not cover the assault. She claims that it merely covers disputes arising out of the production of the show. Does the arbitration agreement cover this claim for personal injury? **Tracy Pemerton v. Jerry Springer, 1995 W.L. 579465 (N.D. Ill. 1995).**

3. Following the murder of Gianni Versace in front of his South Beach home, the FBI offered a reward leading to the "arrest and conviction of Andrew Cunanin." A dock attendant at a marina saw an individual who fit Cunanin's description on a nearby house boat. He notified the authorities, and the FBI surrounded the house boat containing Cunanin. Following a volley of gun shots, Cunanin was found dead inside the vessel. Since Cunanin was never brought to trial, is the dock worker entitled to the reward since he did not provide information leading to the "arrest and conviction" of the fugitive?

4. Turilli operates the Jessie James Museum and contends that the man buried as Jessie James in 1882 was an imposter. He claims that Jessie James lived for many years thereafter under the alias of J. Frank Doulton. Turilli offered a $10,000 reward "to anyone who could prove me wrong." The widow of the desperado's son, maintained that Jessie James was shot and killed by Robert Ford who pleaded guilty to the murder. Ms. James submitted affidavits to Turilli which noted that (**1**) the James Family Bible recited the death of Jessie James in 1882; (**2**) the outlaw's mother often stated that she identified the body of her son; (**3**) a boyhood neighbor of Jessie James swore that he went to the James home right after the shooting and identified the body; and (**4**) Jessie James' own son declared that when he was seven years old, he heard the fatal shot and saw his father die in his mother's arms. Has the daughter-in-law of Jessie James presented sufficient evidence to fulfill the terms of the offer? **Stella James v. Lou Turilli, 473 S.W. 2d 757 (Mo. App. 1971).**

5. Great Entertainment Merchandise (GEM) purchases merchandising rights from various performing artists before they go on tour. Vince Neal of Motley Crue entered into negotiations with GEM to transfer his

merchandising rights to the manufacturer in order for GEM to produce various memorabilia for the upcoming concert tour. In anticipation of the licensing agreement, Neal incorporated a "loan out" company. This type of entity is standard in the music industry so that artists can take advantage of certain tax incentives. Neal then transferred his merchandising rights to the "loan out" company, who in turn, assigned those rights to GEM. GEM paid $1 million to the company based upon 800,000 paid concert attendees. Neal also entered into a contract with GEM agreeing to use his best abilities to discharge the obligations undertaken by the artist. The actual attendance was well below the projected numbers. Therefore, GEM requested that Neal pay back part of the money on the basis that the separate agreement signed by the musician was a guarantee agreement. Neal counters that the clause merely guaranteed that he would use his best efforts to perform for 800,000 attendees. Is Neal responsible to pay back the money on the basis that he guaranteed the obligations of the "loan out" company? **Great Entertainment Merchandising, Inc. v. Vince Neal, 1996 U.S. Dist. Lexis 8973 (N.Y. 1996).**

6. At the start of his employment with Douglas and Lowmenson, Anderson was given an employee handbook which described a progressive disciplinary policy. After three years on the job, Anderson was fired because a box of company pencils were found in his pickup truck. Anderson sued the employer for breach of contract, claiming that they did not follow the progressive disciplinary policies outlined in the handbook for unauthorized possession of company property. These progressive discipline policies merely required a written notice for the first offense. Can an at-will employee be discharged at any time, or is an employer bound by the terms of the employee handbook? **Terry Anderson v. Douglas & Lowmenson Company, 540 N.W. 2d 277 (Ia. 1995).**

SECTION 4.17
INTERNET REFERENCES

The following internet references offer more information on contract law, including breach of contract and remedies.

- **www.law.cornell.edu/topics/contracts.html**
  The Legal Information Institute gives a good overview of contract law with federal and state materials and recent Supreme Court decisions.

- **www.loc.gov**
  The Library of Congress website provides online links to an extensive menu of topics concerning contract law and contains documents, photos, movies, and sound recordings from American history.

- **www.uchastings.edu**
  This reference provides a link to a research project on the nature and enforceability of electronic contracts.

- **www.ilrg.com/forms.html**
  This site gives examples of different types of contracts.

Footnotes:

1. Sophia Bernazzani, *Customer Loyalty: The Ultimate Guide*, HubSpot, https://blog.hubspot.com/customer-success/customer-loyalty (January 16, 2018).

2. *Id.*

3. What Constitutes Acceptance of a Contract Offer?, Nolo.com, http://www.nolo.com/legal-encyclopedia/acceptance-of-contract-offers-32651.html (last visited October 16, 2013).

4. Consideration: Every Contract Needs It, Nolo.com, http://www.nolo.com/legal-encyclopedia/consideration-every-contract-needs-33361.html (last visited October 16, 2013).

5. Commercial Law: Express and Implied Warranties under the Uniform Commercial Code, Cadden and Fuller, LLP, http://www.caddenfuller.com/CM/Articles/Articles34.asp (last visited September 24, 2013).

6. Electronic Signatures and Online Contracts, Nola.com, http://www.nolo.com/legal-encyclopedia/electronic-signatures-online-contracts-29495.html (last visited October 16, 2013).

Acceptance

Agents

Apparent Authority

Bailee

Bilateral Contract

Bill of Lading

Buyer in the Ordinary Course
of Business

Capacity

Clickwrap License

Co-Signer

Consideration

Consumer

Contract

Contract Implied-in-Law

Contracts for Necessities

Counteroffer

Customer Loyalty Program

Destination Contract

Electronic Contract

Electronic Signature in Global and
National Commerce Act

Entrustment

Express Authority

Express Contract

Express Warranty

Firm Offer

Fitness for a Particular Purpose

Gift

Good

Guarantee

Guarantor

Illegal

Illegal Contract

Illusory Promise

Implied Contract

Implied-in-Fact

Implied-in-Law

Lease

Legality

Mailbox Rule

Merchant

Moral Obligation

Obligation of Good Faith

Offer

Past Consideration

Postal Reorganization Act

Pre-Existing Obligation

Preliminary Negotiations

Principals

Quasi-Contract

Quid Pro Quo

Ratification

Risk of Loss

Sale

Sealed Bids

Seller

Shipment Contract

Shrinkwrap License

Silence as Acceptance

Statute of Frauds

Surety

Unenforceable Contracts

Uniform Commercial Code

Uniform Commercial Information
Transaction Act
(UCITA)

Unilateral Contract

Valid Contract

Void Contract

Voidable

Warranty of Merchantability

With Reserve

Without Reserve

CHAPTER 5

BUSINESS TORTS

*That great principle of the common law . . . declares that it is your
duty to use your own rights as not to cause injury to other people.*

—**Sir Charles Williams**
Grey v. North Eastern Rail Co.
48 L.T.R. 905 (1883)
"The Quotable Lawyer"

SECTION 5.1
THE LAW OF TORTS

A **tort** is a private civil wrong committed against another for which the
law provides an award of money damages. That wrong may also give rise
to criminal charges for which the remedy is incarceration. The law of torts
establishes standards of conduct for different types of activities ranging
from driving a car to owning an animal. These standards are established by
either the legislature or by the courts. Matters involving torts are generally
known as personal injury cases. An automobile accident or malpractice
claim are common examples. A person who commits a civil wrong is
labeled a **tortfeasor.**

A **business tort** deals with a variety of non-contractual claims that arise
in a business setting and involve a civil wrong committed by or against an
entity. These wrongdoings generally involve harm to a person or business
asset, such as a firm's business relationships with others or to its intellectual
property. Examples include products liability, interference with contractual
relations, fraud, and defamation.[1]

There are three categories of civil wrongs in a business setting: unintentional, intentional, and strict liability. An **unintentional tort** is conduct
that was not intended or planned by the performer, but whose actions have
harmed another. A driver who negligently operates a motor vehicle thereby
causing an accident is an example of this category. An **intentional tort**
is one that the wrongdoer does on purpose and includes such things as
defamation, invasion of privacy, battery, and false imprisonment. **Strict
liability** is that responsibility imposed upon a business regardless of the
care exercised or the precautions taken to prevent the harm. Such liability
may arise from the ownership of a dangerous animal such as a pet bear or
by selling a defective product such as a new car whose brakes fail.

Recoverable damages include lost wages, medical expenses, harm to property, and pain and suffering.

Statistically, tort cases are more likely than contract claims and in 76% of all jury trials, individuals sued other individuals or businesses. Motor vehicle lawsuits comprised 20% of tort trials, product liability 13%, and medical malpractice 10%.[2] Despite the large number of lawsuits filed each year, most settle before trial.

SECTION 5.2 NEGLIGENCE

Negligence is the most common tort and it deals with an unintentional wrong committed against or by a person or business entity. **Negligence,** generally speaking, is the failure to do what a reasonable person would do under the circumstances. While this definition may seem vague, several principles do emerge. The mere happening of an accident is not negligence. Rather, four elements must be present in order to establish an actionable claim:

1. A duty must be owed;
2. There must be a breach of that duty;
3. The negligence must be the proximate cause of the harm; and
4. The aggrieved party must sustain damages.

The plaintiff has the burden of proving all four elements by the preponderance of the evidence. Suppose Joe Roberts is stopped for a traffic light when the driver of a delivery truck loses control of his vehicle and rams the rear of Joe's car. The force of the impact propels Joe forward, and he sustains a whiplash type injury. Is the truck driver negligent? Yes. The truck driver owed a duty to drive his vehicle carefully and avoid hitting another vehicle. He breached that duty by striking the rear of the Roberts car. Finally, his negligence was the proximate cause of Joe's neck injury causing him to incur medical expenses and conscious pain and suffering.

Common negligence actions in a commercial setting include car accidents, slip and falls on a business premises and malpractice.

SECTION 5.3 DUTY OF CARE

Duty of care establishes the type of behavior a person must exhibit in a given situation. The basic rule is that a person must conform to the standard of care of a "reasonable person under the circumstances." This duty can vary from case to case depending upon the age of the person, his or her expertise, and the specific situation.

A. Standard of Care

Generally, the law does not make a distinction concerning the standard of care between adults of different ages. A 65-year-old man will be held to the same standard of care in driving a car as a person 16-years of age. That standard of care is simply the "average driver."

B. Malpractice

A professional is held to a higher standard of care when he or she is engaged in a professional capacity. This claim is called **malpractice,** and the defendant is held to the standard of care of the average professional. For example, a neurosurgeon who makes a mistake during surgery is held to the standard of care of the average neurosurgeon and not to the standard of care of the average person performing surgery—or even the average physician. The neurosurgeon has been selected because of this individual's specialized skill, so the doctor must possess and utilize the appropriate expertise of the average neurosurgeon.

The following is a sample jury instruction that a judge will deliver to a jury in a medical malpractice case involving a specialist, such as a neurosurgeon:

> "Ladies and gentlemen of the jury, a physician must have the same knowledge and skill and use the same care normally used in the medical profession. A physician whose conduct falls below this standard of care is negligent.

> A physician who professes to be a specialist in a particular field of medicine, such as a neurosurgeon, must have the same knowledge and skill and use the same care as others in that same medical specialty. A specialist whose conduct does not meet this professional standard of care is negligent.

> A physician must also keep informed of the contemporary developments in the medical profession's specialty and must use current skills and knowledge. In other words, a physician must have up-to-date medical skills and knowledge, and if she fails to keep current or fails to use current knowledge in the medical treatment of the patient, the physician is negligent.[3]"

Lawyers and physicians are not the only ones sued for malpractice. Accountants are also target defendants, and such claims occur when an accountant deviates from General Accepted Accounting Principles (GAAP), General Accepted Auditing Standards (GAAS) or rules of the American Institute of Certified Public Accountants (AICPA). If an accountant or auditor is negligent, or violates the rules of standard accounting practices and causes financial harm to a client, she can be held legally responsible.[4] For instance, an accountant commits malpractice if she provides a client with incorrect advice that requires the client to pay additional expenses or fines due to that incorrect accounting advice.[5]

Generally, an accountant must exercise a level of care, skill, and diligence commonly possessed by other members of their profession under like circumstances. Therefore, a successful malpractice action requires the plaintiff to prove: (1) the accountant owed a duty to the taxpayer, (2) there was a breach of that duty, (3) the plaintiff damages are the result of the negligence, and (4) there was a proximate cause between the injury and the duty owned by the accountant.[6]

Let us look at a tax return preparation claim and the elements of a negligence action. The first element of duty is usually memorialized in an **engagement letter** that sets forth the scope of the accountant's duties and responsibilities to the client. Alternatively, the accountant may orally agree to prepare the taxpayer's tax return and then undertakes that task. A breach of duty occurs when the tax preparer makes a significant mistake or omits important information that results in the submission of an incorrect tax return. The third element requires that the negligent failure of the accountant to fulfill her duties be the proximate cause of the harm, and finally, the client must suffer damages as the result of the mistake.[7] These have been calculated to be the difference between what clients would have owed if the tax return had been correctly prepared and what that person did owe as the result of the accountant's malpractice, plus incidental damages.[8]

An accountant does have several defenses to a malpractice action. These include denying that she failed to satisfy the professional standards, or arguing that the failure to satisfy the standards was not the proximate cause of the loss.[9]

C. Children

Children develop differently each year of their lives. There is a vast difference in the motor and intellectual skills between a child of six and a child of twelve. Therefore, minors arc held to a different standard than the average adult. A minor is held to the standard of care of a child of similar age, intelligence, and experience. The exception to this rule is when a child engages in **adult activity**, such as the driving of a car, operating a boat, or the flying of an airplane. In those cases, children are held to the standard of care of the average person.

The age of majority varies from state to state and country to country. In the United States, adulthood can legally begin anywhere between 18 to 21 depending upon the jurisdiction. A youth in Japan, however, achieves majority at 20, while a child in Italy is considered an adult at 18.

DEMERI, V. MORRIS
194 N. J. SUPER. 554 (1983)

An infant party in a negligence trial is entitled to an instruction that a jury must consider his age and intelligence, as well as his experience and capacity to understand and to avoid the danger to which he was exposed in the actual situation. Thus, a child's conduct is to be measured by what can be expected of the average child of the same age, having the same judgmental capacity. An exception to this general rule, however, is that an infant is to be held to an adult standard of care where he engages in an activity which may be dangerous to others and normally is undertaken only by adults. The adult standard is objective; the infant standard is more subjective. The precise issue before the Court is by what standard a jury should evaluate the conduct of a 12-year old child who operates a dirt bike on a public roadway where he is injured in a collision with an automobile?

Kenneth Demeri, the unlicensed infant plaintiff, was riding his unregistered, uninsured motorcycle in Lynn Park, which is owned and maintained by the Borough of Lincoln Park. This park land was regularly used by juveniles and others as a practice course over which to run their dirt bikes. When Kenneth's father observed the boy riding alone, he sent another Demeri child to order the boy home immediately. Kenneth had previously been instructed by his parents never to ride his motorcycle in the park without supervision.

To return home, it was necessary for Kenneth to cross Curtis Drive. Kenneth proceeded to drive across the paved surface of Curtis Drive toward his house and into the path of an oncoming automobile.

At about the same time, an automobile driven by Joseph Morris moved away from its parking place on Curtis Drive. Apparently, Morris had driven out from behind a legally parked car, which partially obscured his vehicle from view. Unfortunately, the predictable did occur: there was a collision between the car and Kenneth's dirt bike toward the middle of Curtis Drive. The impact produced severe and permanent injuries to Kenneth.

The Supreme Court has recognized "that certain activities [like snow skiing] engaged in by minors are so potentially dangerous as to require that the minor be held to an objective standard of care." When an infant engages in an activity normally undertaken only by adults and for which adult qualifications are required, legal fault must be evaluated in the context of the danger implicit in the activity, not the infant's perception of the danger or lack thereof.

Plaintiff contends that riding a dirt bike is a child's activity. Testimony did tend to establish that juveniles regularly used Lynn Park as a practice course for their motorcycles. Regardless of whether riding a dirt bike is an activity generally enjoyed by infants or adults, a dirt bike is a motor vehicle and the incident occurred on a public road. This activity is not only dangerous to the infant driver, but also creates a risk of harm to others. Once any individual chooses to operate a motor vehicle over a public thoroughfare, he must do so with alertness, perception and caution so as not to injure any other person who may be lawfully on the roadway.

The rule is consistent with the realities of modern traffic regulation and control because all drivers have the right to expect reasonable care from other drivers. They are entitled to assume that other persons using the roadway are capable and adult. No driver would have to anticipate that another motor vehicle is being operated by an unlicensed inexperienced infant. Public policy should require that all motor vehicles are to be operated in a uniformly reasonable safe manner on a highway.

Once an infant chooses to operate any motor vehicle over a public road, the standard of reasonable care applies. Children who drive negligently over a public road cannot benefit from their age. All must be judged by the same criterion. The jury will be charged that Kenneth's negligence must be tested by adult standard of reasonable care.

D. Failure to Establish a Standard of Care

Establishing a duty of care is an essential element in every claim for the tort of negligence. This duty can differ depending upon the circumstances. In carrying out the duties of one's trade, a professional is held to a higher standard than an average person and a child is generally held to a lower standard of care than an adult. It is not always possible, however, to establish that a duty of care is owed to a person just because an individual is harmed by the actions or lack of actions of another.

The practice of medicine is a collaborative effort with many physicians frequently providing input on the care of a patient. In this context, each physician owes a duty to exercise care in the rendering of services. Does a duty arise, however, if a treating physician asks a colleague to merely look at a patient's diagnostic films and to provide an opinion? That is the issue in **Ford v. Applegate.**

FORD V. APPLEGATE
2003 WL 22000379 (CAL. APP. 2 DIST. 2003)

Erin Ford appeals a grant of summary judgment in favor of defendant, Gregory Applegate, M.D., in an action for medical malpractice.

In April 1999, Ford, a high school basketball player, fell during a game and injured her knee. Ford was seen by Dr. McKeever for evaluation. Ford underwent an MRI of her right knee. The film was interpreted by Dr. Eto. Dr. Eto's impression was that there were changes in the anterior cruciate ligament suggesting a strain or partial tear.

On July 30, 1999, Dr. McKeever asked Dr. Applegate to look at Ford's film. Dr. Applegate reviewed the MRI and found Ford's "anterior cruciate ligament fully intact." Dr. McKeever included that finding in Ford's medical record. Dr. McKeever then diagnosed Ford's condition as a strain, rather than a tear.

However, Ford, in fact had a partial tear. According to Ford, Dr. Applegate's interpretation led to a delayed diagnosis of the tear, which went from a partial tear to the complete tear of the anterior cruciate ligament.

Ford filed this action against Drs. Applegate and McKeever alleging they were negligent in their diagnosis and treatment, causing her injuries and damages.

Dr. Applegate filed a motion for summary judgment on the ground there was no physician-patient relationship between him and Ford giving rise to a duty of care. Dr. Applegate asserted he never met, saw, examined or treated Ford, he never billed Ford or her insurance company for any care or treatment, he never prepared any medical reports, records or billings in reference to her, and he had no medical chart on her.

Ford contends a physician who is asked to consult in order to assist in making a diagnosis owes a duty of care to the patient and can be sued for medical malpractice.

Negligence is conduct which falls below the standard established by law for the protection of others against unreasonable risk of harm. In the medical malpractice context, liability arises where there is a relationship of physician-patient between the plaintiff and the defendant doctor; the relationship gives rise to the duty of care.

The practice of medicine is a collaborative endeavor. A radiologist, for example, reviews films some clinician has ordered, and a pathologist analyzes a tissue specimen or fluid another doctor has put into a container destined for the laboratory. Such physicians, like other health care providers who engage in serving as consultants in the care of other doctors' patients, as by performing diagnostic services or providing care of one form or another, become subject to liability for lapses committed in such services, if, of course, a physician-patient relationship has come into existence.

No physician-patient relationship arose between Dr. Applegate and Ford, where Dr. Applegate simply provided a colleague with an informal opinion but did not bill for his services, write a report or otherwise undertake to serve as Ford's physician. There is no indication in the record that Dr. Applegate ever billed Ford or her insurance company for any care or treatment. He did not prepare any medical reports, records or billings in reference to her, and he had no medical chart on her. The imposition of liability in these circumstances "would not be prophylactic" but instead counter-productive by stifling efforts at improving medical knowledge, and by extension, patient care.

For these reasons, we conclude that Dr. Applegate's rendering of an informal opinion to a colleague was insufficient to give rise to a physician-patient relationship and a duty of care owed to Ford.

E. Duty to Rescue

Does the law impose a duty upon a person to go to the aid of another? The cases are well documented of people who turn their back on victims of crimes, the injured and the sick. This conduct is morally and ethically reprehensible but is it actionable in a civil lawsuit? Generally, there is no legal duty to aid or protect another.

The law, however, does require a person who harms another or places another in a position of peril to go to that individual's assistance. A legal duty is also imposed where a special relationship exists between the parties. For example, a parent must go to the aid of a child, a spouse must help the other spouse, and an employer must protect an employee.

Must a physician, however, stop and render emergency aid to the victim of a car accident that he or she did not cause? Despite the doctor's specialized training, the answer is no. Physicians are reluctant to become involved because of the fear of being sued for medical malpractice. To encourage healthcare professionals to render emergency help, however, many states have passed **Good Samaritan Statutes,** which impose liability only in the event of gross misconduct.

The following law is an example of a Good Samaritan Statute:

> "Any physician or any other practitioner of the healing arts or any registered nurse, licensed by any state, who happens by chance upon the scene of an emergency or who is present when an emergency occurs and who, in good faith, renders emergency care at the scene of the emergency, shall not be liable for any civil damages as a result of any acts or omissions by such physician or practitioner or registered nurse in rendering the emergency care, except any acts or omissions intentionally designed to harm or any grossly negligent acts or omissions which result in harm to the person receiving emergency care."

This limited immunity also extends to a lay person rendering emergency aid if that individual possesses a current certificate evidencing the successful completion of a course in first aid or basic life support sponsored by the American National Red Cross or a similar organization. A lay person will not enjoy the protection of the Good Samaritan statute if the emergency aid extends beyond one's specialized training. For instance, a person trained in CPR cannot perform open-heart surgery or administer intravenous drugs to regulate the rhythm of the heart.

The Good Samaritan law is created by statute so one must always look at the applicable state law to see how it is phrased and whom it covers. While the protections afforded by these laws are normally limited to those who are medically trained, some legislatures have granted immunity to non-medically trained people when it comes to Automated External Defibrillators or AED devices. These portable units are designed to diagnose and treat certain heart conditions when the heart muscle goes into cardiac arrest. Because these devices come with instructions and are relatively easy to use Pennsylvania, for example, gives immunity to those who attempt to save a person's life by using an AED device even though he or she may not be medically trained. This exception was used in **Atcovitz V. Gulph Mills Tennis Club, Inc.** to try and impose a duty upon a tennis club for not keeping such a life saving device on its premises.

ATCOVITZ V. GULPH MILLS TENNIS CLUB, INC.
812 A.2D 1218 (PA. 2002)

On January 16, 1996, Jerry Atcovitz suffered a stroke, secondary to a heart attack, while playing tennis at the Gulph Mills Tennis Club. Within a minute of his collapse, two tennis club members administered cardiopulmonary resuscitation and called for an ambulance. Approximately ten minutes later, emergency medical technicians arrived and administered a series of defibrillation shocks with an AED and transported Atcovitz to a hospital. Although he survived the incident, Atcovitz sustained severe and permanent injuries.

Atcovitz sued Gulph Mills for negligence. Specifically, they claimed that, "had Gulph Mills possessed an AED device and used it on Atcovitz promptly, his injuries would have been significantly less. In its defense, Gulph Mills asserted that, at the time of Atcovitz's injury, its employees would not have been permitted by law to use an AED.

The court addressed the effect of the "AED Good Samaritan Act," which provides "Good Samaritan civil immunity" for use of an AED in certain instances. It specifically provides immunity for untrained individuals who, in good faith, use an AED in an emergency as an ordinary, reasonably prudent individual would do under the same or similar circumstances. Although the AED Good Samaritan Act was enacted after Atcovitz's injuries, the court found that its passage evinced the Legislature's desire that use of AEDs not be restricted solely to trained professionals.

Here, we must focus our analysis on the threshold element of duty. Only therein may we resolve the fundamental question of whether the plaintiff's interests are entitled to legal protection against the defendant's conduct.

A duty, in negligence cases, may be defined as an obligation, to which the law will give recognition and effect, to conform to a particular standard of conduct toward another. There is a duty if the court says there is a duty; the law, like the Constitution, is what we make it. Duty is only a word with which we state our conclusion that there is or is not to be liability; it necessarily begs the essential question. When we find a duty, breach and damage, everything has been said.

The Legislature's enactments and the ensuing regulations reveal that acquisition, maintenance, and use of an AED, along with AED training

requirements, are highly regulated. Where our lawmakers have so thoroughly considered the statewide application and implications of a subject, this Court must refrain from imposing additional requirements upon that legislation.

Looking first to the EMS Act, the Legislature aspired to assure readily available and coordinated emergency medical services of the highest quality to the people of Pennsylvania. The implication of the Legislature's exclusion of untrained laypersons from the EMS Act and its regulations is to preclude unqualified and untrained individuals from administering emergency medical services using an AED. It would be absurd for the governmental system charged with rendering effective emergency medical care to hinder the delivery of that care using AEDs through the system, while ordinary citizens would be duty-bound to acquire, maintain, and use AEDs free from any regulation by the Department of Health.

The AED Good Samaritan Act, which was adopted two years after Atcovitz sustained his injuries, provides civil immunity for *trained* users of AEDs and requires that "expected users shall complete training in the use of an AED. As an *exception* to that general rule, the AED Good Samaritan Act provides civil immunity to untrained individuals who, *in good faith*, use an AED in an emergency as an ordinary, reasonably prudent individual would do under the same or similar circumstances. Significantly, the AED Good Samaritan Act defines "good faith" as including "a reasonable opinion that *the immediacy of the situation is such that the use of an AED should not be postponed until emergency medical services personnel arrive* or the person is hospitalized."

Thus, the AED Good Samaritan Act merely creates an exception for imposing liability on an untrained individual who uses an AED in limited emergency situations; it does not *authorize* its use by any such individual.

Indeed, the exception applies only to instances where emergency medical services personnel are unavailable. In addition, it does not indicate that the Legislature aimed to dispense with the regulations governing the training and use of AEDs. Simply, the existence of a civil immunity provision for Good Samaritans who use an AED in an emergency situation cannot impose a duty on a business establishment to acquire, maintain, and use such a device on its premises.

The AED Good Samaritan Act does not impose a duty upon Gulph Mills to acquire, maintain, and use an AED. Plaintiff does not cite any other case, statute, or regulation that would have imposed such a duty on Gulph Mills at the time of Atcovitz's injuries in January 1996. Because Gulph Mills did not owe a duty to carry an AED, Appellees could not have established a *prima facie* claim of negligence. We reverse the order of the Superior Court and affirm the trial court's grant of summary judgment in favor of Gulph Mills.

F. Duty of Landowners

What duty does an owner or possessor of land owe to a person who comes upon the premises? The answer will depend on whether the individual is a trespasser, licensee, or business visitor.

A **trespasser** is one who comes upon the premises of another without consent and with no legal right to be on the property. For instance, a burglar is a trespasser. The only obligation a land-owner or possessor of property owes to a trespasser is to avoid injuring the person through willful and wanton misconduct. Suppose Joe Robert fills his pool with piranhas to keep trespassers out of the water. Will Joe be liable if someone climbs over the fence, dives into the water, and is attacked by the man-eating fish? According to **Katco v. Briney,** discussed earlier in this text, the answer is yes. The conduct of Joe Roberts is willful and wanton.

Because of the need to protect very young children, the **attractive nuisance doctrine** has been created to safeguard youngsters who trespass on the land of another that contains an inviting but dangerous condition. For example, if the land contains a dangerous condition that will naturally attract young children to it, the possessor of land owes a duty to eliminate or protect the minor from that risk. A swimming pool is considered such an attraction and property owners are mandated to erect fences around their pools.

A **licensee** is a person who comes on the property of another with the owner's consent or with the legal right to be on the land. The most common type of licensee is a social guest or a person walking on the sidewalk. The owner or possessor of land is liable to a licensee for a defect on the property that the owner or possessor of land knew of or should have known of, and the guest is not likely to discover. For example, if the owner of a house is having the basement steps repaired and fails to warn the licensee of the repairs, the owner is liable if the guest falls. On the other hand, a thief who breaks into the same house and falls down the basement steps will not collect damages from the homeowner, since the failure to warn the thief is not willful and wanton misconduct.

A **business visitor** is one who enters the premises for a business purpose. A person who goes to a department store is a business visitor. In these circumstances, the landowner or possessor of land is liable for a defect that he knew of or should have known of, and the visitor is not liable to discover. While this standard seems to be the same as that owed to a licensee, the difference is that the business establishment owes a duty to make a reasonable inspection of the premises to make sure it is safe for the business visitor.

Businesses open to the public, such as department stores, theaters, and food markets, are particularly susceptible to having debris strewn on the floor. The proprietor of such a business must maintain the premises in a reasonably safe condition. The mere fact that a harmful condition may exist on the property, however, does not establish negligence on the part of the store owner. The injured patron must prove that the dangerous condition existed for such a sufficient period of time that a reasonable inspection would have discovered the problem. For instance, a puddle of milk on the floor of a supermarket that is partially dried, filled with footprints, and contains shopping-cart wheel marks would establish constructive notice on the part of the merchant of the dangerous situation. After all, this condition could only occur after a lengthy passage of time. On the other hand, a puddle of white milk that was not created by the actions of the merchant and is not soiled in any way would indicate a very recent spill for which the supermarket will have no liability.

DUFFY V. KINNAMON
2017 WL 5615772 (CT. APP. MICH. 2017)

Plaintiff was in Defendant's backyard sitting by a fire that had been made in Defendant's fire pit. The fire pit had been constructed that day. The area around the fire pit was covered with gravel. In fact, Plaintiff had helped spread and pat down that gravel the previous day.

On the night she fell, Plaintiff and Defendant were sitting in chairs by the fire pit. At some point, Plaintiff felt too hot and decided to move her chair further away from the fire. Plaintiff stood up, then turned around to grab the arms of the chair to move it. As she leaned over to take ahold of the chair, her feet started sliding backwards on the gravel, down a slight slope, until she lost her balance and fell backwards into the fire pit causing her to sustain significant burns.

Subsequently, Plaintiff sued Defendant. In particular, Plaintiff alleged that Defendant knew or should have known that the gravel immediately adjacent to the fire pit was unstable but failed to warn or protect Plaintiff from the dangerous condition.

Plaintiff argued that the gravel that was on the ground around the fire pit was unstable yet uniform in appearance which created an unreasonably dangerous, and not an open and obvious condition. By the very nature of gravel, it blends together so that an area that is sloped is not readily observable. Consequently, when Plaintiff attempted to move her chair, she slid backwards on the gravel, down the slight slope, lost her balance, and fell into the fire pit.

In a premises liability action, a plaintiff must prove that the defendant owed the plaintiff a duty, which was breached, and was the proximate cause of the plaintiff's injury and damages. The nature of the duty owed by the defendant depends on the status of the plaintiff visitor at the time of the injury. In this case, it is undisputed that Plaintiff was a social guest at Defendant's home so she was a licensee and not a business invitee or an uninvited trespasser. A landowner owes a licensee a duty only to warn the licensee of any hidden dangers the owner knows or has reason to know of, if the licensee does not know or have reason to know of the dangers involved. The landowner owes no duty of inspection or affirmative care to make the premises safe for the licensee's visit. Premises possessors are not insurers charged with a duty to guarantee the safety of all persons who come on their land.

Accordingly, a landowner has no duty to warn or protect a licensee from open and obvious conditions because "the 'open and obvious' danger principle establishes awareness and thus ability to avoid the danger."

A danger is considered "open and obvious" if it is reasonable to expect that an average person with ordinary intelligence would have discovered it upon casual inspection. In this case, the allegedly dangerous condition was the gravel surrounding the fire pit which was uniform in appearance yet unstable and slightly sloped toward the fire pit; thus, when plaintiff attempted to move her chair, her feet slid backward on the gravel toward the fire pit, causing her to lose her balance and fall. Plaintiff knew or had reason to know of the slippery or unstable nature of the gravel because she admittedly had spread it, patted it down, and walked on it before her accident. Plaintiff would have seen that gravel is made of small round stones which make a fluid, non-flat surface and, when it is stepped on, it moves under the feet. She would have also seen that the gravel was not compacted or completely level like a concrete base or patio might be made—regardless of the gravel's allegedly uniform-appearing surface. And to the extent that Plaintiff claims there was any other "hidden danger" associated with the gravel, Plaintiff failed to establish that Defendant knew or had reason to know of it. Further, to the extent that the gravel surrounding the fire pit could be considered a "dangerous condition," it was open and obvious. That is, an average person with ordinary intelligence would have discovered—even at a casual glance—that the pea gravel was not a solid surface; rather, it was a fluid, non-flat, unstable surface made of small round stones about the size of peas.

The defendant's motion for summary disposition is granted.

G. Willful and Wanton Misconduct

Occasionally, a party will be charged with **willful and wanton misconduct.** This is different from negligence, not just in degree but also in kind. Negligence connotes a certain amount of inadvertence. Willful and wanton misconduct goes beyond ordinary negligence and expresses some design or purpose. An individual whose conduct is willful and wanton intends his act but not the resulting harm.[10] As noted by the Restatement Second of Torts:

> "The actor's conduct is in reckless disregard of the safety of another if he does an act or intentionally fails to do an act which it is his duty to the other to do, knowing or having reason to know of facts which would lead a reasonable man to realize, not only that his conduct creates an unreasonable risk of physical harm to another, but also that such risk is substantially greater than that which is necessary to make his conduct negligent."

An example of reckless conduct is an intoxicated driver who kills someone in a motor vehicle accident or a homeowner who sets up a shotgun to protect his property from a thief. The significance of a finding of willful and wanton misconduct is that it gives rise to punitive damages, a sum of money to publish the defendant for the wrongdoing.

H. Dram Shop Liability

A bar, restaurant or tavern has a financial incentive to sell patrons as much liquor as possible. An intoxicated patron, however, creates a risk to both himself and to others. To strike a balance between sales and safety, the courts and legislatures have created **dram shop liability.** This refers to civil liability imposed upon a commercial seller of alcoholic beverages. Basically, the law imposes liability upon a commercial seller of liquor for personal injury caused by an intoxicated customer.[11]

Dram shop is a term of art, meaning a bar, tavern or other establishment where alcoholic beverages are sold. Dram refers to a unit of liquid measure used during colonial times. At common law, a bar had no responsibility for the consequences of serving alcohol to an intoxicated person who later is injured or hurts someone else. First, courts viewed the act of drinking the alcohol, as opposed to the act of selling the liquor, as the proximate cause of the person's intoxication. After all, an able bodied person should be responsible for his own actions. Second, even if the sale of liquor was the proximate cause of the drunkenness, an injury to a third person was an unforeseeable result of the person's intoxication.[12]

As public's awareness of the harm created by furnishing alcohol to irresponsible persons increased, states began to depart from the rule of no-liability through legislative enactments of dram shop statutes. For example, Pennsylvania adopted a dram shop law in 1854 and made it a misdemeanor to provide intoxicating beverages to "any person of known intemperate habits, to a minor, or to an insane person . . . or to any person when drunk or intoxicated."[13]

Pennsylvania's has modified this law over the years. The current legislation provides:

> "No licensee shall be liable to third persons on account of damages inflicted upon them off of the licensed premises by customers of the licensee unless the customer who inflicts the damages was sold, furnished or given liquor or brewed beverages by the said licensee when the customer was visibly intoxicated."

One might wonder how a plaintiff establishes that a bar served liquor to a visible intoxicated patron. That is the issue in the following case.

SCHUENEMANN V. DREEMZ, LLC
34 A.3D 94 (PA. SUPER., 2011)

On November 4, 2006, Brynne Schuenemann ("decedent"), consumed alcohol at Dreemz, a bar in Philadelphia. After leaving Dreemz, the decedent drove her vehicle into a pole, and died minutes after first responders arrived.

Raymond Schuenemann filed a complaint seeking damages against Dreemz for having sold alcoholic beverages to decedent when she was visibly intoxicated under the Pennsylvania Dram Shop Act which prohibits liquor establishments from serving alcohol to visibly intoxicated persons.

A jury trial returned a verdict in favor of plaintiff, awarding damages of $1,964,758.

The Dram Shop Act imposes a duty on liquor licensees to refrain from selling liquor to a visibly intoxicated individual. Thus, where those on whom a duty has been imposed not to serve visibly intoxicated patrons, breach that duty, those persons may be responsible where their actions are found to be a substantial factor in causing an injury. By imposing potential liability on employees of a licensee who are responsible for making the determination of whether a patron is visibly intoxicated, there is a better chance that patrons will not be served when they should not be served. Under the Dram Shop provisions of the Liquor Code, liquor licensees are entrusted with monitoring the patrons to whom they serve alcohol, in order to detect visible signs of intoxication.

Dreemz argues that trial court improperly allowed plaintiff to offer testimony regarding the legal limit for blood alcohol content (BAC). Dreemz asserts that the Vehicle Code, which prohibits individuals with a BAC of over .08 from operating motor vehicles, is a standard pertaining to criminal cases, and had no relevance in the present case. Dreemz contends that testimony that the legal BAC limit in Pennsylvania for operation of a vehicle is .08 was highly prejudicial, and contrary to law prohibiting the introduction of such evidence in civil actions.

The theory behind allowing a blood alcohol level to be admitted into evidence in a civil case is that it is relevant circumstantial evidence relating to intoxication. However, blood alcohol level alone may not be admitted for the purpose of proving intoxication. There must be other evidence showing the actor's conduct which suggests intoxication.

In the present case, the references to the decedent's BAC level were made by plaintiff's expert, Dr. John DiGregorio. Specifically, Dr. DiGregorio testified that the decedent had a BAC level of 0.22 and that the legal limit in Pennsylvania for operation of a motor vehicle is 0.08. Dr. DiGregorio testified extensively about the visible effects of alcohol consumption, including the manner in which alcohol would have impaired the decedent's motor functions, resulting in her exhibiting slurred speech, "wobbling back and forth" and "swaying",

in support of his opinion that the decedent was visibly intoxicated. Moreover, Jasmine Childs, a friend of the decedent, testified that the decedent "bought multiple rounds of alcohol" and while at Dreemz was "loud" "stumbling" and slurring her speech while still buying drinks from the bar. Justin Witt, a friend of the decedent, testified the decedent was "bumping into people," unsteady on her feet, had "glossy . . . almost closing eyes" and was "sluggish" and "sloppy." Dr. DiGregorio testified that the descriptions of the decedent were consistent with the behavior exhibited by a person who is visibly intoxicated. We conclude that the trial court acted within its discretion in admitting as relevant the evidence of the decedent's BAC level. Moreover, in light of the extensive testimony regarding the decedent's conduct and behavior while at Dreemz and her display of visible signs of intoxication, any error resulting from the introduction of testimony about the legal BAC limit for operating a vehicle in Pennsylvania was harmless.

SECTION 5.4
TYLER'S SPORTS BAR AND GRILL

PROBLEM FIVE—A

PARK, BROWN & SMITH, P.C.
ATTORNEYS AT LAW
MEMORANDUM

TO: The Law Clerks

FROM: Peter Smith, Esquire

RE: Estate of Robert Jones v. Tyler's Sports Bar and Grill

As you know, Joe Roberts has an interest in Tyler's Sports Bar and Grill. In order to create an identity, Tyler's only serves poultry that has been specially bred by the Pennsylvania Dutch to reduce its fat content. The chicken and turkey are also served with the skin removed, thereby eliminating unnecessary calories. In any event, Mr. Roberts called me this morning with his latest crisis. It seems that a customer died in the Sports Bar while eating the grilled chicken special, and Tyler's has received a letter of representation from an attorney threatening suit. Roberts conveyed the following facts to me.

Donny Jones was a frequent customer at the restaurant and always ordered the grilled chicken special. Two weeks ago, Jones entered the Sports Bar but seemed out of sorts. His clothes were disheveled and he was unshaven. He staggered to his usual table and reeked of liquor. His normal food order was delivered and Jones bit into a piece of chicken. All of a sudden, Jones seemed to get sick. His face changed colors; he grabbed his throat, and slumped over in his chair. A fellow customer screamed at the sight, and Roberts ran over to the table. The owner checked the customer's vital signs, and noted that Jones' pulse was weak and irregular. Joe immediately called for an ambulance which arrived in minutes. The paramedics' efforts to save Jones, however, were to no avail, and he died. An autopsy determined the cause of death to be an obstruction to the decedent's airway caused by a chicken bone that had become lodged in the decedent's throat. The coroner's report further noted that Jones had a blood/alcohol content of 0.24% which is well above the legal limit for intoxication. Finally, the pathologist opined that it is not unusual for an extremely intoxicated person to choke to death on food.

Joe has learned that a physician was in the restaurant during the incident and did nothing to help out. In fact, Jones was a patient of this surgeon. When questioned by the police as to why he didn't assist the choking victim, the doctor stated that he was eating dinner and was tired after playing a full day of golf in the sun.

The attorney for the Estate of Mr. Jones claims that the bar did not exercise reasonable care to save its customer. It is asserted that not only should Joe have used the "Heimlich" maneuver on the customer, but the restaurant's staff knew that Jones had ordered chicken so the manager should have looked into the decedent's mouth to make sure that nothing was lodged in the customer's throat.

I am not sure if the lawyer also sent a letter to the surgeon about the physician's failure to help his patient. If the attorney does not name the physician in the lawsuit, I will join the doctor into the lawsuit as an additional defendant. At least the owner of Tyler's attempted to help the decedent while the doctor continued to eat his food unconcerned with the health of his patient.

Please discuss the issues and defenses on behalf of all parties. Will the family of the decedent be successful in recovering money from either Tyler's or the doctor?

PROBLEM FIVE—A
ANSWER SHEET

Name _____ **Please Print Clearly**

1. What duties did the bar owe to the decedent?

_____

_____

_____

_____

_____

_____

_____

_____

_____

_____

_____

_____

_____

_____

_____

_____

_____

_____

_____

2. What duty did the surgeon owe to his patient?

_____

_____

_____

_____

_____

_____

_____

_____

3. Who will win the lawsuit? Explain your answer in detail.

_____

_____

_____

_____

_____

_____

_____

_____

_____

SECTION 5.5
BREACH OF DUTY

The second element of a negligence action is quite simple. If a duty is owed, and a person fails to fulfill that obligation, a **breach of duty** has occurred. For example, a property owner owes a duty to a business visitor to make the property safe. This includes the obligation to inspect the premises on a reasonable basis. If a business establishment does not inspect its facility, and a business visitor is injured because a broken bottle or wet spot on the floor is not cleaned up in sufficient time, the store owner has breached its duty of care.

SECTION 5.6
PROXIMATE CAUSE

Proximate cause requires that there be a reasonable connection between the negligence of the defendant and the harm suffered by the plaintiff. The fact that a party is careless and another suffers an injury is not by itself enough to impose liability. Rather, the negligent conduct must be a **substantial factor** in causing the harm. For instance, a surgeon who leaves an instrument in a patient's abdomen following surgery has obviously breached the duty of exercising reasonable medical care. The patient's need for additional surgery to remove the medical instrument would be directly related to the doctor's malpractice.

The driver of a car traveling 90 m.p.h. down the opposite side of the road is negligent. Suddenly, a wheel from an airplane flying overhead falls off and kills the passenger in the speeding automobile. While the driver of the car is operating the vehicle in a negligent fashion, that negligence is not the proximate cause of the passenger's death. The falling wheel from the airplane is the substantial factor in causing the harm.

Obesity has become a major health issue in today's society with nearly twice as many overweight children than there were twenty years ago. McDonald's Corporation aggressively targets youngsters in their marketing campaigns and makes their stores children-friendly in order to entice families to visit their restaurants.

Fast food products offered by McDonald's come at a nutritional price. Supersized french fries weigh in at 610 calories and 29 grams of total fat. A Big Mac tips the scales at 590 calories with 34 grams of fat. Topping off a meal with a Nestle Crunch McFlurry adds an additional 630 calories and 24 grams of fat. However, this information is generally not readily available in the restaurants or on the food wrappers. For the most part, consumers have no idea of the ingredients or nutritional value of what they order.

A class action lawsuit was filed against McDonald's on behalf of overweight children alleging that the fast-food chain is engaged in deception in the making and selling of its products and that this wrongful conduct has caused the minors who consume McDonald's products to harm their health by becoming obese. McDonald's objected to the lawsuit and claimed that the plaintiffs failed to establish a causal connection between their obesity and the consumption of McDonald's fast food products. The court's ruling is contained in **Pellman v. McDonald's Corporation.**

PELLMAN V. McDONALD'S CORPORATION
237 F. SUPP. 2D 512 (S.D. N.Y. 2003)

The plaintiffs have alleged that the practices of McDonald's in making and selling their products are deceptive and that this deception has caused the minors who have consumed McDonalds' products to injure their health by becoming obese.

Americans spend more than $110 billion on fast food each year, and on any given day in the United States, almost one in four adults visit a fast food restaurant.

Today there are nearly twice as many overweight children and almost three times as many overweight adolescents as there were in 1980. Obese individuals have a 50 to 100 percent increased risk of premature death from all causes.

The plaintiffs allege five causes of action as members of a class action of minors who have purchased and consumed McDonald's products. Count III sounds in negligence, alleging that McDonald's acted negligently in selling food products that are high in cholesterol, fat, salt and sugar when studies show that such foods cause obesity and detrimental health effects.

Plaintiffs argue that McDonalds' products have been so altered that their unhealthy attributes are now outside the ken of the average reasonable consumer. They point to McDonalds' ingredient lists to show that McDonalds' customers worldwide are getting much more than what is commonly considered to be a chicken finger, a hamburger, or a french fry.

McDonald's argues that Count III should be dismissed because the plaintiffs may not as a matter of law allege that the unhealthy attributes of McDonalds' products were the proximate cause of their obesity and other health problems.

In order to show proximate cause, a plaintiff must establish that the defendant's conduct was a substantial cause in bringing about the harm. The issue of proximate cause may be determined as a matter of law where no reasonable person could find causation based on the facts alleged in the complaint. E.g., No reasonable person could find probable cause based on the facts in the Complaint without resorting to "wild speculation."

First, the Complaint does not specify how often the plaintiffs ate at McDonald's. The class action proposed by plaintiffs could consist entirely of persons who ate at McDonald's on one occasion. As a result, any number of other factors then potentially could have affected the plaintiffs' weight and health.

Second, McDonald's points out that articles on which plaintiffs rely in their Complaint suggest that a number of factors other than diet may come into play in obesity and the health problems of which plaintiffs complain. Obesity is a complex multifactorial disease developing from interactive influences of numerous factors—social behavioral, physiological, metabolic, cellular, and molecular in addition to cultural and genetic factors.

As a result, in order to allege that McDonalds' products were a significant factor in the plaintiffs' obesity and health problems, the Complaint must address these other variables and, if possible, eliminate them or show that a McDiet is a substantial factor despite these other variables.

Because the Complaint fails to allege that the danger of the McDonalds' products were not well-known and fails to allege with sufficient specificity that the McDonalds' products were a proximate cause of the plaintiffs' obesity and health problems, Count III shall be dismissed. Leave is granted to replead all claims.

SECTION 5.7
DAMAGES

The last element of a claim is **damages.** This is the amount of money awarded to an injured person as the result of the wrongful or improper conduct of the defendant. This recovery may take the form of compensatory and punitive damages.

The purpose of compensatory damages is to make an injured party whole by providing a sum of money that will return the aggrieved party to a position as though nothing had ever happened. These damages must always bear a reasonable relationship to the negligent act of the defendant, and cannot be speculative. In a tort action, the damages should place the injured party in as substantially good a position as that occupied before the injury. These damages, however, are not always easy to quantify. While one may quantify the amount of lost wages, how much is a broken arm worth? Would it matter if the injured party is a painter or professional quarterback?

Reasonable people can differ on the value of a case but the following elements may be considered in arriving at a dollar figure: medical expenses, lost wages, property damages, and pain and suffering.

Pain and suffering is the most controversial of the recoverable items because it is subjective and cannot be calculated with mathematical certainty. The value of each case will also change depending upon the circumstances. For instance, if the victim of a broken arm makes a good recovery after six weeks, the case will have one value. If the injury, however, results in permanent impairment in the person's range of motion with continuing pain upon elevating the arm, it is worth a much larger sum of money.

Punitive damages may be claimed if the conduct of the wrongdoer is outrageous. In that event, the law will punish the party by awarding an additional sum of money to prevent the conduct from ever occurring again. For instance, an automobile accident that occurs because the driver simply failed to see a stop sign is insufficient to give rise to punitive damages. Punitive damages, however, may be awarded if the accident was caused by a driver's intoxication.

Do you believe a punitive damage award of $150 million is excessive for a woman who died of cancer that she developed from smoking low tar cigarettes? That is the issue in **Schwartz v. Philip Morris.**

SCHWARTZ V. PHILIP MORRIS
272 OR. APP. 268 (2015)

Michelle Schwarz began smoking cigarettes in 1964 when she was 18-years old. She attempted to quit smoking numerous times but was unable to do so. In 1976, Defendant introduced a new product, Merit cigarettes. Advertisements for the new brand touted that the cigarettes contain less tar than existing 'full flavor' cigarettes but still tasted like the full-flavor brands. Out of a belief that low tar and nicotine filters are better for you, decedent switched to the low-tar Merit brand. After switching brands, decedent continued to smoke the same quantity of cigarettes—approximately one pack per day—but subconsciously altered her method of smoking. She took longer puffs, inhaled the smoke more deeply, and held it longer in her lungs. At the age of 53, decedent died from a brain tumor that was the result of metastatic lung cancer.

The method of smoking that decedent had adopted after switching to Defendant's low-tar brand was consistent with the behavior of smokers generally. Persons addicted to nicotine in cigarettes tend to develop a certain comfort level of nicotine, and, when smoking cigarettes that contain less nicotine, those smokers are likely to compensate—that is, adjust subconsciously the manner in which they smoke—in order to achieve that comfort level. Compensation causes smokers of low-tar cigarettes to inhale the same levels of tar, the primary carcinogen found in cigarettes, as they would ingest by smoking a full-flavored brand. Defendant was aware of the phenomenon. A primary purpose of defendant's decision to bring low-tar cigarettes to market was to give smokers what one tobacco executive labeled a crutch, that is, a product that enabled smokers to rationalize continued indulgence of a habit that they otherwise would consider to be deadly.

Defendant's behavior with respect to the development and marketing of low-tar cigarettes was but one iteration of a larger pattern of deceiving smokers and the rest of the public about the dangers of smoking. Beginning in the mid–1950s when reports first emerged about a link between smoking and lung cancer and other deadly diseases and enduring throughout decedent's smoking life, Defendant conspired with other cigarette manufacturers to wage a massive disinformation campaign designed to create the perception of uncertainty about the health risks of cigarettes, when in fact research by those same tobacco companies confirmed the adverse health consequences of smoking.

At trial, the jury awarded $168,514 in compensatory damages, and punitive damages of $150 million. The jury heard evidence relating to Defendant's financial condition. According to Plaintiff's expert, Defendant is extremely strong financially. In the several years before trial, its net earnings had been several billion dollars per year. For example, according to the expert, Defendant's earnings in 2010 were $3.3 billion, with net daily earnings for that period at a little over $9 million, and Defendant is worth approximately $50 billion.

On appeal, Defendant contends that the punitive damages award is "arbitrary and excessive. In particular, Defendant asserts that the "record cannot support anything more than a nominal award" of punitive damages and that any amount above a nominal award was arbitrary. Defendant further argues that, even if the jury could award "some non-negligible amount of punitive damages, the amount it did award was excessive."

In a civil case, punitive damages are recoverable only where it has been proven by clear and convincing evidence that the party against whom punitive damages are sought has acted with malice or has shown a reckless and outrageous indifference to a highly unreasonable risk of harm and has acted with a conscious indifference to the health, safety and welfare of others.

If an award of punitive damages is made by a jury, the court shall review the award to determine whether the award is within the range of damages that a rational juror would be entitled to award based on the record as a whole, viewing the statutory and common-law factors that allow an award of punitive damages for the specific type of claim at issue in the proceeding.

In this case, the jury was entitled to conclude that Defendant's conduct was extraordinarily reprehensible. As a result of Defendant's fraud, Plaintiff suffered injury and death. Likewise, Defendant's conduct demonstrated indifference to or reckless disregard for the health or safety of others. Defendant marketed its low-tar brand of cigarettes—a product Defendant knew to have deadly health consequences—to convince smokers that there was a reasonable alternative to quitting smoking. Furthermore, the conduct at issue was not merely an isolated incident; rather, it was one part of a concerted decades-long effort to deceive smokers and the public about the dangers of smoking, and to keep them smoking by falsely representing low-tar cigarettes to be safer and healthier. There was evidence that Defendant's low-tar representations had been made countless times over many years, and that Defendant continued to market cigarettes as "light" or "low tar" until prohibited by law in 2010.

Here, Defendant engaged in fraudulent conduct—it made false representations, either recklessly or knowing those representations were false, with the intent to mislead Michelle Schwarz. And those misrepresentations resulted in Michelle Schwarz's death.

In sum, we conclude that the jury's award of punitive damages was not arbitrary or excessive.

**SECTION 5.8
DEFENSES TO A
NEGLIGENCE ACTION**

Even though a defendant is negligent, an injured party's own conduct may preclude recovery. Two defenses to a negligence action are contributory negligence and assumption of the risk.

Contributory negligence is the failure of the plaintiff to act as a reasonable person under the circumstances. A driver who fails to stop for a red light is negligent. While the operator of the vehicle with the green light has the right of way, that driver may not blindly proceed through the intersection without first looking to the left and right. If the two vehicles collide, and neither driver looked for the other, they are both negligent. Since the individual who went through the red light bears the bulk of the liability, can the other motorist collect damages? No. A plaintiff may not recover if he or she has any degree of contributory negligence, even if that fault is 1%

of the responsibility for the accident. Only a handful of jurisdictions follow this harsh rule such as North Carolina, Virginia, Alabama, Maryland and the District of Columbia.

Most jurisdictions find this principle too harsh and have adopted a modified concept called **comparative negligence.** Basically, as long as the plaintiff's negligence is not greater than that of the defendant, the plaintiff may recover damages, but the verdict will be reduced by the percentage of the plaintiff's negligence. In other words, if the plaintiff is found to be 30% at fault and the verdict is $10,000, the award will be reduced to $7,000.

If the plaintiff and defendant are found to be equally at fault, the plaintiff will receive one-half of the verdict, since the plaintiff's negligence is not greater than that of the other responsible party. If the plaintiff, however, is found to be 51% at fault, the claimant will receive nothing, since his negligence is greater than that of the defendant.

LOPA v. McGEE
373 Pa. Super. 85 (1988)

On September 16, 1983, Mr. Lopa filed a complaint against Maureen and Charles McGee seeking to recover for personal injuries and property damage which he suffered as a result of a motor vehicle accident. Mr. McGee filed a counterclaim to recover property damages arising out of the same incident. The accident occurred at the intersection of Trenton Road and Forsythia Drive South in Levittown, Bucks County. Mr. Lopa and Ms. McGee were approaching the intersection from opposite directions on Trenton Road. As Mr. Lopa proceeded on his motorcycle through the intersection, he was struck by the car driven by Ms. McGee, as it made a left turn. The accident occurred at dusk.

After a non-jury trial, the court found that Mr. Lopa was negligent because his motorcycle headlight was not illuminated so that he was not properly visible. In addition, the judge found that Ms. McGee was negligent because there was sufficient light for her to have seen Mr. Lopa if she had looked carefully and properly. Then, applying the Comparative Negligence Act, the court held that fifty percent of the causal negligence was attributable to Mr. Lopa and fifty percent attributable to Ms. McGee. Having made this assessment, Judge Rufe then found for Maureen and Charles McGee on Mr. Lopa's claim, and for Mr. Lopa on Mr. McGee's claim.

Mr. Lopa does not dispute the trial court's findings of fact; rather, he argues that the only logical conclusion that flows from them is that Ms. McGee was more negligent than he was. We disagree with this contention. The facts as found by the trial court can undoubtedly support the trial court's apportionment of negligence between the parties. The trial court stated: "Although Ms. McGee did not maintain a careful and proper lookout, had

Mr. Lopa been driving with his motorcycle head-light illuminated, he would have been more visible to Ms. McGee. In short, we find that the negligence of Mr. Lopa and Ms. McGee were substantial contributing factors to the accident and that established Mr. Lopa's contributory negligence to be fifty percent. Thus, we see no injustice in finding Mr. Lopa fifty percent negligent." We are unable to ascertain any valid reason that would support our overturning the trial court's apportionment of negligence.

Pennsylvania's Comparative Negligence statute states as follows:

(a) General rule.-In all actions brought to recover damages for negligence resulting in death or injury to person or property, the fact that the plaintiff may have been guilty of contributory negligence *shall not bar a recovery by the plaintiff or his legal representative where such negligence was not greater than the causal negligence of the defendant or defendants against whom recovery is sought*, but any damages sustained by the plaintiff shall be diminished in proportion to the amount of negligence attributed to the plaintiff. 42 Pa. C. S. § 7102

Applying the plain wording of the statute, recovery is barred only when a plaintiff is more negligent than the defendant or defendants. Since Mr. Lopa was fifty percent negligent and Ms. McGee was fifty percent negligent, Mr. Lopa's negligence was not greater than the causal negligence of Ms. McGee. Accordingly, we find that Mr. Lopa is entitled to recover fifty-percent of his damages.

The second defense to a negligence action is **assumption of the risk.** If the plaintiff knows of the danger but voluntarily exposes himself to the harm, the plaintiff will be barred from recovery. For example, if a person jumps over an open manhole instead of walking around it, he will have assumed the risk of injury if he falls into the unguarded hole.

Over the years, a number of lawsuits have been filed for injuries to spectators at sporting events who are hit by flying objects such as baseballs or hockey pucks. This type of claim is generally unsuccessful because the risks are well known and inherent to the event. Most people who attend baseball games are aware that foul balls are hit into the stands on a regular basis. The allure of catching one of these errant balls is also part of the fun of attending the game.

To reinforce the awareness of the danger for purpose of assumption of the risk, the reverse side of an event ticket will contain a warning concerning the danger of flying objects leaving the playing field. The awareness of this danger is reinforced when the announcer repeats the warning over the public address system both before and during the game. For instance, the hockey ticket provided by the Philadelphia Flyers provides on the reverse side:

> Pucks flying into spectator areas can cause serious injury. Be alert when in spectator areas, including after the stoppage of play. If injured, notify an usher for directions to medical station. Ticket holder assumes all risks and dangers of personal injury and all other hazards arising from or related in any way to the event for which this ticket is issued, whether occurring prior to, during or after the event, including, specifically (but not exclusively), the danger of being injured by hockey pucks and sticks, and other spectators or players or by thrown objects. Ticket Holder agrees that the Spectrum Arena Limited Partners, the National Hockey League, Comcast–Spectacor, L.P., the Philadelphia Flyers, the playing teams, the players and the officers, employees and agents of each are expressively released by Ticket Holder from claims arising from or in any way related to the foregoing causes . . .

Before and during the game, the Flyers' announcer also warns fans about the danger of pucks leaving the playing surface and that fans should be vigilant of this risk at all times.

Does a fan, however, assume the risk of injury when she is injured while other fans wildly chase a foul baseball that goes into the stands or by a football that sails over the end zone safety net and into the seats? In other words, should the management of a stadium be liable for failing to protect a fan from the unruly actions of people who will do anything, including knocking people over, in their pursuit of a souvenir ball? This is the issue in the following case.

MITCHELL TELEGA V. SECURITY BUREAU, INC.
719 A.2D 372 (PA. SUPER. 1998)

Mitchell Telega and his wife, Karen, attended a Pittsburgh Steelers football game on December 6, 1992. For approximately two years, the Telegas were season ticket holders whose seats were located in Section 41, the pie-shaped end-zone section of the stadium behind the Steelers' goalpost. During the last quarter of the game, the Steelers' kicker attempted a field goal. The football was catapulted through the uprights of the goalpost, over the stadium net designed to catch it, and into the stands. Mr. Telega, who saw the ball coming his way, stood up in front of his assigned seat, extended his arms, and cleanly fielded the football. When he attempted to sit down, Mr. Telega was thrust from his seat and trampled face first into the cement aisle by aggressive fans who stripped him of the souvenir ball. Mr. Telega suffered numerous injuries from this attack, including facial lacerations, a sprained shoulder and arm resulting in extensive physical therapy, and a broken nose that required surgery.

Prior to this incident, the Telegas and other patrons seated in the end zone section of the stadium lodged complaints with the stadium's Guest Relations Office and security personnel concerning the lack of security and crowd control in their seating area during field goal and extra point attempts. They often complained that the football regularly clears the catch net, lands in the stands, and causes a disturbance among the fans, resulting in a danger to the welfare of the patrons seated in their section.

Appellants filed a complaint asserting a cause of action in negligence against Security Bureau, Inc. alleging that the defendants breached a duty of care owed to Mr. Telega by, failing to supervise security guards at the Stadium and failing to regulate crowd control in the end-zone seating area.

Our courts have long refused to grant recovery for injuries sustained by amusement patrons, which were caused by a risk inherent in the activity in question. The Court has also denied recovery where a spectator at a stockcar race track was struck by one of the racing vehicles while he was standing in the unprotected "pit" area of the track; the patron admitted that his presence in the pit area was unauthorized and that collisions in this area were common.

The question before this Court is whether a spectator will be held to assume as inherent in the game the risk of being attacked by displaced fans if he catches a soaring football. We believe not.

The risk involved here is unlike the risk of being struck by an errant puck while a spectator at a hockey game, falling down or being bumped by other skaters at a roller skating rink, or being hit by a batted ball during baseball tryouts. Contrary to the instant matter, these cases involve risks that are inherent in the activity itself and are specific to the activity at any appropriate venue. They are, therefore, as a matter of law, risks assumed by the spectators and participants who patronize the amusement facilities. It is not a matter of universal knowledge that an onslaught of displaced fans is a common, frequent or expected occurrence to someone catching a souvenir football. Therefore, it cannot be said that the injuries suffered by Mr. Telega resulted from a risk that any spectator would be held to anticipate and against which an amusement facility has no duty to protect. Certainly this matter would compel a different result had Mr. Telega been injured by the aerial football itself rather than the displaced fans intent on obtaining it.

Therefore, the trial court committed an error of law and we must reverse.

SECTION 5.9 IMPUTED NEGLIGENCE

Imputed negligence or **vicarious liability** means that because of a special relationship that exists between the parties, one person can be held liable for the negligence of the other. The classic example of such a relationship is that of employer and employee. Even though the employer has done nothing wrong, he or she will be responsible for the torts of their employees that were committed within the scope of the employment. For example, a bus company will be liable for an accident caused by the negligence of a bus driver. However, the bus company will generally not be liable for the assault of a customer by a bus driver since an assault is beyond the scope of the employment.

An employer will also not be liable for the torts of an **independent contractor.** An independent contractor is one who undertakes to perform the act requested on his own and is not subject to the control of an employer. If a professional sports team charters an airplane to fly the team to its next game, the airline is an independent contractor and not an employee of the sports franchise. The team exercises no control over how to fly the plane, and the team would not be liable for the torts of the pilot if the plane crashes, even though it hired the airline.

JARRAH v. TRUMP HOTELS & CASINO RESORTS, INC.
487 F. SUPP.2D 522 (D. N.J. 2007)

Plaintiffs commenced this personal injury action against Defendants Trump Hotels & Casino Resorts, Inc. ("Trump"), Medical One A.C.E.C., Inc. ("MO"), and Linda A. Erthal ("Erthal").

Trump contracted with MO for MO to operate a medical station on Trump's premise. The contract between Trump and MO stated that:

> "MO shall be solely responsible for the operation of the medical station and is acting as an independent contractor. No relationship of employer and employee is created by this agreement between MO and Trump. Trump shall exercise no control or direction over the methods by which MO and the nurses and physicians who contract with MO perform their work and function."

The contract requires that a registered nurse be on-site for a minimum of 16 hours per day, 7 days per week. In addition, a physician is required to be on-site for a total of 15 hours per week, and on-call 24 hours per day, 7 days per week. MO has the sole responsibility for the selection of physicians and nurses to staff the medical station.

Plaintiff Faud Jarrah ("Faud") was visiting Trump's Casino and Hotel when he complained of dizziness, difficulty moving his left leg and left arm, slurred speech, and inability to hold his bladder. Faud requested emergency medical assistance and was attended to by Erthal. Erthal was an employee of MO; she was not employed by Trump. Erthal performed a medical evaluation on Faud and, after learning that he was diabetic, directed him to sit down and eat. She did not recommend any treatment or arrange for Faud to be transported to a hospital.

After Faud ate, his symptoms continued to worsen. Because of his symptoms, his wife and friend drove him to Lehigh Valley Hospital. In the hospital, Faud discovered that he had actually suffered a stroke. Plaintiffs claim that Erthal's misdiagnosis prevented and delayed him from receiving proper care.

Plaintiffs argue that Trump should be held vicariously liable for the negligence of Defendants MO and Erthal. It is well-settled that when a person engages an independent contractor to do work that is not itself a nuisance, he is not vicariously liable for the negligent acts of the contractor in the performance of the contract. Two exceptions to this general rule exist: (1) where the principal retains control of the manner and means of doing the work subject to the contract; and (2) where the principal engages an incompetent contractor. Plaintiffs claim that Trump is liable because it reserved sufficient control of Defendants MO and Erthal.

Plaintiffs argue that Trump exerted sufficient control over MO and Erthal and that it should be held liable. Plaintiffs claim that the agreement between Trump and MO allows Trump to control the staffing times, staffing levels, competency of staff, staffing selection, follow-up treatment and care, and non-medical office supplies to be used by Medical One in performance of its duties. In addition, Trump requires that its Risk Management Department be promptly notified by MO of any referrals to emergency medical care. Plaintiffs claim that these facts establish that Trump controls MO's manner and means of performing the contract.

The Court is unpersuaded by this argument. The agreement between the parties sets forth the minimum requirement concerning staffing level and qualification. The agreement requires that a registered nurse licensed by the New Jersey Board of Nursing be on-site for a minimum of 16 hours per day, 7 days per week. In addition, a physician is required to be on-site for a total of 15 hours per week, and be on-call 24 hours per day, 7 days per week. MO had the sole responsibility for the selection of physicians and nurses to staff the medical station. As described above, the agreement does not give Trump any control over the manner in which MO practices medicine. Indeed, the agreement specifically provides:

> "MO shall be solely responsible for the operation of the medical station and is acting as an independent contractor hereunder. No relationship of employer and employee is created by this Agreement between MO and Trump. Trump shall exercise no control or direction over the methods by which MO and the nurses and physicians who contract with MO perform their work and function."

The contractual language is unambiguous, and it is clearly intended to establish a minimum level of service that MO must provide. Such requirements apply only to the quality of services provided, and do not transform an independent contractor into an employee. In addition, Plaintiffs failed to produce any evidence showing that Trump was in fact controlling the manner in which MO staff practiced medicine, although it had no contractual right to do so. Thus, the Court concludes that Defendants MO and Erthal are independent contractors, and that Trump is not liable for their alleged negligence.

SECTION 5.10
JOE ROBERTS
V. THE STALLIONS

PROBLEM FIVE—B

PARK, BROWN & SMITH, P.C.
ATTORNEYS AT LAW
MEMORANDUM

TO: All Law Clerks

FROM: Peter Smith, Esquire

RE: Joe Roberts v. The Stallions

For Joe Roberts' birthday, his son obtained a "Press Pass" for his father to attend the Stallions opening football game. Joe was ecstatic since he had never seen Tony play in a live professional football game. Roberts stood on the sidelines next to the Stallions' bench and told everyone that his son was the place-kicker. As a special treat, Tony had arranged for some of the Stallions' cheerleaders to give his father a birthday cheer. During the beginning of the second quarter, the cheerleaders started to sing Happy Birthday to Joe, who was speechless.

Unfortunately, the game was still being played, and the Stallions' 250-pound fullback caught a pass and was pushed out of bounds. The player's momentum carried him into Joe, who had his back to the field as he watched the cheerleaders. Mr. Roberts was violently knocked to the ground and broke his right leg in three places.

Joe Roberts wishes to file suit against the Stallions for negligence in not protecting him against being hit by a football player as he stood on the sidelines. Joe contends the team should not have issued a sideline pass if it was dangerous for an individual to stand there. I am sure the Stallions will argue that Joe assumed the risk of being injured. Does a person normally assume the risk of being hurt by a football player when the spectator is standing ten yards off the field? Based upon **Lowe v. California League of Professional Baseball,** can Joe prevail in a suit against the Stallions since Joe was watching the cheerleaders at the time he was hurt? Are the Stallions responsible for the actions of their cheerleaders in diverting Joe's attention from the game? I suspect the team will argue that the cheerleaders exceeded their duties by engaging in a private cheer. Please refer to **DeFulio v. Spectaguard, Inc.,** which is set forth immediately before this problem, in order to ascertain whether the cheerleaders were acting within the scope of their employment with the Stallions.

LOWE V. CALIFORNIA PROFESSIONAL BASEBALL
56 CAL. APP. 4TH 112 (CAL. 1997)

John Lowe was seriously injured when struck on the left side of his face by a foul ball while attending a professional baseball game. The game was being played at "The Epicenter," home field of the Rancho Cucamonga Quakes.

The Quakes, at their home games, feature a mascot who goes by the name of "Tremor." He is a caricature of a dinosaur, standing seven feet tall with a tail, which protrudes out from the costume. Tremor was performing his antics in the stands just along the left field foul line. Tremor was behind plaintiff and had been touching him with his (Tremor's) tail. Plaintiff was thereby distracted and turned toward Tremor. In the next moment, just as plaintiff returned his attention to the playing field, he was struck by a foul ball before he could react to it. The case was resolved in the trial court by summary judgment entered in favor of the defendant.

In the action, filed after his injury, plaintiff's complaint was styled in a single count, a refreshing example of clear and concise pleading. The key charging allegations were contained in two paragraphs:

1. On said date and some time after the stated time and after the seventh inning, 'Tremor' the Quake's mascot, came up into the stadium in the area where plaintiff and his group were seated. Tremor was accompanied by an usher as he performed antics and entertained the crowd. Tremor is a person who wears a dinosaur costume with a long protruding tail. As John Lowe sat in his assigned seat, he was facing forward and looking toward the playing field when suddenly, and without warning or his consent, his right shoulder was touched by the tail of Tremor's costume. As he turned to his right to see who, or what, was touching him, baseball play had resumed and a batted ball, believed to be a foul ball, hit the plaintiff

on the left side of his face breaking multiple facial bones.

2. The Left Terrace Section, where the plaintiff was seated with his group, is located northwesterly of the left field foul ball territory, and in the direct line of foul balls passing west of the third base line. Tremor's antics and interference, while the baseball game was in play, prevented the plaintiff from being able to protect himself from any batted ball and foreseeably increased the risks to John Lowe over and above those inherent in the sport.

These deposition excerpts provide an insight into how plaintiff was injured:

Q. *Where was the mascot at the time that the foul ball was hit?*

A. Directly behind me.

Q. *How long had the mascot been directly behind you at the time you were hit?*

A. I would say probably two minutes.

Q. *Did any part of the mascot's costume or person touch you before you were hit?*

A. Yes.

Q. *And what or how were you touched by this mascot?*

A. With his tail.

Q. *When did that occur in relationship to when you were hit by the ball?*

A. Well, during that approximate two-minute span he was doing his act. And I felt this bam, bam, bam, on the back of my head and shoulders, and I turned around to see what he was doing.

Q. *And when you turned around and looked, what did you see?*

A. Well, I noticed that he was doing his antics to the crowd that was in the immediate area. And I saw that as he was turning his body, his tail was hitting me.

Q. *Where were you looking at the moment the ball was hit?*

A. I had just turned my head towards the field as the ball arrived.

Q. *And in terms of timing, was it almost instantaneous that you turned your head to the field and got hit?*

A. Yes.

Q. *Where were you looking immediately before you turned your head toward the field?*

A. Up at Tremor.

Q. *And at that time you were looking at Tremor immediately before turning your head back to the field and getting hit, was the reason that you were looking at Tremor that his tail had just tapped you on the shoulder again and you turned around and looked?*

A. Yes.

The dispositive issue in this case then is whether the mascot's antics and their resulting distraction of the plaintiff operated to increase the inherent risks assumed by a spectator at a baseball game. In this regard, it is well established that defendants generally do have a duty to use due care not to increase the risks to a participant over and above those inherent in the sport. The rule is no different in instances involving spectators.

The key inquiry here is whether the risk which led to Plaintiff's injury involved some feature or aspect of the game, which is inevitable or unavoidable in the actual playing of the game. In the first instance, foul balls hit into the spectators' area clearly create a risk of injury. If such foul balls were to be eliminated, it would be impossible to play the game. Thus, foul balls represent an inherent risk to spectators attending baseball games, and such risk is assumed. Can the same thing be said about the antics of the mascot? We think not. Actually, the declaration of the person who dressed up as Tremor, recounted that there were occasional games played when he was not there. In view of this testimony, as a matter of law, we hold that the antics of the mascot are not an essential or integral part of the playing of a baseball game. In short, the game can be played in the absence of such antics. Moreover, whether such antics increased the inherent risk to Plaintiff is an issue of fact to be resolved at trial.

We note further, under the holding in **Neinstein v. Los Angeles Dodgers, 185 Cal. App. 3d 176,** absent any distraction by the mascot, that plaintiff could have assumed the risk. Justice Compton, writing in Neinstein, observed that the plaintiff "voluntarily elected to sit in a seat which was clearly unprotected by any form of screening. She was sufficiently warned of the risk by common knowledge of the nature of the sport. The Dodgers were under no duty to do anything further to protect her from the hazard."

However, in *Neinstein,* there was no mascot bothering the plaintiff and thus distracting her attention from the playing field. Thus, *Neinstein* is readily distinguishable.

Based upon the foregoing analysis, we hold that the trial court improperly granted the motion for summary judgment.

PROBLEM FIVE—B
ANSWER SHEET

Name   **Please Print Clearly**

1. Did Joe Roberts assume the risk of his injuries? Explain your answer.

_____

_____

_____

_____

_____

_____

_____

_____

_____

_____

_____

_____

_____

_____

_____

_____

_____

_____

2. Will the Stallions be held liable for the actions of the cheerleaders?

_____

_____

_____

_____

_____

_____

_____

_____

_____

_____

_____

_____

_____

_____

_____

_____

_____

_____

_____

_____

_____

Generally, parents are not held liable for the torts of their children unless a parent is directly at fault, if the child is acting as the agent of the parent at the time of the harm, or if the parent participates in or encourages the improper act. For instance, a parent will be held liable if he or she leaves a loaded gun on the table and a young child shoots someone with the weapon. Liability attaches because the parent is negligent in leaving the gun unattended and not because of the parental relationship.

Some states have passed laws to hold parents liable for the torts of their children in specific instances. The following statute is the law in Pennsylvania:

23 PA. C.S.A. SECTION 5502—LIABILITY OF PARENTS

Any parent whose child is found liable or is adjudged guilty by a court . . . of a tortuous act shall be liable to the person who suffers the injury to the extent set forth in this chapter.

23 PA. C.S.A. SECTION 5505—MONETARY LIMITS OF LIABILITY

Liability of the parents under this Chapter shall be limited to:

1. The sum of $1,000 for injuries suffered by any one person as a result of the tortuous act or continuous series of tortuous acts.

2. The sum of $2,500 regardless of the number of persons who suffer injury as a result of one tortuous act or continuous series of tortuous acts.

There have been a number of cases where a child has shot another individual, resulting in an increased awareness of a parents' duty to supervise and control their children. From the murders at Columbine High School to the shootings of teenagers walking down the street, the criminal acts by a child against another seem all too common. This raises the questions as to whether a parent can be held liable for the actions of a child under a negligent supervision theory? The Restatement (Second of Torts), which has been adopted by most states, provides:

> "A parent is under a duty to exercise reasonable care so to control his minor child as to prevent it from intentionally harming others or from so conducting itself as to create an unreasonable risk of bodily harm to them, if the parent (a) knows or has reason to know that he has the ability to control his child, and (b) knows or should know of the necessity and opportunity for exercising such control."

Read **Barrett v. Pacheco** which involves the issue of whether a parent may be liable for the actions of a child in shooting a police officer during the commission of a burglary. The court examined the evidence leading up to the event in order to ascertain if the parents failed to properly supervise their child.

BARRETT V. PACHECO
62 WASH. APP. 717 (1991)

At 2 a.m. on May 21, 1987, 14–year–old Arthur Pacheco shot Robert Barrett, a police officer, while committing a burglary at a middle school in Lynnwood. Barrett recovered from his injuries and returned to work as a police officer. Arthur Pacheco pled guilty to first degree assault and second-degree burglary and was sentenced to a juvenile detention center until age 21.

Immediately after the shooting incident, police searched the Pacheco family residence. Arthur's bedroom was locked from the inside, requiring the officer to kick in the door to gain entry. In searching the bedroom, police found a pipe bomb and two large incendiary devices, .22 caliber ammunition rounds, shotgun shells, substances used in making explosives and various Ninja weapons. The officers also found a book and computer printouts on how to make black powder, pipe bombs and other explosives, numerous magazines about Ninjas and pictures of weapons.

On the night of the shooting, Arthur said goodnight to his father around 10 p.m. and went into his bedroom. Both parents worked a graveyard shift, and Arthur's mother had left for work at 10 p.m. At 12:30 a.m., before leaving for work, Arthur's father knocked on his bedroom door. Arthur did not answer, and his father left the house.

The police contacted Arthur's father, Rudolph Pacheco, at work shortly after the shooting. When he learned that his son had shot a police officer, Rudolph stated that he was embarrassed by the "situation" but not surprised.

When Arthur first acquired an interest in guns, his father had enrolled him in a safety course to learn respect for and proper handling of guns and had enforced the rules taught in the class. Arthur owned two .22 caliber rifles, as well as pellet and BB rifles. His father had bought him one of the rifles and was aware that Arthur had purchased one himself. Arthur had been target shooting with his father several times. His father allowed him to shoot his guns only in his presence and only in the country.

In the 6 months preceding the shooting, Arthur had committed three burglaries involving vandalism of a school and two vacant houses. He had also been convicted of attempted theft. Additionally, about a month before the shooting incident, Arthur put a flammable substance down the chimney, causing a fire or explosion which singed his eyebrows and forehead.

When they learned of Arthur's burglaries and vandalism, Arthur's parents imposed severe restrictions on him. Either the parents or a neighbor drove Arthur to and from school. They did not allow him to walk home, and they watched him closely. As punishment, the parents removed Arthur's guns from his room and made them "off-limits." The gun that Arthur used to shoot Barrett was not one of the guns his parents had put away—Arthur had stolen it.

Arthur's parents immediately sought psychological counseling for him after he was arrested for the burglaries. He participated in therapy twice a week. He became interested in skateboarding and began spending time with a group of "good" kids who enjoyed that activity. Two days before the shooting, Arthur's school vice-principal told his mother that Arthur was doing much better in school. According to reports by Arthur's therapist and teachers, he was doing "very well. Arthur had never been in any fights or physical disruptions at school. Neither of his parents had ever seen him act violently toward another person.

Under the doctrine of negligent supervision, parents are liable for the intentional torts of their minor children when: (1) the child has a dangerous proclivity; (2) the parents know of the child's dangerous proclivity; and (3) they fail to exercise reasonable care in controlling that proclivity.

Our Supreme Court first addressed the issue of parental liability for a child's intentional tort against a third person in **Norton, 154 Wash. 241.** In Norton, the guardian of a 5–year–old child brought a negligence action against the parents of a 7–year–old who had struck the other child in the eyeball with a stick. The mother of the 7–year–old admitted that her child had a habit of striking other children with sticks. Additionally, the evidence revealed that the child's father had actually encouraged her attacks on other children. From this evidence, the court determined that there was a sufficient showing of the child's dangerous habit and her parent's knowledge of it to warrant submitting the issue of the parents' negligence to the jury.

The courts have also held a child's dangerous proclivity must be of the same or similar nature as the ultimate tort or crime which injures the victim. In the present case, although Arthur had committed prior delinquent acts, none of them was of the same or similar nature as the

shooting of Barrett. The three burglaries Arthur committed several months before the shooting involved a school and two vacant homes. His other crimes, attempted theft and vandalism, were also property crimes. Significantly, there is no evidence that Arthur was armed with any type of weapon when he committed any of the prior crimes. Thus, Arthur's prior delinquent behavior did not manifest a dangerous tendency to commit the violent assault against Barrett. Nor did Arthur's other prior behavior, including the chimney incident, his night wanderings dressed and equipped as a Ninja, and his possession of Ninja weapons and books, presage his assault on Barrett. Arthur had not committed a violent act during any of these alleged episodes until he shot Barrett. Finally, while we do not condone the Pachecos' laxity in allowing Arthur to keep Ninja weapons, ammunition, and books on dangerous substances and explosives in his room, his possession of these items was also not enough to put his parents on notice that he would assault someone.

In summary, none of Arthur's prior criminal acts or delinquent behavior demonstrate a "dangerous proclivity" that is within the same zone of behavior as the shooting of Barrett. We therefore hold that plaintiffs failed to establish the parental knowledge element of their negligent supervision claim.

SECTION 5.11
INTENTIONAL TORTS

When the wrongdoer purposely sets out to harm another, that conduct gives rise to an intentional tort and may result in the imposition of money damages. Theories of liability include actions for a battery, assault, invasion of privacy, defamation, infliction of emotional distress, and false imprisonment.

Intentional torts are treated more seriously by the courts and verdicts frequently include awards of both compensatory and punitive damages, which sum is to punish the wrongdoer for his actions. Punitive damages are generally not covered by insurance and remain the personal responsibility of the actor.

SECTION 5.12
INFLICTION OF
EMOTIONAL DISTRESS

A person who by extreme and outrageous conduct intentionally or recklessly causes severe emotional distress to another is liable to that person for any bodily harm that may result from the emotional distress. The outrageous conduct must go beyond the bounds of normal decency and be considered as intolerable in a civilized community.

For instance, racial slurs in the workplace can be actionable, or when a physician speaks to a female employee in an unwelcome, "lewd" and "sexual" manner. However, a debt collection agency was found not to have committed the tort of infliction of emotional distress where its employees made six phone calls over a three month period and told the debtor that they were "no better than lying thieves or sponges", that the creditor was going to "sue your asses" or "sue the hell out of you." The court felt that the language used by debt collector's employees was not so atrocious as to be utterly intolerable in a civilized community. Likewise, liability does not extend to mere insults, indignities, threats, annoyances, or petty oppression.

People are very squeamish when it comes to finding unnatural things in food. Over the years, a variety of food cases have arisen in which foreign substances have been found in food ranging from a mouse inside a bottle of soda to finding chewing gum in a salad. **Coca-Cola Bottling Co. v. Hagan** deals with whether two individuals who consumed a can of soda that appeared to contain a condom can succeed in a suit for inflection of emotional distress because they believed they could contact the AIDS virus.

COCA-COLA BOTTLING CO. V. HAGAN
813 SO.2D 167 (FLA. APP. 5 DIST. 2002)

The Plaintiffs, Hagan and Parker, consumed some of the contents of a bottle of Coca-Cola which tasted flat. Upon inspection, it appeared to have a foreign object floating in it which they assumed was a "used condom." Neither investigated nor had the contents of the bottle examined. They did give the bottle to Coca-Cola for analysis. It was inspected and analyzed by a chemist and manager of Coca-Cola Quality Assurance Department. He concluded that although on visual inspection the foreign object appeared to be a condom, it was "to a scientific certainty" a mold.

Recovery of damages for consuming a part of a bottle of Coca Cola containing a mold is possible. However, virtually all of the damages established by the plaintiffs related to their fear they had been exposed to the AIDS virus and we conclude they established no valid basis for this fear.

Hagan and Parker established that after drinking part of the contents of the can of Coke, they were to seek treatment for protection against AIDS, including tests for HIV, immediately and again six months later. They testified they were fearful their possible exposure to AIDS would damage their child care business and reputations. They were embarrassed and humiliated because others knew about their possible exposure to this dreadful disease. They were fearful that they could, in the indefinite future, contract AIDS, and this fear of becoming HIV positive interfered with one Plaintiff's marital relations. Recognizing that the Plaintiffs' fear of contracting AIDS was the basis and essence of their damage claim, the trial court ruled and so instructed the jury that their recovery for emotional distress should be limited to the time beginning with their drinking the Coca-Cola to six months later when they received a negative HIV test. He concluded that after that time, the plaintiffs' fears of contracting AIDS would not be reasonable because there was no scientific basis to substantiate their emotional upset beyond that point.

The fear of AIDS cases in which recovery has been permitted for negligent infliction of emotional distress and upset alone, require as a threshold, a showing by the plaintiff that the fear is reasonable. The great majority of cases say this means the plaintiff must show that the virus was present, and that the contact between the material containing the virus and the plaintiff was a medically and scientifically accepted channel for the transmission of the disease. The plaintiffs failed to establish the foreign item in the bottle was a used condom. But for purposes of argument only, even if they had established that fact, they failed to establish the virus was present. Only a very small percentage of the general population is HIV positive or has AIDS and the mere presence of semen would not be enough.

Without such showings or proofs, a plaintiff's fear of contracting AIDS is unreasonable as a matter of law and not a legally compensable injury. As a matter of public policy, the allowance of such lawsuits without the threshold proofs discussed above could lead to an explosion of frivolous litigation, opening as some courts say a "Pandora's box" of AIDS phobia claims.

We conclude that the judgment being appealed in this case must be reversed because the plaintiffs failed to establish a basis for an award of damages based on fear of getting AIDS.

SECTION 5.13
ASSAULT AND
BATTERY

A **battery** is the intentional touching of the body of another or an object closely associated with the body in an offensive or harmful manner. Mere recklessness or negligence on the part of the actor is insufficient. The tortfeasor must, in fact, have intended to cause the harm.

An offensive touching is as objectionable as a harmful touching. For example, the uninvited touching of the body of another or an unappreciated kiss is as actionable as a punch in the mouth. There are times, however, when an intentional touching will not be deemed a battery. For instance, consent is a defense to a battery which permission may arise by words or implication. A person who engages in sports or play impliedly consents to the usual touching associated with that sport. For example, professional football is a violent sport in which players frequently are injured because of the severity of the impact. If a star running back is injured while being tackled by five members of the opposing team, he cannot sue the opposing players since the tackle is part of the game. The Cincinnati Bengals, however, were required to defend a lawsuit brought by a Denver Bronco who was intentionally hit in the back of the head by a Cincinnati player following an intercepted pass. The court ruled that the general customs of football do not approve the intentional punching or striking of other players. **Jack Hackbart v. Cincinnati Bengals, Inc., 601 F.2d 516 (1979).** Likewise, a hockey player who intentionally strikes another player in the head with a hockey stick commits a battery. Marty McSorley committed such a transgression in October of 2000 while playing for the Boston Bruins. At the end of the game, McSorley purposely struck Donald Brashear on the side of the head with his hockey stick, causing the player to fall to the ice temporarily losing consciousness.

Professional boxing is a violent and vicious sport in which one of the primary goals is to knock out the opponent as quickly as possible. The biting of Evander Holyfield's ear by Mike Tyson during their heavyweight bout, however, was not a usual touching of the sport and would constitute a battery.

A consensual touching may be a battery if the consent is procured by fraud. For example, a party who touches the arms and legs of a woman on the fraudulent misrepresentation that he is a doctor is responsible for a battery.

A person's motives in initiating the touching are also not relevant. A hostile intent or a desire to harm the victim is not required. Rather, it is the intent to bring about a result that establishes a battery. For instance, in **Andrews v. Peters,** a co-employee jokingly tapped the back of the knee of another worker causing her to fall to the ground. While the co-employee did not intend to cause any harm by his prank, he did intend to tap the back of the woman's leg, which constituted a battery.

ANDREWS V. PETERS
330 S. E.2D 638 (CT. APP. N.C. 1985)

The facts, briefly stated, are as follows. The plaintiff, Margaret H. Andrews, was injured when her co-employee, August Richard Peters, III, walked up behind her at work and tapped the back of her right knee with the front of his right knee, causing her knee to buckle. Andrews lost her balance, fell to the floor, and dislocated her right kneecap. Andrews instituted this action against Peters for intentional assault and battery.

Peters alleges that there is no evidence that he intended to injure Andrews. As summarized in Peters' brief:

> [Peters] testified that he did not intend to be rude or offensive in tapping [Andrews] behind her knees. He stated that the same thing had only moments before been done to him by a co-worker and that it struck him as fun. Peters' contention ignores the nature of the intent required for an intentional tort action.

The intent with which tort liability is concerned is not necessarily a hostile intent, or a desire to do any harm. Rather it is an intent to bring about a result which will invade the interests of another in a way that the law forbids. The defendant may be liable, although intending nothing more than a good-natured practical joke, or honestly believing that the act would not injure the plaintiff, or even though seeking the plaintiff's own good. Peters does not deny that he intended to tap Andrews behind the knee. Although tapping Andrews' knee was arguably not in and of itself a harmful contact, it easily qualifies as an offensive contact. "A bodily contact is offensive if it offends a reasonable sense of personal dignity." **Restatement,** Section 19. There is no evidence of consent to the touching. We hold that the trial court did not err in denying Peters' motions for a directed verdict. Vacated and remanded for further proceedings consistent with this decision.

An **assault** is an act intended to put another in fear of an immediate battery. To commit an assault, it is not necessary that the tortfeasor actually intend to cause an offensive or harmful touching upon the body of another. Rather, it is sufficient that the person intends to cause only a fear of such contact. Pointing a gun at a person and saying, "I am going to kill you" is an assault. However, a gunman who points his weapon at another with the warning, "I would kill you on the spot if this gun didn't make so much noise" has not committed an assault. The victim has not been placed in fear of an immediate touching.

The National Highway Traffic Safety Administration has determined that more than 41,000 people die each year in traffic accidents and two thirds of these fatalities are the result of road rage. This recent phenomena defines a situation where an angry driver intentionally harms or threatens another operator or passenger because of some perceived driving indiscretion. According to CNN, there are a number of reasons for road rage. Congested highways cause tailgating and near-collisions, and there is the great urgency for drivers to quickly reach their destinations. Also, some people are transformed from passive citizens into aggressive and discourteous drivers. While criminal charges are the obvious remedy against the aggressive operator, civil lawsuits for assault are finding their way into the courts. The following case is an example.

VETTER V. MORGAN
22 KAN. APP.2D 1 (KAN. CT. APP. 1995)

Vetter was injured when her van ran off the road after an encounter with a car owned by Morgan and driven by Dana Gaither. Vetter stopped her van at a stoplight. Morgan and Gaither drove up beside Vetter. Morgan began screaming vile and threatening obscenities at Vetter, shaking his fist, and making obscene gestures in a violent manner. According to Vetter, Gaither revved the engine of the car and moved the car back and forth while Morgan was threatening Vetter. Vetter testified that Morgan threatened to remove her from her van and spat on her van door when the traffic light turned green. Vetter was frightened and thought Morgan was under the influence of drugs or alcohol. She was able to write down the license tag number of the car. Morgan stated he was trying to amuse his friends, who were laughing at his antics.

When the traffic light changed to green, both vehicles drove forward. According to Vetter, after they had driven approximately 10 feet, the car driven by Gaither veered suddenly into her lane, and she reacted by steering her van sharply to the right. Vetter's van struck the curb, causing her head to hit the steering wheel and snap back against the seat, after which she fell to the floor of the van.

Assault is defined as the intentional threat or attempt, coupled with the apparent ability, to do bodily harm to another, resulting in immediate apprehension of bodily harm. No bodily contact is necessary. There was evidence of a threat in this case. Vetter testified that Morgan verbally threatened to take her from her van. Ordinarily, words alone cannot be an assault. However, words can constitute an assault if together with other acts or circumstances they put the other in reasonable apprehension of imminent harmful or offensive contact with his person. The record is sufficient to support an inference that Morgan's threat and the acts surrounding it could reasonably put someone in Vetter's position in apprehension of imminent or immediate bodily harm. Morgan's behavior was so extreme that Vetter could reasonably have believed he would immediately try to carry out his threat.

The record also supports an inference that Morgan had the apparent ability to harm Vetter. Although Vetter's van was locked and the windows rolled up, the windows could be broken. The two vehicles were only six feet apart, and Morgan was accompanied by two other males. Although Vetter may have had the ability to flee by turning right, backing up, or running the red light, her ability to prevent the threatened harm by flight or self-defense does not preclude an assault. It is enough that Vetter believed that Morgan was capable of immediately inflicting the contact unless prevented by self-defense, flight, or intervention by others. The trial court erred in concluding there was no evidence that Vetter was placed in apprehension of bodily harm. Whether Morgan's actions constituted an assault was a question of fact for the jury.

A person has the right to be left alone. An unwarranted intrusion upon this right constitutes an **invasion of privacy.** Wiretapping a neighbor's telephone, taking improper and revealing photographs of an unsuspecting neighbor in a state of undress, calling a divorced spouse every fifteen minutes, or disclosing private embarrassing facts about another are actionable wrongs.

Truth is not a defense to an invasion of privacy. For example, the disclosure at a party that the host was a prostitute twenty years earlier is highly offensive and a private matter. Even though the information is true, that fact would not protect the disclosing party from liability.

A growing number of employers provide workers with computers and e-mail accounts. These accounts are sometimes monitored by the business to make sure that an employee is not using the e-mail system for personal reasons during working hours or to guarantee that the computers are not being used for improper purposes such as the transmission of harassing or pornographic messages. In **Garrity v. John Hancock Mutual Life Insurance Company,** the court had to decide whether the practice of monitoring the e-mail of employees constituted an invasion of privacy.

GARRITY V. JOHN HANCOCK MUTUAL LIFE INSURANCE COMPANY
2002 WL 974676 (D. MASS. 2002)

Plaintiffs, Nancy Garrity and Joanne Clark, were employees of John Hancock Mutual Life Insurance Company for twelve and two years respectively, until their termination. According to the defendant, plaintiffs regularly received on their office computers, sexually explicit e-mails from Internet joke sites and other parties, including Mrs. Garrity's husband, which they then sent to co-workers. These facts are undisputed: A fellow employee complained after receiving such an e-mail. Hancock promptly commenced an investigation of Plaintiffs' e-mail folders, as well as the folders of those with whom they e-mailed on a regular basis. Hancock determined that plaintiffs

had violated its E-Mail Policy, which states, in relevant part:

- Messages that are defamatory, abusive, obscene, profane, sexually oriented, threatening or racially offensive are prohibited.

- The inappropriate use of E-mail is in violation of company policy and may be subject to disciplinary action, including termination of employment.

- All information transmitted, or contained in the company's E-mail systems is the property of John Hancock. It is not company policy to intentionally inspect E-mail usage. However, there may be situations that necessitate company review of E-mail messages and other documents.

- Company management reserves the right to access all E-mail files.

During Plaintiffs' employment, defendant periodically reminded its employees that it was their responsibility to know and understand the e-mail policy. In addition, defendant warned them of several incidents in which employees were disciplined for violations. Plaintiffs assert that the e-mail policy is almost impossible to locate on Hancock's internet system, and even harder to decipher. In addition, they contend that the reminders sent by Defendant during Plaintiffs' employment did not accurately communicate its e-mail policy. They also dispute Defendant's characterization of the e-mails in question as sexually explicit, or in any way in violation of the policy language. Upon review of the e-mails in question, however, there can be no question that they are sexually explicit within the meaning of defendant's e-mail policy. Regardless, plaintiffs assert that Hancock led them to believe that these personal e-mails could be kept private with the use of personal passwords and e-mail folders. Their complaint sets forth a claim based on invasion of privacy.

Plaintiffs state that "it is uncontested that Ms. Garrity, Mr. Garrity and Ms. Clarke believed that the personal e-mail correspondence they sent and received was private." While that may be true, the relevant inquiry is whether the expectation of privacy was reasonable. Any reasonable expectation on the part of plaintiffs is belied by the record and plaintiffs' own statements. According to deposition testimony, Mrs. Garrity and Ms. Clark assumed that the recipients of their messages might forward them to others. Likewise, Mr. Garrity testified that the e-mails he sent to his wife would eventually be sent to third parties. Although there is a dearth of case law on privacy issues with regard to office e-mail, **Smyth v. Pillsbury Co., 914 F. Supp. 9 (E. D. Pa. 1996)** is instructive here. In Smyth, the court held that even in the absence of a company e-mail policy, plaintiffs would not have had a reasonable expectation of privacy in their work e-mail.

Both Mrs. Garrity and Ms. Clarke admit that they knew Defendant had the ability to look at e-mail on the company's internet system, and knew they had to be careful about sending e-mail. Nevertheless, they claim that their e-mails were private because the company had instructed them on how to create passwords and personal e-mail folders.

Even if Plaintiffs had a reasonable expectation of privacy in their work e-mail, defendant's legitimate business interest in protecting its employees from harassment in the workplace would likely trump plaintiffs' privacy interests. **Title VII of the Civil Rights Act of 1964** requires employers to take affirmative steps to maintain a workplace free of harassment and to investigate and take prompt and effective remedial action when potentially harassing conduct is discovered. Accordingly, Defendant's motion for summary judgment is allowed.

The tort of invasion of privacy may arise in a variety of situations, including:

- Unwarranted publicity;

- Intrusion into a person's private life;

- Disclosure of a private embarrassing fact; and

- Use of a person's name or likeness for another's financial gain.

Invasion of privacy is defined as the right of an individual to be left alone and to lead a life that is free from unwarranted publicity. This right, however, has its limitations. The right of privacy does not forbid the use of information that is of public benefit, nor does it extend to information which the public has the right to know.

Based upon these concepts, the life of a public figure, such as a politician, actor, musician, or athlete, is newsworthy, so great latitude is afforded concerning disclosures of personal information about these famous individuals.

Over the years, a number of cases have arisen where the name, voice or likeness of a well-known person is used to promote a commercial venture without the celebrity's permission. For instance, Johnny Carson successfully sued a toilet manufacturer who dubbed a new product, "Here's Johnny Portable Toilet," after the entertainer's trademark introduction. Bette Midler recovered money from Ford Motor Company when the car manufacturer made a commercial showing a singer doing a Better Midler impersonation. This type of exploitation gives rise to the tort of invasion of privacy, which claim may be advanced by alleging: (**1**) the defendant's use of the plaintiff's identity; (**2**) the use of the plaintiff's name or likeness for the defendant's benefit; (**3**) the lack of consent to use the plaintiff's name or likeness; and (**4**) a resulting injury.

Technology has become an integral part of life. Most people have cell phones that contain the ability to take pictures, computers contain cameras, and monitors have been installed by many businesses to view the streets outside of their business establishments, as well as to monitor the goings on inside the store. These devices have been very helpful solving crimes or in recording accidents to ascertain who was at fault. However, they also have the potential for abuse. **Upskirt voyeurism** is an example in which a small camera is used to look up the skirt of an unsuspecting woman. Generally, cameras are allowed in the workplace when there is a legitimate business reason. However, installing a camera in a private area like a dressing room or bathroom can subject the offender to liability. That is the issue in the next case.

Koeppel v. Spears
808 N. W.2d 177 (Iowa 2011)

Robert Speirs employed Sara Koeppel and Deanna Miller to assist him in his business. The office included a reception area occupied by Koeppel and Miller, an office occupied by Speirs, and a small unisex bathroom.

In October 2005, Speirs noticed Miller's work performance had deteriorated. Speirs decided to monitor Miller's activities at work using a hidden camera. Speirs purchased a security camera, monitor, videocassette recorder (VCR), and video tape. The camera was powered by a nine-volt battery and functioned independently of the receiver and monitor. The receiver, monitor, and VCR were located in Speirs' office. The battery only had a lifespan of a few hours.

Speirs claimed that on December 10, he installed the camera in the reception area of the office to monitor Miller's work station. As a result, he was able to observe the reception area from the monitor in his office. He had no difficulty observing Miller when the equipment was in operation. However, he did not observe any misconduct by Miller and removed the camera after approximately ten days.

On December 26, Speirs claimed he found a hypodermic needle in the office parking lot near the spot Miller parked her car. As a result, he installed the camera inside the hollow base of the shelf in the bathroom. He claimed, however, the equipment did not operate after he placed the camera in the bathroom. Instead, he claimed the monitor in his office produced only static or, at other times, displayed a "no signal" message. After unsuccessfully working with the equipment to produce a picture on the monitor, Speirs claimed he unhooked the monitor and receiver and put them in his desk drawer. Nevertheless, he left the camera in the bathroom and claimed he intended to remove it at work the following day.

The next day, Koeppel discovered the camera in the bathroom. She took photographs of the scene and reported her discovery to the police. The photographs showed the camera angle pointing towards the toilet in the bathroom.

The police investigation uncovered the monitor and receiver located in Speirs' office. The camera was found in the bathroom but was inoperable due to a dead battery. The investigating officers replaced the battery and attempted to operate the monitoring system. They observed a "snowy, grainy, foggy" image on the screen of either the legs or arms of the investigating officer who was inside the bathroom. This image appeared only briefly before the monitor displayed a "no signal" message.

Koeppel filed a claim for invasion of privacy. Speirs moved for summary judgment to dismiss the claim because it did not actually allow him to view or record Koeppel and Miller. Koeppel claimed she produced sufficient evidence of an invasion because Speirs placed the camera in the bathroom with the intent to view her and the camera was operable.

In general, conduct that intrudes on privacy gives rise to liability because it can cause a reasonable person "mental suffering, shame, or humiliation" inconsistent with the general rules of civility and personal autonomy recognized in our society. Importantly, the cause of action for invasion of privacy imposes liability based on a particular method of obtaining information, not the content of the information obtained, or even the use put to the information by the intruder following the intrusion.

We first recognized a cause of action for invasion of privacy in 1956. The first element requires an intentional intrusion into a matter the plaintiff has a right to expect privacy. The next element requires the act to be highly offensive to a reasonable person. We have held that an intrusion upon seclusion occurs when a person intentionally intrudes, physically or otherwise, upon the solitude or seclusion of another or his private affairs or concerns if the intrusion would be highly offensive to a reasonable person.

In this case, the parties do not dispute that placing a camera in a bathroom would be highly objectionable to a reasonable person, nor do they dispute that a bathroom is a place where a reasonable person expects to be left alone. Instead, the parties disagree about the proof necessary to show the act of intrusion occurred. Koeppel argues the installation of the camera in the bathroom with the intent to view is sufficient. Speirs claims he could not be liable for his conduct if the camera could not function to produce an image.

A plaintiff who learns a camera was placed in a private place should not be forced to live with the uncertainty of whether an actual viewing occurred. Such an approach would leave those victims with a reasonable belief that someone could have listened to or seen a private moment without a remedy simply because the device was unable to actually operate to invade privacy at the time it was discovered.

If the fact finder finds from the evidence that the device could have intruded into the privacy of the plaintiff, the element of intrusion is satisfied. The equipment does not need to be operational at the time it is discovered. Instead, the fact finder must only conclude that the equipment could have been operational so as to invade the plaintiff's privacy.

Under the standard we adopt in this case, a reasonable fact finder could conclude the camera was capable of exposing the plaintiff's activities in the bathroom. Importantly, there was evidence the camera was capable of operation, and there was evidence it operated in the past from a different location in the office. This evidence meets the standard and would lead a reasonable person to believe his or her privacy had been invaded.

SECTION 5.15 DEFAMATION

Over two thousand years ago, the Roman Empire expressed its displeasure for the uttering of false statements about another. The Twelve Tablets, the foundation for the ancient laws of Rome, provided: "If any person has sung or composed against another person a song such as was causing slander or insult . . . . he shall be clubbed to death." A case for libel also played a part in the history of this country and the development of the law on defamation. In 1734, John Peter Zenger, a newspaper publisher, was arrested for voicing his opposition to the colonial governor of New York. Zenger's efforts did not go unnoticed. He was tried for seditious libel. He was defended by Andrew Hamilton and the not guilty verdict brought about the principle of freedom of the press.

A statement is **defamatory** if it is false and tends to harm the reputation of another or to lower him in the estimation of the community. There are two categories of defamation: libel and slander.

Libel involves the publication of defamatory matter by written or printed words. **Slander,** on the other hand, is defamatory communication that is verbal or oral in nature. Merely saying something defamatory to the aggrieved party is insufficient regardless of the false nature of the communication. In order for the defamatory comment to be actionable, it must be conveyed to a third person. This is called publication.

In the case of defamation, the truth of the matter communicated is an absolute defense. If the defendant can prove that what was said or written was true, a suit for defamation will fail. The mere expression of an opinion is also not defamatory.

Employers are often thrust into a difficult situation when they are requested to complete a job reference for a prior employee. A poor rating can result in the failure of the worker to obtain the new job. This scenario can trigger a defamation action.

In addition to truth being a defense to defamation, certain situations give raise to the defense of privilege. Privilege exist in two different forms: absolute and qualified. For instance, defamatory statements made in open court or during a debate in a legislative body, such as Congress, enjoy absolute privilege and protect the speakers from being liable for defamation. On the other hand, a qualified privilege exists if the publisher believes that he or she has a duty to speak out, or that to speak out is necessary to protect either his or her interests, or those of third person. Examples of qualified privileges include a job reference provided by a former employer or the reports of a credit agency. This qualified privilege, however, can be lost if statement is made in bad faith.

Kevorkian v. Glass explores the law with respect to the liability of an employer who provides a poor job reference to a potential employer of a former worker.

KEVORKIAN V. GLASS
913 A.2D 1043 (R. I. 2007)

Kevorkian is a licensed practical nurse who began working for the Pawtuxet Village Nursing and Rehabilitation Center (Pawtuxet Village) in 1989. In April 1994, plaintiff was suspended from work for three days for insubordination. Glass, the director of nursing at the center, alleged that plaintiff had failed to dispense necessary medication to patients. Kevorkian disputed her employer's allegation, and, unwilling to continue to work under the shadow of such accusations, she resigned and announced that she had secured new employment elsewhere.

Approximately two years after she resigned, Kevorkian, contacted Mercury Medical, a placement agency for nurses. Mercury Medical asked

Kevorkian if Pawtuxet Village could be contacted for a reference. Kevorkian agreed, and a document entitled "Reference Form" was faxed to Glass. Glass left the document largely incomplete, but she did fill out three parts of it before faxing it back to Mercury Medical. First, she checked a box marked "very good" for the category "appearance;" second, she answered "no" to the question "[W]ould you rehire?" and, finally, she wrote that the reason she would be unwilling to rehire Kevorkian was because of "unacceptable work practice habits."

After Glass submitted the reference form, Kevorkian began attending interviews with prospective employers set up by Mercury Medical. Perplexed that none of those facilities offered to hire her, Kevorkian began to suspect that she had received a poor reference from Pawtuxet Village. When she discovered the contents of Glass' reference, Kevorkian decided to file suit.

Plaintiff filed a one-count complaint alleging that, by using the phrase "unacceptable work practice habits" in the context of a work reference, Defendant had defamed her by "circulating a libelous and slanderous job reference form to prospective employers."

Counsel for Defendant argued that (1) the statement "unacceptable work practice habits" is not capable of a defamatory meaning; and even if the statement is capable of such meaning, and (2) defendant's publication of that statement to Mercury Medical was protected by a statutory privilege set forth in G.L. 1956 § 28-6.4-1(c).

To succeed in an action for defamation, the plaintiff must prove: (1) the utterance of a false and defamatory statement concerning another; (2) an unprivileged communication to a third party; (3) fault amounting to at least negligence; and (4) damages.

General Laws 1956 § 28-6.4-1(c) provides:

> "An employer that, upon request by a prospective employer or a current or former employee, provides fair and unbiased information about an employee's job performance is presumed to be acting in good faith and is immune from civil liability for the disclosure and the consequences of the disclosure. The presumption of good faith is rebuttable upon a showing that the information disclosed was: (1) Knowingly false; (2) Deliberately misleading; (3) Disclosed for a malicious purpose; or (4) Violative of the current or former employee's civil rights under the employment discrimination laws."

In the realm of defamation, privileges exist in two different forms: absolute and qualified. Here, we deal only with the latter. The major difference between the two types of privilege is that a qualified privilege may be lost in situations in which the publication exceeds the scope of the privilege or is the fruit of improper motivation. For example, a qualified privilege may be lost when the publication of an allegedly defamatory statement is induced by spite or ill will-also known as malice. Absolute privileges, on the other hand, are not subject to such limitations. A qualified privilege exists if the publisher makes the statements in good faith and reasonably believes that he has a legal, moral or social duty to speak out, or that to speak out is necessary to protect either his own interests, or those of third person[s], or certain interests of the public.

In **Swanson v. Speidel Corp., 110 R. I. 335 (1972)**, a case factually similar to the matter now before us, we held that a former employer's communication to a prospective employer with regard to the work characteristics of a former employee was protected by a qualified privilege. In that case, we said that: "the public interest requires that the protection of the privilege be accorded to a communication by a former employer to a prospective employer with regard to a former employee's work characteristics where the publisher acts in good faith and has reason to believe that to speak out is necessary to protect his own interests, or those of third persons, or certain interests of the public."

The qualified privilege can be overcome, however, when the plaintiff proves that the person making the defamatory statements acted with ill will or malice.

When it enacted § 28-6.4-1 (c), the General Assembly created a statutory qualified privilege for former employers' communications to prospective employers concerning former employees.

Here, defendant's statement that plaintiff had "unacceptable work practice habits" clearly was covered by the § 28-6.4-1 (c) privilege. The defendant is a former supervisor of plaintiff who, at the request of both plaintiff and a placement agency provided information about plaintiff's

work performance while she was employed at Pawtuxet Village. Clearly, when she received an inquiry about Kevorkian from a prospective employer, Glass had a qualified privilege to reveal her dissatisfaction with plaintiff's work during the time she worked at Pawtuxet Village. Thus, a presumption of good faith attached to defendant's publication and the burden of rebutting that presumption shifted to plaintiff.

Plaintiff argued that defendant's statement was made for a malicious purpose, thereby removing it from the scope of the privilege. However, we conclude that plaintiff did not meet the burden imposed on her by directing the court to specific facts that raise a genuine issue about whether defendant made the publication for a malicious purpose.

After a review of the record, the plaintiff has pointed to no facts that show that defendant's publication of the defamatory remark was motivated by malice toward plaintiff.

We affirm the judgment of the Superior Court, and return the record of this case to it.

Even though a communication is false, an action for defamation will only be successful if the statement actually harms the reputation of another so as to lower the individual in the estimation of the community or to deter others from associating or dealing with that person. Therefore, an individual who believes that he has been defamed must be readily identifiable by and associated with the statement. This is known as the "of and concerning" requirement and creates a problem when a class of people are the subject of the false statement. For instance, if a newspaper publishes an article that the students at a particular college are unruly drunks and bores, the individual students at the school will fail in a defamation action since they are not sufficiently identified in the article.

Likewise, the statement that all politicians are liars and crooks is not actionable since no one individual has been singled out so the "of and concerning" requirement has not been satisfied.

Diaz v. NBC Universal, Inc.
536 F.Supp.2d 337 (S.D. New York 2008)

Plaintiffs have sued as representatives of a class of approximately 400 present and former Special Agents of the New York office of the United States Drug Enforcement Administration. The Complaint alleges that every New York City-based DEA agent was defamed by a false legend that appears on screen at the end of the film. The legend says that Frank Lucas' collaboration with law enforcement led to the conviction of three quarters of New York City's Drug Enforcement Agency.

Defendant NBC Universal, Inc. is in the business of, among other things, producing, releasing and distributing motion pictures to the public. On or about November 2, 2007, Universal released American Gangster to the public. The movie has grossed at least $127,000,000 in profits for the defendant, excluding profits made through secondary businesses.

The film depicts the life of Frank Lucas (played by Denzel Washington), an African American drug kingpin in New York City who was arrested and subsequently convicted of drug trafficking. The film also includes a character identified as Richie Roberts (played by Russell Crowe), a law enforcement official in Essex County, New Jersey. As is common with motion pictures inspired by true events, the Film ends with a standard disclaimer noting that a number of the incidents are "fictionalized," and that "some of the characters have been composited or invented...."

Throughout the film, there are references to corruption among some members of the local police forces in New York City and New Jersey. Several characters depict corrupt narcotics detectives employed by the New York City Police Department (N.Y.PD)—including Josh Brolin, who plays a character identified as Detective Trupo of the NYPD's Special Investigations Narcotics Unit. At no point in the Film is any character identified as a DEA agent; neither is there any suggestion that any federal agent is corrupt.

At one point in the film, law enforcement personnel search Lucas' home. During this scene, Lucas' wife is assaulted, his dog is shot, and hundreds of thousands of dollars are stolen by corrupt law enforcement officials. The film does not identify the people who do these despicable things as DEA agents. The officer who steals the money, however, says that the Feds are going to arrive later and "take everything."

After the Lucas character has been arrested, the film ends with a series of vignettes that purport to show how everything worked out. One of those texts (the "legend") notes that Lucas' cooperation led to "the convictions of three quarters of New York City's Drug Enforcement Agency."

A former special agent from the New York City office of the DEA is currently stationed in Iraq and is a member of the putative plaintiff class. Approximately 20 soldiers stationed in Iraq who saw American Gangster questioned him about the legend. The soldiers all thought the legend referred to Special Agents of DEA, and they asked the former DEA agent how three quarters of the DEA agents based in New York City could be convicted criminals. Although Korniloff told these soldiers that no such thing happened, he felt deeply hurt and embarrassed by the questions, even though he knew the legend was false.

Although the Complaint contains a lengthy description of the many items in the film with which Plaintiffs are dissatisfied, the Complaint identifies only one allegedly defamatory statement: the legend that appears for a few seconds at the end of the film, stating that Lucas' cooperation with authorities after his arrest "led to the conviction of three quarters of New York City's Drug Enforcement Agency."

Hornbook libel law requires that an allegedly defamatory statement must be "of and concerning a particular individual." The Court properly may dismiss an action where the statements are incapable of supporting a jury's finding that the allegedly libelous statements refer to plaintiff.

Under the group libel doctrine, when a reference is made to a large group of people, no individual within that group can fairly say that the statement is about him, nor can the "group" as a whole state a claim for defamation. In order to overcome the group libel doctrine, a plaintiff must demonstrate that the circumstances of the publication reasonably give rise to the conclusion that there is a particular reference to the member.

This suit contains approximately four hundred former and current special agents of the DEA. Plaintiffs concede that neither the legend, nor the movie more generally, ever specifically identifies any of the named plaintiffs, or any other class member, by name. Thus, under New York law, they would appear to be out of court.

SECTION 5.16
FALSE IMPRISONMENT

False Imprisonment is the unlawful detention of a person against his or her will in a specific area. This tort is defined as the intentional and wrongful infliction of confinement against a person's will without consent or legal authority. The confinement may result from acts or words which the person fears to disregard. By implication, it is required that a person being detained be aware of the confinement, and that the actor intended to confine the victim. A simple example includes kidnapping, or the improper imprisoning of a person for a crime that the accused did not commit.

A person detained in a department store who has been falsely accused of stealing merchandise may sue the store for false imprisonment, if the business establishment acted without just cause in its actions.

Louise Ogborn always volunteered to work an extra shift at McDonald's because her mother was ill and had recently lost her job. One night, Ogborn agreed to work overtime but this noble gesture turned into a terrifying ordeal that she will never forget. Ogborn was informed by a store manager that a police officer was on the phone and that she was being accused of stealing a purse from a customer.[14] Read the following case to learn the facts which lead to a multiple million dollar verdict against McDonald's for false imprisonment and other torts.

McDonald's Corp. v. Ogborn
309 S.W.3d 274 (Ky. App., 2009)

Between 1994 and 2004, an unknown individual placed hoax telephone calls to McDonald's and other fast food restaurants, pretending to be a police officer. During that time, he convinced restaurant managers, employees, and third parties to conduct strip searches and sexual assaults at his direction. The caller was successful in accomplishing his perverse hoax more than thirty times at different McDonald's restaurants.

On April 9, 2004, 18-year-old Louise Ogborn had just finished her shift when a manager asked her to work a second shift. Shortly thereafter, an unknown individual telephoned the restaurant and assistant manager Donna Summers answered. The caller falsely identified himself as a police officer and claimed to be investigating a recent theft of a purse at the restaurant. According to the caller, the perpetrator was a McDonald's employee. He described a female suspect which Summers believed fit Ogborn. Ogborn was summoned to the office and informed that she was the subject of an investigation into this theft.

At the instruction of the caller, Summers told Ogborn she had two choices: she could be searched in the office by her managers or at the police station after arrest. After speaking with the caller, Ogborn agreed to be searched in the office. In accordance with the caller's instructions, Ogborn was searched as she was convinced to gradually disrobe.

Without questioning the propriety of doing so, Summers left another man alone in the office with Ogborn, who was naked but for the apron she held in front of herself. That person, acting on the instruction of the caller, forced Ogborn to perform a series of humiliating physical acts, conducted a cavity search of her body, engaged in the additional physical assault of spanking her, and ultimately sexually assaulted her. While Ogborn was detained naked in the office and subjected to these searches, she continuously expressed her objection, asked for her clothes, and requested permission to leave. Her requests evoked some sympathy from her managers but were ultimately denied. After a while, several employees appropriately assessed the caller as a fraud. The hoax having been revealed, the call was terminated.

Ogborn filed suit against McDonald's. Discovery revealed substantial evidence that McDonald's corporate legal department was aware of the many similar previous incidents at its restaurants but chose not to train or warn restaurant employees so as to prevent future incidents. The jury awarded Ogborn $1,111,312 in compensatory damages and $5,000,000 in punitive damages. McDonald's contends that Ogborn's false imprisonment claim fails for two reasons: (1) Ogborn cannot establish that she was physically restrained or threatened; and (2) Ogborn voluntarily consented to be searched, precluding the claim of false imprisonment. We disagree. Ogborn's evidence shows that she was forcibly and unlawfully detained.

Restraint constituting false imprisonment may arise out of words, acts, gestures, or the like, which induce a reasonable apprehension that force will be used if the plaintiff does not submit. On the other hand, submission to the mere verbal direction of another unaccompanied by force, or threats of any character, does not constitute false imprisonment.

McDonald's claims Kentucky has yet to recognize causes of action for negligent failure to warn, train, or supervise its employees as asserted by Ogborn.

Kentucky law recognizes that an employer can be held liable for the negligent supervision of its employees. An employer may be held liable for negligent supervision only if he or she knew or had reason to know of the risk that the employment created.

In Ogborn's case, the evidence clearly allowed the jury to find that McDonald's knew or had reason to know there was a risk that the hoax caller would call another of its restaurants; this was a risk to Ogborn's employment which McDonald's created. The jury found, and we cannot disagree, that but for McDonald's failure to satisfy its duty to supervise or train its employees regarding this particular risk of which it was aware, Ogborn would not have been injured.

SECTION 5.17
TORTIOUS
INTERFERENCE
WITH A CONTRACT

The tort of **interference with a contract** has its origins in a 150-year-old case involving an opera singer who attempted to breach her performance contract with one theater in order to sing at another facility. In **Lumley v. Gye,** the court in England found that liability may attach for the wrongful and malicious interference with a contract.

This cause of action stabilizes business relationships since a party that wrongfully interferes with an existing contract or a future business opportunity may face economic sanctions.

To maintain a viable claim for tortuous interference with a contract, the following five elements must be present:

1. An enforceable contract;

2. The defendant's awareness of that contractual relationship;

3. The defendant's intentional inducement to breach the contract;

4. A wrongful interference by the defendant to breach the agreement; and

5. Actual damages.

VIGODA v. DCA PRODUCTIONS PLUS INC.
741 N.Y.S.2d 20 (2002)

Plaintiffs, as members of a rock band called "Groovelily," entered into a one-year agreement with Defendant DCA Productions Plus Inc. (DCA) to act as Plaintiffs' personal manager in exchange for a percentage of the band's professional revenue.

Defendant's services were to include career counseling in addition to acting as a booking agent. Plaintiffs reserved the right to terminate the agreement, which they did on June 2, 1999. At that time, DCA had already submitted an application on plaintiffs' behalf to have them perform at the Great Lakes Showcase of the National Association for Campus Activities (NACA). For a performer to appear at a NACA showcase, the performer must be represented by an agent who is an NACA member.

After Plaintiffs terminated their agreement with DCA, Plaintiffs advised DCA that they wished to continue with DCA as their booking agent. Following negotiations, however, the parties were unable to agree on terms, and the Plaintiffs signed with another booking agent who had formerly worked for DCA. Under NACA rules, there can only be one booking agent for a performer and an act selected for the showcase may be eliminated if the agency submitting it no longer represents the act. Although NACA had responded to DCA's application on behalf of Plaintiffs with a "Letter of Intent," NACA further required that one signed copy must be received by NACA to guarantee Plaintiffs' appearance at the showcase.

When DCA learned that one of its former employees had become the booking agent for Plaintiffs, DCA informed NACA that DCA no longer represented Plaintiffs. NACA removed Plaintiffs from the showcase. Plaintiffs commenced the present action seeking damages for tortious interference with contractual relations.

Tortious interference with contract requires the existence of a valid contract between the plaintiff and a third party, Defendant's knowledge of that contract, Defendant's intentional procurement of the third party's breach of contract without justification, actual breach and damages. The NACA Letter of Intent was not a binding contract since it contained an explicit condition precedent for the obligations under the contract to arise, namely that it must be signed and returned by a certain date to guarantee Plaintiff's appearance. Even if we were to view the Letter of Intent as having created contractual obligations, Defendants' failure to sign and return it did not constitute a breach of contract. NACA rules required that a performing act only have one agent and that the agent who procured the act's appearance remain as agent. DCA merely informed NACA that Plaintiffs were no longer represented by DCA, a fact created by Plaintiffs. The predictable consequence of Plaintiffs' decision was that NACA removed them from the showcase. DCA breached no contractual duty to Plaintiffs and procured no breach of a contractual relationship between Plaintiffs and NACA.

SECTION 5.18
FRAUD

Consumers, accountants and managers of businesses must be vigilant for **fraud.** From Enron and Worldcom to Bernie Madoff, the news is filed with stories of questionable business practices, misrepresentations and deceit. Fraud, however, is not limited to the business giants of the world. Small companies are also greatly harmed by these wrongs. According to a report by the Association of Certified Fraud Examiners, "The median fraud loss suffered by organizations with fewer than 100 employees was $190,000 per scheme . . . higher than the median loss in even the largest organizations. Small businesses continue to suffer disproportionate fraud losses."[15]

These statistics make small business owners question why they are suffering a greater risk of fraud than their larger counterparts. One explanation is that the small enterprise doesn't think it is at risk and the company tends to trust its employees. Unfortunately, any worker might submit to the temptation of stealing if the proper controls aren't in place. A lavish life style, drugs, high medical bills, and student loans, are just a few of the things that could push a trusted employee over the edge.[16]

Fraud takes many forms and a variety of words are used to describe it such as scam, con, sham, ploy, ruse and swindle.[17] The four basic types of financial fraud are:

- **Embezzlement** - the illegal use of funds by a person who controls those funds such as a store cashier who pockets money from the cash register.
- **Internal theft** - the taking of company assets by employees.
- **Payoffs and kickbacks** - situations in which a worker accepts money or other benefits in exchange for access to the company's business or products.
- **Skimming** - when a worker takes cash and doesn't record the revenue on the books.[18]

Fraud is so harmful that it can have civil and criminal implications. In a civil context, however, fraud is considered to be a legal wrong for which the court may award damages. The essential elements consist of a material representation of a past or existing fact, made with knowledge or reckless ignorance of its falsity, which causes a person to rely upon the representations to his detriment.

Disputes arise with some frequency between parties to the purchase of real estate over hidden defects and conditions. The following case involves a lawsuit for damages as the result of mold that was discovered one month after the sale of a home.

JEFFRIES-BAXTER V. INCOGNITO
2005 WL 2509238 (PA. COM. PLEAS, 2005)

This action arises from the sale of residential property. Roxanne Jeffries–Baxter, instituted a lawsuit against Incognito alleging fraud for failure to disclose the existence of mold.

Sellers decided to sell their home at 511 East Mt. Pleasant Avenue in Philadelphia. Thereafter, Plaintiff expressed an interest to purchase the property. On or about April 24, 2003, Plaintiff entered into a written agreement to purchase the property. The Agreement of Sale obligated Plaintiff to pay the sum of $425,000 to Defendant sellers.

The Agreement contains a clause, which states:

"It is understood that Buyer has inspected the Property before signing this Agreement or has waived the right to do so, and has agreed to purchase the Property in its present condition unless otherwise stated in this Agreement."

Additionally, the Agreement of Sale contained a property inspection contingency clause which the Plaintiff exercised. Plaintiff retained Daniel Banks, P.E. to inspect the property for structural, mechanical and electrical deficiencies. An inspection for hazardous materials, including mold was not performed.

The parties proceeded to settlement on June 30, 2003. In July, Plaintiff allegedly discovered that the property was subject to mold damage and was structurally unsound. Plaintiff alleges that she became ill and noticed water spots on the wall leading down into the basement and in the laundry room. Plaintiff called a plumber who allegedly stated the problem was mold. Plaintiff moved out of the house in August 2003. Thereafter, Plaintiff filed a complaint for fraudulent misrepresentation.

To state a claim for fraudulent inducement, a party must allege (1) a representation, (2) which is material to the transaction, (3) made falsely with knowledge of its falsity or recklessness as to whether it is true or false, (4) with the intent of misleading another into relying on it, (5) justifiable reliance on the misrepresentation, and (6) the resulting injury was proximately caused by the reliance. Fraud is a generic term used to describe "anything calculated to deceive, whether by single act or combination, or by suppression of truth, or suggestion of what is false, whether it be by direct falsehood or by innuendo, by speech or silence, word of mouth or look or gesture." Concealment of a material fact can amount to actionable fraud if the

seller intentionally concealed a material fact to deceive the purchaser. Active concealment of defects known to be material to the purchaser is legally equivalent to an affirmative misrepresentation.

The Restatement (Second) of Torts § 550 provides that a vendor of real property may be liable for failure to disclose "material information" concerning the property. To be liable, the concealment must be intentional and must relate to material information. A misrepresentation or concealment will be considered "material" if "it is of such character that had it not been made . . . the transaction would not have been consummated." Finally, liability for fraudulent concealment exists if a defendant prevents a plaintiff from making an investigation he would have otherwise made.

Sellers claim that Plaintiff failed to satisfy two of the elements necessary to state a claim for fraud, a representation and justifiable reliance. After considering the evidence presented in a light most favorable to the Plaintiff, a jury could reasonably conclude that the Sellers knew that mold existed on the property and failed to disclose same to Plaintiff. According to Plaintiff: 1) the seller resided in the subject home for a short period of time, 2) the wall leading to the basement on the right hand side was freshly painted sometime between Plaintiff's initial "walk through" and settlement on the home, 3) conflicting stories existed as to why the property was being sold, and 4) the conflicting disclosure statements as to the existence of a water problem in the basement area. If proven, a jury could reasonably conclude that the Defendant sellers knew that mold existed and failed to disclose same to Plaintiff. Accordingly, the court finds that genuine issues of material fact exist which preclude the entry of summary judgment.

SECTION 5.19
TRADE
DISPARAGEMENT

The law provides a remedy to someone whose reputation has been damaged by false statements through the tort of defamation. Likewise, the law provides a remedy to an entity whose products or services are disparaged by the false statements of another. This civil wrong has various names such as slander of goods, trade libel, unfair competition or interference with prospective business advantage, but the broader title is **trade disparagement.**[19] This is generally defined as an intentional disparagement of the quality of property, goods or services which results in pecuniary damage.

For example, Coca-Cola sued Proctor and Gamble for trade disparagement over its orange juice. The soda giant sells Minute Maid orange juice while Proctor and Gamble distributes Citrus Hill Select. The defendant's commercials emphasized a "heart of the orange" theme that implied that Citrus Hill Select is made only from the "heart" or cubed center of the orange, which makes its sweeter and better tasting than other juices. Coke's process in making orange juice was almost identical to that of the defendant. The court allowed the claim to proceed and stated that a misrepresentation of quality is an actionable tort.[20]

Congress has also passed legislation on the topic in 15 U.S.C. 1125 which provides:

> "Any person who, on or in connection with any goods or services . . . uses in commerce any word, term, name, symbol, or device, or any combination thereof, or any false designation of origin, false or misleading description of fact, or false or misleading representation of fact, which in commercial advertising or promotion, misrepresents the nature, characteristics, qualities, or geographic origin of his or her or another person's goods, services, or commercial activities, shall be liable in a civil action by any person who believes that he or she is or is likely to be damaged by such act."

SECTION 5.20
PRODUCTS LIABILITY

Nearly everyone has heard of Stella Liebeck and her **products liability** claim against McDonald's over a cup of hot coffee. Lieback was a 79-year-old woman who was scolded by hot coffee that she had placed between her legs in a McDonald's parking lot while attempting to add cream and sugar. She received third degree burns and spent several days in the hospital following skin grafts. The evidence showed that this was not an isolated case but that the fast food chain had received hundreds of complaints from people who had sustained burns as the result of their hot coffee. Stella was awarded almost three million dollars by a jury who found the coffee to be defective because McDonald's brewed the beverage at a temperature that far exceeded the temperature of a normal cup of coffee. This famous case for tort reform is an example of a products liability claim.

To better understand the jury's ruling and the defective nature of the coffee, this is some of the evidence produced at trial:

- McDonald's operations manual required its coffee to be brewed at 180 to 190 degrees Fahrenheit.

- Coffee at this temperature, if spilled, causes third-degree burns within three to seven seconds.

- McDonald's admitted it had known of the risk of serious burns from its scalding hot coffee for more than 10 years. This risk had been brought to its attention through multiple other claims and suits.

- McDonald's quality assurance manager stated that McDonald's coffee, at the temperature at which it was poured into Styrofoam cups, was not fit for consumption because it would burn the mouth and throat.

- McDonald's admitted it did not warn customers of the nature and extent of this risk and could offer no explanation as to why it did not.[21]

Section 402A of the Restatement (2nd) of torts, more commonly known as the law of products liability or strict liability, holds sellers of defective products liable for the harm caused to the user, consumer, or his property. This is the case even though the seller has exercised all possible care in the preparation and sale of the product.

This liability extends to any party along the chain of manufacturing or distribution of a product such as an assembling manufacturer, the wholesaler or distributor, and the retail store. Goods with defects that cause harm to a consumer or user of the product are the subject of products liability suits. While this form of strict liability generally applies to the sale of a good, liability has been extended to the leasing of a good, intangibles such as gas, animals, and writings, including navigational charts.[22]

The law of products liability has developed in response to society's changing attitude towards the relationship between the seller of a product and the consumer. Basically, the courts have abandoned the principle of caveat emptor and have made the supplier of a product a virtual guarantor of its safety. This insures that manufacturers who place a defective product in the marketplace will be responsible for the costs of injuries resulting from the defect rather than by the injured person who is powerless to protect himself.

Defective products include those things that contain a manufacturing defect, lack a proper warning, or contain a defect in the product's design, making it unsafe to a user or consumer.

The law of product liability provides that:

1. One who sells any product in a defective condition unreasonably dangerous to the user or consumer or to his property is subject to liability for physical harm thereby caused to the ultimate user or consumer, or to his property, if

   a. the seller is engaged in the business of selling such a product, and

   b. it is expected to and does reach the user or consumer without substantial change in the condition in which it is sold.

2. The rule stated in Subsection (1) applies although

   a. the seller has exercised all possible care in the preparation and sale of his product, and

   b. the user or consumer has not bought the product from or entered into any contractual relation with the seller.

Over the years, the courts have found the seller of a defective product to include anyone in the chain of distribution from the manufacturer to the retailer. Lessors, such as renters of cars, trucks, or heavy equipment, have also been held to be sellers for purposes of products liability law.

Amazon is the world's largest Internet seller of good and products. A buyer can order just about anything that can be found in a brick-and-mortar store from candy to televisions. While Amazon is a direct seller of many of its advertised products, it also has a cooperative venture with vendors who can independently sell their products with Amazon through a service known as Amazon Marketplace. If a person buys a defective product though Amazon Marketplace, would Amazon be liable as a seller? That is the issue in **Oberdorf v. Amazon.Com, Inc.**, a case of first impression.

OBERDORF V. AMAZON.COM, INC.
2017 WL 6527142 (M.D. PA. 2017)

On January 12, 2015, while walking her dog, Heather Oberdorf suffered severe injuries to her eye when the retractable leash she was using suddenly malfunctioned, snapping backwards and hitting her violently in the face.

Amazon.com is a well-known online retailer. In addition to selling a variety of goods directly to consumers, it also serves as a vehicle through which third parties may independently offer products for sale. This service, known as the "Amazon Marketplace," is currently utilized by more than one million third-party vendors. These third-party vendors decide which products they wish to sell, obtain their stock from manufacturers or upstream distributors, and set their own sales price. They provide a description of the product to Amazon, which Amazon uses to create a listing on its website. Consumers browsing or searching for products on Amazon may be directed to these listings, where they are informed that they are purchasing from an identified third party, and not from Amazon itself. Unless the third-party vendor participates in a special "Fulfillment by Amazon" program, Amazon has no interaction with the third-party vendor's product at any time.

Amazon does, however, maintain some control over the Amazon Marketplace sales process. It serves as the conduit through which payment flows, collecting money from purchasers and directing it to third-party vendors after deducting a fee. It requires third-party vendors, as a condition of utilizing the Marketplace, to agree to conduct all communication with consumers through its messaging platform. It retains the right to edit the content and determine the appearance of product listings. And it imposes rules on how third-party vendors should handle shipping and returns.

Ms. Oberdorf purchased the retractable leash in question on the Amazon Marketplace from a third-party vendor identified as "The Furry Gang." Following the accident, Plaintiffs have apparently been unable to make contact with The Furry Gang or with the manufacturer of the retractable leash.

The Oberdorfs initiated this suit against Amazon. Their Complaint describes the accident as a products liability claim, in that Amazon failed to "provide adequate warnings regarding the use of the subject leash, causing it to be unreasonably dangerous to the intended user at the time it left Amazon's possession." and that the leash was "defectively designed," causing it to be unreasonably dangerous at the time it left the possession of the defendant. Amazon moved for summary judgment.

Pennsylvania has adopted § 402A of the Second Restatement of Torts, which states that:

(1) One who sells any product in a defective condition unreasonably dangerous to the user or consumer or to his property is subject to liability for physical harm thereby caused to the ultimate user or consumer, or to his property if:

    (a) the seller is engaged in the business of selling such a product, and

    (b) it is expected to and does reach the user or consumer without substantial change in the condition in which it is sold.

(2) The rule stated in Subsection (1) applies although

    (a) the seller has exercised all possible care in the preparation and sale of his product, and

    (b) the user or consumer has not bought the product from or entered into any contractual relation with the seller.

This provision creates a products liability regime, whereby a plaintiff may recover against a defendant if he can prove that a product was defectively designed or manufactured, or came with an insufficient warning of its dangers.

Although the Pennsylvania Supreme Court has defined "seller" under § 402A expansively, it has not left that category boundless. In **Musser v. Vilsmeier Auction Co., Inc.**, for example, it held that an auctioneer is not a "seller" for purposes of § 402A. There, the Court first noted the policy behind § 402A—i.e., the "special responsibility for the safety of the public undertaken by one who enters into the business of supplying human beings with products which may endanger the safety of their persons and property, and the forced reliance upon that undertaking on the part of those who purchase such goods"—and then indicated that it would not impose strict liability on a defendant unless that policy was furthered. The auction company merely provided a market as the agent of the seller. It had no role in the selection of the goods to be sold, in relation to which its momentary control was merely fortuitous and not undertaken specifically.

The Pennsylvania Supreme Court has not ruled on whether an online sales listing service like Amazon Marketplace qualifies as a "seller" under § 402A Like an auctioneer, Amazon is merely a third-party vendor's "means of marketing," since third-party vendors—not Amazon—"choose the products and expose them for sale by means of" the Marketplace. Because of the enormous number of third-party vendors and, presumably, the correspondingly enormous number of goods

sold by those vendors, Amazon is similarly "not equipped to pass upon the quality of the myriad of products" available on its Marketplace. And because Amazon has "no role in the selection of the goods to be sold," it also cannot have any "direct impact upon the manufacture of the products" sold by the third-party vendors.

The Amazon Marketplace serves as a sort of newspaper classified ad section, connecting potential consumers with eager sellers in an efficient, modern, streamlined manner. Because subjecting it to strict liability would not further the purposes of § 402A, it cannot be liable to the Oberdorfs under a products liability theory. Therefore, summary judgment will be granted in favor of Amazon on Counts I and II of the Oberdorfs' Complaint.

QUESTIONS FOR DISCUSSION:

1. Should a manufacturer of a microwave be strictly liable for failing to warn a consumer that a cat should not be dried in the appliance?

2. Should a manufacturer of a lawn mower be strictly liable when a person is injured when he uses a lawn mower to trim his hedges?

SECTION 5.21 REVIEW CASES

1. Hustler Magazine featured a "parody" of an advertisement for Campari Liqueur entitled, "Jerry Falwell talks about his first time." While the parody was modeled after an actual Campari advertising campaign, the Hustler ad clearly played to the sexual double entendre of the subject, "first times." Copying the layout of the Campari ads, Hustler's editors chose this conservative religious official as their featured celebrity and drafted an alleged "interview," in which Falwell states that his "first time" was during a drunken incestuous rendezvous with his mother in an outhouse. Falwell sued Hustler Magazine for defamation and infliction of emotional distress. Hustler defended the claim on the basis of the First Amendment and the fact that Falwell is a public figure. Who should win the case? **Hustler Magazine v. Jerry Falwell, No. 87-1278 (U.S. 1986).**

2. Dustin Hoffman is a highly successful and recognizable motion picture actor. He has a strong policy of not endorsing commercial products for fear that he will be perceived in a negative way which would suggest that his career is in decline. Los Angeles Magazine published a photograph of Hoffman as he appeared in the movie "Toostie," and, through

computer software, altered the photograph to make it appear as though the actor was wearing a contemporary silk gown designed by Richard Tyler and high-heeled shoes created by Ralph Lauren. Underneath the picture was the quote: "Dustin Hoffman isn't a drag in a butter-colored silk gown by Richard Tyler and Ralph Lauren heels." Hoffman sued the magazine for invasion of privacy for their commercial use of his name and likeness in a commercial venture. Is the magazine liable for the altered photograph of the actor or is it merely a parody for which no liability would attach? **Dustin Hoffman v. Capital City/ABC, Inc., 33 F. Supp. 2d 867 (1999).**

3. Schick and his father were playing golf with two other people. Schick teed off from the 16th hole and was followed by two other golfers, including his father. Subsequently, Verloito teed off and sliced his drive into the woods on the right, but the ball did not go out of bounds. Schick and his father then walked to their golf cart in front of the tee, assuming that Verloito would play his second shot from the woods. Instead, the golfer unexpectedly hit a second shot from the tee, striking Schick in the face. Did Schick assume the risk of his injuries for being hit by a ball on the golf course? **Jeffrey Schick v. John Verloito, 744 A.2d 219 (N.J. Super. 2000).**

4. Linda Matarazzo attended an Aerosmith concert at Madison Square Garden. She was injured during the concert by an unknown patron who struck her in the nose as she attempted to return to her seat. Matarazzo sued Aerosmith on the grounds that the group's music encourages violence and their concerts attract "crazies" who are particularly drawn to this type of message. Warner Brothers Records was also sued under the theory that Warner Brothers willfully, intentionally, and deliberately aided and abetted Aerosmith in attracting such "crazies" to their concerts by promoting and selling records and tapes of the group's music. Should Aerosmith and Warner Brothers be responsible for the injuries sustained by the plaintiff? **Linda Matarazzo v. Aerosmith Productions, Inc. 1989 W.L. 140322 (S.D. N.Y. 1989).**

5. Debbie Tay had been a frequent guest on the Howard Stern show before her death at the age of 28. She was a topless dancer whose claim of having had sexual encounters with females from outer space earned her the nickname of "Space Lesbian." Tay was cremated and her ashes were given by the family to her friend, Chaunce Hayden, who appeared on the Stern Radio Show with a box containing some of the remains. Stern played prior video clips of Tay's appearances on the program and then shook and rattled the box containing the decedent's remains. Stern even handled some of the bone fragments. These actions prompted a lawsuit by Tay's next-of-kin against Stern

for infliction of emotional distress. Can the family hold Howard Stern responsible for the way he handled the decedent's ashes on his television show? **Jeffrey Roach v. Howard Stern, 653 N.Y.S. 2d 532 (S. Ct. 1996).**

6. Fisher and Segal composed the classic '50s' tune "When Sunny Gets Blue." Dees requested permission to use part of the composition in order to create a comedic version of the song but permission was refused. A few months later, Dees released a comedy tape entitled, "Put It Where the Moon Don't Shine." One cut on the release was, "When Sonny Sniff's Glue." The parody was an obvious take-off on the composers' song and copied the first six of the composition's thirty-eight bars of music—its recognizable main theme. In addition, the remake changed the opening lyrics from "When Sunny gets blue, her eyes get gray and cloudy, then the rain begins to fall," to "When Sonny sniffs glue, her eyes get red and bulgy, then her hair begins to fall." The composers sued Dees for defamation, claiming the new version of the song associated the composition with obscene, indecent and offensive words. Will Dees be responsible for the parody? **Marvin Fisher v. Rick Dees, 794 F.2d 432 (9ᵗʰ Cir. 1986).**

SECTION 5.22 INTERNET REFERENCES

For more information about the topics in this Chapter, see the following Internet sites:

- **www.lawguru.com/auto.html**
  For information on automobile accidents.

- **www.itslegal.com/infonet/injury/injurymain.html**
  Answers to frequently asked questions about tort law, including transportation accidents, injuries to property, medical malpractice, and defamation are provided at this address.

- **www.prairielaw.com/articles/article.asp?channelid= 22&articleid=1371**
  A general overview of the law of personal injury is located at this web address.

- **www.lectlaw.com/tmed.html**
  This site offers practical information about medical malpractice, civil litigation, and standards of care.

- **www.ashcraftandgerel.com**
  A law firm that specializes in tort law has created this website. It provides general information about the subject, and maintains a library of articles on the law of torts, including materials on medical malpractice, and automobile accident litigation.

- **www.legalaidman.com**
  Practical information about personal injury claims, including what to do after an accident and the litigation process, is offered at this website.

- **http://encarta.msn.com/index/conciseindex/17/0170400.htm**
  Encarta Encyclopedia provides an overview of the law of negligence at this address, including the burden of proof in a civil case.

Footnotes:

1. What Are Business Torts?, WiseGEEK, http://www.wisegeek.com/what-are-business-torts.htm (last visited September 25, 2013).

2. Tort, Contract and Real Property Trials, Bureau of Justice Statistics, http://www.bjs.gov/index.cfm?ty=tp&tid=451 (last visited September 25, 2013).

3. 14.10 (Civ) Medical Malpractice—Standard Of Care, Pennsylvania Suggested Standard Civil Jury Instructions, Fourth Edition, Volume II, Chapter XIV, Medical Professional Negligence.

4. Accounting Malpractice, Lawyers and Settlemetns.com, http://www.lawyersandsettlements.com/lawsuit/accounting-malpractice.html (last visited September 25, 2013).

5. *Id.*

6. CPA Malpractice, C.P. Shumann, P.C., http://www.cpschumannco.com/business.asp?subject=109 (last visited September 25, 2013).

7. *Id.*

8. **Thomas v. Cleary, 768 P.2d 1090 (Alaska, 1989).**

9. Kubasek, et. al., "Accountants Liability for Negligence," Dynamic Business Law, Chapter Eleven, McGraw Hill, 2013, page 245.

10. Injury Attorney Explains Willful and Wanton Misconduct, Brien Roche Law, http://www.brienrochelaw.com/tort-law/tort-terms/w/willful-and-wanton-misconduct/ (last visited September 25, 2013).

11. Dram-Shop Liability Law and Legal Definition, USLegal.com, http://definitions.uslegal.com/d/dram-shop-liability/ (last visited September 27, 2013).

12. **Rivero v. Timblin, 2010 WL 7374092 (Court of Common Pleas of Pennsylvania).**

13. *Id.*

14. Restaurant Shift Turns Into Nightmare, ABC News, http://abcnews.go.com/Primetime/story?id=1297922&page=1(last visited September 27, 2013).

15. Fraud and the Small Business, National Federation of Small Businesses, http://www.nfib.com/business-resources/business-resources-item?cmsid=45608 (last visited September 27, 2013).

16. *Id.*

17. A-Z of Fraud, Action Fraud, http://www.actionfraud.police.uk/a-z_of_fraud (last visited September 27, 2013).

18. Lita Epstein, Basic Types of Financial Fraud in Businesses, For Dummies, /hohttp://www.dummies.com/how-to/content/basic-types-of-financial-w-to/content/basic-types-of-financial-fraud-in-businesses.html (last visited September 27, 2013).

19. Commercial Disparagement in Pennsylvania, Wolf Baldwin and Associates, http://www.wolfbaldwin.com/Articles/Commercial-Disparagement-in-Pennsylvania.shtml (last visited September 27, 2013).

20. **Coca-Cola Co. v. Procter & Gamble Co., 822 F.2d 28 (C.A.6 (Ohio), 1987).**

21. The McDonald's Hot Coffee Case, Consumer Attorneys of California, https://www.caoc.org/?pg=facts (last visited September 27, 2013).

22. Products Liability Law: An Overview, Legal Information Institute, http://www.law.cornell.edu/wex/products_liability (last visited September 27, 2013).

KEY TERMS

Adult Activity

Assault

Assumption of the Risk

Attractive Nuisance Doctrine

Battery

Breach of Duty

Business Tort

Business Visitor

Comparative Negligence

Contributory Negligence

Damages

Defamation

Defamatory

Dram Shop Liability

Duty of Care

Engagement Letter

False Imprisonment

Fraud

Good Samaritan Statute

Imputed Negligence

Independent Contractor

Infliction of Emotional
    Distress

Intentional Tort

Interference with a Contract

Invasion of Privacy

Liability of Parents

Libel

Licensee

Monetary Limits of Liability

Negligence

Products Liability

Proximate Cause

Restatement

Slander

Substantial Factor

Title VII of the Civil Rights
    Act of 1964

Tort

Tortfeasor

Tortious Interference with
    a Contract

Trade Disparagement

Trespasser

Vicarious Liability

Willful and Wanton Misconduct

CHAPTER 6

PROPERTY LAW
BY: BARBARA SCHNELLER AND
SAMUEL D. HODGE, JR.

Land is, like any other possession, by natural right wholly in the power of its present owner; and may be sold, given or bequeathed, absolutely or conditionally. But natural law would avail little without the protection of the law.

—Samuel Johnson

SECTION 6.1
INTRODUCTION

Joe Robert and his former college roommate, Carson Peterson, purchased a house in Ocean City as an investment property. Over the past few years, however, Mr. Peterson encountered a streak of bad luck at the casinos and a $50,000 judgment was entered against him by a creditor who had the New Jersey property and its contents listed for Sheriff Sale. Joe's ability to prevent the Sheriff Sale will depend upon how he owns the house and its contents with Mr. Peterson.

Property law deals with those rights and duties that arise out of the ownership or possession of real and personal property. In turn, **real property** consists of the land going from the center of the earth to the heavens and everything permanently attached to the land. For instance, a building, tree or driveway are considered part of the realty. This area of jurisprudence is also known as **real estate** law. **Personal property** is everything else and includes such things as a car, books, clothes, and furniture, as well as bank accounts, stocks, bonds, patents, and copyrights. Property law defines and enforces the rights and responsibilities that accompany these interests in all forms of property.

Property rights are based upon customs and society. Historically, a person living in seclusion did not fret about property rights. When groups of individuals came together, however, they needed to create laws to deal with the benefits of their land. While the issue of property rights receives much attention in modern society, the topic has been debated in the United States since it was created.[1]

Property law has been part of the fabric of this county's legal system since its inception, especially since many settlers could not own land in their home country. Differences among the colonists about following British rules resulted in variances in the law—some desired to follow British customs, while others wanted to discard those traditions. For instance, the ability of women to own land was based on the rights that females living

285

in that colony enjoyed.[2] While Virginia allowed widows to own land, those living in Connecticut had no rights to own property. Yet other colonies required husbands to secure signatures of their wives before title to joint property could be transferred.[3]

The first couple centuries of this country's existence witnessed more than one hundred cases in which the Supreme Court had to decide disputes involving women's rights to property. One of the earliest matters was **Barnes' Lessee v. Irwin** in 1793. This case involved a prenuptial agreement and a wife's interest in property that she inherited. The court upheld the validity of the widow's right to transfer that land through her will. These types of issues demonstrated the importance of property ownership in the many laws enacted and court opinions decided during this country's early history.[4]

The bottom line is that the rights in property offer a number of advantages to the business environment, the economy and society as a whole. Not only do they stimulate economic growth, but nations with sound property laws tend to enjoy more successful economies. Property rights, therefore, have an important role in maintaining a healthy economy.[5]

Property law for the most part is created and enforced by the state in which the property is located.

SECTION 6.2 OWNERSHIP

What is the benefit of property ownership? Not only is the owner able to use and enjoy the land, but equity builds up over time, allowing the property to become a major source of investment. After all, owning a home is a goal of most Americans, and it is believed that through hard work and determination, it's possible to achieve a modicum of success and security.[6] What then is meant by ownership?

Ownership is often viewed as a bundle of rights. Owners have certain rights with respect to their property: they may use it, prevent others from using it, lend it to someone else, sell it, give it away, or destroy it. **Title** refers to the right of ownership. A person who has title to property has all of the rights of ownership. But the idea of title, in a legal context, is more abstract. Courts are often asked to determine who, among several contenders, has ownership rights to a given piece of land. A **quiet title** action is used for this purpose. The court listens to the facts presented by everyone who has a claim to the real property and decides who the owner is, i.e., who has title.

Property can be owned by many types of entities, such as businesses, individuals, partnerships, trusts, cooperatives and even religious or other charitable organizations. It is also subject to division, thereby giving a number of people ownership in the same asset. This has required the creation of specialized terms to explain the ways property may be owned or possessed.

It is customary to use **documents of title** to prove ownership, for example, title to a car, a **"deed"** to a house, or a "bill of sale" for merchandise.

Conveyancing is the term used for the processing and transferring of title between the owner of real estate and the buyer. This transfer generally occurs at a real estate settlement where the seller signs a deed conveying the appropriate interest in the property to a third person. On the other hand, items of personal property are usually conveyed by the mere delivery of the item to another.

Property can be shared with others in a number of ways, so it is important to learn the forms of ownership since it can have a bearing on the rights and obligations of the owners. If the property is owned by more than one person, what happens to that individual's interest upon death? Can one owner transfer her interest to the property without the consent of the other owner? Can the creditor of one owner force the sale of the property to pay the judgment?

The following three methods are the most common forms of ownership and each has its own rules and implications:

A. Sole Ownership

The simplest form of title is **sole ownership** in which one person enjoys the bundle of rights and liabilities that accompany property. A deed to land will reflect this fact by referring to the owner as a single man or single woman. This type of ownership, however, is not limited to real estate. A business owned by one person is labeled a **sole proprietorship** and there is no distinction between the person's personal and business assets. In other words, the liabilities of the business are also the liabilities of the individual. Since the property is owned and controlled by one person, the assets will generally pass upon the owner's death to whomever the owner desires or by intestate succession if there is no will. Interstate succession means that the property will pass to the decedent's heirs according to an established hierarchy. For instance, if there are no children, the property will pass to the surviving spouse. If there are surviving children, the property is divided between the spouse and children.

B. Concurrent Ownership

It is common for people to jointly own assets with one another. The law calls this **concurrent** or **joint ownership** and it occurs when the title to property is shared by two or more people. The most common forms of concurrent ownership are **tenancy in common** and **joint tenancy** with the **right of survivorship.** Both forms give the co-owners essentially equal rights to the property. Each owner, however, has given up the right of exclusivity, meaning one owner cannot prevent his co-owner(s) from using the property.

The difference between a tenancy in common and joint tenancy deals with what happens when one co-owner dies. In a tenancy in common, if one co-owner dies, his share will pass to his heirs. In a joint tenancy, the right of survivorship means that if one co-owner dies, his share will pass to the surviving co-owner. Thus, if Joe Roberts and Peter Christopher have a joint bank account as tenants in common, either of them may make deposits or withdraw funds. If Joe dies, his share will pass to his heirs, usually the family, and Peter will keep his one-half share. If, on the other hand, Joe and Peter are joint tenants with the right of survivorship, and Joe dies, his share will automatically pass to Peter who becomes the sole owner of the bank account. When property is owned concurrently as joint tenants with the right of survivorship, the co-owners forfeit their individual rights to "alienate," or dispose of, the property as they wish at the time of death. The property is automatically transferred to the survivor and does not become part of the estate.

It is sometimes unclear whether property is owned as a joint tenancy or as a tenancy in common. When a dispute arises over the form of ownership, courts scrupulously examine the documents of title to determine what type of ownership was specified by the co-tenants or, if the language is ambiguous, what the parties intended. For example, the Pennsylvania legislature has solved this problem by providing that unless the owners clearly state that the co-tenancy is a "joint tenancy with the right of survivorship," it will be considered a tenancy in common.

As the following case shows, the court's decision on how to classify ownership may be crucial in determining how much a creditor can force a debtor to repay.

University of Montana v. Coe
704 P.2d 1029 (Montana 1985)

This case involves an execution on a bank account to recover student loans under the National Direct Student Loan Program.

The appellant, Mark D. Coe, a former Montana University student, took out a series of student loans under the National Direct Student Loan Program, amounting to $6,437.30. He defaulted on the loans and made only one payment of $20. The University brought suit and obtained a partial summary judgment in the sum of $6,437.30.

Through one of several executions, the University levied against the joint checking account of Mark Coe at the First Bank-Western Montana, Missoula. The savings account was in the name of "Tammerly or Mark D. Coe," which at the time of

execution had a balance of $3,179.23. Tammerly Coe requested the Bank not to release the funds, claiming that the funds did not belong to Mark Coe, but rather belonged to her and to Jordan Coe, brother to Tammerly and Mark. Tammerly Coe and her brother, Jordan contend that they deposited the money in the bank and that their brother, Mark, deposited no funds whatsoever. However, one of the exhibits presented to the District Court was a copy of the signature card of the account which listed the names of Tammerly Coe or Mark D. Coe, along with their addresses, which stated that Mark was "the owner of a joint checking account with his sister." Jordan Coe did not sign this account, nor does his name appear on the signature card though he claims he owns $2,000 of the funds in the account. Jordan alleges he gave that amount to Tammerly for safe keeping on his behalf. Tammerly claims the remainder of the funds, less the $2,000 deposited by her brother Jordan, belong to her and that Mark Coe never made a deposit.

The question is whether this is a joint account or a tenancy in common with no survivor. This Court in **Ivins v. Hardy, 179 P.2d 745,** held that a tenancy in common is created whenever the instrument bringing an estate of two or more persons into existence does not specifically state that the estate created is other than a "tenancy in common." The facts situation concerning the signing of the signature card in **Casagranda v. Donahue** and this case are different. The card signed in the joint account in **Casagranda** specifically said:

> "The undersigned hereby open an account in your bank as joint tenants and not as tenants in common, and, upon the death of either or any of us, all monies then in this account shall be paid to the survivor or survivors as his, her, or their individual property."

Under the facts in **Casagranda,** we held that the savings account became the individual property of respondent upon the decedent's death. Right of survivorship cannot be defeated by the executrix of decedent's estate, and any attempt to satisfy the general devises in a will.

In the case at the bar, the signature card signed by Tammerly D. Coe or Mark D. Coe noted:

> "The undersigned depositor, whose bank account is described on the reverse side, hereby appoints the person(s) whose specimen signature(s) appears above, agent(s) of the undersigned with respect to said bank account with the authority specified in the Bank's posted General Rules and Regulations Governing Bank Accounts."

We find that the major distinguishing characteristic of a joint tenancy as opposed to a tenancy in common is a right of the survivor of each of the co-tenants. We hold, under the facts of this case, that this is a tenancy in common and that the creditor, University of Montana, is entitled to one-half, not the total amount levied against the account currently being held by the Clerk of the Court of the Fourth Judicial District.

SECTION 6.3 **THE JOINT** **BANK ACCOUNT**	**PARK, BROWN & SMITH, P.C.** **ATTORNEYS AT LAW** **MEMORANDUM**

PROBLEM SIX

TO: All Law Clerks

FROM: Peter Smith, Esquire

RE: The Joint Bank Account

Joe Roberts and Donald Feelgood decided to open a joint savings account with their golf partner, Osgood G. Huntingdon, so they could put away their gambling money. Feelgood and Huntingdon informed Joe that they would open the joint account since Joe was busy. Feelgood and Huntingdon signed the bank papers which noted that all three were joint tenants of the account. Nothing further was specified. Joe deposited $5,000 into the account. Feelgood and Huntingdon made similar deposits.

About two weeks later, Huntingdon visited Las Vegas and was quite successful at the slot machines and soon accumulated $500 in quarters. He then cashed in this change for silver dollars so he could play the progressive slot machine. Ten spins later, Huntingdon drew three cherries and won $100,000. He supplied the casino with his social security number and wire-transferred the funds to the newly created bank account. Unfortunately, Huntingdon's luck ran out that evening when he was struck and killed by a car while crossing Las Vegas Boulevard.

Joe was devastated by the news. Mr. Roberts' day grew even bleaker when he was served with a subpoena to appear at a support hearing initiated by a woman who claims that Joe is the father of her five-year-old boy.

Mr. Roberts failed to attend the paternity hearing so the court imposed a retroactive support order for $50,000 and ordered Joe to pay $2,000 a month in future support payments.

Wanting to keep this embarrassing matter from his wife, Joe wrote a check for $54,000 from the joint account. This sum represented the retroactive support obligation and two months of future payments.

When the attorney for the Estate of Osgood Huntingdon learned of the transaction, he sued Roberts to prevent future withdrawals from the account. The lawyer also requested a judgment against Joe for $54,000 which represented the sum our client had already withdrawn from the account. The Estate claimed that Joe was merely entitled to his original $5,000 deposit. In the alternative, the attorney suggests that Joe has a tenancy in common and is only entitled to one-third of the account's balance.

It is our position that Mr. Roberts is a joint tenant with the right of survivorship, thus entitling him to one half of the money at the time of Mr. Huntingdon's death. The remaining 50% should automatically go to Feelgood. Based upon **University of Montana v. Coe,** which is set forth earlier in this Chapter, answer the following questions:

1. Who should win? Please explain your answer.

2. What are the advantages and disadvantages of a tenancy in common?

3. What purpose do you think a joint tenancy with the right of survivorship serves?

PROBLEM SIX
ANSWER SHEET

Name   **Please Print Clearly**

1. Who should win? Please explain your answer.

_____

_____

_____

_____

_____

_____

_____

_____

2. What are the advantages and disadvantages of a tenancy in common?

_____

_____

_____

_____

_____

_____

_____

_____

3. What purpose do you think a joint tenancy with right of survivor serves?

_____

_____

_____

_____

_____

_____

_____

_____

_____

_____

_____

_____

_____

_____

_____

_____

_____

_____

C. Other Kinds of Concurrent Ownership

Married people enjoy a special form of co-ownership designed to protect the marital assets from creditors and to insure an easy transition of the property to the surviving spouse upon a tenant's death. Most states recognize a **tenancy by the entirety,** which is similar to a joint tenancy because it carries the right of survivorship. It differs from a joint tenancy, however, in that neither spouse can convey his or her interest in the property without the other. In other words, each spouse owns 100 percent interest in the property and cannot dispose of the asset without the consent of the other. Because each spouse owns 100 percent of the property, a creditor of one spouse is unable to seize the joint asset. Sophisticated creditors, such as banks and mortgage companies, are aware of this rule and require both spouses to sign the loan documentation, even though only one spouse may receive the money.

Husbands and wives have historically been viewed as one, so in the absence of clear evidence to the contrary, property owned by a married couple is held as a tenancy by the entireties. For instance, a deposit in a bank account which is opened in the name of a "husband and wife," or a "husband or wife" creates a tenancy by the entirety with all of the benefits relating to entirety ownership irrespective of how the joint account is designated.

During the duration of the marriage, either spouse has the presumptive power to act for both, so long as both spouses share in the proceeds. Neither spouse, however, may take the property for his or her sole use unless the other spouse consents. There have been numerous cases over the years where one spouse secretively withdraws money from an entireties bank account and then deposits the funds in a different bank account solely under that person's name. This is a common tactic when a divorce is contemplated. Since this type of unilateral severance works a hardship to the other, the courts have found that the unauthorized transfer destroys the tenancy by the entireties and will order the funds to be divided in half regardless on how the funds were generated. Two elements must exist in order for a court to find that such an "implied mutual agreement" has severed a tenancy by the entireties. A misappropriation by one spouse must occur (the offer), and the other spouse must file a suit for an accounting, division or other appropriate relief (the acceptance).

A handful of jurisdictions, especially in the West, are community property states including Arizona, Idaho, California, Louisiana, Nevada, New Mexico, Texas, Washington and Wisconsin. A community property state regards all property acquired during the marriage, with the exception of that obtained through gift or inheritance, as being owned jointly by the couple. For example, a house or pension in the name of one spouse will be considered the joint asset of both.

As with a tenancy by the entirety, neither spouse can convey separately his or her interest without the consent of the other. In some states, community property will pass to the surviving spouse if one dies. In others, the deceased spouse's interest will pass to his or her heirs. Both a tenancy by the entirety and community property rights will be terminated or severed by a divorce. In that event, property is automatically transferred to a tenancy in common with each owning a one-half interest. These forms of co-ownership apply to both real and personal property.

When a husband and wife own property together, the courts will go out of their way to classify the property as tenancy by the entirety. This tendency is demonstrated by the following case.

OLSON V. CONSTITUTION BANK
423 PA. SUPER. 134 (1993)

We are asked to review the orders of the Court denying to dissolve an attachment by Elizabeth Olson and Robert Olson.

The record discloses that on May 24, 1991, Constitution Bank filed a complaint against the defendant, Robert. Olson, on his guarantee of a loan to Capital Management L.P. in the amount of $251,564.37.

In aid of execution, the plaintiff took Mr. Olson's deposition and learned that he had two accounts with Rorer & Co.: one was co-owned with his wife, Elizabeth and the second was an individual retirement account (IRA). Interrogatories which disclosed that the account with Rorer was designated: "Robert P. Olson Elizabeth Q. Olson JTWROS" and held $159,516.72; and the IRA account was in Mr. Olson's name only and contained $40,995.68. Rorer indicated that all cash and securities in the Olson accounts were in the custody of Paine Webber, Inc., one being "[a] joint account entitled Robert Olson & Elizabeth Olson, J.T.W.R.O.S." Likewise, Merrill Lynch confirmed that the defendant maintained a cash management account co-owned with his wife and captioned: "JTWROS" and valued at $20,545.43.

The plaintiff filed a response asserting that a presumption exists that property held by husband and wife, unless otherwise designated, is a tenancy by the entireties. However, the plaintiff urged that the "presumption" had been "overcome" with the Olsons' electing to title their brokerage accounts as joint tenants with right of survivorship (JTWROS), and, as such, "they could not now seek to insulate these accounts from Mr. Olson's lawful creditors."

The case law appears established in that the type of ownership which is created in property when a husband and wife are involved, regardless of how the relationship is denominated and in the absence of clear and convincing evidence to the contrary, is as tenants by the entireties. Where property or an account is placed in the names of a husband and wife, a gift and the creation of an estate by the entireties is presumed even though the funds used to acquire the property were exclusively those of the husband. The placing of the property in both names, without more, creates an estate by the entireties. *It is their actual marital status and not necessarily the words stated or omitted in the instrument that determines their right to take as tenants by the entireties.* In order to overcome the presumption that an estate by the entireties exists and that a complete gift ensued there from, there must be clear and convincing evidence to the contrary. The same principles apply whether real estate, personal property or stocks and securities are involved.

A deposit in a bank account, in a checking account or in a savings account, which is opened or registered in the name of a husband and wife, or of a husband or wife, *creates a tenancy by the entireties, irrespective of whether the money deposited is payable to husband and wife or to husband or wife, or is denominated a joint account or a joint tenancy.*

When we align the facts with the applicable law, we find that Mr. Olson opened accounts with Paine Webber and Merrill Lynch under the legend: "Robert Olson & Elizabeth Olson, J.T.W.R.O.S." At the moment Olson opened the accounts, *he was married* to the individual named as a co-owner of the funds and this coalesced with the legal unities to establish a tenancy by the entireties.

As the accounts, from their inception, were jointly established by the husband for himself and his wife, the creditor/Constitution Bank has no present interest in such estates by the entireties. Should the wife survive the husband she will become the absolute owner of the accounts, in which the creditor will have no interest. On the other hand, if the husband survives the wife, he will become the owner of the property by survivorship, and it will be subject to all of his debts as any other property or estate of his would be.

D. Encumbrances

As a sole owner or co-owner, it is possible to give up one or more of the rights of ownership. In property law, this is called an **encumbrance.** An encumbrance is any right or interest that someone has in another's real property. For example, if a homeowner rents her house, she has given the tenant the rights of possession and use during the term of the lease. The title to the real property therefore encumbered: she still owns the house but no longer has all of the rights of ownership because she has given some to the tenant for the term of the lease. Another example is a mortgage or lien on a property. For instance, a bank obtains an interest in the parcel of land until the loan is repaid and a business or person who makes improvements to the land of another obtains a mechanics lien until the work is paid in full.

E. Easements

An **easement** is the granting of a nonpossessory right to use a part of the land by an entity that does not own the land. A common example is the grant of an easement to a utility company to bury gas, electric and telephone lines on the owner's property. Easements run with the land on transfer, so they constitute restrictions on the property and the new owner must honor the easement. Easements can be formed in a number of ways, including by contract, deed or implication.

F. Adverse Possession

Adverse possession is an archaic principle that is deeply rooted in American jurisprudence. One hundred and fifty years ago, adverse possession was a method that plantation owners employed to claim ownership over runaway slaves. The principle is still part of the law, but adverse possession is currently applied to real estate and squatters who take possession of an abandoned property, fix it up and stay in the home for an extending period of time in order to claim that the property is now theirs.[7]

Adverse possession permits a person who possesses land owned by another for an extended period of time to claim legal ownership to the land. The laws of each state vary but Pennsylvania requires possession for twenty one years.[8] For instance, if a neighbor erects a fence two feet onto an adjacent landowner's property and the landowner says nothing about the intrusion, he could lose ownership to the strip of lane after twenty one years.

A typical adverse possession law mandates that the following requirements be present:

- Open and Notorious. The person seeking adverse possession must occupy a parcel of land in a manner that is obvious.

- Exclusive. The property must be occupied solely by the individual trying to claim ownership by adverse possession.

- Hostile. The occupation must be adverse to the interests of the owner.

- Statutory Period. Occupation of the property must continue for the statutory period.

- Continuous and Uninterrupted. The above requirements must be satisfied concurrently during the time period.[9]

**SECTION 6.4
PERSONAL PROPERTY**

Various legal terms are used to describe items of personal property. **Chattel,** an old English word for cattle, has come to mean all forms of personal property: tangible or intangible. **Tangible personal property** refers to a physical object. Personal property that is both tangible and movable is called a **good.** An automobile is an example of a good. **Intangible property** gives the owner a right rather than a physical object of independent value. For example, the owner of a share of stock in a company has certain rights, such as the right to receive dividends and the right to vote for the corporation's officers. But there is no physical object that goes with it, aside from the stock certificate that says the investor owns a share of the corporation. Other forms of intangible personal property include patents, trademarks, and copyrights.

SECTION 6.5
ACQUIRING TITLE TO
PERSONAL PROPERTY

Personal property may be acquired by purchase, gift, production or possession.

A. Purchase

The most common way to acquire ownership of personal property is to purchase it. A **purchase** is the transfer of title from one owner to another for payment or compensation. State law governs the purchase and sale of goods as noted in Chapter Two. The states have adopted Article 2 of the **Uniform Commercial Code,** a lengthy catalog of rules that details the rights and responsibilities of sellers and buyers of goods. Federal and state laws, including the Securities Exchange Act and Articles 3 and 4 of the Uniform Commercial Code regulate the purchase and sale of intangibles.

B. Gift

Personal property may also be acquired by gift, a transfer of title to property without payment or compensation. A **gift** may be made **inter vivos,** which means while the donor is alive, or it may take effect upon death under the terms of a will or the laws of inheritance. There are three requirements for an inter vivos gift to be valid: **(1)** the donor must intend to make a gift of the property; **(2)** the donor must deliver the property to the donee; and **(3)** the donee must accept the property. If the gift is valid, all the rights of ownership pass from the donor to the donee. For example, a gift is completed when a person hands a present to another during the holiday season and the recipient takes the package.

A **gift causa mortis** is the transfer of personal property made in contemplation of one's approaching death. It requires the same elements of a normal gift plus the fact that it was done by the donor in anticipation of imminent death. A gift causa mortis is revocable anytime prior to the donor's death and the gift fails if the person recovers. For instance, if a heart attack victim tells his best friend to take his gold Rolex watch moments before he dies, the gift is complete at that time and the time piece does not pass under the decedent's will. Also, no writing or consideration is necessary to support a gift causa mortis. Because of the chances of fraud, however, proof of a gift causa mortis must be clear and convincing.

C. Production

Personal property may also be acquired by **production.** A person who takes scraps of fabric and creates a quilt owns the quilt because she has created or produced it by her labor. Similarly, the author of a book owns the copyright to the book because she has produced it. She may, however, transfer those rights to a publisher in order to have the book published.

D. Possession

Possession is another means of acquiring personal property. Historically, if one captured or killed a wild animal, he acquired title to the animal. If, however, he captured or killed the animal while he was trespassing on someone else's property, the owner of the land would acquire title to the animal. Today, state gaming statutes typically provide that the state owns and retains title to the wild animals captured or killed within its borders unless the animal was hunted or trapped pursuant to state laws regulating hunting, trapping, and fishing.

E. Abandoned Property

If personal property has been abandoned by its owner, title may be acquired by anyone who finds it. **Abandoned property** is that which has been discarded and the owner has no intention of claiming it. Abandoned property also includes property that was lost and its owner has given up all attempts to find it. An example would be a broken television put out for trash collection by its owner and then a junk dealer picks it up and repairs the television set. The junk dealer is now the lawful owner of the repaired television set. As with wild animals, if the abandoned property was discovered while the finder was trespassing, the landowner will acquire title to the property.

Abandonment of property requires intent plus an act that manifests a conscious purpose and intention of the owner neither to use nor to retake the property into his possession. An intention to discard property may be inferred from convincing evidence or it may be shown by conduct inconsistent with an intention to continue the use or ownership of the asset. The actual motive behind the abandonment is not a factor. Mere nonuse of the item, or lapse of time without claiming the property, however, is not enough to constitute abandonment.

F. Treasure-Trove

An exception to this rule protecting the rights of landowners is the doctrine of **treasure-trove.** This form of property carries with it the thought of antiquity; the treasure must have been hidden or concealed so long as to indicate that the owner is probably dead or unknown. Treasure trove is money, gold, silver, or bullion that has been found buried in the earth or hidden in a private place. If the owner of the treasure-trove is unknown, the finder will acquire title as against the owner of the land where it is found.

G. Lost Property

If property has merely been lost or mislaid, the person who lost or misplaced the item retains title. **Lost property** is that which the owner has involuntarily and accidentally parted with and does not know where to find it. If someone finds lost property, he does not acquire title to it as against its rightful owner. The finder will, however, have better title to the property than anyone other than the rightful owner. For example, the finder of a wallet that contains identification must return it to the rightful owner, or be guilty of conversion. If the wallet contains no identification, but the owner learns that the wallet has been found and requests that it be returned, the finder must do so.

Most states have statutes that govern lost property. These statutes typically provide that if a finder of lost property turns it over to the appropriate authority and the loss is advertised, then the finder will acquire title to the property if the item is not claimed. This is the case even against the original owner if its rightful owner does not claim the property within a specified period of time.

Does a police officer who finds a bundle of money obtain ownership of the cash? This is the issue in **In re Funds in Possession of Conemaugh Tp. Sup'rs, 753 A.2d 788 (Pa. 2000)** where the court noted that police officers are held to a higher standard than ordinary citizens. It is part of an officer's duties to guarantee the protection of lost property and to investigate whether the item is evidence of a crime and whether the owner can be located. If the law permitted a police officer to retain lost property, then the law enforcement official might be encouraged by such a policy to conduct a sham or less than complete investigations in order to insure that no crimes would be unearthed and the true owners would never be located.

H. Mislaid Property

Mislaid property has been voluntarily and intentionally placed somewhere by the owner and forgotten. This would occur if someone leaves a textbook in the back seat of a friend's car and can't remember where he left it. The friend does not acquire title to the book but becomes an involuntary bailee and has a duty to take care of the book for the owner.

A most unusual case involving property rights occurred when Barry Bonds hit his record breaking 73rd homerun in 2001. Because of the obvious value of this historic ball, a wild melee occurred in the stadium to retrieve the valuable souvenir. One man had the ball in his glove but was attacked by other fans. This caused the ball to dislodge, where it was retrieved by another person. A dispute then arose as to which of the two men owned the ball. The matter ended up in court where the judge had to apply a King Solomon like ruling to determination ownership.

POPOV V. HAYASHI
2002 WL 31833731 (CAL. SUPERIOR 2002)

In 1927, Babe Ruth hit sixty home runs. On October 7, 2001, Barry Bonds hit number seventy three. That accomplishment set a record which, in all probability, will remain unbroken.

Many people who attended the game came prepared for the possibility that a record setting ball would be hit in their direction. Among this group were Alex Popov and Patrick Hayashi. Barry Bonds came to bat in the first inning. Bonds swung at a slow knuckleball. The ball sailed over the right-field fence and into the arcade [and] landed in the glove worn by Popov. A crowd of people began to engulf Mr. Popov [and] he was thrown to the ground while attempting to complete the catch. Eventually, Mr. Popov was buried face down on the ground under several layers of people.

At some point the ball left his glove. Mr. Hayashi was [also] involuntarily forced to the ground. While on the ground he saw the loose ball. He picked it up, and put it in his pocket. We will never know if Mr. Popov would have been able to retain control of the ball had the crowd not interfered with his efforts to do so.

Prior to the time the ball was hit, it was possessed and owned by Major League Baseball. At the time it was hit, it became abandoned property. The first person who came in possession of the ball became its new owner.

Mr. Popov has clearly evidenced an intent to possess the baseball. The question is whether he did enough to reduce the ball to his exclusive dominion and control. Were his acts sufficient to create a legally cognizable interest in the ball?

Mr. Hayashi argues that possession does not occur until the fan has complete control of the ball. The custom of the stands creates a reasonable expectation that a person will achieve full control of a ball before claiming possession. Mr. Popov has not established by the preponderance of the evidence that he would have retained control of the ball and after any incidental contact with people or objects. Consequently, he did not achieve full possession. The reason we do not know whether Mr. Popov would have retained control of the ball is not because of incidental contact. It is because he was attacked.

Where an actor undertakes significant but incomplete steps to achieve possession of a piece of abandoned personal property and the effort is interrupted by the unlawful acts of others, the actor has a legally cognizable pre-possessory interest in the property. Our problem is that Mr. Popov was set upon by a gang of bandits, who dislodged the ball from his grasp. Recognition of a legally protected pre-possessory interest, vests Mr. Popov with a qualified right to possession and enables him to advance a legitimate claim to the baseball. It does not, however, address the interests of Mr. Hayashi [who] was a victim of the same bandits that attacked Mr. Popov. The difference is that he was able to extract himself from their assault and he discovered the loose ball. When he picked up and put it in his pocket, he attained unequivocal dominion and control. While Mr. Hayashi appears to have done everything necessary to claim full possession of the ball, the ball itself is encumbered by the interest of Mr. Popov.

An award of the ball to Mr. Popov would be unfair to Mr. Hayashi. It would be premised on the assumption that Mr. Popov would have caught the ball. That assumption is not supported by the facts. An award of the ball to Mr. Hayashi would unfairly penalize Mr. Popov. It would be based on the assumption that Mr. Popov would have dropped the ball. That conclusion is also unsupported by the facts.

Both men have a superior claim to the ball as against the world. Each man has a claim of equal dignity as to the other. The principle at work here is that where more than one party has a valid claim to a single piece of property, the court will recognize an undivided interest in the property in proportion to the strength of the claim.

The court, therefore, declares that both plaintiff and defendant have an equal and undivided interest in the ball.

SECTION 6.6
BAILMENTS

A **bailment** occurs when the owner of personal property gives possession of the item to someone else, usually for a particular purpose. The owner is called the **bailor,** and the person temporarily in possession of the item is the **bailee.** The bailor continues to have title to the property but has given up some of the rights of ownership, possession and use to the bailee.

Bailments can be placed into three categories: (**1**) for the sole benefit of the bailor, e.g., when someone takes care of a friend's dog as a favor; or when a friend forgets her gloves at another's house; (**2**) for the sole benefit of the bailee, e.g., when someone lends a car to a friend so the friend may get to work; and (**3**) for the mutual benefit of the bailor and the bailee, e.g., renting a car, taking clothes to the cleaner, or shipping a package. Mutual benefit bailments are the most common. Typically one party receives monetary compensation for supplying a good or service to the other. Such a bailment occurs when a person leaves a car at a parking garage. A bailment, however, only transfers possession and not ownership in the property. The transfer does not provide the person who takes possession of the asset, with the right to use it. For instance, a parking garage employee may not use a patron's car to run an errand.

Bailments have three elements: (**1**) the item must be personal property; (**2**) the property is delivered into the possession of another; and (**3**) the property is delivered pursuant to an agreement, which may be either expressed or implied.

Although the rights and responsibilities of the bailor and bailee may be specified in an agreement, there are certain rights and duties implied by law. The bailee has the right to temporarily possess and use the property for the purposes of the agreement. In addition, the bailee has a right of compensation. Usually the amount of compensation will be expressed in the agreement. For example, if a customer takes a jacket to the cleaners, the shop owner will be entitled to the cost of providing the cleaning service. Even if the amount of compensation is not expressly agreed upon, the bailee will have the right to receive a reasonable amount if it is a mutual benefit bailment. If the bailor does not pay the bailee's fee, the bailee may retain possession of the item until the bill is paid. This is called a **bailee's lien.** Thus, the cleaner can keep the jacket until the bill is paid, or a gas station may retain a car until the repair bill has been satisfied.

A bailee also has certain duties with respect to the item. For instance, the bailee has the duty to take reasonable care of the item. If the bailee fails to exercise reasonable care of the property entrusted to him, he will be liable for damages. The bailee also has the duty to return the item at the end of the bailment.

If there is an express agreement between parties, the bailee can limit her liability, either by a set dollar amount or by type of risk. For example, when one takes film to be developed, it is common for the developer to limit its liability to the replacing of the film if the film is lost or destroyed. This type of limitation of liability is generally valid if it is conspicuous, and the bailor has notice of the limitation.

A bailor also has certain rights and responsibilities with respect to the bailment. The bailor has the right to have the property returned in the same condition or as altered, pursuant to the terms of the agreement. Any service provided by the bailee must be performed in a workmanlike manner. The bailor is responsible to notify the bailee of any known or discoverable defects in the property. If the bailor fails to do so, she will be responsible for any injuries that result. For example, if someone rents a car with defective brakes, and the renter is injured in an accident as a result of that defect, the car rental company would be liable for the injuries.

Municipalities, businesses, and property owners have become very protective of their parking areas. Many have contracts with towing services to remove any vehicle which has been parked in a spot without authorization. What kind of bailment arises when a car is towed to a storage facility because it was illegally parked and is damaged while in the possession of the bailor or towing company? That is the issue in **Hadfield v. Gilcrest.**

HADFIELD V. GILCHRIST
538 S.E.2D 268 (S. C. 2000)

Gilchrist owns a motor vehicle towing service and maintains a storage facility for the retention of the towed vehicles.

Hadfield went to retrieve his Lincoln Continental from the parking spot where his wife parked the vehicle. The parking spot was on private property owned by Allen Saffer. Hadfield's wife parked the vehicle on Saffer's property without permission. The vehicle was not in the parking spot when Hadfield arrived as Saffer had called Gilchrist to have the vehicle removed.

Gilchrist towed Hadfield's car to his storage facility. Gilchrist maintained a chain link fence around the storage area and had an employee on the lot around the clock. The employees' duties included periodically leaving the office to check on the storage area which was some distance away from the office.

Upon Hadfield's arrival to pick up his car, he paid the fees. When he went to the storage area to collect his vehicle, Hadfield discovered the vehicle had been extensively vandalized. The vandals entered the storage area by cutting a hole in the fence.

Hadfield's attempts to persuade Gilchrist to pay for the damages were futile. Hadfield left the vehicle on Gilchrist's lot as he could not afford to repair it. After more than 60 days elapsed, Hadfield sold the vehicle for $1,000.

A bailment is created by the delivery of personal property by one person to another in trust for a specific purpose.

Bailments are generally classified as being for **(1)** the sole benefit of the bailor; **(2)** the sole benefit of the bailee; or **(3)** the mutual benefit of both. Bailments which benefit only one of the parties, the first and second classifications, are often described as gratuitous.

A gratuitous bailment is one in which the transfer of possession or use of the bailed property is without compensation. For instance, a gratuitous bailment arises if the bailment is undertaken as a personal favor.

By contrast, a bailment for the mutual benefit of the parties arises when one party takes the personal property of another into his or her care or custody in exchange for payment or other benefit.

Although a bailment is ordinarily created by the agreement of the parties, the agreement of the parties may be implied, and the bailment may arise by operation of law. Such a constructive bailment arises when one person has lawfully acquired possession of another's personal property, other than by virtue of a bailment contract, and holds it under such circumstances that the law imposes on the recipient of the property the obligation to keep it safe and redeliver it to the owner.

Gilchrist argues he towed the vehicle pursuant to the **Charleston Municipal Ordinances,** and the ordinances are for the sole benefit of the vehicle owners. Accordingly, he contends, the relationship created is a gratuitous bailment. We disagree.

We conclude a constructive bailment, for the mutual benefit of Hadfield and Gilchrist, was created.

After finding a bailment for mutual benefit exists in this case, we must determine whether Hadfield is entitled to damages.

The degree of care required of a bailee for mutual benefit is the degree of care which would be exercised by a person of ordinary care in the protection of his own property.

The burden of proof in this case rests first upon the bailor, Hadfield, to prove a prima facie case. He must show: **(1)** the goods were delivered to the bailee in good condition; and **(2)** they were lost or returned in a damaged condition. When the bailor, Hadfield, has so proven, the burden is then shifted to the bailee, Gilchrist, to show that he has used ordinary care in the good's storage and safekeeping.

Hadfield testified regarding the "nice" condition of his vehicle prior to it being towed, and the damage to his vehicle. Thus, Hadfield made out his prima facie case. The burden then shifted to Gilchrist to show that he used ordinary care in protecting the vehicle while in his care.

Gilchrist impounded the cars in a storage lot surrounded by a chain link fence. The person on duty spent time in the office and only visited the storage lot to check on it. The vandal cut a hole in the fence and broke into six to eight cars on the night in question. The fact the guard was not on duty at the impound lot and, considering the only other security for the vehicles was the chain link fence, the trial judge could have concluded Gilchrist failed to exercise ordinary care.

We rule that where a city ordinance is utilized as the legal justification for taking possession of a vehicle on private property, the entity lawfully acquiring possession of the property becomes a constructive bailee as a matter of law. We also conclude the burden of proof in a constructive bailment case rests first upon a bailor to prove a prima facie case and, once so proven, the burden shifts to the bailee to show the use of ordinary care in the storage and safekeeping of the property. Accordingly, the order of the lower court is affirmed in favor of the plaintiff and he is awarded $4,030 in damages.

Pennsylvania has enacted legislation dealing with the removal of a motor vehicle that has been illegally parked on private property. That law is contained in the Motor Vehicle Code which provides:

(b)(1) No person shall park or leave unattended a vehicle on private property without the consent of the owner or other person in control of the property except in the case of emergency or disablement of the vehicle, in which case the operator shall arrange for the removal of the vehicle as soon as possible.

(b)(2) The provisions of this subsection shall not apply to private parking lots unless such lots are posted to notify the public of any parking restrictions and the operator of the vehicle violates such posted restrictions.

(c) The owner or other person in possession of any property on which a vehicle is parked or left unattended in violation of the provisions of subsection (a) may remove or have removed the vehicle at the reasonable expense of the owner of the vehicle. Such person who removes or has removed a vehicle left parked or unattended in violation of the provisions of subsection (b) shall have a lien against the owner of the vehicle, in the amount of the reasonable value of the costs of removing the vehicle plus the costs of storage. If storage charges arc not set by the municipality, a maximum of $25 per day may be charged for storage.

SECTION 6.7
REAL PROPERTY

Real property consists of land and everything attached to the land. Thus, the owner of a parcel of real estate owns the land itself, any minerals such as oil, ore, or gems located under the ground, the air space above the land, and the buildings, plants and trees attached to the land. Ownership comprises the bundle of rights that allow someone to possess, use, exclude others, encumber or alienate the real estate. There might be a sole owner or there may be co-owners who share the rights of ownership.

The purchase of a home has certain inherent problems. Disputes frequently arise as to what was included in the sale. When the buyers looked at a home before they agreed to purchase it, an elegant crystal chandelier hung in the foyer. At the time of settlement, however, the chandelier had been replaced by a plastic fixture. The seller refuses to give the buyers the chandelier claiming that it is a family heirloom worth several thousand dollars. The buyers maintain that the fixture was part of the realty since it was on display at the time the home was inspected. Who is correct? The answer will depend on whether the item is real or personal property. If the item is found to be real property, it will be part of the sale.

In a commercial setting, real property consists of such things as the land and buildings in which the business operates, warehouses, storage facilities, factories, and offices.[10]

SECTION 6.8 ESTATES IN REAL PROPERTY

The word **estate** is used in the law of real property to refer to a person's interests or rights concerning land.

A. Fee Simple

There are several types of estates; the most common is **fee simple absolute.** Its name derives from the same root as "fief" or "feudalism" because the concept of fee land ownership descends from the feudal system. Originally, the term denoted land that was held by a "free holder" in exchange for certain rights or duties paid to the superior lord. In fact, the property system used today—estates in land and tenancy—evolved from the feudal systems in England and France.

The fee simple absolute estate is the most complete form of ownership of real property. It includes the rights to possess, use, exclude others, encumber and alienate the property. It is not, however, totally unrestricted ownership because the government still retains certain rights in privately owned property.

For example, the government has the right to regulate an owner's use of the property through zoning laws that prescribe which areas of a community may be used for residential, commercial, or industrial purposes. Although the owner of the land owns the airspace above it, the United States government has passed various statutes that allow the public to use that airspace for air traffic and commerce.

The government also has the right to tax real property. Typically, each parcel of property is taxed based on its value. If the owner does not pay the tax, the government will place a tax lien on the property. The tax lien is a form of encumbrance that allows the government to have the property sold at a sheriff's sale to satisfy the unpaid tax bill.

The government has the right of **eminent domain** which is the right to take private property for a public purpose. However, the Fifth and Fourteenth Amendments to the United States Constitution require the government to pay just compensation to the private property owner whose land is taken by eminent domain.

The power of eminent domain should be exercised only in the mode and manner, prescribed by the legislature and the taking must be for a public purpose with just compensation. A government entity, however, is forbidden from taking a person's land for the purposes of conferring a private benefit on another citizen and the government is not allowed to take property under the mere pretext of a public purpose, when its actual purpose is to bestow a private benefit. A recent controversy in this area is whether a governmental entity may take property on behalf of a private party who plans on using the land for a public purpose. That was the issue in **Kelo v. City of New London, 545 U. S. 469 (2005)** where the Supreme Court ruled that the use of the powers of eminent domain to advance redevelopment by a private developer and to increase tax revenues for an economically distressed area met the "public use" requirement of the Constitution.

As for condemned property owned by a commercial establishment, the income from the business operation is not one of the factors that go into calculating the value of the property for the public taking. Instead, the fair market value of the land is the proper measure of damages. The owner, however, may receive business dislocation damages if that business cannot be relocated without substantial loss of patronage.

Other than the fee simple absolute, there are lesser estates in which the title holder of the real property does not enjoy the unrestricted right of ownership. These include the **fee simple defeasible** and the **life estate.** The fee simple defeasible estate, also known as a conditional or qualified fee, conveys all of the rights of ownership so long as the owner complies with a certain condition. For example, if an owner gives her real estate to a church to be used for church purposes, the church receives all of the rights of ownership but the use of the property is restricted to church purposes. If the church attempts to use the property for any other reason or attempts to alienate the property, the real estate will revert back to the original owner, or her legal heirs if she is no longer living. The owner, therefore, is said to retain a **reversionary interest** in the property.

B. Life Estate

A **life estate** conveys an ownership interest that is limited to the life of the person holding it. The holder of the life estate has all the rights of possession, use, and exclusivity. When that person dies, however, the estate reverts back to the original owner or his heirs or other grantees. They hold the future interest in the property, called the **remainder.**

For example, a person may convey property to her children while retaining the right to reside in the home as long as she wants. Such an interest, however, must be done through a deed which carves out the life estate for the grantor.

The remaindermen have the right to receive the property without diminution in value. This right imposes a duty on the life tenant not to allow or commit waste, through the deterioration, destruction, or material alteration of the property. **Waste** may include cutting timber for more than household purposes, removing subsurface minerals, and not maintaining the property. If the life tenant commits waste, the remaindermen may seek an injunction to prevent the wasteful conduct.

C. Estate at Sufferance and at Will

An **estate at sufferance** refers to the lowest interest one can have in real property. This term deals with a person who retains possession of real estate with no title. For example, a tenant who continues to remain in the property after a lease has expired will be considered to have an estate at sufferance. If the tenant pays rent after the expiration of the lease and the landlord accepts that rent, this acceptance converts an estate at sufferance into an estate at will. An **estate at will** is an estate created not by the consent, but by the doctrine of laches or actions of the owner in accepting the rent.

D. Condominium and Housing Cooperatives

In recent times, new terms have been coined to describe interests in real estate. For example, a **condominium** refers to a multiunit structure where the resident owns the unit that he or she occupies together with an interest in the common areas. Usually, these units are run by a condominium association that levies monthly fees against the owners for the upkeep of the common areas. Condominiums will also have bylaws that govern the operation of the association and establish rules and regulations that the owners of the units must follow for the common good. On the other hand, a **housing cooperative** is an entity that owns real estate but allows a person to use the premises. The resident does not own the unit that he or she occupies and no deed is issued. Rather, the housing cooperative issues stock to the resident which gives the person the right to occupy one housing unit, to use the common amenities, and the resident has a say in the operation of the cooperative. This type of estate is very similar to a lease. Also, the housing cooperative will meet and decide if a perspective resident is to their satisfaction.

E. Leases

A leasehold estate is commonly called a **lease.** As mentioned earlier, a lease is an encumbrance upon the property; the landlord is the owner of the property and he has a fee simple absolute estate, but the landlord has given the tenant the exclusive right to possess and use the property.

In Pennsylvania, a lease for a term of more than three years must be in writing. As for which party is required to make the repairs to the leased premises, one must examine the written lease since that document will usually specify who is responsible for the repairs. For example, the lease may specify that all repairs under $100 are the responsibility of the tenant and all other repairs are the responsibility of the landlord unless caused by the conduct of the tenant. If the contract is silent on the issue or if the parties are operating under an oral lease, the owner of the property is usually responsible for those things that are attributable to ordinary wear and tear. On the other hand, if the tenant causes the damage, the renter may be responsible to fix it.

Many states have enacted **housing codes** that set minimal standards for apartments. Example provisions include providing heat between October and May, providing hot and cold water, and exterminating insects and rodents. Tenants also have obligations under a housing code, such as the disposing of trash in a sanitary manner.

**SECTION 6.9
LEASEHOLD ESTATES**

The rights and responsibilities of the **lessor** (landlord) and the **lessee** (tenant) are usually specified by a written lease agreement. Even in the absence of a written lease, the law provides certain rights and responsibilities. The tenant receives the rights to exclusively possess and use the real estate by the landlord's covenant of quiet enjoyment. In other words, the landlord promises that he will not disturb the tenant's possession and use of the property. If the landlord, or anyone working for the landlord, unreasonably disturbs the tenant's enjoyment of the property, the tenant will have the right to sue for damages, or the lessee may elect to terminate the lease under the doctrine of constructive eviction. A constructive eviction occurs whenever the landlord breaches its duties to the extent that the tenant's use and possession of the premises is impossible or extremely difficult. A landlord may enter the premises for reasonable purposes, such as to do maintenance and repair, but many leases require the landlord to give the tenant reasonable notice of such entry unless there is an emergency.

A residential tenant also has the right to insist that the premises be fit for human habitation. This right is contained in the landlord's **implied warranty of habitability,** which the law requires to be a part of all residential leases. This warranty, however, does not apply to leases of property for commercial purposes. Lack of heat during winter months, no hot or cold running water, a substantial leak in the roof or pest infestation to the extent it may injure the health of the residents, are examples of defects which render the premises uninhabitable. If the premises are not habitable, a constructive eviction has occurred, allowing the tenant to sue the landlord for damages or recission of the lease.

Many states have passed statutes that provide additional remedies for a breach of the warranty of habitability. These remedies include withholding rent and placing money into an escrow account, or repairing the defect and deducting the cost of the repairs from the rent. Before engaging in these self-help remedies, the tenant is usually required to give the landlord notice of the problem and an opportunity to repair it. In addition, many local housing ordinances provide that a violation of building and housing codes constitutes a breach of the warranty of habitability.

JOHNSON V. SCANDIA ASSOCIATES, INC.
717 N.E.2D 24 (IND. 1999)

Scandia Associates, Inc. owns and operates an apartment complex through its agent Oxford Management, Co. Terri Johnson sued Scandia and Oxford after suffering physical injuries caused by an electric shock she received when simultaneously touching two kitchen appliances while cooking in her apartment.

Asked whether a warranty of habitability is implied in the residential leasehold contract, we hold that a landlord could be found liable to his tenant on a breach of implied warranty, at least where there was a housing code and city inspectors had cited the landlord with multiple violations.

A warranty is a promise relating to a past or existing fact that incorporates a commitment by the promisor that he will be responsible if the facts are not as manifested. Habitability means reasonably fit for occupation as a dwelling. Thus, when a landlord warrants habitability, the warranty is an affirmative declaration of the apartment's fitness for habitation, that is, as a dwelling place.

When a landlord enters a lease agreement with her tenant, she voluntarily confers certain rights upon the tenant, such as possession and quiet enjoyment for a specific term. She does this in consideration of the tenant's promise to pay rent,

not to waste the property, and not to "holdover" beyond the term. The landlord agrees to this legal relationship after balancing the costs and benefits, and the same is true for the tenant.

In light of these considerations, we conclude that a warranty of habitability is a landlord's promise to convey to a tenant an apartment suitable for living, and breach of which promise occurs when a landlord fails to tender a suitable apartment.

When a landlord warrants his property to be suitable for living and then breaches that promise by conveying an unsuitable apartment, the tenant's remedy may take several forms, including conveyance of a suitable property, recision and reformation of the agreement while the tenant retains possession, recision of the contract, or damages at law.

Johnson complains that her apartment was not suitable for living because its fixtures unexpectedly released an electric current and, second, that her injuries were foreseeably caused by the breaching condition. She does not allege whether the defect was present at the time of entry or arose after taking possession, nor does she have any contention about giving Scandia notice of the defect.

Indiana's law governing the landlord-tenant relationship has developed a warranty of habitability. The warranty derives from the agreement between the tenant and the landlord and may be express or implied. The existence of an implied warranty may be proven through evidence of the parties' course of dealing or performance and by evidence of ordinary practices in the trade. Where the warranty is express, consequential damages for injury to the person may be available as a remedy.

Where the warranty is implied-in-fact, however, consequential damages may not be awarded because personal injury is outside the parties' contemplation. Johnson's complaint does not aver facts tending to show that Scandia warranted the apartment's habitability or that her injury was reasonably foreseeable within a warranty of habitability.

For these reasons, we find in favor of the defendants.

The tenant's right to use and possession, however, are not unlimited. The tenant may not create a nuisance that would interfere with other tenants' rights of quiet enjoyment. The tenant also has a duty not to commit waste by abusing, destroying, or altering the premises. If the tenant causes a problem that renders the premises uninhabitable, it will be the tenant's responsibility to repair it.

The primary right of the landlord is to receive rent; if the tenant does not pay it, the landlord may evict the renter. Most states require the landlord to give the tenant notice (frequently 30 days) to vacate the premises. If the tenant does not move out, the landlord may sue. If the tenant has no defense, such as breach of the implied warranty of habitability, the court will order the tenant to vacate the premises within a reasonable time (e.g., 10-30 days). If the tenant still refuses to move out, the landlord may request the sheriff to forcibly remove the tenant from the premises.

The tenant has a corresponding duty to pay rent for the term of the lease, which means that if the tenant leaves before the term has expired, she is still responsible to pay the rent, unless the landlord is able to lease the premises to someone else. The landlord has a duty to mitigate damages by attempting to lease the property; if he is unable to find a suitable new tenant, however, the original tenant will be liable for the rent until the end of the lease term.

In a residential lease, the landlord has a duty to maintain and repair the premises pursuant to the warranty of habitability. If a defective condition renders the property unfit for human habitation and causes an injury to the tenant or a guest, the landlord will be liable.

The law also imposes upon the landlord a duty to maintain common areas in a reasonably safe condition. A common area is used by some or all tenants—sidewalks, parking lots, entrance ways, halls, stairs, and elevators, and remains under the control of the landlord. If a tenant or guest is injured in a common area because the landlord has failed to maintain it in a safe condition, the landlord is liable for negligence. Some written leases contain an **exculpatory clause,** which provides that the landlord is not liable for injuries sustained upon the leased premises, whether due to the landlord's negligence or some other cause. Exculpatory clauses are not enforceable in residential leases because they violate the public policy that people need a safe place to live. In commercial leases, however, exculpatory clauses may be enforceable if the tenant is aware of and knowingly agrees to the clause.

Dean v. Gruber deals with a landlord's duty to make repairs under an oral lease.

DEAN V. GRUBER
978 S.W.2D 501 (MO. APP. 1998)

On November 15, 1993, Ms. Dean fell and sustained injuries while walking down the driveway at 5139 Swope Parkway. At the time, she was visiting her sister, Cynthia Gorman. Ms. Dean claims that her fall was caused by a loose handrail.

Approximately four months prior to Ms. Dean's fall, Ms. Gorman rented the single-family dwelling from Mr. Gruber. The lease was a verbal month-to-month agreement. Gorman states that the only entrance to the premises was the driveway and, because of the condition of the driveway, the lack of lighting at night, and the slope of the driveway, it was necessary to use the handrail to enter and exit the residence. Gorman also states that she noticed the handrail was loose shortly after moving in, and reported the problem to Gruber's employees, but that no repairs were made. Additionally, Ms. Gorman stated that at the time of the verbal rental agreement, she and Gruber agreed that all repairs would be made by the landlord. Gruber's employees were at the house to repair the plumbing, a toilet, a screen door, and a clogged basement drain.

Gruber stated that he was not aware that the hand railing was loose or in a dangerous condition until

after Dean's fall, and that "at no time during the tenancy of Cynthia E. Gorman did she report . . . any dangerous condition of the hand railing, driveway or lighting, of which plaintiff complains" and at no time did he "promise Gorman to fix or repair any reported dangerous condition of the hand railing."

The general rule is that a landlord does not owe a duty to his tenant, and is not liable for personal injuries received by a tenant or by a tenant's invitee, caused by dangerous conditions of the premises. Exceptions to the rule include: (**1**) when the landlord had knowledge of a dangerous condition, which condition is not discoverable by the tenant, and the landlord fails to make disclosure; (**2**) when the injury occurs in a common area; and (**3**) when a landlord is responsible for making repairs, but negligently fails to do so. The tenant argues that exceptions two and three are applicable here.

This was a single-family home with a driveway which is for the exclusive use of the tenant of the homeowner and her invitees. The driveway was not a common area used by more than one tenant. Thus, the common area exception to the general rule of landlord non-liability is inapplicable.

Next, Dean contends that Gruber maintained control of the premises such that he was responsible for making repairs. A landlord is under no obligation to a tenant to repair unless there is a contract which creates a duty to repair. However, where the landlord retains partial control over the leased premises for the purpose of making repairs, the landlord is then obligated to make such repairs and to keep the premises in a reasonably safe condition for the intended use.

Although Dean contends that when she rented the premises from Gruber they agreed that he would make all repairs, such evidence alone does not create a duty. There must be something more from which a jury could infer that under the agreement the tenant gave up and surrendered his right to exclusive possession and control and yielded to the landlord some degree or measure of control and dominion over the premises.

Determination of whether the amount of control a landowner exerts is sufficient to incur liability turns largely on the extent to which the landowner permits the tenant to treat the premises as belonging to the tenant. Viewing all the factual inferences in favor of Dean, there are no facts alleged which would allow a jury to infer Gruber's control of the premises that would demonstrate a duty for him to make repairs. Gruber did not retain a key, or reserve the right to inspect the premises, except with the permission of the tenant. The fact that Gruber may have made repairs to the property prior to the injury does not establish control absent other evidence. There is no assertion of general supervision by Gruber over the premises in order to make the repairs. As a result, the trial court correctly determined that Gruber was entitled to judgment as a matter of law. Judgment affirmed.

SECTION 6.10
ACQUIRING TITLE TO REAL PROPERTY

There are several ways to acquire title to real property: by gift, adverse possession, or purchase. One may acquire title by gift, either inter vivos or testamentary. For an inter vivos gift, a deed will be prepared transferring title to the land from the donor to the donee. As with personal property, a valid gift requires the donor to intend to give the property, that the donor delivers it, and that the donee accepts it. Because real property cannot be delivered physically, delivery of the deed is the symbolic transfer of possession.

A. Testamentary Gift

A **testamentary gift** of land is one given by a will. For example, a parent may leave real property to a child by will. If the owner of real estate dies without a will, the property will be given to the decedent's legal heirs. This is called intestate succession. If there are no legal heirs, the property will be transferred to the state under a doctrine called **escheat,** which means that real property lacking an individual competent to inherit it, the property will revert to the state.

B. Adverse Possession

Title to real property may be acquired by **adverse possession.** Adverse possession requires a person claiming title to the real estate to possess and use it for a statutory period of time which varies from 5 to 30 years, depending on the state. There are five elements required to acquire title by adverse possession; the claimant's use must be: (**1**) adverse or hostile, which means that the claimant is using the property without the owner's permission; (**2**) actual, meaning the claimant is using the real estate in an appropriate fashion; (**3**) open, visible or notorious, which means that the claimant's use of the land is visible to the community to see; (**4**) exclusive, which signifies the claimant is asserting the right to exclude others (the land is not being used by the public at large); and (**5**) continuous for the statutory period, meaning that the claimant has continued to use the land for the statutory period without being ejected by the rightful owner.

To prevent adverse possession, the record owner must affirmatively act to interrupt the adverse possessor's use of the property. The owner cannot sit passively by, knowing of the adverse use. For example, a homeowner who erects a fence 5 feet onto his neighbor's property may end up owning that extra piece of land if the trespass goes unchallenged for the appropriate number of years. In Pennsylvania, the law requires that the possession be uninterrupted for 21 years and possession of the property must be visible. In other words, the use of the land must be open for all to see. Nevertheless, adverse possession does not apply to the land owned by the government.

C. Purchase

By far, the most common way to acquire title to real property is to **purchase** it. The legal process of purchasing a home usually begins when the buyer and seller enter into an Agreement of Sale for the purchase of real property.

The Agreement of Sale specifies how much money is to be paid for the property and when the money is to be paid. In addition, the agreement presumes that the buyer will secure financing. The mortgage contingency clause provides that if the buyer is unable to secure financing, she may terminate the agreement and receive a full refund of any deposit that has been given to the seller or the realtor, as the seller's agent. After both parties have signed the agreement, the buyer will apply for a mortgage with a bank or mortgage company. If the lender approves the application, it will lend the money to the buyer at settlement. The collateral or security for the loan is a mortgage on the real estate purchased by the buyer. A **mortgage** is a lien that allows the lender to have the property sold at a foreclosure sale if the buyer does not repay the loan. A mortgage holder can also insist that its interests in the property be protected. For instance, it is common for a mortgage company to require that the owner pay the real estate taxes into an escrow account that will be maintained by the mortgage company to insure that the taxes are paid currently.

The agreement normally provides that the seller will convey good and marketable fee simple title to the buyer. A title is marketable if it is free from reasonable doubt as to its validity or if it conveys all the rights of owner-ship. A title that is encumbered by liens would not be marketable unless the liens were removed.

After the agreement is signed, the buyer will usually arrange for a search of the title by a lawyer, or more commonly, by a title insurance company, to be sure that the seller can convey a marketable fee simple title. If the seller cannot convey such a title, the buyer may terminate the agreement and re-ceive a full refund of his deposit money.

The agreement will specify what items are attached to the property as fix-tures and are therefore included in the sale. If any of these items are not to be included in the sale, or if there are additional items which are to be included, the parties must state this either in the "Special Clauses" section or by an addendum or rider to the agreement.

A standard agreement will generally provide for remedies in the event the buyer defaults. If the buyer breaks the agreement and refuses to purchase the property for a reason other than the buyer's inability to obtain financing or the seller's inability to convey marketable title, the seller's most com-mon remedy is to keep the buyer's deposit money as liquidated damages. Liquidated damages are an amount of money agreed upon as damages prior to a breach of the contract. In this case, it is the amount of the buyer's deposit. If the seller breaches the agreement by refusing to convey the prop-erty to the buyer, the buyer's usual remedies are either: to seek specific performance, which is to sue the seller to convey the property; or to rescind the contract, which is to sue the seller for a return of his deposit and any other money expended to perform his duties under the agreement (such as a loan application fee).

If all goes smoothly after the agreement is signed, the buyer can obtain a mortgage loan, and the seller can convey marketable title, at which point, the parties will have a closing or settlement, the consummation of the trans-action. The buyer will pay the purchase price to the seller, and the seller will deliver a deed, which conveys fee simple title to the buyer. At that point, all the rights and responsibilities of ownership will belong to the buyer.

SECTION 6.11
ZONING

As our country, particularly the more populated cities began to develop in a haphazard way, the desire for orderly planning arose. As a result, local gov-ernments, often with input from the citizens, created codes which specified areas for development as residential, commercial and industrial areas. This process is known as **zoning** and is defined by the federal government as the public regulation of land and building use to control the character of a place. One may remember that at one time in Philadelphia, no building was allowed to be taller than the hat of William Penn on the top of City Hall. This is known as a height restriction.

After a landmark decision by the United States Supreme Court in 1926 found that zoning codes were constitutional, these codes began to be adopted in many communities. Although similar, there were, and still are, differences to reflect the character of the city or town and what a good scheme is for a specific area.

The different designations are further divided. For instance, within the Residential Districts, some places are limited to single family dwellings while others permit multi-family units, including duplexes and apartments. Likewise, the Industrial Districts are divided into light and heavy uses. The amount, area, or lot size, is also specified within each district.

A. Nonconforming Use

One problem with these codes is what to do with uses of property that were already in place when the new regulations were adopted, but are now in conflict with the zoning classification. In order to protect the property rights of these owners, they are permitted to continue their existing use, and to pass it on to family or purchasers of their property. This is referred to as a nonconforming use. Often the codes provide that if a **nonconforming use** ceases for a certain period of time, usually from one to three years, that non-conforming use is lost. The property must then confirm to the new zoning code designation.

B. Variance

In addition to nonconforming uses, a zoning board is created to hear cases where the owner of property can show that for some reason related to the property, such as shape, size, or type of building, the owner cannot conform to the code. The board is then empowered to give that property owner a **variance** to permit a use not designated in the code. The standards for a variance are usually strict and never granted just because the property owner would make more income by not complying with the code.

C. Spot Zoning

From time to time, a legislative body, such as City Council or the Township Commissioners, adds to or changes the code. They also shift zoning classification when changes to a neighborhood or new uses occur. The legislative body cannot make such changes for just one property as a favor to the owner. The area in question must be large and the change must be in keeping with the surrounding area. Otherwise, the change may be challenged as **spot zoning** which is not permitted. Zoning and land use planning are supposed to go together. Most large cities have a compre-hensive plan which is prepared by professional land planners who staff a planning commission. Smaller towns have planning boards made up of citizens from the area that perform a particular task.

There has been a movement with gasoline service stations to expand their product offerings to more than the sale of gasoline. A number of establishments have converted their gas stations into mini-markets. This simple conversion can run afoul of laws in the areas which are not zoned for such a use. That is the issue in **Atlantic Richfield Company v. Harrisburg Zoning Hearing Board** where the court had to decide if a mini-mart is just an expanded use of a gas station which previously sold candy bars, cigarettes and sodas to its customers.

ATLANTIC RICHFIELD COMPANY V. HARRISBURG ZONING HEARING BOARD
18 D. & C. 3D 564 (PA. COM. PL. 1981)

Food and fuel, the prime participants in our unprecedented inflationary spiral, are locked in a territorial conflict which, impinging on certain zoning restrictions, necessitates a judicial delineation. Apparently feeling that "fill her up" should apply to tummy as well as tank, the Atlantic Richfield Company seeks to expand its service station at Second and Verbeke Streets in the city of Harrisburg into a mini-market. The zoning administrator denied its application for a permit. An appeal from his decision was denied by the zoning hearing board and the matter is now before this court.

The zoning hearing board based its denial on the principal grounds that to permit Atlantic Richfield to operate a grocery store would add a second nonconforming use to the property. Since 1923 when the gasoline and service station began operation, the area has become more restrictive and is now classified an RPO zone which permits only residential and professional offices. Following marketing studies which identified this location as desirable as a convenience store, appellant proposed to remove the auto lifts, close off the service bay, delete the service and repair functions entirely and convert the building into a 24 hour mini-market having only self-service gas pumps.

The applicant contends that its proposal is permissible under the Codified Ordinances of Harrisburg which provide that a nonconforming use may continue as the "same" use or be "expanded" into other portions of the building for increased trade. We cannot see the operation of the proposed grocery store as a continuation of the same use. Since its inception, this station has been operated as a traditional full-service gas station. While there have been incidental sales in the office portion of the building of such items as cigarettes, soda, candy, flashlight batteries, aspirin and a limited supply of snacks, they were merely offered as a convenience for motorists and can be viewed only as incidental to the primary purpose of providing gasoline and auto repairs and service. While you can buy a hot dog and a cup of coffee at Penn State's Beaver Field, it's still a football stadium and not a restaurant. In **Reinert v. Weisenberg Zoning Board, 48 Pa. Commonwealth Ct. 519 (1980),** an applicant who "merely worked on and tinkered with his own automobiles and those of his friends without charge" was not permitted to claim this nonconforming use entitled him to establish a complete automobile repair shop. If more is needed, one need only consider the extensive physical alterations proposed for the conversion of the property to a grocery store.

The applicant also asserts that its proposal is simply an expansion of a previous nonconforming grocery use. This argument would be attractive if the use as an existing grocery store had been established. Appellant did present testimony that 15 percent of its current sales are of non-gasoline items, although inspection by the zoning officer throws this into serious doubt. Nor can we accept appellant's projection that a full grocery store line as it contemplates would result only in a 22 percent total sales ratio of nongasoline items. The oil industry is not noted for its philanthropic gestures and one can hardly imagine all this bother for an anticipated 7 percent increase in sales.

The past sales of non-gasoline items do not, under the evidence, justify or create a presumption that they were always part and parcel of the primary use. It appears that they were really incidental sales, made in the fashion of the old time gasoline stations, which are now being transformed into an argument that the grocery store was always there, you just couldn't see it. The policy of the law is to restrict closely nonconforming uses and to strictly construe provisions which provide for their continuance.

And finally a nonconforming use cannot be expanded unless applicant's proposed use will not be detrimental to or tend more greatly to alter the character of the neighborhood. The zoning hearing board, acting with proper discretion, determined that the introduction of a convenience grocery store would defeat the recent efforts to upgrade the neighborhood. The board cited substantial rehabilitative and restorative efforts being undertaken in this district. The existence of these efforts combined with the neighboring corridor of various "commercial" enterprises including two grocery stores obviates the need for a retail enterprise in this particular neighborhood.

The board was also justifiably concerned about the safety, health and welfare of the citizens. It found that existing traffic patterns on North Second Street create a significant flow of automobiles particularly "circuit" riders who parade around this area and would be further attracted by the presence of an all-night convenience store.

For all the above reasons, we feel that the board committed no error of law; hence, no mini-market.

| Section 6.12 Review Cases | 1. Chavez conveyed his interest in a piece of real estate to himself and his spouse as tenants by the entirety after a lawsuit had been filed against him by Premier Property. Later that year, a judgment was entered against Chavez for $190,000. When Premier learned of the transfer, it moved to set aside the conveyance as being a fraudulent conveyance to defeat the rights of a creditor. Can a debtor transfer property to the other spouse in anticipation of the entry of future judgment in order to defeat the rights of the creditor? **Premier Property Management Inc. v. Claudia Chavez, 728 N.E.2d 476 (Ill. 2000).** |

2. Bloomfield Club Recreation Association sued the builder of a housing complex for breach of implied warranty of habitability with respect to certain commonly held facilities within their residential development. The builder had created a declaration of covenants agreed to by each homeowner when they purchased their homes that granted each owner

a right of easement to use the common areas, including the clubhouse in the development. The homeowner, however, said the clubhouse was uninhabitable because of defective workmanship. Does the implied warranty of habitability apply to non-residential construction, such as a clubhouse or is it limited to an occupied residence? **Bloomfield Club Recreation Association v. The Hoffman Group, Inc., 712 N.E.2d 330 (Ill. 1999).**

3. Hamilton and Morris were guests at a dinner party where alcoholic beverages were served throughout the evening. Hamilton removed her wrist watch and placed it on the kitchen counter. About midnight, the lights in the house went off and Hamilton left the kitchen. Morris saw the watch on the counter and picked it up so that it would not be misplaced. Unfortunately, Morris could not remember where she put the watch for safekeeping. Hamilton sued Morris, alleging that Morris was the bailee of the watch and that she negligently lost it while it was in her possession. Morris, however, contended that she was a gratuitous bailee and only owed a slight duty of care. Was a bailment created when Morris took possession of the watch? If so, what type of bailment was created, and will Morris be responsible for losing the watching? **Andrea Morris v. Marsha Hamilton, 302 S.E.2d 51 (Va. 1983).**

4. During his lifetime, the decedent had a romantic relationship with Sharon Clark. During the winter months, they traveled to Florida with a camper. They continued this ritual on an annual basis. The trailer was registered in both of their names. The decedent also maintained a bank account in which he added Clark's name to the account. That account, however, did not have survivorship language on the signature card in the event of the death of Mr. Donahue. How much of the decedent's property is Clark entitled to with respect to the trailer and bank account? **Estate of John Donahue v. Sharon Clark, 692 N.Y.S.2d 225 (N.Y. App. 1999).**

5. Rodman was an employee of the Horse Shoe Casino. As an employee, she was required to park her car in an employee's parking lot. One night, her car was stolen from the Casino lot. Employees of the casino were required to park their vehicles in this special lot and they were forbidden to park in the guest parking lot which was much closer to their place of employment. What type of bailment was created and who should win the case? **Robinson Property Group, Ltd. v. Debra Rodman, 1998 Miss. LEXIS 359 (Miss. 1998).**

SECTION 6.13
INTERNET REFERENCES

For more information on the materials in this Chapter, see the following sites on the Internet:

A. Real Estate

- **www.propertymart.net**
  This company site provides information about real estate, including advertisements about available properties and various related links.

- **www.realtor.com**
  Realtor.com helps prospective home buyers find houses for purchase all over the country. The site also has a reference library relating to real estate matters and offers information about buying, selling, and other important issues regarding real property.

- **www.realestate.com**
  This site discusses home buying, selling, and financing. Specific information is offered on the real estate professional, lending services, appraisers, and service providers.

- **www.vamch.com/reinfo.html**
  This site provides a detailed glossary of real estate and mortgage terms.

- **www.parealtor.org**
  The Pennsylvania Association of Realtors maintains this site devoted to real estate news, consumer information, and updated information regarding real estate legislation.

- **www.legalwiz.com/contract**
  An attorney explains the basics of the real estate contract at this site.

- **www.yahoo.com/Government/Law/Property**
  Yahoo's search engine on property law is located at this address, and a person can use it to search through many subjects concerning real estate. For instance, a person can learn about the disposition of property by will.

B. Intellectual Property

- **www.expresssearch.com/inventor**
  Information about the patent process is offered at this site.

- **www.patentcafe.com**
  This site offers information about patents, including articles and frequently asked questions on the topic; it also discusses other intellectual property issues, such as trademarks and copyrights.

- **www.patents.com**
  The law firm of Oppedahl & Larson, LLP, maintains this site which is dedicated to information on intellectual property.

C. Estate Planning

- **http://evans-legal.com/dan**
  Information relating to estate planning is provided at this address, and issues discussed include wills, trusts, and inheritance tax.

- **www.virginiaweber.com/eplan.htm**
  This site provides answers to frequently asked questions about estate planning.

- **www.estateattorney.com**
  Articles and information about decedent's estate and estate planning is offered at this site, which is maintained by a Pennsylvania estate-planning attorney.

D. Leasing

- **www.pa.landowners.org**
  The Pennsylvania Landowners' Association maintains this site which provides information about the organization and current articles of interest dealing with land for rent.

- **www.nolo.com/encyclopedia/articles/lt/agreement_faq.html**
  Nolo's Legal Encyclopedia provides general information about leases and rental agreements at this address.

Footnotes:

1. Introduction to Property Rights: A Historical Perspective, University of Illinois Extension, http://urbanext.illinois.edu/lcr/propertyrights.cfm (last visited September 28, 2013).

2. Property Law, Law Library of Congress, http://memory.loc.gov/ammem/awhhtml/awlaw3/property.html (last visited September 28, 2013).

3. *Id.*

4. *Id.*

5. Kayla Lowe, The Importance of Property Rights, Yahoo! Voices, http://voices.yahoo.com/the-importance-property-rights-2195928.html?cat=3 (last visited September 28, 2013).

6. Julia Hanna, How Property Ownership Changes Your World View, Harvard Business School, May 28, 2007, http://hbswk.hbs.edu/item/5649.html (last visited September 28, 2013).

7. *Adverse Possession Making a Comeback*, Mortgage Marvel, http://www.mortgagemarvel.com/industrynews/adverse-possession-making-a-comeback/ (last visited January 23, 2018).

8. *Adverse Possession*, Legal Dictionary, https://legaldictionary.net/adverse-possession/ (last visited January 23, 2018).

9. Adverse Possession, Real Estate and Property Law, Justia, https://www.justia.com/real-estate/docs/adversepossession. html (last visited January 23, 2018).

10. Jean Murray, Real Property, About.com, http://biztaxlaw.about.com/od/glossaryr/g/realproperty.htm (last visited October 19, 2013).

KEY TERMS

Abandoned Property
Adverse Possession
Bailee
Bailee's Lien
Bailment
Bailor
Charleston Municipal Ordinances
Chattel
Concurrent Ownership
Condominium
Conveyancing
Deed
Documents of Title
Easement
Eminent Domain
Encumbrance
Escheat
Estate
Estate at Sufferance
Estate at will
Exculpatory Clause
Fee Simple
Fee Simple Absolute
Fee Simple Defeasible
Gift
Gift Causa Mortis
Good
Habitability
Housing Code
Housing Cooperative
Implied Warranty of
Intangible Property
Inter Vivos
Joint Ownership

Joint Tenancy
Lease
Lessee
Lessor
Life Estate
Lost Property
Mislaid Property
Mortgage
Nonconforming Use
Ownership
Personal Property
Possession
Production
Property
Purchase
Quiet Title
Real Estate
Real Property
Remainder
Reversionary Interest
Right of Survivorship
Sole Ownership
Sole Proprietorship
Spot Zoning
Tangible Personal Property
Tenancy by the Entirety
Tenancy in Common
Testamentary Gift
Title
Treasure-Trove
Uniform Commercial Code
Variance
Waste
Zoning

CHAPTER 7

WHITE COLLAR AND OTHER BUSINESS CRIMES

The real significance of crime is in its being a breach of faith with the community of mankind.

—**Joseph Conrad**
Lord Jim, 1990

SECTION 7.1
INTRODUCTION

Stealing, lying, and cheating; that neatly summarizes the crimes that can be perpetrated in a business environment. A single scam, however, can be so harmful that it can devastate an enterprise, wipe-out a person's life savings, or cost investors billions of dollars, or as in case of Enron, which accomplished all three.[1]

The types of **crimes** that can be committed against the business venture are numerous, so it may be useful to categorize those offensives in terms of who commits them: employees; non-employees, including customers, and cybercriminals; and those who steal from a company without entering the business property.[2]

Some businesses have criminal culpability and routinely perpetrate a number of crimes that injury the public; financially, socially, and environmentally. Corporate offenses, or as more commonly dubbed, white collar crimes, and are perpetrated by the owners, principals, directors, officers and workers as part of their business operations. These crimes include such things as bribery, fraud, blackmail, insider trading, Ponzi schemes, racketeering and money laundering.[3] The losses from just a few of the top corporate frauds, such as Tyco, Adelphia, and Enron, dwarf the financial losses from all street robberies and burglaries put together. Health care fraud alone costs the nation between $100 billion to $400 billion annually. And, one cannot forget the less publicized crimes such as auto repair fraud, a $40 billion a year enterprise, securities fraud, and so on.[4]

White-collar crime, as opposed to street crime, acquired its name because the offenses were perpetrated by criminals who dress in business shirts, as opposed to blue-collar workers who are engaged in industrial or low paying jobs. Many of the criminals charged with white collar crimes are classified as middle or upper class. Their offenses do not usually encompass crimes of violence but involve unethical activities, fraud and financial theft.[5] For instance, the robbing of a bank would not be an example of white collar crime, but a bank teller taking money from the register would be.[6]

Some of the largest white collar crimes in history include:

- Bernard Madoff and his $465 billion Ponzi scheme in which he sought investments from wealthy people and businesses, and then used other funds to pay off existing patrons who wanted money rather than profits and then pocketing the difference for himself.

- Allen Stanford and Stanford International Bank, sold $8 billion in certificates of deposits to investors, with the promise of very high returns that never materialized. In reality, more than $1 billion was diverted into personal loans for Stanford, who falsely asserted that the bank's assets grew from $1.2 billon to $8.5 billon.

- Bernard Ebbers, CEO of WorldCom, who became rich from the holdings in this telecommunication company while executives used fraudulent accounting practices to hide WorldCom's declining earnings by portraying a false picture of financial growth. The loss was placed at $3.8 billion.[7]

This Chapter will explore white collar and other business crimes and will examine several of the constitutional rights commercial enterprises have against unwarranted governmental intrusion, such as the law of search and seizure or the right against self-incriumination.

SECTION 7.2 AN OVERVIEW OF CRIMINAL LAW

As a general rule, an individual can engage in any type of conduct that he or she wishes unless the law specifically prohibits those actions. The legislature, however, will intercede whenever necessary to regulate and prohibit conduct that society deems inappropriate.

A **crime** is an offense against society as determined by the legislature or considered a public wrong that carries the punishment of imprisonment or some other public sanction. The types of crimes number in the thousands, and specific definitions will vary from jurisdiction to jurisdiction. The offense is investigated by law enforcement officials who usually file the criminal charges against the accused, and a governmental agency, such as the District Attorney or United States Attorney, prosecutes the defendant. These crimes range from felonies to summary offenses.

The United States Department of Justice maintains statistics on the categories of crimes committed each year in this country. The most frequently charged offenses deal with non-violent crimes and make up about three-fourths of all **arrests.** Drug trafficking and other drug-related crimes constitute the single largest category of all arrests and make up 36%

of the total arrests made in the United States. Violent crimes account for one-fourth of all arrests and assault and robbery lead this category. The Southern states have the highest rate of violent crimes and account for 42% of all such crimes committed in this country.

Crimes against businesses retard economic prosperity. Some people, however, consider these types of offenses to be "victimless" crimes because of the perception that commercial entities can absorb the losses or have insurance.[8]

Burglary, robbery, shoplifting, employee theft, and fraud costs businesses billions of dollars annually. Crime can be particularly harmful to small commercial establishments, which lose both customers and employees when crime and fear take their toll on a neighborhood. A small business is especially vulnerable because they often fail to have preventative measures in place to prevent the crimes. A survey performed by the Small Business Administration determined that 13% of the businesses surveyed had been the victims of a crime, less than half used any type of security measures, and many crimes, particularly employee theft, went unreported.[9] For instance, when small businesses are victims of crime, they often change their hours of operation, raise their prices to cover the losses, relocate outside of the community, or simply close.[10] As for crimes by employees, they are 15 times more likely to steal from an employer than customers do and shoplifting costs vendors $9.5 to $11 billion annually.[11]

SECTION 7.3 CRIMES

Crimes against businesses take many forms and include burglary, trespass, embezzlement, robbery, receiving stolen property, electronic fencing, retail theft, identify theft and conspiracy.

A. Burglary

According to the FBI, more than two million burglaries occur each year and two-thirds of these offenses are of residential structures. Burglars invade homes primarily during the day through forcible entry while business structures are usually entered at night. The average loss per illegal entry is a little more than $1,700. The Northeast has the fewest number of burglaries while the South has the highest rate for these crimes. As for what month has the highest burglary rate, that distinction goes to July. February has the fewest.

The definition of burglary has changed over time. At common law, **burglary** was defined as the breaking and entering of a building at night with the intent of committing a felony. Since the purpose of this law is to allow people to be secure in their homes, should it matter whether the offense occurs during the day or night? The modern definition of burglary provides that a person is **guilty** of this crime if he enters a building or occupied structure with the intent to commit a crime unless the premises are open to the public. The distinction of committing the crime between the day or night has been eliminated, as well as the requirement of breaking and entering. For instance, a person who enters a business premise while it is closed to steal something commits the crime of burglary.

By way of comparison, England defines burglary as the entry into "any building, part of a building, inhabited vehicle or vessel with the intent to steal, cause grievous bodily harm, criminal damage, or to commit rape."

Burglary is a crime in and of itself and does not require the substantive offense to be committed. For example, if a person breaks into a home to steal a rare painting, but the painting is no longer there, the individual is still guilty of burglary.

The following case deals with whether a person commits burglary when he breaks the lock on a door to enter a structure without permission while standing in the courtyard entrance to four business establishments.

PEOPLE V. CRAWFORD
2013 WL 3006957 (CAL. APP. 2 DIST., 2013)

In September 2010, David Knowlton lived in West Hollywood, which sat behind a small business compound. The commercial building housed four businesses. A 15–foot wall was attached to the building and surrounded the compound, with a locked eight-foot gate. The businesses shared a patio/courtyard.

Knowlton woke up to the sound of repeated banging on what he thought was a dumpster. Fifteen minutes later, he heard a "creaking" sound like nails being pulled from wood. He looked out his window, but he did not see anyone. He continued to hear banging and the sound of plaster being hit with something heavy. Suddenly, Knowlton saw a man wearing a Fedora hat and dark clothes walk "briskly" by the window. Knowlton called 911.

Sheriff Deputies Egan and Tiwari responded to a dispatch of a possible burglary in progress. They received information that two men were trying to break in at the back of the location. They saw appellant walking in their direction, wearing dark clothing. Appellant dropped a "bundle of items"

on the ground. He was sweating profusely and breathing heavily.

Deputy Egan asked appellant where he was coming from. He replied, "The door was open and I was just checking the lock." Appellant was handcuffed and placed in a patrol car. Deputy Egan retrieved the items that appellant had dropped. He found a pair of dark gloves, a hat, and a dark shirt. Deputies [also] found a crowbar in shrubbery near the driveway. They observed extensive damage to a metal gate at the back of the compound. Both deputies noticed that appellant had stucco dust on his shoes.

At the close of the prosecutor's case, defense counsel argued that the structure was not a "building" because it had no roof over the courtyard. Furthermore, even if the structure was a building, there was no evidence that appellant made entry onto the premises. In response, the prosecutor argued that the structure containing the four businesses was attached by four walls and a roof and was designed to contain people or shelter property. It did not matter whether the courtyard was covered.

Burglary requires proof of entry into certain structures with the intent to commit a felony. Here, there is ample evidence showing that appellant committed burglary. He was practically caught red-handed. He was walking away from the scene as deputies arrived. He dropped a pair of dark gloves, a dark shirt, and a hat similar to the witness's description of the man he saw. He had plaster dust on his shoes when he was apprehended. He had burglary tools in his vehicle, which was parked close to the scene, and his crowbar was found near the driveway.

Appellant argues that the courtyard is not a "building". We are not convinced. It has long been the rule that a building is any structure which has walls on all sides and is covered by a roof. Here, the courtyard was an integral part of the building. The businesses were encompassed by a 15–foot wall, where the only entry was through the eight-foot gates at the front and rear of the compound, which were locked to protect against thieves.

Here, the building owner testified that the locked gate provided access to the four business suites, through the shared courtyard. A metal plate was installed in the stucco doorjamb so that an assailant could not reach the lock. The broken lock was found inside the gate to the compound. The jury could infer from this evidence that some part of appellant's body, or some instrument he was using, entered the compound and resulted in the damaged lock being found inside the gate and courtyard.

How would you answer the following questions?

1. If a person breaks into a truck to steal the radio, does it constitute burglary?

2. If a person enters a mobile office to assault the occupants, is this burglary?

3. If a person enters a department store while it is open in order to steal a coat, is this burglary?

B. Criminal Trespass

Has a person committed a crime if he or she purposely comes onto the land of another but has no intent to commit a crime? For example, is it a crime if a person climbs over a fence of a business property to go hunting on that land?

Criminal trespass laws have been enacted to protect the unlawful intrusion onto real estate. The crime occurs when a person enters the land of another without permission or with no legal right to be there. For instance, some states make it a crime if a person:

1. Enters, gains entry by subterfuge or surreptitiously remains in any building or occupied structure, or breaks into any building or occupied structure or separately secured or occupied portion thereof; or

2. Knowing that he is not licensed or privileged to do so, enters or remains in any place as to which notice against trespass is given by:

   i.   actual communication to the actor;

   ii. posting in a manner prescribed by law or reasonably likely to come to the attention of intruders;

   iii. fencing or other enclosure manifestly designed to exclude intruders; or

   iv. an actual communication to the actor to leave school grounds as communicated by a school, center or program official, employee or agent or a law enforcement officer.

This crime is not usually considered that serious and is classified as a misdemeanor.

C. Theft Related Crimes

Consider the following cases to ascertain if there is a common thread. In 1980, two men rigged the Pennsylvania State Lottery by placing counterfeit balls in the machine ensuring that 666 would be the winning number. A bank clerk mistakenly deposited ten thousand dollars into a customer's checking account which was promptly withdrawn by the recipient. A person gives his ATM card to a co-worker to withdraw $20 from his checking account as a loan. Instead, the co-worker withdraws $500. Have you figured it out? The common thread is that they are all examples of theft-related offenses.

The Federal Bureau of Investigation determined that there is an estimated loss of $9.4 billion dollars in property each year. In fact, in 2015, there were more than five and one-half million larceny related crimes in the United States, with the average amount taken of $929 per offense. These figures represent a very sizable portion of the total crimes committed during the year with theft related offenses ranging from larceny to receiving stolen property.

1. Larceny

Larceny is the taking and carrying away of property that belongs to another without the owner's consent and with the intention of depriving the owner of the goods permanently. Because this crime requires the person to take possession of and carry away the item, the offense does not apply to real estate or intangible property.

Most people have heard of the terms "petit larceny" and "grand larceny." The distinction between these crimes merely involves the value of the item stolen. For instance, Virginia classifies a theft of something having a value of $200 or more as grand larceny while an item with a value of less than $200 is petit larceny.

2. Embezzlement

Embezzlement is the act by which someone takes ownership of property that has been entrusted to him with the fraudulent intent to deprive the owner of the property. For instance, embezzlement occurs when a bank teller fraudulently changes the deposits so she can take some of the money. While embezzlement is closely aligned with theft, there is a critical difference. An embezzler is lawfully entrusted with the property as opposed to a thief who improperly obtains possession of the asset.

Embezzlement has no financial boundaries. The amount taken can be small or large. The crime can be as minor as a store clerk pocketing a few dollars from the register to executives of a large company falsely transferring millions of dollars of corporate funds into their personal bank accounts. Depending upon the scale of the wrongdoing, embezzlement may be punishable by large fines and jail time.[12]

3. Robbery

Robbery consists of all of the elements of larceny with one additional requirement. The taking must be accomplished by force or the threat of force.

The Federal Bureau of Investigation reports that most robberies occur on streets and highways and firearms are used almost half of the time. The average dollar value of the items taken per robbery is $1,230.

4. Receiving Stolen Property

A person commits the crime of **receiving stolen property** if he or she intentionally obtains or disposes of property of another knowing that it has been stolen, or believing that it has probably been stolen.

Generally, the person prosecuted for receiving stolen property is the "fence" and not the original thief. The thief cannot be convicted of receiving stolen property he already has in his possession.

The government has the burden of proving each element of this crime. Knowledge that the item was stolen can be established by circumstantial evidence; however, that knowledge may not be inferred solely from the unexplained possession of recently stolen merchandise. The test of knowledge is a subjective one, and the operative question is whether the defendant knew from the circumstances surrounding the possession that the property had been the subject of a theft.[13] For instance, a person who purchases a 48 inch, high definition television from the back of a truck for $100 is going to be hard pressed to convince the fact finder that the buyer did not suspect the item was stolen.

What type of knowledge must a person have that an item was stolen, in order to be convicted of receiving stolen property? That is the issue in **People v. Cabrera**

PEOPLE V. CABRERA
2017 WL 6506210 (CT. APP. CALIF. 2017)

In July 2011, someone stole more than 40 electronic items, including several laptop computers, computer towers, projectors, and speakers, from Cogswell Elementary School. Around August 2011, Defendant's brother and roommate, Anthony Cabrera, received several of the stolen items from one of his friends. In September 2011, El Monte Police Department officers traced one of the stolen computers to Defendant's home after she and Anthony used it to access the internet. Three officers went to Defendant's home to investigate the theft of the stolen items. Defendant initially refused to allow the officers to enter her home, but retrieved for them a Dell laptop that had been stolen from the school. When the officers told Defendant, they were looking for a Hewlett Packard (HP), and not a Dell, computer, she told them there was another computer in her kitchen. Defendant then signed a consent-to-search form, allowing the officers to enter the kitchen to retrieve the other computer. Inside the kitchen, the officers found an HP computer with a keyboard and mouse attached. As the officers left the kitchen, they saw a projector that had been reported stolen from the school sitting in plain sight on a table in the living room. The officers retrieved the HP computer, keyboard, mouse, and projector.

After leaving Defendant's home, the police obtained a warrant to search the rest of the home for additional items that were stolen from the school. When they executed the search warrant, the officers found the following items that had been reported stolen: two Sony speakers, a Linksys internet router, a scanner, a computer keyboard, a computer mouse, two sets of headphones, and two Dell computer towers. All the items were found in the living room, where Anthony slept. The speakers were found inside an armoire that had Anthony's name written on it, and the other items were found inside a cardboard box at the foot of Anthony's bed.

The officers arrested Defendant and Anthony on suspicion of receiving stolen property. During a jailhouse interview, Anthony told the police that his friend gave him the electronic items to "hold on" to for about a month and a half. Anthony believed the items had been stolen when he received them. He stored most of the items in the living room, and he set up the HP computer in the kitchen for him and Defendant to use.

After she was arrested, Defendant told the police that she first saw the HP desktop computer, the Dell laptop, the projector, and a cardboard box containing other electronic items inside her living room after she returned from school one day. When she asked Anthony where the items came from, he told her that his friend had stolen them from a school.

To sustain a conviction for receiving stolen property, the prosecution must prove (1) the property was stolen; (2) the defendant knew the property was stolen; and, (3) the defendant had possession of the stolen property.

Defendant does not dispute that the first two elements of the crime of receiving stolen property are satisfied with respect to all of the property recovered from inside her home. Instead, she contends the evidence establishes she possessed only the two computers she admitted to the police she had used, and the court therefore erred in finding she also possessed the other stolen electronic items found inside her home. Specifically, she argues she could not have constructively possessed the items recovered from her living room because they were under Anthony's exclusive control.

To establish the third element of the crime of receiving stolen property, the requisite possession of the stolen property may be either actual or constructive, and need not be exclusive. Physical possession also is not required, as it is sufficient if the defendant acquires a measure of control or dominion over the stolen property. However, mere presence near the stolen property in and of itself is insufficient evidence of possession to sustain a conviction for receiving stolen property.

Here, the court properly found Defendant actually or constructively possessed all of the stolen property recovered from her home. Defendant admitted she used the Dell laptop computer, the HP desktop computer, the keyboard, and the mouse. Thus, there is no dispute she actually possessed those items.

The evidence also supports an inference that Defendant constructively possessed the other items found inside her home. While she was in custody, Defendant told the police she first saw the Dell and HP computers as well as the video projector and a cardboard box containing other electronic items in her living room after she came home from school one day. When Defendant asked her brother where the items came from, he told her that they had been stolen from the local elementary school. Despite knowing the items were stolen, Defendant did not report the theft, and took no steps to remove the stolen items from her home. The fact that Defendant was aware that the stolen items were being stored in her living room was sufficient to support a finding that she constructively possessed those items.

---

5. Electronic Fencing

As a sign of our dependence on the Internet, states have added the offense of **electronic fencing.** This crime occurs when one uses the Internet to sell property gained through unlawful means. This variation of receiving stolen property is demonstrated by Illinois Public Act No. 94-179 which provides:

> "A person commits the offense of electronic fencing when he or she uses or accesses the Internet with the intent of selling property gained through unlawful means knowing that the property was stolen. A person who unknowingly purchases stolen property over the Internet does not violate this provision."

This crime is aimed at penalizing those who take possession of stolen merchandise. The court looks at the circumstances behind the transaction to decide the criminal intent of the person who obtained the goods.

6. **Retail Theft**

According to the National Crime Prevention Council, **retail theft** is committed by people of every age, race, sex, social and economic background, and about 25% of those who get caught are between the ages of 13 and 17. The offense is so commonplace that it costs businesses about $10 billion dollars a year. Customary tools of the trade include umbrellas, baby carriages, newspapers and diaper bags. When questioned as to why the person committed this crime, a common response is that the individual was bored and had nothing better to do or that peer pressure played a role in this crime.[14]

Common synonyms for this illegal activity are "five-finger discounts" and shoplifting. A person is guilty of this offense if he carries away or transfers any merchandise offered for sale with the intention of depriving the merchant of such items without paying the retail value for the product. Retail theft also encompasses the altering of a label or price tag in order to purchase the product at a discounted price or the removal or destruction of a security tag with the intent of depriving the merchant of the full purchase price. In a number of jurisdictions, retail theft statutes provide more severe penalties for theft from retail businesses than for theft from other parties.

7. **Identity Theft**

Identity theft is a recent phenomenon that involves using the victim's personal information to obtain a financial advantage such as the misappropriation of a credit card or money from a bank account. Criminals have even assumed the unsuspecting person's identity to obtain a fraudulent driver's license or to apply for a job. In fact, the United States Postal Authority estimates that nearly 10 million people are the victims of identity theft at the cost of about 5 billion dollars.

In 1998, Congress enacted the **Identity Theft and Assumption Deterrence Act** by making it a crime to misuse the personal identifying information of another. A number of states have followed suit by passing similar legislation. For example, Wisconsin provides that: "Whoever intentionally uses or attempts to use any personal identifying information or personal identification documents of an individual to obtain credit, money, goods, services or anything else of value without the authorization or consent of the individual and by representing that he or she is that individual, is guilty of a felony."

It is not necessary to break into someone's home to steal a person's private information. For instance, some thieves engage in "shoulder surfing" which involves watching an unsuspecting victim punch in a password on an automated teller machine or by listening in on a conversation while the person discloses a credit card number over the telephone. Some criminals even engage in "dumpster diving" by looking through discarded trash for copies of checks, or credit card statements. A recent expansion of this crime has occurred with the Internet. People frequently receive spam e-mails requesting personal information under a false pretense and people unwittingly provide that data.[15]

Has a robbery been committed if a person places a finger inside his jacket pocket and points it at a teller when he demands money or if a criminal is hitting papers off of a teller's desk but never brandishes a weapon or threatens bodily harm? Consider the following case:

BIRDSONG V. COM.
347 S.W.3D 47 (KY., 2011)

On June 21, 2005, with a bandana over his nose and mouth, Ronald Birdsong ran into the Fifth Third Bank in Lexington, Kentucky. He burst through the gate separating the teller area from the customer line. He moved the gate forcefully enough to create a loud bang when the gate hit the wall. And, the gate locked behind him. The tellers hid under the counter. Birdsong ordered them to "get up" and "give him the money." In doing so, he pulled a printer off the shelf under the counter near the tellers.

One teller arose and opened the drawers. Birdsong emptied the drawers. When the teller told him he had all of the money, Birdsong ran toward the exit. Unable to unlatch the gate leading to the customer area, he leapt over the gate and on to a nearby table, overturning a computer monitor in due course. Birdsong fled from the bank.

The police released a still photograph of the perpetrator from the bank's surveillance camera.

Subsequently, they received a tip implicating Birdsong.

At trial, one teller testified Birdsong screamed at them to "get up," "give me the money," and "open the drawers." She said Birdsong was really loud. And, she complied with his orders because she was afraid of him based on his tone of voice. He screamed at her. The second teller confirmed Birdsong did not make any explicit verbal threats against them or brandish a weapon.

Birdsong argued he did not use force or threaten the use of force during the crime; therefore, the jury could not find him guilty of robbery. The Commonwealth argued Birdsong's behavior constituted an implied threat to use force against a person and this was sufficient for a robbery.

A person is guilty of robbery when, in the course of committing theft, he uses or *threatens the use of physical force on another person* with intent to accomplish the theft. Thus, the question for this

Court is whether aggression toward inanimate objects in the presence of others during a theft sufficiently "threatens the use of physical force on another person."

The American Heritage Dictionary defines "threaten" as "To express a threat against." Moreover, a "threat" is "An expression of an intention to inflict pain, injury, or one regarded as a possible danger."

We cannot say it was clearly unreasonable for the jury to find Birdsong threatened the use of physical force on another person. Birdsong entered the bank wearing a bandana. He caused a loud noise when he entered the teller area by slamming the gate into the wall. He gave orders to the tellers in a loud voice. He pulled a printer onto the floor from a shelf near where the tellers hid under the counter. It was not unreasonable for the jury to conclude Birdsong expressed an intention to inflict pain or injury or that his behavior indicated danger or harm. Moreover, it is clear from the tellers' testimony that they were afraid of Birdsong, that they "regarded [him] as a possible danger."

The defendant's conduct must be objectively menacing. Consideration of the victim's fear is subjected to an objective test of whether a reasonable person in the teller's position would have perceived a threat of harm based on the defendant's conduct.

We opine a jury can find a defendant guilty of robbery when the defendant demands money and in making the demand, acts aggressively toward inanimate objects nearby. While the victim's or victims' perception of the aggressive behavior as a personal threat to him is not controlling, it is a factor the jury can consider in the totality of the circumstances. Therefore, we affirm Birdsong's convictions for robbery.

D. Conspiracy

In July of 2004, the FBI shocked the American public by indicting the chairman of Enron Corporation and other officers for perpetrating one of the largest corporate frauds in this country's history. They were charged with overseeing a massive scheme to "cook the books" and to create the illusion that Enron was a robust, growing company with limitless potential when Enron was an increasingly troubled business kept afloat only by a series of deceptions." The charged crimes for this deception were **conspiracy** and fraud.[16]

Labeled by the court as the "darling of the modern prosecutor's nursery," conspiracy is an all encompassing crime that allows the government to file charges against anyone who has participated in the planning or committing of a crime and to hold each liable for the actions of the other. For example, the following is Pennsylvania's definition of a conspiracy:

A person is guilty of conspiracy with another person or persons to commit a crime if with the intent of promoting or facilitating its commission he or she:

1. agrees with such other person or persons that they or one or more of them will engage in conduct which constitutes such crime or an attempt or solicitation to commit such crime; or

2. agrees to aid such other person or persons in the planning or commission of such crime or of an attempt or solicitation to commit such crime.

3. No person may be convicted of conspiracy to commit a crime unless an **overt act** in pursuance of such conspiracy is alleged and proved to have been done by him or by a person with whom he conspired.

4. It is a defense that the actor, after conspiring to commit a crime, thwarted the success of the conspiracy, under circumstances manifesting a complete and voluntary renunciation of his criminal intent.

Conspiracy is a separate crime from the actual offense that is to be committed. The agreement to commit the crime does not have to be in writing and can be informal. In fact, a mere tacit understanding is sufficient and each participant becomes the agent of the other for purposes of criminal responsibility.

Conspiracy is a common charge filed by the Federal Government in order to prosecute terrorists who plan to harm people of this country or to incite others to carry out such attacks.

Abu Ghayth was a disciple and spokesperson for Al Qaeda and is married to a daughter of Osama bin Laden. He gained worldwide attention after the 9/11 attacks by appearing in two videos defending the attacks and threatening repercussions because of the United States invasion of Afghanistan.[17] Ghayth was eventually captured and tried in the United States for conspiracy to kill Americans. The following is his case.

United States v. Ghayth
2017 WL 4287796 (Ct. App. 2nd Cir. 2017)

Abu Ghayth is an Islamic cleric of Kuwaiti descent who delivered speeches at Al Qaeda training camps and guesthouses in the months leading up to September 11, 2001, in which he urged Al Qaeda recruits to pledge their loyalty to bin Laden and fight for jihad. He also participated in numerous Al Qaeda recruiting and propaganda videos that aired in the months following the September 11 terrorist attacks. He was detained abroad and charged with conspiracy to murder

Americans, and conspiracy to provide material support to terrorism. After a jury trial, he was convicted on all counts.

The gravamen of Abu Ghayth's appeal is that he could not commit any of the charged crimes because he lacked specific knowledge of any particular plot and did not participate in a specific terrorist act.

To establish the existence of a criminal conspiracy, the government must prove that the conspirators agreed on the essence of the underlying illegal objectives, and the kind of criminal conduct in fact contemplated. The government need not prove that the defendant knew every unlawful objective of the conspiracy, every detail of its operation, or the identity of every co-conspirator.

The court's instructions properly conveyed those requirements. It explained to the jury: "What is necessary is that the defendant has participated in the conspiracy with knowledge of its unlawful purpose, and with an intent to aid in the accomplishment of its unlawful objective," i.e., the murder of Americans. It added that the "defendant, with an understanding of the unlawful nature of the conspiracy, must intentionally have engaged, advised, or assisted in the conspiracy for the purpose of furthering any of its illegal objectives." It then defined the illegal objective of the conspiracy, murder.

The instructions did not require the jury to find that Abu Ghayth intended to kill a specific person or plan a specific plot, because the killing of Americans was the "essential nature" of the illegal objective, and Abu Ghayth was charged only with conspiracy to commit that act.

Abu Ghayth challenges the sufficiency of evidence to support the crimes of conspiracy to murder Americans. He essentially characterizes himself as a religious figure that was present among known terrorists without killing anyone or participating in the execution or planning of any specific act of terror.

The government had no need to show that he possessed knowledge of any particular plot to kill Americans or that he had the specific intent to carry out such a plot. Its burden was to prove that he had knowing participation or membership in the scheme and some knowledge of its unlawful aims and objectives. In other words, the jury only had to find that Abu Ghayth knew of Al Qaeda's objective to kill Americans and intended to participate.

The proof of this knowledge is overwhelming. Abu Ghayth joined the criminal conspiracy by seeking out Osama bin Laden in Afghanistan and pledging his services to Al Qaeda as a religious scholar and orator. He participated in the conspiracy by delivering speeches with bin Laden, including on the day after the September 11 attacks and in advance of the shoebomb plot. These speeches threatened and urged the killing of Americans, for example, by evoking the "Storm of Airplanes" and "our war with the United States," and promised further deadly attacks. The fact that Abu Ghayth may not have known the logistics is of no moment. The defendant joined the conspiracy and is equally complicit by reason of his knowledge of the plan's general scope, if not its exact limits.

Abu Ghayth's words in his speeches served as "the very vehicle of a crime" by aiding in the commission of terrorist acts. He told Muslims it was their duty to fight for Al Qaeda, urged them to pledge loyalty to bin Laden, and threatened future attacks against "new American targets ... at the time that we pick, and the place that we pick, and the method that we pick." Far from "pure speech," Abu Ghayth's words provided material support to Al Qaeda by spreading its message to the world and encouraging others to join its terrorist cause.

For the foregoing reasons, and finding no merit in Abu Ghayth's arguments, we hereby affirm the judgment of the district court.

SECTION 7.4
KATHY'S PURSE
SNATCH

PARK, BROWN & SMITH, P.C.
ATTORNEYS AT LAW
MEMORANDUM

PROBLEM SEVEN—A

TO: All Law Clerks

FROM: Peter Smith, Esquire

RE: Kathy Robert's Criminal Charges for Robbery

Kathy Roberts has gotten herself into trouble once again. She was recently arrested for robbery and my investigation has revealed the following. Kathy was experiencing withdrawal from her opioid addiction. She needed to immediately obtain Oxycodone to feed her habit but she had no money. Not knowing what to do, she began wondering the streets looking for a dealer. She was turned down wherever she went because she had no money.

Somehow, she ended up in Rittenhouse Square and was sitting on a bench shaking with her arms wrapped around herself and sweating profusely. A kind elderly lady approached Kathy and asked her if she needed help. Kathy said in a whisper, "Yeah I do. Please give me your money." The Good Samaritan thought that she heard Kathy incorrectly, so she asked Kathy to repeat herself. Kathy stood up and said in a louder voice, "Look ma'am, I am very sorry, but I urgently need some money and I need it now! Please, just give me the money from your handbag." The woman opened her handbag and Kathy snatched the wallet, causing the lady to drop her bag. The lady was so started that she took a step backwards, lost her balance, and fell onto the sidewalk, breaking her arm. Kathy did not know what to do, panicked and ran away.

The police apprehended Kathy about one-hour later, when they found her about two blocks from the scene. Kathy was sitting on the curb stoned. A search of Kathy's clothes found the elderly lady's driver's license, three hundred dollars in cash and a handful of pills. Our client was arrested for robbery and taken to the Juvenile Detention Center. I was eventually able to secure her release pending trial.

I am a realistic and know that Kathy has a major problem. There is no question that she committed theft by taking the money, but I do not know if she also committed robbery, which can result in a ten year jail sentence. I was able to find the following case which should be of some help. Please read **Missouri v. Coleman** and let me know if you think Kathy committed robbery.

Missouri v. Coleman
2014 WL 48154 (Miss. Ct. App. 2104)

On October 6, 2012, Appellant walked into a branch office of Bank Star One wearing sunglasses. He walked up to teller Maria Rothove, rested his forearm on the counter, leaned slightly forward, handed Rothove a plastic grocery sack, and said, "I need you to do me a favor. Put the money in this bag." He spoke in a low, serious tone. Rothove took the bag, opened her drawer, and put $1,472.00 in the bag. While this was going on, the assistant branch manager, Sharon Holland, approached. When she was a few feet from Rothove, Appellant told her, "Ma'am, stop where you are and don't move any farther." Holland complied with those instructions. Rothove handed Appellant the bag of money, and he ran out of the bank.

Appellant was eventually arrested and charged with robbery. Appellant was tried, found guilty and sentenced to ten years imprisonment. On appeal, Appellant challenges the sufficiency of the evidence to support his conviction for robbery.

A person commits the crime of stealing if he or she appropriates property or services of another with the purpose to deprive him or her thereof, either without his or her consent or by means of deceit or coercion. The offense of stealing is transformed into the greater offense of robbery when the stealing is accomplished forcibly. A person forcibly steals, if, in the course of stealing, the person uses or threatens the immediate use of physical force upon another person for the purpose of preventing or overcoming resistance to the taking of the property or compelling the owner of such property or another person to deliver up the property. Thus, in order to support a robbery conviction, there must be evidence establishing beyond a reasonable doubt that the defendant used physical force or threatened someone with the immediate use of physical force in order to accomplish the theft.

Appellant contends that the evidence did not support a finding that he used physical force or threatened anyone in the bank with the immediate use of physical force during the incident and that the evidence, therefore, does not support his conviction for robbery. The State concedes that Appellant did not actually use any physical force during the incident but maintains that the evidence supports a finding that Appellant threatened Rothove and/or Holland with the immediate use of physical force. Accordingly, the sole question on appeal is whether the evidence was sufficient to establish beyond a reasonable doubt that Appellant threatened the immediate use of physical force against one or both of the two ladies in order to compel Rothove to give him the money in her drawer and/or to prevent resistance to his taking of the money.

To support a conviction for robbery based upon the threatened use of physical force, there must be evidence of some affirmative conduct on the part of the defendant, beyond the mere act of stealing, which communicates that he will "immediately" employ "physical force" if the victim fails to deliver up the property or otherwise resists his taking of the property. The threat of physical harm need not be explicit; it can be implied by words, physical behavior or both. Appellant made only two statements while in the bank. While handing Rothove a plastic bag, he stated, "I need you to do me a favor. Put the money in this bag." And when Holland approached, he told her, "Ma'am, stop where you are and don't move any farther." Both statements were made in a low, serious tone.

The State argues that the statements made by Appellant are indistinguishable from handing a teller a note saying, "This is a holdup." Contrary to the State's contention, however, these comments are readily distinguishable. "The expression 'holdup,' in its ordinary significance, means a forcible detention of the person held with the intent to commit robbery and implies the necessary force to carry out that purpose." Thus, the use of the term itself implies possession of a weapon and the willingness to use force. The ordinary meaning of the terms and phrases used by Appellant do not convey a similar message.

Whether a defendant has impliedly threatened the immediate use of physical force for the purpose of overcoming resistance to the taking of property is determined by the defendant's actions rather than the reactions and perceptions of the putative victim. Thus, a conviction for robbery requires evidence beyond a reasonable doubt that the defendant communicated, through affirmative conduct and/or words, an intent to immediately use physical force if the victim fails to deliver up the property or otherwise resists his taking of the property.

As his verbal statements are insufficient to support a finding of a threat of physical force, we are left to consider whether Appellant's actions and nonverbal communication add enough to the situation for a trier of fact to infer beyond a reasonable doubt that he threatened Rothove and/or Holland with the use of immediate physical force. Multiple security cameras recorded Appellant's actions inside and outside the bank. None of it reflects Appellant ever placed a hand in a pocket or otherwise made any type of physical gesture that could be interpreted as intending to indicate that he had a weapon or was poised to attack. He walked into the bank with his arms swaying freely at his side, walked up to the counter, placed one arm on the counter, leaned slightly on it, handed Rothove a plastic bag, and then spoke with her. After receiving the money, Appellant turned and walked quickly out of the bank and then ran away. In short, Appellant's body language does not support a finding beyond a reasonable doubt that Appellant threatened anyone with the immediate use of physical force.

There must be some affirmative conduct on the part of the defendant, beyond the mere act of stealing, which communicates that he will immediately employ "*physical force*" if the victim resists the taking of the property. If, as the State argues, no affirmative conduct is required, then virtually all stealing other than by means of deceit will be the same as robbery. In other words, appropriating the property of another with the purpose to deprive the other thereof by means of coercion becomes essentially meaningless if virtually all verbally coercive conduct is treated as robbery.

For these reasons, we hold that the evidence was insufficient to support a finding beyond a reasonable doubt that Appellant, either explicitly or implicitly, threatened Rothove or Holland with the immediate use of physical force. As his conviction for robbery is, therefore, not supported by sufficient evidence, it must be vacated.

PROBLEM SEVEN—A
ANSWER SHEET

Name   **Please Print Clearly**

1. Has Kathy committed the crime of robbery?

2. Explain your answer based upon the holding in **Missouri v. Coleman.**

SECTION 7.5
WHITE-COLLAR CRIME

Illegal actions perpetuated in a business setting are generally classified as **white-collar crimes.** It has been estimated that the dollar loss from this offense is larger than all other crimes put together. In fact, the figure has been placed at a staggering $400 billion dollars a year and the frequency of crime is on the rise. While there is no one exact definition for this offense, the Federal Bureau of Investigation has defined white collar crime as ". . . those illegal acts which are characterized by deceit, concealment, or violation of trust and which are not dependent upon the application or threat of physical force or violence." This catch-all phrase includes computer fraud, health care fraud, securities fraud and insider trading, counterfeiting, theft of trade secrets, embezzlement, and tax evasion. The problem is so pervasive that the FBI estimates that white-collar crime accounts for 4% of all reported crime with the majority of these offenses being for fraud, counterfeiting, and forgery. The National White Collar Crime Center has determined that one in every three American households has been victimized by white-collar crimes. While individuals are the largest group of victims, businesses, financial institutions, governments, religious organizations, and other public entities have all been victimized.

Because of the difficulty and expense in uncovering white-collar crime, as well as the public's low tolerance for corporate wrongdoing, the state and federal governments have become more aggressive in prosecuting these cases. Some legislative bodies have even increased the penalty for white collar crime by imposing mandatory jail time. California is an example of a state that now imposes a minimum jail sentence for anyone convicted of economic or white collar crime. The rationale for this mandate is discussed in **People v. Alejandro.**

PEOPLE V. ALEJANDRO
28 CAL. 4TH 481 (CAL., 2002)

On April 18, 1997, a complaint was filed charging defendant with the theft of a trade secret. It was further alleged that the loss exceeded $2.5 million. Defendant pleaded no contest to the theft charge, a charge based upon evidence that he had printed out confidential design specifications for certain computer chips on the last day of his employment as an electrical engineer at Digital Equipment Corporation. Defendant objected to the potential application of **Section 1203.044** to his sentence.

Defendant stands convicted of theft, specifically a violation of **Section 499c,** which provides: "Every person is guilty of theft who, with intent to deprive or withhold the control of a trade secret from its owner, or with an intent to appropriate a trade secret to his or her own use or to the use of another, does any of the following: steals, takes, carries away, or uses without authorization, a trade secret."

The trial court determined that **Section 1203.044** applies to such a theft. This statute, entitled The

Economic Crime Law, requires that a defendant who is convicted of certain theft offenses and is granted probation shall be sentenced to at least 90 days in the county jail as a condition of probation.

The Legislature declared in enacting **Section 1203.044:** "Major economic or white collar crime is an increasing threat to California's economy and the well-being of its citizens. The Legislature intends to deter that crime by ensuring that every offender, without exception, serves at least some time in jail. White collar criminals granted probation too often complete their probation without having compensated their victims or society. Probation accompanied by a restitution order is often ineffective because county financial officers are often unaware of the income and assets enjoyed by white collar offenders. Thus, it is the Legislature's intent that the financial reporting requirements of this act be utilized to achieve satisfactory disclosure to permit an appropriate restitution order. White collar criminal investigation and prosecutions are unusually expensive. These high costs sometimes discourage vigorous enforcement of white collar crime laws by local agencies. Thus, it is necessary to require white collar offenders to assist in funding this enforcement activity."

We observe that the term "white collar crime" is a relatively broad one and is not limited to losses involving cash or cash equivalents. It generally is defined as "a nonviolent crime usually involving cheating or dishonesty in commercial matters. Examples include fraud, embezzlement, bribery, and insider trading." **Black's Law Dict. (7th ed., 1999).** The Legislature has applied the term "white collar crime" to fraud and embezzlement in **Section 186.11,** a statute that provides for enhanced prison terms for recidivists committing these offenses when the offense involves a pattern of "taking more than one hundred thousand dollars." Like the crime of theft, fraud and embezzlement are not limited to the unlawful acquisition of cash or cash equivalents. Indeed, frequently fraud and embezzlement simply are methods by which a charged theft is accomplished.

Because the crime of theft includes a wide range of property and the term "white collar crime" has a broad meaning, we find it improbable that the Legislature intended to address only the theft of cash or cash equivalents in adopting The Economic Crime Act. It is far more reasonable to conclude that the Legislature intended the provision to apply to all thefts of property of a particular value. Any other interpretation would permit many white collar thieves to continue to receive light probationary sentences and to evade strict restitution requirements. From the usual meaning of the terms used in **Section 1202.044,** the purpose of the enactment, and the Legislature's parallel use of the same terms in other statutes, one must conclude that **Section 1203.044** is not limited to thefts of cash or cash equivalents.

We find it clear from the words employed in **Section 1203.044** and the declaration of intent accompanying its enactment, that **Section 1203.044** does not apply solely to thefts of cash or cash equivalents, but rather that it addresses thefts of property, including trade secrets, exceeding specified values.

A. Bribery

Do the words "payola" or "kickback" sound familiar?" These terms refer to the crime of **bribery.** This crime is the act of offering something of value to another with the intent of influencing that person's opinion or to have something done in return by that entity. Bribery arises in a number of contexts such as influencing a juror's vote, paying a police officer to disregard a traffic ticket or influencing the awarding of a contract. Over the years, a number of politicians have been convicted of this crime. For instance, Congressman Randy Cunningham resigned from Congress in 2005 after pleading guilty to taking more than $2 million in bribes from government contractors. One of the most famous bribery cases, however, involved a sting operation known as Abscam. The FBI set up a dummy business which was said to represent an Arab Sheik that offered bribes to a variety of politicians to influence their actions. The result of this undercover investigation was the conviction of seven members of Congress, a member of the New Jersey legislature, and several members of Philadelphia City Council for bribery.

B. Money Laundering

In the fall of 2005, House Majority leader Tom DeLay resigned from Congress after being indicted by a **grand jury** for illegally funneling campaign contributions to the Republican National Committee. His alleged crime was **money laundering.**

Money laundering is not something new. Some say the term originated with organized crime's ownership of laundromats during the days of Al Capone. Criminals were in possession of large sums of cash from extortion, prostitution, and gambling. They needed to show a legitimate source for these funds so this was accomplished by purchasing legitimate businesses that could commingle the illegal earnings with the revenues received from these businesses. Laundromats were chosen because they were cash businesses, so the crime naturally became known as money laundering.[18]

This crime is contained in a Federal statute entitled the **Money Laundering Control Act.** The basic design of money laundering is to conceal the real source of illegally obtained money by having a third party claim ownership to the currency. This is a frequent tool used by terrorists, drug traffickers, organized crime, and corrupt politicians, so that the source of illegally obtained money cannot be traced.

The statute is rather complex and the following is part of the federal law:

Whoever with the intent:

a. to promote the carrying on of specified unlawful activity;

b. to conceal or disguise the nature, location, source, ownership, or control of the property believed to be the proceeds of specified unlawful activity; or

c. to avoid a transaction reporting requirement under state or federal law;

conducts or attempts to conduct a financial transaction involving property represented to be the proceeds of specified unlawful activity, or property used to conduct or facilitate specified unlawful activity, shall be fined, or imprisoned for no more than 20 years, or both.

A person charged with money laundering does not have to commit the crime which generated the illegal revenue. Rather, the charge applies to the person who disposes of the cash or hides its true origination. **U.S. v. Awada** demonstrates this point.

U.S. v. Awada
425 F.3D 522 (C. A. Minn., 2005)

Awada was indicted following an investigation into a large-scale gambling ring operated by Douglas Sabby. Sabby was a bookmaker, taking bets on various sporting events. Concerned that the assets of his illicit activity would come to the attention of the federal government, Sabby took pains to veil his gambling operation. For instance, Sabby's cellular telephone was not registered in his name, and he would pay and collect from his bettors through intermediaries.

Sabby testified that, because most illegal gamblers do not want to leave a paper trail, they would generally pay him in cash. However, one bettor, John Boss, found himself several hundred thousand dollars in debt to Sabby, and tired of the scrutiny associated with making large-sum withdrawals from his financial accounts to pay Sabby in cash. Sabby accommodated Boss by letting Boss write several checks, made out to "cash." Boss gave Sabby a number of $5,000 checks made out in this fashion at the same time. Sabby did not have a bank account of his own, as he sought to hide the assets of his enterprise.

Sabby was a patron of Awada's bar and restaurant. Awada was one of Sabby's bettors, and thus knew he was a bookmaker. Sabby brought several of the $5,000 checks from John Boss to Awada's bar, seeking to have Awada cash them. The checks were not endorsed by Sabby, and no marking on the checks connected Sabby to them. Awada had never met Boss, the person from whose account the checks were drawn. Awada cashed Boss's checks as requested by Sabby, commingling them with his legitimate business proceeds when he later deposited them into his business account. Awada was subsequently indicted for twelve counts of money laundering.

To sustain a money laundering conviction, the government must prove that the defendant conducted a financial transaction designed to conceal the proceeds of a "specified unlawful activity." The transaction or transactions that created the criminally-derived proceeds must be distinct from the money laundering transaction, because the money laundering statutes criminalize transactions in proceeds, not the transactions that create the proceeds.

After reviewing the evidence, we are convinced that Awada was properly convicted. The **indictment** specifies the unlawful activity from which the criminal proceeds derived was "an illegal gambling business." Conducting an illegal gambling business is a felony under federal law, and thus is a predicate offense sufficient to support the "specified unlawful activity" element of the crime of money laundering. The money laundering allegations concerned *proceeds* of the illegal gambling business; they did not comprise the illegal gambling business. Further, the record contains more than sufficient evidence that an illegal gambling business did exist. Sabby and many of his accomplices testified that Sabby conducted a large-scale, long-running, bookmaking operation.

Money laundering is a financial transaction crime involving the proceeds of some other crime; there is absolutely no requirement that a money laundering defendant also be involved in the underlying crime. That Awada was not a conspirator in Sabby's gambling ring does not exempt him from liability for laundering the proceeds of that illegal activity.

Awada further asserts that the evidence at trial was insufficient as to the scienter element of the crime. We disagree. The government was required to prove that Awada performed financial transactions (the check cashing) knowing that the transactions were designed "to conceal or disguise the nature, the location, the source, the ownership or the control of the proceeds of the specified unlawful activity." Although Awada never directly admitted such knowledge and Sabby testified that he never made his concealment plan explicit, reasonable jurors could infer Awada was aware of what he was doing. Awada knew Sabby was a bookmaker since Awada himself placed bets with Sabby. Awada cashed a number of $5,000 checks for Sabby, all of which were from an unknown third party, made out to "cash," and not endorsed by Sabby. Even Awada himself admitted that he suspected the checks came from one of Sabby's losing customers. Accordingly, we find that a jury could reasonably conclude that Awada knew he was laundering the funds of Sabby's gambling enterprise, and that the transactions were undertaken with the intent to conceal the nature of that enterprise.

C. Insider Trading

Many people have heard of **insider trading** and the news contains stories about this problem. For instance, the former CEO of Qwest Commutations was convicted of this charge for selling the company's stock at a profit of $176 million before the firm's financial collapse. And, who can forget the well publicized case against the CEO of Enron Corporation because of that firm's accounting fraud that showed tremendous profits which were not an accurate reflection of the firm's financial status. Even Martha Stewart was involved in an insider trading scandal, in her case concerning the sale of ImClone stock. So, what is this crime?

According to the Securities and Exchange Commission, insider trading occurs when corporate insiders, such as officers, directors, and employees, buy or sell stock in their own companies. Illegal insider trading, however, refers to the buying or selling of a security, in breach of a relationship of trust and confidence, while in possession of information that has not yet been made public about the stock.[19]

Examples of insider trading complaints filed by the SEC include:

- Corporate officers, directors, and employees who traded the corporation's securities after learning of significant, and confidential corporate developments;

- Friends, business associates, family members, and other "tippees" of such officers, directors, and employees, who traded the securities after receiving confidential information;

- Employees of law, banking, brokerage and printing firms who were given confidential information in order to provide services to the corporation and then traded those securities;

- Government employees who learned of such confidential information because of their employment by the government; and

- Other persons who misappropriated, and took advantage of confidential information concerning their employers.

Because insider trading undermines investor confidence in the securities markets, the SEC has treated the detection and prosecution of insider trading as one of its enforcement priorities.[20]

There are two theories of insider trading: the **"classical theory"** and the **"misappropriation theory."** The classical theory imposes liability on corporate insiders who trade on the basis of confidential information obtained by reason of their position within the business. This responsibility is based on the idea that a corporate insider breaches a duty of trust and confidence to the stockholders of the corporation. On the other hand, the misappropriation theory, imposes liability on "outsiders" who trade on the basis of confidential information obtained by reason of their relationship with the person possessing such information, usually a person on the inside of the corporation. Liability under the misappropriation theory is based on the notion that the outsider breaches "a duty of loyalty and confidentiality" to the person who shared the confidential information with him. Not only are the insider and outsider forbidden from trading on the basis of the confidential information they have received, they are also forbidden from **"tipping"** such information to someone else who, being fully aware that the information is confidential, does the trading. In other words, the people are forbidden from doing indirectly what they are forbidden from doing directly.[21]

Assume for a moment that Tyler's Sports Bar and Grill has concluded that it can dramatically increase its revenues by putting a microbrewery in its business establishment. This project will cost $250,000, so Tyler's needs a loan for this expenditure. The problem is that the bar's financial statements will not justify the loan. The expenses exceed the revenues which is why Tyler's wants to install a microbrewery. The solution is to change the financial statements to reflect larger revenues. Joe Roberts reasoned that it is only the bank and not the government who will receive the inaccurate information. Also, the bar will have no trouble repaying the loan so everything will work out. Well, things didn't play out exactly as Roberts planned. The bank requested backup documentation to support the loan application. They wanted to see the bar's tax returns and daily revenue logs. Has Roberts and the bar done anything criminal by "cooking the books?"

It is a federal crime to make a false statement to a financial institution in order to secure a loan. The offense is **making a false statement to a bank.** The law provides that anyone who knowingly makes a false statement of a material fact or overvalues property for the purposes of inducing a bank to take action shall be guilty of this offense. The penalty is a fine not to exceed $1,000,000 or imprisonment of a term not to exceed 30 years, or both.

In order to be convicted, the government must prove (1) that the defendant made a false statement or willfully overvalued land, property, or security, and (2) made the statement for purposes of influencing the action of financial institution upon application, commitment, or loan. These statements can be made orally or in writing, and whether the bank relied upon the false information is irrelevant. It is enough that the false statements are of the type that would disturb the balance of facts that would otherwise be available to the bank. The justification for this federal law is that false statements given to insured banks have the potential to mislead the government's auditors charged with maintaining the federal standards. After all, the government's interest in maintaining the vitality of its federal deposit insurance programs for banks mandates that all material false statements violate the federal law, even when they are given with the knowledge, consent or duplicity of a bank officer.[22]

Does the making of a false statement to the bank require that the false declaration be material and relied upon by the financial institution? That is the issue in the next case.

UNITED STATES V. TAYLOR
808 F.3D 1202 (CT. APP. 9TH CIR. 2015

Lloyd Taylor appeals his conviction of making false statements to a bank. These convictions arose out of a tax evasion scheme in which Taylor used multiple false identities to open bank accounts in order to obtain cashier's checks to buy gold. The

bank discovered the scheme and reported it to federal authorities.

Taylor's scheme began in the 1980s when he used the identities of children who had died before receiving social security numbers, and who would have been approximately the same age as Taylor. At trial, the government introduced evidence that Taylor obtained Florida driver's licenses, which he subsequently renewed, and voter registration cards, using the stolen identities.

According to the evidence, Taylor used these false documents to open various bank accounts, including checking accounts at Wells Fargo and Wachovia. In 2009, Taylor, using one of his false identities, purchased four cashier's checks from Wells Fargo Bank, in the total amount of $250,000. Around the same time, again using a false identity, he purchased two cashier's checks from Wachovia Bank, in the amount of $98,050. To obtain the cashier's checks, Taylor provided various forms of false identification. To pay for these cashier's checks, he used funds drawn from checking accounts he had opened at each bank, also using false identities.

The law provides, in relevant part:

> "Whoever knowingly makes any false statement or report ... for the purpose of influencing in any way the action of ... any institution the accounts of which are insured by the Federal Deposit Insurance Corporation ... upon any ... commitment ... or application for ... a guarantee ... shall be guilty of an offense against the United States. **18 U.S.C. § 1014**."

It is undisputed that Taylor made false statements of his identity to open accounts, withdraw funds, and obtain cashiers' checks from insured banks. A cashier's check is a commitment within the meaning of **18 U.S.C. § 1014**.

Prior to 1997, most circuits had held that § 1014 reached only those false statements that were "material," that is, having "the capacity to influence the lending institution" with respect to a decision involving the bank's funds. The Supreme Court in **United States v. Wells, 519 U.S. 482 (1997)**, rejected the materiality requirement, holding that materiality of a false statement is not an element of § 1014. The **Wells** Court relied on the plain text of § 1014, which contains no mention of materiality, as well as on the legislative history of the statute, to determine that there is no materiality requirement.

If a false statement violates the statute even if it cannot influence any financial decision, then there can be no requirement of risk of financial loss. Because materiality is not an essential element of § 1014, it would be nonsensical for us to require the government to nonetheless prove that the financial institution faced a risk of financial loss.

We, therefore, hold that proof of a risk of loss to a financial institution is not required for conviction of making a false statement in violation of § 1014.

D. Bankruptcy Fraud

Have you ever heard of **"bankruptcy fraud?"** Bankruptcy offers protection to a debtor by offering a fresh start or the ability to repay the obligations over a period of time. An entity that is overwhelmed with debts can turn to the bankruptcy courts for help in which assistance comes in a variety of ways. A **Chapter 7 bankruptcy** is known as a straight bankruptcy because it extinguishes or liquidates the debts. A bankruptcy trustee will collect all of the non-exempt property of the debtor and pay the creditors with those proceeds. The person will then be discharged in bankruptcy which means that the debts have been extinguished so the person can start over with a clean slate. A business, however, may not wish to liquidate its assets and go out of business. A **Chapter 11 bankruptcy** is known as reorganization and allows the debtor to regain solvency by seeking an adjustment of the obligations, either by reducing the debts or by extending the time for repayment. This allows the entity to stay in business while repaying the debts under a court approved plan. A **Chapter 13 bankruptcy** is known as a wage earner's plan since it allows individuals with regular income to develop a plan to repay all or part of their debts. The advantage of this bankruptcy is that it allows individuals to save their homes from foreclosure.[23]

Unfortunately, not all those who seek bankruptcy protection are honest in their disclosures. The Department of Justice estimates that 10 percent of all bankruptcy petitions contain some element of fraud. This undermines public confidence in the system, and taints the reputation of honest citizens seeking protection under the bankruptcy statutes.

The crime of **bankruptcy fraud** covers this situation and provides:

A person who having devised a scheme or artifice to defraud:

1. Files a bankruptcy petition;

2. Files a document in a bankruptcy proceeding; or

3. Makes a fraudulent representation, claim, or promise concerning a bankruptcy

shall be fined or imprisoned not more than five years, or both.

Bankruptcy fraud takes several forms: (1) when a debtor conceals assets to avoid forfeiting them, (2) when individuals file false or incomplete bankruptcy forms; (3) when a person files numerous times, either by using real information in several states or by using false information; or (4) when a court-appointed trustee is bribed. The FBI has primary investigative jurisdiction over bankruptcy frauds.[24]

E. RICO

RICO stands for the **Racketeer Influenced and Corrupt Organizations Act** passed by Congress in 1970 to eliminate the influence of organized crime. This legislation is commonly used by the victims of white collar crimes, such as mail and wire fraud.[25] The purpose of the law is to exclude the access of organized crime and racketeering into business operations in interstate commerce. The statute, however, is sufficiently comprehensive to target the illegal activities of any enterprise affecting interstate or foreign commerce.[26]

RICO prohibits anyone from investing, acquiring, or participating in the affairs of a business through a pattern of racketeering activities. This was believed to happen through organized crime's utilization of money and power gained from illegal means, such as loansharking, theft, gambling, fencing of property, and the importation and distribution of illegal drugs.[27]

In creating this legislation, Congress wanted to strengthen the legal weapons and evidence gathering abilities against organized crime by crafting new remedies against those engaged in organized activities. RICO provides substantial criminal and civil remedies to both the government and private citizens injured by reason of a violation of this law. The prohibited racketeering activities include a vast array of both federal and state offenses and allow for treble damages.[28]

The target of the legislation has recently undergone a change and is now used to prosecute corruption in organized labor, gangs and corrupt government officials. The magic of the law is that it allows the government to prosecute both the criminals and their leaders. Under the statute, if a group is involved in other illegal action, such as corruption or prostitution, the organizers can be convicted of racketeering—even if they didn't personally sell the drugs or accept the bribe.[29]

A conviction under RICO requires the defendant to have engaged in two or more instances of racketeering and the criminal must have directly invested in, maintained, or participated in a criminal enterprise affecting interstate or foreign commerce.[30]

Examples of such activities are varied and include any act or threat involving murder, kidnapping, gambling, arson, robbery, bribery, extortion, dealing in obscene matter or a controlled substance, bribery, counterfeiting, mail and wire fraud, obstruction of justice, retaliating against a witness, money laundering, sexual exploitation of children, trafficking in counterfeit phonograph records, DVDs, computer programs or motion pictures, embezzlement from union funds, and fraud in the sale of securities.

A pattern of racketeering requires at least two acts of racketeering activity, one of which occurred after the effective date of the law and the last one occurring within ten years after the commission of a prior act of racketeering.

An example of a RICO conviction involved charges against eleven of America's major tobacco companies. These defendants were found guilty of nearly 150 counts of mail and wire fraud in a continuing "pattern of racketeering activity" with the "specific intent to defraud" under the Racketeer Influence Corrupt Organizations Act. The case charged that the tobacco companies engaged in "a pattern of racketeering activity" geared to "deceive the American public about the health effects and addictiveness of smoking cigarettes." The court found that the defendants had embarked upon a decades-long scheme to defraud smokers by falsely denying the adverse health effects of smoking; that nicotine and smoking are addictive; and that the firms had manipulated cigarette design so as to guarantee nicotine delivery levels that created and sustained addiction.[31]

F. Mail and Wire Fraud

Consider the following e-mail that Mary received from a friend:

> Hi Mary,
>
> I am sorry that I didn't inform you about my trip to London but right now, I am stranded and need help to get back home. I am writing from an internet café. I can't believe it but I was robbed on my way back to the hotel. The robbers took my bag containing my wallet, phone, air plane ticket and other valuables.
>
> Can you lend me $2,500, or any amount you can spare, so that I can sort out my hotel bill and other expenses? My flight is in 6 hours and I am desperate. I promise to pay you back with interest as soon as I am home. I was told by the police that the safest way to receive the money is through Western Union. If you can help, send the money by following these directions. You can get a list of Western Union money transfer agents closest to you by entering your full address at the following link:
>
> www.westernunion.com/info/agentLocatorLookup.asp
>
> As soon as you transfer the money, please email me with the transaction code. I will need it to pick up the money from Western Union. I will check back in a couple of hours to get the transfer details. Thanks again and I really appreciate your help.
>
> Love David

Welcome to the world of e-mail fraud and a common scheme that is perpetrated upon unsuspecting people as the result of a friend's email account being hacked into by a criminal.

Federal law requires that the government demonstrate the following elements to make out a case of mail or wire fraud: 1) a scheme to defraud, 2) which involves the use of the mails or a wire communication, 3) for the purpose of executing the scheme.

Important facts to understand about this offense:

- The mail or electronic communication is not essential to the fraud.

- Referring to the scheme once in a phone conversation may subject the person to prosecution.

- The defendant does not have to directly mail or wire something fraudulent. It is sufficient if the scheme causes an alleged victim to mail or wire something of value.

- Each electronic communication or mailing will constitute a separate wire or mail fraud count.

- If an employer is perpetrating a fraudulent scheme and an employee does something related to that scheme such as mailing envelopes, that worker can be charged with aiding and abetting even if he or she did not know what was in the envelopes and was not otherwise involved in the fraud.[32]

The Department of Justice discourages the prosecution of a scheme if it is an isolated case, in which event the parties should settle their dispute by civil or criminal litigation in state court. Serious consideration, however, will be given to the prosecution of any deception which is directed at defrauding a class of people, with a substantial pattern of conduct.[33]

**SECTION 7.6
CRIMINAL LIABILITY
FOR BUSINESS
ENTITIES**

Even though corporations are distinct entities from their stockholders, officers and employees, a general rule has emerged that corporations can be liable for the criminal acts of its employees committed within the scope of their employment and with the intent to benefit the business. Criminal liability arises under the doctrine of **respondeat superior.** This result is only logical since a corporation is not a natural person who can engage in actions independently. It can only act through the efforts of agents and employees.

The scope of a corporation's criminal responsibility can only be determined by looking at the laws in the particular jurisdiction where the offense occurred. For instance, Congress may impose criminal liability on a corporation for the mere doing of the proscribed act wholly unrelated to actual or constructive knowledge of the event. Application of this principle is found in the public welfare crimes, such as distribution of harmful drugs, or narcotics, where injury to the public comes from the act or thing without regard to the antecedent circumstances, motivation or conduct. The actions also don't have to be by a top executive. The corporation may be criminally bound by the acts of subordinates or even menial employees.[34]

A corporation can be convicted of a crime when the offense is committed by an agent acting within the scope of her employment such as a bar employee serving alcohol to a minor. An employee is acting within the scope of her authority if: (1) the employee has authority to do the particular corporate business which was conducted criminally; (2) the employee was acting, at least in part, in furtherance of the corporation's business interests; and (3) the corporate management has authorized, tolerated, or ratified the criminal acts.

Criminal liability has been found even where the corporation has published instructions and policies which are violated by the employee. Such instructions and policies when violated by its employees do not insulate the entity from criminal liability. Instead, the corporation must place the acts outside the scope of a worker's employment by adequately enforcing its rules.[35] A corporation can also be criminally responsible for the actions of its employees and agents even if it expressly instructed the person not to engage in that criminal conduct, so long as the agent acted within the scope of his or her authority.[36]

STATE V. ZETA CHI FRATERNITY
696 A.2D 530 (N.H., 1997)

The defendant, Zeta Chi Fraternity, appeals its conviction on the charges of selling alcohol to a person under the age of twenty-one.

The defendant, a corporation and fraternity at the University of New Hampshire, held a "rush" at its fraternity house to attract new members. Andrew Strachan, a 19-year-old guest at the fraternity party, testified that at some point during the evening he learned that beer was available from a soda machine. He made his way to an apartment in another part of the fraternity house where the machine was located, waited in line with three or four other people, and purchased three to five cans of beer. Strachan also testified that he noticed someone making change for the machine. The fraternity's secretary testified that the fraternity members voted not to provide alcohol at the rush and that

they moved the vending machine that contained beer to a separate apartment in another part of the fraternity house for the rush. He also testified, however, that the fraternity had control over the vending machine and its proceeds and that only fraternity members would have an interest in making change for the machine.

The defendant argues the evidence was insufficient to convict it of selling alcohol to a person under the age of twenty-one. Specifically, the defendant contends that the testimony of the State's sole witness that he bought beer from the vending machine was uncorroborated; that even if the jury could find that beer was purchased from the machine, the State failed to prove that the defendant was responsible for the sale; and that the State failed to prove that the defendant acted recklessly.

The defendant argues that the State failed to prove that the defendant caused alcohol to be sold to Strachan. The defendant asserts that because the fraternity voted not to provide beer at the rush and the soda machine was moved from the main area in the fraternity house to a separate apartment at the back of the house, the defendant did not have control over the machine, and, therefore, could not have caused the sale of alcohol from the machine. Essentially, the defendant is arguing that the individuals responsible for making the beer available for sale to Strachan were not acting on behalf of the corporation or within the scope of their authority. We begin by noting that the only defendant in this case is a corporate entity. A corporation is a jural person, but not a person in fact. It is an artificial creature, acting only through agents. A corporation may be held criminally liable for criminal acts performed on its behalf by agents or employees acting within the scope of their authority or employment. The criminal conduct need not have been performed, authorized, ratified, adopted or tolerated by the corporation's directors, officers or other high managerial agents in order to be chargeable to the corporation.

In fact, a corporation can be convicted for actions of its agents even if it expressly instructed the agents not to engage in the criminal conduct. The agents, however, must have been acting within the scope of their actual or apparent authority. Actual authority can be either express or implied. Express authority exists when the principal explicitly manifests its authorization for the agent to act. Implied authority is the "reasonable incident or construction of the terms of express authority or results from acquiescence by the principal in a course of dealing by the agent. Apparent authority, on the other hand, exists where the principal so conducts itself as to cause a third party to reasonably believe that the agent is authorized to act. It is the rare case in which the corporate leadership explicitly authorizes its agents to engage in criminal conduct.

Evidence at trial indicates that the defendant had control over the apartment in which the vending machine was located, even though it had voted to make the apartment separate from the fraternity house. More importantly, however, witnesses testified that the defendant had control over the soda machine; that only the defendant had an interest in the proceeds from the machine; that only fraternity members had keys to the apartment in which the machine was located; that someone was making change for the machine; and that no one would have an interest in making change except a member of the fraternity. We believe that from these facts the jury could reasonably have found that an agent of the defendant sold beer from the vending machine and that this agent was acting on behalf of the corporation and within the scope of his authority.

The defendant next argues that the evidence was insufficient for the jury to find that the defendant acted recklessly, the mens rea charged in the indictment. Because the defendant is a corporation, its mental state depends on the knowledge of its agents.

The corporation is considered to have acquired the collective knowledge of its employees and is held responsible for their failure to act accordingly.

In this case, the jury could reasonably have found that the defendant acted recklessly from the facts that about 150 guests, many of them under the age of twenty-one, were at the rush party that had been widely publicized on campus; that it was the defendant's vending machine; that only fraternity members had keys to the apartment in which the machine was located; that party guests gained access to the machine; that someone was making change; and that a number of people were waiting in line to use the machine.

SECTION 7.7
TYLER'S LIQUOR
PROBLEM

PARK, BROWN & SMITH, P.C.
ATTORNEYS AT LAW
MEMORANDUM

PROBLEM SEVEN—B

TO: All Law Clerks

FROM: Peter Smith, Esquire

RE: Criminal charges
for underage
drinking

Joe Roberts called about a problem at his business establishment. Criminal charges have been filed against Tyler's Sports Bar and Grill for underage drinking, and Joe is really upset because the bar does everything it can to prevent this from happening. These are the facts.

Tyler's has an aggressive policy against underage drinking and it posts signs throughout the bar warning people under 21-years of age not to order drinks. The employee's manual devotes three pages to the topic, including the rule that all young people in the bar must be carded. In fact, employees are told in no uncertain terms that if he or she serves alcohol to a person under 21, the worker will be fired. Employees are also required to attend classes on how to spot underage drinkers. These policies are then reinforced in the monthly staff meetings Mr. Roberts holds on bar issues.

Last Friday night, Tyler's was lively and filled to capacity. People were standing five deep at the bar and the tables were stuffed with extra chairs to accommodate the overflow crowd. The reason for the packed house was that Tyler's was sponsoring a mechanical bull riding contest, and people came from all over for the $5,000 cash prize that was being offered to the winner of the event. A sports talk show was also broadcasting live from the bar and several sporting events were being shown on the large screen televisions. It was sheer madness. Tyler's had never had a crowd like this before.

Tyler's was understaffed and the bar was having trouble keeping up with the food and beverage orders. Joe's wife had volunteered to help in the kitchen and Tony Roberts, Joe's oldest son, happened to be in town so Tony was asked to help out. Tony had been trained as a bartender a few years earlier and had helped his dad once or twice before.

During the evening, Tony waited on a table which ended up containing some acquaintances from college. Tony had not seen them for years so he spent a few minutes talking about mutual friends and classes they had taken together. Tony didn't bother to card his former classmates because he knew they were of proper age. After all, they had all graduated from college together two years earlier and Tony had gone to a few bars with some of them while in school. These individuals turned out to be great customers. They ordered food and drinks continually and several participated in the bull riding contest. Tony even introduced Mr. Roberts to his former college friends and told his father about some of their college pranks. Mr. Roberts wished the guests well and thanked them for patronizing Tyler's. However, he excused himself because Joe wanted to keep an eye on the customers to make sure no one was intoxicated and to insure that the younger customers were being carded.

About one o'clock in the morning, investigators from the state's liquor control board paid a surprise visit and carded everyone. Much to the horror of Mr. Roberts, two of the people at the table containing his son's friends were underage. It turns out that one of Tony's former classmates was brilliant and had started college at age 14. The state investigators discovered that this individual and his girlfriend were only 20-years old. The police immediately arrested the two patrons and Tyler's received a criminal citation for serving liquor to minors. Mr. Roberts told me that he assumed his son had carded the people at the table so he did not personally inquire about their ages.

Our client is devastated by the bad press the arrests have generated. Tony has even told the state investigators that he would accept full responsibility for what happened that night, stating that the bar and his father were faultless. Nevertheless, the corporation has been criminally charged for the violations.

North Dakota v. Smokey's Steakhouse, Inc. is the only case I could find even remotely on point. I know it is from a different state but the law is very similar to the one in this jurisdiction. Please let me know if Tyler's Sports Bar and Grill is criminally liable for the innocent mistake.

North Dakota v. Smokey's Steakhouse, Inc.
478 N. W. 2d 361 (N.D., 1991)

Smokey's Steakhouse, Inc., appealed from a judgment of conviction for allowing a person under the age of twenty-one to remain on the premises where alcoholic beverages were being sold. We affirm.

Smokey's is a restaurant and bar located in West Fargo. During an inspection of the premises, members of the West Fargo Police Department found Patricia Ingberg and Nicole Huether, both age twenty, in separate parts of the bar portion of the business. The women were arrested for being in a bar while underage.

Smokey's was cited and a trial was held at which the arresting officers and the two women testified. Both women stated that they were in the bar portion of Smokey's premises, that no Smokey's employee asked them for proof that they were of legal age, and that they were served an alcoholic beverage purchased by another patron. Accordingly, the court found Smokey's guilty of a single count of violating section 5-02-06, NDCC.

Smokey's contends that the State offered insufficient proof of the offense because a corporate defendant cannot be convicted for the willful criminal act of an employee acting outside the scope of her employment. Specifically, Smokey's argues that Loretta Frison intentionally served her underage sister, Patricia Ingberg. There is no culpability requirement in the statute under which Smokey's was convicted. A corporation can be convicted of a strict liability crime when the offense is committed by an agent acting within the scope of her employment. An employee is acting within the scope of her authority, for criminal law purposes, if: (1) the employee has authority to do the particular corporate business

which was conducted criminally; (2) the employee was acting, at least in part, in furtherance of the corporation's business interests; and (3) the corporate management has authorized, tolerated, or ratified the criminal acts. A corporation is not insulated from criminal liability merely because it published instructions and policies which are violated by its employee; the corporation must place the acts outside the scope of an employee's employment by adequately enforcing its rules. Whether the corporation's enforcement measures are adequate is a question of fact.

Here, one of the employees working at the time of the police inspection, Loretta Frison, was the sister of Patricia Ingberg, one of the two minors the police found in the bar portion of Smokey's. Frison said she was not aware that her sister was underage. As a bartender, Frison was employed to serve alcoholic beverages and to determine the ages of patrons of the bar. While a supervisor testified that all Smokey's employees are instructed not to serve minors or to allow them to remain on the premises, no evidence of measures taken to enforce those instructions was offered. No employee checked the age of either Ingberg or Huether. The women arrived separately and were not together in the bar. Both women admitted being in the bar in excess of five minutes and receiving alcoholic beverages purchased by another patron. The trial court could infer from this, and other, evidence that Frison was not acting willfully when her underage sister and another minor were allowed to remain in the bar. The court could also infer that Smokey's had inadequately enforced its policy against serving minors so that the act of any employee who allowed Ingberg and Huether to remain on the premises without proving that they were of legal age was an act done within the scope of employment. The evidence is sufficient to sustain the conviction.

Smokey's also contends that it was entitled to the statutory defense under section 5-01-08.2, NDCC, which provides:

> The establishment of the following facts by a person making a sale of alcoholic beverages to a person not of legal age constitutes prima facie evidence of innocence and a defense to any prosecution therefore:
>
> 1. That the purchaser falsely represented and supported with other documentary proof that he was of legal age to purchase alcoholic beverages.
>
> 2. That the appearance of the purchaser was such that an ordinary and prudent person would believe the purchaser to be of legal age to purchase alcoholic beverages.
>
> 3. That the sale was made in good faith and in reliance upon the representation and appearance of the purchaser in the belief that the purchaser was of legal age to purchase alcoholic beverages.

Smokey's argues that the fact that Nicole Huether appeared to be of legal age entitles it to this statutory defense. Smokey's misreads the statute. Reading the statute as a whole, it is clear that the three subsections do not present separate defenses. The false representation described in subsection (1) and the appearance of the purchaser described in subsection (2) are necessary elements of the good-faith sale described in subsection (3). All three subsections must be satisfied in order to qualify for the single statutory defense established in section 5-01-08.2, NDCC. Neither Ingberg nor Huether made a false representation to an employee of Smokey's; neither woman was asked for proof that she was of legal age to be in a liquor establishment. The trial court properly concluded that Smokey's was not entitled to use the "good faith" statutory defense.

The judgment of the county court is affirmed.

PROBLEM SEVEN—B
ANSWER SHEET

Name _____   **Please Print Clearly**

1. Can Tyler's beat the charges by showing the many steps that the bar uses to prevent underage drinking?

_____

_____

_____

_____

_____

_____

_____

_____

_____

_____

_____

_____

_____

_____

_____

_____

_____

2. Will we be successful in asserting that we have a defense under Section 5-01-08.2? Afterall, Tony honestly believed that the patrons were of proper age.

_____

_____

_____

_____

_____

_____

_____

_____

_____

3. Please explain what you think will be the outcome of the case against Tyler's Sports Bar and Grill.

_____

_____

_____

_____

_____

_____

_____

_____

_____

**SECTION 7.8
POLICE
INVESTIGATION**

Following the reporting of a crime, the police must ascertain the identity of the perpetrator, in order to prosecute the criminal and to bring that person to justice. How the police conduct their investigation, however, will depend upon the offense and its surrounding facts.

Generally, when a crime is reported, the police are dispatched to the scene. After all, there is a possibility that the police can immediately apprehend the suspect, or the victim may need immediate medical assistance. A crime scene unit is often dispatched to secure the scene and to locate the evidence. This will include assessing the crime scene, taking pictures, and preserving the evidence.[37]

If no one saw the crime being committed, a detective may be assigned to conduct the investigation, especially if the offense was serious or complicated. This person will be in charge of a team of investigators whose goal is to develop a list of suspects and to find the culprit. While the list of witnesses is being developed, the crime scene unit will be collecting the forensic evidence such as fingerprints, bullet casings and bodily fluids in order to send them to the lab for analysis.[38] At some point, the investigation may require the police to question suspects and to conduct searches of a home, car or person. While justice demands that the culprit be apprehended, the government must not violate the constitutional rights of a suspect or business entity. In this regard, two provisions of the Constitution come into play, the Fourth and Fifth Amendments.

**SECTION 7.9
QUESTIONING OF A
SUSPECT**

Part of the **Fifth Amendment** provides that "no person…shall be compelled in any criminal case to be a witness against himself." This provision is part of the **Bill of Rights** and protects an individual from being forced to give a testimony that could inculpate the person in a crime or subject someone to a fine, penalty or forfeiture. This guarantee has application to both when the police want to question a suspect or when a person is questioned at trial.

A sole proprietor is the owner of the business, so that person would enjoy the full benefits of the Constitution in the event that the police investigate the business. Likewise, an employee or officer of a corporation enjoys the protections of the **Fifth Amendment** against self-incrimination that applies to custodial interrogation.[39] Can the business, however, invoke the Fifth Amendment when asked to produce the corporation's books?

Custodial interrogation by the police is considered inherently coercive so the Supreme Court has mandated specific procedures to be followed in obtaining statements. More specifically, the Fifth Amendment provides the basis for the **Miranda Warnings**. Basically, the police have to remind a suspect that under the Fifth Amendment, he or she has no obligation to talk to the law enforcement official and that the individual has the right to have an attorney present before the questioning can commence. The warnings, however, only apply when the person is in custodial interrogation. In that event, the police must inform the suspect that he or she has the right to remain silent, that anything he or she says can and will be used against the individual in court, and the accused has the right to have a lawyer present during the questioning. If the accused cannot afford counsel, the government will supply an attorney for free.

Custodial interrogation has been defined as "questioning initiated by law enforcement officers after a person has been taken into custody or otherwise deprived of his or her freedom of action in any significant way." Custody is much broader than being incarcerated for purposes of the Miranda Warnings. A suspect must be told of his right to remain silent if his freedom of movement or liberty is significantly restricted. In practical terms, the issue is whether the suspect is free to walk away from the interrogation. If not, the suspect must be read his rights. For example, the president of a firm who is questioned in his office by several police officers is in custody for purpose of the Miranda Warnings. Interrogation, on the other hand, involves more than merely asking the suspect questions about routine information such as the person's name and address. The questions must focus on the crime to trigger the reading of the warnings.

Generally, corporate records are not protected by the Fifth Amendment even if they will incriminate the owner of the business.[40]

Would an independent accountant who has prepared the tax returns of a business be allowed to assert the Fifth Amendment in refusing to produce the requested business records? That is the issue in the following case.

U.S. v. MARRA
2005 WL 2474873 (N.J. 2005)

On September 12, 2005, Marra appeared before this Court to Show Cause why [this accountant] should not be compelled to obey an IRS summons served on him in the investigation of Kenneth Reiher. Reiher is being investigated to determine whether he "committed any offense under the Internal Revenue laws by filing false returns to evade Federal income taxes. Specifically, the summons calls for the production of:

All books, records, bank statements, cancelled checks, deposit tickets, work-papers,

financial statements, correspondence and other pertinent documents furnished by or on behalf of the above named client(s) for the preparation of state and federal income tax returns and for any other entity in which either or both of them have a financial interest.

The Government contends that Marra is "the accountant, tax preparer and record-keeper" for Reiher. As such, he is the custodian of corporate records. Thus, the Government argues that Marra has no privilege to withhold the documents it seeks. Marra has declined to produce the records, arguing that any such production or attendant testimony could incriminate him, and asserting his Fifth Amendment privilege against self-incrimination.

The issue is whether Marra is a custodian of corporate records, to whom a Fifth Amendment privilege is unavailable, or whether he can personally assert a Fifth Amendment privilege in refusing to turn over the books and records of a taxpayer and several corporate entities under investigation by the IRS.

A corporation has no Fifth Amendment privilege to refuse to produce its records. Accordingly, this Court finds that Marra is a custodian of corporate records because he is a "person having possession, custody, or care" of the books and records pertaining to Reiher and the corporations at issue.

Marra argues the act of producing documents responsive to the IRS summons could incriminate him based on the thought-processes necessary for selecting documents responsive to the subpoena as compelled testimony. Here, Marra is not under investigation; he is not being asked to produce personal documents; and the Government presumably knows that Reiher and the corporations filed the tax returns.

It is clear that the IRS summons seeks whatever documents Marra has that were used in the preparation of the tax returns. The IRS has authority to audit taxpayers by comparing returns with supporting documentation. The IRS's requests for production here are tailored to accomplish its investigation of Reiher's potential tax liability. Marra is not under investigation.

However, assume *arguendo,* that in preparing Reiher's tax returns, Marra engaged in some alleged wrongdoing, where the Fifth Amendment might attach. Indeed, Marra's argument has seemingly evolved in this direction. The privilege against self-incrimination extends to protect the private papers and personal effects of the person asserting it. This statement obviously applies to the taxpayer. A custodian of corporate records cannot assert the privilege against self-incrimination with regard to the production of corporate records, but may assert the Fifth Amendment on a question-by-question basis with regard to any attendant testimony.

A blanket or general assertion of a Fifth Amendment privilege is improper. Instead, an individual claiming the privilege must raise the privilege with respect to each question posed and each document sought. Marra's Motion to Stay enforcement of the IRS summons must be denied.

**SECTION 7.10
COMMONWEALTH V. CHRISTOPHER**

PROBLEM SEVEN—C

**PARK, BROWN & SMITH, P.C.
ATTORNEYS AT LAW
MEMORNDUM**

TO: All Law Clerks

FROM: Peter Smith, Esquire

RE: Commonwealth v. Peter Christopher In Court Identification

Kathy Roberts often stays after school to work out in the gym. The wrestling team is usually there practicing but they were away at a match on the evening in question.

Kathy was so busy exercising that she didn't notice the presence of a stranger—at least not until it was too late. Kathy first realized that she wasn't alone when she looked up and saw what appeared to be a shark staring back at her. When she looked again, she realized it was a man with a tattoo of a shark on his left shoulder. The strange thing was that he was wearing a ski mask. Before she had time to realize what was happening, she was assaulted and her pocketbook was stolen.

Kathy was extremely troubled by the incident. She could not stop thinking about the tattoo, since she knew she had seen the image before. To her shock and amazement, Kathy realized that she knew her assailant. It was her next door neighbor, Peter Christopher. He had a tattoo of a shark on his shoulder, and he intensely disliked her family.

Ms. Roberts reported her suspicions to the police and their investigation led to the arrest of Peter Christopher on a variety of criminal charges. During the second day of trial, the District Attorney requested Peter Christopher to stand before the jury and remove his shirt so the panel could ascertain whether the defendant had a tattoo of a shark on his shoulder. The defense vigorously objected to this in-court identification, claiming that it would violate Christopher's Fifth Amendment rights against self-incrimination. The issue before the court concerns these identifying marks on the defendant's shoulder. The Fifth Amendment guarantees that no person shall be compelled to testify against himself. According to **Morgan v. State,** can the District Attorney compel Christopher to remove his shirt to show the jury his shoulder? Why would this type of incourt identification violate (or not violate) the Constitution?

GLENMORE MORGAN V. STATE OF MARYLAND
558 A.2D 1226 (MD. APP., 1989)

We are called upon to decide whether requiring a defendant to don an article of clothing in the courtroom in front of the jury so that the jury may see if the article of clothing fits violates his privilege against self-incrimination under the 5th Amendment.

In the case before us, Glenmore Morgan, defendant, was charged with possession of cocaine with intent to distribute, possession of cocaine and possession of controlled paraphernalia. During a jury trial, the court required the defendant to put on a jacket seized by officers of the Montgomery County Police Department pursuant to a search warrant.

At the time the search warrant was executed, defendant and two other men were present in the living room of the residence. After the two other men retrieved their coats, Morgan queried, "What about my jacket?" When asked by the police if a jacket located on the loveseat in the living room was his, Morgan hesitated before responding, "No." Police search of the jacket revealed a small quantity of cocaine, a beeper, keys to the residence and a key to a safe in the kitchen. During a search of the safe, the police discovered bottles of inositol powder, several baggies, razor blades, measuring spoons, a box containing a grinder, and twenty-three grams of cocaine. Morgan was convicted on all charges.

The Fifth Amendment of the United States Constitution provides: "No person . . . shall be compelled in any criminal case to be a witness against himself." Defendant contends that the court's order requiring him to put on the jacket in front of the jury violated his constitutional right against compelled self-incrimination.

The Court of Appeals in **Andrews v. State** upheld a trial court order restraining Andrews from shaving his head or facial hair until the conclusion of this trial. Purportedly, he had changed his appearance immediately after the crime in question by shaving his head and beard. The trial court order was designed to prevent the defendant from defeating "legitimate avenues of identification" by disguising his appearance.

In **Schmerber v. California, 384 U.S. 757 (1966),** the Supreme Court stated that the privilege against compelled self-incrimination "protects an accused only from being compelled to testify against himself or otherwise provide the State with evidence of a testimonial or communicative nature . . ." Requiring a defendant to put on an article of clothing, simply does not constitute an act compelling a testimonial or communicative response. The fact that an article of clothing fits may give rise to a inference of ownership, which under the facts of any given case could be incrimination, is not a communicative response from the defendant.

By granting the prosecutor's request to order the defendant to don the coat in the presence of the jury, the trial court compelled the defendant to disclose nothing of his personal knowledge. This is not communication within the meaning of the Fifth Amendment. Moreover, it is of no consequence that the defendant declined to take the stand to testify on his own behalf; his physical display simply does not constitute "testimony."

In this case, the trial court order requiring defendant to don a coat, which admittedly contained incriminatory evidence, to determine whether it fit him did not constitute a compulsion to elicit communicative or testimonial evidence from the defendant.

Judgment affirmed.

PROBLEM SEVEN—C
ANSWER SHEET

Name   **Please Print Clearly**

1. According to **Morgan v. State,** can the District Attorney compel Christopher to remove his shirt to show the jury his tattoo? Explain your answer.

2. Why would this type of in court identification violate or not violate Christopher's constitutional rights? Explain your answer.

_____

_____

_____

_____

_____

_____

_____

_____

_____

_____

_____

_____

_____

_____

_____

_____

_____

_____

_____

SECTION 7.11
SEARCH AND SEIZURE

A truck driver delivering cargo was stopped by the police for a traffic violation. A drug-detecting dog was walked around the commercial vehicle while another officer wrote the traffic ticket. The canine soon became agitated alerting the police to the presence of drugs. A search of the trailer yielded several hundred pounds of marijuana. Is there anything unconstitutional with allowing a police dog to randomly walk around a commercial vehicle. This example raises the issue as to what constitutes a police search.

The **Fourth Amendment** prohibits unlawful **search and seizure** and requires that all warrants be issued upon probable cause. This protection against over-zealous police conduct usually requires a police officer to appear before a judge to establish **probable cause** for the issuance of a **search warrant.** Probable cause, however, is not defined in the Constitution. Over the years, the courts have determined probable cause to exist when the information on which the warrant is based is such that a reasonable person would believe that what is being sought will be found in the location to be examined. The judge, however, may consider the opinion of an experienced law enforcement officer in making the probable cause determination for a search warrant. An affidavit based on mere suspicion, or stating a conclusion with no supporting facts, however, is insufficient. If the court is satisfied that sufficient evidence exists to issue a warrant, that document must be specific as to the location and evidence that is the subject of the search warrant.

The general test to determine whether a warrant is needed by the police to conduct a lawful search and seizure is to ascertain whether the person had a **reasonable expectation of privacy.** If the entity enjoyed a reasonable expectation of privacy, a warrant must be obtained before the search can be undertaken. For example, a person has an expectation of privacy that the police will not search his private locker at work, but the police would not need a warrant to seize a gun that a person is brandishing while walking down the street.

Businesses do not enjoy the same protections against unlawful search and seizure as do individuals. For instance, the police have the right to inspect the premises of "closely regulated" industries without a warrant in certain situations. The justification is that a business enterprise has a reduced expectation of privacy that is outweighed by the government's need to conduct warrantless inspections in particular situations.[41] For instance, the courts have allowed warrantless searches for purposes of a fire inspection of warehouse, a liquor store, a gun dealer's storeroom, and an OSHA safety inspection. However, an investigative search may not be employed as a subterfuge to avoid the burden of establishing probable cause to support a criminal investigative search required by the Fourth Amendment.

AMVETS POST NO. 711 V. RUTTER
863 F. SUPP.2D 670 (N.D. OHIO, 2012)

The Smoke Free Act requires all public places and places of employment in Ohio to prohibit smoking. The law's purpose is to "protect all workers and the public from exposure to secondhand smoke in workplaces and public places." The Act provides that upon receipt of a report of violation, the Department of Health may investigate the violation.

On April 7, 2011, after notifying plaintiff of a complaint of an alleged violation of the Smoke Free Workplace Act, [the Department of Health] conducted an on-site investigation. Plaintiff twice attempted to refuse defendant's entry onto the premises: first, at the door, and, second, just inside the door. Defendants then proceeded to search behind the bar and in places not normally accessible to non-members.

The Fourth Amendment protects [t]he right of the people to be secure in their persons, houses, papers, and effects, against unreasonable searches and seizures, and no warrants shall issue, but upon probable cause. While the bulk of Fourth Amendment law is in the criminal context—when police are searching for contraband or other evidence of criminal activity—the Amendment also protects against unwarranted searches in the context of non-criminal investigations.

The Supreme Court has held, however, that when the business at issue is closely regulated, legislative schemes that provide for warrantless administrative inspections can be permissible. The Court has reasoned that an "owner or operator of commercial premises in a 'closely regulated' industry has a reduced expectation of privacy." Thus, where the privacy interests of the owner are weakened and the government interests in regulating particular businesses are heightened, a warrantless inspection of commercial premises

may well be reasonable within the meaning of the Fourth Amendment.

The so-called administrative exception to the warrant requirement requires that the business at issue be "closely regulated." It is well-established that liquor permit holders have a reduced expectation of privacy, as the liquor industry is highly regulated.

The Court laid down a three-factor test for warrantless inspections of heavily regulated business: First, there must be a "substantial" government interest that informs the regulatory scheme pursuant to which the inspection is made. Second, the warrantless inspections must be "necessary to further [the] regulatory scheme." Finally, "the statute's inspection program, must provide a constitutionally adequate substitute for a warrant."

Because medical studies have conclusively shown that exposure to secondhand smoke from tobacco causes illness and disease, smoking in the workplace is a statewide concern and, it is in the best interests of public health that smoking of tobacco products be prohibited in public places and places of employment.

The second factor looks to whether warrantless inspections are necessary. The court recognizes the necessity for warrantless inspections because advance knowledge of an impending health inspection would provide restaurant owners with the opportunity to take temporary remedial measures designed to mask or conceal violations.

The third factor measures whether the regulatory scheme provides a constitutionally adequate substitute for the warrant procedure. The Supreme Court determined that the regulations at issue complied with this third requirement because the statute stated that inspections would be made on a regular basis, set forth clear standards for compliance, and stated who was authorized to conduct an inspection.

Ohio's Smoke Free Act authorizes warrantless administrative searches to protect its citizens against the well-documented dangers from secondhand smoke. The Act, therefore, does not violate plaintiff's Fourth Amendment rights. Because defendants have not violated plaintiff's constitutional rights, they are entitled to dismissal of plaintiff's complaint.

Section 7.12
The Raid of Tyler's Sports Bar and Grill

Problem Seven—D

Park, Brown & Smith, P.C.
Attorneys at Law
Memorndum

To: All Law Clerks

From: Peter Smith, Esquire

Re: The Raid of Tyler's Sports Bar and Grill

I received a frantic call from Joe Roberts about a surprise raid of Tyler's Sports Bar and Grill by the Liquor Control Board. The bar has been open for about three months and is doing quite well. Joe has been fanatical about making sure the bar is run properly. He meets with his staff regularly about following proper procedures and in making sure than no one under 21 is served liquor.

Nevertheless, agents from the Liquor Control Board entered his premises unannounced and seized all of his video surveillance tapes without a warrant. They also took Tyler's books and records in order to audit them. Apparently, this surprise visit was the result of a car accident that occurred about two miles from the bar when an 18-year old man's car struck a tree, killing him instantly. A toxicology screening revealed that his blood/alcohol level was .25 so the agents think that the decedent may have been drinking at Tyler's right before the fatal collision.

Roberts thinks it is absurd for the agents to presume that Tyler's Sports Bar and Grill had anything to do with the accident. He claims that they had no probable cause for the search and should have gotten a search warrant. Joe is also upset because the raid was carried out on a very busy Saturday night and the bar was filled with patrons who witnessed the raid. Not only is our client humiliated, but he has no idea what the tapes with show and he does not want the books and records audited. At the end of our conversion, Joe said, "I have to tell you something." He then proceeded to explain that Kathy and her friends were in the bar on the night of the accident. It was

Kathy's 17th birthday and he wanted to keep an eye on her and her friends. Therefore, he threw a party for Kathy at Tyler's Sports Bar and Grill. He made sure than none of them had anything improper to drink because of their age. However, he gave them pitchers of Shirley Temples, and on the video, he is concerned that it will look like he was serving them alcohol.

I am troubled that the Liquor Control Board would carry out such a search without a warrant. After all, the Fourth Amendment does apply to commercial establishments. However, I did find **Pinney v. Phillips** and it gives me some concern. Please read the case and let me know your thoughts on whether the actions of the Liquor Control Board were proper. I need to file a motion seeking the return of the evidence, so I am going to need an analysis of our client's problem in view of the case.

PINNEY V. PHILLIPS
230 CAL. APP.3D 1570 (1991)

Pinney, a licensed electrical contractor, is the owner of an electrical contracting business named Telco, Inc. (Telco). Investigators for the Registrar received information that Pinney's father-in-law, Donald Virgil Tonelli, was being prosecuted for receiving stolen property and that stolen construction equipment had been used on one of Pinney's construction sites. Tonelli and Pinney were owners, partners, or license qualifiers in a number of companies licensed by the Registrar. Pinney was given a letter by the Registrar requesting that Pinney produce the business records for the company.

[In response], the Registrar received a letter from an attorney retained by Pinney advising that Pinney would not be appearing at the scheduled time [with the records]. The Registrar then sought the revocation of the license issued to Telco.

The Registrar contends Pinney's Fourth Amendment right to be free of unreasonable searches was not violated by the demand for the records. It is contended that no warrant was required to inspect the records because the electrical

contracting industry falls within the "closely regulated" business exception to the Fourth Amendment's warrant requirement. By accepting a license in a closely regulated industry such as contracting, there is an implied consent that a contractor will comply with the requirements of the Contractor's License Law. Consequently, the failure to produce them constitutes grounds for discipline.

Pinney counters that the electrical contracting business does not fall within the pervasively regulated industry exception. The inspection of his business records is therefore subject to the requirements of the Fourth Amendment.

The inspection of business premises is commonplace in our society. Virtually all businesses, without regard to their character, are subject to inspection of their premises to ensure compliance with fire, health and safety regulations. In addition, businesses of particular types are subject to inspection of business records required by law to be kept and of the materials used or produced in their operation. The concern is with the extent to which the Fourth Amendment limits the manner in which such inspection programs may be conducted.

The Supreme Court of the United States long has recognized that the Fourth Amendment's prohibition on unreasonable searches and seizures is applicable to commercial premises, as well as private homes. An owner or operator of a business thus has an expectation of privacy in commercial property, which society is prepared to consider to be reasonable. This expectation exists not only with respect to traditional police searches conducted for the gathering of criminal evidence but also with respect to administrative inspections designed to enforce regulatory statutes. An expectation of privacy in commercial premises, however, is different from, and indeed less than, a similar expectation in an individual's home. Thus, unlike searches of private homes, which generally must be conducted pursuant to a warrant in order to be reasonable under the Fourth Amendment, legislative schemes authorizing warrantless administrative searches of commercial property do not necessarily violate the Fourth Amendment.

Nevertheless, administrative searches generally require warrants....except in certain carefully defined classes of cases, the nonconsensual entry and search of property are governed by the warrant requirement of the Fourth Amendment. One of those carefully defined classes of cases is comprised of what has become known as the "closely regulated" business exception. Certain industries have such a history of government oversight that no reasonable expectation of privacy could exist for a proprietor over such an enterprise. When this exception applies, the warrantless inspection of commercial premises may pass constitutional muster. Because the owner or operator of commercial premises in a closely regulated industry has a reduced expectation of privacy, the warrant and probable-cause requirements, which fulfill the traditional Fourth Amendment standard of reasonableness

for a government search, have lessened application in this context. Rather, we conclude that, as in other situations of special need, where the privacy interests of the owner are weakened and the government interests in regulating particular businesses are concomitantly heightened, a warrantless inspection of commercial premises may well be reasonable within the meaning of the Fourth Amendment.

A closely regulated business is one where the pervasiveness and regularity of the government's regulation reduces the owner's expectation of privacy in his business records. The duration of a particular regulatory scheme is an important factor, but it is not always essential that there be a long-standing history of regulation.

Although statutes governing contractors were first enacted over 60 years ago, we do not find the contracting industry to be a closely regulated one. Our review of cases holding various industries to be pervasively regulated discloses that all of them concern licensed businesses engaged in activities which have a high risk of illegal conduct or of serious danger to the public such that frequent, unannounced inspections are essential for the protection of the public or for the enforcement of the statutory purpose. These exceptions for heavily regulated businesses are just that: exceptions. They involve licensed businesses engaged in activities which have a high risk of illegal conduct or of serious danger to the public. A warrantless search is permitted in those instances where it is necessary to regulate businesses that are likely to give rise to public danger or well-known evils. But contractors in general and electrical contractors in particular are not engaged in any such activities.

The theory of the closely regulated business exception is that inspection and visitation by agents of the government are so regular and frequent that the licensee has no reasonable expectation of privacy. In the words, some industries are so heavily regulated that government inspections are held constitutionally permissible, without notice, warrant, or individualized suspicion of wrongdoing. Business owners in the heavily regulated industries are presumed to know that they are subject to the periodic inspections which are specified by and regularly carried out pursuant to enabling legislation. But that theory has no application to ordinary contractors. Indeed, if electrical contracting is a closely regulated industry, then all licensed businesses would fall within the exception and the exception would swallow the rule.

The Registrar has failed to demonstrate that the requisite pervasiveness and regularity of the regulations are associated with the contracting industry. Therefore, it is not a closely regulated one for purposes of the Fourth Amendment. That exception, therefore, does not justify the compulsory production of contractors' records without legal process.

PROBLEM SEVEN—D
ANSWER SHEET

Name _____   **Please Print Clearly**

1. Were the actions of the Liquor Control Board in conducting the raid of Tyler's Sports Bar and Grill without a search warrant proper? Please explain your answer.

_____

_____

_____

_____

_____

_____

_____

_____

_____

_____

_____

_____

_____

_____

_____

_____

_____

_____

2. Do you think that the Liquor Control Board had probable cause to search the bar?

_____

_____

_____

_____

_____

_____

_____

_____

_____

_____

_____

_____

_____

_____

_____

_____

_____

_____

_____

SECTION 7.13
PROBLEM CASES

1. Three packages containing more than $500,000 fell out of the back of an armored truck. Morant, an individual walking down the street, retrieved and carried away the bags. The money was not returned immediately nor were the police notified that the money had been located. A couple of days later, the armored truck company posted a $75,000 reward, and Morant came forward with the money in order to claim the reward. Has this individual committed the crime of theft by retaining the money until a reward was posted?

2. The police suspected that Gindlesperger was growing marijuana in his basement. An officer aimed a thermal detection device at the home from the street in order to measure the heat emissions coming from the defendant's house. The temperature of the home was felt to be consistent with marijuana production activities. Did the warrantless search of the house, with a thermal detection device, constitute an unlawful search and seizure? **Commonwealth of Pennsylvania v. Gregory Gindlesperger, 706 A.2d 1316 (Pa. Super., 1997).**

3. The police set up a road block as part of a program to interdict drunk drivers. Schavello, who was driving towards the road block, made a U-turn in order to avoid police contact. He was then stopped by the police a short distance away, and alcohol was detected on his breath. Schavello failed a field sobriety test and was arrested for driving under the influence of alcohol. Is avoiding a road block sufficient probable cause to stop a motor vehicle when it makes a U-turn without any further suspicion by the police of illegal activity? **Commonwealth of Pennsylvania v. Schavello, 734 A.2d 386 (Pa., 1999).**

4. The manager of an apartment building was making yearly repairs and maintenance inspections. The date of these inspections were posted throughout the building. During his examination of one of the units, the manager observed drugs on the kitchen table and immediately contacted the police. The manager then led the officers into the apartment with a pass key. The police observed five plastic bags containing crack cocaine on the kitchen table. Based upon their observations, one officer left the apartment in order to obtain a search warrant. The other officer remained behind and arrested Davis when he entered the apartment. The lease agreement provided: "Landlords and anyone allowed by the landlord may enter the leased unit after first notifying tenant." Was the entry by the police into the apartment without a search warrant legal? **Commonwealth of Pennsylvania v. Curtis Davis, 743 A.2d 946 (Pa. Super., 1999).**

SECTION 7.14
INTERNET REFERENCES

To learn more information about the topics in this chapter, see the following internet references:

A. Criminal Law

- **www.talkjustice.com**
  A person is able to post messages at this location about the criminal justice system and can access Cybrary, an online library which provides 12,000 links to different websites relating to criminal justice.

- **www.law.indiana.edu/law/crimlaw.html**
  This site by Indiana University School of Law in Bloomington allows a user to download short speeches about different aspects of criminal law, such as double jeopardy and being called as a witness.

- **www.thebestdefense.com**
  Information about specific crimes and the process of a criminal case is offered at this criminal law firm's website.

- **www.usdoj.gov**
  The United States Department of Justice provides information on criminal justice programs and initiatives, as well as other information on the United States criminal justice system.

- **www.fbi.gov**
  The Federal Bureau of Investigation's site provides information and statistics on crime, including FBI investigations, international crime, wiretapping, electronic surveillance, and economic espionage.

B. Miranda Warnings

- **www.courttv.com/legalhelp/lawguide/criminal/91.html**
  This site provides general information about Miranda Warnings and its history.

C. Search and Seizure

- **www.supreme.findlaw.com/constitution/amendment04/**
  The Constitutional Law Center provides a variety of information relating to the law of Search and Seizure at this site, including the history, cases, and statutes concerning this Amendment.

Footnotes:

1. White Collar Crime, FBI, http://www.fbi.gov/about-us/investigate/white_collar

2. Dave Hendrickson, List of Three Crimes That Affect Businesses, Chron, http://smallbusiness.chron.com/list-three-crimes-affect-businesses-64360.html (last visited September 28, 2013).

3. Julian Hermida, Corporate Crime, http://www.julianhermida.com/contcorporate.htm (last visited September 28, 2013).

4. Russell Mokhiber, Twenty Things You Should Know About Corporate Crime, http://www.alternet.org/story/54093/twenty_things_you_should_know_about_corporate_crime (last visited September 28, 2013).

5. What is Corporate Crime, wiseGEEK, http://www.wisegeek.com/what-is-corporate-crime.htm (last visited September 28, 2013).

6. *Categories and Examples of Business Crime*, Lumen, https://courses.lumenlearning.com/workwithinthelaw/chapter/categories-and-examples-of-business-crime/ (last visited January 23, 2018.)

7. 10 Biggest White-Collar Crimes In History (and How They Were Unravelled), Business Pundit, December 14, 2009, http://www.businesspundit.com/white-collar-crimes-history-and-how-they-were-unravelled/ (last visited September 28, 2013).

8. Business Crime Prevention Report, The Sonoma County Economic Development Board, http://www.sonoma-county.org/edb/pdf/2002/bcp_report.pdf.

9. Martin Bressler, *The Impact of Crime on Business: A Model for Prevention, Detection and Remedy*, Journal of Management and Marketing Research, http://www.aabri.com/manuscripts/09202.pdf (last visited January 23, 2018.)

10. Workplace Safety-Small Business Crime Prevention, Philadelphia Police Department, http://www.ppdonline.org/prev/prev_work_smallbiz.php.

11. Small Business Security Tips: Internal Employee Theft Prevention, ADT Security Services, Inc.

12. Embezzlement, Investopedia, http://www.investopedia.com/terms/e/embezzlement.asp.

13. Barnett v. State, 834 N.E. 2d 169, (Ind. App., 2005).

14. Shoplifting Statistics & Tactics: 75% of Adults Are Guilty of the Five Finger Discount, The People's Media Company, http://www.associatedcontent.com/article/183545/shoplifting_statistics_tactics_75_of.html.

15. Identify Theft and Identify Fraud, www.usdoj/gov/criminal/fraud/idtheft.html.

16. *Sulaiman Abu Ghaith*, Wikipedia, https://en.wikipedia.org/wiki/Sulaiman_Abu_Ghaith (last visited January 23, 2018.)

17. Former Enron Chairman and Chief Executive Kenneth L. Lay Charged with Conspiracy, Fraud, and False Statements, Department of Justice, July 8, 2004.

18. Billy Steel, Money Laundering—A Brief History, http://www.laundryman.u-net.com/page 1_hist.html.

19. Insider Trading, Securities and Exchange Commission, http://www.scc.gov/answers/insider.htm.

20. *Id.*

21. **S.E.C. v. Yun, 327 F.3d 1263 (C.A. 11th Fla., 2003).**

22. **U.S. v. Greene, 670 F. Supp. 337 (M.D. Fla., 1987).**

23. See: http://www.uscourts.gov/bankruptcycourts/bankruptcybasics/process.html.

24. White-Collar Crime, Operation Targets Bankruptcy Fraud, http://www.fbi.gov/page2/oct2006/bankruptcy 101806.htm.

25. Jeffrey E. Grell, Greel on RICO, http://ricoact.com/ crime (last visited September 28, 2013).

26. Organized Crime and Racketeering, Department of Justice, http://www.justice.gov/usao/eousa/foia_reading_room/usam/title9/110mcrm.htm (last visited September 28, 2013).

27. Gregory M. Wasson, Pattern of Racketeering Activity" Under the Racketeer Influenced and Corrupt Organizations Act (RICO), American Jurisprudence Proof of Facts 3d Database updated September 2013.

28. Wesley Kobylak, Civil action for damages under 18 U.S.C.A. § 1964(c) of the Racketeer Influenced and Corrupt Organizations Act (RICO, 18 U.S.C.A. §§ 1961 et seq.) for injuries sustained by reason of racketeering activity, 70 A.L.R. Fed. 538.

29. Jim Schaefer, The RICO Act: What does it mean?, Detroit Free Press, December 16, 2010, http://www.freep.com/article/20101216/NEWS05/12160551/The-RICO-Act-What-does-mean? (last visited September 28, 2013).

30. Racketeer Influenced and Corrupt Organizations Act (RICO), Nolo.com, http://www.nolo.com/legal-encyclopedia/content/rico-act.html (last visited September 28, 2013).

31. Ronald A. Goodbread, RICO Convictions of Major Tobacco Companies Affirmed, The Daily Washington Law Reporter, May 12, 2011, http://www.dwlr.com/blog/2011-05-12/rico-convictions-major-tobacco-companies-affirmed (last visited September 28, 2013).

32. *Id.*

33. Mail Fraud and Wire Fraud, Department of Justice, http://www.justice.gov/usao/eousa/foia_reading_room/usam/title9/43mcrm.htm (last visited September 28, 2013).

34. Standard Oil of Texas v. United States, 307 F.2d 120 (1962).

35. *How Do the Police Investigate Crimes*, FindLaw, http://criminal.findlaw.com/criminal-law-basics/how-do-the-police-investigate-crimes.html (last visited January 24, 2018.)

36. *Id.*

37. **State v. Smokey's Steakhouse, Inc., 478 N.W. 2d 361 (N.D., 1991).**

38. **Dietz, et al., Corporations, 18B Am. Jur. 2d Section 1841.**

39. Kevin Johnson, Sole Proprietorship and the Fifth Amendment, Chron, http://smallbusiness.chron.com/sole-proprietorship-fifth-amendment-15334.html (last visited September 28, 2013).

40. *Id.*

41. **Com. v. Eagleton, 402 Mass. 199, 521 N.E.2d 1363 (Mass., 1988).**

KEY TERMS

Arrest

Bankruptcy Fraud

Bribery

Burglary

Chapter 7 Bankruptcy

Chapter 11 Bankruptcy

Chapter 13 Bankruptcy

Classical Theory

Conspiracy

Crime

Criminal Trespass

Custodial Interrogation

Electronic Fencing

Embezzlement

Fifth Amendment

Fourth Amendment

Grand Jury

Guilty

Identity Theft

Identity Theft and Assumption
Deterrence Act

Indictment

Insider Trading

Larceny

Making a False Statement

Misappropriation Theory

Miranda Warnings

Money Laundering

Money Laundering Control Act

Overt Act

Probable Cause

Racketeer Influenced and Corrupt
Organizations (RICO)

Reasonable Expectation of Privacy

Receiving Stolen Property

Respondeat Superior

Retail Theft

Robbery

Search and Seizure

Search Warrant

Theft

Tipping

White-Collar Crime

CHAPTER 8

REMEDIES AVAILABLE IN COURT

SECTION 8.1
AN OVERVIEW

Carnegie Melon University received $1.17 billion dollars as the result of a patent infringement, a company was given $956 million dollars because of a misrepresentation concerning the value of stock and a patient was awarded $900 million dollars as the result of improper care rendered at a nursing home.[1] These damage awards are nothing new in the United States. In fact, lawsuits are considered part of doing business as a large corporation, especially considering they are target defendants. However, it is a misperception to believe that lawsuits only happen to big businesses. Almost 70% of lawsuits involve entities with less than one million dollars in revenue a year and 33% of small business owners have been sued or threatened with a lawsuit.[2]

When a business enters into a contract, it is anticipated that the other party will fulfill the terms of the agreement in good faith. Unfortunately, this does not always happen for a multitude of reasons. Nevertheless, if a party fails to correctly perform its contractual obligations, that entity can be sued for breach of contract relying on this basic principle – whenever a legal wrong is committed, there must be a legal remedy. The court will fashion a proper legal or equitable remedy to correct the wrong inflicted by the nonperforming party's actions.[3] This means of seeking legal redress is termed a **judicial remedy**.

A judicial remedy is a way of restoring the party to the status quo or placing that person in the same position as if the contract had not been breached or if the accident had never occurred. This relief may be ordered by a judge, awarded by a jury, entered into by agreement of the parties, or determined by operation of law. Some remedies require that certain acts be done or prohibited; others involve the payment of money, while still others mandate a court's determination of the rights of the parties.[4] **Monetary compensation** is a major and most common reason people file lawsuits, but it is not the only motive. Suits are also filed to obtain injunctions, recissions of contracts and other forms of equitable relief.

For instance, if you enter into a contract for a company to put a new roof on your house for $5,000 and the workers leave after one day and never return, the roofing company has breached the contract. You are now forced to find another company to finish the task, but the new roofer charges $6,000 to complete the repairs. In order to restore you to the status quo for the breach of contract, the damages would be $1,000.

This chapter will discuss the remedies a party may seek through court intervention and will include a discussion of damages, and those remedies available in equity.[5]

The American legal system has its origin in English common law which had two different kinds of courts – courts of law and courts of equity. **Remedies at law** were considered the main vehicle for seeking redress for civil wrongs, such as a breach of contract or a tort. The primary damages are monetary and are classified as compensatory, punitive, nominal and liquidated.[6] On the other hand, the **courts of equity** were viewed as the court of last resort when the remedy in the court of law was insufficient or unfair.

When remedies at law are inadequate, a party may seek **equitable relief.** Some scholars refer to this principle as the *irreparable harm* requirement. Developed in the Chancery Court of ancient England, **equity** allows the court to fashion a remedy to do what is just where traditional rules of law would produce an unfair result. Equitable remedies may either prohibit one from performing specified acts or require specific actions to be taken by a party. This relief can include an injunction to force employees to return to work or specific performance to require a party to go through with the sale of a unique item, such as a Picasso painting. The forms of equitable relief include restitution, reformation, injunctions, declaratory judgments, and specific performance. A party who violates an equitable decree may be held in contempt of court and be subject to the payment of fines and possible imprisonment.

JUDICIAL REMEDIES	
LAW	**EQUITY**
Compensatory	Injunction
Punitive	Reformation
Nominal	Restitution
Liquidated	Declaratory Judgment
	Specific Performance
	Recission

While there is a constitutional right to trial-by-jury in lawsuits at common law, no corresponding right exists in equity cases. Recently, however, the courts have started to disregard the distinction between these two categories of remedies, and award both legal and equitable relief in the same piece of litigation. Since the concept of equity attempts to do what is right, the courts have developed maxims or guiding principles in decided matters. One of the oldest doctrines is that a person who requests the court to exercise its equitable powers must come before the judiciary with clean hands and keep them clean throughout the course of the proceeding.

This principle is demonstrated in **United States v. Parlavecchio.** This case involves a fight over the frozen sperm of a reputed New York mobster. Mr. Parlavecchio, an inmate at Allenwood Federal Correctional Institution, was part of a conspiracy to funnel seminal fluids to his wife so that she could conceive his child through artificial insemination. After Mrs. Parlavecchio pled guilty to participating in the scheme, she requested the court to exercise its equitable powers by ordering the government to return the sperm of her imprisoned spouse to her. The court refused to intercede because the wife was part of the illegal activity and did not have clean hands.

UNITED STATES V. PARLAVECCHIO
192 F. SUPP. 2D 349 (M.D. PA., 2002)

On December 13, 2000, a federal grand jury returned a 10-count indictment charging John Alite, Antonino Parlavecchio and Maria Parlavecchio with conspiracy. John Alite and Maria Parlavecchio pled guilty to Count 6 and Antonino Parlavecchio, the husband of Maria Parlavecchio, pled guilty to Count 7 of the indictment. Mrs. Parlavecchio was sentenced to a one-year term of probation.

On February 1, 2002, Mrs. Parlavecchio filed a motion for return of property pursuant to **Federal Rule of Criminal Procedure 41(e).** The presentence report filed in this case reveals that the following facts are undisputed. In furtherance of the conspiracy, Mrs. Parlavecchio provided toiletries, foodstuffs and cryogenic sperm preservation kits to her husband through Troy Kemmerer who was employed as a correctional officer at the prison. It was part of the conspiracy that in exchange for receiving $5,000, Mr. Kemmerer would obtain the sperm kits from Mrs. Parlavecchio and deliver the kits to Mr. Parlavecchio. Mr. Parlavecchio would then fill the sperm preservation kits with his seminal fluids and the kits would be returned to Mr. Kemmerer who would transport the kits from the prison to Mrs. Parlavecchio. Mrs. Parlavecchio would thereafter transport the kits or cause them to be transported to a Park Avenue Fertility Clinic in New York City. On or about October 2, 2000, Mrs. Parlavecchio directed that the seminal fluids be forwarded to her gynecologist. One of the purposes of the conspiracy was to enable Mrs. Parlavecchio to conceive a child by her husband through artificial insemination.

Federal Rule of Criminal Procedure 41(e) provides:

Motion for Return of Property. A person aggrieved by an unlawful search and seizure or by the deprivation of property may move the district court for the return of the property on the ground that such person is entitled to lawful possession of the property . . .

A basic principle applicable to this case is that one requesting the court to exercise its equitable powers must come into court with "clean hands." **Gaudiosi v. Mellon, 269 F. 2d 873 (3d Cir., 1959).** No principle is better settled than the maxim that he who comes into equity must come with clean hands and keep them clean throughout the course of the litigation, and that if he violates this rule, he must be denied all relief whatever may have been the merits of his claim. The Court of Appeals in Gaudiosi further stated that "[p]ublic policy not only makes it obligatory for courts to deny a plaintiff relief once his unclean hands are established but to refuse to even hear a case under such circumstances."

Mrs. Parlavecchio is not entitled to equitable relief. The ultimate crime in this case was bribery, i.e., the illegal payment of money in exchange for receiving seminal fluids from Mrs. Parlavecchio's husband. The fruits of the crime for Kemmerer was the cash he received. From the other perspective, the fruits of the crime for Mrs. Parlavecchio were the seminal fluids she obtained in exchange for the cash she paid. Each of the parties to the illegal transaction gained something to which they were not legally entitled and which was the result of the criminal activity: Kemmerer received the cash and Mrs. Parlavecchio received the seminal fluids.

To permit Mrs. Parlavecchio to recover the illegally obtained seminal fluids would constitute judicial approval of her criminal activities and reward her for her crime. We will not use our equitable powers to aid a wrongdoer. Mrs. Parlavecchio's motion for return of property will be denied.

SECTION 8.2 COMPENSATORY DAMAGES

The purpose of **compensatory damages**, as is set forth in **Bayer v. Neiman Marcus Group, Inc.**, 861 F.3d 853 (Ct. App. 9th Cir. 2017), is the classic form of damages intended to redress the specific loss that a person has suffered by reason of the defendant's wrongful conduct. To that end, compensatory damages may include not only out-of-pocket expenses but other monetary harms, such as impairment of reputation, personal humiliation, mental anguish and suffering. In light of this purpose, compensatory damages are measured by the harm the defendant has caused the plaintiff.

A. Tort

In a tort action, the damages should place the injured party in as substantially good a position financially, emotionally, and physically as he or she occupied before the injury. Such damages, however, may be difficult to quantify. The most obvious damages include the recovery of out-of-pocket expenses, such as:

1. medical expenses; **2.** lost wages; and **3.** property damage.

It is without question that a person can recover the medical expense incurred for the accident related injuries as well as whatever wages are lost by being out of work while the recovery process takes place. The claimant may also recover any property damage, such as the cost to have a damaged car repaired. These items when added together form what is known as the out-of-pocket expenses. However, has the person been fully compensated for his injuries from the tort?

Another item of recovery, known as **pain and suffering,** is allowed in personal injury actions and is the most controversial because of its subjective nature. For instance, the person is entitled to be compensated for the anguish and discomfort he has had to endure because of his injuries.

Pain and suffering is not as easy to calculate as other forms of damages that can be reduced to a mathematical certainty. Pain and suffering is subjective, and the value of each case will vary depending upon the circumstances. For instance, if the injured party makes a speedy recovery with no ill effects, his pain and suffering will be worth far less than if he suffers from the residuals of the incident for the rest of his life. As a rule of thumb, it is not uncommon to see a claimant receive three to ten times the out-of-pocket expenses in the form of pain and suffering damages.

Damages in a contract action should place the injured party in the position he or she would have occupied had the contract not been breached. The damages must be demonstrated with reasonable certainty. In other words, the compensation for the injury must be a foreseeable result of the breach, and one the parties could reasonable have foreseen at the time the contract was created.[7] In other words, the plaintiff is entitled to receive the benefit of its bargain. Suppose Joe Roberts contracts with Dr. Jones to purchase the physician's boat for $20,000. On the day Joe learns that Jones breached the contract, the market value of the boat is $22,000. Joe is entitled to the difference between the contract price and the market price, or $2,000. What if Joe can purchase a comparable boat for $21,500 within a reasonable time after the breach? He would be entitled to the difference between the cover or purchase price and the contract price or $1,500.

Joe Roberts is also entitled to any **special damages** that were caused by the breach. Special damages are limited to those losses that are foreseeable, reasonably certain, and unavoidable. For example, if Dr. Jones knew that Joe needed the boat for a charter-fishing business, which business has generated profits of $10,000 each summer for the past five years, the physician will be responsible for Joe's lost profits.

If Joe is the breaching party, what can the aggrieved seller recover? Suppose the contract price was still $20,000, but the boat's market value had slipped to $19,000 on the scheduled date of contract performance. Jones' lost benefit would be the difference between the contract price and the market price or $1,000. If the seller can resell the boat, the damages will be the difference between the contract price and the resale price.

When an established entity is harmed, damages are determined by looking at the diminution in value of the business because of the wrongful conduct. This is measured by calculating the loss of profits after deducting for the expenses that would have been incurred if the contract had been performed.[8]

Establishing the damages incurred by a new business creates unique problems because there is not a history of revenue and profits to examine. Evidence of expected profits is too uncertain and remote to calculate with certainty. Thus, recovery for lost profits from a transaction is generally not granted, even if the defendant's actions prevented the business from opening up.[9]

The following case illustrates the problem with collecting special damages. Even though a party clearly breaches a contract, unless that defendant has knowledge of the circumstances from which such damages might arise, items like lost profits can not be recovered.

SUTTLE V. LANDSTAR INWAY, INC.
2009 WL 1297470 (S.D., TEX.)

Suttle and Dai are partners in G & B. In April 2006, Plaintiffs purchased the CNC Machine at issue in this case for $10,000 "as-is, where-is, with all faults." Plaintiffs bought this machine from Delphi Automotive North America (Delphi) in an online auction. Plaintiffs did not physically see the machine before they bid on and purchased it. They did, however, view several photos of the CNC Machine. Plaintiff Dai then contacted Avxa Freight Logistics (Avxa) to arrange for the transportation of the CNC Machine from Delphi's Dayton, Ohio location to G & B's address in Houston, Texas. On October 13, 2006, Landstar transported the CNC Machine from Delphi to G & B. The shipping document completed by Delphi declares that the machine's extended value is $10,000. Plaintiffs allege that Landstar failed to adequately tarp the CNC Machine for transportation and that, during transport, the machine sustained rain damage which made it "unsafe and unmarketable."

Defendant contends that Plaintiffs' claims for damages in the form of lost profits and lost income are claims for special damages and are not recoverable under the facts of this case.

Plaintiffs had entered into an agreement with and had paid Defendant to protect and cover the machine with a tarp from weather elements and other debris while transporting the machine from one destination [Dayton] to another [Houston] for them. Additionally, Plaintiffs owned the CNC Machine at issue as they had purchased it several months earlier in an auction.

Defendant contends that Plaintiffs cannot recover damages for lost profits or lost income because Defendant did not have notice of these special damages prior to or at the time the bill of lading was issued. General damages are those that are foreseeable at the time of contracting. Special damages are those unusual or indirect costs that, although caused by the defendant's conduct in a literal sense, are beyond what one would reasonably expect to be the ordinary consequences of a breach. Typically, a plaintiff cannot recover special damages in a breach of contract action absent actual notice to the defendant of special circumstances from which such damages might arise.

When Dai contacted Avxa to arrange for the shipment of the CNC Machine, he only provided Avxa with the machine's physical size and weight. Plaintiffs never provided Avxa or Defendant with actual notice of the intended use of the CNC Machine prior to or at the time the bill of lading was issued. It was not until Plaintiffs submitted their (lawsuit) that they asserted a claim for special damages, specifically lost profits on the operation of the CNC Machine. Accordingly, the Court finds that Plaintiffs' claim for special damages must fail.

SECTION 8.3
PUNITIVE DAMAGES

Punitive or **exemplary damage** is exactly what its name implies. A sum of money is awarded to punish the wrongdoer and to send a message to others not to engage in the same type of conduct. Punitive damages, however, should not exceed the amount needed to adequately punish the wrongdoer and serve as an example to that entity and others.[10] This punitive penalty is a United States doctrine that has not gained recognition in other parts of the world.

A. Contract Actions

Contract damages are to compensate an injured party for those losses caused by the breach and not to punish the breaching party. Generally, punitive damages are not available in breach of contract actions, even when the contract is maliciously or intentionally breached.[11]

B. Tort Actions

Punitive damages are more commonly awarded in tort actions where the defendant has engaged in outrageous, malicious, or gross misconduct. For example, an automobile accident that occurs as the result of a party's mere negligence in going through a traffic light is insufficient to give rise to punitive damages. In order for punitive damages to be awarded, the accident would have had to be caused by the defendant being intoxicated, the driver intentionally going through a red light, or the wrongdoer driving at a speed far in excess of the speed limit in a school-crossing zone.

To provide an example of a jury instruction involving a punitive damage claim, the following is the standard jury charge in Pennsylvania:

> "If you find that the conduct of the defendant was outrageous, you may award punitive damages, as well as any compensatory damages, in order to punish the defendant for his conduct and to deter the defendant and others from committing similar acts.
>
> A person's conduct is outrageous when it is malicious, wanton, willful, or oppressive, or shows reckless indifference to the interests of others."[12]

Punitive damage awards are unpredictable and can be staggering, since the jury is allowed to consider the net worth of the defendant in their calculations. According to a CNN survey of jury verdicts, a California jury punished Philip Morris by awarding a lung cancer patient 28 billion dollars, and a Missouri jury ordered a pharmacy to pay over 2 billion dollars to a woman with ovarian cancer whose medication was diluted by the drugstore. The record for punitive damages, however, was rendered in Florida where a 144 billion-dollar punitive damage award was entered against the tobacco industry.

An award of punitive damages is the exception rather than the rule. The New York Times published a study analyzing verdicts across the country. The article noted that punitive damages are awarded in only four percent of the cases and they are proportionate to the amount of compensatory damages.

State governments have the authority to regulate punitive damages and the Due Process Clause prohibits the imposition of grossly excessive or arbitrary awards against a tortfeasor. In fact, the Supreme Court has established the following guidelines to consider when looking at a punitive damage award: (1) the degree of reprehensibility of the defendant's misconduct; (2) the disparity between the actual or potential harm suffered by the plaintiff and the punitive damages award; and (3) the difference between the punitive damages awarded by the jury and the civil penalties authorized or imposed in comparable cases.

MULHERON V. PHILADELPHIA EAGLES
2013 WL 211349 (D.N.J., 2013)

This matter comes before the Court upon the Philadelphia Eagles Motion to Dismiss.

Plaintiff was injured during a Philadelphia Eagles game she attended on December 2, 2010. During that game, a fight broke out in which Plaintiff played no role. The combatants tumbled down upon Plaintiff and allegedly caused Plaintiff serious injuries. She seeks compensatory and punitive damages.

Plaintiff's Complaint names the Eagles and Aramark and is based upon purported violations of the Pennsylvania Dram Shop Act. The claim alleges that the Eagles and Aramark "served, sold, or gave alcoholic beverages to Defendants, Richard Roe and Jane Doe . . . while they were visibly intoxicated," after which Richard Roe and Jane Doe "began fighting, pushing, rumbling, and were careless, negligent and grossly negligent and fell on Plaintiff, causing her serious injuries."

The Eagles assert that Plaintiff's request for punitive damages should be dismissed because they are legally barred. Punitive damages cannot be awarded unless Plaintiff can prove that the Eagles' "actions were of such an outrageous nature as to demonstrate intentional, willful, wanton or reckless conduct" and that it would be appropriate to punish the Eagles for such action. Punitive damages must be proven by a preponderance of the evidence.

The key inquiry is whether the facts in Plaintiff's complaint, taken as true for purposes of this motion, support a finding that she is entitled to punitive damages under Pennsylvania law. Plaintiff must allege that the Eagles "actions were of such an outrageous nature as to demonstrate intentional, willful, wanton or reckless conduct." Here, Plaintiff has failed to plead facts which could plausibly lead to a successful action for punitive damages. There is simply nothing in the facts of the Complaint which indicates or alleges that the Eagles were *intentional, willful, wanton or reckless*. Those claims simply fail to allege any facts which would support a finding that the Eagles were engaged in conduct based upon an "evil motive or reckless indifference to the rights of others." The portions of the claims that seek punitive damages are stricken without prejudice as to all defendants. Leave to amend is granted so that Plaintiff may plead facts which support a finding that punitive damages exist.

The Eagles [also] contend that they cannot be held liable under Pennsylvania's Dram Shop Act because Plaintiff has failed to plead that the Eagles are a licensee under the act. In order to sustain a claim under Pennsylvania's Dram Shop Act, a Plaintiff must prove that the licensee served a third party who was "visibly intoxicated." In this case, Plaintiff alleges that the Eagles "served, sold, or gave alcoholic beverages" to the unnamed defendants "while they were visibly intoxicated, in violation of the Pennsylvania Dram Shop Act. . . ." The Court finds that statement to be a conclusory allegation which is otherwise unsupported by any other facts in the complaint. That claim, alone, constitutes nothing more than a "threadbare [recitation] of a cause of action's elements, supported by mere conclusory statements." "Visibly intoxicated" has a legal significance under the Dram Shop Act. The facts of the complaint, however, do not indicate any basis for that legal conclusion. As such, the Court dismisses Plaintiff's Dram Shop Claim without prejudice as to both named Defendants in that claim. Leave to amend this claim is granted.

SECTION 8.4
NOMINAL DAMAGES

Have you ever heard of a verdict of one dollar? **Nominal damages** arise when a technical wrong has been committed but no actual harm has resulted. Courts will acknowledge the legal rights of the complaining party, but will award a trivial or nominal sum of money to the injured party. It is as if the court or jury is saying "Technically, a tort has been committed but so what?" By awarding normal damages, the fact finder is reinforcing the principle that the defendant's conduct is contrary to established law.

For example, if a motorist carelessly opens a car door into the side of a parked vehicle, causing a small dent on an already blemished and rusty 1995 Chevy, a cause of action for negligence can be successfully maintained. However, it is likely that the court will award a token sum of money or nominal damages since there has been no real harm to the aging automobile.

One of the better known cases involving nominal damages arose in a suit filed by the defunct United States Football League or USFL against the NFL for a violation of the Sherman Antitrust Act. The floundering USFL claimed damages of 567 million dollars which, when trebled according to antitrust laws, would total more than 1.7 billion dollars. Following a 48 day trial, the jury returned with a verdict of $1 which was then multiplied by 3 to arrive at an award of $3. While the jury believed that the NFL was technically guilty of an antitrust violation, the fact finders were not impressed that the USFL would have survived under any circumstance.

The following case involves a suit between ESPN and the National Baseball League over the breach of contract by the television network not to show baseball games on Sunday nights in September. The case discusses the burden of proof in showing damages with the necessary certainty.

ESPN, Inc. v. Office of the Commissioner of Baseball
76 F. Supp. 2d 416 (S.D. N.Y., 1999)

ESPN breached its 1996 telecasting agreement with Baseball when it preempted six baseball games scheduled for Sunday nights in September 1998 and September 1999 without the prior written approval of Baseball. ESPN broadcast NFL football games rather than the previously scheduled baseball games on those six nights.

Baseball claims that it has been damaged in an amount "believed to exceed millions of dollars" as a result of ESPN's breach of the 1996 Agreement.

ESPN seeks to preclude Baseball from introducing testimony of its alleged monetary damages. ESPN contends that "there is no factual basis to support any claim for monetary damages arising from these perceived injuries, and that such claims are the product of speculation and guesswork."

It is well-established that a plaintiff must prove the existence of damages with certainty in order to recover for breach of contract. Although it is true that "[w]hen the existence of damage is certain, and the only uncertainty is as to its amount, the plaintiff will not be denied recovery of substantial damages," but even then the plaintiff must show "a stable foundation for a reasonable estimate" of damages.

During discovery, ESPN served Baseball with interrogatories regarding its claims for monetary damages. Among other things, ESPN asked Baseball to "state the amount of monetary damages you seek in this action and explain the basis for the computation of your claim." Baseball responded as follows: "Baseball has not quantified the amount of damages it has sustained by reason of ESPN's willful refusal to carry baseball games as required by the 1996 Agreement."

Nowhere in its response does Baseball set forth any specific dollar amount of monetary damages other than its estimate that damages are "believed to exceed millions of dollars."

Finally, this Court held oral argument on ESPN's motion to preclude damages evidence. During that argument, this Court specifically asked counsel for Baseball whether Baseball had any "concrete proof of monetary harm." Counsel for Baseball was unable to show "any loss of sponsorship, any loss of advertising, or any loss of ancillary sales or ticket sales." As counsel for Baseball conceded: "We have not shown specific losses your Honor, we agree with you there. What we have said is we believe it did affect us."

Baseball has failed to adequately demonstrate either the fact of damages or the amount of damages. Put simply, Baseball's subjective belief that the amount of damages is "significant" does not meet any of the required proofs set forth under New York law. To the contrary, under New York law, a claim of damages for loss of reputation and future profits must be "reasonably certain."

Although Baseball is not entitled to an award of money damages, it may still receive nominal damages. It is a well-settled tenet of contract law that even if the breach of contract caused no loss or if the amount of the loss cannot be proven with sufficient certainty, the injured party is entitled to recover, as nominal damages, a small sum fixed without regard to the amount of the loss, if any. Accordingly, I will instruct the jury that if Baseball proves its breach of damages claim, it is entitled to an award of nominal damages.

SECTION 8.5
LIQUIDATED DAMAGES

The parties to a contract can agree in advance on the amount of damages that will be paid in the event of a default or breach of contract. These amounts are known as **liquidated damages** and are appropriate when the damages are uncertain or difficult to prove. The stipulated sum should be a reasonable forecast of the damages, although the plaintiff may end up recovering more or less than the actual loss.

As noted in the Restatement 2d of Contracts:

> "Damages for breach by either party may be liquidated in the agreement but only at an amount that is reasonable in the light of the anticipated or actual loss caused by the breach and the difficulties of proof of loss. A term fixing unreasonably large liquidated damages is unenforceable on grounds of public policy as a penalty."

If the liquidated amount is unreasonable and grossly disproportionate to the actual loss, a court may refuse to uphold the agreement. The fact that the actual damages suffered by the aggrieved party end up being less than the damages specified in the contract is not fatal so long as the stipulated sum was reasonable at the time the contract was formed. Liquidated damages clauses have even been enforced when no real damages have been suffered.

A common example of a liquidated damages clause is contained in an Agreement of Sale for real estate. Such a clause requires the forfeiture of the buyer's deposit or down payment in the event of a default by the purchaser. The following is a sample liquidated damages clause:

> "In the event of a breach of this agreement by the Buyer, all deposits and other sums paid by the Buyer on account of the purchase price shall be retained by the Seller as liquidated damages for such breach."

Air travel is the subject of several liquidated damage clauses unilaterally imposed by the governments of the world to stimulate the expansion of airline routes to all parts of the globe. This protection was created by the **Warsaw Convention,** which limits the recovery of compensatory damages in personal injury actions against an airline in international travel. Most countries have agreed to be bound by the terms of this Convention which was originally created in 1929 and amended several time since then. As the Supreme Court noted:

> "The cardinal purpose of the Warsaw Convention is to achieve uniformity of rules governing claims arising from international air transportation. The Convention signatories, in the treaty's preamble, specifically 'recognized the advantage of regulating in a uniform manner the conditions of . . . the liability of the carrier.' To

provide the desired uniformity, the Convention sets out an array of liability rules which, the treaty declares, 'apply to all international transportation of persons, baggage, or goods performed by aircraft.' The Convention describes the areas of air carrier liability; personal injuries, baggage or goods loss, destruction, or damage, and damage occasioned by delay, the conditions exempting air carriers from liability, the monetary limits of liability and the circumstances in which air carriers may not limit liability."[13]

Limitations on recovery have also been imposed for property damage claims such as those that result from lost or damaged luggage.

Additional protection can be obtained by purchasing insurance from a private company. Such insurance is not affected by the limitation of the carrier's liability under the Warsaw Convention, any tariff, or the plane ticket.

Would an airline be allowed to limit its liability for damages for a domestic flight between two U.S. cities? That is your next assignment, since the firm has received a new case on this issue. As usual, Mr. Smith will provide you with more information.

SECTION 8.6
ROBERTS V.
EASTCOAST AIRLINES

PROBLEM EIGHT—A

PARK, BROWN & SMITH, P.C.
ATTORNEYS AT LAW MEMORANDUM

TO: All Law Clerks

FROM: Peter Smith, Esquire

RE: Limitation of Liability of an Airline for Lost Luggage

Joe Roberts is a big fan of "The King." While a youth, Mr. Roberts spent some of his time in Nashville because of his love of music. One night, he went to hear the cover band, "Love Me Tender" at a bar in the rural countryside. The lead singer looked familiar but Joe couldn't place him. Our client waited around until the group was finished their set and approached the singer. "You are great!" exclaimed Joe as he asked the singer for an autograph. To his amazement, the musician gave Joe his guitar and autographed it with the name, "The King."

Two years ago, our client's guitar was appraised by Sotheby's, the famous auction house, for $50,000.

Joe recently booked a trip sponsored by fans of "The King." For a mere $200, a person can travel to Memphis and visit the spots where "The King" grew up, owned his famous home, and recorded his tunes. After booking the trip, our client received the travel tickets from East Coast Airlines. This start-up company offers inexpensive plane fares because it utilizes retired pilots and offers a "no-frills" operation. Joe checked his guitar at the airline counter along with the rest of his luggage. During the flight, however, the plane encountered unexpected turbulence which caused the baggage in the cargo bay to shift, crushing the guitar.

Joe is devastated by the damage to the valuable instrument and wishes to sue the airline for $50,000. East Coast, however, claims that its liability is limited to $2,500.

I have reviewed the plane ticket and found the following notice on the reverse side:

Notice of Baggage Liability Limitation

Liability for loss, delay or damage to checked baggage is limited as follows, unless a higher value is declared in advance and additional charges are paid: $2,500 per passenger.

This limitation of liability seems unjust considering the airline's negligence and the actual value of the musical instrument. The terms of the Warsaw Convention are not applicable to this case since this flight was purely domestic. My preliminary research has uncovered an old case on point. Please read **Martin v. Transworld Airlines, Inc.** in order to ascertain whether the limitation of liability clause asserted by East Coast Airlines is enforceable.

MARY MARTIN V. TRANS WORLD AIRLINES, INC.
280 A.2D 642 (PA. SUPER., 1972)

Mary Martin brought suit to recover $2,200, the stipulated value of wearing apparel contained in a piece of luggage which was lost in transit when the plaintiff was traveling on Defendant's airline from New York City to Pittsburgh.

The Plaintiff had checked her baggage at the East side terminal at 42nd Street, New York City, and then proceeded to the airport. The agent of the

Defendant gave the plaintiff a baggage claim check which recited on its front: "Baggage checked subject to the tariffs indicating limitations of liability contained therein." A similar notice was also printed on the airline ticket.

In addition to the above notices, there were notices posted in bold-face type and prominently displayed in the baggage wells at the East Side terminal and at the airline ticket counter and also at the passenger boarding gates which bore the following notation:

> "Tariff regulations limit airline liability for baggage to actual value not to exceed:
>
>   Domestic $250
>   International $495
>
> unless higher valuation declared in advance and appropriate charges paid."

Similar signs were posted at the Pittsburgh airport in the baggage wells, at the ticket counter, and at boarding gates.

The Plaintiff did not declare any valuation on any of her luggage. One bag was missing. She had testified that she didn't read the small print on her ticket and the baggage check, didn't see the posted signs, and had no knowledge of the limitations. Mary Martin denied knowledge of the limitations, although in her profession as a singer, she was a seasoned traveler.

Under the Civil Aeronautics Act, an airline Carrier may, by tariff, limit its liability and such tariff is valid even though loss of property is the result of the company's negligence. The tariff provisions are part of the contract, and it is the duty of the passenger to declare the higher valuation and pay the higher rate if he wished protection in excess of the limited amount.

This Court held in a similar case:

> "The requirement that a passenger must be offered a fair opportunity to choose between higher or lower liability before an interstate carrier can limit recovery for loss of baggage to an amount less than the actual loss sustained does not require that the passenger be actually informed that a choice of rates is available.

> The appellant had ample opportunity to discover there was a choice of rates available. The baggage check which she received made reference to the tariff regulations under which the baggage was transported. In addition, the appellee had signs posted in the bus terminal referring to the limitations of liability for checked bags and advising how travelers could increase their protection."

Unlimited liability or even common law liability for negligence would seriously affect the economic life of a transportation industry already subsidized by government to insure its healthy operation. Unlimited liability would be an open invitation to fraud. It should be noted that the United States courts have never permitted airlines to limit their liability with regard to injury and death actions on domestic flights. The Civil Aeronautics Board has always permitted limitations on baggage liability. The Second Circuit Court has held that tickets must be delivered to the traveler "in such a manner as to afford him a reasonable opportunity to take protection against the limited liability."

Even if we were to hold that notice on the baggage check and ticket was in too small print to bring notice home to the traveler, it would not dispose of the conspicuous signs in the baggage wells, ticket office, and the boarding gates, which not only gave notice of the filing of tariffs but advised of the right to file for a higher valuation. In addition, the record shows Martin was a seasoned traveler and had many opportunities to see the posted signs, and it is highly unlikely that she had no knowledge of the value limitation on luggage and her choice to pay a fee for higher valuation. A person may not be heard to say she did not see what should have been clearly visible to her.

This record had overwhelming evidence that such notice was given to Martin. Therefore, judgment is entered in favor of the plaintiff and against the defendant in the amount of $250, the amount as limited by the filed tariff.

ANSWER SHEET
PROBLEM EIGHT—A

Name   **Please Print Clearly**

1. Are such liquidated damage clauses enforceable?

2. What policy considerations support the enforcement of such clauses?

_____

_____

_____

_____

_____

_____

_____

3. What is required for the clause to be enforced?

_____

_____

_____

_____

_____

_____

_____

_____

_____

_____

SECTION 8.7 INJUNCTION

An **injunction** is an equitable order issued by the court directing a person to do something (**mandatory injunction**) or to refrain from doing something (**prohibitory injunction**). Injunctions are further classified as permanent, preliminary, and **temporary restraining orders ("TRO")**.

A. Permanent Injunction

A **permanent injunction** is the final resolution of a dispute issued after a full hearing of all relevant factors. In granting this type of injunction, the court will evaluate the adequacy of a remedy at law, the enforceability of the decree, and the comparative hardship to the parties.

B. Preliminary Injunction

A **preliminary injunction** is granted as an emergency measure before a full hearing on the merits of the dispute can be held. The plaintiff must provide notice to the defendant of the proceeding, and the court will conduct an informal hearing to review the issue. If the plaintiff demonstrates that irreparable harm will result without such an order, the court will grant the temporary injunction to maintain the status quo prior to a final determination of the dispute.

C. TRO

A **TRO** is an ex parte injunction, or an injunction granted without notice to the defendant. Because the court initially only hears the plaintiff's side of the case, it will grant the order if the need for relief is so urgent that there is no time for a hearing. The plaintiff must also establish that an irreparable harm will occur. Since there is no notice to the defendant, the court weighs factors more heavily against the plaintiff. These proceedings must be followed by a full hearing on the merits of the dispute.

Injunctive relief is a tool frequently used by employers or the government to regulate the conduct of employees on strike. For instance, a prohibitory injunction can be obtained to limit the number of pickets at a facility or to prohibit violent conduct of striking employees.

Does a court of equity, however, have the power to order striking employees to return to work? In the absence of a law or provision in the collective bargaining agreement to the contrary, the court will not order striking workers to return to the job place unless the health, welfare and safety of the public is threatened.

The following case deals with whether McDonald's, the fast food giant, can obtain an injunction prohibiting its landlord from leasing empty space to an International House of Pancakes franchisee, since the lease between the landlord and McDonald's prohibited the using of the shopping center space for the operation of another "fast food" restaurant.

McDonald's Corp. v. Rappaport
532 F. Supp. 2d 264 (Mass., 2008)

McDonald's Corporation asserts that the Highlander Plaza shopping center is violating a restrictive covenant contained in a lease between McDonald's and the shopping center. Specifically, McDonald's challenges Highlander Plaza's legal authority to lease space to an International House of Pancakes franchisee for the operation of an IHOP on the premises.

Defendants own Highlander Plaza, a shopping center which has located within it a variety of stores and restaurants. In 1993, McDonald's entered into a twenty-year lease with Defendants to open a new McDonald's restaurant in the shopping center. The lease contains a covenant not to compete provision that restricts the landlord as follows:

> "Landlord covenants and agrees that no property within two (2) miles of the perimeter of the Demised Premises shall, during the term of this Lease be leased, or occupied as a so-called fast food restaurant, food service establishment, drive-in or walk-up eating facility."

In 2007, the Ground Round restaurant in Highlander Plaza closed. Defendants entered into an agreement to lease the space to Salem Pancakes, Inc., a company that intended to operate an IHOP franchise.

McDonald's sought to enjoin Defendants permitting the installation of an International House of Pancakes restaurant on the premises.

The standard for issuing a permanent injunction requires the court to find that (1) Plaintiffs prevail on the merits; (2) Plaintiffs would suffer irreparable injury in the absence of injunctive relief; (3) the harm to plaintiffs would outweigh the harm the Defendant would suffer from the imposition of an injunction; and (4) the public interest would not be adversely affected by an injunction.

This court must determine the coverage of the restrictive covenant in the lease. McDonald's asserts that the restrictive covenant applies to all "food service establishments," arguing that the words "so-called fast food" modify only "restaurant." Defendants assert that the covenant applies only to "fast food" restaurants, with the phrase "so-called fast food modifying all of the elements that follow [in the clause]."

At trial, Defendants presented compelling evidence that the Parties intended the clause to restrict Highlander Plaza's ability to lease property in the shopping center to other "fast food" restaurants only, not all "food service establishments." As a result of such evidence, this court concludes that the restrictive covenant applies to fast food only.

Specifically, Defendants demonstrated that McDonald's originally sought a broad restrictive covenant, one that prohibited Highlander Plaza from renting to all other food service establishments. During negotiations, however, Highlander Plaza did not accept such a sweeping covenant. Gary Markoff, counsel for Highlander who participated in the negotiations, stated that Highlander was trying to "give as narrow an exclusive as possible." As a result, Highlander only agreed to restrict its ability to lease to other fast food restaurants. After negotiations, McDonald's accepted the narrower restriction. Accordingly, Markoff added "so-called fast food" to modify the entire covenant:

The evidence is more than sufficient for this court to conclude that the clause applies only to fast food. In addition, however, restrictive covenants are restraints on the alienability of land, and traditional rules governing these restraints add further support to this conclusion. The Supreme Court of Massachusetts has noted that restrictions on land are disfavored, and they in general are to be construed against the grantor and in favor of freedom of alienation. More specifically, any ambiguity in a restrictive covenant must be resolved in favor of the "freedom of land from servitude," meaning the less restricted use.

Here, a narrower interpretation of the covenant results in increased alienability of the premises. Although the lease does not define "so-called fast food," the Parties do not dispute that IHOP is a full service, family style restaurant.

Because the restrictive covenant in the lease applies only to fast food restaurants, and IHOP is not a fast food restaurant, the covenant did not prohibit Defendants from leasing the former Ground Round space to the IHOP franchisee, Salem Pancakes. Accordingly, Plaintiff's request for injunctive relief is DENIED.

SECTION 8.8
RESTITUTION

Defining **restitution** is difficult because there is no one definition for this remedy. It is commonly accepted that unjust enrichment is the key element for these types of claims. In other words, a person who has been unjustly enriched at the expense of another is mandated to make restitution to the aggrieved party. The purpose of this remedy is to give back the gains the defendant improperly obtained in a transaction.[14]

This remedy has the advantage of either returning the property that is in the defendant's possession to the injured party or providing monetary relief. Money damages are measured by the sum that the defendant has been unjustly enriched. Not only must the defendant return the aggrieved party to the status quo, but the wrongdoer must also return any profits that he has earned by the use of the property.

THOMAS MITCHELL V. WILLIAM MOORE
729 A.2D 1200 (PA. SUPER., 1999)

Thomas Mitchell and William Moore first met in 1980; the two men quickly developed a romantic relationship. Moore resided in Elverson, Pennsylvania and Mitchell in South Carolina. In the spring of 1981, Mitchell accepted Moore's invitation to spend his "off season" at Moore's Chester County farm. By 1985, Mitchell had permanently moved to Elverson, where he resided at

Moore's farm without paying rent. Among other things, Mitchell took care of the farm animals. In 1990, Mitchell enrolled at Penn State University for graduate studies. As a result of his academic schedule, he was unable to maintain the farm. Soon thereafter, the parties' relationship soured; Mitchell moved out of Moore's residence in June of 1994.

In 1995, Mitchell sought restitution for the services he rendered to Moore throughout the thirteen years the two men lived together on the farm. In his complaint, Mitchell alleged that Moore had: promised him compensation for his services rendered to maintain and operate his farm, agreed to compensate him for his help in running an antique cooperative (co-op) that Mitchell had purchased, and promised him future compensation and the devise of property in a will and codicil.

Mitchell's claim for restitution lies upon the theory of unjust enrichment. Where unjust enrichment is found, the law implies a contract, which requires the defendant to pay to the plaintiff the value of the benefit conferred. The elements necessary to prove unjust enrichment are:

1. benefits conferred on defendant by plaintiff;

2. appreciation of such benefits by defendant; and

3. acceptance and retention of such benefits under such circumstances that it would be inequitable for defendant to retain the benefit without payment of value.

Both parties concur that when Mitchell moved into Moore's home on a full-time basis, Moore paid many of Mitchell's bills, including car payments, card charges, and phone bills. Moreover, Moore claims that Mitchell became part of his own family; Mitchell, himself, admits to having celebrated all the major holidays with Moore's immediate family and received gifts from them on special occasions.

In order to prove that the defendant had been unjustly enriched by plaintiff's actions and services, there must be convincing evidence that plaintiff's services were not gratuitous.

We first note that Mitchell had complete access to a large farm house where he lived rent-free. The amount of benefits that plaintiff received from living at Moore's farm rebuts any presumption that the benefit conferred upon Moore was unjust.

Furthermore, the defendant testified that the plaintiff himself suggested that he move in with the defendant because he could not afford to rent an apartment on his own. He, as well as the defendant, thought such potential living arrangement would give the two men more time to foster their relationship. In fact, upon learning of plaintiff's potential job opportunity in nearby Lancaster, Pennsylvania, the defendant anticipated that the two parties would be able to grow closer in a permanent "live-in" situation—another indication that there existed no expectation of payment for plaintiff's voluntary work on the defendant's farm.

While Mitchell would characterize the nature of the parties' relationship as a type of business venture between partners, the evidence indicates a very different aspect of their lives. As Mitchell, himself, testified, he had a "romantic or sexual aspect to his relationship with Dr. Moore." Furthermore, the parties conducted themselves around the home like parties in a loving relationship; they shared household chores, cooked dinners for each other, bestowed gifts upon one another, attended events together, and shared holidays and special occasions with Moore's family.

After a review of the record in this case, we cannot find that the defendant benefited unjustly from plaintiff's services.

**SECTION 8.9
RECISSION AND
REFORMATION**

A contract can be **rescinded** if it is voidable, such as those agreements procured through misrepresentation, fraud, duress, undue influence, or impossibility. In that case, each party must return the property they have received from the other.

Suppose, however, that the contract between the parties is valid but it fails to express the real intent of the parties because of a mistake or ambiguity in language. In that event, a party can seek the equitable remedy of **reformation** in order to modify the written agreement to reflect their real intentions.

For example, suppose a seller orally agrees to transfer 120 acres of land to a buyer, but the written deed conveys only 100 acres. The buyer can request that the court reform or change the contract to reflect the sale of 120 acres of land. The remedy of rescission is not easily granted. A court must be satisfied with the fact that the breach of contract is material and willful, or at least substantial and fundamental enough to strongly defeat the object of the parties in making the contract. The aggrieved party must also show that the normal remedy for breach of contract in the form of monetary damages, is inadequate. Rescission has the effect of canceling the contract, thereby excusing future performance and requiring the return of all monies advanced.

Would a house that is reputed to be haunted allow the buyer to rescind the sale? That is the issue in **Stambovsky v. Ackley.** Where the condition created by the seller materially impairs the value of the contract and is peculiarly within the knowledge of the seller or is unlikely to be discovered by the buyer, nondisclosure of a material fact constitutes grounds for recission.

STAMBOVSKY V. ACKLEY
572 N.Y.S. 2D 672 (N.Y., 1991)

Plaintiff, to his horror, discovered that the house he had contracted to purchase was widely reputed to be possessed by poltergeists, reportedly seen by defendant seller and members of her family on numerous occasions over the last nine years. Plaintiff promptly commenced this action seeking rescission of the contract of sale.

The unusual facts of this case, clearly warrant a grant of equitable relief to the buyer who, as a resident of New York City, cannot be expected to have any familiarity with the folklore of the Village of Nyack. Not being a "local," plaintiff could not readily learn that the home he had contracted to purchase is haunted. Whether the source of the spectral apparitions seen by defendant seller are parapsychic or psychogenic, having reported their presence in both a national publication (Readers' Digest) and the local press, defendant is estopped to deny their existence and, as a matter of law, the house is haunted. More to the point, however, no divination is required to conclude that it is defendant's promotional efforts in publicizing her close encounters with these spirits which fostered the home's reputation in the community. The house was included in a five-home walking tour of Nyack and described in a November 27 newspaper article as "a riverfront Victorian (with ghost)." The impact of the reputation thus created goes to the very essence of the bargain between the parties, greatly impairing both the value of the property and its potential for resale.

From the perspective of a person in the position of Plaintiff, a very practical problem arises with respect to the discovery of a paranormal phenomenon: "Who you gonna' call?" as a title song to the movie "Ghostbusters" asks. Applying the strict rule of caveat emptor to a contract involving a house possessed by poltergeists conjures up visions of a psychic or medium routinely accompanying the structural engineer and Terminix man on an inspection of every home subject to a contract of sale.

The doctrine of caveat emptor requires that a buyer act prudently to assess the fitness and value of his purchase and operates to bar the purchaser who fails to exercise due care from seeking the equitable remedy of rescission. It should be apparent, however, that the most meticulous inspection and the search would not reveal the presence of poltergeists at the premises or unearth the property's ghoulish reputation in the community. Therefore, there is no sound policy reason to deny Plaintiff relief for failing to discover a state of affairs which the most prudent purchaser would not be expected to even contemplate.

Where a condition which has been created by the seller materially impairs the value of the contract and is peculiarly within the knowledge of the seller or unlikely to be discovered by a prudent purchaser exercising due care with respect to the subject transaction, nondisclosure constitutes a basis for rescission as a matter of equity.

In the case at bar, Defendant seller deliberately fostered the public belief that her home was possessed. Having undertaken to inform the public-at-large, to whom she has no legal relationship, about the supernatural occurrences on her property, she may be said to owe no less a duty to her buyer. Where, as here, the seller not only takes unfair advantage of the buyer's ignorance, but has created and perpetuated a condition about which he is unlikely to even inquire, enforcement of the contract is offensive to the court's sense of equity. Application of the remedy of rescission is entirely appropriate to relieve the unwitting purchaser from the consequences of a most unnatural bargain.

SECTION 8.10
DECLARATORY
JUDGMENT

If a person's rights are uncertain or disputed, an aggrieved party may request the issuance of a **declaratory judgment** to clarify the uncertainty. As the court noted in **Chanos v. MADAC, LLC, 903 N.Y.S.2d 506 (N.Y., 2010)**, "the primary purpose of a declaratory judgment is to stabilize an uncertain or disputed jural relationship with respect to present or prospective obligations."

For example, suppose a twice-married man dies, leaving life insurance to his "wife" without specifying which spouse is the recipient of the insurance. Either his former spouse or his current wife may request a declaratory judgment in order to ascertain who is entitled to the property. When the court renders a decision on the issue, it will be a final determination of the problem between the parties. Courts are also specific about the conditions that must exist before they will entertain a declaratory judgment. An actual case or controversy must be present that requires court intervention.

HOLMAN V. HOLMAN
2014 WL 2548088 (N. D. ALABAMA 2014)

This case began when Sun Life Assurance Company of Canada (Sun Life) filed a Request for Declaratory Judgment against Cathy Holman and Ella Holman.

Therein, Sun Life asserted that Cathy Holman and Ella Holman had made competing claims to the benefits of Jerry Holman's (the Decedent) life insurance policy which was obtained through his employment with Liberty National Life Insurance Companies, Inc. (Liberty National), and which was insured by Sun Life.

Ella Holman alleged that Sun Life and/or its agents failed to change the beneficiary designation under the Policy from Cathy Holman, the Decedent's ex-wife, to Ella Holman, his wife at the time of his death, pursuant to the Decedent's alleged instructions. Ella Holman further asserted that Sun Life and/or its agents misrepresented to her and the Decedent that the requested designation change had been made.

According to the undisputed facts asserted by Cathy Holman, Ella Holman (Jerry Holman's widow) and Cathy Holman (Jerry Holman's ex-wife and the mother of his adult disabled daughter) have made competing claims for the life insurance proceeds under the Policy. At the time of Jerry Holman's death, Cathy Holman was the sole named beneficiary of the Policy, and Jerry Holman never changed the designated beneficiary under the Policy. Jerry. Holman had named Ella Holman as the beneficiary of three other insurance policies, and she has received payment under each of those other policies; she also received other benefits since his death, including his retirement, his profit-sharing plan, and his pension and thrift plan. There is no evidence of any beneficiary designation naming Ella Holman

as beneficiary under the Policy. Further, it is undisputed that the signature on the designation of beneficiary form for the Policy is Jerry Holman's signature.

Jerry Holman worked for Liberty National as a life insurance agent for 20 and served as a district manager for Liberty National. Because of his job, Jerry Holman was familiar with life insurance and how it works and knew the requirements for naming a policy beneficiary. Ella Holman learned that she was not the named beneficiary of the Policy and that Cathy Holman was the designated beneficiary one week after Jerry Holman's death. Nevertheless, she filed a claim for the Policy benefits. Her asserted reason for doing so was that a few days after she and Jerry Holman married, he told her that he had told the office manager/secretary at Liberty National to get the necessary papers to change the beneficiary designation of any policies and mail them. She also based her belief that she was entitled to the benefits on discussions she had with Jerry Holman about how she would pay bills after he passed away. The implication was that Jerry Holman thought he had changed all beneficiary designations from Cathy Holman to Ella Holman, but in actuality, the beneficiary designation under the Policy was not changed; Jerry Holman never gave Ella Holman any indication that the beneficiary designation under the Policy had not been changed to her. However, Ella Holman never saw him sign a change of beneficiary form. The only change of beneficiary form by Jerry Holman that Ella Holman had been shown named Ella Holman as beneficiary for his profit sharing and retirement plan, his pension plan and his thrift plan.

Cathy Holman asserts that she is entitled to summary judgment because the undisputed evidence is that she is the sole named beneficiary of Jerry Holman's life insurance policy at issue. The evidence of record indeed establishes that Cathy Holman is the sole named beneficiary of the Policy. The Designation of Beneficiary for the Security Plan executed by Jerry Holman shows Cathy Holman as beneficiary of the Policy. Ella Holman admitted in her deposition that the beneficiary designation form completed by Jerry Holman had Cathy Holman's name on it as beneficiary. While Ella Holman has expressed her belief that Jerry Holman changed the beneficiary of the Policy to her (Ella Holman), she has not come forth with any proof that he actually did so. Further, Jerry Holman worked for more than 20 years in the insurance business and was familiar with life insurance policies and the requirements for designating beneficiaries or changing beneficiary designations. It is clear that while Jerry Holman changed the beneficiary designations from Cathy Holman to Ella Holman for his profit sharing and retirement plan, his pension plan and his thrift plan, he did not change the beneficiary designation for the Policy. Cathy Holman remained the designated beneficiary under the Policy, despite the subsequent divorce of Cathy Holman and Jerry Holman.

Based on the foregoing, the motion for summary judgment of Cathy Holman be granted and that she be awarded the $211,000 in life insurance proceeds from the Policy.

QUESTIONS FOR DISCUSSION:

1. What do you think would have been the results if the designated beneficiary merely stated "my wife" without providing a specific name? Would the policy proceeds be given to the decedent's ex-wife when the policy was taken out or the wife of the decedent at the time of his death?

2. Do you think status and process played any role in **Holman v. Holman**? In other words, do you think the court wanted to give some money to the former wife because of the special needs child?

SECTION 8.11
SPECIFIC
PERFORMANCE

Specific performance is an equitable remedy for breach of contract that is used when money damages are inadequate to make the aggrieved party whole. If a court orders specific performance, it simply tells a defendant to do that which he or she has contractually promised to do. Courts generally prefer to award money damages for a breach of contract. Nevertheless, the court will enforce the terms of a contract by requiring performance when the goods are unique and cannot be purchased elsewhere.

Montanile v. Botticelli deals with whether the sale of rare baseball cards is the type of item that gives rise to the equitable remedy of specific performance.

MONTANILE v. BOTTICELLI
2009 WL 196423 (E.D., VA.)

Montanile brought suit against Botticelli for events originating with Botticelli's unsuccessful attempt to purchase vintage baseball cards from Montanile. Montanile's complaint claimed that Botticelli had her falsely arrested and then maliciously prosecuted.

On or about July 16, 2006, Botticelli ordered six vintage baseball cards from Montanile, at the cost of $7,800. Montanile insured and shipped the cards to Botticelli via UPS on August 30, 2006. Botticelli declared that he never received the cards. Montanile alleges that UPS failed to properly deliver the package. She states that she told Botticelli she had filed a claim for the misplaced package with UPS and that the matter would be settled civilly by a refund when UPS remitted the funds.

Botticelli met with the police department in Fair-fax County, Virginia and secured a warrant for Montanile's arrest. He accused Montanile of obtaining money by false pretenses. Montanile was subsequently arrested, jailed for two weeks in New Jersey, and then extradited to Virginia, where she was released after posting bail. The charges against her were ultimately dismissed. Montanile seeks $5 million in compensatory damages and $5 million in punitive damages against Botticelli.

Botticelli submitted a Counterclaim against Montanile requesting specific performance of their agreement. The Counterclaim alleges that Montanile paid Botticelli for the six baseball cards with a check in the amount of $7,820, which Montanile cashed. For weeks, Botticelli did not receive the cards. He e-mailed Montanile numerous times and requested a tracking number for the shipment. Montanile responded first by telling Botticelli that his shipment was still being processed, then that the package was scheduled to ship later in the week, and later, when Botticelli threatened to ask for a refund, that she was waiting "for payments to clear our bank" and that the package should have been on its way.

When, approximately six weeks after ordering the baseball cards, Botticelli told her that he was planning to meet with the police because he had not received the cards and Montanile was ignoring his e-mails and phone calls, Montanile told him that the package had not yet shipped because she was still waiting for one card to arrive. The next day, Montanile e-mailed Botticelli to tell him that the package had shipped. The following day, Botticelli received a sealed, empty box. He e-mailed Montanile to request an immediate refund. Montanile never delivered the baseball cards and did not refund the $7,820. Botticelli alleges that Montanile never actually possessed the baseball cards.

Botticelli's claim for specific performance requests the tender of the six rare baseball cards he ordered in the condition in which they were advertised at the time of sale. Montanile moved to dismiss the Counterclaim. This motion is before the Court.

Botticelli's counterclaim requests specific performance of the agreement that he and Montanile reached: that he would pay $7,820 for six vintage baseball cards. He claims to have no adequate remedy at law because the baseball cards are rare, highly unique, and specialized goods. Botticelli requests "specific performance of the agreement . . . that Plaintiff tender the six rare baseball cards in the condition advertised at the time of sale."

Specific performance is an equitable remedy that may be considered where the remedy at law is inadequate and the nature of the contract would allow specific enforcement without great practical difficulties. A remedy at law is not adequate if it is partial; instead, an adequate remedy at law must reach the end intended, and actually compel a performance of the duty in question. Specific performance is addressed to the reasonable and sound discretion of the court. A contract must be complete and certain and the essential elements of price and terms of sale must have been agreed upon before a court of equity will specifically enforce the contract.

Here, Botticelli has alleged that the parties entered into a "valid and enforceable agreement for the sale, delivery and purchase of the six rare baseball cards," that he performed by paying for the cards, and that Montanile failed to perform by never sending him the cards. Looking at the face of the Counterclaim, it appears that Botticelli has pled a claim for specific performance.

Montanile suggests that the issue is "moot" because she will reimburse the defendant as soon as UPS pays her the insurance proceeds for the lost baseball cards. Montanile's promise that she will refund Botticelli's money at some point in the future does not serve to make the issue of specific performance moot. First, Botticelli's claim requests specific performance, not a refund. Second, he has pled facts sufficient to allege that Montanile did not perform the contract. Montanile's statement that she will refund the payment at some indefinite point in the future-depending on the outcome of a pending insurance dispute-has no bearing whatsoever on the merits of Botticelli's claim, which alleges that a breach of contract has already occurred. Montanile's statement that Botticelli will be reimbursed after UPS pays her does not make Botticelli's claim against her moot. The Court will not dismiss the claim for specific performance.

For the foregoing reasons, the Court will deny Plaintiff's Motion to Dismiss Defendant's Counter-claim.

SECTION 8.12
MICROBREWERY
PURCHASE

PARK, BROWN & SMITH, P.C.
ATTORNEYS AT LAW
MEMORANDUM

PROBLEM EIGHT—B

To: All Law Clerks

FROM: Peter Smith, Esquire

RE: Purchase of a Microbrewery

It has been a dream of Joe Roberts to install a microbrewery at Tyler's Sports Bar and Grill. While it requires a significant investment of capital, making beer on the premises is the rage among beer drinkers and will attract more customers to the bar.

Recently, Joe was approached by his nephew, Marcus Roberts, about equipping the bar with a microbrewery. It turns out that Joe was very fond of Marcus and helped raise him since Marcus' father died at an earlier age. Marcus worked for a bar in Florida that recently went out of business. He told Joe that he could help Roberts fulfill his dreams of making craft beer. The nephew explained that the equipment for a microbrewery costs about $1 million, and it can produce 30 barrels of beer at a time. One barrel makes about 31 gallons of brew, which translates to 320 12-ounce glasses.

Roberts did some quick calculations and realized the potential boom to Tyler's business. The only problem was the capital investment to buy the equipment. The bar was still paying off the loan to open the establishment, so Joe could not afford a $1 million purchase. The nephew said not to worry. Marcus just so happened to be involved in the sale of a microbrewery in Florida and he was selling the contents of the business, including the equipment to make craft beer. This included all of the mashing, fermentation, cooling, cleaning, and packaging equipment that Tyler's would need. More importantly, the equipment could be purchased used for $200,000.

Roberts was intrigued but he knew nothing about the brewing process or the equipment needed to make craft beer. Marcus said that he had undergone extensive training on the process as part of his past employment at the bar in Florida. The nephew even quipped that he would teach his uncle how to operate the equipment and would finance the purchase which would allow Tyler's to pay back the money over a ten-year period. Joe was floored by the generous offer but knew that Tyler's could not afford to pay any more than $200,000, and even that was a stretch. The nephew said that he would take care of everything and Joe should consider the deal done. The parties hugged and Joe told Marcus that his father would have been very proud of him.

Joe set out to reconstruct the bar to accommodate the brewing equipment based upon a design supplied by the nephew. After several months of remodeling, Tyler's was ready to proceed and Joe told his nephew the exciting news. A few hours later, Marcus appeared at the bar and said that he needed Joe to sign some papers so that the nephew could remove the equipment from the property of the Florida brewery and transport it to Pennsylvania for installation. Joe was in the middle of making food for the Friday night's very busy happy hour so he just signed the document without reading it. After all, Marcus knew that Tyler's Sports Bar and Grill could not pay more than $200,000 and he trusted his nephew.

A few weeks later, the equipment arrived, and the nephew along with a crew of 3 men, had the microbrewery up and operating in no time. Marcus even spent three additional days showing the staff of Tyler's how to make craft beer.

Everything was going marvelously until Joe received a certified letter from Fidelity Finance Company. The letter explained that Fidelity had purchased the loan contract from Marcus and directed Tyler's Sport Bar and Grill to make the monthly payments of $4,080 to them. Joe had no idea what Fidelity was talking about so he called the loan officer. At this time, Joe leaned that the contract was for $300,000 with an interest rate of 15%. Joe vigorously protested saying that Tyler's was only obligated to pay $200,000 and that no interested rate was assigned to the loan. The loan officer then read off the list of itemized charges. While it was true that Tyler's was being charged $200,000 for the equipment, there was a $50,000 expense for the removal of the equipment from the Florida bar and installation of the microbrewery at Tyler's. Transportation charges were $10,000 and licensing fees and taxes paid to Pennsylvania amounted to another $40,000. Joe angrily protested but the finance company responded that Joe should take up the matter with his nephew. After all, the loan officer retorted, the finance company had purchased the $300,000 note in good faith and Tyler's had to pay the contract price of $4,080 a month. This amounted to a total payment over the life of the loan of $489,600.

Joe's nephew has skipped town and no one knows where he is hiding. I never liked the kid and I don't know why Joe trusted him so much. My idea is to sue the finance company for reformation of the contract. I want the court to reform the contract price on the agreement to be $200,000 and eliminate all of the other charges. I found the following case. Please read it and let me know if you think we would be successful in getting a court to reform the agreement.

KISH v. NUSTURA
190 OR. APP. 458 (2003)

Defendant Nustura is the personal representative of the estate of her father, Laszlo Szender. In early 1990, Szender's health was failing. His health problems led him to seek a buyer for a 24-unit apartment complex that he and his wife lived in. Szender, a native Hungarian, never learned to read or write English.

Plaintiff was interested in buying the apartments and began to negotiate with Szender to purchase them. Plaintiff eventually agreed to buy the apartments for $600,000. Most aspects of their initial agreement were memorialized in a letter that plaintiff wrote to Szender. The letter, after it was modified by the parties, provided that plaintiff was to pay Szender a down payment of $40,000, monthly payments of $2,000 for ten years, and a final payment of $90,000. The letter also provided that Plaintiff was to assume a $230,000 mortgage on the apartments. After further negotiations, Plaintiff agreed to several additional provisions that Szender requested. They included Plaintiff's acceptance of the apartments "as is" and a provision that entitled Szender and his wife to live in their apartment rent free for ten years after the sale. Plaintiff also agreed to prepare a written contract that accurately reflected her and Szender's letter and oral agreement. Both Plaintiff and Szender signed the contract on January 29, 1991.

The written contract did not, however, accurately reflect the parties' oral agreement. It gave only Szender-not Szender and his wife-the right to live in their apartment rent free. It also provided that the interest payments that Plaintiff made on the mortgage would apply to the $600,000 purchase price for the apartments. That change meant that the amount that Plaintiff paid to Szender would not equal the agreed amount of $370,000. The change was never discussed with Szender. Plaintiff did not present Szender with the contract until the day that the parties signed it, and she did not translate it for him. Plaintiff continued to represent to Szender that the written contract accurately reflected their agreement.

Over the next seven years, Plaintiff made payments to Szender that totaled $630,000. During that period, the Szenders lived in their apartment rent free. Mr. Szender died in 1998. After his death, Plaintiff demanded that Mrs. Szender pay rent to live in the apartment. Mrs. Szender subsequently moved out of her apartment. Plaintiff then brought an action for specific performance of the contract. Defendant alleged counterclaims, including a claim for reformation of the contract. The court reformed the contract to include Mrs. Szender as a beneficiary of the ten-year, rent-free period on the apartment and to provide that the interest payments on the mortgage were not to be counted as payments toward the $600,000 purchase price.

To obtain reformation of a contract, a party must prove by clear and convincing evidence (1) that there was an antecedent agreement to which the contract can be reformed; (2) that there was a mutual mistake or a unilateral mistake on the part of the party seeking reformation and inequitable conduct on the part of the other party; and (3) that the party seeking reformation was not guilty of gross negligence. Clear and convincing evidence is evidence that makes a fact in issue highly probable. Clear describes the character of unambiguous evidence, whether true or false; convincing describes the effect of evidence on an observer.

The range of misconduct termed inequitable is quite broad, varying from the most egregious and concrete, such as fraud, to somewhat less egregious misconduct, sometimes described as over-reaching or sharp practice. Inequitable conduct includes a party's silence where that party knows that the other party is materially mistaken as to a writing's scope and effect, but remains silent, hoping to take advantage of the other's mistake.

Plaintiff and Szender agreed that Plaintiff would purchase the apartment complex by paying Szender $370,000 and assuming a $230,000 mortgage, for a total purchase price of $600,000. Szender and his wife were also to live in their apartment rent free for ten years. Although the written contract deviated from the parties' agreement, Szender did not learn of the differences before he signed the contract because he could not read the contract and did not have anyone translate it for him. Instead, he relied on Plaintiff's assurances that the written contract accurately reflected the parties' earlier agreement.

Szender trusted Plaintiff because they were both Hungarian immigrants and were friends. For several months before the parties signed the contract, Plaintiff represented to the Szenders and others that the Szenders would have the right to live in their apartment for ten years and never gave Szender any reason to believe that the interest payments Plaintiff made on the mortgage would count toward the purchase price. Szender spoke hardly any English, and neither his wife understood English well enough to translate the contract. Plaintiff was the only person at the signing who could have translated the document and Mr. Szender trusted her. Plaintiff took advantage of Szender's trust in her and his inability to read or speak English. Plaintiff presented Szender with the written contract the day that the parties signed it and told him that it represented their prior agreement when she knew that it did not. That was not mere silence with the knowledge that Szender was materially mistaken as to the contents of the contract; it was an active misrepresentation. Because of his misplaced trust in Plaintiff, Szender signed the contract believing that it conformed to their prior agreement. Defendant has established by clear and convincing evidence that plaintiff was aware of Szender's mistaken belief that the contract conformed to their prior agreement and has therefore proved the second element of her claim for reformation.

A party seeking reformation must establish that the mistake that the party seeks to reform in a contract was not the product of the party's gross negligence. For conduct to amount to gross negligence, it must go beyond mere oversight, inadvertence, or mistake and, instead, must amount to a degree of inattention that is inexcusable under the circumstances. Gross negligence is a fact-intensive inquiry to determine if a party's inattention is excusable. A party's failure to read a contract, standing alone, generally is insufficient to constitute gross negligence.

Here, Szender's failure to have the document translated into Hungarian is akin to a failure to read the document. Although that failure was perhaps negligent, it does not amount to inexcusable inattention under the circumstances. In fact, the circumstances indicate that Szender's failure to have the document translated was excusable. He was presented with the contract the day that he was to sign it. The contract was written in English, a language that he could not read. Plaintiff, who spoke Hungarian, told him that the contract reflected their prior agreement. Although Szender should have reviewed the contract with the aid of a translator or a lawyer who spoke Hungarian before signing it, he did not do that because he trusted Plaintiff. That failure, under the circumstances, does not amount to gross negligence. We therefore conclude that the trial court correctly reformed the parties' contract.

PROBLEM EIGHT—B
ANSWER SHEET

Name _____   **Please Print Clearly**

1. Do you think we can convince the court to reform the contract so that Tyler's does not have to pay the large monthly payments? Please explain your answer in detail based upon an analysis of our facts and the holding in **Kish v. Nustura**.

_____

_____

_____

_____

_____

_____

_____

_____

_____

_____

_____

_____

_____

_____

_____

_____

_____

_____

2. Is there anything from the chapter on contract law that can help us?

_____

_____

_____

_____

_____

_____

_____

_____

_____

_____

_____

_____

_____

_____

_____

_____

_____

_____

_____

SECTION 8.13
PROBLEM CASES

1. The New York Yankees told the City of New York that the team was going to play it's home opening series with the Detroit Tigers in Denver instead of at Yankee Stadium. The City of New York filed for injunctive relief to prevent the implementation of that agreement with the City of Denver. The facts show that after extensive renovations to Yankee Stadium were made by the City, it was discovered that there were certain structural flaws in the bleachers in right and left field. Additional permanent repairs were scheduled to be made between the close of the last baseball season and the opening game of the new season. Those plans were done with the approval of the Yankees. Nevertheless, the Yankees requested a guarantee that the repairs would be completed in a timely manner at the start of the new baseball season. The City stated that under the worse case scenario, only 1,000 to 2,000 seats would be unavailable for the Yankees' home opener. Nevertheless, this information led to the Yankees scheduling it's home opener in Denver. Is the City of New York entitled to an injunction to prevent the Yankees from playing in Denver even though the repairs had not been completed but only 2,000 seats would have been unavailable for the Yankees home opener? **City of New York v. New York Yankees, 458 N.Y.S. 2d 486 (N.Y., 1983).**

2. Brett Michaels and Pamela Anderson Lee sought a Temporary Restraining Order to prevent the dissemination of a videotape in which Michaels and Lee had a registered copyright. The videotape showed the two high profile plaintiffs engaging in sexual intercourse. Internet Entertainment Group, Inc., claimed that it obtained the videotape from a purported "agent" of Michaels, who allegedly sold the tape to the Internet Entertainment Group for $15,000. Will Michaels and Lee be successful in blocking the distribution of the tape since IEG obtained a copy of the videotape from a third person? Will the distribution of the tape cause irresponsible harm? **Pamela Lee Anderson v. Internet Entertainment Group, Inc. 5 F. Supp. 2d 823 (C.D. Cal., 1998).**

3. The State of Washington enacted an "Erotic Sound Recordings Statute" which subjected all distributors of sound recordings to civil and criminal proceedings for distribution to minors of "erotic material." A number of recording artists filed a declaratory judgment against the state in an attempt to have the court determine that the statute violated their substantive due process right. Is a declaratory judgment a proper action in order to invalidate a statute which is believed to be unconstitutional? **Soundgarden v. Bikenberry, 871 P. 2d 1050 (Wash., 1994).**

4. Star Magazine published an article about Rodney Dangerfield entitled, "Vegas Casino Accuses Candy Shack Funnyman; Rodney Dangerfield Swills Vodka by the tumblerful, smokes pot all day and uses cocaine."

Dangerfield sued Star Magazine for defamation and requested punitive damages. The purpose of punitive damages is to punish the wrong-doer, and this is accomplished by awarding money based on the net worth of the defendant. Star Magazine's statement of operation for the fiscal year reflected a net loss. Dangerfield, however, argued that the financial condition of Star's parent owner is relevant to the tabloid's financial condition and should have been disclosed to the jury. Is the comedian correct? **Rodney Dangerfield v. Star Editorial, Inc., 25 Media L. Rep. 1379 (9th Cir., 1996).**

SECTION 8.14 INTERNET REFERENCES

For more information on nominal damages, see the following internet reference:

- **www.seyfarth.com/practice/labor/articles/ll_1221.html**
  An article about a Supreme Court decision regarding nominal damages is located at this address.

Footnotes:

1. Margaret Cronin Fisk, Largest U.S. Jury Verdicts of 2012, Bloomberg, January 17, 2013, http://www.bloomberg.com/news/2013-01-18/largest-u-s-jury-verdicts-of-2012-table-.html (last visited September 28, 2013).

2. Maria Valdez Haubrich, Is Your Small Business at Risk of Being Sued?, Grow Smart Biz, http://www.networksolutions.com/smallbusiness/2012/10/is-your-small-business-at-risk-of-being-sued/ (last visited September 28, 2013).

3. Trudie Longren, *Differences Between Legal Remedies & Equitable Remedies of Contract Law*, Chron, http://smallbusiness.chron.com/differences-between-legal-reme-dies-equitable-remedies-contract-law-66084.html (last visited January 24, 2018.)

4. *Id.*

5. Remedies: An Overview, Legal Information Institute, Cornell University Law School, http://www.law.cornell.edu/wex/remedy (last visited September 28, 2013).

6. *Id.*

7. Damages – Generally, Pennsylvania Suggested Standard Civil Jury Instruction, Fourth Edition, Volume II, Chapter XIX – Contracts, revised December 2012.

8. Joesph Bassano, et. al., Loss of Business, 25 C.J.S. Damages Section 167, Database updated September 2013.

9. **Tillett v. Lippert, 275 Montana 1 (1996).**

10. Dietz, et. al., Certainty- Profits From New Business, 22 Am. Jur.2d Damages Section 445, Database updated August 2013.

11. 24 *Williston on Contracts* § 65.2 (4th ed.)

12. Punitive Damages – General Instructions, Pennsylvania Suggested Standard Civil Jury Instructions, Fourth Edition, Volume 1, Revised December 2012.

13. **El Al Israel Airlines, Ltd. v. Tsui Yuan Tseng,** 525 U.S. 155, 119 S.Ct. 662 (1999).

14. **Board of Trustees, Sheet Metal Workers' Nat. Pension Fund v. Illinois Range, Inc., 71 F.Supp.2d 864 (N.D. Ill., 1999).**

KEY TERMS

Compensatory Damages

Declaratory Judgment

Equitable Relief

Equity

Exemplary Damage

Injunction

Judicial Remedy

Liquidated Damages

Mandatory Injunction

Monetary Compensation

Nominal Damages

Pain and Suffering

Permanent Injunction

Preliminary Injunction

Prohibitory Injunction

Punitive Damages

Recission

Reformation

Rescinded

Restitution

Special Damages

Specific Performance

Temporary Restraining Order (TRO)

Warsaw Convention

Part Three
Corporate Governance

Creating a new enterprise requires more than a good business plan and the ability to work hard. Multiple laws and regulations influence how the entity is formed and operated. Decisions with legal implications include whether to form a corporation or sole proprietorship and whether the entity can use a certain logo or name. Legal issues, however, do not stop with the formation of the business. The entrepreneur is confronted with a myriad of decisions in the daily operation of the venture that have legal implications and are subject to government regulations. These range from the benefits that must be offered to an employee to the information that is required to be disclosed if the enterprise wishes to sell its stock. And, these laws and rules only become more complex if the business wishes to sell its products outside of the United States.

Corporate governance is the term applied to the structure and process for running a business. This part of the book will discuss some of the laws and regulations that influence business decisions.

Chapter Nine will discuss the various types of entities that can be selected in starting a business. While it is common knowledge that the business can be formed as a sole proprietorship, partnership or corporation, a number of other more exotic choices exist such as the family limited liability partnership and sub-chapter S corporation. This chapter will also explore some of the laws that regulate the business operation such as the Securities Act of 1933 and the Dodd Frank Act.

Chapter Ten will explore employer and employee relations and will look at the differences between an employee and an independent contractor. Other issues will include the hiring, retention and supervision of workers, workplace hazards and employee benefits.

Chapter Eleven will provide an introduction to international law. While half of the net profits of large businesses come from international trade, there are a number of risks involved in global transactions such as a change in the leadership of the foreign government and economic or currency risks. A number of organizations and alliance between counties have also been forged in an attempt to increase trade and to make international transactions more uniform. These range from the United Nations to the World Trade Organization.

Chapter Twelve will examine intellectual property and cyberlaw issues. The four types of intellectual property: patents, copyrights, trademarks, and trade secrets will be discussed along with the unique issues involving business transactions conducted electronically such as domain names and e-contracts.

CHAPTER 9

CORPORATE GOVERNANCE AND BUSINESS ORGANIZATIONS
BY: S. JAY SKLAR AND SAMUEL D. HODGE, JR

Remind people that profit is the difference between revenue and expense. This makes you look smart.

—Scott Adams

SECTION 9.1 CORPORATE GOVERNANCE

Corporate governance is a multidimensional subject that is defined as the structure by which businesses are controlled. It involves the structure and process for running the organization including the relations among the officers, Board of Directors, shareholders, and other stakeholders. Good corporate governance fosters sustainable economic development by enhancing the operation of firms and increasing their productivity and access to capital.[1]

Corporate governance is based upon ideals such as managing the business with integrity and fairness, being open in dealings with others, providing the necessary disclosures, following the laws, answerability to the stakeholders and dedication to running the operation in an ethical manner. The managers of the enterprise must also separate corporate funds and personal funds while running the business.[2]

Five principles for good corporate governance include:

1. **Ethics:** establish and maintain a clear ethical pathway for operating the entity;

2. **Align Business Goals:** fashion goals, arrived at through proper stakeholder decision making models;

3. **Strategic Management:** maintain an effective strategy which is geared towards stakeholder value;

4. **Organization:** form an entity structured to achieve sound corporate governance; and

5. **Reporting:** establish reporting systems designed to provide transparency and accountability.[3]

This approach to sound corporate governance recognizes that the interests of the shareholders are not always equal, but it does not mean that those with a larger interest in the business are more important than the minority owners. In fact, proper corporate governance requires that all interest parties should be treated equally.[4]

This Chapter will explain the different types of business entities that can be used to run an enterprise and will explore some of the legislative pronouncements that have been enacted to ensure fairness in the business world.

SECTION 9.2
TYPES OF ENTITIES

An entrepreneur is an individual who manages a business, assuming the risks in order to make a profit. Starting a business can also have its benefits such as: being your own boss, maintaining your own schedule, and making money doing something you desire to do. However, a successful entrepreneur requires proper planning, creativity and hard work.[5]

On the other hand, a business enterprise is centered on an entity in which the owner plans to utilize in order to make a profit and succeeding in the business world. These entities are created by entrepreneurs who generally have the expertise required to launch the business, possess an idea about a product or service and know how it can be used to create a customer base and turn a profit.[6]

The U.S. Small Business Administration lists the following qualities commonly associated with being a successful entrepreneur:

- **Comfortable with taking risks:** Entrepreneurship involves uncertainty, and if a person is adverse to uncertainty, then entrepreneurship may not be the best fit.

- **Independent:** Entrepreneurs cannot be afraid of rejection.

- **Persuasive:** If you cannot persuade others, you may find entrepreneurship to be challenging.

- **Ability to negotiate:** A business person must be able to negotiate everything from leases to contract terms.

- **Creativity:** Entrepreneurs must be able to think creatively and be able to take advantage of new opportunities.

- **Support by others:** A strong support system is needed.[7]

The most common business organizations include the sole proprietorship, a partnership and a corporation. Hybrid forms consist of a limited partnership, a limited liability partnership, a family limited liability partnership, a subchapter **S corporation** and a limited liability corporation. Each form has its own advantages, disadvantages and tax consequences. Choosing the correct form of organization is a critical first step and should be made in consultation with an attorney and accountant. Considerations include the cost in bringing the business to life, the liability of its owners, management issues and dissolution. The reader needs to keep in mind that no one form is automatically "better" than any other. They each have aspects that might be appropriate at a particular time in the development of a business.

The Internal Revenue Service defines a **sole proprietor** as someone who owns an unincorporated business by himself or herself. The sole proprietorship, or business trader, is not a separate entity and the identity remains that of the business owner who controls the operation of the enterprise. The businesses that operate under this type of structure are endless and can include a vendor selling food from a truck at a University to a lawyer or accountant.

A. Creation

The sole proprietorship is the least expensive, most simple and common business to form. It has one owner who usually operates the *unincorporated* business under his or her name. There can be many employees but only one owner who has personal liability for all of the business debts and obligations. A sole proprietorship is also not expensive to establish. The owner does not need the permission of a governmental agency in order to open the business but may be required to obtain a business license or permit in the county of operation. The status of a sole proprietor arises automatically from the business operations. In fact, an entrepreneur may already be engaged in a **sole proprietorship** without knowing it. If the individual is a computer programer or freelance writer, for example, he or she is a sole proprietor.[8]

A sole proprietor usually signs contracts in his or her name, because the entity has no independent identity under the law. The owner will usually have customers issue checks in the owner's name, even if the business goes by a fictitious name. Sole proprietors often mix personal and business assets, something that a different business form cannot do. Sole proprietors do not adhere to formalities such as voting and meetings and they can bring lawsuits in their own name. A business can also begin as a sole proprietor and change to a more complex entity like a corporation as the business develops.[9] The owner may be required to file a **fictitious name registration** if the entrepreneur wishes to do business under a name other than his or her own which is not being used by another entity. An example of a fictitious name registration would be Joe Roberts doing business at Tyler's Sports Bar and Grill.

B. Liability

The sole proprietorship has the greatest risk to the owner since the liability for the debts of the business is unlimited and the entrepreneur's personal assets can be seized to satisfy the business obligations. The entrepreneur may attempt to limit the exposure of personal assets to the creditors by holding all property jointly with the spouse. As one may remember from the chapter on Property Law, the assets of a husband and wife are considered owned as tenancy by the entireties and cannot be seized by a creditor for the debts of one spouse. The owner may also reduce the risk of suit from a customer who is injured on the premises or by use of a defective product sold by the merchant by obtaining the appropriate liability insurance.

C. Tax Implications

The simplicity of the sole proprietorship is further evidenced by the fact that the owner keeps all of the profits from the business operation and pays personal income tax on them on what is known as a Schedule "C." A separate tax return is not filed as is done with a corporation so there is no issue of double taxation. The opportunity to raise capital, however, is limited to the owner's personal resources or by obtaining a loan.

D. Termination

The business operation terminates whenever the owner stops doing business and no separate forms have to be filed with the government putting the company out of business. Since the owner is the business, it terminates upon the proprietor's death.

SECTION 9.4 PARTNERSHIP

A **partnership** is an association of two or more people to carry on a business as co-owners. The partners will share in the profits and losses of the enterprise on an equal basis unless there is an agreement setting forth some other arrangement. This type of enterprise is defined by state law and is not limited to individuals. It can include corporations, groups of people or companies. As defined by the Internal Revenue Service:

> "A partnership is the relationship existing between two or more persons who join to carry on a trade or business. Each person contributes money, property, labor or skill, and expects to share in the profits and losses of the business."

A. Creation

No magic words are needed to create a partnership and the parties do not need a written agreement even though that is strongly recommended in order to avoid conflicts over the business operation. In fact, a partnership can arise by implication. For instance, two or more people who join together to operate a business may be deemed to have formed a partnership regardless of their intent or failure to realize that a partnership has arisen.

Three essential elements are examined to determine if a partnership has been created:

1. The sharing of profits and losses by two or more people is prima facie evidence of a partnership. In other words, the law will assume that a partnership has been created if there is a sharing of profits. The burden then shifts to the persons involved in the business to show that they were not partners;

2. A joint ownership of the assets of the business; and

3. An equal right in the management of the enterprise.

The following case discusses the elements that create the existence of a partnership when a written agreement has not been made setting up the partnership.

HILLME V. CHASTAIN AND C & H CUSTOM CABINETS, INC.
75 S.W.3D 315 (MO. APP. S.D. 2002)

Chastain appeals from the order finding that a partnership existed between Chastain and Hillme.

A partnership is defined as an association of two or more persons to carry on as co-owners of a business for profit. A partnership has also been judicially defined as a contract of two or more competent persons to place their money, effects, labor and skill, or some or all of them, in lawful commerce or business and to divide the profits and bear the loss in certain proportions. The partnership agreement may be written, expressed orally, or implied from the acts and conduct of the parties. The intent of the parties is the primary factor for determining whether such a relationship exists. The required intent necessary to find a partnership existed is not the intent to form a partnership, but the intent to enter into a relationship, which in law constitutes a partnership.

A partnership agreement may be implied from conduct and circumstances of the parties and the parties are not required to know all the legal implications of a partnership. A voice in the management of the partnership business, a share of the profits of the partnership business, and a corresponding risk of loss and liability to partnership creditors are all indications of a partnership.

The record shows that Chastain and Hillme had each worked for a period of time at Classic Cabinets, a cabinet making shop. Hillme had worked there for about four years and had eight or nine years experience in cabinet making. Chastain

had also worked for the same concern and for the most part performed staining, finishing and installation work.

In April of 1997, Chastain and Hillme made the decision to go into business together. Hillme testified that they both agreed to divide the workload, profits, expenses, and losses equally, that is on a "50/50" basis. No written partnership agreement was executed. Each drew a flat and equal amount of pay each week. According to Hillme, any money left over they agreed to let accumulate in the partnership account.

Hillme wrote a check for the purchase of plywood and Chastain also contributed monies for the venture. Chastain rented a building and purchased some woodworking equipment. He also negotiated the rent for the building. Both spent time cleaning the building and prepared to move into the building. Hillme purchased furnace parts to heat the building. Both contributed tools and equipment to the business. A business insurance policy was obtained. The parties named the business "C & H Custom Cabinets." The "C" stood for Chastain's last name and the "H" stood for Hillme's last name.

During the day-to-day operation, Chastain ran errands and applied stain and finish to cabinets. Hillme's time was generally spent building the cabinets. Chastain was also in charge of paying bills and scheduling installations. A checking account for the business was opened at "Central Bank." The name shown on their checks was

"C & H Cabinets." It was Hillme's understanding that as business partners, they were both owners of the jointly held account at the bank. Both issued checks from the account and each carried the concern's checkbook on occasion.

In 1997, Chastain and Hillme decided their business required a cargo trailer for hauling cabinets to the installation site. They discussed the purchase and both went to a vehicle dealer to select one. According to Hillme, it was his understanding that the cargo trailer was to be paid out of the partnership account. A bank loan was initially obtained for the purchase of the cargo trailer. Both Chastain and Hillme personally signed the note for the loan. Unbeknownst to Hillme, title to the cargo trailer was placed in Chastain's name only. Hillme also stated that it was not until after his lawsuit had commenced that he had found out how the title to the cargo trailer was held.

Hillme further testified that in October of 1998, a Dodge pickup truck was purchased. Hillme related that funds generated by the partnership were used for this purpose and he understood that the vehicle was to be a partnership vehicle. According to Hillme, Chastain informed him that once the 1994 pickup truck was paid for, the partnership would buy Hillme a pickup truck. However, the pickup truck was not titled in the name of the business. Rather, it was titled in Chastain's name. Once again, Hillme testified it was only after the lawsuit was filed that he first learned that the pickup truck was titled solely in Chastain's name.

According to Hillme, Chastain showed him the business records for 1997 and gave Hillme tax documents for the 1997 tax year so that Hillme could file his individual return. Each of the parties claimed half of the business expenses, such as utilities, and each claimed half of the gross income. At trial, Chastain claimed that Hillme was a subcontractor and then an employee. Significantly, Chastain's 1997 tax return did not show that he had paid Hillme either as an employee or as a

contract laborer. Indeed, as previously set out for the tax year involved, Chastain split the expenses of the business with Hillme.

Eventually, disagreements over management caused Hillme to open his own cabinet making business some time in 1999. By then Hillme had become aware of Chastain's claims that they were not partners.

In his appeal, Chastain maintains the trial court erred in finding that a partnership existed between himself and Hillme. Chastain asserts that Hillme failed to demonstrate the necessary elements of a partnership, such as co-ownership of business assets, mutual rights of control of the business, an agreement in fact, and the right to share in profits and duty to share in losses. We disagree.

While each evidentiary factor standing alone may not show a partnership, it is clear that the combination of the following probative factors is supportive of the trial court's conclusion that a partnership was created by Chastain and Hillme in 1997.

The factors we note are the following: The name of the business was based on each party's last name, all of the advertising included each party's name and home telephone number, the day-to-day operation of the business relied on each one's specialized skills—Hillme's greater experience in cabinet making and Chastain's accounting and management skills, and each party co-signed the note for the cargo trailer. Additionally, Hillme had a voice in the management of the partnership. This is evidenced by his "veto" of using partnership assets for the construction of an additional shop building. Furthermore, during the first year of the partnership in 1997, each divided equally the income and expenses generated through the business.

We cannot say that the trial court erred in finding that a partnership existed between Chastain and Hillme. Sufficient evidence in the record supports the trial court's judgment. The trial court's judgment is affirmed.

B. Management

The Partnership Agreement usually sets forth the rights and duties of the partners. If there are no provisions in the agreement to the contrary, the law imposes certain rights and duties between the partners. For instance, all partners have an equal right to participate in the management of the business' affairs. This right, however, can be limited or altered by the partnership agreement whereby one or more partners may have a greater role in the operation of the enterprise. A majority vote is usually needed for the approval of most daily operational aspects of partnership operations, but unanimous consent of the partners may be required for certain significant actions, such as the admission of a new partner or the purchase of a major asset. The following is a partial listing of some of these types of circumstances:

- Altering the essential nature of the partnership business

- Amending the partnership agreement

- Admitting new partners

- Entering into a wholly new business

- Assigning partnership property for the benefit of creditors

- Disposing of partnership goodwill

- Entering a confession of judgment or submitting a claim to arbitration

- Engaging in any action that would make it impossible to carry out the partnership's business

As for the duty of loyalty and good faith dealings, each partner has the duty to devote his or her time, skill and energy to the partnership's business. This is not a separately commensurable activity, unless otherwise agreed. Basically, the partners' "pay" is their share of the profits. The partnership books and records must also be made available to all partners.

Partners act in a fiduciary relationship to each other. This requires the utmost degree of trust and loyalty among them and they must act for the benefit of the partnership and not for their individual benefit. As the court stated in **Leff v. Gunter 33 Cal.3d 508 (1983):**

A partnership establishes a fiduciary relationship, and partners are held to the standards and duties of a trustee in their dealings with each other. In all proceedings connected with the conduct of the partnership, every partner is bound to act in the highest good faith to his co-partner and may not obtain any advantage over him in the partnership affairs by the slightest misrepresentation, concealment, threat or adverse pressure of any kind.

C. Liability

Like the sole proprietorship, the partners have unlimited liability for the debts of the business. Each is liable for the full debts of the business. A creditor, however, must first seek satisfaction of the debt out of the partnership assets. If this fails to satisfy the obligation, the creditor may then advance a claim against any single partner or all of the partners for the remaining partnership obligations. This is known as **joint and several liability.** While it may seem unfair that the creditor can go after one partner over another, the owner who pays a partnership debt may sue the other partners for reimbursement. This is known as **indemnification.**

Each partner is also an **agent** for the partnership and other partners. This means that one partner can bind the others on business matters with third parties even if those actions exceed the person's authority. For instance, a partner who buys a car in the partnership's name will bind the other partners to that contract, even if the partnership agreement states that no one partner may make a purchase for the business that exceeds $1,000 without the consent of the others.

D. Taxation

A partnership is not a taxable entity. Rather, the profits of the business are apportioned to each partner who pays personal income tax on his or her share. The partnership, however, is required to file an **information return** each year with the Internal Revenue Service, showing such things as income, deductions, gains, and losses but it pays no taxes. Rather, the partnership "passes through" the profits or losses to the individual partners who file a Schedule K-1. In this way, each partner includes his or her share of the partnership's income or loss on that person's personal tax return. On the other hand, partners are not employees and are not issued a W-2 tax form.

E. Termination

When certain events occur, the partnership will **terminate** such as at the expiration of the term of the partnership, the business objectives have been reached or the partners by agreement terminate the operation. For instance, the partnership agreement can provide that the business will operate for a set period of time at which point it will terminate. If no fixed time is specified, the partnership is one at will in which any partner at any time can dissolve the business without violating the agreement. The following is a sample clause in a partnership agreement concerning the termination of the business:

> "The term of this partnership shall continue from the date of this Agreement until the death, retirement, or withdrawal of all partners or until the partnership is terminated as provided in this Agreement."

A change in the relationship of the partners that signals an unwillingness or inability to carry on the partnership, dissolves that relationship and leads to a termination of the entity. Such a termination is a two-stage process. The first step is the **dissolution** process, which means that a partner ceases to be associated with the venture and the second step is known as the **winding up**. This involves the collecting and distribution of the partnership assets. At the completion of the winding up, the partnership's existence is terminated.

As a sole proprietorship terminates upon the death of the owner, a similar principle applies to a partnership. The original partnership will automatically terminate upon the death of any owner.

There is also a distinction between the power to dissolve the partnership and the right to dissolve the business. Since a partnership is a voluntary agreement to act together, any partner has the power to dissolve the partnership but may not have the right to terminate the business without incurring legal liability to the others.

If liquidation occurs following the death of a partner, there is a fiduciary duty upon the remaining partners to act without delay and act in good faith to the estate of the deceased partner.

The intent to dissolve must be communicated to all partners. This notice can be made by word or act.

The leaving partner must give notice to third parties who have dealt with the partnership, if he or she wants to be relieved from the future obligations of the remaining partners. Actual notice must be given to all those who have extended credit to the partnership, otherwise a public notice is sufficient.

After dissolution and notice, the partners cannot create new obligations for the partnership. Instead, the partnership moves to the second step in the termination process known as winding up. Current obligations must be concluded and the business wound up, i.e. collect assets, pay debts and accounts of each partner for the value of their interest.

Once the assets of the partnership have been accumulated, they are distributed in the following order:

- Third party creditors are paid first.

- Refund of loans made to or for the firm by the partners is then made.

- The capital contributions made by the partners are refunded.

- The balance of the assets is distributed to the partners in proportion to their shares in the venture.

Savvy business partners usually provide for a **Buy-Sell Agreement** in their partnership agreement, which document creates a process in advance, on how the remaining partners are to buy out the leaving partner. Procedures for calculating value and payout method are predetermined. In case of death of a partner, this agreement can also provide for life insurance to be used to pay the estate of the deceased partner, the value of that person's interest.

Like many small businesses, Joe Roberts and Donald Feelgood did not enter into a written partnership agreement concerning the creation and operation of Tyler's Sports Bar and Grill. If they had signed such an agreement, it would look like the following:

THIS PARTNERSHIP AGREEMENT is entered into between the following:

Joseph Roberts, 2605 Sandy Road, Philadelphia, Pa. and Donald Jones, 1534, Rydal Street, Philadelphia, Pa.

The above-named persons agree that they shall be become partners in business and conditions of this partnership are as follows:

1. The partnership's name shall be: Tyler's Sports Bar and Grill.

2. The principal place of business of the partnership shall be: *523 Water Avenue, Philadelphia, Pa.*

3. *Purpose*—The business of the partnership is to sell food and alcoholic beverages.

4. *Term*—The partnership shall continue until dissolved by mutual agreement of the partners.

5. *Capital contribution and distribution of profits and losses shall be as follows:*

   > *Joseph Roberts $10,000*
   > *Donald Jones $10,000*

   The profits and losses of the partnership shall be divided between the partners equally.

6. *Control*—Each partner shall have equal rights in the management and conduct of the business.

7. *Dissolution*—In the event of retirement, bankruptcy, or death of a partner, the remaining partners shall have the right to continue the business under the same name.

PARK, BROWN & SMITH, P.C.
ATTORNEYS AT LAW
MEMORANDUM

PROBLEM NINE—A

TO: All Law Clerks

FROM: Peter Smith, Esquire

RE: Purchase of a Microbrewery

As was discussed in Chapter 8, Joe Roberts was approached by his nephew, Marcus Roberts, about equipping Tyler's Sports Bar and Grill with a microbrewery. Marcus worked for a bar in Florida that went out of business. The nephew explained that he was involved in selling the contents of the business including the equipment to make craft beer. This included all of the mashing, fermentation, cooling, cleaning, and packaging equipment that Tyler's would need and the equipment could be purchased used for $200,000.

Roberts was intrigued but he knew nothing about the brewing process or the equipment needed to make craft beer. Marcus said that he had undergone extensive training on beer making as part of his previous employment. The nephew even quipped that he would teach his uncle how to operate the equipment and would finance the purchase, which would allow Tyler's to pay back the money over a ten-year period. The nephew said that he would take care of everything and Joe should consider the deal done at $200,000.

Joe modified the bar to accommodate the brewing equipment. After several months of construction, Joe told his nephew that he was ready to proceed. A few hours later, Marcus appeared at the bar and said that he needed Joe to sign some papers so that the nephew could remove the equipment from the Florida brewery and transport it to Pennsylvania for installation. Joe signed the document on behalf of Tyler's Sports Bar and Grill without reading it, since he trusted his nephew who knew of the bar's limited abilities to finance the transaction.

A few weeks later, the equipment arrived, and the nephew along with a crew of three men, had the microbrewery up and running in no time. Marcus even spent three additional days showing the staff of Tyler's how to make craft beer. The brew tasted great and Joe started to put the beer into kegs for sale to his customers.

Everything was sailing along until Joe received a letter from Fidelity Finance Company. The letter explained that Fidelity had purchased the sales contract for the equipment from Marcus and directed Tyler's Sport Bar and Grill to make the monthly payment of $4,080 to them. Joe had no idea what Fidelity was talking about so he called the loan officer. At this time, Joe learned that the contract was for $300,000 with an interest rate of 15%. Joe vigorously protested, saying that Tyler's was only obligated to pay $200,000 and that no interested rate was assigned to the loan when he had signed the loan documentation.

The loan officer read off the list of itemized charges in the signed document. While it was true that Tyler's was being charged $200,000 for the equipment, there was an additional $50,000 expense for the removal of the equipment from the Florida bar and installation of the microbrewery at Tyler's. Transportation charges were $10,000 and licensing fees and taxes paid to the Pennsylvania Department of Revenue amounted to another $40,000. Joe angrily protested but the finance company responded that Joe should take up the matter with his nephew. After all, the loan officer retorted, the finance company had purchased the $300,000 promissory note in good faith and Tyler's had to pay the contract price of $4,080 a month for ten years. This amounted to a total payment over the life of the loan with interest of $489,600. Our law firm has filed an action to rescind the contract but another issue has arisen.

Dr. Feelgood, the investor who put up the money for the bar, claims that Joe had no right to enter into the purchase of the equipment for making craft beer without his permission. He has also taken the position that there is no written contract between him and Joe establishing a partnership, so he is disavowing that he is Joe's partner in the venture. If you remember from Chapter 1, Joe and Dr. Feelgood had an oral agreement to open the bar together. Joe would run the establishment and the doctor would put up the money.

Please read **Hofer v. St. Clair and Beam** and let me know if you think there is a valid partnership. I told Joe that he needed a written agreement spelling out the rights and duties between Roberts and Feelgood before the bar was opened but he did not listen to me. The next question is whether Joe had the authority to bind the partnership to the purchase of the equipment.

HOFER V. ST. CLAIR AND BEAM
298 S.C. 503 (1989)

The plaintiff, Donald Hofer, brought this action for breach of contract to sell real property against Defendants, James St. Clair and Fred Beam.

Hofer was an engineer with the merchant marines. He alternated between four month periods of time at sea and four months at his home in South Carolina. During the periods Hofer was in South Carolina, he was very active in the real estate market purchasing and leasing residential property for investment. While he was at sea, his parents had a Power of Attorney to transact business for him.

St. Clair and Beam were partners in Rock Hill Paint and Repair. This partnership does insurance construction repair work. St. Clair and Beam were also active in the residential real estate market, buying and leasing property for investment.

In the early part of 1984, Hofer was in South Carolina. Through a local real estate agent, Hofer became aware that St. Clair and Beam were interested in selling several pieces of rental property they owned. When Hofer expressed an interest in the properties to the Realtor, the agent scheduled a meeting between Hofer, Hofer's mother, Beam and himself. As a result of this meeting, Hofer made offers on the three pieces of property which form the basis of this action.

St. Clair made counteroffers on behalf of himself and Beam. The negotiating process consisted of several offers and counteroffers over the period of approximately a week, at the end of which Hofer and St. Clair met at the real estate agent's office. During this meeting, all of the changes to the original contracts were initialed and signed by St. Clair. Hofer left the meeting with the original contracts, and proceeded to a mortgage company, suggested by St. Clair, to make an application for financing.

Shortly after this meeting, Hofer returned to sea. Approximately one week later, Mrs. Hofer became aware one of the properties did not have a heat pump as was represented on a form Hofer had received from the real estate agent. Mrs. Hofer called St. Clair to question him about the discrepancy and demanded he either pay for the installation of a heat pump or reduce the purchase price of the property by the cost of such an installation. St. Clair told Mrs. Hofer her son could either buy the property, as it was, for the agreed upon price, or "the deal was off." Mrs. Hofer stated she could not agree to buy the property for the same price in a condition different from that represented to her son.

Several days later, Hofer's father contacted Beam to settle the misunderstanding. Beam told Hofer's father "the deal was off." The defendants failed to convey the properties to Hofer, and sold them to a third party. Hofer brought suit for breach of contract.

The case was referred to a Referee who found that: a partnership existed between the defendants; St. Clair entered into binding contracts for sale of partnership properties; St. Clair had the actual authority to bind the partnership in these contracts; the defendants breached the agreements in failing to convey the properties to Hofer and by conveying them to another; Mrs. Hofer did not repudiate the contract by raising the question of the absence of the heat pump; and Hofer suffered damages in the amount of $15,050.00. This appeal by St. Clair and Beam followed.

The Uniform Partnership Act defines a partnership as "an association of two or more persons to carry on as co-owners of a business for profit." S.C. Code Ann. § 33–41–210 (1987). The lower court found the defendants were operating a partnership, called Rock Hill Paint & Paper, the business of which was, in part, the ownership, purchase and sale of rental real estate properties. These findings are amply supported by the record.

A partnership existed between St. Clair and Beam. Hofer testified that during his initial meeting with Beam to view the property, Beam gave him a card for Rock Hill Paint and Repair with the names "Fred and Jim" on it. Hofer testified Beam referred on many occasions during this meeting to his "partner," Jim, and to Rock Hill Paint & Repair. Both Beam and St. Clair admitted at trial they were partners in Rock Hill Paint & Repair. The evidence also supports the lower court's finding that the business of the partnership was, in part, to purchase, sell, lease and hold real estate for investment. The evidence showed the rental income from the properties at issue, and other jointly owned properties, was shown on the tax returns and books of Rock Hill Paint and Repair.

South Carolina Code Ann. § 33–41–310(1) and (2) (1987) states:

> "(1) Every partner is an agent of the partnership for the purpose of its business and the act of every partner, including the execution in the partnership name of any instrument, for apparently carrying on in the usual way the business of the partnership of which he is a member binds the partnership, unless the partner so acting has in fact no authority to act for the partnership in the particular matter and the person with whom he is dealing has knowledge of the fact that he has no such authority.
>
> (2) An act of a partner which is not apparently for the carrying on of the business of the partnership in the usual way does not bind the partnership unless authorized by the other partners."

Section 33–41–310 sets out two ways in which one partner may bind the partnership. First, if a partner has the actual authority to bind the partnership, that partner's acts will bind the partnership. Second, even if a partner lacks the actual authority to bind the partnership, when a partner is apparently carrying on the business of the partnership in the usual way, and the one with who he is transacting business does not know the partner lacks actual authority; the partner's acts will bind the partnership.

The lower court found that St. Clair had the actual authority to bind the partnership to the contracts for the sale of partnership land. The evidence showed that in the course of this transaction St. Clair made counteroffers, signed a listing agreement and a management agreement on behalf of both of the partners. In the past, St. Clair had alone executed contracts for the sale of partnership property and other partnership contracts on behalf of both partners.

The lower court's finding that St. Clair had the actual authority to bind the partnership is supported by the record. For the foregoing reasons, the opinion of the lower court is affirmed.

PROBLEM NINE—A
ANSWER SHEET

Name   **Please Print Clearly**

1. Despite Joe and Dr. Feelgood not having a written partnership agreement, do you think a partnership was created over Tyler's Sports Bar and Grill?

_____

_____

_____

_____

_____

_____

_____

_____

_____

_____

_____

_____

_____

_____

_____

_____

_____

2. Dr. Feelgood is trying to claim that Joe had no authority to enter into the contract on behalf of the partnership. Therefore, he claims that Mr. Roberts should be solely liable for the promissory note. What do you think?

_____

_____

_____

_____

_____

_____

_____

_____

_____

_____

_____

_____

_____

_____

_____

_____

_____

SECTION 9.6
LIMITED PARTNERSHIP

A **limited partnership** is a business entity that consists of one or more general partners and one or more limited partners who are also referred to as silent partners. This form of enterprise is generally used to raise revenue since the liability of the limited partner is restricted to that person's investment and the limited partner has no say in the management of the operation. This type of entity is common in real estate development projects and the film industry.

There are many advantages to a limited partnership, such as:

- **Protection of assets:** A limited partnership offers liability protection up to the amount of the person's investment in the business entity.

- **Pass-through taxation.** The income paid to a limited partner is not taxed at the business level. Rather, the profits and losses go on the person's individual tax return.

- **Investment potential:** Additional revenue can be generated by adding more limited partners.

- **Full oversight:** The limited partner does not have to worry about running the company. That is the sole responsibility of the general partners.[10]

A. Creation

This business form requires the filing of a **Certificate of Limited Partnership** with the state that contains the name of the partnership along with the words "limited partnership" in the title. The names and business addresses of each general partner will also be listed in the certificate.

B. Management

The business must be run by the general partners without the active participation from the limited partners. Generally, the limited partners are investors and remain in the background with the daily day-to-day business operations.

C. Liability

The liability of a limited partner is restricted to that person's investment. The general partners, however, continue with unlimited liability. This benefit can be lost by a limited partner if that individual becomes involved in the affairs of the business. In that event, the person will have unlimited exposure.

If the limited partnership is organized in an improper manner and the limited partners discover this fact and fail to withdraw or amend the certificate, the limited partner can be held personally liable by the partnership's creditors.

D. Dissolution

A limited partnership is dissolved for the same reasons, and in much the same manner, as a general partnership. However, the death or bankruptcy of a limited partner does not dissolve the partnership.

SECTION 9.7
LIMITED LIABILITY
PARTNERSHIP

The **limited liability partnership** (LLP), a relatively new concept, is a hybrid between a partnership and corporation. It has been designed specifically for professionals, such as lawyers, doctors and accountants, to avoid personal liability for the malpractice of the other partners. Not all states, however, recognize this type of entity.

A. Creation

This business form must be registered with the state as a limited liability partnership and the name of the business must include a designation like company, limited, or limited liability company. For instance, it is common to see the firm use the initials "LLP" in order to notify others of the nature of the **organizational form.** In addition, the company is required to file a certificate of annual registration each year.

B. Management

Unlike a limited partner, those in a limited liability partnership manage the business on a routine basis.

C. Liability

The major advantage of this business form is that the partners are not personally liable for the malpractice claims of the other partners, and in some states, are not liable for the debts of the partnership. This is why it is called a hybrid, since its owners enjoy the immunity of stockholders of a corporation.

When more than one partner is negligent, such as when a claim is made against a negligent partner and that person's supervisor, there is a question as to how liability is to be shared. Some states provide for proportionate liability, i.e. a separate determination of the negligence of each partner.

CHAMBERLAIN V. IRVING
2006 WL 3290446 (CONN. SUPER., 2006)

This is a breach of contract action brought by Henry and Mary Chamberlain against the defendant, attorney Charles J. Irving. The plaintiffs filed their complaint alleging that the defendant's bill for $13,680 breached the fee agreement, which stated that fees were not to exceed $1,000. On May 30,

2006, the defendant filed an answer alleging that he was a limited liability partner at all times.

General Statutes § 34-327(c) provides in relevant part: "[A] partner in a registered limited liability partnership is not liable . . . for any debts, obligations and liabilities . . . arising in contract . . . arising in the course of the partnership business while the partnership is a registered limited liability partnership." This statute protects partners in a registered limited liability partnership from personal liability.

To establish that he is not personally liable under this statute, the defendant submits as evidence (1) the firm's certificate of standing with the secretary of state indicating the firm's existence as a registered limited liability partnership; (2) an affidavit from Garon Camassar, a partner of the law firm, attesting that the defendant practiced law as a partner during the time period at issue in the present case; and (3) an assortment of pleadings and other papers filed on the plaintiffs' behalf during the course of representation, all bearing the firm's name, "Irving, Dubicki & Camassar, LLP."

Also submitted is the fee agreement between the parties written in the form of a letter addressed to the plaintiffs. It states in relevant part: "To confirm our office discussion . . . it is my understanding that, should you decide to engage the services of this *law firm, we* would be representing each of you . . . Legal fees would be charged at the rate of $125.00 per hour for partners' time and $75.00 per hour for *associate attorneys'* time . . . Should you see fit to engage the services of this law firm, I would look forward to working with you in this matter." At the top and centered, the agreement's letterhead contains the following in bold, conspicuous letters: "IRVING, DUBICKI & CAMASSAR." Below the firm name is: "ATTORNEYS & COUNSELORS AT LAW," followed beneath by the firm's address.

The plaintiffs' memorandum in opposition prints out that there is no "LLP" designation in the fee agreement. Henry Chamberlain states that he never met with attorneys Camassar and Dubicki, that he was unaware that he was dealing with a limited liability partnership, and that the defendant never "specifically represented" to him that he was a limited liability partner.

The court finds first that there is no genuine issue as to whether the defendant's firm represented the plaintiffs under the fee agreement. The agreement's terms-its words and their context-give rise to no conclusion other than that the firm, not the defendant individually, is agreeing to provide legal representation. The letterhead's omission of "LLP" is insignificant for that reason. Second, nowhere does § 34-327 condition its protection of partners on whether a third party knows that he or she is dealing with a limited liability partnership. This entitles the defendant to judgment as a matter of law.

For the above foregoing reasons, the defendant's motion for summary judgment is hereby granted.

SECTION 9.8 FAMILY LIMITED LIABILITY PARTNERSHIP

There are millions of family businesses, and some of the most difficult decisions involve how a family handles money, property and other family investments. A possible solution for families with substantial assets or real estate holdings is a **Family Limited Partnership**. When used correctly, this type of entity can be very profitable and save families large amounts of money in gift and estate taxes. It also offers protection from creditors and flexibility not provided by other trusts since it can be amended or changed.[11]

A **family limited liability partnership** (FLLP) is a relatively new phenomenon in which the partners are related to each other. This type of partnership is recommended by a number of tax professionals as an estate planning tool especially for a client who has a great deal of wealth. Basically, the owner transfers the specified assets or property to the partnership made up of family members. The owner then supervises the partnership as the general partner and the family members are the limited partners. In this way, the property is removed from the person's estate even though the previous owner continues to use and manage the property. In addition to the obvious estate planning benefits, the family limited partnership offers significant income tax savings. By adding children as partners and splitting partnership income with them, family taxes may be reduced. For instance, many small businesses are established as sub-chapter S corporations. This allows the owners to bypass the profits of the business on the corporate tax return and pass them through to the owner's personal return. If, however, the owner establishes an FLLP, the general partner can split the income with his or her children, thereby reducing his personal tax obligation.[12] The owner, however, cannot transfer income to children younger than 14 because any income over $1,600 in that case will be taxed at the top tax rate of the parents.[13]

SECTION 9.9 CORPORATION

A **corporation** is a separate and distinct entity apart from its owners. This allows the corporation to own assets, borrow money, hire employees and enter into contracts. By being its own person, the owners of the business, known as stockholders, are able to reduce their personal exposure for the debts and liabilities of the corporation.

A. Creation

A corporation is a creature of state law and those wanting to form a corporation are required to file **Articles of Incorporation** with the appropriate state office and pay a fee. The following information must be included in the Articles of Incorporation:

- Corporate Name

- Nature and Purpose

- Duration

- Capital Structure

- Internal Organization

- Registered Office

The name of the business is an important marketing tool for the business and great care is usually exercised in its selection. That name, however, cannot be the same or similar to an existing corporation or mislead the nature of the corporate business. The name must also end with a corporate denominator, such as inc., co. or corp. For instance, if Tyler's was created as a corporation, it would be identified as Tyler's Sports Bar and Grill, Inc.

The nature and purpose requirement can usually be set forth as "for all legal purposes" in order not to restrict the corporation in the future as to the type of business it will conduct.

The duration of the corporation can be for a specific term of years or perpetual.

Capital structure refers to the classes and numbers of shares of stock that will be issued by the new entity.

Internal organization refers to the management structure of the company and the registered office is the address within the state where the corporation can be served with legal process and papers are to be mailed.

Once this information is ascertained and the Articles of Incorporation form is completed, it is signed by the **incorporators** and sent to the appropriate state office. The papers will then be processed and the incorporators will receive a **Certificate of Incorporation.** This is the corporation's "birth certificate."

If Tyler's Sports Bar and Grill had been created as a corporation, the following would be an example of the Articles of Incorporation:

ARTICLES OF INCORPORATION
Tyler's Sports Bar and Grill, Inc.

We, the undersigned, persons acting as incorporators under the Pennsylvania Business Corporation Act, adopt the following Articles of Incorporation for such Corporation:

Article I

The name of the corporation is: *Tyler's Sports Bar and Grill, Inc.*

Article II

The purpose for which the corporation is organized is to engage in all aspects of the sale of food and alcoholic beverages. The corporation shall further have unlimited power to engage in and do any lawful act concerning any and all lawful business for which corporations may be organized under the Pennsylvania Business Corporation Act and any amendments thereto.

The corporation shall have authority to issue One Hundred Thousand (100,000) shares of stock which stock shall be of one class only, which shall be common, voting stock.

Article IV

The address of the corporation's initial registered office shall be:

1500 John F. Kennedy Boulevard, Philadelphia, Pa. 19102

The corporation's initial registered agent at such address shall be:
Peter Smith, *Esquire*

Article V

The names and addresses of the Incorporators are:

Joseph Roberts, 2605 Sandy Road, Philadelphia, Pa.
Donald Jones, 1534, Rydal Street, Philadelphia, Pa.

In Witness Whereof, Joseph Roberts and Donald Jones of Tyler's Sports Bar and Grill, Inc., have executed these Articles of incorporation and say: That they are all incorporators herein; that they have read the above and foregoing Articles of Incorporation; know the contents thereof and that the same is true to the best of their knowledge and belief, excepting as to matters herein alleged upon information and belief and as to those matters they believe to be true.

B. Continuity

Since the corporation is its own person, its status is not changed by the death or sale of stock by a shareholder.

C. Management

A corporation can engage in any act or enter into any contract available to a natural person in order to accomplish the purposes for which it was created. The corporation has express powers as delineated in the Certificate of Incorporation, By-Laws and resolutions of the Board of Directors. A corporation also has the implied power to perform all acts reasonably appropriate and necessary to carry out its corporate purposes.

Responsibility for the overall management of the corporation is with the **Board of Directors** who are elected by the shareholder. In turn, the Board of Directors selects the **corporate officers,** such as the president or treasurer, who are responsible for the day-to-day operation of the business. The **Directors,** however, have a duty to supervise the activities of the **officers** selected by them to run the corporation.

The members of the Board of Directors are fiduciaries of the corporation. However, no single director can bind the corporation. The Board holds formal meetings with recorded minutes that must be in compliance with the firm's by-laws. The Board can also delegate some of its functions to an Executive Committee of the Board, and various committees can be formed to deal with a specific issue such as compensation, auditor selection and nominating new members to the Board.

Directors cannot use corporate funds or inside information to their own advantage. These problems usually arise in the areas of competing with the corporation, usurping a corporate opportunity, doing business with the corporation, abusing minority shareholders or seizing control of the corporation.

The **Business Judgment Rule** guides the conduct of the Directors. They must use their best judgment in making decisions for the corporation. However, they are not insurers of the corporation's business success. If a decision is made that does not turn out well for the corporation, generally there is no cause of action against the directors, if they exercise their best judgment even if a "wrong" decision was made.

D. Liability

The **shareholders** own the corporation but they are not personally liable for the payment of corporate debt in the absence of a personal guarantee. Their only risk is the investment made in the corporation in the nature of purchasing stock in the business. While shareholders are not personally responsible for corporate debt or corporate actions, a Court could find responsibility by **piercing the corporate veil.** This occurs when there is fraud, under capitalization, intermingling of the business assets or disregarding the corporate entity such as what might occur when the business commingles the business assets with those of the stockholders.

Shareholders must approve major changes in corporate authority, such as amendments to the Articles of Incorporation, and they must approve a merger or dissolution or the sale of a substantial part of the corporate assets.

A shareholder has the right to inspect and copy the corporate books and records but such an inspection can be limited if it is for the purpose of corporate espionage, trade secret violations or harassment.

E. Taxation

The major disadvantage of a corporation is one of **double taxation.** Federal and state governments tax the corporate profits. However, the share of profits or dividends passed on to shareholders is taxed again on their personal tax returns.

The following case deals with an attempt to pierce the corporate veil in order to hold the stockholders liable for the debts of the business.

GILBERT V. JAMES RUSSELL MOTORS, INC.
812 SO.2D 1269 (ALA. CIV. APP., 2001)

James Russell Motors, Inc. ("JRM"), sued G & W Auto Sales, Inc. ("G & W"), and John Gilbert and his wife Lori Gilbert, who were shareholders of G & W. In its complaint, JRM sought to pierce G & W's corporate veil and impose on the Gilberts personal liability for G & W's debt to JRM. The trial court entered a judgment that pierced the corporate veil, and held the Gilberts both liable for the actions of the corporation.

In December 1997, the Gilberts and Lee Wood formed G & W to buy and sell automobiles. Wood contributed his experience in the automobile trade; Wood had exclusive responsibility for buying and selling the used automobiles. The Gilberts contributed $22,000 in initial capital, and they later contributed an additional $3,600 to G & W to pay taxes.

Wood obtained business licenses for G & W, and he began buying and selling automobiles. The

Gilberts opened two business bank accounts in the name "G & W Auto Brokers." G & W used one account for its regular business operations and the other account for a tax account. After all of these actions were taken, the Gilberts contacted an attorney about incorporating the business.

On February 4, 1998, the Gilberts and Wood executed articles of incorporation. The articles of incorporation named Lori Gilbert, John Gilbert, and Wood as the incorporators of G & W. On February 5, 1998, the Gilberts and Wood filed G & W's articles of incorporation thereby forming G & W Auto Brokers, Inc.

On February 5, 1998, the date of G & W's incorporation, the shareholders held a corporate meeting, at which they adopted bylaws and elected officers. The minutes of the first shareholders' meeting indicate that stockholder certificates were delivered to G & W's shareholders. G & W's corporate minutes further reflect that the shareholders elected John Gilbert as president, Wood as vice president, Lori Gilbert as treasurer, and Michelle Wood as secretary.

On or about April 29, 1998, Wood, on behalf of G & W, took possession of three motor vehicles from Steve Dyas Autoshine, Inc., the predecessor to JRM. The total amount of G & W's transaction with Steve Dyas Autoshine was $24,275. G & W satisfied $7,600 of that amount. A balance remained of $16,675; that balance is the basis of this litigation.

Wood testified at his deposition that the Gilberts were not aware of the transactions between G & W and Steve Dyas Autoshine. Wood had accepted the three automobiles from Steve Dyas Autoshine and had sold the automobiles to individuals; Wood did not pay Steve Dyas Autoshine for the three automobiles. It does not appear that Wood actually deposited the money he received for the sale of those automobiles into either of G & W's bank accounts. Wood's testimony further indicates that on more than one occasion, Wood took money from G & W without the Gilberts' knowledge. In doing so, Wood accepted cash for automobiles he sold from G & W's stock, but he did not deposit that money into either of G & W's bank accounts. Wood also admitted that he lied to the Gilberts about transactions that did not actually take place.

A corporation is a legal entity that exists separate from its shareholders, and its actions and obligations are to be considered separately from those of its shareholders. The corporate structure is intended to protect shareholders and officers from liability arising from the operation of the corporation. The ability to pierce a corporate veil and impose personal liability on the corporation's shareholders furnishes a means for a complainant to reach an individual upon a cause of action that otherwise would have existed only against the corporation. Piercing the corporate veil to impose personal liability on a corporation's shareholder is not a power that is exercised lightly.

The Alabama Supreme Court has set out the following circumstances in which it would be appropriate to pierce the corporate veil: 1) where the corporation is inadequately capitalized; 2) where the corporation is conceived or operated for a fraudulent purpose; or 3) where the corporation is operated as an instrumentality or alter ego of an individual or entity with corporate control.

The Gilberts argue that the record contains no evidence indicating that G & W was a "sham" corporation; they also argue that JRM presented no evidence of fraud on their part. G & W was created to buy and sell. The evidence suggests that G & W did in fact buy used automobiles and sell them to various businesses and individuals, including JRM. JRM argued to the trial court that G & W was created for a fraudulent purpose, namely to protect the Gilberts from liability that might arise from wrongful acts by Wood. However, the use of the corporate form to shield shareholders from personal liability is not a fraudulent purpose. In the absence of fraud, the corporate structure protects an individual from liability for the actions of the corporation. A legitimate primary purpose of any corporation is to limit the liability of its shareholders. JRM presented no evidence indicating that the Gilberts engaged in any fraudulent conduct. We agree that JRM presented no evidence to support a conclusion that the Gilberts had a fraudulent purpose in their conception of, or in their operation of, G & W.

JRM also argued that G & W did not comply with corporate formalities required by the Alabama Business Corporation Act. The evidence indicates without dispute that G & W was operated in accordance with its stated purpose, that of buying and selling used automobiles. In addition, the record contains evidence indicating that G & W was formed and registered in compliance with the provisions of the Alabama Business Corporation Act; that articles of incorporation and bylaws were adopted, that officers were elected, that common stock was issued, that corporate meetings were held, and that corporate records were maintained.

The trial court received into evidence G & W's articles of incorporation, its bylaws, and minutes of the initial shareholders meeting, bank-account records, tax records, and employment-withholding records. Our supreme court has affirmed a judgment refusing to pierce a corporate veil even though the shareholders had failed to comply with all corporate formalities. Our review of the documents presented suggests that G & W substantially met the requirements of a corporate entity.

We cannot say the evidence regarding G & W's compliance with corporate formalities is sufficient to demonstrate that the Gilberts operated G & W as a "sham" corporation, or that the evidence supports a conclusion that G & W's corporate veil should be pierced on this basis.

The Gilberts also argue that they did not operate G & W as an alter ego or instrumentality of themselves. In order to prove that G & W was an alter ego or instrumentality of the Gilberts, JRM would have to present evidence indicating: 1) that the Gilberts had complete control and domination of G & W's finances, policy, and business practices, so that at the time of the challenged transaction G & W had no separate mind, will, or existence of its own; 2) that the Gilberts misused that control; and 3) that the Gilberts' misuse of that control was the proximate cause of harm or unjust loss to JRM.

JRM presented evidence indicating that it dealt only with Wood when it engaged in business with G & W. The Gilberts and Wood testified that Wood conducted the day-to-day operations of G & W. The evidence in the record indicates that, by having sole check-writing authority, the Gilberts controlled only the expenditures from G & W's bank accounts; the record indicates that Wood made many, if not all, of the deposits into G & W's bank accounts. No evidence indicates that the Gilberts knew of Wood's inappropriate activities with regard to the business or that they condoned those activities. The evidence in the record does not support a conclusion that the Gilberts had complete control of G & W, that they misused any control that they did have, or that any misuse they allegedly exerted proximately caused harm to JRM. We cannot say that the record contains evidence that would support a piercing of G & W's corporate veil for that reason.

We agree with the Gilberts that the evidence in the record is not sufficient to support an order piercing the corporate veil so as to impose personal liability on the Gilberts. We must reverse the judgment of the trial court.

SECTION 9.10
SUBCHAPTER S
CORPORATION

A corporation can choose to be treated as an "S Corporation" as that term is defined by the Internal Revenue Code. The distinction for this type of corporation is that the profits are passed on directly to the shareholders and taxed to them, as profits would be in a partnership. Since the corporation pays no taxes, this type of entity eliminates the issue of double taxation that normally arises with a corporation.

In order to form a Subchapter S corporation, several qualifications must be met. The corporation must be a domestic corporation formed in a particular state and the entity must be a stand-alone company. In other words, it may not be a member of an affiliated group of corporations. The shareholders must be individuals, estates or certain trusts and there are a maximum number of shareholders allowed. Currently, that number is 100 and no shareholder can be a non-resident alien. If these conditions are met, the business can file Form 2553 with the Internal Revenue Service. This form is known as an Election by a Small Business Corporation and requires each shareholder to sign the form consenting to the business being treated as a Subchapter S corporation.

A **limited liability company** is a new but popular type of business venture that does exactly what its name implies; it offers limited liability to its owners like a corporation who are also known as members. It is less formal than a corporation in that the business does not have to maintain minutes and hold formal meetings of its owners.

A. Creation

To form a limited liability company (LLC), the Articles of Corporation must include information similar to corporate Articles of Incorporation. The business name must also include the designation at the end of LLC. For jurisdictional purposes, an LLC is a citizen of every state where its members are citizens.

The "owners" of the business are known as members and depending upon the state, they can be a sole owner, two or more individuals, corporations or another LLC. Unlike shareholders in a corporation, however, an LLC is not taxed separately. Instead, all profits and losses are "passed through" to each member of the entity. In turn, the profits and losses are listed on the members' personal tax returns, just like partners.[14]

Many states do not require operating agreements for this type of entity. Such an agreement, however, is recommended for multi-member LLCs because it structures the company's finances, and offers rules for a smooth operation. For instance, an operating agreement frequently contains the percentage of interests of the members, allocation of profits and losses, and member's rights and responsibilities.[15]

B. Advantages and Disadvantages

A limited liability company is a hybrid form of a business enterprise that offers the limited liability of the corporation with the tax advantages of a partnership. In addition, the members of the venture are taxed as a sole proprietorship, unless they elect to be taxed as corporations.

Members of the limited liability company decide how to operate the business but an operating agreement does not need to be in writing. In a member managed LLC, all owners participate in management. In a manager managed LLC, the members designate a group of persons (member or not) to run the firm.

According to Franchise Consultants, Inc., **franchises** account for about 50% of all retail sales in the United States and employ more than 15 million people. Entrepreneurs like them because the franchise has instant name recognition and assistance in running the business. People immediately know what is sold at McDonald's or Dunkin Donuts and the retailer receives start up training and advertising help. What then, is a franchise? It is an arrangement in which the owner of a trademark, trade name or copyright allows another to offer its products for sale or use in a geographic area. The key parties to this arrangement are the **franchisor** or owner of the business idea, and **franchisee**, or owner of the store offering the item to the public.

Several types of franchise arrangements have emerged over the years. A **distributorship** involves a manufacturing concern that licenses a dealer to sell its product, such as an automobile dealership. A **chain style business operation** is one in which the franchisee operates the business under the name of the franchisor and must follow standardized methods of operation. This is the classic fast food operation such as McDonald's or Burger King. The last is a **manufacturing** or **processing plant franchise** where the franchisor provides the franchisee with an essential ingredient or formula to make a particular product, such as a Coca Cola bottling plant.

The franchise agreement is a contract and is governed by state and federal statutes that regulate these types of contracts. For example, the Automobile Dealers Franchise Act and the Petroleum Marketing Practices Act deal with problems that can arise in automobile and gasoline franchise operations. The Federal Trade Commission also requires the (1) disclosure of material facts to all prospective franchisees in the business arrangement at the earlier of the first face-to-face meeting or ten business days before any money is paid or an agreement is signed in connection with the investment, and (2) the franchisor must give investors a copy of its standard-form franchise and related agreements at least five business days before their signing.

The franchise agreement is important because it spells out the terms of the relationship including the payment for the franchise, the purchase of products from the franchisor and the costs for advertising. The agreement will also discuss whether business premises are to be leased or purchased, the location of the franchise, sales quotas, record keeping responsibilities, and employee training. The franchiser may even require the franchisee to buy supplies from the franchisor.

There are several factors that can cause the termination of a franchise arrangement. For instance, the franchise contract may have a set term, such as ten years, and there can be a "termination for cause" clause that allows the franchise license to be revoked such as for none payment of fees to the franchisor, failure to follow the rules established by the home office or upon the death, disability or insolvency of the franchisee.

The franchisor and franchisee must also act in good faith and fairly deal with each other at all times. This is the issue in the following case.

SHERMAN V. MASTER PROTECTION CORP.
2002 WL 31854905 (CAL. APP. 6 DIST. 2002)

Master Protection Corporation (MPC) is in the business of selling and servicing fire protection equipment under the trade name "FireMaster." In 1987, Michael Sherman purchased an MPC franchise for $40,000, and in 1991, he purchased a second franchise for $60,000. The franchise agreements provided that the purchase price was equivalent to the approximate gross sales from the previous year. In each case, Sherman signed a promissory note for the entire purchase price. The franchise agreements gave the franchisee the right to sell and service FireMaster fire extinguishers to MPC's customers within particular geographical territories, and to use MPC's trade name and service mark. In addition, MPC agreed to provide certain support services to its franchisees. The franchise agreements provided that the franchisee could sell or assign its rights under the agreement to a bona fide purchaser, subject to MPC's right to approve such a sale. When Sherman purchased his franchises, MPC's portable fire extinguishers were all sold and serviced by franchisees operating under territorial franchises similar to those purchased by Sherman.

In 1994, MPC management decided to phase out the franchise program in favor of an employee-based service operation. MPC did not inform its franchisees of this decision. A phase-out plan was drafted whereby MPC would stop selling new franchises and would repurchase existing franchises only at the "end" of the phase-out and only if necessary to keep the franchises from reselling to others. In January of 1995, MPC established a field service employee program and began hiring increasing numbers of employees to perform field services, including the sales and servicing of fire extinguishers formerly referred exclusively to the franchisees. MPC projected that its future mode of doing business would be with a "100% employee based field work force."

Sherman filed this complaint containing five causes of action: 1) violation of franchise investment law; 2) breach of the franchise agreement; 3) breach of the implied covenant of good faith and fair dealing; 4) breach of fiduciary duty; and 5) fraud.

As to the second cause of action for breach of the franchise agreements, the court found that MPC had breached the agreements when its employees sold and serviced fire extinguishers within Sherman's territories "resulting in a misappropriation of work." The court fixed damages at $11,697.49. As to the third cause of action for breach of the implied covenant of good faith and fair dealing, the trial court found that MPC's decision to phase out the franchise program was more than simply a decision not to sell any more franchises. It also involved a decision to make it difficult for franchisees to sell or assign their franchises, a decision not to repurchase any of the franchises and a decision to replace the franchisees with employees. The trial court found this conduct constituted a breach of the implied covenant of good faith and fair dealing. The trial court further found that as a result of MPC's conduct, "[Sherman's] franchises have become unsalable." The court awarded damages of $258,679, representing the purchase value of the franchises based on the gross sales for the previous year, as per the parties' franchise agreement.

MPC contends that there was no wrongful conduct shown that was contrary to any express or implied term of the franchise agreements. MPC argues that nothing in the franchise agreements guaranteed the longevity of the franchise program or prevented MPC from making what was essentially a business decision to discontinue the franchise program and move to an employee-based operation. Therefore it could not be a breach of the covenant of good faith and fair dealing to do so since the covenant exists merely to prevent one contracting party from unfairly frustrating the other party's right to receive *the benefits of the agreement actually made.* These principles, MPC argues, prevent a finding of a breach of implied covenant because MPC did not act contrary to any provision in the contract.

Breach of a provision in the contract, however, is not a necessary prerequisite to finding a breach of the covenant of good faith and fair dealing. Rather, the question is whether the conduct, even though not expressly prohibited, is nevertheless "contrary to the contract's purposes and the parties' legitimate expectations. The covenant of good faith is implied as a supplement to express contractual covenants to prevent a party from engaging in conduct that frustrates the other party's rights to the benefits of the agreement.

Here, the evidence showed that one of the intended benefits of purchasing a franchise was to build equity for resale. The franchise agreements provided for a right to sell the franchise and further provided that MPC had the right of first refusal. The franchisee was required to meet minimum increases in annual sales, and the purchase price of the franchise at any given time was determined based on the previous year's approximate gross sales. Thus, the agreements clearly contemplated that the franchises would increase in value over time. In 1992, MPC's President, Robert Wiles, issued a mission statement to all franchisees emphasizing MPC's "commitment to fair and ethical dealings with our . . . franchise owners."

MPC argues that the court erred by finding that the phasing out of the franchise program was a breach of the covenant of good faith and fair dealing. This somewhat misstates the court's finding. The wrongful conduct found by the trial court was "more than simply a decision not to sell any more franchises." Rather, it was the way MPC went about implementing its decision. Without informing its franchisees of a management decision

affecting their livelihood, MPC began hiring increasing numbers of employees to perform field services within the franchised territories and in competition with the franchisees. MPC made it difficult for franchisees to sell or assign their franchises. In addition, MPC refused to repurchase franchises. The court found that such conduct was a breach of the covenant of good faith and fair dealing in that it frustrated plaintiff's expectations and injured "plaintiff's right to receive the fruits and benefits of his franchise agreements." We believe this falls within the legal parameters of the theory of breach of the covenant of good faith and fair dealing.

The court found that MPC's conduct rendered Sherman's franchises "unsalable," and awarded Sherman damages representing the "full amount of the probable sales value of [Sherman's] franchises, but for Defendant's conduct." This amount was the equivalent of the previous year's gross annual sales, which was the method of setting the price of an MPC franchise as per the parties' franchise agreement. MPC argues that "unsalability" was an erroneous legal standard on which to base an award of damages.

The court's finding that Sherman's franchises had become "unsalable" was supported by substantial evidence in the record. Other franchise owners testified that they had made efforts to sell their franchises back to MPC or to employees of MPC, with no success. In some cases, MPC discouraged the buyers or blocked the sales by withholding approval. Sherman testified that he was not aware of any franchise owner in the San Jose area who had been able to resell his franchise since 1994. Out of eight or nine franchise owners in this area, there were only three left and none of the others had gotten anything for their franchises.

Sherman offered to sell his franchises to a number of MPC field service employees, whose response was to laugh at him. They told him "FireMaster doesn't want the franchise program any more. Sherman's expert witness testified that in his opinion, Sherman's franchises were not saleable because the franchise system was being phased out, because MPC was no longer selling franchises or repurchasing them, and because MPC was in fact competing with its own franchisees by supporting its employee system.

MPC's principal argument regarding damages is that the court erred in awarding damages representing the full value of the franchises because the franchises were not worthless and in fact continued to produce income for Sherman. Uncontroverted evidence, including Sherman's testimony, showed that the income produced by the two franchises had steadily increased over the years, in spite of MPC's phase-out plan. In 1999, the year upon which the court based its damages award, income from the two franchises was at a record high. Even if MPC's conduct in moving to an employee-based system may have rendered Sherman's franchises unmarketable, the franchises continued to have some value as income-producing assets. According to MPC, it was therefore error to award Sherman the full value of the assets while he retained the assets and the benefit of the income they continued to produce. Such an award, MPC argues, resulted in an impermissible double recovery.

The damages award was only a double recovery, however, if it represented the full fair market value of the franchises. The evidence showed that it did not. The amount awarded by the trial court was derived from the formula set forth in parties' franchise agreement-one times gross sales for the previous year. There was no evidence that this corresponded to fair market value.

The trial court, having found that the franchisor had wrongfully refused to buy back the franchise at this amount, and having found that the franchisor had essentially rendered the franchise unmarketable to others at any price, assessed damages based on the customary formula. Under the circumstances, the court's use of the formula in the franchise agreements was reasonably based in the evidence.

The judgment is affirmed.

Section 9.13 Tyler's Sports Bar and Grill Franchise

Park, Brown & Smith, P.C. Attorneys at Law Memorandum

Problem Nine—B

To: All Law Clerks

From: Peter Smith, Esquire

Re: The Franchise

The installation of the microbrewery at Tyler's Sports and Grill has been very successful. The customers love the craft beer and the bar is jammed most nights. People are also crazy about the entertainment that Tyler's offers, which is centered on a sports theme, such as the mechanical bull and a dog who catches any ball tossed his way. The food is also a hit. Each item is named after a famous Philadelphia athlete. For instance, the Weinzburger is made from beef grown in North Dakota and the Embiid Pulled Pork sandwich is huge and can be dunked into a boat of spices from Cameroon. The Giroux Fries are offered in a cone shaped like the Stanley Cup and the Charley is a milkshake named after Charley Manuel.

Dr. Feelgood brought a group of friends to the restaurant and they went wild over the concept. They asked Joe and the doctor about opening another Tyler's Sport Bar and Grill in South Philadelphia near the stadium complex. Roberts contacted me about the idea and I suggested that he and Feelgood franchise the business. I crafted the appropriate franchise agreement and the parties have signed on the dotted line.

The agreement mandates that the new business be run the same way as the original bar, and Joe has given them all of his secret food recipes. He has also taught them how to make craft beer whose taste is unique to Tyler's. The franchise agreement further requires that the business be named Tyler's Sport Bar and Grill, be operated in accordance with Tyler's Standards of Operation and be opened for a ten year period within two miles of the stadium complex in South Philadelphia. All of the decorations inside and outside the bar must be the same as those at the original restaurant. The agreement also allows Tyler's to terminate the contract at any time if the franchisee cease operations of their Tyler's Sports Bar and Grill; and further provides, that upon termination, the franchisee will cease their use of any procedures and techniques associated with the franchisor and not open another restaurant or bar for a 5 year period within 5 miles of the stadium complex. The franchisor also has the right to reposes the equipment for making the craft beer. This is a penalty that the franchisee will be required to pay for their being taught how to install and operate the microbrewery.

The franchisee hired a French trained chef to run the new bar but after a few months, he started to change the items on the menu. For instance, he introduced a line of health foods, such as steamed cauliflower, low fat cheese fries and tofu burgers. This prompted our firm to send a letter telling the franchisee that they were in violation of the contract and to please go back to the original Tyler's menu and format.

Mr. Roberts just called and said that he drove by the new bar on the way to a 76ers game and discovered that the business had removed all references to Tyler's Sport's Bar and Grill and had renamed the bar "The Grand Slam." He also looked at the menu posted outside of the bar, and it is the same menu offered at Tyler's Sports Bar and Grill. This is a clear breach of contract and constitutes a termination of the franchise agreement. We need to stop the bar's operation immediately and to obtain possession of the beer brewing equipment. It is my thinking that we file a preliminary injunction barring the franchisee from continuing the operation of "The Grand Slam" and to enforce the restricted covenant of not being able to open a bar for five years and within a five mile radius of the stadium complex. I will sue the owners of the franchise at a later date for money damages.

Please read **Rita's Water Ice v. S. A. Smith Enterprises** and let me know if you think we will be successful in obtaining a preliminary injunction.

RITA'S WATER ICE V. S. A. SMITH ENTERPRISES
2011 WL 101694 (E.D. PA. 2011)

Rita's Water Ice Franchise Company, and Shirley and Jeffrey Smith entered into a franchise agreement, titled "Rita's Water Ice Franchise Agreement." On July 29, 2010, pursuant to the terms of the Franchise Agreement, the Smiths transferred their interest in the Franchise Agreement to S. A. Smith Enterprises.

Pursuant to the Franchise Agreement, Defendants paid Plaintiff $35,000 and agreed to pay Plaintiff a royalty fee of six-and-a-half percent of estimated gross sales. In addition, Defendants agreed to operate a Rita's Franchise for ten (10) years in accordance with Plaintiff's Standards of Operation, which required, among other things, that Defendants adhere to product and service quality standards, comply with operation and preparation methods, maintain, refurbish and modify store premises and equipment as needed and/or directed by Plaintiff, and allow Plaintiff to enter the Franchise premises to ensure Defendants' compliance with these standards. Defendants also agreed to purchase and install certain fixtures and equipment including Plaintiff's "proprietary batch machine."

In exchange, Plaintiff granted Defendants the right to operate a Rita's Franchise as well as the right to use confidential and proprietary information regarding the establishment and operation of a Rita's store. The confidential and proprietary information that comprises the System includes Rita's recipes, food preparation, and business and management practices.

The Franchise Agreement provides for a term of ten (10) years, with an option for Plaintiff to terminate it unilaterally under certain conditions. The Franchise Agreement provides that Plaintiff may terminate the Agreement at any time if Defendants cease operation of their Rita's Franchise.

The Franchise Agreement provides that, upon termination, Defendants will cease their use of any confidential methods, procedures and techniques associated with the franchise. It also provides that, upon termination, Plaintiff may purchase from Defendants "the "dasher" and "door" of each batch machine used in the operation of the Franchised Business for One–Hundred Dollars ($100) per machine. Finally, the Franchise Agreement provides that, upon its termination, Defendants will adhere to the restrictions of a "non-compete clause." The relevant portion of the Franchise Agreement states:

> "Franchisee covenants that Franchisee shall not, for a continuous uninterrupted period commencing upon the expiration

or termination of this Agreement, regardless of the cause for termination, and continuing for two (2) years thereafter, either directly or indirectly, for itself, or through, on behalf of, or in conjunction with any person, persons, partnership, corporation or limited liability company, own, maintain, operate, engage in, act as a consultant for, perform services for, or have any interest in any retail business which: (a) (i) is the same as, or substantially similar to, a Rita's shop; (ii) offers to sell or sells any product or products which are the same as, or substantially similar to, any of the Proprietary Products; or (iii) offers to sell or sells any product or products which are the same as, or substantially similar to, any of the products offered by a Rita's shop."

On July 19, 2010, Defendants, without providing notice to Plaintiff, ceased operation of their Rita's Franchise. Plaintiff alleges that this act is a breach of the Franchise Agreement. In a letter dated August 19, 2010, Plaintiff exercised its option pursuant to the Franchise Agreement to repurchase the "dasher" and "door" of Rita's proprietary batch machine. Shortly after Defendants stopped operating their Rita's shop, they began operating a similar business at the same location under the name "Pearly's Sweet Creative Desserts." Plaintiff alleges that this action violates the non-compete clause contained the Franchise Agreement.

Pearly's Sweets sells soft serve ice cream, Pearly's Italian ice, "Pearlatis" and "Pearly's Shakes." Rita's offers frozen custard, Italian ice, "Gelatis," and "Misto Shakes." The Court finds that soft serve ice cream are products competing with those of Plaintiff.

By its Motion for a Preliminary Injunction, Plaintiff seeks to enforce the restrictive covenant contained in Franchise Agreement, which would enjoin Defendants from continuing to sell competing products at Pearly's Sweets.

In order to obtain a preliminary injunction the moving party must show: (1) a reasonable probability of success on the merits; (2) irreparable harm if the relief sought is not granted; and (3) that the harm to the moving party outweighs the possible harm to the non-moving party. As a form of injunctive relief, the grant of a preliminary injunction is "an extraordinary remedy," which should be granted only in "limited circumstances.

Based on the testimony, the Court finds that Plaintiff is entitled to injunctive relief. Under Pennsylvania law, a covenant not to compete is enforceable if the application of the covenant is reasonably limited in both time and territory.

Defendants argue that the non-compete clause is unenforceable because it is unreasonable in both time and territory. The time duration and geographic scope of the restrictive covenant contained in of the Franchise Agreement are two years and three miles, respectively. The Court finds the two-year time duration and three-mile geographic scope of the covenant to be reasonable under Pennsylvania law. The restrictive covenant here is intended to give the franchisor, the opportunity to establish a new franchise in the area while there is still customer loyalty and brand recognition in place.

The Court heard testimony that it would take Plaintiff "multiple years" to establish another franchise in the territory in which Defendants' Franchise has been located. A two-year restrictive covenant would be necessary to give Plaintiff the opportunity to establish a new franchise in this location. In addition, Pennsylvania courts have upheld non-compete clauses with longer durations. Therefore, the two-year time duration of the non-compete clause is reasonable under Pennsylvania law. The three-mile geographic scope of the non-compete clause is also reasonable. Having established that the restrictive covenant at issue is enforceable under Pennsylvania law, Plaintiff has demonstrated a reasonable probability of success on the merits of its claim. This factor favors granting injunctive relief.

Irreparable injury results when a former franchisee competes against a franchisor in breach of a restrictive covenant contained in the parties' franchise agreement. A franchisor has an interest in retaining an established customer base in an area where it has established a franchise location. A franchisor's business reputation is irreparably harmed when a former franchisee continues to operate at a franchise location after the expiration of a franchise agreement in violation of a noncompete clause. Here, Plaintiff is irreparably harmed by Defendants' operation of a competing business, Pearly's, is in violation of the non-compete clause contained in the Franchise Agreement.

Since Plaintiff has shown a reasonable probability of success, the Court will grant Plaintiff's Motion for a Preliminary Injunction.

ANSWER SHEET
PROBLEM NINE—B

Name   **Please Print Clearly**

   1. Has the franchisee breached the franchise agreement?

_____

_____

_____

_____

_____

_____

_____

_____

_____

_____

_____

_____

_____

_____

_____

_____

2. Will we be successful in obtaining a temporary injunction?

_____

_____

_____

_____

_____

_____

_____

_____

_____

3. Will the terms of our restrictive covenant barring the franchisees from opening another restaurant for five years and within five miles of the stadium complex be enforced?

_____

_____

_____

_____

_____

_____

_____

_____

_____

_____

_____

_____

SECTION 9.14 LAWS REGULATING BUSINESSES

Businesses are subjected to a great number of rules and regulations. This corporate governance requires that they be vigilant of these legal mandates when selling products, offering stock to the public or when determining the compensation for the officers of the enterprise. A number of the best business practices have been created in response to a scandal or an economic collapse. One must keep in mind, however, that since Donald Trump assumed office, he has slowed the rule-making process with the avowed goal of deregulating businesses, regardless of the reason for a particular rule. For instance, he has ordered government agencies not to create any new regulatory costs on businesses, despite the benefit, and to not create any new regulations unless the government first repeals two old ones.[16] The long term impact of this policy change is uncertain. However, one must remember this initiative by the President when considering government regulations.

The following are some of the traditional legislative initiatives affecting businesses.

A. The Laws to Regulate the Sale of Securities

The **Securities and Exchange Commission** ("SEC") was created following the Great Depression and it protects investors and regulates capital formation. The laws governing securities in the United States are based upon a simple principle: all investors should have access to the same information about an investment before buying it, and for as long as they own it. This insures that investors have similar knowledge when buying, selling, or holding a security. It is only through timely and accurate information that people can make proper investment decisions.[17]

With a staff of almost 4,000 employees scattered throughout the United States, the SEC is responsible for the interpretation of federal securities laws; to oversee the inspection of securities firms, brokers, investment advisers, and ratings agencies; to oversee private regulatory organizations in the securities, accounting, and auditing fields; and to coordinate U.S. securities regulation with federal, state, and foreign authorities.

For instance, these goals have led to a variety of remedial actions such as the required disclosure of facts concerning the offering of listed securities, the regulation of trading of listed securities, the investigation of securities fraud, the regulation of securities dealers, the supervision of mutual funds and to recommend administrative sanctions for violations of securities laws.

It should be noted that consistent with President Trump's goal of deregulation and a business friendly attitude, the SEC has imposed fewer penalties for violations of the securities laws with the fewest enforcement cases since 2013.[18]

The following is an overview of some of the important legislation that is within the purview and enforcement of the SEC.

1. Securities Act of 1933

The **Securities Act of 1933** authorizes the SEC to regulate the trading of listed securities, investigate securities fraud, regulate securities dealers, supervise mutual funds and recommend administrative sanctions for violations of the various securities laws.

Additional authority has been given to the SEC over the years such as: expansion of authority over securities fraud cases, the power to sanction those who violate foreign securities laws, and the authority to exempt persons or securities from the requirements of securities laws.

After the collapse of the Enron Company and the revelation of massive accounting fraud and misleading corporate financial reports, Congress enacted the **Sarbanes-Oxley Act.** Described by President Bush as "the most far reaching reforms of American business practices since the time of Franklin Delano Roosevelt," the law seeks to enhance corporate responsibility, enhance financial disclosures, and combat corporate and accounting fraud.

The Sarbanes-Oxley Act only applies to publicly traded companies and seeks to increase corporate accountability through a number of initiatives, such as the requirement that the CEO and CFO of a firm must certify the validity of financial statements and there can be no personal loans to officers and directors. The law also provides more protection for corporate whistle-blowers, and extends the Statute of Limitations for securities fraud to two years after discovery or five years after violation, whichever is earlier.

The Securities Act of 1933 also governs the initial sales of securities by a business and mandates that all information concerning the issuance of securities must be made available to the public.

A **security** is defined in the Act to include such investments as a note, stock, bond, and evidence of indebtedness, certificate of interest or participation in any profit sharing agreement. For our purposes, however, it is best to think of a security as stocks and bonds issued by a corporation.

If a corporation wants to "go public" or sell stock to the public, it must file a **Registration Statement** with the SEC. In turn, a prospective investor in the business is provided with a **prospectus** with information similar to the Registration Statement. The SEC does not recommend any security for purchase. Rather, its job is to make sure a prospective investor has all of the information needed to make an informed decision as to whether to buy the security.

The Registration Statement must provide information as to the significant provisions of the security, how the proceeds of the sale are to be used, the registrant's property, the management of the company and compensation arrangements, a certified financial statement and a listing of pending lawsuits. There is a twenty-day waiting period after registration before a sale can take place.

It is a violation of the Securities Act of 1933 to intentionally defraud investors by misrepresenting or omitting facts in a Registration Statement or prospectus. Liability is also imposed on anyone who is negligent in failing to discover the fraud, such as the accountants, lawyers, and underwriters hired by the firm.

Defenses to a violation of the Act include such things as the false statement or omission was not material and the buyer knew of the misrepresentation but bought the stock anyway.

The SEC has broad powers and can impose both criminal and civil penalties. Criminal penalties consist of imprisonment, fines or both while civil remedies include damages and injunctions against any further sales of the securities. In addition, a person who purchases a security as a result of false or omitted statements in the prospectus can sue to recover those losses.

2. Securities Exchange Act of 1934

While the Securities Exchange Act of 1933 focuses on the original offerings of a security, the **Securities Exchange Act of 1934** regulates the subsequent sale of securities and requires the registration of security exchanges, brokers, and dealers of the markets in which securities are traded. This is known as the secondary market and would include the regulation of the New York and American Stock Exchanges.

As for the Act itself, it prohibits the use of any manipulative or deceptive device in violation of the SEC rules. In fact, **Rule 10b-5** prohibits the commission of fraud in connection with the purchase or sale of any security and provides:

"It shall be unlawful for any person . . . by the use of any means or instrumentality of interstate commerce, or of the mails or of any facility of any national securities exchange:

1. To employ any device, scheme, or artifice to defraud,

2. To make any untrue statement of a material fact or to omit to state a material fact necessary in order to make the statements made, in the light of the circumstances under which they were made, not misleading, or

3. To engage in any act, practice, or course of business which operates or would operate as a fraud or deceit upon any person, in connection with the purchase or sale of any security."

The Securities and Exchange Commission is also concerned with **insider trading** and aggressively pursues these types of cases. The SEC defines illegal insider trading as the buying or selling of a security, in breach of a fiduciary duty or other relationship of trust and confidence, while in possession of non-public information about that security.

When officers and directors are privy to information others do not possess, they cannot take advantage of this information so material information about the company must be disclosed to the public before an insider can buy or sell that security.

The key to liability is whether the insider's information is material such as the fraudulent trading in the stock by a broker, a dividend change (up or down), sale of corporate assets, a newly discovered process or product, a significant change in financial position and potential litigation.

Insider trading also encompasses **tipping,** which refers to the practice of buying or selling of securities by a person who is "tipped," with non-public information in a stock or bond. The SEC has used several legal theories to establish liability for such insider trading.

The **Tipper/Tipee Theory** deals with someone who acquires inside information as the result of a corporate insider's breach of that person's fiduciary duty to the corporation.

On the other hand, the **Misappropriation Theory** deals with an individual who wrongfully obtains or misappropriates inside information and trades on it for that person's own benefit. In essence, the individual is considered to have stolen the information belonging to another.

In order to reduce the potential for insider trading, the SEC requires corporate insiders, who trade in their own securities, to report those trades to the Commission. A corporate insider includes a company's officers and directors, as well as any beneficial owners of more than ten percent of a class of the company's equity securities.

The SEC has also issued a regulation to prevent **short swing profits.** This rule requires company insiders, who buy and sell their firm's securities within a six-month period, to return any profits made from those transactions to the business.

Insider trading retards investor confidence in the integrity of the securities markets. Therefore, the SEC, by its own admission, considers the detection of insider trading as one of its top priorities. In fact, the Commission will issue a reward to any individual who provides information leading to the recovery of a civil penalty from an inside trader, from a person who "tipped" information to an inside trader, or from an individual who controlled an inside trader.

Penalties can include the Commission's filing of a civil enforcement action or the request of a fine not to exceed three times the amount of the profit gained or lost avoided as a result of a violation or in a criminal prosecution by the Department of Justice.

Have you heard of a **Bitcoin?** This electronic currency can be exchanged without using a bank or money transfer system.[19] It is not backed by any real currency like gold nor is it regulated by a banking authority. Instead, it is digital money very much like cash but for the Internet. Bitcoin is a mobile application that sets up an internet wallet that lets the user exchange the credits with others in the place of hard currency. An increasing number of consumers and enterprises are adopting this digital currency. In fact, as of 2013, the value of Bitcoins in the marketplace exceeded $1.5 billion and millions of dollars in this digital currency are being used every day.[20]

While Bitcoin is the result of the digital age, is it subject to the traditional rules involving currency? In **Securities and Exchange Commission v. Shavers,** the court had to decide in a case of first impression whether a Bitcoin is security subject to the Securities Act of 1933 and the Exchange Act of 1934.

SECURITIES AND EXCHANGE COMMISSION V. SHAVERS
2013 WL 4028182 (E.D. TEX., 2013)

The question currently before the Court is whether or not it has subject matter jurisdiction over this action pursuant the Securities Act of 1933 and the Exchange Act of 1934.

Shavers is the founder and operator of Bitcoin Savings and Trust ("BTCST"), formerly known as First Pirate Savings & Trust. According to the facts stated by the SEC, Shavers made a number of solicitations aimed at enticing lenders to invest in Bitcoin-related investment opportunities.

Bitcoin is an electronic form of currency unbacked by any real asset and without specie, such as coin or precious metal. It is not regulated by a central bank or any other form of governmental authority; instead, the supply of Bitcoins is based on an algorithm which structures a decentralized peer-to-peer transaction system. Bitcoin was designed to reduce transaction costs, and allows users to work together to validate transactions by creating a public record of the chain of custody of each Bitcoin. Bitcoin can be used to purchase items online, and some retail establishments have begun accepting Bitcoin in exchange for gift cards or other purchases. The value of Bitcoin is volatile

and ranges from less than $2 per Bitcoin to more than $260 per Bitcoin.

Beginning in November of 2011, Shavers began advertising that he was in the business of "selling Bitcoin to a group of local people" and offered investors up to 1 % interest daily "until either you withdraw the funds or my local dealings dry up and I can no longer be profitable". During the relevant period, Shavers obtained at least 700,467 Bitcoin in principal investments from BTCST investors, or $4,592,806 in U.S. dollars, based on the daily average price of Bitcoin when the BTCST investors purchased their BTCST investments. The BTCST investors who suffered net losses (compared to investors who received more in withdrawals and purported interest payments than they invested in principal), collectively lost 263,104 Bitcoin in principal, that is $1,834,303 based on the daily average price of Bitcoin when they purchased their BTCST investments, or in excess of $23 million based on currently available Bitcoin exchange rates.

The SEC asserts that Shavers made a number of misrepresentations to investors regarding the nature of the investments and that he defrauded investors. However, the question currently before the Court is whether the BTCST investments in this case are securities as defined by Federal Securities Laws. Shavers argues that the BTCST investments are not securities because Bitcoin is not money, and is not part of anything regulated by the United States. Shavers also contends that his transactions were all Bitcoin transactions and that no money ever exchanged hands. The SEC argues that the BTCST investments are both investment contracts and notes, and, thus, are securities.

The term "security" is defined as any note, stock, treasury stock, security future, security-based swap, bond or investment contract. An investment contract is any contract, transaction, or scheme involving (1) an investment of money, (2) in a common enterprise, (3) with the expectation that profits will be derived from the efforts of the promoter or a third party. First, the Court must determine whether the BTCST investments constitute an investment of money. It is clear that Bitcoin can be used as money. It can be used to purchase goods or services, and as Shavers stated, used to pay for individual living expenses. The only limitation of Bitcoin is that it is limited to those places that accept it as currency. However, it can also be exchanged for conventional currencies, such as the U.S. dollar, Euro, Yen, and Yuan. Therefore, Bitcoin is a currency or form of money,

and investors wishing to invest in BTCST provided an investment of money.

Next, the Court looks at whether there is a common enterprise. To show a common enterprise, the Fifth Circuit requires interdependence between the investors and the promotor, which "may be demonstrated by the investors' collective reliance on the promotor's expertise even where the promotor receives only a flat fee or commission rather than a share in the profits of the venture." That interdependence is established in this case because the investors here were dependent on Shavers' expertise in Bitcoin markets and his local connections. In addition, Shavers allegedly promised a substantial return on their investments as a result of his trading and exchanging Bitcoin. Therefore, the Court finds that there is a common enterprise.

Finally, the Court considers whether there is an expectation that profits will be derived from the efforts of the promotor or third party. The Court finds that this prong is also met. At the outset, Shavers allegedly promised up to 1% interest daily, and at some point during the relevant period the interest promised was at 3.9%. Clearly any investors participating in the BTCST investments were expecting profits from the efforts of Shavers.

Therefore, the Court finds that the BTCST investments meet the definition of investment contract, and as such, are securities.

B. The Laws to Regulate Financial Institutions

The Great Recession, which extended from December 2007 to June 2009, started with the bursting of an $8 trillion dollar housing bubble. The resulting financial losses caused dramatic reductions in consumer spending, reduction in buying by the public, combined with the chaos in the financial markets, led to a breakdown in business investment. Massive unemployment followed and there was a decrease of 8.4 million jobs in the U.S. work force.[21]

This development led to the enactment of comprehensive regulations involving the financial markets known as the Dodd-Frank Wall Street Reform and Consumer Protection Act. This law, which is more commonly called the **Dodd-Frank Act,** places a number of restrictions on the financial industry with the intention of preventing another collapse like Lehman Brothers.[22]

The Act, passed in 2010, protects consumers from improper bank loans and mortgage practices. The law is complex with 16 major areas of reform and it is hundreds of pages in length.[23] Its primary thrust is to prevent excessive risk-taking that caused the financial meltdown of the Great Recession. These rules are designed to build a safer, more stable financial system: one that will hopefully provide a foundation for economic growth and job creation. Dodd-Frank also offers protections for American families by creating a new consumer watchdog to prevent mortgage companies and other lenders from exploiting them.[24]

These are some of the areas of regulation:

1. **Regulate Credit Cards, Loans and Mortgages**

    The tasks of the many different agencies were consolidated into the **Consumer Financial Protection Bureau**. This agency watches over credit reporting agencies, credit and debit cards, and consumer loans. It also safeguards consumers in real estate transactions by requiring them to understand risky mortgage loans and it forces lenders to confirm a borrower's employment, income, and credit history.[25]

2. **Compensation of Executives**

    If a company seeks shareholder approval of an acquisition, merger, or proposed sale of substantially all of a company's assets, a disclosure must be made by the person soliciting the **proxies** of any agreement to make "golden parachute" payments to the executive officers of the company or buyer. Businesses will also be required to create independent compensation committees that require consideration of the sources of compensation for the director, such as consulting, advisory or other compensatory fees paid by the company.[26]

3. **Credit Rating Agencies Review**

    The **Office of Credit Ratings** was established under the direction of the SEC to regulate credit rating agencies, such as Moody's and Standard & Poor's. This was done because a number of people believed that these agencies had been responsible for over-valuing derivatives and mortgage-backed securities.[27]

4. Federal Insurance Office

The Dodd-Frank Act created the **Federal Insurance Office** ("FIO") and gave it the power to oversee all aspects of the insurance market and to monitor the degree to which underserved communities and consumers have access to affordable non-health insurance products. In addition, FIO serves as an advisory member of the Financial Stability Oversight Council, assists with administration of the Terrorism Risk Insurance Program, and provides advice to the Secretary on important insurance matters.[28]

5. Repeal of the Dodd Frank Act

On June 8, 2017, the House of Representatives voted to repeal the Dodd-Frank Act by approving a bill known as the Financial Choice Act, which scales back or removes a number of the postcrisis banking rules.[29] The bill has been sent to the Senate for further action.

C. Antitrust Laws

Antitrust laws are designed to prevent or control trusts, cartels and other monopolies that restrict free trade and competition. The goal of these laws is to make businesses compete fairly and to prevent price fixing. Premised on the idea that free trade helps the economy, the laws forbid several types of restraint of trade. This targeted conduct falls into several areas: agreements between or among competitors, contractual arrangements between sellers and buyers, and the pursuit or maintenance of monopolies and mergers.[30] The major antitrust laws are as follows:

1. The Sherman Antitrust Act

The **Sherman Antitrust Act** was the first law enacted to prohibit monopolies and trusts. A trust was an instrument by which stockholders in different corporations transferred their shares to a single set of trustees. In consideration of the transfer, they received a certificate giving the stockholders a portion of the earnings of the managed companies. These trusts, however, came to control a number of major industries, and constituted monopolies because they were run by the same trustees and destroyed competition.[31]

The Sherman Act allowed the government to sue the trusts in order to break them up. As was noted, any combination "in the form of trust or otherwise that was in restraint of trade or commerce among the several states, or with foreign nations" was declared illegal. Persons forming such combinations were subject to fines of and criminal prosecution.[32]

The thrust of this law is to prevent the unreasonable collection of market power, either by a single entity or a group of entities that gain "market power" through anticompetitive agreements. Market power arises when consumers have few alternatives to the seller's product, thereby allowing the merchant to establish terms based upon the maximization of profits rather than by competitive pressures.

The legislation attempts to accomplish these objectives by prohibiting restraint of trade and monopolies which are the subject of the first two sections of the law. Section 1 of the Sherman Antitrust Act deals with unreasonable restraint of trade and prohibits every contract, combination or conspiracy in restraint of trade in interstate commerce. To establish a claim under this section, one must demonstrate a concerted action on the part of the defendant and an unreasonable restraint of trade. To show a concerted action, the claimant must show a "conscious commitment to a common scheme designed to achieve an unlawful objective."[33]

Section 2 prohibits monopolies, and two elements must be demonstrated: possession of a monopoly in the relevant market that provides the ability to set prices and exclude competition, and a willful acquisition or maintenance of that power as opposed to merely acquiring market dominance through proper competitive means or through events beyond its control.[34]

2. The Clayton Antitrust Act

In 1924, Congress passed additional antitrust legislation in the form of the **Clayton Antitrust Act.** This law was an effort to prohibit certain actions that lead to anti-competitiveness such as price discrimination, price fixing, mergers, and unfair business practices.[35] Unlike the Sherman Antitrust Act, which used general language and a broad approach to antitrust issues, the Clayton Act was aimed at specific anticompetitive practices which had been found by the courts to be outside the reach of the original legislation, but which Congress deemed dangerous to free competition and commerce.[36]

The Clayton Act allows a person, who can show that he or she has been harmed by reason of any antitrust violation, to file a private lawsuit in the federal courts for treble damages plus reasonable attorneys' fees and a court order prohibiting future violations.[37]

C. The Robinson Patam Act

The **Robinson Patam Act** was enacted during the depression to ban discriminatory pricing practices in sales transactions. The Act forbids different prices being charged to various purchasers, solely on the basis that the buyers are of different sizes. The ban is supposed to assist smaller businesses who may be at a competitive disadvantage when they must compete against larger buyers who purchase larger amounts of the product. For instance, the law may come into play if larger retailers are being sold merchandise at a lower rate than other buyers may obtain them.[38]

Very simply, the Robinson Patam Act prohibits sellers in interstate commerce from charging different buyers different prices for goods of "like grade and quality." The Act applies only to the sale of goods and only when the sale is of goods purchased for resale within the United States and not those sold for export.[39] A violation may be defended by showing that the different prices signify only the cost of the seller's manufacture or delivery; or, that the seller is trying either (1) to meet the prices of another vendor or (2) to enable the buyer to competitive with the buyer's competition.[40]

One issue that arises is whether a seller may charge a different price in a geographic area based upon local competition. Anheuser-Busch lowered its prices for Budweiser in the St. Louis area in the 1950s, enabling it to capture a significant segment of that market area. The company was accused of illegal price discrimination but the count found in favor of the beer company, because the brewery was simply engaging in normal competition; Anheuser-Busch was meeting the price in the St. Louis market. Much later, this practice became known as the **"Starbucks Effect."** It has been shown that whenever Starbucks opens stores in an area, coffee sales increase overall in that area, and local vendors—Starbucks' competitors—end up doing better than they were before Starbucks' arrival.[41]

SECTION 9.15
REVIEW QUESTIONS

1. Jones, Jackson and Daly are lawyers. Each was a sole proprietor of his own law practice and shared an office suite. They each paid one-third of the rent, photocopier, fax and cost of a receptionist to answer their telephones. Each had his own telephone number and stationary, paid his own secretary, postage and all other expenses associated with the law practice. They each kept all fees earned individually and did not share fees with the others. When a client called the office, the receptionist would answer, "Law office of Jones, Jackson, or Daly" depending on whose line rang. One day, they were having lunch together and Jones said they might be able to make more money if potential clients believed they were partners. Jackson and Daly agreed so they changed their stationary to read "Jones, Jackson and Daly—Attorneys at Law." Each kept his own telephone number, but if someone called the receptionist, she would answer "Jones, Jackson and Daly—Attorneys at Law, how may I direct your call?" They each still paid one-third of the rent, photocopier, fax and receptionist expenses and continued to keep the fees each earned. One day, Ellie Vator came into the law suite and asked to see a lawyer in regard to a recent motor vehicle accident

in which she sustained serious injuries. The receptionist directed her to Mr. Jackson who handled negligence cases and he agreed to represent her. Unfortunately, Mr. Jackson did not file Ellie's lawsuit within the appropriate Statute of Limitations and her case was dismissed by the court. Ellie wants to bring a legal malpractice case to collect damages for her loss as the result of Jackson's negligence. Can Ellie successfully sue Jones and Daly as partners of Mr. Jackson? Can Ellie sue the law partnership of "Jones, Jackson and Daly—Attorneys at Law." Do Jones and Daly have any legal redress against Jackson?

2. Bob is the Deputy Assistant Associate Vice-President of Intergalactic Industries. One day his boss, Big Joe, called Bob into his office and told him that because Intergalactic lost a big government contract, he had to let Bob go. Big Joe was sorry but he had no alternative. However, Bob had back vacation pay and would be given a severance package of $100,000 to ease his transition to another job. About a week later, Bob saw an ad in the Business Journal for a new franchise seeking franchisees for a business venture known as "Roadkill Restaurants." Bob was interested. He always wanted to own a restaurant but he did not have the education or knowledge as to how to fulfill this dream. What questions should Bob ask Roadkill? Should Bob talk to anyone else other than Roadkill? What information is Roadkill required by FTC regulations to provide Bob? What advantages are there for Bob in obtaining a Roadkill franchise as opposed to staring his own restaurant?

3. Joe and Diane, a married couple, started a business selling left socks. At first, they sold the socks out of a cart they pushed down the street, but the business prospered and they opened a store. They then incorporated the business under the name "Left Socks, Inc." As the years went by, they expanded and at their death, they operated six retail outlets selling left socks. They left the business to their two sons and daughter and the business grew into 25 stores. Eventually, the three children died. Each son had two sons and the daughter had one daughter. These children inherited their parent's share. They all worked in the business and were members of the Board of Directors. They received a salary for the work they did and dividends for the shares they owned each year. One day, the four male cousins who owned two-thirds of the shares in the business decided to fire their female cousin who owned one-third of the shares. Then they removed her from the Board of Directors, decided not to declare any dividends and raised their own salaries to compensate for the lack of dividends. What action can their cousin take to get her position back? What can she do to get back on the Board of Directors? Can she compel her cousins to authorize the payment of a dividend? Will she be successful in her efforts?

4. Westside Sand, Inc. is a corporation and Gerald Webber is the president and stockholder of the business. An agent for Westside Sand Company purchased materials from P&L Construction Materials for use by Westside Sand Company. When the business defaulted on the payment of the bill, suit was instituted against Webber in his personal capacity. The evidence demonstrated that the agent never informed P&L that she was buying the materials for Westside Sand, Inc. Since the identity of Westside Sand, Inc. was not disclosed by the agent to P&L at the time of the purchase, does that make the president of Westside personally liable for the corporate debt? **Deroche v. P&L Construction Materials, Inc., 554 So.2d 717 (Ct. App. La., 1989).**

5. A&M Records sued M.V.C. Distributing Corporation and Donald Merry for the unauthorized duplication and distribution of musical recordings. Merry ran the business. These pirated or bootlegged tapes were reproductions of the original records marketed under a different record label. The record companies attempted to pierce the corporate veil of M.V.C. in order to hold Merry personally liable as a corporate officer for the music piracy. Is the officer of a business personally responsible for the improper or illegal actions of a corporation? **A&M Records, Inc. v. M.V.C. Distributing Corp., 574 F.2d 312 (6th Cir., 1978).**

SECTION 9.16
INTERNET REFERENCES

For more information about topics discussed in this chapter, see the following Internet sites:

A. Starting a Business

*   **www.businesstown.com/gettingstarted/index.asp**
    This site provides a step by step process of starting a small business.

*   **www.irs.ustreas.gov/bus_info/index.html**
    The IRS offers this site in order to provide tax information for businesses.

*   **http://aol.toolkit.cch.com**
    This is a comprehensive site providing news updates and information on planning, starting, and financing a business.

B. Starting an Internet Business

*   **www.buildyourhomebiz.com**
    Those interested in starting an Internet business may find this address helpful since it offers articles, advice, and answers to frequently asked questions about the topic.

C. Limited Liability Companies

- **www.llc-usa.com**
  This site is dedicated to those interested in limited liability companies. Several links are provided to resources on the topic.

- **www.llcweb.com**
  General information about limited liability companies is contained at this site.

Footnotes:

1. Corporate Governance, International Finance Corporation, http://www.ifc.org/wps/wcm/connect/Topics_Ext_Content/IFC_External_Corporate_Site/Corporate+Governance (last visited October 5, 2013).

2. Lisa Mary Thomson, What Is Corporate Governance?, http://articles.economictimes.indiatimes.com/2009-01-18/news/28462497_1_corporate-governance-satyam-books-fraud-by-satyam-founder (last visited October 5, 2013).

3. Best Corporate Governance Practice, Applied Corporate Governance, http://www.applied-corporate-governance.com/best-corporate-governance-practice.html (last visited October 7, 2013).

4. *Id.*

5. Is Entrepreneurship For You?, SBA.gov, http://www.sba.gov/content/entrepreneurship-you (last visited October 5, 2013).

6. Tyler Lacoma, *What Is a Business Enterprise?*, bizfluent, https://bizfluent.com/about-6721330-business-enterprise-.html (last visited January 29, 2018.)

7. Is Entrepreneurship For You?, Supra.

8. *Id.*

9. The Basics of Sole Proprietorships, Entrepreneurs, http://www.entrepreneur.com/article/77798 (last visited October 5, 2013).

10. *Limited Partnerships*, Incorproate.com, https://www.incorporate.com/limited_partnership.html (last visited January 29, 2018.)

11. Stephanie Morrow, *FLP: What is a Family Limited Partnership and How Can It Save Your Family Money?*, Legal Zoom, https://www.legalzoom.com/articles/flp-what-is-a-family-limited-partnership-and-how-can-it-save-your-family-money (last visited January 29, 2018.)

12. Kiara Ashanti, What Is a Family Limited Partnership (FLP) – Pros & Cons, Money Crashers, http://www.moneycrashers.com/family-limited-partnership-flp/ (last visited October 5, 2013).

13. *Id.*

14. Limited Liability Company, SBA. gov, http://www.sba.gov/content/limited-liability-company-llc (last visited October 5, 2013).

15. *Id.*

16. *An Assessment of the White House's Progress on Deregulation*, The Economist, October 14, 2017, https://www.economist.com/news/business/21730170-donald-trump-has-blocked-new-regulations-ease-repealing-old-ones-will-be-harder.

17. The Investor's Advocate: How the SEC Protects Investors, Maintains Market Integrity, and Facilitates Capital Formation, Securities Exchange Commission, http://www.sec.gov/about/whatwedo.shtml (last visited October 5, 2013).

18. Akin Oyedele, *Wall Street's Top Watchdog Is Gong Soft Under Trump*, Business Insider, November 15, 2017, http://www.businessinsider.com/trump-sec-regulation-jay-clayton-2017-11 (last visited January 29, 2018.)

19. Emily Stephenson and Brett Wolf, Regulators, Bitcoin Group Discuss Digital Currency, Reuters, August 26, 2013, http://w.reuters.com/article/2013/08/26/us-financial-regulation-bitcoin-idUSBRE97P0OO20130826 (last visited October 25, 2013).

20. Frequently Asked Questions, Bitcoin, http://bitcoin.org/en/faq (last visited October 25, 2013).

21. The Great Recession, State of Working America, http://stateofworkingamerica.org/great-recession/ (last visited October 5, 2013).

22. Mark Koba, Dodd-Frank Act: CNBC Explains, May 11, 2012, http://www.cnbc.com/id/47075854 (last visited October 5, 2013).

23. *Id.*

24. Wall Street Reform: The Dodd-Frank Act, The White House, http://www.whitehouse.gov/economy/middle-class/dodd-frank-wall-street-reform (last visited October 5, 2013).

25. Kimberly Amadeo, Dodd-Frank Wall Street Reform Act, About.com, http://useconomy.about.com/od/criticalssues/p/Dodd-Frank-Wall-Street-Reform-Act.htm (last visited october 5, 2013).

26. David S. Huntington, Summary of Dodd-Frank Financial Regulation Legislation, The Harvard Law School Forum on Corporate Governance and Financial Regulation, http://blogs.law.harvard.edu/corpgov/2010/07/07/summary-of-dodd-frank-financial-regulation-legislation/ (last visited October 5, 2013).

27. Kimberly Amadeo, Dodd-Frank Wall Street Reform Act, About.com, *supra.*

28. Federal Insurance Office, U.S. Department of the Treasury, http://www.treasury.gov/about/organizational-structure/offices/Pages/Federal-Insurance.aspx (last visited October 5, 2013).

29. Geoff Bennett, *House Passes Bill Aimed at Reversing Dodd-Frank Financial Regulations*, National Public Radio, https://www.npr.org/2017/06/08/532036374/house-passes-bill-aimed-at-reversing-dodd-frank-financial-regulations (last visited January 29, 2018.)

30. Antitrust Law, The Free Dictionary by Farlex, http://legal-dictionary.thefreedictionary.com/Antitrust+Law (last visited October 5, 2013).

31. The Sherman Antitrust Act, LINFO, http://www.linfo.org/sherman.html corpgov/2010/07/07/summary-of-dodd-frank-financial-regulation-legislation/ (last visited October 5, 2013).

32. Sherman Anti-Trust Act (1890), www.ourdocuments.com, http://www.ourdocuments.gov/doc.php?flash=true&doc=51 (last visited October 5, 2013).

33. Acme Markets, Inc. v. Wharton Hardware and Supply Corp., 890 F. Supp. 1230 (D.N.J., 1995).

34. Great Western Directories, Inc. v. Southwestern Bell Telephone Co., 63 F.3d 1378 (C.A.5 (Tex.), 1995).

35. Clayton Antitrust Act, Investopedia, http://www.investopedia.com/terms/c/clayton-antitrust-act.asp (last visited October 5, 2013).

36. John Bourdeau, et. al., 54 Am. Jur. 2d Monopolies and Restraints of Trade § 138, Database updated August 2013.

37. Richard M. Steuer, Findlaw, http://corporate.findlaw.com/business-operations/executive-summary-of-the-antitrust-laws.html (last visited October 5, 2013).

38. What is the Robinson-Patman Act, WiseGEEK, http://www.wisegeek.com/what-is-the-robinson-patman-act.htm (last visited October 5, 2013).

39. Janice E. Rubin, Discriminatory Pricing and the Robinson-Patman Act: Brief Overview, Including Some Exceptions, CRS Report for Congress, http://congressionalresearch.com/RS21337/document.php (last visited October 5, 2013).

40. *Id.*

41. G. Stolyarov II, The Robinson-Patman Act and Cases Regarding Price Discrimination in the United States, Yohoo! Voices, http://voices.yahoo.com/the-robinson-patman-act-cases-regarding-price-671960.html?cat=37 (last visited October 5, 2013).

KEY TERMS

Agent

Antitrust Laws

Articles of Incorporation

Bitcoin

Board of Directors

Business Judgment Rule

Buy-Sell Agreement

Certificate of Incorporation

Certificate of Limited Partnership

Chain Style Business Operation

Corporate Governance

Corporate Officers

Corporation

Consumer Financial Protection Bureau

Clayton Antitrust Act

Dodd-Frank Act

Directors

Dissolution

Distributorship

Double Taxation

Family Limited Partnership

Family Limited Liability Partnership

Federal Insurance Office (FIO)

Fictitious Name Registration

Franchise

Franchisee

Franchisor

Incorporators

Indemnification

Information Return

Insider Trading

Joint and Several Liability

Limited Liability Company

Limited Liability Partnership

Limited Partnership

Manufacturing Franchise

Misappropriation Theory

Officers

Office of Credit Ratings

Organizational Form

Partnership

Piercing the Corporate Veil

Processing Plant Franchise

Prospectus

Proxies

Registration Statement

Robinson Patam Act

Rule 10b-5

S Corporation

Sarbanes-Oxley Act

Securities Act of 1933

Securities and Exchange Commission (SEC)

Securities Exchange Act of 1934

Security

Shareholders

Sherman Antitrust Act

Short Swing Profits

Sole Proprietor

Sole Proprietorship

Starbucks Effect

Terminate

Termination

Tipper/Tipee Theory

Tipping

Winding Up

CHAPTER 10

EMPLOYMENT LAW*

SECTION 10.1
INTRODUCTION

Steve Backup, a bartender at Tyler's Sport Bar and Grill, was called into Joe Robert's office because he had served liquor to an underage patron. Following a reprimand by Joe, Backup stormed out of the office and slammed the glass office door shut casing it to shatter. A piece of glass struck the bartender severely cutting his hand. Surgery was required to fix a ruptured tendon and to sew the wound shut. Backup could not work for six months so her requested that the bar pay his medical bills and lost wages. Robert's denied the claim noting that the injury was Backup's fault when he slammed the door shut out of anger and not work related. The employee then filed a worker's compensation claim and the judge ruled in his favour agreeing that the injury was work related.[1]

Managers have always had tough, demanding jobs, but in recent years, the law has added complicated, frustrating new expectations. The threat of lawsuits, like Pierce's, has become an important consideration in management decision-making. As union strength has declined, government rules and court decisions protecting employees have expanded. Those increased legal protections, a volatile economy, downsizing, decreased employer-employee loyalty, and other forces have led to unprecedented levels of employee litigation.

Rapidly changing technology is enhancing employee efficiency, but it too brings new litigation risks:

> Most of us have probably seen and maybe are also guilty of the daring and increasingly dangerous practice of "driving while dialing." This means cruising down the highway or zipping around city streets while chatting on a cell phone. Now, with the increasing popularity of PDAs (personal digital assistants), such as Palm Pilots and pocket PCs, some people are beginning to boldly master tapping the screens of the PDAs (as they sit in their laps) with one hand, and clutching the wheel with the other.

SECTION 10.2
SELECTION OF
AN EMPLOYEE

The nature of the selection (hiring) process and the laws governing it depend on the type of relationship the employer decides to build with the worker. The traditional, stable model of long-term direct employer—employee relationships now is often replaced with new, flexible, nontraditional staffing arrangements including outsourcing and employee leasing, along with the use

---

* **This Chapter is reprinted from McAdams, Chapter 12, Employment Law 1: Employee Rights, Eighth Edition, Law, Business and Society, McGraw Hill Publishing Company.**

of freelancers, temporary agencies, and professional employer organizations. (Firms save money and increase expertise by contracting with these PEOs to administer the firms' human resource services.) These new contingent workers, along with **independent contractors,** who are increasingly relied on to perform specific, shorter-term, nonrecurring jobs, permit employers to rapidly and inexpensively inflate or shrink their work forces as competitive and regulatory conditions change. The bad publicity and bad feelings associated with downsizing can be reduced with greater reliance on temps, and the cost savings can be large. Employers who choose to provide health and retirement benefits for their traditional employees need not do so for their contingent workers. Nor must they withhold income, Social Security, Medicare, and unemployment taxes. With fringe benefit costs reaching 40 percent of total compensation and averaging $15,000 (including payroll taxes) per employee, shrinking benefits has become an important consideration for many firms.[2]

The impact of many legal themes discussed in this chapter depends, initially, on whether the worker in question is considered, as a matter of law, an **employee** whether, long-term or contingent, or an independent contractor. That is, when an enterprise hires, for example, a trucker, programmer, or service technician, is that person an employee or an independent operator under contract to the organization but not, legally, a part of that organization?

The dominant test in settling the employee—independent contractor question is one of control. Where a worker's performance is controlled by an employer, or where the employer has the right or the ability to control that work, the worker is likely to be considered an employee. A business that hires an independent contractor generally is not required to comply with a wide range of employment and labor law standards that would apply were the worker an employee. Thus, a business must provide unemployment insurance, workers' compensation coverage, minimum wages, and so on to employees, but generally would not need to do so for independent contractors.

Microsoft agreed in 2000 to pay $97 million to settle federal lawsuits involving independent contractors and other contingent workers who won a long court battle to establish that they were entitled to employee benefits.[3] That coverage was especially important in the Microsoft case because it entitled many of the workers to very valuable Microsoft stock options. Basically, the Ninth Circuit Federal Court of Appeals found that the freelancers did the same work as Microsoft employees, and thus, had to be treated the same for benefit purposes despite the fact that the workers had signed contracts acknowledging their temp status and agreeing that they had no right to participate in the benefit plans.[4] The U.S. Supreme Court declined to review that ruling.[5] One of Microsoft's strategies to deal with the worker classification problems was to enact a new policy providing that temporary employees could not work for more than one year before taking a hiatus of at least 100 days.[6]

In conventional employer—employee relationships, contingent deals, and in some cases, independent contractor arrangements, a growing variety of potential legal problems have emerged.

- *Resume fraud:* HireRight, an Internet-based company, reviewed about 200,000 job applicants in one year and concluded that 80 percent of résumés are misleading, 20 percent list fraudulent degrees, and 40 percent have inflated salary histories.[7] Another study found that 13 percent of college students falsified their résumés even before beginning their careers.[8]

- *Background checks:* The 9/11/2001 attacks and the duty to provide a safe workplace have dramatically increased employers' attention to background and security checks. A recent survey found that about 80 percent of companies conducted criminal background checks in 2003, up from 51 percent in 1996, while credit checks increased to 35 percent from 19 percent in the earlier survey.[9]

- *Inappropriate questions:* About 21 percent of 1,000 workers in a national survey said they had been asked inappropriate questions in a job interview.[10] Often these questions, such as "How old are you?" and "Are you married?" raise discrimination concerns. The questions themselves are not technically unlawful, but discrimination based on the answers to those questions would be illegal. But what about the enormous array of awkward, intrusive, but nondiscriminatory interview questions that might leave the candidate feeling uncomfortable if not wronged? For example:

  > Following a job interview this year, Megan Johnson sent a handwritten thank-you note on fine stationery. But she didn't make the impression she intended. "You aren't a Republican, are you?" asked the hiring manager during a follow-up phone call. Ms. Johnson was stumped until she remembered the small blue elephant with an upturned trunk engraved along the upper margin of her note card.[11] The elephant was, in fact, supposed to represent good luck, but Johnson did not get the job. Furthermore, she cannot sue the company because questions about politics break no employment laws.[12]

- *Noncompete clauses:* In November 2002, Frank Cumbo and 10 colleagues left a New York temporary staffing agency to start a competing business. Two months later, their former employer sued all 11 for unfairly attempting to solicit business from its clients.[13]

Cumbo says he and the others built their new business from scratch and took no information with them. The lawsuit is pending at this writing. To address problems like these, employers sometimes require employees and new hires to sign agreements providing that they will neither pass trade secrets to others nor work for a competitor for a specified period. Cumbo and his colleagues had not signed such a pact, but a recent survey found that 30 percent of companies now require employees to sign non-compete agreements, and 51 percent require nondisclosure agreements.[14]

• *Arbitration:* New hires are sometimes expected to sign agreements specifying that disputes with the employer will be settled by arbitration rather than by litigation. Employers like arbitration because they view it as less adversarial than a trial—faster, cheaper, and more consistent. Often employees see arbitration as stacked in favor of corporate interests and as a denial of the fundamental right of access to the legal system. Sherri Warner is one of those:

> When Sherri Warner claimed a former employer sexually harassed her, the California secretary had to abide by a legal agreement requiring any claims to go to arbitration instead of court. Warner lost her arbitration case, but that was just the beginning of her problems. Warner's lawyer says she was then required to pay her former boss's legal fees. After three years of hearings, the total bill came to more than $200,000. . . .[15]

An important 2001 U.S. Supreme Court decision in the **Circuit City** case generally upholds the enforceability of legitimate, equitable employment arbitration agreements.[16] The federal government's anti-discrimination agency, the **Equal Employment Opportunity Commission,** however, retains authority to file lawsuits to secure damages for employees despite arbitration agreements that might prevent the employee herself from suing.[17]

Historically, a job applicant's previous performance record was an important ingredient in the hiring decision, but legal difficulties have significantly reduced the usefulness of the standard reference letter. Employers fear that providing references may lead to defamation claims (*slander* when spoken; *libel* when written) by former employees.

Many state courts, however, recognize what is labeled a **qualified privilege** as a defense in an employment-related defamation suit. The privilege applies where the one communicating the statement and the recipient share a legitimate, business-related interest in the information conveyed. Thus, references, internal employee evaluations, and the like are protected in most states from defamation claims in the absence of malice or extreme recklessness. Similarly, a number of states have passed statutes protecting legitimate reference communications from defamation claims. Nevertheless, some recent court decisions appear to have eroded the qualified privilege a bit, leading many employers to "play it safe" by limiting their references to strictly factual details such as the date of hire, date of departure, and job title.

Broadly, a successful **defamation** suit requires the following conditions:

1. A false statement.

2. The statement must be "published" to a third party.

3. The employer must be responsible for the publication.

4. The plaintiff's reputation must be harmed.

Truth is a complete defense in defamation cases, and firms that avoid second-hand information, personal issues, and potential discrimination themes such as age are likely not to have problems. A mistake, however, can be expensive.

SECTION 10.3
LONDON V.
TYLER'S SPORTS
BAR AND GRILL

PROBLEM TEN—A

PARK, BROWN & SMITH, P.C.
ATTORNEYS AT LAW
MEMORANDUM

TO: All Law Clerks

FROM: Peter Smith, Esquire

RE: The Mechanical Bull

I know that you will find this hard to believe, but the owners of Tyler's Sports Bar and Grill have another legal dilemma. When the bar opened, Joe Roberts hired an outside security firm named Armed Services Security to maintain order at the premises. In this way, he did not have to find and train a security staff, a task that he knew nothing about. Joe turned to Armed Services Security, which was run by a former major in the army who only hired ex-military police officers and specialized in security for bars and nightclubs.

Tyler's entered into a contract with the outside firm for a two-year period. Armed Services Security agreed to supply at least four veteran security guards each night and the document specified that the agency "shall be considered an independent contractor at all times."

Tyler's caters to all tastes, so in its quest to be a success, it leased a mechanical bull in order to appeal to the country and western crowd. This machine operated ride simulated the bucking experience of a rodeo bull made so popular in the movie Urban Cowboy.

Because the machine was dangerous and required a lot of skill to use, Tyler's has a firm policy that no one who appears to be intoxicated could ride the bull.

One night, a group of Dallas Cowboy fans appeared at the bar and became obnoxiously drunk. The leader of the group, Willie London, was very loud and kept bad mouthing the Philadelphia sports fans as being losers. This bantering eventually led to a dare. The Cowboy fan taunted everyone in the bar that he could ride the mechanical bull longer than anyone else and offered $1,000 to any person who could beat his time riding the bull.

The bar patrons immediately lined up to ride the mechanical device. After 25 attempts by people to stay on the bull, one person was able to ride the mechanical bull for the required time. Not to be outdone, London staggered up to the bull and attempted to get on. Boastfully, he shouted to his friends to turn up the setting for difficulty to the highest speed. The bar manager overheard this order and realized that the customer was drunk so he signaled to the security guards to remove him from the bull. When London refused the requests to dismount, the manager told the security guards to forcible remove him. Four guards then violently grabbed the Cowboy fan and throw him to the floor. The customer landed awkwardly and broke his hip and wrist.

Mr. Roberts informed me this morning that Tyler's has been sued for the injuries sustained by the patron. The owner doesn't understand the claim and read me the language in the security guards' contract that says the security guards shall be considered "independent contractors." Joe looked up the law on the Internet and found a series of comments that an employer is not liable for the actions of an independent contractor. I went to the bar later in the day and took a statement from the bar manager. I am concerned about the fact that the manger was the one who told the guards to forcible remove the Cowboy fan from the mechanical bull.

Please read the following case and let me know whether you think that Tyler's will be liable for the actions of the security guards.

FIFTH CLUB, INC. V. RAMIREZ
196 S.W.3D 788 (TEX., 2006)

Fifth Club, Inc. operates a nightclub known as Club Rodeo. David West, a certified peace officer, was hired as an independent contractor by Fifth Club to provide security at the nightclub. Late one night, Roberto Ramirez arrived at Club Rodeo after several hours of drinking. Ramirez and his brother tried to enter the club but were denied admission by the doorman, allegedly because they were intoxicated. The doorman signaled to West and another parking lot security officer to escort Ramirez and his brother out of the club's entrance. West allegedly grabbed Ramirez, slammed Ramirez's head against a concrete wall, knocking him unconscious, and then struck him several times. The altercation resulted in multiple injuries to Ramirez, including a fractured skull. Ramirez claims Fifth Club is vicariously liable for West's conduct in spite of his independent contractor status because it controlled West's security activities. Fifth Club contends there is legally insufficient evidence it retained sufficient control over West's security activities to make it vicariously liable for his conduct.

Generally, an employer has no duty to ensure that an independent contractor performs its work in a safe manner. However, an employer can be held vicariously liable for the actions of an independent contractor if the employer retains some control over the manner in which the contractor performs the work that causes the damage. One who entrusts work to an independent contractor, but who retains the control of any part of the work, is subject to liability for physical harm to others for whose safety the employer owes a duty to exercise reasonable care, which is caused by his failure to exercise his control with reasonable care.

A right of control requires more than a general right to order the work stopped or resumed, to inspect its progress or to receive reports, to make suggestions or recommendations, which need not necessarily be followed, or to prescribe alterations and deviations. Such a general right is usually reserved to employers, but it does not mean that the contractor is controlled as to his methods of work, or as to operative detail. There must be such a retention of a right of supervision that the contractor is not entirely free to do the work in his own way.

Employers can direct when and where an independent contractor does the work and can request information and reports about the work, but an employer may become liable for the independent contractor's tortious acts only if the employer controls the details or methods of the independent contractor's work to such an extent that the contractor cannot perform the work as it chooses.

In this case, there was no evidence that Fifth Club gave more than general directions to West or that it retained the right to control the manner in which West performed his job. Fifth Club's action in directing West to remove Ramirez from the premises did not rise to the level of directing how the work was to be performed or directing the safety of the performance because West retained the right to remove Ramirez by whatever method he chose. Fifth Club, therefore, cannot be held vicariously liable for West's conduct.

Because the character of West's work for Fifth Club alone does not impose employer liability, we conclude Fifth Club is not vicariously liable to Ramirez.

**PROBLEM TEN—A
ANSWER SHEET**

Name   **Please Print Clearly**

1. By ordering the security guards to remove the Cowboy fan from the
   bull, did the security guards become transformed from independent
   contractors to employees of the bar?

2. Will the bar be liable for the injuries sustained by Mr. London?

SECTION 10.4
LIABILITY

Once hired, what happens when employees make mistakes or engage in misconduct on the job that hurts others? Must the employer bear the loss in these situations? Job classification is an important first question in determining company liability for workers' job-related injuries, injuries to others, and crimes. An enterprise ordinarily will not be liable for the acts of its independent contractors. Employers, on the other hand, often bear legal responsibility for employees' accidents or wrongs. That liability often springs from the doctrine of respondeat superior), a form of **vicarious liability** (sometimes called *imputed liability*).

Employer liability for employee injuries, accidents, or wrongs is largely dependent on whether the employee was on the job at the time of the incident in question. As explained later in the chapter, employers are generally liable, under **workers' compensation** statutes, for injuries to employees regardless of the cause of those injuries if they occurred within the **scope of employment** (on the job). Likewise, employers will be held liable under vicarious liability/respondent superior reasoning for harm to third parties caused by the intentional or negligent acts of their employees when those acts occur within the scope of employment. A finding of employer liability, of course, does not excuse the employee from her liability, but the vicarious liability/respondent superior reasoning does have the potential effect of opening the employer's deeper pockets to the plaintiff. The central inquiry in assigning employer liability lies in the scope of employment question; that is, broadly, did the accident happen while the employee was on the job? The following questions ordinarily determine whether the harm occurred within the scope of employment:

1. Was the employee subject to the employer's supervision?

2. Was the employee motivated, at least in part, by a desire to serve the employer's business interests?

3. Did the problem arise substantially within normal working hours and in a work location?

4. Was the act in question of the general kind the employee had been hired to perform.

In a 1991 case, **Mary M. v. City of Los Angeles,**[18] the city was held liable under the doctrine of respondent superior for a sexual assault committed by a police officer. At 2:30 AM on October 3, 1981, Sergeant Leigh Schroyer was on duty, in uniform, carrying a gun, and patrolling in his marked police car. He stopped Mary M. for erratic driving. She pleaded not to be arrested. He ordered her to enter his patrol car and took her to her home. He entered her home and said that he expected "payment" for not arresting her. He raped her and was subsequently sentenced to a term in state prison. Mary M. sued the City of Los Angeles. The general inquiry was whether Schroyer was acting within the scope of his employment during the rape episode. The jury found for Mary M. and awarded $150,000 in damages. The Court of Appeals reversed, saying that Schroyer was not acting within the scope of his employment. The case went to the California Supreme Court. The city argued that Schroyer was acting on behalf of his own interests rather than those of the city, and that the city had not authorized his conduct. Therefore, Schroyer could not have been acting within the scope of employment. However, the court said that the correct question was not whether the rape was authorized but whether it happened in the course of a series of acts that were authorized. The court reversed, saying that a jury could find the city vicariously liable (imputed to the principal from the agent) given the unique authority of police officers in our society. The City was therefore held liable for the sexual assault committed by a police officer.

QUESTIONS FOR DISCUSSION:

1. Gonzalez, working for Land Transport, was driving his employer's tractor-trailer behind Nichols, who was driving his pickup. Gonzalez followed at an unsafe distance and twice attempted to pass in no-passing zones. Nichols responded with "predictable obscene gestures." While both drivers were stopped at a red light, Gonzalez left the company truck and attacked Nichols with a rubber-coated metal cable and a knife.

   Gonzalez was convicted of assault. Nichols sued Land Transport.

   a. What is his claim?

   b. Decide the case. Explain. See **Nichols v. Land Transport, 233 F.3d 21 (1st Cir., 2000).**

2. Williams, Hemphill, Dixon, and Osborne, while driving in Chicago, noticed some pizza boxes on top of a car parked in front of the Italian Fiesta Pizzeria. Dixon and Hemphill jumped out, discovered the boxes were empty, dropped them, and reentered their Jeep. Hall, a driver for Italian Fiesta, observed Dixon and Hemphill, yelled at them to return the pizza boxes, and then followed them in his vehicle. Dixon turned the wrong way onto a one-way street and Hall followed. Dixon then collided with another vehicle. Williams died and Hemphill was injured. Italian Fiesta was subsequently sued on negligent hiring and vicarious liability claims. The negligent hiring claim was rejected by the judge, but the vicarious liability theme was allowed to proceed to trial. The defendants provided evidence showing the pizzeria specifically informed employees that they were not to attempt to recover stolen property or punish perpetrators. Rather, the pizzeria's policy

was for supervisors to contact police. Further, drivers were not penalized if property was stolen.

    a. What was the central issue in this case?

    b. Decide the case. Explain. See **Williams v. Hall, 681 N.E. 2d 1037 (Ill. App., 1997).**

3. What policy justifications support the imposition of liability on an employer for the wrongs of an employee operating within the scope of employment?

<table>
<tr>
<td>

**Section 10.5
Hiring, Retention,
Training and
Supervision**

</td>
<td>

In recent years, employers' potential liability for employee wrong has been significantly expanded by a line of cases finding employers liable for **negligence in hiring an employee** or retaining an employee who subsequently causes harm to a third party, or for careless training or supervision. Typically, the employer is liable on negligence grounds for hiring or retaining an employee whom the employer knew or should have known to be dangerous, incompetent, dishonest, or the like where that information was directly related to the injury suffered by the plaintiff. The case that follows examines the law of negligent hiring, supervision, and retention.

</td>
</tr>
</table>

Yunker v. Honeywell, Inc.
496 N.W. 2d 419 (Minn. App., 1993)

Honeywell employed Randy Landin from 1977 to 1979 and from 1984 to 1988. From 1979 to 1984 Landin was imprisoned for the strangulation death of Nancy Miller, a Honeywell co-employee. On his release from prison, Landin reapplied at Honeywell. Honeywell rehired Landin as a custodian in Honeywell's General Offices facility in South Minneapolis in August 1984. Because of workplace confrontations, Landin was twice transferred, first to the Golden Valley facility in August 1986, and then to the St. Louis Park facility in August 1987. Kathleen Nesser was assigned to Landin's maintenance crew in April 1988. Landin and Nesser became friends and spent time together away from work. When Landin expressed a romantic interest, Nesser stopped spending time with Landin. Landin began to harass and threaten Nesser both at work and at home. At the end of

June, Landin's behavior prompted Nesser to seek help from her supervisor and to request a transfer out of the St. Louis Park facility. On July 1, 1988, Nesser found a death threat scratched on her locker door. Landin did not come to work on or after July 1, and Honeywell accepted his formal resignation on July 11, 1988. On July 19, approximately six hours after her Honeywell shift ended, Landin killed Nesser in her driveway with a close range shotgun blast. Landin was convicted of first-degree murder and sentenced to life imprisonment.

Jean Yunker, as trustee for the heirs and next-of-kin of Kathleen Nesser, brought this wrongful death action based on theories of negligent hiring, retention, and supervision of a dangerous employee. Honeywell moved for summary judgment and, for purposes of the motion, stipulated that it failed to exercise reasonable care in the hiring and supervision of Landin. The trial court concluded that Honeywell owed no legal duty to Nesser and granted summary judgment for Honeywell.

The issue is whether Honeywell had a duty to Kathleen Nesser to exercise reasonable care in hiring, retaining, or supervising Randy Landin? In determining that Honeywell did not have a legal duty to Kathleen Nesser arising from its employment of Randy Landin, the district court analyzed Honeywell's duty as limited by its ability to control and protect its employees while they are involved in the employer's business or at the employer's place of business.

Negligent hiring and negligent retention do not rely on the scope of employment but address risks created by exposing members of the public to a potentially dangerous individual. These theories of recovery impose liability for an employee's intentional tort, an action almost invariably outside the scope of employment, when the employer knew or should have known that the employee was violent or aggressive and might engage in injurious conduct.

Minnesota first explicitly recognized a cause of action based on negligent hiring in **Ponticas** in 1983. **Ponticas** involved the employment of an apartment manager who sexually assaulted a tenant. The Supreme Court upheld a jury verdict finding the apartment operators negligent in failing to make a reasonable investigation into the resident manager's background before providing him with a passkey. The court defined negligent hiring as predicated on the negligence of an employer in placing a person with known propensities, or propensities which should have been discovered by reasonable investigation, in an employment position in which, *because of the circumstances of the employment,* it should have been foreseeable that the hired individual posed a threat of injury to others.

Honeywell argues that under **Ponticas** it is not liable for negligent hiring because, unlike providing a dangerous resident manager with a passkey, Landin's employment did not enable him to commit the act of violence against Nesser. This argument has merit, and we note that a number of jurisdictions have expressly defined the scope of an employer's duty of reasonable care in hiring as largely dependent on the type of responsibilities associated with the particular job. **Ponticas** rejected the view that employers are required to investigate a prospective employee's criminal background in every job in which the individual has regular contact with the public. Instead, liability is determined by the totality of the circumstances surrounding the hiring and whether the employer exercised reasonable care. The court instructed that [t]he scope of the investigation is directly related to the severity of the risk third parties are subjected to by an incompetent employee. Although only slight care might suffice in the hiring of a yardman, a worker on a production line, or other types of employment where the employee would not constitute a high risk of injury to third persons, when the prospective employee is to be furnished a passkey permitting admittance to living quarters of tenants, the employer has the duty to use reasonable care to investigate his competency and reliability prior to employment.

Applying these principles, we conclude that Honeywell did not owe a duty to Nesser at the time of Landin's hire. Landin was employed as a maintenance worker whose job responsibilities entailed no exposure to the general public and required only limited contact with co-employees. Unlike the caretaker in **Ponticas,** Landin's duties did not involve inherent dangers to others, and unlike the tenant in **Ponticas,** Nesser was not a reasonably foreseeable victim at the time Landin was hired.

Honeywell did not breach a legal duty to Nesser by hiring Landin because the specific nature of his employment did not create a foreseeable risk of harm, and public policy supports a limitation on this cause of action. The district court correctly determined that Honeywell is not liable to Nesser under a theory of negligent hiring.

In recognizing the tort of negligent hiring, **Ponticas** extended established Minnesota case law permitting recovery under theories of negligent retention.

The difference between negligent hiring and negligent retention focuses on when the employer was on notice that an employee posed a threat and failed to take steps to ensure the safety of third parties. The Florida appellate court has provided a useful definition:

Negligent hiring occurs when, prior to the time the employee is actually hired, the employer knew or should have known of the employee's unfitness, and the issue of liability primarily focuses upon the adequacy of the employer's pre-employment investigation into the employee's background. Negligent retention, on the other hand, occurs when, during the course of employment, the employer becomes aware or should have become aware of problems with an employee that indicated his unfitness, and the employer fails to take further action such as investigating, discharge, or reassignment.

The record contains evidence of a number of episodes in Landin's post imprisonment employment at Honeywell that demonstrate a propensity for abuse and violence toward co-employees.

While at the Golden Valley facility, Landin sexually harassed female employees and challenged a male coworker to fight. After his transfer to St. Louis Park, Landin threatened to kill a coworker during an angry confrontation following a minor car accident. In another employment incident, Landin was hostile and abusive toward a female coworker after problems developed in their friendship. Landin's specific focus on Nesser was demonstrated by several workplace outbursts occurring at the end of June, and on July 1 the words "one more day and you're dead" were scratched on her locker door. Landin's troubled work history and the escalation of abusive behavior during the summer of 1988 relate directly to the foreseeability prong of duty. The facts . . . show that it was foreseeable that Landin could act violently against a co-employee, and against Nesser in particular.

This foreseeability gives rise to a duty of care to Nesser that is not outweighed by policy considerations of employment opportunity. An ex-felon's "opportunity for gainful employment may spell the difference between recidivism and rehabilitation," but it cannot predominate over the need to maintain a safe workplace when specific actions point to future violence. Our holding is narrow and limited only to the recognition of a legal duty owed to Nesser arising out of Honeywell's continued employment of Landin. It is important to emphasize that in reversing the summary judgment on negligent retention, we do not reach the remaining significant questions of whether Honeywell breached that duty by failing to terminate or discipline Landin, or whether such a breach was a proximate cause of Nesser's death. These are issues generally decided by a jury after a full presentation of facts.

We affirm the entry of summary judgment on the theories of negligent hiring and supervision, but reverse the summary judgment on the issue of negligent retention.

QUESTIONS FOR DISCUSSION:

1. What did the court mean when it said that "negligent hiring and negligent retention are based on direct, not vicarious, liability"?

2. Why did the court reject the negligent supervision claim?

3. Why did the court reject the negligent hiring claim?

SECTION 10.6
MINIMUM WAGE

A note was passed to President Franklin D. Roosevelt in 1936 from a young girl:

> I wish you could do something to help us girls. We have been working in a sewing factory, getting our minimum pay of $11 a week. Today, 200 of us girls have been cut down to $4, $5 and $6 a week.[19]

Roosevelt reportedly remarked that something needed to be done about child labor. The Depression and its tragic suffering, even of those working hard, shattered many Americans' faith in the free market and led to government intervention including, in 1938, the **Fair Labor Standards Act** (FLSA), which is directed to these major objectives:

1. The establishment of a minimum wage that provides at least a modest standard of living for employees.

2. A flexible ceiling on hours worked weekly, the purpose of which is to increase the number of employed Americans.

3. Child labor protection.

4. Equal pay for equal work regardless of gender.

Pat Williams of Shreveport, Louisiana, lost her home gas service in April 2001 because, according to *The Wall Street Journal,* a $477 payment was overdue. She works for $5.55 per hour in her daytime nursing assistant job and $5.15 per hour in her evening cleaning job. She is a 46-year-old mother of three. She reports having been able to live comfortably and even indulge herself occasionally while working minimum wage jobs 20 years ago. Why is she unable to have a similarly comfortable life today with her current minimum wage jobs? *The Wall Street Journal* answered:

> There's little wonder why. As a longtime low-wage worker, Ms. Williams has felt the sting of one of the most profound shifts in American economic policy during the past 20 years: a mounting disdain for the minimum wage.

> This sea change began when Ronald Reagan swept into office. From 1950 through 1982, the minimum wage was allowed to fall below 45 percent of the average hourly wage in the U.S. in only four separate years. Since 1982, the minimum wage has never reached 45 percent, and it currently stands at 36 percent of that benchmark.[20]

Many politicians and economists, however, fear that a minimum wage increase from the current federal requirement would unfairly drive up the cost of doing business and reduce the number of entry-level jobs.

Some evidence supports that view, but other studies have found that a higher minimum wage does not harm job growth. For example, in the 17 states and the District of Columbia that have minimum wages above the federal required level, job growth appears to have been at least as strong as growth in the states with the federal minimum wage.[21]

The most interesting recent development in this area is the "living wage" movement. Since 1994, more than 100 communities have passed laws aimed at pushing wages high enough to lift families above the federal poverty line. The laws typically apply only to companies contracting to provide goods and services to the cities, although some cover city employees as well. Santa Fe, New Mexico, may have the most aggressive living wage plan. All Santa Fe businesses with more than 25 employees must pay $8.50 per hour, increasing to $10.50 by 2008.[22] Critics fear that businesses will lay off staff to fall below the 25 threshold, others will decline to expand, while others will simply leave. A 2002 study found, however, that the higher minimums have been effective in reducing poverty despite some increase in unemployment.[23]

Vickey Ramsey, a former Wal-Mart assistant manager, was working 48 hours per week, but most of that time was occupied by stocking shelves and doing other tasks normally performed by hourly workers. Ramsey was moved to an hourly role at her request, but she sued Wal-Mart for classifying her as a manager in order, she claimed, to avoid paying **overtime.**[24] At this writing in 2005, Wal-Mart is facing some 30 overtime lawsuits.[25] Wal-Mart is not alone. A New Jersey appeals court ruled that Pepsi improperly failed to pay overtime to delivery truck drivers and others whom the company had classified as "outside" salespeople.[26] Disneyland paid $1.7 million to settle claims that it unlawfully failed to pay workers for their time spent getting into and out of costumes and for time spent wearing costumes before reaching the work site.[27]

In general, workers are entitled to FLSA protections, including the minimum wage and overtime (normally time and one-half for hours over 40 per week), but certain occupational classes are exempt; that is, those workers are not entitled to FLSA protections. In response to corporate pleas for relief from lawsuits, the Bush administration approved a 2004 revision of overtime rules. While still complicated, the new rules attempt to clarify the murky distinction between exempt and nonexempt employees.

At the simplest level, nearly all workers making less than $23,660 per year will be nonexempt (entitled to time and one—half overtime pay), whereas very few of those making $100,000 or more will be entitled to that pay. The tens of millions in between may or may not receive overtime depending on some rather vague rules. Those who fall in one of the following classes may, after close analysis of their duties, prove to be exempt from the overtime protections: executives, administrators, professional/creative workers, computer professionals, and outside salespeople. Some workers such as police officers, firefighters, and better-paid blue-collar workers are expressly granted the right to overtime pay. Others, such as insurance adjusters, dental hygienists, pharmacists, and journalists, are expressly exempt and thus not entitled to overtime. Critics say millions of workers will be ineligible for overtime pay under the new rules, but at this writing, the impact is unclear.

QUESTION FOR DISCUSSION:

1. Answer this person's complaint: "I work at a business that offers overtime. There are two employees, myself and one other, who do the same job. The other person is always offered overtime, and I'm left working regular hours only. Is there a law that requires an employer to equally distribute overtime? Is there some place I can complain to?"[28]

**SECTION 10.7
WORKPLACE
HAZARDS**

An illegal Mexican immigrant, Jose Alatorre, took a job for $8.75 an hour as a welder at a dairy farm in the California Central Valley. He was 22. On his first wedding anniversary, (February 22, 2001) his wife asked him to stay home, but he said he had to go to work for the morning to repair a machine. The farm's 1,700 cattle produced 200,000 gallons of waste per day. That day the waste pump clogged. Alatorre went down a 30-foot shaft, was overcome by hydrogen sulfide gas, plunged head first into standing manure, and drowned. Another worker died trying to rescue him.

At the time of their deaths, *The New York Times* reported that the two men's lungs were packed with cow manure, and they had eight pennies and one dime in their pockets. In telling Alatorre's story, the *Times* reported on his first encounter with his wife-to-be: It was not a promising pickup line. "I don't own a car, I'm not legally here, and I don't earn much money," he said, flashing a smile. "It's up to you." Angelica Acevedo Hernandez followed Jose Alatorre onto the dance floor.[29]

Perhaps we are not surprised to learn that the American workplace is particularly hazardous for Mexican workers. The Associated Press recently studied Mexican workplace deaths:

- The workplace death rate for Mexicans in a number of western and southwestern states is four times that of the average for United States–born workers in those states.

- Mexican death rates are rising while the U.S. workplace grows safer overall.

- "Though Mexicans often take the most hazardous jobs, they are more likely than others to be killed even when doing similarly risky work . . . These accidental deaths are almost always preventable and often gruesome: Workers are impaled, shredded in machinery, buried alive. Some are as young as 15."[30] Government officials note, however, that the most recent data show, for the first time, a decline in workplace deaths among foreign-born Hispanics.[31]

Although Mexicans working in America are significantly at risk, the total American workplace has gradually become safer because of tighter rules, improved workplace technology, and the shift to service industry jobs. Here is the data:

- Nationwide workplace deaths in 2003 totaled 5,559, up from 5,534 in 2002,[32] but the rate of fatalities remained at 4.0 per 100,000 workers, and the fatality rate fell some 11 percent from 1998 to 2003.[33]

- Injuries and illnesses continued their steady decline with a 2002 rate of 5.3 injuries and illnesses per 100 workers, down from 6.7 in 1998.[34]

- In fiscal year 2004, the federal government found nearly 87,000 workplace violations of its rules, a 9.5 percent increase over the previous five years, with serious violations up by 3 percent in one year and willful violations up by 14 percent during that year.[35] Of course, that increase might reflect more effective government oversight.

SECTION 10.8 OCCUPATIONAL SAFETY AND HEALTH ACT

The **Occupational Safety and Health Act** imposes a general duty on most employers to provide a workplace free of "recognized hazards causing or likely to cause death or serious physical harm to employees." Employers have an absolute duty to remove any serious and preventable workplace hazards that are generally recognized in the industry and are known to the employer or should be known to the employer. That general duty is then supplemented with numerous, detailed, and demanding specific standards. A federal agency, the **Occupational Safety and Health Administration (OSHA),** is responsible for ensuring safe workplaces.

OSHA, through the secretary of labor, promulgates and enforces health and safety standards that identify and seek to correct specific workplace hazards and problems. These can range from exposure to cancer-causing agents (such as the chemical benzene), to the surprisingly commonplace problem of one worker restarting a machine while another is servicing it, to mundane requirements for sanitary toilet facilities in agricultural jobs.

A battle is inevitable when OSHA considers new workplace safety measures. A pair of safety issues demonstrates some of the competing considerations in determining whether further government intervention is needed.

Repetitive motion and overexertion injure about 1.8 million workers annually.[36] These musculoskeletal injuries, such as carpal tunnel syndrome and back strains, total one-third of all workplace injuries and cost billions of dollars.[37] Employers often try to address those problems via ergonomics, "the science of fitting the job to the worker."[38] In response to the many injuries and their high costs and after 10 years of study commencing with the George Bush Senior administration, OSHA issued new ergonomics standards at the close of the Clinton administration in 2000 that were intended to provide strict rules for adapting workplaces to employee practices (for example, changing the height of a workstation or slowing down a production line). However, with the backing of the Bush administration, Congress repealed those rules in 2001 after the business community complained about the cost of compliance.

The government had estimated that the rules would cost about $4.5 billion annually[39] and save $9 billion,[40] but business groups said the costs could balloon to $125 billion.[41] A new plan was issued in 2002 to replace the mandatory rules with voluntary guidelines, but OSHA in 2003 asserted its general duty power to once again issue ergonomics citations in high-hazard workplaces such as nursing homes and grocery chains. OSHA has indicated that citations will be directed only to employers with high injury rates who do not make a good faith effort to address those problems.

"Going postal" has become, probably unfairly, a readily recognizable shorthand expression for **violence in the workplace.** Workplace homicides, the third leading cause of on-the-job deaths, increased to 631 in 2003 from 609 in 2002.[42]

With other workplace deaths declining steadily and national overall murder rates falling precipitously in recent years, we must wonder what accounts for rather steady or, in some years, increasing workplace homicides. Stress from job insecurity, deadlines, tight work spaces, overwork, and so on seem to be ongoing problems. In a recent survey, 42 percent of office workers said yelling and verbal abuse happened frequently in their offices.[43]

But should OSHA assert its authority? Do we need new rules to curb workplace violence? Would those rules prove effective? Can management take steps to reduce workplace tensions? OSHA, at least during the Bush years, is unlikely to take an activist stance except for situations like ergonomics, where some industries clearly can improve their safety measures. Indeed, in 2004 OSHA levied a $2,500 fine and cited a Dallas janitorial firm that allegedly failed to protect employees who worked at night in Dallas Area Rapid Transit stations.[44]

Employers may seek both permanent and temporary **variances** (exceptions) from OSHA standards. A permanent variance may be granted only if the workplace will be as safe as if the standard were enforced. A temporary variance permits additional time to put in place the necessary compliance measures. Employees have a right to a hearing to contest variances.

OSHA has adopted an **employee hazard communication standard** to protect employees from the dangers associated with chemicals and other toxins in the workplace. Chemical manufacturers and importers must develop material safety data sheets for all chemicals. Employers must then label all chemical containers so that employees will know about the chemical and its dangers, and employers must educate employees about chemical hazards and how to deal with them.

Businesses must maintain records listing and summarizing injuries, illnesses, and deaths on the job. A summary of those records must be posted at the job. Notice of any OSHA citations of imminent dangers on the job must also be posted at the job site. OSHA reformed and simplified the record-keeping process effective in 2002. Some smaller companies, especially in non-hazardous activities, do not need to meet the record-keeping requirements.

OSHA's most publicized **enforcement** mechanism is the unannounced on-site inspection. Inspections arise at the initiative of the agency itself or at the request of employees or their representatives. The inspections must be conducted in a reasonable manner during working hours or other reasonable times, and ordinarily they must not be announced in advance. Employers can demand a warrant prior to inspection. With proper justification, warrants can easily be secured from a federal magistrate. Employer and employee representatives may accompany the inspector.

To enhance efficiency, OSHA practices a targeted, site-specific inspection plan designed to identify the workplaces most likely to have safety and health problems. The targeted sites are those that reported at least 14 injuries or illnesses for every 100 full-time workers where lost workdays or restricted activity resulted. OSHA explains its enforcement policy at its Web site:

> OSHA seeks to assist the majority of employers who want to do the right thing while focusing its enforcement resources on sites in more hazardous industries, especially those with high injury and illness rates. Less than 1 percent of inspections, about 300, came under the agency's Enhanced Enforcement Program, designed to address employers who repeatedly and willfully violate the law. Outreach, education, and compliance assistance enable OSHA to play a vital role in preventing on-the-job injuries and illnesses.[45]

Citations may be issued if violations are discovered during the inspection process. Immediate, serious threats can be restrained with a court order. Following a citation, the employer may ask to meet with an area OSHA official to discuss the problem. Often a settlement emerges from these meetings. Failing a settlement, the employer can appeal to the independent OSHA Review Commission and thereafter to the federal court of appeals. Violations may lead to fines and/or imprisonment.

The business community criticizes OSHA for unfairly increasing the cost of production by imposing inflexible and overzealous expectations. Labor organizations and job safety advocates, on the other hand, see OSHA as a timid, faltering safety shield. The AFL—CIO estimates that OSHA can inspect each American workplace only once each century.

Concerns about workplace deaths led *The New York Times* to conduct an eight-month investigation of OSHA enforcement policy. The *Times* concluded that OSHA officials had not fulfilled their promises to aggressively pursue the worst of workplace safety wrongs:

> Over a span of two decades, from 1982 to 2002, OSHA investigated 1,242 of these horror stories—instances in which the agency itself concluded that workers had died because of their employer's "willful" safety violations. Yet, in 93 percent of those cases, OSHA declined to seek prosecution. What is more, having avoided prosecution once, at least 70 employers willfully violated safety laws again, resulting in scores of additional deaths. Even these repeat violators were rarely prosecuted.[46]

When, if ever, should managerial misjudgments, carelessness, and indifference be treated as crimes with serious penalties including imprisonment? Or does the market, in most cases, provide an effective, just method of addressing workplace deaths? Consider the criminal prosecution that emerged from the aforementioned case of Jose Alatorre and a would-be rescuer who, while working, drowned in cow manure at the bottom of a 30-foot-deep sump hole. California officials decided to charge dairy manager Patrick Faria with involuntary manslaughter in the Alatorre episode. Faria was not on the site when the workplace deaths occurred, but officials reportedly had "indications that he knew the dangers of the shaft."[47] A newspaper account summarized the prosecution view:

> As a volunteer county firefighter, he aced the test on safety in confined spaces. But he hadn't relayed that information to his workers, prosecutors say, and did not supply them with proper fans to ventilate the air or a harness to extract a stricken worker. Faria could have hired a professional crew to clean the pump for about $600, according to prosecutor Gale Filter, instead of sending down three low-wage dairy hands. "It's about money, M-O-N-E-Y," Filter told the grand jury that indicted Faria.[48]

SECTION 10.9
WORKERS'
COMPENSATION

Korey Stringer, a 27-year-old Pro Bowl tackle, died of heatstroke complications on August 1, 2001, after going through a preseason Minnesota Vikings workout. Normally, when an employee is injured or dies on the job, the employee or the estate may not sue for damages. Rather, recovery is limited to the fixed sum provided for by the workers' compensation statute, regardless of fault. Stringer's family, however, filed a wrongful death suit trying to hold the Vikings and various individuals responsible for negligence, intentional infliction of emotional distress, and other wrongs in responding to Stringer's heatstroke. The Vikings argue that the Stringer suit is barred by the state workers' compensation law. Minnesota is one of a number of states, however, that recognizes an exception to **workers' compensation** exclusivity provisions in cases of gross negligence by the defendants. At this writing, the Minnesota Supreme Court has agreed to review the case after two lower court defeats for the Stringer family.[49]

Early in the twentieth century, the states began enacting workers' compensation laws to provide an administrative remedy for those, like Stringer, who are injured or killed on the job. Previously, employers' superior financial resources and various technical legal defenses meant that employees often could not successfully sue to recover damages for their on-the-job injuries. Thus, all states now provide some form of workers' compensation not requiring a lawsuit. Workers or their families simply apply for compensation based on illness, injury, or death. Typically, the system is governed by a state board or commission. Most decisions are routine and are accomplished by completing the necessary forms. Often a claims examiner will verify the nature and severity of the injury. In return for the ease and predictability of the system, however, workers and families are, by law, denied the right to sue, barring unusual circumstances such as gross negligence (as alleged in the Stringer case).

In most states, employers are compelled to participate in workers' compensation, depending on state law, either by purchasing insurance privately, by contributing to a state-managed fund, or by being self-insured (paying claims directly from their own funds). Firms with good safety records are rewarded with lower premium payments. A benefits schedule specifies the sum to be awarded for the injury (or death) in question. The amount of the award is normally a percentage of the worker's salary either for a specified period or indefinitely, depending on the severity of the injury. Injury benefits normally amount to one-half to two-thirds of regular wages. Death benefits ordinarily are tied to the wages of the deceased.

Certain employment classifications such as agriculture may be excluded from workers' compensation, but about 90 percent of the labor force is covered. Most on-the-job injuries are covered, but those that are self-inflicted (including starting a fight) and others such as those springing from alcohol or drug use may not be.

In general, injuries, illnesses, and deaths are compensable where the harm (1) *arose out of the employment,* and (2) *arose in the course of employment.* Proof of employer negligence is not required, and the traditional defenses such as contributory negligence are not available to the employer. Thus, workers' compensation provides a form of no-fault protection in the workplace. Workers give up the right to sue, and employers participate in an insurance system that recognizes the inevitability of workplace harm.

Although workers' compensation recovery is the exclusive remedy for workplace injury, illness, or death, some jurisdictions allow litigation in cases of intentional torts and/or gross negligence.

Notwithstanding its no-fault character, workers' compensation has generated many lawsuits. For example, Manuel Guico had worked for two years in an Excel meat packing plant until he was fired after sustaining an injury on the job. Guico's knife slipped, cutting his thumb and a finger, and causing an 11 percent permanent partial disability. Guico had repeatedly been told to wear his steel-mesh gloves and mesh apron whenever he was using his knife, but he was not doing so when he was injured. Guico applied for and received workers' compensation benefits. Excel appealed to the courts but lost when the Nebraska Supreme Court ruled that Excel failed to show that Guico was willfully negligent.[50]

QUAKER OATES CO. V. CIHA
552 N.W.2D 143 (IOWA, 1996)

In May 1991, petitioner Bradley Ciha was employed by defendant Quaker Oats Company at its Cedar Rapids plant as an area maintenance supervisor. Ciha's normal workweek at Quaker Oats was Monday through Friday. On a typical weekend including Saturday and Sunday, Ciha was not on duty and was not expected to be on call to drive to the plant for emergency maintenance purposes.

While preparing dinner at his home on Sunday, May 26, Ciha was contacted through a company electronic paging device. He was informed that several large cooling fans at the plant were malfunctioning. Ciha responded to the breakdown by electing to drive his motorcycle to the plant to remedy the problem himself. To reach the plant, Ciha drove a direct route on Johnson Avenue. After reaching the plant without incident, he personally remedied the problem by cooling the fans with an air hose. At approximately 5:45 pm, Ciha telephoned his wife and informed her that she could resume dinner preparations because he was about to return home.

Ciha drove a different route from the plant to home than he drove earlier from his home to the plant. The return-home route was on Ellis Road and was admittedly not the most direct route from the plant to Ciha's home. The Ellis Road route was scenic and subject to less traffic and traffic signals than the direct route Ciha commonly drove from home to the plant.

On his return trip from the plant to home along Ellis Road, Ciha was involved in a serious motor vehicle accident in which he suffered a broken neck and was rendered a quadriplegic.

Following the accident, Ciha was admitted to St. Luke's Hospital in Cedar Rapids until he requested transfer to a specialized care facility, Craig Hospital, located in Englewood, Colorado.

In addition to the health care Ciha received while at Craig, the hospital also provided Kim specialized training in order for her to be able to care for Ciha upon his return home.

Ciha was discharged from Craig Hospital on September 14, 1991, to his home in Cedar Rapids. Since his discharge, Kim has performed necessary, extensive home nursing services. Ciha requires assistance in dressing, changing urine bags, and transferring between his wheelchair and his bed. At night, he must be repositioned in bed one to four times in order to prevent him from developing pressure sores.

Ciha first returned to work at Quaker Oats in January 1992 in a new position as materials supervisor. In this position, he works at a computer (with the aid of an adaptive device and telephone headset) in the company's purchasing department. In his position as materials supervisor, he receives the same base salary, not including raises, as that of an area maintenance supervisor. Ciha no longer has the same opportunity, however, to earn overtime as he had as an area maintenance supervisor.

In order to return to work, Ciha relied on the county's disabled persons transportation service to and from Quaker Oats. Based on the hours of the transportation service, however, Ciha was not able to return to work full-time.

Ciha was readmitted to Craig for one week in March 1992 for a comprehensive evaluation. A driving specialist from the hospital concluded Ciha would need to purchase a specially modified van in order to be able to drive independently. At some time thereafter, Ciha purchased the recommended van.

Many of Ciha's medical expenses from the accident were paid for through a group health and accident insurance plan available to Ciha through his employer Quaker Oats. However, there were significant limitations in coverage under the group plan. For example, in addition to a lifetime cap on medical expenses, the group plan did not provide Ciha coverage for necessary home health care services, home modifications, or motor vehicle conversions.

In November 1991, Ciha filed a claim for permanent partial disability benefits with the Iowa Industrial Commissioner's Office against his employer, Quaker Oats.

In Iowa, every employer, not specifically excepted by the provisions of Iowa Code shall provide, secure, and pay compensation according to the provisions of this chapter for any and all personal injuries sustained by an employee arising out of and in the course of the employment.

To obtain such compensation, an injured employee has the burden of proving by a preponderance of the evidence that his injuries arose out of and in the course of his employment. An injury arises "out of" the employment when there is a causal relationship between the employment and the injury.

Quaker Oats contends Ciha did not sustain his injury in the course of his employment because the injury was sustained away from the employer's premises and while Ciha was on his way home from the plant. The employer relies on the well-established "going and coming" rule, which generally provides, "[A]bsent special circumstances, injuries occurring off the employer's premises while the employee is on the way to or from work are not compensable."

Under the "going and coming rule," Ciha admittedly did not sustain an injury in the course of his employment: He was injured while driving his motorcycle home from the Quaker Oats plant.

There are, however, several exceptions to the going and coming rule. The first exception to the going and coming is the "special errand" exception. Under the exception, if an employee is on a special errand or mission for his or her employer at the time of the injury, the injury is held to have arisen in the course of employment.

After considering all arguments raised by the parties, we believe substantial evidence supports the commissioner's conclusion that Ciha was on a special errand at the time of his injury.

In answer to the question "whose business was the employee pursuing at the time of the injury?" the answer must be Quaker Oats' business. The fact that Ciha was contacted on Sunday while he was on duty was truly "special." It was unusual, sudden, and unexpected.

Notwithstanding our conclusion that the special errand exception to the going and coming rule applies in the present case, Quaker Oats contends Ciha had "deviated" from his trip home from the plant to such an extent that he abandoned his employment at the time of the accident. The commissioner and district court rejected this argument, and we do the same.

In concluding Ciha did not deviate from his special errand, the commissioner stated, Ciha testified that he often took the Ellis Road route home because it was more scenic, it had less traffic, it had fewer stoplights, and the actual difference in miles between this route and the more direct route was minimal. Ciha's call to his wife from the plant to start the grill for their meal shows that his purpose was to return home, and that he had no other destination other than to return to his residence. The record does not show a deviation from the course of the employment.

Affirmed.

QUESTIONS FOR DISCUSSION:

1. The Iowa Supreme Court in *Quaker Oats* (and most courts in workers' compensation cases) required a two-part showing that the injury must "arise out of" and "in the course of" employment.

   a. Explain those two standards.

   b. Must an employee be engaged in a prescribed task in order to be "in the course of employment?" Explain.

   c. Why did the court conclude that Ciha was on a "special errand?"

2. Fernandez, a waitress at Tyler's Sports Bar and Grill, left her job drunk and was seriously injured in a crash while riding as a passenger in a car driven by another employee. The crash came within one hour of leaving work. Her intoxication led to her decision to ride with her intoxicated coworker. Fernandez sought workers' compensation. She claimed that Joe Roberts required her to socialize with male customers when not serving food or taking food orders and to generate at least two drinks per hour from customers. Weight staff were not required to drink, but most consumed six to eight drinks per night, if not more. Did Fernandez's injury arise out of and in the course of employment so that she can recover workers' compensation? Explain. See **2800 Corp. v. Fernandez, 528 N.W.2d 124 (Ia., 1995).**

3. Joseph Smyth, a college mathematics instructor, was killed while driving his personal auto home from work. At the time, Smyth had

student papers with him, which he intended to grade that evening. He often worked at home. Many faculty members took work home in the evenings. However, the college did not require that practice. Indeed, the college neither encouraged nor discouraged working at home. The widely adopted "going and coming rule" provides that employees injured while commuting to and from work, in general, are not covered by workers' compensation.

a. Should Smyth (and other teachers) be exempted from the going and coming rule, thus permitting recovery by Smyth's family? Explain. See **Santa Rosa Junior College v. Workers' Compensation Appeals Board and Joann Smyth, 708 P.2d 673 (Cal., 1985).**

b. Would you reach a different conclusion had a student been accompanying Smyth? Explain.

4. Casimer Gacioch worked at a Stroh Brewery. The company provided free beer at work. When he began work in 1947 he drank only three to four beers on the weekend. He was fired in 1974, by which time he was drinking 12 bottles of beer daily. After Gacioch's death, his wife sought workers' compensation benefits. The evidence indicated that Gacioch had a predisposition to alcoholism but was not an alcoholic at the time he was hired. How would you rule on the widow's workers' compensation claim? Explain. See **Gacioch v. Stroh Brewery, 466 N.W. 2d 303 (Mich. Ct. of Appeals, 1991).**

SECTION 10.10 RIGHTS OF PRIVACY

Do we have a **"right to privacy"** on the job? Increasingly, employers are engaging in an array of testing and monitoring procedures both before and after hiring. Drug testing, integrity tests, personality tests, spying, television and computer monitoring of work performance, and so forth are routine personnel practices in many firms. Employers have an interest in these strategies not only to hire better employees and improve productivity but also to protect coworkers, reduce insurance claims, and shield consumers from poor products and service. On the other hand, job applicants and employees often feel "Big Brother" looking over their shoulders, as corporate critic Barbara Ehrenreich argues:

Only a person of unblemished virtue can get a job at Wal-Mart—a low-level job, that is . . . A drug test eliminates the chemical miscreants; a detailed "personality test" probes the job applicant's horror of theft and willingness to turn in an erring coworker.

Extreme submissiveness to authority is another desirable trait. When I applied for a job at Wal-Mart, I was reprimanded for getting something wrong on this test: I had agreed only "strongly" to the proposition, "All rules have to be followed to the letter at all times." The correct answer was "totally agree."[51]

Do employers' financial goals justify policies that significantly reshape employee lives—especially their off-the-job lives? Should employers be able, for example, to require employees to lose weight or to quit smoking? One study of large employers finds 11.5 percent of the population accounting for 80 percent of health costs, with the chronically ill being particularly expensive.[52] Many employers offer wellness programs and various incentives to encourage employees to achieve more healthful lifestyles. Now some are going further by firing workers who refuse to take nicotine tests to prove they do not smoke. Others are beginning to charge higher insurance rates for those who fail to meet weight and health standards. The law offers only limited protection for employees. About half the states offer some form of "smoking discrimination" protection, and the federal **Health Insurance Portability and Accountability Act (HIPAA)** generally forbids discrimination based on health status or conditions.

And what about "office romance?" Changing cultural patterns have made the workplace a primary venue for romance and marriage. A 2003 poll found 47 percent of office workers had had an office romance and 19 percent more would like to do so.[53] Managers, however, are increasingly concerned about those relationships. More than one-third of 558 companies surveyed in 2001 said employees involved in office romances could be fired, up from 27 percent taking that position in 1998.[54] Managers are concerned about productivity and fairness, but perhaps the bigger fear is the possibility of sexual harassment charges.

SECTION 10.11 DRUG TESTING IN THE WORKPLACE

Drug testing in the corporate workplace is simply a fact of life, especially for blue-collar workers. Most *Fortune* 500 companies use some form of drug testing, although some companies, including Hewlett-Packard, have found so few job applicants testing positive that drug testing is not cost-effective for them. Regardless of the severity of the risk, many companies feel they must engage in drug testing to protect themselves against liability claims should an impaired employee cause harm and to comply with the federal **Drug-Free Workplace Act.**

The Drug-Free Workplace Act of 1988 applies to employers who have contracts of $100,000 or more with the federal government or who receive aid from the government. Those employers are required to develop an anti-drug policy for employees. They must provide drug-free awareness programs for employees, and they must acquaint employees with available assistance for those with drug problems, while also warning them of the penalties that accompany violation of the policy. The act requires employees to adhere to the company policy and to inform the company within five days if they are convicted of or plead no contest to a drug-related offense in the workplace.

Broadly, employment-based alcohol and drug testing occurs in six circumstances: (1) pre-employment screening, (2) routine physical examinations, (3) "reasonable suspicion" testing, (4) post accident testing, (5) random testing, and (6) follow-up testing.[55]

1. Ordinarily, private-sector, pre-employment testing is lawful although some state and local laws may impose restrictions. In general, public-sector employers have less drug testing latitude because of constitutional limitations, but when challenged in court, those programs have generally been approved.

2. Drug testing as a part of periodic physical examinations is generally lawful if properly conducted. To avoid legal problems, employers should notify job applicants and current employees of drug testing in association with physicals.

3. Reasonable suspicion is something less than probable cause and means that the employer has evidence, such as lapses in performance that would justify a drug test. Such tests, given a sound factual foundation and even-handed application, ordinarily are permissible.

4. Post accident testing involves employees who have been involved in a serious on-the-job accident. Such tests normally are permissible.

5. Selecting employees at random, without notice, for drug testing can be very effective in deterring drug use, but the practice raises significant legal questions. Some states explicitly forbid random testing, except for safety-sensitive jobs such as those in transportation. The Supreme Court has upheld such testing for public sector employees where public safety is involved and for those having access to particularly sensitive information.[56]

6. Follow-up testing is used for employees who are returning from drug or alcohol rehabilitation. The testing acts as an incentive for recovering drug users to remain "clean." All states permit follow-up testing, but employers should create contracts with rehabilitating employees to establish testing arrangements.

Drug use as a societal problem is undeniable, but critics are concerned that personal rights may be trampled in our zeal to attack substance abuse. Some of the doubts are that the tests (1) are often unreliable, (2) invade employee privacy, and (3) do not measure actual job impairment.

Challenges to drug testing ordinarily spring from the following claims and defenses:

1. **Federal constitution:** The Fourth Amendment to the United States Constitution forbids unreasonable searches and seizures. Thus government officials ordinarily cannot conduct a search without individualized

suspicion—that is, without probable cause. Certain exceptions, however, have been recognized in cases involving safety, national security, athletic participation, and other special needs. Remember that the Constitution protects us from the government, not from private-sector employers (with limited exceptions).

2. **State constitutions:** Many state constitutions offer privacy protection, but court decisions, to date, have generally not extended those protections to private-sector employers. On the other hand, certain states, such as California and Massachusetts, explicitly offer constitutional protection to private-sector employees.

3. **Federal statutes:** Drug testing could violate Title VII of the Civil Rights Act of 1964 or the **Americans with Disabilities Act** if the testing fails to treat all individuals equally. The ADA protects *recovering* drug addicts and those erroneously believed to be drug users.

4. **State and local statutes:** Historically, most state and local drug testing legislation placed limits on that testing; but in recent years, fears about drug use in the workplace and often intense business community lobbying have, in some cases, relaxed those testing restraints.

5. **Common law claims:** Some of the more prominent judge-made (common law) claims that might provide a challenge to drug testing include invasion of privacy, defamation (dissemination of erroneous information about an employee), negligence (in testing or in selecting a test provider), intentional infliction of emotional distress, and wrongful discharge.

A McDonald's manager in Elmira, New York, began an affair with a McDonald's employee in another town. They exchanged "steamy" messages by voice mail. An Elmira coworker retrieved the messages and played them for the manager's wife and boss, whereupon the manager was fired. He filed suit claiming violations of a federal wiretapping law and a state eavesdropping statute.[57] The case was settled out of court.

Nearly 75 percent of major U.S. companies monitor their employees on the job,[58] and misconduct can result in severe sanctions. Dow Chemical, for example, fired 50 employees and disciplined over 200 more after discovering widespread use of its computers to receive pornography.[59] Employees are, of course, concerned about privacy, while employers' worries include reduced productivity and company liability for criminal or tortuous conduct (such as sexual harassment or defamation). Electronic oversight is gradually altering the workplace:

> At New York law firm Akin & Smith LLC, paralegals, receptionists, and clerks clock in by placing a finger on a sensor kept at a secretary's desk. "It keeps everyone honest," says Derek T. Smith, a managing partner at the firm.[60]

In general, employers can lawfully monitor workers' attendance, performance, e-mail, use of the Internet, and so on; but uncertainty remains. Certainly the prudent course of action is to expect employees to sign an agreement such as the following language from the Principal Financial Group employee handbook:

> The corporation's electronic mail system is business property and is to be used for business purposes. The corporation reserves the right to monitor all electronic mail messages.[61]

The primary federal legislation, the **Electronic Communications Privacy Act,** prohibits private individuals and organizations from intercepting wire, oral, or electronic communications. The act provides for two exceptions, however: (1) prior consent by one of the parties to the communication, and (2) employer monitoring in the "ordinary course of business" by telephone or other device furnished by a provider of wire or electronic communication service. Thus workplace monitoring of phone calls (except for purely private conversations), workplace computers, voice mail, e-mail, and Internet use are all likely to be considered lawful at this point if approached in a reasonable manner.

The case that follows is one of the few judicial examinations of privacy and monitoring. The plaintiff, Smyth, was an **at-will employee** meaning that he did not have an employment contract for a specified period. Under the law of Pennsylvania, where the case took place, at-will employees could be fired for any reason unless the discharge violated public policy. The **Smyth** case examines whether an e-mail interception amounts to an invasion of privacy and is thus a violation of public policy.

Smyth v. Pillsbury Co.
914 F. Supp. 97 (E. D. Pa., 1966)

Plaintiff claims he was wrongfully discharged from his position as a regional operations manager by the defendant. Presently before the court is the motion of the defendant to dismiss. Defendant maintained an electronic mail communication system ("e-mail") in order to promote internal corporate communications between its employees. Defendant repeatedly assured its employees, including plaintiff, that all e-mail communications would remain confidential and privileged. Defendant further assured its employees, including plaintiff that e-mail communications could not be intercepted and used by defendant against its employees as grounds for termination or reprimand.

In October 1994, plaintiff received certain e-mail communications from his supervisor over defendant's e-mail system on his computer at home. In reliance on defendant's assurances regarding defendant's e-mail system, plaintiff responded and exchanged e-mails with his supervisor. At some later date, contrary to the assurances of confidentiality defendant, acting through its agents, servants, and employees, intercepted plaintiff's private e-mail messages made in October 1994. On January 17, 1995, defendant notified plaintiff that it was terminating his employment effective February 1, 1995, for transmitting what it deemed to be inappropriate and unprofessional comments over defendant's e-mail system in October 1994.

Plaintiff claims that his termination was in violation of "public policy, which precludes an employer from terminating an employee in violation of the employee's right to privacy as embodied in Pennsylvania common law." In support for this proposition, plaintiff directs our attention to a decision by our Court of Appeals in **Borse v. Piece Goods Shop, Inc., 963 F.2d 611 (3d Cir., 1992).** In **Borse,** the plaintiff sued her employer alleging wrongful discharge as a result of her refusal to submit to urinalysis screening and personal property searches at her workplace pursuant to the employer's drug and alcohol policy. After rejecting plaintiff's argument that the employer's drug and alcohol program violated public policy encompassed in the United States and Pennsylvania Constitutions, our Court of Appeals stated "our review of Pennsylvania law reveals other evidence of a public policy that may, under certain circumstances, give rise to a wrongful discharge action related to urinalysis or to personal property searches. Specifically, we refer to the Pennsylvania common law regarding tortious invasion of privacy."

In the case before us we find that plaintiff has failed to state a claim upon which relief can be granted. In the first instance, unlike urinalysis and personal property searches, we do not find a reasonable expectation of privacy in e-mail communications voluntarily made by an employee to his supervisor over the company e-mail system notwithstanding any assurances that such communications would not be intercepted by management. Once plaintiff communicated the alleged unprofessional comments to a second person (his supervisor) over an e-mail system, which was apparently utilized by the entire company, any reasonable expectation of privacy was lost. Significantly, the defendant did not require plaintiff, as in the case of a urinalysis or personal property search, to disclose any personal information about himself. Rather, plaintiff voluntarily communicated the alleged unprofessional comments over the company e-mail system. We find no privacy interests in such communications.

In the second instance, even if we found that an employee had a reasonable expectation of privacy in the contents of his e-mail communications over the company e-mail system, we do not find that a reasonable person would consider the defendant's interception of these communications to be a substantial and highly offensive invasion of his privacy. Again, we note that by intercepting such communications, the company is not, as in the case of urinalysis or personal property searches, requiring the employee to disclose any personal information about himself or invading the employee's person or personal effects. Moreover, the company's interest in preventing inappropriate and unprofessional comments or even illegal activity over its e-mail system outweighs any privacy interest the employee may have in those comments.

In sum, we find that the defendant's actions did not tortiously invade the plaintiff's privacy and, therefore, did not violate public policy. As a result, the motion to dismiss is granted.

QUESTIONS FOR DISCUSSION:

1. Why did the court reject Smyth's invasion of privacy claim?

2. Why did Pillsbury win even though it repeatedly promised employees that the e-mail system would be private and would not be used against employees?

3. In your opinion, should on-the-job e-mail messages be free from employer monitoring? Explain.

4. Does an employer have the right to search the office of an employee? Explain.

5. What if the employer provides a locker for the employee and allows the employee to provide a lock? Explain.

SECTION 10.12 EMPLOYEE BENEFITS AND INCOME MAINTENANCE

Have we reached that uncomfortable and perhaps socially destabilizing moment when the generous benefits (health insurance, life insurance, pensions) we have come to expect from our jobs are beginning a permanent decline? For decades employers used benefits to attract and retain the best employees, but the economic downturn in recent years forced employers to shift benefit burdens to employees by raising insurance deductibles and co-pays, for example. Indeed, from 2001 to 2003, nearly 9 million Americans lost their employer-provided health insurance, although most of those people subsequently moved to publicly subsidized plans such as Medicare.[62] At this writing, prosperity has returned to a considerable extent, but the benefit cuts have not been restored; and the future for improvements, especially in the prized but highly expensive health care area, does not look promising for employees. Benefits add 22 percent in value to the average employee's paycheck.[63] We prize the security of knowing that we will be shielded in the event of a health catastrophe. But can we sustain that comfort in this intense global market? A 2004 study found that a majority of surveyed companies are not raising benefits, and the small number who are increasing perks are doing so only slightly.[64] Further, *The Wall Street Journal* anticipates that any future growth in benefits will be in work/personal life balance, involving matters such as elder and child care rather than the stratospherically expensive health care costs.[65]

Even as benefits decline, American employees try harder. Almost 40 percent of us work more than 50 hours per week, and we have the stingiest vacation policies among industrialized nations with vacation allocations averaging about 10 days after three years on the job, as compared with Australia, for example, where four weeks are required by law.[66] Yet more, Expedia.com found that vacations for 2004 were expected to decline by 10 percent from 2003 as at least 20 percent of Americans report that they feel guilty about taking vacation.[67]

Meanwhile, the unmarried subset of the working population is increasingly aggressive in its pursuit of legal and economic benefits equal to those of families. Married employees have enhanced health care plans and unemployment benefits, for example, and differential treatment on the job allegedly is commonplace. The American Association for Single People receives complaints from singles:

> In the workplace, singles are expected to put off summer vacations so married colleagues can visit Disney World while their kids are out of school. Married people get family leave and special dispensations to work at home, while singles often feel chained to their desks.[68]

QUESTION FOR DISCUSSION:

1. Are single people wronged at work and in the American economy, generally?

Perhaps the most notable legally mandated insurance benefit is the **Consolidated Budget Reconciliation Act (COBRA),** which requires employers with 20 or more employees to permit departing employees to retain group health coverage at their own expense for up to 18 months as long as they are not terminated for gross misconduct.

The **Family and Medical Leave Act (FMLA)** requires up to 12 weeks of unpaid leave in any 12-month period for family needs such as the birth or adoption of a child, caring for a child or parent, or for the employee's own serious illness. Employees taking leave are entitled to reinstatement to the same or equivalent job. The law applies to all companies employing 50 or more workers and covers about 50 percent of the workforce. The business community has opposed the FMLA from the beginning, and experience with the law has not decreased that opposition, as *The Wall Street Journal* reported:

> While the act is helping employees, it's leaving many employers frustrated. They say the vague definition of what can trigger time off and the right of employees to take leave in increments—weeks, days, even hours—at different times make the law ripe for abuse. What's more, many human resource administrators believe employees sometimes use the law for bogus or questionable reasons. Among employers, this has earned the FMLA the nicknames "the Slacker's Protection Act" and the "Far More Leave Than Anyone Intended Act."[69]

But one FMLA advocate reminds us; FMLA has made an extraordinary difference in the lives of over 50 million Americans who haven't had to choose between their jobs and caring for a family member.[70]

In any case, only 16.5 percent of the workforce took leave under the FMLA in 2000,[71] and the FMLA has had no impact on males' propensity to take leave, while new mothers are taking leaves only slightly more frequently than before the FMLA.[72] Financial considerations often make FMLA leaves unattractive, but California has addressed that problem by becoming the first state to require private employers to provide *paid* time off. The program is paid for by employee payroll deductions and allows up to six weeks of leave at 55 percent of wages up to $728 per week.

SECTION 10.13 UNEMPLOYMENT COMPENSATION

The tragedy of the Depression, when up to 25 percent of the workforce was unemployed, led in 1935 to the passage of the Social Security Act, one portion of which provided for an unemployment insurance program. Today, all 50 states and the federal government are engaged in a cooperative system that helps protect the temporarily jobless. The system is financed through a payroll tax paid by employers.

The actual state tax rate for each employer varies, depending on the employer's *experience* ratings—the number of layoffs in its workforce. Thus employers have an incentive to retain employees.

Rules vary by state, but in general, employees qualify for **unemployment benefits** by reaching a specified total of annual wages. Those losing their jobs must apply to a state agency for unemployment compensation, which varies by state. Benefits may be collected up to a specified maximum period, usually 26 weeks. During that time, those collecting compensation must be ready to work and must make an effort to find suitable work. Workers who quit or who are fired for *misconduct* are ineligible for unemployment compensation. The episodes that follow illustrate the foolish and often funny cases where compensation has been denied:

- The Swiss Valley Farms dairy worker who led her coworkers in an after-hours swim in the cheese vat (filled with water at the time)."[73]

- The bored production worker who removed her underwear, put the garment on the production line, and asked a supervisor if he "wanted to sniff them."[74]

- The sheriff's department dispatcher who was dismissed for refusing to remove her tongue stud. The dispatcher had initially been granted benefits, but she lost on appeal when the stud caused her to slur her words as she pleaded her case to the administrative law judge.[75]

The **Worker Adjustment and Retraining Notification Act (WARN)** requires firms with 100 or more employees to provide 60 days notice if they lay off one-third or more of their workers at any site employing at least 150 workers, drop 500 employees at any site, or close a plant employing at least 50 workers. A General Accounting Office study concluded, however, that the law had been ineffectual, with half of plant closings not covered by the law.

Some employers began to adopt pension plans for their employees by the late 1800s. Comprehensive protection for pension rights did not arrive until 1974, when Congress approved the **Employee Retirement Income Security Act (ERISA),** under which the government regulates pension funds to help ensure their long-term financial security by reducing fraud and mismanagement. ERISA requires that fund managers keep detailed records, engage in prudent investments, and provide an annual report that has been certified by qualified, impartial third parties.

ERISA also establishes strict *vesting* rights (the point at which the employee has a nonforfeitable right to the funds) to ensure that employees actually receive the pensions to which they are entitled. Employer contributions typically vest after three years or in a six-year, graduated system. Broadly, pensions take two forms: defined benefit plans and defined contribution plans. **Defined benefit** pensions are the traditional form of company-sponsored and company paid plans that provide specified monthly payments upon retirement. Defined benefit plans provide security for employees who remain with a firm for many years; but for those changing jobs, benefits will likely be smaller. **Defined contribution plans,** such as the popular 401(k), specify in advance the "match" the employer will provide to go with the employee's own contributions and allow the employee a menu of investment options in which to place that retirement money; but they make no promises about the amount that will be paid upon retirement. Defined contribution plans often are attractive to employees because the money vests quickly and follows the employee who changes jobs. ERISA requires that defined benefit fund managers diversify their investments for greater safety, putting no more than 10 percent of the plan's funds in the employer's stock. Defined contribution plans, in general, have no such limit under the law. Defined benefit plans were once the norm in the business community, but defined contribution plans are now much more common. The latter are less expensive to manage, they shift the risk from employer to employee, and they are free of some ERISA requirements.

ERISA established the **Pension Benefit Guaranty Corporation (PBGC),** which insures defined benefit plans to protect retirees in the event that their employer's pension fund fails. The PBGC, which is funded by company contributions, guarantees that vested persons will be paid up to a specified maximum if their plan cannot meet its obligations.

But even the PBGC-protected defined benefit pensions will eventually be at risk if company contributions to the PBGC fund are not significantly increased. As costs go up, however, can American companies compete successfully with lower-cost foreign competition? Can we afford the generous promises we have made to retirees? Will we see, in the decades to come, something of a generational battle between the young and the old about how big a slice of American wealth each will receive?

Unlike defined benefit plans, defined contribution arrangements are not covered by the PBGC. Thus the more relaxed and, in some ways, highly desirable 401(k) holds some big risks for employees, as we have learned in this era of corporate scandals.

Tens of thousands of employees at Enron, World-Com, and other financially devastated corporations lost most of their retirement savings in 2001–02 largely because their 401(k) plans were heavily invested in their employers' stock. Enron shares fell from a high of $90.56 in August 2000 to 36 cents in late November 2001, after the firm's alleged financial corruption became public.[76] Enron's 401(k) plan lost an estimated $850 million in two months. One employee explained his personal loss:

> "I feel like I've been betrayed," said Roy Rinard, 54, a veteran lineman at Enron subsidiary Portland General Electric in Oregon. "I have lost my savings, my plans for the future, everything." He lost the lion's share of his retirement account—once valued at more than $470,000—because he says he invested in Enron stock on the advice of plan administrators . . . His lawyer valued Rinard's 401(k) at about $40,000.[77]

That sense of betrayal, if not outrage, doubtless is exacerbated by the news that Enron executives cashed out more than $1 billion in company stock when it was near its peak value, and 600 key employees received $100 million in bonuses just before the energy giant collapsed.[78] Enron reached a $356 million settlement in 2005 with about 20,000 current and former employees, but Enron assets available after its bankruptcy suggest that claimants are likely to receive only 15–20 percent of the settlement.[79]

Congress and President Bush promised new laws to reduce the likelihood of future, huge employee retirement losses. At this writing, changes have been limited, but two prominent rules are in place: (1) Participants in **401(k)** and similar retirement plans must receive 30 days' notice of any "blackout" periods when they cannot buy, sell, or borrow from their plans, and (2) corporate executives are forbidden from selling their company stock during blackout periods when employees are locked out of transactions involving their 401(k) holdings. Reform zeal has now cooled, but perhaps it should be so because employees doubtless must bear part of the risk, and more rules are likely to reduce efficiency and competitiveness.

In some ways, a more tragic but less spectacular retirement threat than Enron and WorldCom has been visiting hundreds of thousands of retirees across America in recent years. Many companies under tremendous financial pressure have been forced, in most cases entirely legally, to reduce or withdraw health care benefits that had once been promised to workers. Health care costs have been, for many companies, their most rapidly increasing cost of doing business. Consider GM's rather astonishing health care burdens for both its retirees and its current employees:

> Health care is one of the single biggest costs GM faces each year—representing about $1,400 per vehicle produced. The company's health plans cover 1.21 million employees, retirees, and their dependents. For 2003, the company reported that it spent $4.8 billion, or about $3,966 per person, for health care benefits.[80]

Companies feel they have no choice but to expect retirees to pay more of their own health care costs, but the retirees must endure a humiliating and frightening struggle for survival when the money they expected is no longer there. Richard Bruce, a retired Sears manager, paid $95 a month nine years ago for health care coverage for himself and his wife. As Sears' subsidy has fallen from 75 percent to less than 50 percent of his medical insurance premium, Bruce must now pay over $450 per month to maintain his coverage.[81]

In a sense, only demographics and a changing economy are to blame. Many employers simply have too many retirees to support in this era of long life spans, huge medical costs, and a highly competitive world economy. Bethlehem Steel, for example, employs 13,000 people but has 74,000 retirees.[82]

SECTION 10.14
UNEMPLOYMENT
CASE

PROBLEM TEN—B

PARK, BROWN & SMITH, P.C.
ATTORNEYS AT LAW
MEMORANDUM

To: All Law Clerks

From: Peter Smith, Esquire

Re: The Unemployment Claim

Joe Roberts called with the following unemployment compensation question. Walter Robinson, his best bartender on the busy evening shift, quit his job at Tyler's Sports Bar and Grill when his wife became seriously ill and was unable to care for their nine children. Mr. Robinson said that he had to be at home in the evenings to care for his family. The employee did ask Joe to be moved to the day shift but Joe was unable to accommodate the request due to commitments to other employees. Upon learning that day work was unavailable, Mr. Robinson ripped off his apron, and told Joe in no uncertain terms what he could do with the job. At first, Joe was sympathetic to the bartender's plight but there was nothing he could do under the circumstances.

Now, Joe is angry since the employee left without giving notice, and the bar had to pay other employees overtime to work the bar at night.

Mr. Roberts has just received notice from the Unemployment Compensation Board that the bartender has filed a claim for unemployment compensation benefits claiming that he had no recourse but to quit his job in order to take care of his family. Joe wants to fight the claim and desires to know who is right in this dispute.

Please read **Draper v. Unemployment Compensation Bd. of Review** and let me know who you think should win the case. Please write a memo explaining the law and your conclusions so that I can present it to Mr. Roberts.

DRAPER V. UNEMPLOYMENT COMPENSATION BD. OF REVIEW
718 A.2D 383 (PA. CMWLTH., 1998)

The issue presented is whether Joseph Draper (Claimant) terminated his employment with Frankel Chevy Buick, Inc. (Employer) for reasons of a necessitous and compelling nature, thus entitling him to benefits under the Unemployment Compensation Act. Because he did not, the decision of the Unemployment Compensation Board of Review (Board), which denied benefits, is affirmed.

The relevant facts are as follows. Claimant was employed as a department manager for Employer until August 22, 1997, at which time he resigned in order to move to Virginia. At that time, Claimant's ill 95-year-old mother lived in Virginia with his sister, but his sister was becoming increasingly unable to care for his mother. Claimant purchased a home in Virginia and moved his mother into his home where she is now cared for by Claimant and his wife. In addition to his sister, Claimant also has two brothers in Virginia, but Claimant testified that neither of them is capable of taking care of his mother.

Claimant subsequently filed for unemployment compensation benefits with the Interstate Claims Office on the grounds that, although he voluntarily quit his job with Employer, he did so for a necessitous and compelling reason, i.e., the necessity to move to Virginia to take care of his mother. The Interstate Claims Office denied the claim, and a hearing was held before a referee on March 10, 1998.

At the March 10 hearing, Claimant testified as follows in response to questions from the referee:

Q. All right. Now, Mr. Draper, tell me clearly when you realized your mother couldn't live with your sister down in Virginia any longer. Rather than quitting your job in Pennsylvania why didn't you bring your mother up here to live?

A. Well, I had made plans to just go down there.

Q. Why did you decide to go to Virginia rather than bringing your mother up to Pennsylvania?

A. Well, Virginia is where I thought I was going to find myself a job, and because all my family is here also.

Q. What I'm asking you, sir, is why didn't you bring your mother to Pennsylvania instead of you resigning your job to move to Virginia.

A. Sir, here in Virginia I had purchased my property, and I wanted to be here with [my mother] and I felt this was where I was going to be located.

By decision dated March 12, 1998, the referee denied benefits. Claimant appealed to the Board, which affirmed on May 6, 1998, adopting the opinion of the referee.

Claimant argues that caring for his ill mother constituted a necessitous and compelling reason for terminating his employment and moving to Virginia. The Board acknowledges that domestic circumstances can indeed rise to the level of necessitous and compelling reasons for terminating one's employment, but argues that the facts of this case do not support such a conclusion.

A claimant who voluntarily terminates his employment yet seeks to receive unemployment compensation benefits bears the burden of proving that he quit for cause of a necessitous and compelling nature. Cause of a necessitous and compelling nature is such cause as results from overpowering circumstances that produce both real and substantial pressure to terminate employment and that would compel a reasonable person to terminate employment. Cause of a necessitous and compelling nature may arise from purely domestic circumstances and need not be related to a claimant's employment situation. The question of whether quitting one's employment to care for an ill parent constitutes cause of a necessitous and compelling nature must be decided on the specific facts of each individual case. A claimant who terminates his employment to care for a chronically ill parent cannot be said to have done so for cause of a necessitous and compelling nature unless he has given the employer an opportunity to accommodate him, has explored alternative options for care of the parent, or has considered the possibility of relocating the parent so that he can continue his employment.

In this case, we find it likely that Claimant did in fact move to Virginia primarily because he wanted to take care of his ill mother, and such a commitment is certainly laudable. However, this does not entitle Claimant to unemployment compensation benefits absent evidence that Claimant explored other options less drastic than quitting his job, such as purchasing a home in Pennsylvania in which to care for his mother or asking Employer for a leave of absence or some other accommodation. Had Claimant presented evidence that he explored such options and found them to be fruitless, then his termination of employment and move to Virginia might have been found "necessitous and compelling." Not having done so, we conclude that the Board did not err in concluding that Claimant failed to sustain his burden of proving that he terminated his employment for cause of a necessitous and compelling nature.

Accordingly, the order of the Board is affirmed.

PROBLEM TEN—B
ANSWER SHEET

Name   **Please Print Clearly**

1. Please tell me the law about quitting one's job because of a medical issue.

_____

_____

_____

_____

_____

_____

_____

2. What do you think the outcome of the unemployment compensation case will be? Please explain your answer.

_____

_____

_____

_____

_____

_____

_____

_____

**SECTION 10.15
AT-WILL EMPLOYEES**

Catherine Wagenseller, an Arizona nurse, her boss, Kay Smith, and some co-workers joined a Colorado River rafting trip where Wagenseller declined to participate in a "Moon River" skit in which the group allegedly "mooned" the audience. Likewise, Wagenseller did not join Smith in the heavy drinking, "grouping up," public urination, and similar behaviors that allegedly marked the trip. Despite favorable job evaluations preceding the trip, Wagenseller's relationship with Smith deteriorated following the trip, and eventually she was terminated. Wagenseller, an at-will employee, sued claiming that she was wrongfully discharged. An **at-will employee,** by definition, is not under contract for a definite period of time, and as such can be fired at any time. Wagenseller, however, argued that Arizona should adopt the *public policy exception* to the at-will doctrine. She claimed that she was fired because she refused to engage in behaviors that might have violated the Arizona indecent exposure statute. The state Supreme Court agreed with Wagenseller by finding in the statute a public policy favoring privacy and decency. The case was returned to the trial level, giving Wagenseller the opportunity to prove that her refusal to violate state public policy by engaging in public indecency led to her dismissal.[83]

The **Wagenseller** decision is an exception to the long-standing American rule that at-will employees can be fired for good reasons, bad reasons, or no reason at all. Of course, the employee is likewise free to quit at any time. Furthermore, both employer and employee freely entered the bargain understanding its terms, and thus the court should, in general, enforce those terms, Critics, however, argue that the doctrine ignores the historic inequality of bargaining power between employers and employees. In recent decades the at-will rule has been softened in most states by legislative and judicially imposed limitations. Statutory exceptions to the at-will rule include our labor laws protecting union workers and the equal employment opportunity laws that forbid the dismissal of an employee for discriminatory reasons.

An increasing number of court decisions provide grounds for dismissed at-will employees to claim that they have been **wrongfully discharged.** Those judicial decisions were often provoked by transparently unjust dismissals including, for example, whistle-blowers who exposed their employers' misdeeds and employees who declined to commit perjury on behalf of their employers. Those judicial limitations to the at-will doctrine fall into three categories: (1) express or implied contracts, (2) an implied covenant of good faith and fair dealing, and (3) the tort of violating an established public policy, as in **Wagenseller.** Additional tort claims may substitute for or supplement wrongful discharge claims.

1. **Express or implied employment contracts:** A number of states have adopted a contract protection for at-will employees that arise, typically, either from the employee handbook or from employer conduct and oral representations. The notion here is that the courts will recognize a contract based either on language in the handbook or on such assurances of continued employment as routine promotions, no notice of poor performance, longevity, and oral communications.

2. **Implied covenant of good faith and fair dealing:** A few state courts have held that neither party to a contract may *act in bad faith* to deprive the other of the benefits of the contract. For example, Bruce Rubenstein gave up his job with Arbor Mortgage and took an at-will position with Huntington Mortgage with the understanding that he would be manager of a new branch office in central New Jersey. After a few weeks, however, Huntington decided on a downsizing strategy that included not opening the new branch. Rubenstein was offered a job as a loan originator, but he declined. He sued Huntington asserting, among other things, that Huntington had breached the covenant of good faith and fair dealing. Rubenstein believed that Huntington knew of the possibility of downsizing before hiring him. The court agreed that Rubenstein may have had a viable claim for breach of the implied covenant of good faith and fair dealing if the facts, at trial, proved to be as Rubenstein alleged.[84]

3. **Public policy:** Most states have now adopted some form of public policy (the general preference of the citizenry) exception providing that a dismissal is wrongful if it results from employee conduct that is consistent with the will of the people as expressed in statutes, constitutions, and the like. Those exceptions are established case by case, and they differ from state to state. In addition to the whistle-blowing and perjury situations noted, the exception often protects, for example, those fired for pursuing a lawful claim (like workers' compensation) and those fired for fulfilling a civic responsibility (like jury duty).

Dismissed employees are increasingly turning to a variety of tort actions (often labeled *tag-along torts*) to enhance potential financial recovery, including punitive damages. Those tort possibilities include, among others, defamation, intentional infliction of emotional distress, interference with contract, and invasion of privacy. The following case raises public policy and false imprisonment tort claims following an employment termination.

BARRERA V. CONAGRA, INC.
244 F.3D 663 (8TH CIR., 2001)

Manuel Barrera appeals from the district court's order granting summary judgment to ConAgra, Inc., and Swift & Co. (collectively, Swift), on Barrera's claims of retaliatory discharge in violation of public policy and false arrest and imprisonment.

On June 14, 1996, Barrera, a Mexican national who speaks very little English, was fired from his job on the cut floor of Swift's hog processing plant in Marshalltown, Iowa, after allegedly violating a company policy against eating in the employee locker room. Barrera was asked to report to human resources, where Swift alleges that he threatened the lives of several employees.

Barrera contends that he was fired in retaliation for filing a worker's compensation claim related to a slip-and-fall accident that occurred on or about March 22, 1996. He alleges that Swift staged the incident in the locker room as a pretext for his termination and that he was actually fired prior to the time he reported to human resources and before the alleged threats were made. Barrera also denies threatening to kill anyone at Swift, although he concedes that he may have threatened, depending on the translation, to "kick their asses" or "spank their buttocks."

In Iowa, an employer's ability to discharge an employee is limited when the discharge clearly violates the well recognized and defined public policy of the state. Discharge in retaliation for filing a worker's compensation claim clearly violates Iowa's public policy. To prevail on a retaliatory discharge claim, Barrera must establish (1) that he engaged in a protected activity; (2) that he suffered an adverse employment action; and (3) that there existed a causal connection between the protected activity and his termination.

We agree with the district court's conclusion that Barrera failed to produce evidence sufficient to raise a genuine issue of material fact regarding causation. As the court noted, other than the timing of the discharge, Barrera produced "almost no evidence" that his termination was in any way related to his worker's compensation claim. Under Iowa law, the fact that Barrera was fired after filing a worker's compensation claim is not alone sufficient to prove causation.

Iowa law demands, rather, that Barrera produce evidence demonstrating that his worker's compensation claim was the determinative factor in Swift's decision to terminate his employment. Barrera's version of the facts, however, suggests nothing more than rude and callous behavior on Swift's part. We conclude that the grant of summary judgment on Barrera's first claim was proper.

Affirmed.

QUESTIONS FOR DISCUSSION:

1. Why did Barrera lose this lawsuit?

2. The criminal harassment charges against Barrera were dropped, and the court noted that Barrera (according to his account) was the victim of "rude and callous" behavior by Swift.

3. Given this version of the facts, does it appear that Swift had legitimate grounds for dismissal?

4. If not, should Barrera have prevailed in this appeal? Explain.

5. Schuster worked, in an at-will relationship, for Derocili for 15 months, during which time she claims he touched her inappropriately and made numerous sexual comments despite her repeated rejections of those behaviors. Schuster received bonuses and good evaluations, but in a meeting between Schuster, Derocili, and Schuster's direct supervisor, Goff, she was fired for poor performance. Schuster's sexual harassment complaint with the Delaware Department of Labor was rejected as unsubstantiated. She sued Derocili for breach of contract, but the trial court dismissed that complaint. She appealed.

   a. Does Schuster have a legitimate wrongful discharge claim? Explain.

   b. Does she have any other plausible causes of action? Explain. See **Schuster v. Derocili, 775 A.2d 1029 (Del. S. Ct., 2000)**.

6. Gilmartin took a job as station manager at a Texas television station. He was hired on a year-to-year basis under an oral agreement providing that his employment would continue as long as his work was satisfactory. Gilmartin was subsequently blamed for declining profits, and he was fired. Gilmartin sued. In his pleadings, Gilmartin said that he was informed of his annual salary, vacation time, and possible future raises, that his contract was to be renewed from year to year contingent on satisfactory performance, and that a commitment by KVTV for one to three years was "very doable." He was also told that a written agreement was not necessary. Was Gilmartin wrongfully discharged? Explain. See **Gilmartin v. KVTV-Channel 13, 985 S.W.2d 553 (Ct. App. Tex., 1998)**.

7. IBP operates a large hog-processing plant in Storm Lake, Iowa. IBP prohibits possession of "look-alike drugs" on company property. An employee, Michael Huegerich, was randomly and lawfully inspected as he was entering the plant. The inspection revealed an asthma medication, Maxalert, which was identical in appearance to an illegal street drug, "speed." Maxalert contained the stimulant ephedrine. The pills actually belonged to his girlfriend and were in his possession by accident. Huegerich was terminated for possessing a look-alike drug in violation of company policy. Huegerich admitted that he was generally aware of IBP drug policies, but since he was a transfer from another IBP division, he had not gone through the company orientation program where new employees are advised of the policy against look-alike drugs. About six months after his dismissal, two IBP employees told Huegerich that they had heard

he was fired for possessing speed. Huegerich then sued IBP for, among other claims, wrongful discharge and defamation. At trial, Huegerich provided no evidence as to how, when, and from whom the IBP employees had heard that he was terminated for possession of speed. The district court found for Huegerich in the amount of $24,000 on the wrongful discharge claim and $20,000 on the defamation claim. The court said that IBP was guilty of negligent discharge in failing to inform Huegerich about its drug policy. IBP appealed to the Iowa Supreme Court. Iowa law recognizes the doctrine of at-will employment with "narrow" exceptions for public policy violations and where a contract is created by an employer's handbook. Decide. Explain. See **Huegerich v. IBP, 547 N. W. 2d 216 (Iowa S.Ct., 1996).**

8. Freeman, a television anchorperson employed by KSN, gave birth to her second child. On the day she returned from the hospital, she was notified that she had been dismissed. Six weeks later, she became unable to lactate. She sued KSN for wrongful discharge, tortious interference with contract, and negligent infliction of emotional distress. Decide. Explain. See **Freeman v. Medevac Mid-america of Kansas, Inc., 719 F. Supp. 995 (D. Kan., 1989).**

**SECTION 10.16
IMMIGRATION**

Immigration is vital fuel for America's economic and cultural growth, but immigration is also a source of deep divisions in national opinion—especially since September 11, 2001. Thirteen percent of the nation's workers are immigrants, both legal and illegal.[85] About 700,000 legal immigrants enter the United States each year, and another 300,000 arrive illegally or overstay their visas.[86] In total about 30 million immigrants live in the United States, and an estimated 8.0 million of those are here illegally.[87]

About one-half of the nation's farm workers and 9 percent of restaurant employees are illegal immigrants.[88] A recent federal study found that immigrants provide a $10 billion annual boost to the American economy, and immigrants, over a lifetime, are no greater drain on public money for welfare and the like than are native-born citizens.[89] Without heavy immigration in the 1990s, unemployment probably would have been so low that wages and prices would have spiraled upward, threatening inflation.[90] A steady influx of highly skilled workers has been vital in maintaining high-tech growth.

Foreign workers seeking permanent residence in the United States on the basis of employment must have an offer of a permanent, full-time job. If so, the employer and the foreign national employee apply to the appropriate state Department of Labor for *labor certification,* which affirms that no one is available for the job and the hiring will not harm wages and working conditions in similar jobs. Some exceptions are provided for people in occupations where shortages exist and for those with exceptional abilities.

In hiring those already in the United States, federal immigration law, including the 1986 Immigration Reform and Control Act, requires employers to verify that each new hire is a U.S. citizen, a permanent resident, or a foreign national with permission to work in this country. To meet this requirement, employers must complete an employment eligibility verification form (I–9) for each new employee. New employees must present documents establishing the employee's identity and eligibility to work in the United States. The employer must examine the documents and complete the I–9 if the documents appear legitimate. Of course, employers cannot knowingly hire illegal immigrants, but neither can they discriminate against legal immigrants because of national origin and similar factors.

SECTION 10.17 REVIEW QUESTIONS

1. In general, employers are forced to bear (or at least share) the legal burden for their employees' negligent conduct on the job. Why do we force employers to bear that responsibility? Should we do so? Explain.

2. Abplanalp, a five-year employee of Com-Co Insurance, signed an employment agreement including a restrictive covenant providing that, should he leave Com-Co, he would not use Com-Co customer lists or solicit business from Com-Co clients for three years. Abplanalp moved to Service Insurance, where he sold insurance to some friends and relatives. He did not sell to any other persons whom he came to know while working for Com-Co. Abplanalp was sued by Com-Co for violating the restrictive covenant. Decide. Explain. See **Com-Co Insurance Agency v. Service Insurance Agency, 748 N.E.2d 298 (Ill. App. Ct., 2001).**

3. Many companies refer to credit reports when investigating job applicants. The Fair Credit Reporting Act requires employers to notify applicants if they are rejected because of information in a credit report.

   a. In your judgment, does evidence of failure to pay debts constitute useful information in the job selection process? Explain.

   b. Is the use of that information an "invasion of privacy" as you understand it? Explain.

4. A group of Fargo, North Dakota, nurses were paid a sub-minimum wage for their "oncall" time. When on call, the nurses were required to be able to report to their hospital within 20 minutes, they were required to provide a phone number where they could be reached, and they were not to consume alcohol or drugs. After being called, nurses returned to regular pay. In three years, 36 of the 135 nurses who sued had been called in more than once. The nurses sued the hospital for violating the Fair Labor Standards Act's minimum wage provision. Decide. Explain. See **Reimer v. Champion Healthcare Corp., 258 F.3d 720 (8th Cir., 2001).**

5. Simons, an engineer at the CIA, downloaded child pornography on his workplace computer. The computer was to be used only for work. The pornography was discovered by a search of employee computers. Simons was then convicted of receiving and possessing child pornography. Simons appealed on Fourth Amendment grounds. Decide. Explain. See **United States v. Simons, 206 F.3d 392 (4ᵗʰ Cir., 2000); cert. den. 122 S. Ct. 292 (2001).**

6. Guz, a longtime Bechtel employee, was dismissed during what Bechtel said was a business slump. Bechtel's personnel policy included a provision saying employees "may be terminated at the option of Bechtel." Guz sued for wrongful dismissal claiming, among other things, that Bechtel breached an implied contract to be terminated only for good cause, and that Bechtel breached the implied covenant of good faith and fair dealing. A lower court concluded that Guz's promotions, raises, favorable performance reviews, together with Bechtel's progressive discipline policy and Bechtel officials' statements of company practices supported Guz's position. Bechtel appealed. Decide. Explain. See **Guz v. Bechtel National Inc., 8 P.3d 1089 (Cal., 2000).**

7. Sharon Kay Riddle sought workers' compensation claiming she had been totally and temporarily disabled by mental stress caused by the implementation of a no-smoking ban in the electronics manufacturing plant of her employer, Ampex. Riddle had smoked one to two packs per day for 24 years. Following the plant-wide ban, Riddle took leave and was diagnosed as suffering from major depression, nicotine dependence, and posttraumatic stress disorder. The administrative law judge found that Riddle had established three of the statutory requirements for her workers' compensation claim, but that she had failed to establish the fourth, which provided that work-related stress disabilities are not compensable if they are based "in whole or in part, upon facts and circumstances that are common to all fields of employment" and that the "facts and circumstances" were "not unique to [claimant's] employment." Riddle appealed the unfavorable ruling to the Colorado Court of Appeals. Is she entitled to workers' compensation? Explain. See **Riddle v. Ampex Corporation, 839 P. 2d 489 (Colo. App. Ct., 1992).**

8. As discussed in this chapter, many recent judicial decisions have afforded at-will employees much-improved protection against unfair dismissals. A special area of concern is whether at-will employees can be dismissed for off-duty conduct. The decisions are split, but the trend seems to be toward greater respect and protection for employee privacy. Nonetheless, companies still retain broad latitude to dismiss.

For example, an employee convicted of selling drugs would most likely not be protected by the courts from a company dismissal.

Virginia Rulon-Miller, an IBM salesperson, had been dating another IBM employee, Matt Blum, for several years. Her supervisors were aware of the relationship. Blum left IBM to join a competitor, QYX, and he moved from San Francisco to Philadelphia. QYX transferred him back to San Francisco, and he and Rulon-Miller resumed dating. Again, her superiors were aware of the relationship, and one mentioned that he didn't "have any problem" with her romance. Rulon-Miller did well in her sales role and was promoted to a management position, where she continued to do well, as evidenced by a $4,000 raise. Nonetheless, one week after receiving notice of the raise, Rulon-Miller was either dismissed (her version) or "transferred" (the company's version). IBM felt her romance and her concern for the success of Blum created a conflict of interest. Despite being an at-will employee, Rulon-Miller argued that she was protected by IBM's written policies that detail those circumstances under which an employee's private life can become a company issue. She filed suit, claiming wrongful discharge. Decide. Explain. See **Rulon-Miller v. IBM, 1 BNA IER Cases 405, 162 Cal. App.3d 241 (1984).**

9. Terrell was employed by Red Giant Foods as a forklift driver. Terrell's supervisor, Rowsey, had received reports from employees that Terrell was drinking on the job. Rowsey later observed Terrell drinking in his car, parked on company property during the noon break. An hour later, Rowsey entered the unoccupied, unlocked car and found beer. Subsequently, Terrell was terminated for violating company policy against drinking on the job. Terrell filed suit.

    a. What claim(s) would Terrell raise?

    b. Decide. Explain. See **Terrell v. Rowsey and Red Giant Foods, 647 N. E.2d 662 (Ind. App. Ct., 1995).**

10. In most drug testing cases, courts have balanced the employee's privacy interests against the employer's need for information. What business justifications are likely to be most persuasive to a court reviewing the legality of employee drug testing?

11. Millions of workers can be regarded as telecommuters. As such, they bring new legal problems to the workplace. As a manager, what legal difficulties would you want to anticipate and protect against as more and more of your employees work off-premises and often from his or her own homes?

12. A reader sent the following story to a newspaper question and answer forum:

> I was fired recently by my employer, an architecture firm, immediately after serving for one month on a federal grand jury. From the moment I informed my boss, I was harassed, and told I was not putting the company first. I was told to get out of my jury service, "or else." I was fired exactly one week after my service ended.[91] Was the dismissal of this at-will employee lawful? Explain.

13. Katherine Born and Rick Gillispie were employed by a Blockbuster Video store in Iowa. Blockbuster maintained a policy that forbade dating between supervisors and their subordinates. Born and Gillispie were dismissed for violating the policy. They denied that they were romantically involved and filed suit for wrongful dismissal. Under Iowa law, an at-will employee can be discharged at any time for any reason, but Iowa law does recognize the public policy exception. To prevail in this lawsuit, what must the plaintiffs show about Iowa law? See **Katherine Born and Rick Gillispie v. Blockbuster Videos, Inc., 941 F. Supp. 868 (S. D. Ia., 1996).**

14. A pregnant employee at a retail store was operating a buffing machine when propane gas that powered the machine led to a carbon monoxide buildup, causing the worker and others to be taken to a hospital. The worker's fetus sustained oxygen deprivation, resulting in injuries including abnormal motor functions, cerebral palsy, and a seizure disorder. The worker sued on negligence grounds for her child's injuries. The employer defended by arguing that workers' compensation provides the exclusive remedy in such situations. Does workers' compensation bar the child's suit? Explain. See **Snyder v. Michael's Stores, Inc., 945 P.2d 781 (Cal. S. Ct., 1997).**

15. Lang, a white male working in a factory, called a black coworker such names as "watermelon" and "buckwheat." The coworker told Lang to stop. Lang continued the racist name-calling and his coworker then called Lang a "cracker" and a "honkey." Later, while Lang was talking with his supervisor, the coworker twice struck Lang, who then filed a workers' compensation claim.

    a. Is Lang entitled to workers' compensation?

    b. What is the key issue? Explain. See **Redman Industries v. Lang, 326 Or. 32 (Sup. Ct. Or., 1997).**

16. LaTourette worked for a California college and was attending a conference for work purposes when he suffered a heart attack. He underwent various operations including bypass surgery, subsequent to which he died in the hospital from a bacterial infection. His estate sought

workers' compensation, claiming that his heart attack was a response to job stress. Is his estate entitled to workers' compensation? Explain. See **LaTourette v. Workers' Compensation Appeals Board, 72 Cal. Rptr.2d 217 (Sup. Ct. Cal., 1998).**

SECTION 10.18

INTERNET REFERENCES

The following internet references offer more information on employment law:

- **http://dir.yahoo.com/Government/Law employment_Law Driving while Dialing**
  This site provides an extensive employment law database.

- **http://www.toolkit.cch.com/tools/indcon_m.asp**
  A sample of independent contractor agreements can be reviewed at this site.

- **www.employlaw.com**
  This site offers an overview on employment law.

- **www.dol.gov**
  The U.S. Department of Labor home page may be accessed at this site.

- **www.dol.gov/esa/minwage/america.htm**
  More information can be learned about the state minimum wage laws at this reference.

- **www.dol.gov/esa/regs/compliance/whd/fairpay/main.htm**
  Details about the new overtime rules are contained at this internet reference.

- **www.osha.gov**
  This is the internet address for the OSHA home page.

- **www.osha.gov/comp-links.html**
  OSHA standards may be accessed at this site.

- **http://ergo.human.cornell.edu**
  This site contains advice on measures to reduce repetitive stress problems for students.

- **www.wcrinet.org**
  The Workers' Compensation Research Institute may be accessed at this site.

- **www.questdiagnostic.com**
  More details on drug testing results is available at this reference.

- **www.hrlawindex.com/email/email.html**
  This reference offers more information on e-mail and privacy.

- **www.dol.gov/esa/whd/fmla**
  More information about the Family Medical Leave Act is contained at this site.

- **http://uscis.gov/graphics/formsfee/forms/i-9.htm**
  This site offers an introduction to the I–9 requirements.

Footnotes:

1. Power, Kinder, & *Sweeney*, "Employee Strikes Door in Anger but Receives Workers' Comp," *Rhode Island Employment Law Letter, May 1999*.

2. Craig J. Cantoni, "The Case against Employee Benefits," *The Wall Street Journal*, August 18, 1997, p. A14.

3. "Microsoft Settles Federal Lawsuit," *Des Moines Register*, December 13, 2000, p. 8C.

4. **Donna Vizcaino v. Microsoft Corporation, 120 F.3d 1006 (9 Cir., 1997).**

5. **Microsoft Corporation v. Donna Vizcaino, 522 U.S. 1098 (1998).**

6. Staff Reporter, "Microsoft Says Temps Must Take a Hiatus after Working a Year," *The Wall Street Journal*, February 22, 2000, p. A32.

7. Sally Richards, "Résumé Fraud: Don't Lie to Get That Job!" *High Technology Careers Magazine* **[http://www.hightechcareers.com/doc699nextstep699.html]**.

8. "Lying on Résumés: Why Some Can't Resist," *Dallas Morning News*, December 22, 2001, p. 8A.

9. Kris Maher, "The Jungle," *The Wall Street Journal*, January 20, 2004, p. B8.

10. Carlos Tejada, "They Asked What?" *The Wall Street Journal*, March 27, 2001, p. A1.

11. Kris Maher, "The Jungle," *The Wall Street Journal*, September 28, 2004, p. B10.

12. Maher, "The Jungle," p. B10.

13. Kris Maher, "The Jungle," *The Wall Street Journal*, June 8, 2004, p. B4.

14. Maher, "The Jungle," p. B4.

15. Stephanie Armour, "College Grads Confront Tough Job Market," *USA TODAY*, June 12, 2001, p. 1B.

16. **Circuit City Stores, Inc. v. Adams, 532 U.S. 105 (2001).**

17. See Sidney L. Gold and Hyman Lovitz, "Arbitration Agreements Don't Supersede Authority to Recover Damages," *The Legal Intelligencer*, June 6, 2002, p. 6.

18. 814 P.2d 1341 (Cal. S. Ct., 1991).

19. Jenny B. Davis, "Still Working after All These Years," *ABA Journal*, October 2001, p. 67.

20. Rick Wartzman, "As Officials Lost Faith in the Minimum Wage, Pat Williams Lived It," *The Wall Street Journal*, July 19, 2001, p. A1.

21. For a study involving 12 of the higher minimum wage states, see Gwendolyn Bounds, "Argument for Minimum-Wage Boost," *The Wall Street Journal*, July 27, 2004, p. B3.

22. Editorial, "Living in Santa Fe," *The Wall Street Journal*, July 9, 2004, p. A10.

23. Associated Press, "Study Shows 'Living Wage' Helping to Reduce Poverty," *Waterloo/Cedar Falls Courier*, March 14, 2002, p. A2.

24. Ann Zimmerman, "Big Retailers Face Overtime Suits as Bosses Do More 'Hourly' Work," The Wall Street Journal, May 26, 2004, p. A1.

25. Zimmerman, "Big Retailers Face Overtime Suits," *Id.*

26. Michael Orey, "Lawsuits Abound from Workers Seeking Overtime Pay," *The Wall Street Journal*, May 30, 2002, p. B1.

27. Associated Press, "Disney Workers Win Pay Ruling," *Des Moines Register*, April 8, 2001, p. 2K.

28. "Call the *Courier*," *Waterloo/Cedar Falls Courier*, February 4, 2001, p. C1.

29. David Barstow, "California Leads in Making Employer Pay for Job Deaths," *The New York Times*, December 23, 2003, p. A1.

30. Justin Pritchard, "Mexican Worker Deaths Rise in U.S. Even as Safety Improves," *Des Moines Register*, March 14, 2004, p. 1D.

31. "OSHA Enforcement Focuses on the Triple Bottom Line," *U.S. Newswire*, November 22, 2004.

32. Leigh Strope, "U.S. Workplace Deaths Up Slightly in 2003," *Des Moines Register*, September 23, 2004, p. 8C.

33. "OSHA Enforcement Focuses on the Triple Bottom Line," supra.

34. "OSHA Enforcement Focuses on the Triple Bottom Line," supra.

35. "OSHA Enforcement Focuses on the Triple Bottom Line," supra.

36. Robert J. Grossman, "Making Ergonomics," *HR Magazine*, April 2000, p. 36.

37. Grossman, "Making Ergonomics," *Id.*

38. Grossman, "Making Ergonomics," *Id.*

39. Bloomburg News, "Poultry, Grocery Firms Face Ergonomic Rules," *Los Angeles Times*, June 12, 2002, Part 3, p. 4.

40. "U.S. Repeated Trauma Rates Decline for Third Straight Year," *CTDNEWS Workplace Solutions* for Repetitive Stress Injuries 8, no. 1 (January 1999).

41. Diane E. Lewis, "Voluntary Ergonomic Proposal Released, Business Cheers Plan; Foes Say It Lacks Teeth," *The Boston Globe*, April 6, 2002, p. C1.

42. "OSHA Prepares to Turn the Spotlight on Workplace Homicides," *Security Director's Report*, January 2005.

43. Daniel Costello, "Incidents of 'Desk Rage' Disrupt America's Offices," *The Wall Street Journal*, January 16, 2001, p. B1.

44. "OSHA Prepares to Turn the Spotlight," supra.

45. "OSHA Facts, December 2004" [http://www.osha.gov/as/opa/oshafacts.html].

46. David Barstow, "U.S. Rarely Seeks Charges for Deaths in Workplace," *The New York Times*, December 22, 2003, p. Al.

47. Justin Pritchard, "Mexican Workers More Likely to Die on the Job," *Marin Independent Journal*, April 14, 2004 **[www.marinij.com].**

48. Pritchard, "Mexican Workers More Likely to Die on the Job," *Id.*

49. **Stringer v. Minnesota Vikings, 686 N. W.2d (Minn. Ct. App., 2004); Stringer v. Minnesota Vikings, 2004 Minn. LEXIS 752 (Minn. S. Ct.).**

50. **Guico v. Excel Corp., 619 N.W.2d 470 (Neb. S. Ct., 2000).**

51. Barbara Ehrenreich, "Two-Tiered Morality," *The New York Times*, June 30, 2002, sec. 4, p. 15.

52. Bernard Wysocki Jr., "Companies Get Tough with Smokers, Obese to Trim Costs," *The Wall Street Journal*, October 12, 2004, p. B1.

53. Sue Shellenbarger, "Getting Fired for Dating a Coworker: Office Romance Comes under Attack," *The Wall Street Journal*, February 19, 2004, p. D1.

54. Shellenbarger, "Getting Fired for Dating a Coworker," *Id.*

55. Littler and Mendelson, *The 1996 Employer* (San Francisco: Littler, Mendelson, Fastiff, Tichy & Mathiason, P.C., 1996), p. 860.

56. See, e.g., **National Treasury Employees Union v. Von Raab, 109 S.Ct. 1385 (1989).**

57. Frances A. McMorris, "Is Your Office Voice Mail Private? Don't Bet on It," *The Wall Street Journal*, February 28, 1995, p. B1.

58. "Does Your Boss Watch You Work?" *Des Moines Register*, June 18, 2000, p. 3D.

59. Associated Press, "Study: Employers Monitoring Internet Use of a Third of Online U.S. Work Force," Waterloo/Cedar Falls Courier, July 10, 2001, p. B5.

60. Kris Maher, "Big Employer Is Watching," *The Wall Street Journal*, November 4, 2004, p. B1.

61. Mark P. Couch, "Eyes Are on Your E-Mail," *Des Moines Register*, January 26, 1997, p. 1G.

62. *Hartford Courant*, "Study Finds Millions Lost Health Insurance at Work," *Waterloo/ Cedar Falls Courier*, August 3, 2004, p. D6.

63. Kathy Chu, "Good Times Return, Not Benefits," *The Wall Street Journal*, June 30, 2004, p. D2.

64. Chu, "Good Times Return, Not Benefits," *Id.*

65. Chu, "Good Times Return, Not Benefits," *Id.*

66. Joe Robinson, "Vacation Deficit Disorder," *Des Moines Register*, August 1, 2003, p. 9A.

67. Robinson, "Vacation Deficit Disorder," *Id.*

68. Jeffrey Zaslow, "The Singles Lobby: Unmarried People Seek Economic Perks Enjoyed by Couples," *The Wall Street Journal*, June 24, 2004, p. D1.

69. Sara Munoz, "Leadership (A Special Report); A Good Idea, but . . . : Some Businesses Complain That the Family and Medical Leave Act Should Be More Aptly Named the Slackers Protection Act," *The Wall Street Journal*, January 24, 2005, p. R6.

70. Munoz, "Leadership (A Special Report)," *Id.*

71. Munoz, "Leadership (A Special Report)," *Id.*

72. Knight Ridder Newspapers, "Study: New Parents' Leave Is Unchanged," *Waterloo/ Cedar Falls Courier*, February 21, 2003, p. A10.

73. Patt Johnson, "Getting the Boot," *Des Moines Register*, May 4, 2003, p. 1D.

74. Johnson, "Getting the Boot." *Id.*

75. Clark Kauffman, "Stud-Wearing Dispatcher Gets a Tongue-Lashing," *Des Moines Register*, March 20, 2004, p. 1A.

76. Liz Pulliam Weston, "Betting It All on Company Stock Is Risky Business," *Los Angeles Times*, November 30, 2001, p. I.

77. James T. Madore, "Enron Employees See 401(k)s Wiped Out," *Newsday*, November 30, 2001, p. A75.

78. "Enron: Deconstructing the Energy Giant's Fall," *The Scotsman*, January 11, 2002, p. 5.

79. Ellen Schultz, "Enron Settles with Employees Who Lost Retirement Money," *The Wall Street Journal*, July 12, 2005, p. A8.

80. Lee Hawkins Jr., "GM's Liabilities for Retiree Health Top $60 Billion," *The Wall Street Journal*, March 11, 2004, p. A3.

81. Sandra Guy, "Coverage Causes Pain," *Chicago Sun-Times*, June 20, 2002, p. 47.

82. Kristine Henry, "Steel Workers' Benefits in Peril," *Baltimore Sun*, July 10, 2002, p. 1A.

83. **Wagenseller v. Scottsdale Memorial Hospital, 710 P.2d 1025 (Az. S. Ct., 1985).**

84. **Rubenstein v. Huntington Mortgage Company, N. J. Supp.Ct., App.Div., 1997.** For a journalistic account of the case, see Pitney, Hardin, Kipp, and Szuch, "Employers Must Be Cautious about Failing to Disclose Business Plans That Will Affect the Jobs of New Hires," *New Jersey Employment Law Letter, September 1997.*

85. Laura Parker, "USA Just Wouldn't Work without Immigrant Labor," *USA TODAY*, July 23, 2001, p. 1A.

86. Parker, "USA Just Wouldn't Work," *Id.*

87. Miriam Jordan, "Arizona Limits Illegal Immigrants' Access to Benefits," *The Wall Street Journal*, November 4, 2004, p. A4.

88. Deborah Kong, "Illegal Immigrants Abound in Some Jobs," *Des Moines Register*, March 22, 2002, p. 1A.

89. Mark Siebert, "Immigrants Aid Economy, Study Shows," *Des Moines Register*, February 18, 2001, p. 3B.

90. Adam Ninklewicz, "Keeping the Hive Humming," *BusinessWeek*, April 24, 2000, p. 50.

91. *Washington Post*, "The Boss Can't Fire You for Doing Your Civic Duty," Waterloo/ Cedar Falls Courier, May 26, 1999, p. C8.

KEY TERMS

Americans with Disabilities Act

At-Will Employee

Circuit City

Citations

Consolidated Budget Reconciliation Act (COBRA)

Defamation

Defined Benefit

Defined Contribution Plan

Drug-Free Workplace Act

Drug Testing

Electronic Communications Privacy Act

Employee

Employee Hazard Communication Standard

Employee Retirement Income Security Act (ERISA)

Enforcement

Equal Employment Opportunity Commission

Family and Medical Leave Act (FMLA)

Fair Labor Standards Act

Health Insurance Portability and Accountability Act (HIPAA)

Immigration

Independent Contractor

Minimum Wage

Negligence in Hiring an Employee

Occupational Safety and Health Act

Occupational Safety and Health Administration (OSHA)

Overtime

Pension Benefit Guaranty Corporation (PBGC)

Qualified Privilege

Right to Privacy

Scope of Employment

Unemployment Benefits

Unemployment Compensation

Variances

Vicarious Liability

Violence in the workplace

Worker Adjustment and Retraining Notification Act (WARN)

Workers' Compensation

Wrongfully Discharged

CHAPTER 11

INTERNATIONAL LAW
BY: MICHAEL VALENZA, ESQ.,
SAMUEL D. HODGE, JR.
AND KEVIN FANDL

"Insofar as international law is observed, it provides us with stability and order and with a means of predicting the behavior of those with whom we have reciprocal legal obligations."

—J. William Fulbright

SECTION 11.1 CORPORATE GOVERNANCE AND GLOBALIZATION

The major forces shaping corporate governance and world peace are those dealing with **globalization** and international trade. The potential role for business entities in this environment is the result of three things— economic integration, transition to a more democratic regime, and global governance networks. These interests have led to advancements in productivity across the globe and offer new opportunities in developing and developed nations.[1]

This impetus for increased globalization is partially the result of changes in transportation, communications, and computer technology. Multinational businesses manufacture goods in many countries and sell to people around the world. Money, technology and materials move quickly across the borders of countries and ideas, finances, and cultures flow more freely. As a result, laws, social movements, and economies are developing at the international level.[2]

Law has traditionally been the province of individual countries, whose courts and law enforcement officials administer and enforce the rules. By contrast, international law has been relatively weak with few effective enforcement powers. But globalization is changing the face of the law and creating new worldwide legal institutions and norms. International business law is developing rapidly, as nations implement standardized rules and legal practices. For instance, governments and courts are establishing international rules for bankruptcy, intellectual property, and many other areas of corporate law.

SECTION 11.2 INTERNATIONAL LAW

A caveat is in order before examining the traditional notions of international law and the role of the United States in world order. President Trump's "America First" policy has posed unprecedented challenges to international norms. This position appears to be driven by the belief that international law does not demonstrate American values. Rather, it endangers American institutions because this country's prestige, peace and success were not being advanced by exiting foreign policy.[3] From threatening to pull out of the North American Free Trade Agreement to actually withdrawing from the Iran deal on nuclear armament and Paris Climate Accord, the Trump Administration has put the world on notice that it is not business as usual.

International law deals with the rules, principles and customs that govern the dealings between sovereign states and the obligations and protections of the citizens of one country towards the people of other states. There has never been a formal law making body, like a world legislature, for international law so it has developed piecemeal through accords, agreements, **charters,** compromises, conventions, memorandums, protocols, treaties, tribunals, and other forms of understandings.[4]

Historically, the foundation of international law was established during the European Renaissance, though its origins are deeply steeped in early history and can be traced back to cooperative agreements between societies in the ancient Middle East.[5] Hugo Grotius, however, is dubbed the father of international law and his book, *De Jure Belli ac Pacis,* which translates to *The Law of War and Peace,* blends the ideas of natural law and positivism. The most distinguishing feature of his work was his belief in the freedom of the seas.[6]

The early advocates of international law interjected principles of the Bible, the *jus gentium* of the Romans, or law derived from the many different laws of the many cultures conquered by the Ancient Romans, and the doctrines of the Roman Catholic Church.[7] The phrase international law was first used in the early 19th century by Jeremy Bentham of England. Until then, it was known as the Law of Nations.[8]

The evolution of modern international law has progressed along two distinct, but sometimes overlapping, tracks. On the one hand, there are the political and organizational affairs of nation states. The second track involves the commercial activities of countries and private business entities. Many law texts distinguish these categories as being covered by either public international law or private international law.

A. Public International Law

Public international law deals with those relationships between and among nations, as evidenced through treaties, conventions, and adherence to the rules and policies of international organizations. For instance, a **treaty** is an agreement between two or more countries, and it may be further classified as bilateral or involving two states, or multilateral, meaning that more than two countries are parties to the arrangement. Since treaties are established by the particular nations involved, they only apply to those countries which are parties to the agreement. In the United States, the word treaty may only be properly applied when the agreement has been ratified by the Senate. On the other hand, **a convention** is an agreement negotiated usually by members of international organizations, which resulting document is then open to adoption by member states and other nations.

Another form of international arrangement is the **protocol,** an agreement on a matter considered to be of less significant impact than the subject of a convention. There are literally thousands of such treaties, conventions, and protocols in effect and they serve to create a substantial body of international law applicable to those nations that have made them part of their system of jurisprudence. Membership in international organizations may also create legal obligations and responsibilities by virtue of the charters of such organizations. Human rights and equal rights for men and women are, for example, guaranteed by the UN Charter.

B. Private International Law

Private international law is generally used to refer to the laws applicable to private parties in their business affairs when those entities are citizens of different nations. Issues of jurisdiction (a court which has the power to exercise control over a dispute), conflicts of laws (which nation's laws will apply to a dispute), and enforcement (whether judgments and arbitration awards will be enforceable in jurisdictions other than where the judgments are rendered) will always, absent agreement of the parties, be implicated in these disputes. As a consequence of the potential for irreconcilable differences between the involved legal systems, trading nations sought the creation and acceptance of trade practices.

C. Lex Mercatoria

The international norms that were created by commercial entities became known as **lex mercatoria** or law merchant. These norms were applied and enforced by the merchants themselves to their transactions. The lex mercatoria eventually became a part of the English common law and was applied to international commercial transactions until partially replaced in the nineteenth century by various multilateral treaties. Nations in addition to England also incorporated elements of lex mercatoria into their domestic laws such that there continued to be a more or less common approach to international commercial affairs.

SECTION 11.3 INTERNATIONAL NORMS

Unlike U.S. domestic law, where law is established by statute as well as court decisions, international law is usually established by treaty or by custom. As noted previously, treaties are agreements between specific nations to bind themselves to certain commitments. If these treaties are registered with the **United Nations** (UN), they can be enforced by the court of the UN, the International Court of Justice. Treaties cover a variety of subjects, from human rights to nuclear disarmament and are generally respected by the countries to those agreements.

In addition to treaties and customs, state practices may also serve as a source of international law. Known commonly as **customary international law,** this law exists as a result of the practices of a country or countries, rather than by a treaty or statute. The fact that a country adheres to a certain norm combined with their belief that the norm should be followed as law, may establish that norm as customary international law and prevent the jurisdiction from deviating from that standard. That form of international law is discussed in the *Paquete Habana* case that follows.

One of the earliest U.S. cases invoking recognition of international law arose out of the events of the Spanish-American War. The case, known as **The Paquete Habana,** involved the seizure of two Spanish fishing vessels by an American naval ship off the coast of Cuba. The Paquete Habana and The Lola, with civilian crews of three and six fishermen respectively, were seized while returning to Cuba, which was a Spanish territory at the time. The fishing vessels were unarmed and not participants in any of the on-going hostilities between the U.S. and Spain. The owners of the fishing vessels brought claims against the U.S. Government for the value of their seized vessels and cargoes. The U.S. Supreme Court, in 1900, issued its ruling in favor of the ship owners and stated:

> "By an ancient usage among civilized nations, beginning centuries ago, and gradually ripening into a rule of international law, coast fishing vessels, pursuing their vocation of catching and bringing in fresh fish, have been recognized as exempt, with their cargoes and crews, from capture as prize of war . . .

> The doctrine which exempts coast fishermen with their vessels and cargoes from capture as prize of war has been familiar to the United States from the time of the War of Independence.

> Since the English orders of council of 1806 and 1810 . . . in favor of fishing vessels employed in catching and bringing to market fresh fish, no instance has been found in which the exemption from capture of private coast fishing vessels, honestly pursuing their peaceful industry, has been denied by England, or by any other nation . . .

> International law is part of our law, and must be ascertained and administered by the courts of justice of appropriate jurisdiction, as often as questions of right depending upon it are duly presented for their determination. For this purpose, where there is no treaty, and no controlling executive or legislative act or judicial decision, resort must be had to the customs and usages of civilized nations; and, as evidence of these, to the works of jurists and commentators . . .

> Upon the facts proved in either case . . . [those of both The Paquete Habana and of The Lola] . . . it is the duty of this court, sitting as the highest prize court of the United States, and administering the law of nations, to declare and adjudge that the capture was unlawful, and without probable cause; and it is therefore, in each case, Ordered, that the proceeds of any sale of her cargo, be restored to the claimant, with damages and costs."

The codification of the lex mercatoria has been supplemented by a more active participation of governments in recognition of international legal norms of not only commercial enterprises but also nation states. Numerous laws have been enacted by Congress and many treaties and multilateral conventions have been signed by the United States that incorporate general international legal principles into U.S. law. A full listing of such laws is not feasible, but several do deserve mention, as they have had broad application to U.S. businesses and commerce.

A. The Harter Act

The responsibility for lost or damaged goods is an important issue in maritime law. The law for the most part is governed by the Carriage of Goods by Sea Act. Congress passed this legislation to stop the owners of vessels from disclaiming liability through contracts of carriages.[9]

The **Harter Act** applies to the transportation of goods not subject to the Carriage of Goods by Sea Act (COGSA), including the time before loading of the goods and after discharge and carriage between U.S. ports unless the bill of lading expressly makes COGSA applicable to such shipments. The Harter Act makes void any clause in a bill of lading which attempts to eliminate the vessel's owner of liability for loss or damage to cargo arising from negligence in loading, care and delivery or clauses that attempt to lessen the ship owner's obligation to provide a seaworthy vessel for the carriage and delivery of cargo. It does, however, relieve a ship owner of liability for errors in navigation or management of the vessel if the owner exercises due care to make the vessel seaworthy.[10]

For example, in 1892, Congress passed the Harter Act, which set forth the liability of ocean carriers for cargo losses (replaced by the Carriage of Goods by Sea Act, when the shipment is between a U.S. port and a foreign port, leaving the **Harter Act** in place as to shipments between two U.S. ports).

B. The Warsaw and Montreal Conventions

The United States became a signatory nation to the **Warsaw Convention,** which dealt with the liability of airlines in international travel and capped their exposure at a set dollar amount for injuries to passengers and luggage. This protection was needed in the 1920's to allow the fledgling airline industry to expand around the world. In 1999, the Warsaw Convention was amended by the **Montreal Convention** which expanded the liability of airlines to about $150,000 a person without the need to show fault and by giving more protection to air travelers for such things as lost baggage.

The new law, however, refuses to recognize an award of money for psychiatric injury unless inseparably linked to the physical injury.[11] The Montreal Convention also increases the maximum liability of airlines for lost baggage to $1,685 per passenger and mandates that airlines fully compensate flyers for the cost of replacement items purchased until the baggage is delivered up to the cap of a maximum of $1,685.

C. The Foreign Sovereign Immunities Act

The **Foreign Sovereign Immunities Act** of 1976 (FSIA) is a law that imposes restrictions on suing a foreign sovereign nation and its agencies or instrumentalities in the courts of the United States. This law is the primary method to institute a lawsuit against a foreign sovereign in the United States. It also imposes specific procedures for the service of process of foreign sovereigns, as well as the attachment of property in order to collect a judgment.[13]

The basic premise of this law is that foreign sovereigns are immune from suit in the United States unless the action falls under a specific exception enumerated in the statute. If the foreign sovereign is not immune, the federal district courts have exclusive jurisdiction over the lawsuit. Once a foreign-sovereign asserts immunity, the plaintiff has the burden of producing evidence to show that there is no immunity and that the court has jurisdiction over the claim. For instance, a sovereign is not immune from suit if it is engaging in commercial activity, such the renting of a house that it owns for investment purpose to a lessee.[14]

The Foreign Sovereign Immunities Act codified the immunity of foreign governments in U.S. courts. The language of this Act, however, specifies that foreign governments are not immune when conducting commercial activities.

D. The Foreign Trade Antitrust Improvements Act

The **Foreign Trade Antitrust Improvements Act ("FTAI"),** enacted by Congress in 1982, makes it illegal when anti-competitive conduct outside of the U.S. has a direct, substantial, and reasonable foreseeable impact on Commence within the United States, or on the business of U.S. exporters outside of this country.

Though awkwardly phrased, the law seeks to make clear to American exporters and to firms doing business abroad that the Sherman Act does not prevent them from entering into business arrangements, however restrictive or anticompetitive, as long as those arrangements only affect only foreign markets. The legislation itself provides in the first section a broad general rule that the Sherman Act "shall not apply" to conduct involving foreign trade or commerce. It then carves out limited exceptions. For instance, FTAIA restores the Sherman Act's applicability to two categories of foreign anticompetitive business practices: (1) foreign anticompetitive conduct "involving . . . U.S. import trade or import commerce"; and (2) foreign anticompetitive conduct that "has a direct, substantial, and reasonably foreseeable effect" on this country's domestic or import commerce or trade.[15]

In 1982, Congress passed the **Foreign Trade Antitrust Improvements Act.** This law made it illegal when anti-competitive conduct outside of the

U.S. has a direct, substantial, and reasonably foreseeable impact on commerce within the U.S., or on the business of U.S. exporters outside the U.S.

E. The Foreign Corrupt Practices Act

This country also enacted the **Foreign Corrupt Practices Act (FCPA),** which makes it illegal for U.S. companies and their agents to bribe foreign officials. The FCPA, as well as many other enactments, represent examples of the extraterritorial effect of certain U.S. laws, that is, those laws that apply to U.S. citizens and sometimes non-citizens outside of the U.S., even when the prohibited conduct is not illegal in the country where performed.

The passage of the Foreign Corrupt Practices Act was the result of a series of publicized efforts on the part of U.S. business interests to secure favored contracts in countries where bribery of public officials was done, even if the process was not legal. The FCPA was intended to reach such conduct through prosecution in the federal courts. No matter where the conduct of the U.S. party takes place, the person violating the Act is subject to the reach of the FCPA. Exactly what conduct is covered by the FCPA is addressed in **USA v. David Kay and Douglas Murphy.** The opinion of the federal district judge in dismissing charges of FCPA violations is also instructive on the importance of legislative history in the interpretation of statutes that are not ideally clear.

UNITED STATES OF AMERICA v. KAY AND MURPHY
200 F. SUPP.2D 681 (S.D. TEX., 2002)

Defendants Douglas Murphy and David Kay are charged with violations of the Foreign Corrupt Practices Act of 1977 ("FCPA"). The indictment alleges that the Defendants, as president and vice president of American Rice, Inc. ("ARI"), made improper payments to officials in Haiti to reduce customs duties and sales taxes owed by ARI to the Haitian government.

The FCPA prohibits payments to a foreign official to "obtain or retain business" . . . The question before the Court, therefore, is whether payments to foreign government officials made for the purpose of reducing customs duties and taxes fall under the scope of "obtaining or retaining business" pursuant to the text of the FCPA. Defendants contend that the FCPA does not prohibit such payments. Rather, the FCPA

only prohibits payments made to "obtain or retain business," which, according to Defendants, limits the scope of the FCPA to payments to secure new business or to renew existing business. Here, Defendants argue that they did not make the alleged payments to Haitian officials to obtain new business or to renew existing business, as ARI had already established its business in Haiti and made the payments to reduce customs duties and taxes on incoming goods. The Government responds that the FCPA applies, without any textual limit, to all bribes made for the purpose of obtaining or retaining business. The Government further argues that Defendants' payments to reduce customs duties and sales taxes were essential to ARI to be able to conduct business in Haiti and, thus, the payments constituted prohibited payments made to retain business.

In applying criminal laws, federal courts must follow the plain and unambiguous language of the statute. Reviewing the "obtain or retain business" language, the Court determines that the FCPA is ambiguous under these circumstances. Therefore, the Court turns to an analysis of the legislative history of the FCPA. Congress enacted the FCPA to stop bribery of foreign officials by domestic corporations.

In the course of enacting the FCPA, Congress rejected two bills that would have broadened the scope of the FCPA's prohibited activities . . . Congress rejected these proposals in favor of the phrase "obtain or retain business" as found in the current version of the FCPA.

In response to business concerns that the FCPA placed American businesses at a competitive disadvantage in the foreign marketplace, Congress amended the FCPA. These amendments included exceptions for . . . "routine governmental action" . . . The House also sought to amend the FCPA to prohibit payments for "procurement of legislative, judicial, regulatory, or other actions in seeking more favorable treatment by a foreign government." Congress rejected this proposed amendment in favor of the original statutory language.

In response to the Organization for Economic Cooperation and Development Convention on Combating Bribery of Foreign Officials in International Business Transactions ("the OECD Convention"), Congress again amended the FCPA . . . [but] . . . again declined to amend the "obtain or retain business" language in the FCPA.

Given the foregoing, counts one through twelve of the indictment are hereby dismissed.

**SECTION 11.4
JOE ROBERT AND
SCARE AIRLINES**

**PARK, BROWN & SMITH, P.C.
ATTORNEYS AT LAW
MEMORANDUM**

PROBLEM ELEVEN—A

TO: All Law Clerks

FROM: Peter Smith, Esquire

RE: Joe Roberts v. Scare Airline

Joe Roberts had to go to Munich, Germany with Banner, the bar's preforming dog, so the pooch could receive additional training. The problem is that Joe is terrified of flying and experiences severe panic attacks. Dr. Feelgood gave his partner a prescription for Lexipro, a heavy-duty tranquilizer, to take before and during the flight as well as a letter indicated that he could take Banner on the plane as a service dog to keep Joe calm. Roberts loves the dog and Banner has a calming influence on him.

When Joe arrived at the airline counter, he was told that Banner could not accompany him in the main cabin of the aircraft because the Canine was not properly certified as a service dog. Joe told the airline of his panic attacks and that he needed Banner to sit next to him on the plane. He even showed the check-in attendant the letter from Dr. Feelgood but she summarily dismissed it by noting that the letter was not a valid service dog certification. Roberts then offered to buy Banner a first class tickets but the agent would not budge in her position. She said that Banner had to be checked-in with the baggage, so a cage was produced by the airline and Banner was led away.

Joe was devastated and did not know what to do. Roberts immediately felt the start of a panic attack so he went to a bar near his gate and ordered one drink after another to settle his nerves. By the time his flight was called for boarding, Roberts was inebriated. Then, as soon as he sat down in his seat, Joe popped a couple of Lexipro into his mouth and washed them down with a glass of Vodka. About one hour into the flight, Joe had a bad reaction to the combination of pills and alcohol and had a seizure. The flight was diverted to Newfoundland and Joe was taken off the plane and transported to the hospital. Unfortunately, Banner continued on the flight to Germany where no one was present to take possession of the pooch when the plane landed.

The next day, Joe awakened in the hospital and remembered that Banner was on the flight to Germany. He called the airline but no one was able to find Banner at the Munich airport. This news caused Joe to experience another panic attack and the doctors had to give him a shot to knock him out for a few hours. Joe was discharged later that day and unhappily retuned to Philadelphia. The next morning, Joe received a call from the airline noting that Banner was found safe and sound at the animal holding area in the Munich airport. Roberts was told that the dog would be put on the next flight back to Philadelphia and Joe could pick up the dog at 10 a.m. at the customs office.

Joe went to the customs office as directed but was not reunited with Banner until 2 p.m. The dog seemed out of sorts from the experience, did not greet Joe and was dehydrated. It took about one week before Banner was back to himself.

Roberts is furious and wants to sue the airline on behalf of both himself and the dog. If the airline had merely allowed the dog to board the plane, Joe maintains that none of the problems would have occurred. Roberts wants to recover for his panic attack on board the plane, his subsequent hospitalization, the anguish and mental suffering suffered by the dog and Joe's anguish until the dog was found.

Please read the following case and let me know if you think Joe will be successful in any part of his claim against the airline. Both the United States and Germany have agreed to the terms of the Montreal Convention.

OJIDE V. AIR FRANCE
2017 WL 4402569 (S.D. NEW YORK 2017)

On May 23, 2016, Plaintiffs, Angelia Ojide and her son, Joshua, traveled from John F. Kennedy International Airport to Nigeria, with a layover in Charles De Gaulle International Airport in Paris, France. Plaintiffs checked four bags at the check-in counter at JFK, one of which contained Joshua's medically prescribed nutrition. At Charles De Gaulle, Defendant Air France compelled Plaintiffs to check a carry-on bag that contained a smaller amount of Joshua's medically prescribed nutrition.

Upon plaintiffs' arrival in Nigeria, all five bags were missing; because Plaintiffs had none of Joshua's medication, and Joshua subsequently suffered from dehydration. The bags did not arrive for at least three days; as a result, Angela "had to hurriedly depart Nigeria and return to the United States," causing Plaintiffs to miss Angela's father's—and Joshua's grandfather's—burial. The bags never arrived in Nigeria, and they were delivered to Angela's home on May 31, 2016, allegedly in "severely damaged condition."

The Montreal Convention applies to all international carriage of persons, baggage, or cargo performed by aircraft. The United States, France, and Nigeria are all signatories to the Montreal Convention. An action for damages that occurs "in the carriage of passengers, baggage, and cargo" must be brought subject to the Montreal Convention.

Under the Montreal Convention, an airline "carrier is liable for death or bodily injury of a passenger upon condition only that the accident which caused the death or injury took place on board the aircraft or in the course of any of the operations of embarking or disembarking. To bring a claim, a plaintiff must establish that "(i) there has been

an 'accident'; (ii) resulting in 'bodily injury'; and (iii) the incident took place while on board the aircraft or during the operations of embarking or disembarking."

Article 19 of the Montreal Convention establishes carrier liability for "delay in the carriage by air of passengers, baggage or cargo. Damages under this provision are limited to Special Drawing Rights per passenger."

Plaintiffs' alleged injuries include dehydration, deprivation of food, and various forms of emotional distress. None of these is a "bodily injury" as defined under Article 17 of the Montreal Convention. Neither dehydration nor food deprivation are "bodily injuries" under the Convention. **Vumbaca v. Terminal One Grp. Ass'n L.P., 859 F. Supp. 2d 343 (E.D. N.Y. 2012)** (holding that no physical injury was alleged when the plaintiff claimed she suffered from "dehydration, headache, nausea, disgust, hunger, thirst, and discomfort"). Nor may Plaintiffs recover for emotional distress under the Convention. **E. Airlines, Inc. v. Floyd, 499 U.S. 530, 552 (1991)** (holding that "an air carrier cannot be held liable under Article 17 when an accident has not caused a passenger to suffer death, physical injury, or physical manifestation of injury"). And because neither dehydration nor food deprivation are bodily injuries, the emotional distress alleged did not arise from a qualifying injury. Furthermore, even if Plaintiffs plausibly claimed an injury, nowhere do they allege that it was caused "on board the aircraft or in the course of any of the operations of embarking or disembarking," as required to establish liability under the Convention. Montreal Convention, art. 17, § 1. As such, this claim is dismissed.

ANSWER SHEET
PROBLEM ELEVEN—A

Name

Please Print Clearly

1. Does the Montreal Convention apply to this case?

_____

_____

_____

_____

_____

_____

_____

_____

_____

_____

_____

_____

_____

_____

_____

_____

_____

_____

2. Can Joe recover the damages he seeks in this case? Please discuss the various claims that apply to Roberts and Banner

_____

_____

_____

_____

_____

_____

_____

_____

_____

_____

_____

_____

_____

_____

_____

_____

_____

_____

Section 11.5 International Organizations as Sources of Law

International organizations, in addition to domestic governments, non-governmental trade organizations and business entities, play a role in formulating international legal principles and rules that govern the community of nations. These organizations, whose charters typically encompass the development of friendly relations among states and the promotion of basic human rights, also facilitate the implementation of the international legal norms which they create. Membership in these organizations ordinarily means adherence to their charter principles.

A. United Nations

The United Nations is the most extensive international organization, both in its geographic and member nation coverage and in the number of multilateral agreements it has produced. Created in 1945 to replace the largely ineffective League of Nations, the goals of this body are to prevent war, to safeguard fundamental human rights, to maintain the obligations arising from treaties and other sources of international law, and to promote social progress and better standards of life.

The United Nations consists of six principal divisions: the General Assembly, the Security Council, the Economic and Social Council, the Trusteeship Council, the International Court of Justice and the Secretariat.

Each country that belongs to the United Nations is represented in the **General Assembly** which has been referred to as a "parliament of nations" since it meets regularly to discuss world issues. Article 10 of the UN Charter provides the General Assembly with the authority to adopt resolutions, which are recommendations on matters within the scope of the Charter. The UN General Assembly is also primarily responsible for analyzing legal matters of interest to the group and in formulating international conventions. These legal activities are delegated to the International Law Commission and the Sixth (Legal) Committee of the General Assembly. Subjects covered by these law committees have included matters such as trade relations, the exploitation of the seas, and genocide. The committees typically draft proposed conventions that are then submitted to the General Assembly for consideration.

The real power in the United Nations rests with the **Security Council,** an organization of 15 countries, whose purpose is to maintain international security and peace. There are five permanent members of this important Council: the United States, Russia, China, France and England. The remaining members are selected by the General Assembly and serve two-year terms. This group has the power to impose economic sanctions, order an arms embargo, or even to dispatch troops to an area.

The **International Court of Justice (ICJ),** also known as the World Court, is the main judicial arm of the United Nations. This court is located in The Hague, Netherlands, and its role is to apply international law to legal disputes in an attempt to settle controversies. It also gives advisory opinions on legal questions referred to it by authorized United Nations and other specialized agencies. The court consists of 15 judges who are selected by the Assembly and the Security Council.

The court functions as a place where member nations may seek binding rulings on such issues as boundary disputes, offshore maritime claims, and claims to the continental shelf resources. For example, ICJ cases handled in 2007 pertained to territorial and maritime disputes involving mainly Central and South American nations. Not all disputes will be heard by the ICJ, however, because the court's jurisdiction is dependent upon its acceptance by the parties involved.

Only countries which have accepted the jurisdiction of the World Court may be parties to contentious cases. In this regard, the Court is competent to hear a dispute only if the countries concerned have accepted its jurisdiction in one of the following ways:

- by entering into a special agreement to submit the dispute to the Court;

- by virtue of a jurisdictional clause, i.e., typically, when they are parties to a treaty containing a provision, whereby, in the event of a dispute of a given type or disagreement over the interpretation or application of the treaty, one of them may refer the dispute to the Court; or

- through the reciprocal effect of declarations made by them whereby each has accepted the jurisdiction of the Court as compulsory in the event of a dispute with another State having made a similar declaration.

Despite the good intentions of this judicial body, very few cases are brought before the World Court. From its inception in 1945 until 2008, only 137 cases have been entered on the Court's General List.

The United States enjoys an uneasy relationship with the World Court and has actually withdrawn as a member of that organization. This country will only submit to the court's jurisdiction on a case-by-case basis. For instance, the United States, to the chagrin of many countries, has withdrawn from an agreement signed by President Clinton to establish an International Criminal Court because it is concerned that the court can be used as a mechanism to bring charges against the United States for war crimes. The court has also criticized the United States justice system for its handling of Mexican defendants who have been accused of committing crimes in which the death penalty can be imposed. The United States was rebuked for not allowing these foreigners to talk to their consular officials following arrest in violation of the Vienna Convention on consumer relations.

Medellin v. Texas provides an example. Jose Medellin, a Mexican national, was convicted and sentenced to death for participating in the gang rape and murder of two teenage girls in Houston. Medellin raised a post-conviction challenge arguing that the state had violated his rights under the Vienna Convention, a treaty to which the United States is a party. Article 36 of the Vienna Convention gives any foreign national detained for a crime the right to contact his consulate. After his petition was dismissed by the United States Supreme Court, Medellin's case returned to the Texas Court of Criminal Appeals. Medellin's argument rested in part on a ruling of the International Court of Justice (ICJ) holding that the U.S. had violated the Vienna Convention rights of 51 Mexican nationals, including Medellin, and that their convictions must be reconsidered. Medellin argued that the Vienna Convention granted him an individual right that state courts must respect. Medellin also cited a memorandum from the President of the United States that instructed state courts to comply with the ICJ's rulings by rehearing the cases. Medellin argued that the Constitution gives the President broad power to ensure that treaties are enforced, and that this power extends to the treatment of treaties in state court proceedings.[16]

The Texas Court of Criminal Appeals rejected each of Medellin's arguments and dismissed his petition. The court said that rulings of the ICJ are not binding on state courts. The Texas court stood by its position that allowing Medellin to raise the Vienna Convention issue after his trial would violate state procedural rules, and that those rules were not supplanted by the Convention. The President had no authority to order the enforcement in state court of an ICJ ruling, because that would imply a law-making power not allocated to him by the Constitution.

The Court upheld the rulings of the Texas Court of Criminal Appeals in a 6-3 opinion written by Chief Justice John G. Roberts. The Court held that the signed Protocol of the Vienna Convention did not make the treaty self- executing and, therefore, the treaty is not binding upon state courts until it is enacted into law by Congress. Furthermore, Chief Justice Roberts characterized the presidential memorandum as an attempt by the executive branch to enforce a non-self executing treaty without the necessary Congressional action, giving it no binding authority on state courts.[17]

The UN has also established specialized tribunals for the purpose of handling such matters as war crimes and genocides that occurred in Bosnia-Herzegovina and in Rwanda. These tribunals, empowered by the Security Council of the UN, prosecute crimes by individuals whereas the ICJ limits its jurisdiction to nation parties.

B. Customs Unions

A **customs union** is an international association organized to relieve or eliminate customs restrictions on goods traded between member countries and to establish a standard tariff policy toward nonmember nations.[18]

1. European Union

Following the two World Wars, a number of European leaders thought that the only way to establish a lasting peace was to reconcile the two chief belligerent nations–France and Germany–both economically and politically. In 1950, the French Foreign Minister proposed a union for all of Europe, the first step of which would be the integration of the coal and steel industries. The following year, the European Coal and Steel Community (ECSC) was set up when six nations, Belgium, France, West Germany, Italy, Luxembourg, and the Netherlands signed the Treaty of Paris. The ECSC was a tremendous success and within a few years it was decided to combine other elements of the countries' economies. In 1957, the Treaties of Rome created the European Economic Community (EEC) and the six member counties agreed to eliminate trade barriers among themselves by forming a common market. In 1967, these countries merged into the European Community (EC), creating one Commission, a single Council of Ministers, and the body known today as the European Parliament. About 25 years later, the Treaty of Maastricht established the foundation for additional cooperation in foreign and defense policy, in judicial and internal affairs, and in the creation of an economic and monetary union–including a common currency. This further integration created the **European Union (EU).**

Today, the European Union consists of 28 nations, and a number of other countries are seeking entry.

The European Union is a powerful political and economic force that has torn down the geographic barriers of many European countries. Its goal is to promote a common market in which people, money, goods and services can move unimpeded among member countries. This organization represents almost one-half billion people, which makes it the third largest population behind China and India. Its citizens no longer need passports to travel between countries and a single currency, the Euro, has been established.

The EU has established common institutions such as a Council, which represents national governments, the European Parliament, which represents the people of member nations, and the European

Commission, an independent body that represents the European interests as a whole–to legislate specific matters in a democratic fashion involving the joint interest of participating countries at a European level. The United States is not a member of the European Union but it has maintained a Mission to that organization since 1961.[19]

The U.S. has a strong strategic partnership with the EU reflected in our close cooperation on regional crises and conflicts, and our extensive collaboration on a broad range of global challenges from counter-terrorism to nonproliferation. The U.S. and EU have significant trade and investment relations.

The United Kingdom shocked the world in 2016 by voting to leave the European Union in March 2019. This development is called **Brexit**. Part of the reason for the exit is the unhappiness by the conservative population with the influx of European immigrants into the nation in return for the free trade of goods. The economic impact of this decision to withdraw remains to be seen, and questions remain as to whether other countries will follow the United Kingdom's lead.

2. The African Union

The **African Union ("AU")** consists of 55 countries in Africa and is loosely based upon the European Union model. The member nations work closely with each other despite their differences in geography, history, race, language, and religion in an attempt to improve the political, economic, and social conditions for the one billion individuals who live on the African continent. A goal of the AU is to protect Africa's many cultures, some of which have existed for thousands of years.[20]

The African Union tries to enhance every facet of government and human life on the continent. It works to deliver safe food and water, and provide adequate housing to the poor, particularly in times of adversity. It examines the causes of these issues, such as famine, drought, crime, and war. Unfortunately, the countries have a high degree of people that suffer from HIV, AIDS, and malaria, so the AU attempts to provide treatment to the affected and offers education to prevent the spread of these diseases.[21]

3. The European Court of Justice

The **European Court of Justice** is the supreme judicial authority of the EU and retains jurisdiction over EU legal matters that cover not just the relationships among the EU member states but also those non-EU business enterprises that operate within the EU. Once the ECJ has issued a ruling, the authority to implement and enforce the ruling is then within the control of the judicial branches of the individual member states.

C. Free Trade Agreements

A free trade agreement (FTA) is a treaty between two or more countries focused on the liberalization of trade between members of that agreement. Members of FTAs receive preferential access to the markets of member states, allowing them to export goods in many cases with no tariffs, making their exports more competitive on those foreign markets. In more recent FTAs, non-goods elements have been included in such agreements, including trade in services, intellectual property, government procurement, and related issues.

Members of the WTO are bound by a rule known as Most Favored Nation, which requires those countries to share any trade benefit that it offers to one country with all members. In other words, countries cannot selectively apply benefits to certain trading partners—they must extend those benefits to all members. FTAs are an exception to this rule. An FTA allows a country to grant benefits to one or several countries that it does not extend to other members. The hope is that these FTAs serve as steps toward broader reduction in trade barriers over time; however, there is some concern that FTAs are rapidly expanding, while the WTO's role in trade diminishes.

1. North American Free Trade Agreement

The North American Free Trade Agreement (NAFTA) went into effect in 1994. This agreement provides for the reduction, and eventual elimination, of almost all trade tariffs on goods moving among the three members: the United States, Canada, and Mexico. NAFTA also provides for the elimination of trade barriers, increased competition through market access, protection of intellectual property rights, and other aspects of trade liberalization.

NAFTA has established the world's largest free trade area, which now consists of 450 million people, producing $17 trillion worth of goods and services.

The immediate advantage of NAFTA is that it lifted tariffs on the majority of goods made by the three member nations. The agreement also calls for the gradual elimination, over a period of 15 years, of most remaining barriers to cross-border investment and to the movement of goods and services among the countries.[22]

Trade between the United States and its member partners has increased since the agreement went into effect. For instance, U.S. goods and services trade with NAFTA totaled $1.6 trillion in 2009 and exports amounted to $397 billion. The United States had

$918 billion in total trade with NAFTA countries in 2010. Exports totaled $412 billion and goods imported into the United States amounted to $506 billion.[23]

NAFTA has made two land ports in Texas among the busiest in the country with deliveries of a multi-trillion-dollar cumulative gross domestic product for its member nations. The Agreement, however, is not without its critics. Unions and consumer-advocacy groups argue that NAFTA has had a negative impact in Mexico and the United States. They claim that resulting outsourcing and lower wages have hurt the United States' domestic economy and that Mexico's rural industries have been destabilized. It is asserted that that the Agreement has resulted in a loss of United States manufacturing and shipping jobs, and NAFTA has forced Mexican agricultural workers into other sectors or caused forced them to immigrate illegally to the United States.[24]

The future of NAFTA is on shaky grounds. Soon after President Trump's election, he indicated that he is going to renegotiate the Agreement to make it more favorable to the United States with the goal of decreasing this country's trade deficit. This is not a surprising development, considering that during his election campaign, Trump labeled the deal "the single worst trade deal ever approved in the United States."[25] Considering that many Republican members of Congress support free trade, the outcome of the President's threat to withdraw could be difficult to implement. As the Agreement is current constructed, Trump's plans to build the much touted border wall between the United States and Mexico through the imposition of tariffs that Mexico must pay would violate NAFTA. The bottom line is that if the United States alters the terms of NAFTA or withdraws from the Agreement, consumers would face higher costs for goods or products brought into the United States, and American firms could lose access to critical foreign markets.[26]

2. **Association of Southeast Asian Nations**

The **Association of Southeast Asian Nations** or **ASEAN** was created by Indonesia, Malaysia, Philippines, Singapore, and Thailand in 1967, to stimulate economic growth, cultural development and social progress in Southeast Asia and to promote regional peace and stability. The organization was subsequently joined by Brunei, Darussalam, Vietnam, Lao PDR, Myanmar, and Cambodia. ASEAN represents almost 500 million people, and has trade of about $850 billion. It too has created a free trade area in order to provide a competitive edge by operating as a single unit. This is done through the elimination of tariff and non-tariff barriers among its member countries. According to the European Union, ASEAN is its second largest trading partner, accounting for 11.7% of ASEAN trade. Because of ASEAN's global impact and regional success, it has been labeled one of the world's most influential organizations, and an "emerging powerhouse."[27]

3. Central America and Dominican Republic Free Trade Agreement

On August 5, 2004, the United States entered into the **Central America and Dominican Republic Free Trade Agreement (CAFTA-DR)** with five Central American countries, Costa Rica, El Salvador, Guatemala, Honduras, Nicaragua and the Dominican Republic. This agreement is the first free trade agreement between the United States and a group of smaller developing countries. CAFTA-DR creates new economic opportunities by eliminating tariffs, opening markets, reducing barriers to services, and promoting transparency. It is facilitating trade and investment opportunities among the participating countries and furthering regional integration.[28]

Central America and the Dominican Republic make up the third largest U.S. export market in Latin America, behind Mexico and Brazil. United States exports to the countries of this agreement were worth $19.5 billion in 2009. Combined total two-way trade during the same year between the United States and Central America and the Dominican Republic was $37.9 billion.[29]

4. United States-Israel Free Trade Agreement

The United States and Israel entered into a free trade Agreement in 1975. The **United States-Israel Free Trade Agreement ("FTA")** serves as the foundation for expanding trade and investment between the United States and Israel by reducing barriers and promoting regulatory transparency.[30] A major advantage of this FTA is that American products are able to compete on an equal basis with goods from Europe, which have free access to Israel's domestic markets.[31] Because of the success of the United States-Israel FTA, Israel is among America's 12 largest export markets per capita. Despite their small population of less than 8 million people, making them the 96th highest in the world, Israel is among the U.S.'s 25 largest export markets by value, ahead of much larger nations like Russia, Spain and Argentina.[32]

In addition to these trade agreements, over 575 other FTAs have been proposed and 379 are in force around the world as of 2013. Each country on average is a member of at least six free trade agreements. As of the time of publication, one of the most wide-ranging FTAs in terms of membership and covered issues is the Trans-Pacific Partnership, which is still under negotiation. More information about this agreement can be found on the web site of the U.S. Trade Representative, which is the U.S. agency responsible for trade negotiations: www.ustr.gov.

D. World Trade Organization

Twenty-three nations came together at the end of World War II to establish a stable trade and financial regime that would reduce the likelihood of another war. The creation of institutions to stabilize currencies, stem financial crises, and lock countries together in trade relations would make military action much more costly for potential aggressor nations. The result was the creation of the World Bank to finance economic development and the International Monetary Fund to stabilize currencies. The proposed trade organization that would accompany these two institutions never came into existence due to disagreement in the U.S. congress. However, a set of trade rules known as the General Agreement on Tariffs and Trade (GATT) was established as an interim measure to provide a uniform set of trade rules and to encourage countries to lower trade barriers.

This set of rules guided trade until 1994, when it was updated as the GATT 1994, which included the establishment of an organization to oversee the implementation of those rules. This **World Trade Organization** (WTO) is now the only major entity in existence to regulate international trade, including setting the rules for trade between countries, providing a forum to resolve disputes between countries, and pushing countries to further reduce or eliminate barriers to trade. The WTO has 164 members as of 2016.

One of the key features of the WTO is its dispute settlement system, which allows countries to lodge complaints against unfair trade practices by other countries. The WTO facilitates consultations between the countries first and, if these fail to resolve the dispute, they establish a panel of experts to arbitrate the dispute. Decisions of the WTO are only recommendations made to countries to adjust their trade practices. However, failure to adequately implement a WTO decision may lead the WTO to authorize the prevailing party to retaliate by raising tariffs or otherwise penalizing imports from the violating country. This ability to authorize retaliation makes the WTO dispute settlement process an effective tool to protect fair trade.

The **Agreement on Trade Related Aspects of Intellectual Property Rights** or **TRIPS** is said to be the most comprehensive international agreement on intellectual property rights in the world. Countries who are members of the WTO are automatically bound by the agreement. TRIPS covers most types of intellectual property such as patents, copyright, trade secrets, trademarks, geographical indications, industrial designs, and exclusionary rights over new plant varieties.[33]

Some of the more important parts of TRIPS concerns patent protection. In this regard, parties to the agreement are required to make patents available for all inventions, in all fields of technology without discrimination even though the law does not define what is meant by an invention.[34] Inventions are to be protected by a patent for 20 years, whether it is for a product or a process. However, to qualify for a patent, the invention has to be "new", it must be an "inventive step" and it must have "industrial applicability." A nation can refuse to issue patents:

- for inventions whose commercial exploitation needs to be prevented to protect human, animal or plant life or health;

- for diagnostic, therapeutic and surgical methods for treating humans or animals;

- for certain plant and animal inventions.[35]

In the United States, the decisions rendered by the WTO dispute resolution bodies are not binding on the courts. The decisions however are not without some weight. The following is an example of the weight afforded to a WTO ruling.

HYUNDAI ELECTRONICS CO., LTD. ET AL. V. UNITED STATES OF AMERICA
53 F. SUPP.2D 1334 (CT. INT'L. TRADE, 1999)

The U.S. Department of Commerce had issued an antidumping order (an increased tariff to compensate for the sale of the product in the U.S. at below fair market value) against Korean manufacturers of DRAM semiconductors. Federal Regulations allow the Commerce Department to lift the anti-dumping order if it is determined that the offending party has not sold the product at less than foreign market value for at least three consecutive years and that it is "not likely" that the offending party will make a below foreign market sale in the future (the only two of the regulations at issue). The court found that plaintiff LG Semicon had failed to meet the first test. As to plaintiff Hyundai, the Department of Commerce was not assured regarding the future of that party's conduct and refused to lift the anti-dumping order.

Hyundai argued that the satisfaction of the "not likely" standard is an unreasonable requirement given the circumstances of the chip marketplace, which is subject to periodic downturns during which dumping of chips is commonplace. Plaintiff LG Semicon argued that the "not likely" standard espoused by Commerce also violates the international law obligations of the U.S., as those obligations are expressed by the WTO. In a semiconductor dumping case filed with the WTO, a panel ruled that the "not likely" standard promulgated by Commerce violates WTO rules.

On this latter question of whether a WTO report constitutes precedent, Judge Goldberg of the U.S. Court of International Trade wrote:

> As an initial matter, the WTO report itself has no binding effect on the court. **In Footwear Distributors and Retailers of America v. United States, 852 F. Supp.1078 (1994),** the court was confronted with a claim that an adopted

GATT panel decision should govern the outcome of the case. Upon thorough review, the Footwear Distributors court reasoned that the response to a panel report is the prerogative of the executive branch, not the judiciary, because it implicates political decisions.

The WTO panel report does not constitute binding precedential authority for the court. Of course, this is not to imply that a panel report serves no purpose in litigation before the court. To the contrary, a panel's reasoning, if sound, may be used to inform the court's decision.

**SECTION 11.6
SCOPE OF
INTERNATIONAL
TRANSACTIONS**

One would be hard-pressed to find any nation that does not conduct some level of international political and commercial relations; even countries as isolated as North Korea and Myanmar (Burma) engage in international trade. Then, there are those nations that, as a result of the absence of natural resources and manufacturing capacity, have commerce restricted to the receipt of foreign assistance. Yet, even these nations participate in multinational agreements. Trade, whether conducted directly by governments, or by commercial businesses, has expanded exponentially in recent times. And, while international business was long the arena of large corporations and trading companies, advances in transportation and the internet have brought together participants from distant nations to conduct business activities that previously could never be accomplished.

The catch-word of the new millennium is **"globalization,"** and the pioneers of this process are global businesses supported by governments to deregulate and liberalize world markets and re-define the legal rules that govern commercial relationships. An emerging aspect of globalization is the changed perception of national boundaries and domestic laws. Global competition has led to mergers and acquisitions on an international scale. Technology transfers have expanded the reach of businesses beyond domestic markets and in a manner that could hardly have been envisioned 20 years ago. Countries have re-defined their roles as members of regional or common markets.

For instance, the European Common Market has been transformed into the European Union with an integration of currency, banking and other legal aspects. The United States and Canada formalized a free trade zone which has been expanded to include Mexico, and now has more than 500 million regional customers as part of the North American Free Trade area. India and the People's Republic of China have liberalized their laws regarding foreign investment and have added two trillion more individuals to the global marketplace. This process has engaged an ever-increasing movement of goods, services, and information across national boundaries. Some nations have, to an extent, kept pace with these economic developments by establishing elements of a world legal order and incorporating these elements into their domestic legal systems. Other nations have, however, been slow to adhere to international legal principles, thus requiring international businesses to remain vigilant regarding where and how they should conduct their businesses. Many global business activities remain subject to multiple risks. While the international legal environment has become the focus of multinational conventions and agreements intended to manage some aspects of this risk, the global business community itself has developed mechanisms intended to encourage commerce and at the same time reduce, if not eliminate, the risks entailed in moving the goods, services, and information across boundaries.

SECTION 11.7
RISKS OF
INTERNATIONAL
COMMERCE

Small businesses control international business by contributing 97% of the products to the number of exports. These organizations are able to take advantage of the significant growth opportunities in international trade, but not without overcoming a number of challenges and risks. Small businesses must overcome these potential problems in order to be successful and earn a return on investment faster.[36]

The main risks associated with international trade include foreign exchange risks and political risks. These hazards may sometimes make it difficult to maintain constant and reliable revenue.[37]

A. Political Risks

Political risks occur when a nation's government unexpectedly alters its policies, which negatively affect the foreign company. These changes can include trade barriers which act to restrict or prevent international trade. For instance, governments may ask for additional funds or tariffs in consideration for the ability to export items into their country. Quotas and tariffs are employed to protect local companies from foreign competition. These extra charges can have a large bearing on the profits of a business because it either cuts income as the result of a tax on exports or restricts the amount of revenues that can be generated. While the number of trade barriers has decreased due to free-trade agreements and other comparable measures, the daily changes in the laws of foreign countries can affect the profits and overall success of a company doing business in another nation.[38]

For example, the **Trading with the Enemy Act,** passed by Congress to restrict trade with nations at war with the United States, was repealed in 1977, but replaced with a prohibition against trading with Cuba and North Korea. Also, Congress passed the **International Emergency Economic Powers Act (IEEPA)** that grants authority to the President to place restrictions on trade and international financial transactions during peacetime as well as wartime. For example, trade and travel to Libya had been banned until a 2007 loosening of those restrictions, and sales of computer equipment and other sensitive products to numerous countries have been prohibited. As a direct response to the terrorist attacks of September 11, 2001, Congress passed the **Patriot Act** which, while granting extensive authority to the U.S. Government to freeze foreign assets held in the U.S. pending IEEPA investigations, also requires U.S. financial institutions to maintain detailed records and to report transactions made by certain individuals and groups.

Expropriation, or nationalization, is the taking of property by a foreign government without adequate compensation. This is a serious risk that businesses and individuals face when investing in foreign lands. For example, Fidel Castro and his government confiscated the property of a number of U.S. business enterprises in Cuba following the 1959 Revolution which, in fact, is partially responsible for the long-standing animosity between the two countries.

Unlike the Due Process Clauses of the Fifth and Fourteenth Amendments to the United States Constitution, which prohibit governmental takings of property without payment of fair compensation, seizures of property by foreign governments may be considered a legitimate exercise of sovereignty. Whether or not compensation is paid to the former property owners will generally be determined by whether the seizing power adheres to a traditional theory of legitimizing seizures upon payment of compensation, or whether the seizure is made in defiance of the international norm that takings are linked to some degree of compensation. In the latter instance, the question arises as to what, if any, recourse may be had in response to seizures without compensation. For instance, there have been a series of decisions involving nationalization of business interests by Iran that illustrate the distinction made between the two theories. The more prevalent view is that sovereign nations have an absolute right to take private holdings within the country but must pay reasonable compensation for that taking. The less prevalent view is that full compensation is not required. While most of the arbitration panels of the Iran-United States Claims Tribunal have followed the more prevalent view, other panels have provided for lesser amounts of compensation.

B. **Economic/Currency Risks**

Commercial transactions involve the movement of capital from one country to another. This often requires the transfers of funds, whether physically or electronically, between financial institutions. These types of transfers experience a variety of problems. Exchange rates may fluctuate, and restrictions may be imposed by governments upon the movement of funds from one country to another. Also, some currencies do not have convertible value in the international marketplace and are unacceptable as a medium for exchange. Regardless of currency risks, the income tax implications of foreign operations are always a part of the profit calculus.

Of particular interest to the Internal Revenue Service are pricing issues related to the movement of goods, services, and capital across international borders. Moreover, the examination of transfer pricing arrangements has also been given greater attention by many non-U.S. tax jurisdictions. Transfer pricing arrangements entail income allocation between entities in different tax jurisdictions. This could result in an unjustified allocation by a multinational company of greater levels of income to a low tax jurisdiction. Each country in which profits are earned will be interested in taxing the full value of those profits, and when the full value of profits that should have been created domestically has instead been understated, the taxpayer company should be prepared to explain and defend how and why its pricing and profit methodology has been applied.

C. Transaction Risks

The sale of goods moving across national boundaries is subject to the risks of non-payment to a seller and non-delivery to a buyer. Parties may not wish to do business by the payment of cash or with the use of open account terms because of the risks of non-payment and non-delivery. Goods moving long distances may be subject to harsh transportation conditions and to loss or theft of goods. Most trade in goods still involves ocean transport, and the risks inherent in such transport have, in most nations, been subject to the limitations of carrier liability set forth in the laws governing ocean transportation. The **Carriage of Goods by Sea Act,** for example, provides significant protection to ocean carriers against claims made by the owners of cargoes arising from loss or damage to their goods. The carrier, absent failure to ship goods on seaworthy vessels or absent misdelivery or nondelivery of goods, will ordinarily be held harmless for claims made by shippers and consignees. This very effective degree of carrier protection makes it imperative for those parties that would otherwise bear the risk of loss to secure pertinent transport insurance.

D. Legal Risks

Those business entities engaging in foreign commerce will encounter a variety of legal systems in the global marketplace. Whether these legal systems are based upon the English common law, French civil law, religious codes, or some combination of these, one can be assured that inherent differences, however subtle, will provide numerous opportunities for legal disputes.

In the United States alone there is a separate body of law for each of the 50 states and each territory. In addition, there is a separate body of federal law, some of which is enforceable only within the United States, but other portions of which have been given extraterritorial effect; that is, some federal laws apply to U.S. citizens and business entities outside of the U.S.

Substantive differences in domestic and foreign law, in traditional areas such contract law and as complex as antitrust law, require careful attention when engaging in trans-national business activities. One example of how businesses may find themselves in uncharted legal territory is created by the principle of **pre-contractual liability.** This principle is rarely studied in American schools because it is not generally recognized as part of our system of jurisprudence. Pre-contractual liability encompasses a duty to negotiate in good faith and a duty to proceed with negotiations in accordance with prior representations and promises. Since most nations other than the U.S. have some form of pre-contractual obligations and liability as part of their legal systems, legal consequences may arise even in the absence of a final written contract.

Another example of potential contractual risk involves the question of whether a contract may be enforceable even if not reduced to writing. The study of contract law will include a discussion of the statute of frauds, a doctrine that has been incorporated in the laws of every state. Application of this doctrine requires that some contracts, including those for sales of goods worth more than $500 will be unenforceable if not in writing. Yet, the contract laws of many nations, as well as the **Convention on the International Sale of Goods (CISG),** provide that there will be many international contracts that are clearly enforceable, even if not reduced to writing, because the statute of frauds is not widely followed outside the U.S. For example, Article 11 of the CISG states: "A contract of sale . . . need not be concluded in or evidenced by writing and is not subject to any other requirement as to form. It may be proved by any means, including witnesses."

Section 11.8 Protecting Against the Risks of International Transactions

Recognition of the risks connected to international business transactions is only the first step in the process of risk avoidance, if not risk prevention. While opportunities to do business exist around the world, the risks attendant to doing business in different locations will differ significantly from country to country. What may work in one country might not always work in another jurisdiction, and what might work with respect to one business opportunity might not be subject to duplication elsewhere.

It is, therefore, important for the business entrepreneur to select how to do business from the several available models: sales/direct exporting, agency sales/indirect exporting, licensing, joint ventures/subsidiary, direct investment/subsidiary, and direct investment/branch facility.

Regardless of the choice of business model, all such international transactions will be subject to contract law principles. Consequently, an understanding of international contract law is critically important.

SECTION 11.9
PRINCIPLES OF
FOREIGN CONTRACT
LAW

Consider the following facts: a Pennsylvania company negotiates a contract to sell machine parts to a firm in Helsinki, Finland. The Pennsylvania firm manufactures the parts at its Chicago factory, and ships the items from Chicago to Germany where the parts are assembled into printing presses. The presses are then sold by the Finnish company to a publishing house in Australia, where the presses are found to be defective because the parts manufactured in Chicago were not made to specifications. The Australian publishing company makes claim against the Finnish company and the Finnish company claims against the Pennsylvania company. Which country's laws will apply to these transactions? What happens if more than one body of law could apply? What happens when the laws differ from one country to another? One of the legal risks inherent in such a geographically complex transaction is known as **conflicts of law,** or whose laws should apply to a transaction, and the applicable rules used to address these conflicts are themselves complex and sometimes irreconcilable.

A. United Nations Convention on Contracts for the International Sale of Goods

In the U.S., these contracts prior to 1988 were subject to Article Two of the Uniform Commercial Code. In Finland, Germany, and Australia, there would also be differing versions of commercial law. In order to impose uniformity and a level of certainty involving international disputes involving the sale of goods, some seventy-nine nations, including the United States, conducting a significant percentage of international trade, have signed the **United Nations Convention on Contracts for the International Sale of Goods,** thereby replacing their own contract laws with the provisions of the CISG when the transactions are between companies located in nations that have signed the convention.

This CISG has been labeled the most successful attempt to unify commercial laws at the international level. This purpose of the CISG is to reduce obstacles to international trade, especially those involving choice of law issues, by establishing even-handed and modern substantive rules, governing the rights and obligations of those involved with international sales contracts. Currently, this treaty applies to more than two-thirds of the sale of goods in international trade.[39]

As noted by the United Nations, the Convention creates a set of rules governing the formation of contracts between merchants for the international sale of goods, the obligations of the buyer and seller, remedies for breach of contract and other aspects of the contract. These rules, however, do not apply to consumer transactions. This Convention also allows the parties to avoid the uncertainty of whose conflicts of law principles should apply to a transaction. The fore-going hypothetical contracts (Pennsylvania firm and Finnish company in the first one, and Finnish company and Australian business in the second) would only involve application of the CISG if the particular parties to the contracts have places of business in those countries that have signed the CISG, or if the contracts themselves specified that the CISG would apply.

In order to resolve the uncertainty of which body of law will apply in international transactions, the parties may include dispute resolution provisions in their agreements. Such provisions would include choices of the country in which the matter will be heard, how legal disputes would be decided, what body of law would be applied to those disputes, and how court judgments or arbitration awards would be enforced.

B. Comity

While the full faith and credit clause of the United States Constitution provides that the judgments rendered in any of the states in this country must be honored in every other state, this constitutional requirement is not extended to the decisions of the courts of other nations, nor would U.S. judgments necessarily be enforced outside of this country. **Comity** is the concept that represents the international equivalent of full faith and credit. This international principle allows a country to recognize the laws and judgments of another jurisdiction as a matter of courtesy but not as a right. Generally, as long as the laws of another country are not contrary to public policy or prejudicial to the interests of the forum jurisdictions, the laws will be upheld.

There is no guarantee, however, when conducting international business transactions and in seeking to enforce U.S. court judgments in other lands, that those judgments will be enforced. Any expectation that the results of court proceedings in one nation will be honored in another must be based upon existing treaties or the incorporation of the comity principle in national law by either statutory enactment or judicial construction. For example, in 1895, the Supreme Court in **Hilton v. Guyot, 16 S. Ct. 139,** was faced with deciding whether a judgment secured in France by a French citizen in an action against a U.S. defendant would be enforceable in a U.S. court without the case being retried. The Supreme Court stated:

> No law has any effect, of its own force, beyond the limits of the sovereignty from which its authority is derived. The extent

to which the law of one nation, as put in force within its territory, whether by executive order, by legislative act, or by judicial decree, shall be allowed to operate within the dominion of another nation, depends upon what our greatest jurists have been content to call "the comity of nations." Although the phrase has been often criticized, no satisfactory substitute has been suggested.

Comity, in the legal sense, is neither a matter of absolute obligation, on the one hand, nor of mere courtesy and good will, upon the other. But it is the recognition which one nation allows within its territory to the legislative, executive or judicial acts of another nation, having due regard both to international duty and convenience, and to the rights of its own citizens or of other persons who are under the protection of its laws.

The consideration of the rights of its own citizens was the focus of a more recent decision reached by a federal district court in California. Unlike the Hilton case which involved a purely commercial matter without U.S. constitutional implications, the **Yahoo! Inc. v. La Ligue Contre le Racisme et l'Antisemitisme** litigation questioned the enforceability of a foreign judgment when that judgment results in an alleged impermissible restriction on the First Amendment freedom of speech. In 2000, a French court held Yahoo! Inc. criminally liable offering Nazi memorabilia on Yahoo's auction site in France. Sales of Third Reich materials were violations of the French Criminal Code. The French trial court, after ruling that it had jurisdiction over Yahoo because the auction website could be accessed by French citizens, issued orders imposing financial penalties. More significantly, however, the court also ordered Yahoo to restrict access to the site and to warn French users to leave the site whenever it contains prohibited items for sale.

Yahoo! filed a declaratory judgment action in a federal district court in California seeking to challenge the legality and enforceability of the French judgment. The district court ruled that it had personal jurisdiction over the French citizens and that the French interim orders would be an impermissible restriction on Yahoo's First Amendment rights. On appeal, the Ninth Circuit Court of Appeals, while upholding the jurisdictional rulings, held that the Yahoo's declaratory judgment action was not ripe because there had been no effort made by the French parties to enforce the French orders. And, on the question of Yahoo's First Amendment rights, the Ninth

Circuit was clear that such a right could not be enforced in France as to French citizens but was to be limited to the U.S. The decision of the federal district court and the French tribunal demonstrate the unpredictability of comity.

There is one other convention worthy of mention. In 1970, the United States ratified the **New York Convention on Recognition and Enforcement of International Arbitral Awards,** thus embracing a policy encouraging the arbitration of international disputes. Currently, more than 130 nations have adopted this Convention, which requires all signatory nations to recognize arbitration agreements made by contracting parties and to enforce the results of these proceedings unless procured by fraud, misconduct, clear error, or are decisions that exceed the panel's authority.

SECTION 11.10 DOCUMENTARY TRANSACTIONS

Another method utilized to protect a seller's expectation of payment and a buyer's expectations of delivery is the **documentary sale.** This process involves the operations of a transit carrier and the separate contractual promise of payment made by a bank. Upon receipt of goods by a carrier, e.g., air transport or ocean transport, the carrier generates an irrevocable **bill of lading** that operates as a receipt for the goods, title to the goods, and a contract for transporting the goods. Whichever party possesses the bill of lading owns and controls the goods. The buyer will, as a stated requirement in the underlying sales agreement, have already secured a letter of credit issued by its bank. The letter of credit contains a promise by the bank to make payment to the seller upon receipt by the bank of the bill of lading. When the bill of lading is forwarded to the buyer's bank, title to the goods has been transferred to the bank. The bank will then issue a payment to the seller in accordance with the terms of the underlying transaction.

The process of moving goods from one country to another will sometimes result in loss or damage to the goods being shipped. Fungible goods may deteriorate if arrival at the destination is delayed. Heavy seas may cause damage to goods in the holds of cargo vessels. Operators of loading equipment or ocean and air transports may, by their negligence, cause cargo losses. When goods are handed over to a domestic transport carrier, issues of liability are ordinarily subject to the law of bailment. A **bailment** is the physical transfer of goods by the owner (bailor) into the hands of another party (bailee), for safekeeping or for some other purpose consistent with the terms of the bailment. Typically, the carrier in possession of the goods is responsible for the return of the goods to the bailor or delivery of those goods without damage to the designated recipient.

The customary domestic bailment rules do not, however, apply in transnational shipments. In order to make international commerce financially feasible, it was necessary to provide some manner of protection to the carriers against claims made by the owners of their cargos. Without some measure of protection, the carriers could simply not have afforded to operate without charging substantially higher fees, thus making commerce that much more difficult. And, as these transactions always involved transportation between the ports of different countries, these trading nations recognized the need to create uniformity in the rules applied to their commerce. What emerged were the **Hague Rules,** which have now been codified in many nations, and in the United States as the Carriage of Goods by Sea Act. While this law imposes upon the ocean carrier a duty to exercise due diligence in shipping goods on a seaworthy vessel and in delivering the goods to the named consignee, the law also limits the liability of ocean carriers when loss or damage occurs based both upon the cause of the loss and in the amount of loss. While such limitations result in reduced shipping costs, they also make it incumbent upon sellers and buyers to purchase the pertinent type and amount of transport insurance to protect against in-transit losses.

When the parties to a sales contract negotiate the terms, the resulting agreement will place the risk of loss on either the buyer ("shipment" contract) or seller ("destination" contract) while the goods are in transit. If the carrier is deemed not liable for the loss, the parties will be responsible for the loss based upon their contractual allocation of risk.

SECTION 11.11
INCO TERMS

As a further element of contract uniformity and in the interest of eliminating variations in contract interpretation, the **International Chamber of Commerce** has published the International Rules for the Interpretation of Trade Terms, a set of trade term definitions that have been generally accepted in the global business marketplace. When contract parties incorporate the **Incoterms,** or international commercial terms, as part of their agreements, they add a measure of uniformity to those agreements and the expectation that courts will adhere to these usual and customary trade term definitions.

The following is an example of how the Incoterms have been accorded general acceptance. Shared Imaging, a U.S. company, purchased MRI equipment from Neuromed, a German company. The sales contract specified that the sale was "CIF" but there was no explanation in the contract regarding the meaning of the CIF term. The MRI machine was damaged while in transit, and Shared Imaging received an insurance payment from St. Paul Guardian Insurance Company. St. Paul then filed a subrogation action against Neuromed in federal district court.

St. Paul Guardian Ins. Co. v. Neuromed Medical Systems & Support, GmbH
2002 U.S. Dist. Lexis (S.D. N.Y., 2002)

The parties concede that pursuant to German law, the U.N. Convention on Contracts for the International Sale of Goods ("CISG") governs this transaction because (1) both the U.S. and Germany are Contracting States to that Convention, and (2) neither party chose, by express provision in the contract, to opt out of the application of the CISG . . .

"CIF," which stands for "cost, insurance and freight," is a commercial trade term that is defined in *Incoterms 1990,* published by the International Chamber of Commerce, ("ICC"). The aim of INCOTERMS, which stands for international commercial terms, is "to provide a set of international rules for the interpretation of the most commonly used trade terms in foreign trade . . ." INCOTERMS are incorporated into the CISG through Article 9(2) which provides that, "The parties are considered, unless otherwise agreed, to have impliedly made applicable to their contract or its formation a usage

of which the parties knew or ought to have known and which in international trade is widely known to, and regularly observed by, parties to contracts of the type involved in the particular trade concerned." INCOTERMS defines "CIF" (named port of destination) to mean the seller delivers when the goods pass "the ship's rail at the port of shipment." The seller is responsible for paying the cost, freight and insurance coverage necessary to bring the goods to the named port of destination, but the risk of loss or damage to the goods passes from seller to buyer upon delivery to the port of shipment . . . Thus, because (1) Neuromed's risk of loss of, or damage to, the MRI machine under the contract passed to plaintiff upon delivery of the machine to the carrier at the port of shipment and (2) it is undisputed that the MRI machine was delivered to the carrier undamaged and in good working order, Neuromed's motion to dismiss for failure to state a claim is hereby granted.

Section 11.12
Intellectual
Property in
the Global
Environment

Physical goods are by no means the only products that form the substance of international contracts. Intellectual property has become an increasingly larger and more problematic component of global commerce. Patent rights, trademarks, copyrighted material, and trade secrets, the sum total of intellectual property, have become the substance of legitimate international licensing agreements and, sometimes, the stuff of illegal pirating and gray market transactions.

Recognition of intellectual property rights (IPRs) in the global marketplace is by no means a recent phenomenon. The **Paris Convention for the Protection of Industrial Property,** providing basic rights of protection of patents and trademarks, dates back to 1883, and has been adopted by the United States and some 170 other nations. The rights granted by the Paris Convention are in addition to those granted by signatory nations' domestic patent and trademark laws, and signatory nations must give the same protections to foreign parties as they give to their domestic patent and trademark applicants. In 1978, the **Patent Cooperation Treaty** went into effect and it created uniform procedures that allow patent applications to be filed initially as an international application, then to be followed by individual country applications.

The **Berne Convention for the Protection of Literary and Artistic Works** originated in 1886. It has been amended many times, but always aims at protecting rights of authorship. Works first published in the United States are given protection virtually world-wide through this international convention. A second international agreement, the **Universal Copyright Convention,** to which the United States is a signatory, provides recognized protection for not only literary and scientific writings, but also sculpture, visual arts, music, and cinematographic works.

The business model that has been developed to govern the legitimate transfer of IPRs is the license agreement. The owner of the IPR (the licensor) grants to a licensee the right to use the licensor's patent, trademark, copyright or other know-how in return ordinarily for a fee or royalty. The cost of operation in the geographic area subject to the license is borne by the licensee. Licensing arrangements permit the owner of the IPR to do business in multiple locations without incurring any additional production/distribution costs.

Inherent in the transfer of IPRs are risks associated with violations by the licensee of the standard confidentiality obligations and non-competition agreements. Additional problems may be caused to IPR owners should the governments where the licensees operate not enforce the legal and contractual rights of the licensors.

SECTION 11.13
TRIPS

Lax enforcement of IPRs in many countries led to the **Agreement on Trade-Related Aspects of Intellectual Property Rights (TRIPS),** which became effective on January 1, 2000. TRIPS require all signatory nations, including all members of the World Trade Organization, to enforce the Paris and Berne Conventions and to create minimum standards for protection of IPRs.

IPR protection and enforcement had already existed in the industrialized nations, so TRIPS was aimed essentially at attempting to secure protective IPR action in the developing nations and the newer industrializing economies. While TRIPS provides a mechanism for signatory countries to avoid compliance where, for example, health issues are concerned, the goal of securing protection of IPRs has had at least some support where in the past there was minimal enforcement.

SECTION 11.14
COMPARATIVE LAW

Comparative law is a comparison of the different legal systems of the world. This type of study is important because it helps the business entrepreneur better grasp and provide solutions for legal issues which are global in nature.[40]

There are hundreds of different legal systems in the world but three dominate: common law, civil law and Islamic law. These systems reflect the great variances in the historical and cultural experiences of the countries.

A. Civil Law

The **civil law system** originated in ancient Rome and spread throughout Europe with the domination of the Roman Empire. This system was based upon codes which set forth the laws to govern the people. Examples included the Napoleonic Code, the German Civil Code and the Italian Civil Code.[41]

This type of legal classification is found all over the world and is the dominate legal. It is premised on concepts, categories, and rules derived from Roman law, with some influence of canon law, and largely altered by local custom or culture. The civil law tradition places more focus on individual freedoms, and promotes cooperation between human beings.[42] The laws can be found in constuitions or statutes.

B. Common law

A distinct legal system of laws developed in the British Empire during the middle ages known as **common law.** This type of law does not ordinarily rely on compilations of legal rules and statutes. Rather, it is premised on the customs and traditions of the people as determined by a judge. The system is largely premised on precedent, or judicial decisions that have been rendered in prior similar cases. These rulings are maintained over the years through court records and books of court cases. Common law acts in an adversarial system, a contested proceeding between opposing parties in which a judge moderates. This system accounts for the law in the United States and Great Britain.[43]

C. Islamic Law

Islamic law refers to the principles that guide those of the Muslim faith as interpreted from the Koran, which is considered the word of God, and the teachings of Mohammed. Islamic law is best known for its deterrent punishment which is the foundation of the Islamic criminal system, and for discrimination against women.[44] Another important attribute is that there is no clear separation of church and state. The religion of Islam and the government are one and the same. Islamic law is ruled controlled, and regulated by the Islamic religion.[45]

Islamic law is also known as the Law of Sharia and it is controlled by religion. It applies to all public and private behavior such as hygiene, diet, sexual conduct, and child rearing. Islamic law is prevalent in the countries of the Middle East, as well as Central and South Asia, covering about twenty per cent of the world's population.[46]

SECTION 11.15
THE FUTURE OF
INTERNATIONAL LAW

The end of the Cold War in the closing decades of the twentieth century may have generated a sense of security and personal well-being that is noticeably absent in the opening years of the twenty-first century. The ethnic and religious conflicts of the 1990's have multiplied in the first decade of the 2000's. Rwanda, Bosnia, and other less extensive conflicts, have been joined by the Congo, Afghanistan, Iraq, Darfur, Sri Lanka, and many others. And, after years of public debate over whether global warming is or is not real, there is finally a consensus that action must be taken to curtail fossil fuel emissions, as well as to preserve what continental forests remain uncut, and somehow end the degradation of the world's oceans through pollution and over-harvesting. Recognition that the plight of refugees, the spread of AIDS/HIV, depletion of the ozone layer, international terrorism, and air and water pollution are matters of international proportion and require international solutions, may also lead to the appreciation of the need for global legal remedies.

SECTION 11.16
TYLER'S SPOILED
WINE

PROBLEM ELEVEN—B

PARK, BROWN & SMITH
ATTORNEYS AT LAW
MEMORANDUM

To: All Law Clerks

FROM: Peter Smith, Esquire

RE: The Spoiled Shipment of Wine

Tyler's Sport's Bar and Grill ordered twenty cases of vintage wine from a winery in Southern France. The contract called for the wine to be shipped "CIF" aboard a vessel leaving Nice and arriving at the Port of Philadelphia on the Delaware River two weeks later. When Joe Roberts uncorked the first bottle soon after the shipment arrived, he discovered that all of the wine had spoiled. A sample bottle had been tested prior to shipment and no problem was detected. Roberts is now wondering what, if any, legal action he may take to recover the cost of the wine.

Please answer the following questions for Tyler's Sports Bar and Grill.

1. In what court and against what parties may Tyler's bring the action for the spoiled wine?

2. Based upon which laws will this matter proceed?

3. Who do you believe will win the lawsuit?

PROBLEM ELEVEN—B
ANSWER SHEET

Name   **Please Print Clearly**

1. In what court and against what parties may Tyler's bring the action for the spoiled wine?

_____

_____

_____

_____

_____

_____

_____

_____

_____

2. Based upon which laws will this matter proceed?

_____

_____

_____

_____

_____

_____

_____

_____

3. Who do you think will win? Please explain.

1. In 1967 a Houston-based U.S. manufacturer of drilling equipment contracted with a German ocean towing company to have the German company tow a barge carrying drilling equipment from the Gulf Coast to Italy. A storm in the Gulf of Mexico caused damage to the drilling equipment when the German towboat captain failed to secure the equipment properly. The contract contained a forum selection clause (London Court of Justice), a choice of law clause (English law), and a hold harmless clause, protecting the German company against negligence claims (enforceable in England but not in Florida). The U.S. company filed suit against the German company and the towboat in the federal district court in Tampa, Florida. Does the federal court have subject matter jurisdiction? Does the court have personal jurisdiction over the German company? Should the forum selection, choice of law, and hold harmless provisions of the contract be enforced? Why was the towboat made a party defendant? **M/S Bremen v. Zapata Off-Shore Company, 407 U.S. 1 (1972).**

2. A Canadian manufacturer of wood shingles entered into an oral agreement to sell 88 truckloads of cedar shakes to a U.S. company. After accepting only 13 truckloads, the U.S. company refused further deliveries of shakes. The Canadian company filed a lawsuit against the U.S. company, claiming the profit lost on the rejected 75 truckloads. The U.S. company raised the statute of frauds as a defense to the claims presented by the Canadian company. Which party should prevail on the statute of frauds issue? What international convention should apply in this case? **GPL Treatment, Ltd. v. Louisiana-Pacific Corp., 894 P. 2d 470 (Or. Ct. App. 1995), aff'd. 914 P. 2d 682 (Or., 1996).**

3. A Pennsylvania manufacturer of farm tractors has received a purchase order from a buyer in Japan. The standard wait period before all of the import approvals are secured by the Japanese buyer is longer than the Pennsylvania seller wishes to incur. The Japanese buyer offers to make the pertinent inquiries in Japan in order to reduce the wait time. This process will cost the seller $50,000 for the necessary political influence to move the approval and paperwork on an expedited basis through the proper trade ministry channels. The buyer has however agreed to share the cost. Will the proposed $25,000 share payment violate the Foreign Corrupt Practices Act?

4. A Hong Kong exporter (C-ART) has contracted to sell and ship goods to a New York Merchandising Company (NYMCO). C-ART hands the goods over to Hong Kong Islands Line (HKIL), an ocean carrier, for shipment to California. HKIL issues to C-ART a bill of lading stating that the goods are to be delivered only to the party holding the original bill of lading. The original bill of lading was retained by

C-ART pending payment by NYMCO. Upon arrival in California, HKIL delivered the goods to a NYMCO agent upon the agent's presentation of a corporate guaranty but not the original bill of lading. When C-ART could not recover the contract price from NYMCO due to NYMCO's bankruptcy, C-ART files suit against HKIL. Will C-ART be successful? **C-ART, Ltd. v. Hong Kong Islands Line America, S.A., 940 F.2d 530; 1991 U.S. App. LEXIS 17414.**

SECTION 11.18
INTERNET REFERENCES

For more information about international law, see the following internet sites:

A. International Court of Justice

- **www.icj-cij.org**
  The International Court of Justice provides decisions, recent cases, and general information at this site.

B. United Nations

- **www.un.org**
  This is the United Nations' official site, and it offers general information, materials on international law, humanitarian affairs, peace and security, human rights, economic and social development, as well as conferences and events, about the UN's work around the world.

C. Other International Organizations

- **www.usitc.gov**
  The International Trade Commission's web site is located at this address and provides news releases, tariffs, and trade resources.

- **www.wto.org**
  This is the World Trade Organization's official site which discusses intellectual property and environmental issues, trade policy, and dispute settlement.

- **www.ita.doc.gov**
  The International Trade Administration maintains this address and provides information about trade rights, tariffs, exports, and answers to frequently asked questions.

- **www.nato.int**
  The North Atlantic Treaty Organization's (NATO) official site is maintained at this location.

- **www.europa.eu.int/index-en.htm**
  This is the European Union's site, giving news, basic information about the European Union, its policies, and its institutions.

- **www.dfait-maeci.gc.ca/nafta-alena/menu-e.asp**
  To learn background information about NAFTA, the text of that agreement, as well as information on dispute settlement, trade agreements, and answers to frequently asked questions, visit this address.

D. Foreign Corrupt Practices Act

- **www.tannedfeet.com/Business/Importing_and_Exporting/Foreign_Corrupt_Practices_Act/foreign_corrupt_practices_act.html**
  This site offers an explanation of the Foreign Corrupt Practices Act.

- **www.abanet.org/cle/articles/turza.html**
  An article about the Foreign Corrupt Practices Act, is maintained at this address including information about the elements of a violation and an introduction to due diligence.

E. Miscellaneous

- **http://august1.com/pubs/dict/**
  This site provides an international law dictionary.

- **http://www.state.gov**
  The United States government maintains a site that discusses doing business abroad.

- **http://www.unidroit.org**
  UNIDROIT maintains a site that explains its functions and role in international transactions.

- **http://www.jus.uio.no/lm/eu.contract.principles.1998**
  Principles of **European Contract Law** may be accessed at this location.

- **http://www.lexmercatoria.com**
  This is the address for the Lex Mercatoria website.

- **http://cisgw3.law.pace.edu**
  More information about the Convention on Contracts for the International Sale of Goods is located at this reference.

- **http://www.unzco.com/basicguide**
  Information on **documentary transactions** may be accessed at this site.

Footnotes:

1. Lee A. Tavis, Corporate Governance and The Global Social Void, 35 Vand. J. Transnat'l L. 487, March, 2002.

2. Globalization, Global Policy Forum, http://www.globalpolicy.org/globalization.html (last visited October 8, 2013).

3. Jack Goldsmith, *The Trump Onslaught on International Law and Institutions*, Lawfare, March 17, 2017, https://www.lawfareblog.com/trump-onslaught-international-law-and-institutions.

4. International Law, Business Dictioctary.com, http://www.businessdictionary.com/definition/international-law.html (last visited October 7, 2013).

5. Historical development, International Law, Encyclopedia Britannica, http://www.britannica.com/EBchecked/topic/291011/international-law/233496/Historical-development (last visited October 7, 2013).

6. Harold Damerow, International Law, Union County College, http://faculty.ucc.edu/egh-damerow/int_law.htm (last visited October 7, 2013).

7. *Id.*

8. *Id.*

9. Carriage of Goods by Sea Act – COGSA, Perry and Neblet, P.C., http://perryneblett.com/cogsa.asp (last visited October 7, 2013).

10. Harter Act Law and Legal Definition, USLegal.com, http://definitions.uslegal.com/h/harter-act/ (last visited October 7, 2013).

11. *Montreal Convention*, Wikipedia, https://en.wikipedia.org/wiki/Montreal_Convention (February 4, 2018.)

12. *Id.*

13. Charles Camp, Knowledgeable Foreign Sovereign Immunities Act Lawyer, http://www.charlescamplaw.com/international-dispute-resolution/foreign-sovereign-immunities-act/ (last visited October 7, 2013).

14. **Peterson v. Royal Kingdom of Saudi Arabia, 332 F.Supp.2d 189 (D.D.C., 2004).**

15. **Minn-Chem, Inc. v. Agrium Inc., 657 F.3d 650 (C.A.7 (Ill.), 2011).**

16. **552 U.S. 491 (2008).**

17. *Id.*

18. Customs Union, The Free Dictionary by Farlex, http://www.thefreedictionary.com/customs+union (last visited October 7, 2013).

19. European Union, US Department of State, http://www.state.gov/p/eur/rt/eu/ (last visited October 7, 2013).

20. Katherine Richard, African Union, About.com, http://geography.about.com/od/africamaps/a/African-Union.htm (last visited October 7, 2013).

21. *Id.*

22. North American Free Trade Agreement (NAFTA), CBC.gov, http://www.cbp.gov/xp/cgov/trade/trade_programs/international_agreements/free_trade/nafta/(last visited October 7, 2013).

23. North American Free Trade Agreement, Office of the United States Trade Representative, http://www.ustr.gov/trade-agreements/free-trade-agreements/north-american-free-trade-agreement-nafta (last visited October 7, 2013).

24. Julián Aguilar, Twenty Years Later, Nafta Remains a Source of Tension, The Texas Tribune, http://www.nytimes.com/2012/12/07/us/twenty-years-later-nafta-remains-a-source-of-tension.html?_r=0 (last visited October 7, 2013).

25. *North American Free Trade Agreement*, Wikipedia, https://en.wikipedia.org/wiki/North_American_Free_Trade_Agreement (February 4, 2018.)

26. Eric Bradner, *Trump to Begin Renegotiating NAFTA with Leaders of Mexico, Canada*, CNN, January 22, 2017, https://www.cnn.com/2017/01/22/politics/trump-renegotiate-nafta/index.html.

27. *Association of Southeast Asian Nations*, Wikipedia, https://en.wikipedia.org/wiki/Association_of_Southeast_Asian_Nations (February 4, 2018.)

28. Dominican Republic-Central America-United States Free Trade Agreement, Office of United States Trade Representative, http://www.ustr.gov/trade-agreements/free-trade-agreements/cafta-dr-dominican-republic-central-america-fta (last visited October 7, 2013).

29. *Id.*

30. Israel Free Trade Agreement, Office of the United States Trade Representative, http://www.ustr.gov/trade-agreements/free-trade-agreements/israel-fta (last visited October 7, 2013).

31. Mitchell Bard, Free Trade Agreement, Jewish Virtual Library, http://www.jewishvirtuallibrary.org/jsource/US-Israel/FTA.html (last visited October 7, 2013).

32. *Id.*

33. Trade-Related Aspects of Intellectual Property Rights (TRIPS), Patent Lens, http://www.patentlens.net/daisy/patentlens/415.html (last visited October 7, 2013).

34. *Id.*

35. Agreement on intellectual property rights relating to trade and pharmaceutical patents, Summaries of EU Legislation, http://europa.eu/legislation_summaries/internal_market/single_market_for_goods/pharmaceutical_and_cosmetic_products/l21168_en.htm (last visited October 7, 2013).

36. Carrieanne Larmore, 10 International Business Risks and Challenges for Small Businesses, Yahoo! Voices, http://voices.yahoo.com/10-international-business-risks-challenges-for-7526598.html (last visited October 7, 2013).

37. What Risks Do Organizations Face When Engaging In International Finance Activities?, Investopedia, February 26, 2009, http://www.investopedia.com/ask/answers/06/international financerisks.asp (last visited October 7, 2013).

38. *Id.*

39. Harry M. Flechtner, United Nations Convention on Contracts for the International Sale of Goods, Audiovisual Library of International Law, http://untreaty.un.org/cod/avl/ha/ccisg/ccisg.html (last visited October 7, 2013).

40. Comparative Law and Legal Definition, USLegal.com, http://definitions.uslegal.com/c/comparative/ (last visited October 7, 2013).

41. Emilia Powell and Sara Mitchell, The International Court of Justice and the World's Three Legal Systems, The Journal of Politics, Vol. 69, No. 2, May 2007, page 397.

42. What is the Civil Law, LSU Law Center, http://www.law.lsu.edu/index.cfm?geaux=clo. whatis (last visited October 7, 2013).

43. The Common Law and Civil Law Traditions, The Robbins Collection, University of California at Berkeley School of Law, http://www.law.berkeley.edu/library/robbins/ CommonLawCivilLawTraditions.html (last visited October 7, 2013).

44. Islamic Law Definition, Duhaime.org, http://www.duhaime.org/LegalDictionary/I/ IslamicLaw.aspx (last visited October 7, 2013).

45. *Id.*

46. Islamic Law, Legal Glossary, http://www.legal-glossary.org/islamic-law/ (last visited October 7, 2013).

Agreement on Trade-Related
    Aspects of Intellectual
    Property Rights (TRIPS)
Association of Southeast
    Asian Nations (ASEAN)
Bailment
Berne Convention for the
    Protection of Literary
    and Artistic Works
Bill of Lading
Brexit
Carriage of Goods by Sea Act
Central America and Dominican
    Republic Free Trade
    Agreement (CAFTA-DR)
Charter
Civil Law System
Comity
Common Law
Comparative Law
Conflicts of Law
Convention
Convention on the International
    Sale of Goods (ISG)
Customary International Law
Customs Union
Documentary Sale
Documentary Transactions
European Contract Law
European Court of Justice
European Union
Expropriation
Foreign Corrupt Practices Act
    (FCPA)
Foreign Sovereign Immunities Act
Foreign Trade Antitrust
    Improvements Act (FTAI)
General Assembly
Globalization

Hague Rules
Harter Act
Incoterms
International Chamber of
    Commerce
International Court of Justice (ICJ)
International Emergency
    Economic Powers Act
    (IEEPA)
International Law
Islamic Law
Lex Mercatoria
Montreal Convention
New York Convention on
    Recognition and Enforcement
    of International Arbitral
    Awards
Paris Convention for the Protection
    of Industrial Property
Patent Cooperation Treaty
Patriot Act
Pre-contractual Liability
Private International Law
Protocol
Public International Law
Security Council
The African Union (AU)
Trading with the Enemy Act
Treaty
United Nations
United Nations Convention on
    Contracts for the International
    Sale of Goods
United States-Israel Free Trade
    Agreement (FTA)
Universal Copyright Convention
Warsaw Convention
World Trade Organization

CHAPTER 12

INTELLECTUAL PROPERTY AND CYBERLAW

Questions: What do the terms copyright, trade secret, domain name, and cybersquatting have in common?

Answer: They refer to intellectual property protections.

The idea of protecting the creative talents of people can be traced back to Article One of the United States Constitution, which provides:

> "To promote the progress of science and useful arts by securing for limited times to authors and inventors the exclusive right to their respective writings and discoveries."

The basic tenet of this **Copyright Clause** is that inventors, authors, and others should be able to enjoy the benefits of their works for a set period of time, after which the intellectual property becomes part of the public domain for all to use freely. This benefits society because it "yields a rich and varied cultural menu for its citizens. Indeed, one can say that copyright protection is a necessary ingredient for ensuring cultural wealth in our societies."[1]

In broad terms, **intellectual property** is something created by the mind which is then protected from the unauthorized use by others. This ownership right creates a limited monopoly in the protected property.[2] Intellectual property law can be likened to that involving the law of tangible property since both consists of a bundle of rights granted to the property owner. The law of intellectual property, however, is separate from tangible property.[3] While the right of exclusive possession is the basis for protecting real and personal property, the same is not true for intellectual property. The latter provides a monetary incentive to those who create works for the public good by regulating there use by others in order to insure the creators are compensated for their efforts.[4]

Licensing violations are among the most common types of intellectual property infringements, as well as plagiarism, software piracy, and corporate espionage. Intellectual property rights are protected by a variety of organizations and treaties such as the World Intellectual Property Organization (WIPO), World Trade Organization (WTO), United Nations Commission on International Trade Law (UNCITRAL), and Trade-Related Aspects of Intellectual Property Rights (TRIPs).[5]

There are four types of intellectual property: patents, copyrights, trademarks, and trade secrets. They are discussed in the following sections.[6]

<table>
<tr>
<td>

SECTION 12.2
COPYRIGHT LAW

</td>
<td>

A **copyright** is a form of legal protection given to the creator of an original work and the recognized symbol for copyright is ©. This protection can be obtained in both unpublished and published works. Examples of such artistic endeavors include the writing of a book, song, computer program, video game or musical work. Whenever a person composes a poem, makes a drawing or produces a movie, that individual automatically owns the copyright to the creative piece.[7]

</td>
</tr>
</table>

The owner of a copyright enjoys a number of valuable property rights, including the exclusive ability to reproduce and distribute copyrighted materials, display or perform the work publicly, or create a derivative product, such as the development of a screenplay from a novel. Surprisingly, it is not necessary to register the materials with the United States Copyright Office in order to secure legal protection. **Federal registration** merely creates an official record of the copyright. Protection takes effect as soon as the work of authorship is recorded in some fashion–from writing it down on a piece of paper to storing the information on a computer disc.

The copyright law only applies to the specific mode or manner in which information or an idea has been created. This is known as the "**form of material expression**." A copyright does not protect the idea or technique created by the protected work. For instance, Wonder Woman comic books are copyrighted, which limits their reproduction or use without the permission of the copyright owner. The copyright also restricts the ability of another person to create a similar comic book featuring a woman with superpowers. However, the copyright offers no protection to an artist who wishes to create a work about another female character with special powers in general, for instance, a soldier who has robotic abilities.[8]

The unauthorized distribution of a copyrighted work constitutes an **infringement** and allows the registered owner of the copyright to seek legal redress, including the recovery of monetary damages, attorneys fees, and court costs. A willful violation of a copyright, such as the "bootlegging" of music for resale or counterfeiting expensive handbags may also result in criminal prosecution.

The **Copyright Act** does allow a person to use protected materials without permission under very limited circumstances. One such exception is called **"fair use"**, and permits the utilization of a copyrighted work for the restricted purpose of criticism, comment, news reporting, teaching, scholarship, or research. The standard for judging whether the purpose of a copyrighted work is a "fair use" is based upon four factors:

1. The purpose and character of the use, including whether such application is of a commercial nature or is for non-profit educational purposes;

2. The nature of the copyrighted work;

3. The amount and substantiality of the portion used in relation to the copyrighted work as a whole; and

4. The effect of the use upon the potential market for the copyrighted work.

A book review or the quoting of a passage from a book for a term paper would be an example of "fair use" of copyrighted material. However, the photocopying of this text book for resale to other students would be a copyright infringement.

As noted by the United States Copyright Office the distinction between fair use and infringement may not always be clear and easily defined. There is no magic amount of words, lines, or paragraphs that may safely be used without permission. Also, merely acknowledging the source of the copyrighted material does not substitute for obtaining permission.[9]

The 1961 Report of the Register of Copyrights on the General Revision of the U.S. Copyright Law provides a series of examples that courts have regarded as fair use: "quotation of excerpts in a review or criticism for purposes of illustration or comment; quotation of short passages in a scholarly or technical work, for illustration or clarification of the author's observations; use in a parody of some of the content of the work parodied; summary of an address or article, with brief quotations, in a news report; reproduction by a library of a portion of a work to replace part of a damaged copy; reproduction by a teacher or student of a small part of a work to illustrate a lesson; reproduction of a work in legislative or judicial proceedings or reports; incidental and fortuitous reproduction, in a newsreel or broadcast, of a work located in the scene of an event being reported."[10]

The safest approach is to always obtain permission from the copyright owner before using copyrighted material. The Copyright Office, however, is unable to grant this permission. When it is not possible to obtain consent, the utilization of copyrighted items should be avoided unless the doctrine of fair use would clearly apply to the situation.[11]

Is it a copyright violation for Kinko's to copy excerpts from various books for a college course without obtaining the publisher's permission, or is this an example of fair use for an educational purpose? That is the issue in the next case.

BASIC BOOKS, INC. V. KINKO'S GRAPHICS CORP.
758 F. SUPP. 1522 (S.D. N.Y., 1991)

Plaintiffs, all major publishing houses, brought this suit against Kinko's alleging copyright infringement pursuant to the Copyright Act.

More specifically, plaintiffs allege that Kinko's infringed their copyrights when Kinko's copied excerpts from books, whose rights are held by the plaintiffs, without permission and sold the copies for a profit.

Kinko's admits that it copied the excerpts without permission, compiled them into course "packets," and sold them to college students. Kinko's claims their use of the excerpts was a "fair use." This court finds that defendant did violate the Copyright Act. This court hereby awards plaintiffs damages in the amount of $510,000.

There are 12 instances of copyright infringement, which vary in length from 14 to 110 pages, were copied from books previously published by the plaintiffs, compiled packets with excerpts and distributed by Kinko's. Kinko's neither sought nor obtained permission to copy any of these works. Each packet has a cover page, printed with the Kinko's logo, "Kinko's Copies: Professor Publishing," the name of the course and professor, the designated packet number, and a price listing. On the inside cover is a sheet entitled "Education and Fair Use: The Federal Copyright Law."

The fair use of a copyrighted work for purposes such as criticism, comment, news reporting, teaching, scholarship, or research, is not an infringement of copyright. In determining whether the use made of a work in any particular case is a fair use the factors to be considered shall include (1) the purpose and character of the use, including whether such use is of a commercial nature or is for nonprofit educational purposes; (2) the nature of the copyrighted work; (3) the amount and substantiality of the portion used in relation to the copyrighted work as a whole; and (4) the effect of the use upon the potential market for or value of the copyrighted work.

This case involves multiple copying. The copying was conducted by a commercial enterprise which claims an educational purpose for the materials. The copying was just that—copying—and did not interpret them or add any value to the material copied, as would a biographer's or critic's use of a copyrighted quotation or excerpt.

Most contested instances of copyright infringement are those in which the infringer has copied small portions, quotations or excerpts of works and represents them in another form, for example, a biography, criticism, news article or other commentary. In this case, there was absolutely no literary effort made by Kinko's to expand upon or contextualize the materials copied. The excerpts were merely copied, bound into a new form, and sold. The use of the Kinko's packets, in the hands of the students, was no doubt educational. However, the use in the hands of Kinko's employees is commercial. There are no absolute rules as to how much of a copyrighted work may be copied and still be considered a fair use. This court finds that the portions copied were critical parts of the books copied; since that is the likely reason the college professors used them in their classes.

This factor, amount and substantiality of the portions appropriated, weighs against defendant. In this case, the passages copied ranged from 14 to 110 pages, representing 5.2% to 25.1% of the works. In one case Kinko's copied 110 pages of someone's work and sold it to 132 students. Even for an out-of-print book, this amount is grossly out of line with accepted fair use principles. Kinko's has 200 stores nationwide, servicing hundreds of colleges and universities which enroll thousands of students. This court finds that Kinko's copying unfavorably impacts upon plaintiffs' sales of their books and collections of permissions fees.

In this case an important additional factor is the fact that defendant has effectively created a new nationwide business by usurping plaintiffs' copyrights and profits. This cannot be sustained as its result is complete frustration of the intent of the copyright law which has been the protection of intellectual property and, more importantly, the encouragement of creative expression.

SECTION 12.3
TRADEMARK
INFRINGEMENT

A **trademark** includes any word, name, symbol, device, or any combination, used or intended to identify and distinguish the goods or services of one vendor from those of the others, and to indicate the source of the goods or services. Although federal registration of a trademark is not required, there are several benefits, including notice of the registrant's claim of ownership of the mark and exclusive right to use it in connection with the items listed in the registration.[12]

Trademarks are usually words, logos, phrases, and symbols utilized by sellers to identify their goods. However, shapes, sounds, fragrances and colors may also be protected.[13]

Examples of well-known trademarks are the McDonald's golden arches, the mascot from the Philadelphia Phillies, the Nike slogan, "Just Do It," the Nike swoosh and the name I Pad. These names or symbols are associated with one specific company and allow consumers to recognize a particular brand or company.

Trademarks come in all sizes and shapes and can be designed to replicate the personality of a company. Types of trademarks include:

- **Brand names** like Chick-A-Filet and Old Spice for Men.

- **Product names** like the Whopper or Android.

- **Company logos** like the Nike "swoosh" and Volkswagen symbol.

- **Slogans** such as Kentucky Fried Chicken's "Finger Licking Good," and Federal Express' "When There is No Tomorrow."

- **Words in a stylized font** like Pepsi and Coke.

- **Product shapes** like the Coca-Cola bottle and Apple iPod.

- **Sounds** like the MGM lion and Harlem Globetrotter's Theme, "Sweet Georgia Brown."

- **Fictitious characters** such as the talking gecko at Geico and Colonel Sanders.

- **Symbols** like the NBC peacock and the Starbucks woman.[14]

Federal trademark law is regulated by the **Lanham Act,** which defines a **trademark** as a word, name, symbol or slogan, which identifies the origins of a product or service from those of a competitor. The recognized symbol for trademark is™. For instance, "Scotch" is a trademark for tape manufactured by 3M, and "Crest" is a form of toothpaste distributed by Proctor and Gamble. Four interconnected circles is the symbol for Audi automobiles, and "You deserve a break today" is a slogan registered to McDonald's. These trademarks are synonymous with a specific product and its reputation in the market place. Only the owner of a trademark may use the name or symbol on the product it was intended to identify.

Two requirements must be satisfied in order for a mark to be eligible for trademark protection: it must be used in interstate commerce and it must be distinctive. The Lanham Act defines a trademark as one used in commerce, or registered with a bona fide design to be utilized it in commerce. The second element, that a mark be distinctive, requires that the goods be identified as belonging to one entity as opposed to another.[15]

A **trademark infringement** occurs when there is a likelihood of confusion as to the source, origin, or sponsorship of a product in a commercial environment. Elements that will be examined in order to determine whether there is a likelihood of confusion between the products include:

1. Product similarity, including sight, sound, and meaning;

2. Strength of the trademark as demonstrated by the amount of consumer recognition and degree of advertising;

3. Evidence of actual confusion among consumers; and,

4. Similarities of channels used to market or sell the product.

Pepsi could not market a soda line called "Koka-Kola" and feature a polar bear sipping the soft drink. This would constitute a trademark infringement because of the obvious likelihood of confusion with Coca-Cola. Similarly, a fast-food restaurant specializing in fried chicken could not open a store named Kansas Fried Chicken and feature an elderly gentleman with a beard advertising the product under the banner "KFC."

Trademarks are categorized according to their inherent distinctiveness and degree of protection afforded by the law. In descending order of importance, these marks are: (**1**) fanciful, (**2**) suggestive, (**3**) descriptive, and (**4**) generic.

A **fanciful mark** consists of made-up words which serve as a product's brand name, such as Kodak, Sunoco, Cisco, and Pepto-Bismol. Because these marks are inherently distinctive, they receive the greatest protection against infringement.

A **suggestive mark** requires imagination in order to figure out the nature of the product which the mark represents. Ocean Spray, Handiwipes, Orange Crush, and Chicken of the Sea are examples of words which do not easily disclose the nature of the product which they represent. Through advertising, however, the public is able to associate the mark with a specific product. This category of trademark is also considered inherently distinctive and entitled to protection.

A **descriptive mark** does not identify the source of the goods. Rather, it describes some feature or characteristic of the product, such as Instant

Hot, Quick Print, All Season, or No-Fat. This type of mark will not receive protection unless the term has achieved a secondary meaning. That distinction occurs when the public recognizes a particular mark as an indicator of quality. For instance, Rita's Water Ice has achieved a secondary meaning that everyone associates with water ice, even though Rita is a person's first name, which would not normally be protected.

A **generic mark** enjoys no protection under the **Lanham Act,** since it merely describes a type of product regardless of its source. Examples include shredded wheat, pub, aspirin, cellophane, and orange juice.

It is not always easy to figure out which category is the proper fit for a mark, which frequently forces a party to seek court intervention when a trademark infringement is suspected.

McDonald's is the largest advertiser in the United States and has created a number of names that start with Mc such as "McNugget" and "McMuffin." Would a hotel that names itself "McSleep Inn" be infringing upon a McDonald's trademark? That is the issue in **Quality Inns International, Inc. v. McDonald's Corporation**.

QUALITY INNS INTERNATIONAL, INC. v. McDONALD'S CORPORATION
695 F. SUPP. 198 (D. CT. MD. 1988)

On September 21, 1987, Quality Inns International, Inc. announced a new chain of economy hotels to be marketed under the name "McSleep Inn." The response of McDonald's Corporation was immediate. It demanded that Quality International not use the name "McSleep" because it infringed on McDonald's family of marks that are characterized by the use of the prefix "Mc" combined with a generic word.

McDonald's alleges a trademark infringement. It contends that "McSleep Inn" is likely to cause confusion and that Quality International selected the word deliberately to trade on the goodwill and reputation of McDonald's.

Quality International claims that there is no likelihood of confusion. McDonald's marks have been developed in the fast-food business and do not preclude the use of "McSleep Inn" in lodging.

McDonald's is the largest single brand advertiser in the United States. McDonald's has achieved an extremely high awareness in the minds of the American public. In 1977, McDonald's began advertising a fanciful language called "McLanguage" that featured the formulation of words by combining the "Mc" prefix with a variety of nouns and adjectives. In television advertising, Ronald McDonald is shown teaching children how to formulate "Mc" words, and he used words such as McService, McPrice, McFries and McBest.

In a consistent vein, McDonald's has coined "Mc" words for many of its products and services. McChicken, Chicken McNuggets, Egg McMuffin or Sausage McMuffin, McHappy Day, McFortune Cookie, McFeast, and McSnack are but some of the many words. It has obtained trademark registrations for all of these.

The trade name for Quality International's new economy line of hotels, McSleep Inn, is the brainchild of its CEO, Robert Hazard. He wanted a name that conveyed thrift and consistency so he selected "McSleep." He said that "Mc" is from the Scottish surname conveying thrift. He denied that his selection was an imitation of McDonald's. For the reasons given, the Court does not credit this testimony.

In presenting his idea of McSleep Inns to the Board of Directors for approval, Hazard described the new product in terms not only suggestive of McDonald's advertising but openly modeled on the McDonald's concept. The marketing promise of McSleep is "a consistent, convenient, quality product at a low price." The name McSleep should help consumers instantly identify the product for what it is—a consistently clean, quality product at a low price.

The final factor contributing to the Court's belief that Mr. Hazard had McDonald's in mind when he selected the name McSleep is the evidence that Mr. Hazard's thinking was not limited to the one-word McSleep, but rather a family of words, all created by using the prefix "Mc" with a generic word. In the Spring of 1987, when he instructed his attorneys to register and protect the name McSleep, he also directed registration of the names "McSuite" (which he intended to use for two rooms at McSleep Inn).

Trademark law gives the owner of a mark the right to preclude a use by a junior owner of a mark that causes or is likely to cause confusion, mistake, or deceives an appreciable number of typical consumers into believing that some sponsorship, association, affiliation, connection, or endorsement exists between the owner of the senior mark and the owner of the junior mark. There are but two elements that must be established for entitlement, from which all permutations of the cause of action are derived: the senior owner of the mark must demonstrate (1) the adoption and use of a mark and his entitlement to enforce it, and (2) the adoption and use by a junior user of a mark that is likely to cause confusion that goods or services emanate from the senior owner.

McDonald's golden arches and the McDonald's logo rank among the strongest marks, enjoying instant recognition among virtually all members of society. As part of its promotion, McDonald's created a language that it called "McLanguage" from which it developed a family of marks for its products such as McChicken, McNugget, McPizza, as well as marks outside the food area related to its business such as McStop, McKids, and McShuttle.

The central question is whether the use of McSleep Inn is likely to cause confusion so that an appreciable number of the public attribute the product and services of McSleep Inn to McDonald's.

With the announcement of McSleep Inn, the questions from the press and the industry as to whether Quality International would be infringing on the marks of McDonald's were instantaneous. The message directed to Quality International by reporters and potential customers was "what will McDonald's think?" When officers and employees of Quality International first became aware of the new product and name, they raised the same questions. A survey revealed that over 30 percent confused the name McSleep Inn with McDonald's, a level which the Court concludes is substantial.

For the reasons given, the Court concludes that the name McSleep Inn is likely to cause an appreciable number of the public to be confused by believing that McSleep Inn is sponsored, associated, affiliated, connected, or endorsed by McDonald's. Therefore, the Court will find trademark infringement.

Section 12.4
Patent

A **patent** is a right given by the government to an inventor "to exclude others from making, using, offering for sale, or selling the invention throughout the United States or importing the invention into the United States" for a specified period in exchange for the public disclosure of the invention when the patent is granted.[16]

George Washington granted the first patent to Samuel Hopkins in 1790 for an invention to make fertilizer. Since that time, the United States Patent and Trademark Office has licensed more than 6,000 patents ranging from a light bulb to a computer.[17]

U.S. patent law notes that "processes, machines, articles of manufacture, and compositions of matter are patentable." This phrase seems to apply to every type of invention. To a large extent, this is accurate. The United States has one of the broadest standards for determining what is patentable in the world.[18]

An invention can only be patented if it is "new." This means that an invention may not be registered if certain public disclosures of the invention have been made. The law is rather complicated in this area, but an invention may not be registered if:

- The invention was known to others before it was "invented" by the person seeking patent protection;

- The invention was described in a publication more than one year before the filing date; or

- The invention was used publicly, or offered for sale more than one year prior to the filing date.[19]

The one year period after the first public disclosure or offer for sale during which a patent application must be filed is rigidly applied. If an inventor does not file for patent protection within this period, the creator will lose all rights to obtain patent protection on the invention.[20]

The inventor is the only one who may apply for a patent and it can be obtained for a new and nonobvious process, machine, article of manufacturing, composition of matter or an improvement to any of these things. You cannot patent laws of nature, a physical phenomenon an abstract idea, a literary, dramatic, musical, and artistic work and things that are offensive to public morality. For applications filed on or after 1995, utility patents are good for 20 years from the date the patent was first filed subject to the payment of appropriate maintenance fees for the patent.[21]

Section 12.5
Trade Secrets

Two employees of Coca-Cola recently tried to sell the secret Coke recipe to Pepsi.[22] The exact formula to make this famous beverage is one of the best-kept **trade secrets** in the world. While most of the elements are known, the things that give Coca-Cola its taste is a secret blend of ingredients called "Merchandise 7X." This formula has been a secret since Coca-Cola was first invented and is known by only two persons within the company. The only written record of the formula is kept in a secured vault at a bank, which can only be opened upon a resolution from the Company's Board of Directors.[23]

Many businesses besides Coca-Cola have highly guarded trade secrets or confidential information that provides them with a business advantage. Those in the manufacturing, industrial and commercial markets are most apt to have trade secrets, which can vary from a formula or recipe to software.[24]

Some of the top trade secrets include the formula for Coca-Cola, the Big Mac special sauce, Doctor Pepper, and the KFC chicken recipe, the WD-40 formula, Google's algorithm, Krispy Kreme Doughnuts, Twinkies, and Listerine.[25]

So, what is a trade secret? It is defined as any confidential business information which gives a business a competitive advantage. Trade secrets encompass manufacturing, industrial or commercial secrets. The unauthorized use of a trade secret by someone other than the holder is considered an unfair practice and a violation of the law.[26]

Trade secrets include sales and distribution methods, advertising strategies, lists of suppliers and clients, and manufacturing processes. While what information constitutes a trade secret will depend on the circumstances of each case, unfair practices with respect to secret information include industrial or commercial espionage, breach of contract and breach of confidence.[27]

SECTION 12.6
TRADEMARK DILUTION

Trademark infringement provides a clear remedy when someone adopts a name that is confusingly similar to a competing product. Can a merchant, however, utilize a well-known name to promote an unrelated product line? Coca-Cola is famous as a leading manufacturer of soft drinks. Enormous sums of money are spent to promote the consumption of this beverage. A clothing manufacturer hoping to cash in on the Coca-Cola name develops a line of jeans called "Coca-Cola Blue." There is little chance of a consumer confusing the sale of pants with the purchase of a Diet Coke. Nevertheless, Coca-Cola can maintain that its image is being diluted by the sale of an unrelated product that uses the name Coca-Cola on the grounds that the clothing line could blur the public's instantaneous recognition of the beverage manufacturer.

This type of problem is remedied by the **Federal Trademark Dilution Act,** which was enacted to protect the owner of a famous mark from dilution regardless of the likelihood of confusion between the products.

In determining whether a name is distinctive and famous, the courts may consider such factors as:

A. The degree of distinctiveness of the mark;

B. The duration and, extent of use of the mark;

C. The duration and extent of advertising the mark;

D. The geographic extent of the trading area in which the mark is used;

E. The channels of trade for the goods or services;

F. The degree of recognition of the mark in the trading areas used by the mark's owner and against whom the injunction is sought;

G. The nature and extent of use of similar marks by third parties; and

H. Whether the mark was registered.

Congress limited the application of the Federal Trademark Dilution Act to only those marks that are famous such as Pepsi, McDonald's, and Nike. An important advantage of the law is that the owner of the famous mark does not have to show actual competition between its product and that of the defendant. In other words, a firm that improperly uses a famous mark in an unrelated industry has still violated the law. For example, a clothing manufacturer that creates a line of summer dresses called Pepsi Lite has diluted the trademark of the soda company even though clothing has nothing to do with a soft drink.

The Federal Trademark Dilution Act defines dilution to mean the "lessening of the capacity of a famous mark to identify and distinguish goods or services, regardless of the presence or absence of (1) competition between the owner of the famous mark and other parties, or (2) likelihood of confusion, mistake, or deception."

Must there be proof of an actual economic injury to the trademark, or is a technical violation of the Act sufficient to trigger the awarding of damages? That was the issue in a 2003 case that reached the Supreme Court of the United States. Victor Mosley opened a woman's lingerie and adult gift store named "Victor's Little Secret" much to the chagrin of Victoria's Secret. Mosley advertised the store's opening in a weekly magazine with the following advertisement: "GRAND OPENING. Just in time for Valentine's Day!" The ad featured "Intimate Lingerie for every woman," "Romantic Lighting," "Lycra Dresses," and "Adult Novelties/Gifts." The lingerie giant filed a lawsuit against Mosley for using a name that would tarnish and dilute the famous Victoria's Secret mark. The United States Supreme Court was unimpressed with the claim and found that a violation of the Act requires a showing of actual dilution of the mark, and not just the likelihood of dilution. This burden can only be established by objective proof of an injury to the economic value of the trademark.

To counter this decision and its high burden of proof, Congress revised the Federal Trademark Dilution Act in 2006 to make it clear that a plaintiff needs only show that the a defendant's mark is *likely* to cause dilution or blurring by tarnishment of a famous mark, regardless of the presence or absence of actual or likely confusion of competition or of an actual economic injury.

Most people can immediately identify Louis Vuitton products and their design. In fact, the French company spends millions of dollars each year to advertising the uniqueness and sophistication of its luxury handbags and accessories. Also, no one would question the company's aggressive efforts to prevent others from infringing on their trademark by making "spin-offs" or counterfeit copies of their products. Louis Vuitton prominently displays a notice on its website that it has a zero tolerance policy against counterfeiting. For example, in 2004, there were over 13,000 legal actions, more than 6,000 raids, over 947 arrests and the seizure of fake printing cylinders.[28] However, is it a trademark violation for a company to manufacture and distributes dog toys and bones called "Chewy Vuitton"? That is the issue in the following case.

LOUIS VUITTON MALLETIER S.A. v. HAUTE DIGGITY DOG, LLC
507 F.3D 252 (C.A. 4TH, 2007)

Louis Vuitton Malletier (LVM) manufactures luxury handbags and accessories and commenced this action against Haute Diggity Dog, LLC, a corporation that sells pet products alleging trademark infringement. Haute Diggity Dog manufactures plush toys on which dogs can chew. The particular Haute Diggity Dog chew toys in question are small imitations of handbags that are labeled "Chewy Vuiton" and mimic LOUIS VUITTON handbags.

Haute Diggity Dog, LLC, sells a line of pet chew toys and beds whose names parody elegant high-end brands of products. These include–Chewy Vuiton (LOUIS VUITTON), Chewnel No. 5 (Chanel No. 5), Furcedes (Mercedes), Jimmy Chew (Jimmy Choo), Dog Perignonn (Dom Perignon), Sniffany & Co. (Tiffany & Co.), and Dogior (Dior). Haute Diggity Dog's "Chewy Vuiton" dog toys loosely resemble miniature handbags and undisputedly evoke LVM handbags of similar shape, design, and color. In lieu of the LOUIS VUITTON mark, the dog toy uses "Chewy Vuiton"; in lieu of the LV mark, it uses "CV"; and the other symbols and colors employed are imitations, but not exact ones, of those used in the LVM Multicolor and Cherry designs.

To prove trademark infringement, LVM must show that Haute Diggity Dog's use is likely to cause confusion. To determine whether the "Chewy Vuiton" product line creates a likelihood of confusion, we have identified several nonexclusive factors to consider: (1) the strength or distinctiveness of the plaintiff's mark; (2) the similarity of the two marks; (3) the similarity of the goods or services the marks identify; (4) the similarity of the facilities the two parties use in their businesses; (5) the similarity of the advertising used by the two parties; (6) the defendant's intent; and (7) actual confusion. These factors are not always weighted equally, and not all factors are relevant in every case.

Because Haute Diggity Dog's arguments with respect to the factors depend on whether its products are successful parodies, we consider first whether Haute Diggity Dog's products are indeed successful parodies of LVM's marks.

For trademark purposes, a parody is defined as a simple form of entertainment conveyed by juxtaposing the irreverent representation of the trademark with the idealized image created by the mark's owner. A parody must convey two simultaneous-and contradictory-messages: that it is the original, but also that it is not the original and is instead a parody. This second message must not only differentiate the alleged parody from the original but must also communicate some articulable element of satire, ridicule, joking, or amusement. Thus, a parody relies upon a difference from the original mark, presumably a humorous difference, in order to produce its desired effect.

When applying the criteria to the facts of this case, the "Chewy Vuiton" dog toys are successful parodies of LVM handbags and the LVM marks and trade dress used in connection with the marketing and sale of those handbags. The pet chew toy is obviously an irreverent, and indeed intentional, representation of an LVM handbag, albeit much smaller and coarser.

At the same time, the "Chewy Vuiton" dog toy is not the "idealized image" of the mark created by LVM. The differences are immediate, beginning with the fact that the "Chewy Vuiton" product is a dog toy, not an expensive, luxury Louis Vuitton handbag. Thus, "Chewy Vuiton" is not Louis Vuitton ("Chewy" is not "LOUIS" and "Vuiton" is not "VUITTON," with its two Ts); CV is not LV; the designs on the dog toy are simplified and crude, not detailed and distinguished. In short, the Haute Diggity Dog "Chewy Vuiton" dog toy deliberately conjures up the famous LVM marks and trade dress, but at the same time, it communicates that it is not the LVM product.

We conclude that the criteria are amply satisfied and that the "Chewy Vuiton" dog toys convey "just enough of the original design to allow the consumer to appreciate the point of parody," but stop well short of appropriating the entire marks that LVM claims.

Finding that Haute Diggity Dog's parody is successful, however, does not end the inquiry into whether "Chewy Vuiton" creates a likelihood of confusion. Haute Diggity Dog concedes that its marks are designed to be somewhat similar to LVM's marks. But that is the essence of a parody-the invocation of a famous mark in the consumer's mind, so long as the distinction between the marks is readily recognized. While a trademark parody necessarily copies enough of the original design to bring it to mind as a target, a successful parody also distinguishes itself and, because of the implicit message communicated by the parody, allows the consumer to appreciate it.

The differences are sufficiently obvious and the parody sufficiently blatant that a consumer encountering a "Chewy Vuiton" dog toy would not mistake its source or sponsorship on the basis of mark similarity. It is obvious that a "Chewy Vuiton" plush imitation handbag, which does not open and is manufactured as a dog toy, is not a Louis Vuitton handbag. LVM markets Louis Vuitton handbags through high-end fashion magazines, while "Chewy Vuiton" products are advertised primarily through pet-supply channels. "Chewy Vuiton" toys and Louis Vuitton products are neither sold nor advertised in the same way.

Recognizing that "Chewy Vuiton" is an obvious parody and applying the factors, we conclude that LVM has failed to demonstrate any likelihood of confusion. Accordingly, we affirm the judgment in favor of Haute Diggity Dog on the issue of trademark infringement.

**PARK, BROWN & SMITH, P.C.
ATTORNEYS AT LAW
MEMORANDUM**

PROBLEM TWELVE—A

To: All Law Clerks

FROM: Peter Smith, Esquire

RE: Tyler's Sports Bar and Grill Hermit Fries

Joe Roberts has come up with an idea for the bar. He wants to offer some low-calorie items, such as sweet potato fries that he will bake instead of deep fry. He wishes to flavor them with Old Bay seasoning, since the crab fries from Chickie's and Pete's are such a hit and provide a unique flavor. Roberts wants to call the new offering "Hermit Fries" and use a drawing of a crab wearing a baseball hat as the logo.

He has heard that Chickie's and Pete's is very protective of its Crab Fries logo and that they have registered it as a trademark. Joe does not want to run into a problem but believes the idea does not compete with or cause any confusion with the famous Chickie's and Pete's product. After all, he is selling sweet potato fries and not French fries. Therefore, he has contacted our firm to find out if Tyler's can proceed with naming the sweet potato fries, "Hermit Fries" and use the logo of the crab wearing a baseball cap.

I have found a case involving Chickie's and Pete's and a suit that it brought against a restaurant who sold crab fries. Please read **CPC Properties, Inc v. Dominic, Inc.** and let me know what I should tell Joe.

CPC PROPERTIES, INC V. DOMINIC, INC.
2013 WL 4457338 (E.D. PA. 2013)

Plaintiff owns and licenses all intellectual property associated with the "CHICKIE'S & PETE'S" network of restaurants, including the CRAB FRIES® trademark. Since 1978, CHICKIE'S & PETE'S restaurants have used the CRAB FRIES® trademark on menus, signs, and packaging in order to sell their seasoned French fries. Plaintiff has spent millions of dollars in marketing and promotion centered on this trademark and has gained media and public recognition and goodwill as a result.

Recently, Dominic began to use an image of a crab next to the word "FRIES" in an advertisement for its seasoned French fries, and on both its take-out and in-house menus. On August 3, 2012, CPC sued Dominic for trademark infringement.

CPC alleges that the overall commercial effect of using an image of a crab next to "FRIES" is the same the effect of using the word "CRAB" next to "FRIES," and that prospective purchasers will equate Dominic's image with CPC's trademarked good. CPC alleges that using the image of a crab falsely indicates to potential customers that the parties' restaurants are affiliated in some manner or that CPC approved Dominic's use of the image to sell seasoned French fries. Therefore, CPC alleges, Dominic's use of the image violates CPC's exclusive trademark.

CPC alleges a violation of the Lanham Act: statutory trademark infringement. To prevail on a Lanham Act trademark infringement, a plaintiff must demonstrate three elements: (1) the mark it seeks to protect is valid and legally protectable, (2) the plaintiff owns the mark and (3) the defendant's use of the mark is likely to create confusion concerning the origin of goods or services associated with the mark. To establish the first two elements, a plaintiff may show that the mark is federally registered and has become incontestable. A trademark is considered incontestable once the owner files affidavits stating that the mark is registered, the mark has been continuously used for five consecutive years, and that there is neither a pending proceeding nor an adverse decision that challenges ownership. CPC has alleged that it has validly registered and owns four variations on the CRAB FRIES® trademark that it has continuously used the trademark for over five consecutive years, and thus that it is incontestable. Therefore, CPC has established the first two elements of its Lanham Act claims.

CPC must also establish that Dominic's use of the image of a crab next to "FRIES" on its menus and in its advertising is likely to create confusion as to the origin of Dominic's seasoned fries. The use of a word or image creates a likelihood of confusion when consumers viewing the mark would probably assume that the product or service it represents is associated with the source of a different product or service identified by a similar mark. The Third Circuit has set out a number of factors, collectively referred to as the **Lapp** factors, to determine whether the use of a mark is likely to cause such confusion. *See* **Interpace Corp. v. Lapp, Inc., 721 F.2d 460 (3d Cir.1983).** However, in a case such as [as] this, where products are directly competing, and the marks are clearly very similar, a judge should feel free to consider only the similarity of the marks themselves.

The Complaint makes numerous allegations that, accepted as true, demonstrate the similarity of the directly competing marks, and thus demonstrate a likelihood of confusion. First, the parties are competing because both parties occupy the restaurant market in the Philadelphia area. The parties sell substantially similar seasoned fries at their restaurants.

Second, the Complaint states that CPC's trademark "CRAB FRIES®", which it has continuously used for at least thirty-five years, is essentially equivalent to Dominic's use of the image of a crab next to "FRIES." Third, the Complaint alleges that Dominic's use of the similar mark will cause customers to mistakenly attribute the properties and reputation of Plaintiff's seasoned French fries to those of the defendant. The undisputed facts support a finding of likelihood of confusion. The Complaint further alleges that CPC has suffered substantial and irreparable injury. Thus, CPC has established that Dominic committed statutory trademark infringement.

CPC's Complaint also alleges violations of the Pennsylvania anti-dilution statute based on Dominic's use of a picture of a crab near the word FRIES. The Pennsylvania anti-dilution statute states, "[t]he owner of a mark which is famous in this Commonwealth shall be entitled to an injunction against another person's commercial use of a mark or trade name if such use begins after the mark has become famous and causes dilution of the distinctive quality of the mark."

To establish a violation of the dilution statute, the plaintiff must prove that: (1) the plaintiff is the owner of a mark that qualifies as a "famous" mark in light of the totality of factors; (2) the defendant is making commercial use in interstate commerce of a mark or trade name; (3) the defendant's use began after the plaintiff's mark became famous; and (4) Defendant's use causes dilution by lessening the capacity of the plaintiff's mark to identify and distinguish goods or services.

CPC has satisfied these four elements by alleging facts, accepted as true by this Court, that support each of the elements. First, CPC alleges that it owns the CRAB FRIES® trademark. The Complaint states that the mark is famous in the City of Philadelphia and throughout Pennsylvania, and that it has acquired this fame in large part due to CPC's extensive advertising efforts. CPC further notes that CHICKIE'S & PETE's was named the "Best Sports Bar in North America" by ESPN Mobile, and that all of the CHICKIE'S & PETE'S locations that offer CRAB FRIES® prominently feature the trademark on signage and menus. Considering these factors, CPC has demonstrated the fame of the trademark in Pennsylvania. Second, the Complaint states that the trademark has been used in Philadelphia and in the surrounding geographical areas since 1978. Third, the Complaint states that Dominic's use of the mark began after the mark became famous. Fourth and finally, CPC alleges that Dominic wrongfully and intentionally implied an affiliation between Dominic and CPC and lessened the capacity of the mark to identify and distinguish CHICKIE'S & PETE'S seasoned fries. This fact, accepted as true by the Court, establishes both likely and actual trademark dilution. Defendant's use of the crab image near the word "FRIES" violates Pennsylvania statutory anti-dilution law.

CPC has established a trademark infringement under the Lanham Act and trademark dilution in violation of Pennsylvania law.

PROBLEM TWELVE—A
ANSWER SHEET

Name   **Please Print Clearly**

1. What are the elements needed to make out a Lanham Act trademark infringement?

2. If Tyler's sells Hermit fries, have they committed a trademark infringement under the Lanham Act?

3. If Tyler's sells Hermit Fires, have they committed a trademark dilution in violation of Pennsylvania law?

_____

_____

_____

_____

_____

_____

_____

_____

_____

_____

_____

_____

_____

_____

_____

_____

_____

_____

SECTION 12.8
DOMAIN NAMES

The **Internet** has had a profound impact on society with more than one billion users each day. Billions of dollars in business is also transacted annually, a development called e-Commerce. Internet sales are skyrocketing. In 2016, online sales of physical goods alone were $360.3 billion, and are projected to surpass $603.4 billion in this country by 2021. What is surprising is that the United States lags behind several other countries in terms of e-commerce sales as a percentage of total retail sales. For instance, 20 percent of China's retail sales occurred via the internet, as opposed to only 8.1 percent in the United States.[29]

The name of a business has very important marketing implications and can determine the success or failure of a business venture. With the growing popularity of the internet, companies strive to obtain a **domain name** or website that is identical to or similar with their product line or business identity. After all, logic dictates that a customer will try to locate a website by logging onto a name that is similar to the name of the company that the customer is seeking to find.

A. Domain Names

A **domain name** is an identification label that provides a field of administrative autonomy, authority or control within the Internet. A domain name usually represents an Internet Protocol (IP) resource, such as a home or office computer, utilized to access the Internet, a server computer hosting a web site, or the web site itself, or any related service communicated by the Internet.[30]

It is estimated that more than 252 million domain names have been registered worldwide, and these cyberspace addresses are the equivalent of physical street addresses. Aboutdomains.com notes that a domain name is an entity's own cyber-estate that has value depending upon its contents and address. Every domain name contains two or more elements separated by periods or "dots." The last part of the address is the top level domain and includes abbreviations such as .com, .net, .org, .edu, .biz, .info, .mil, and .gov. These designations are made according to the purpose of the website. For instance, ".edu" is associated with an educational institution, and ".gov" refers to a governmental affiliation. The information to the left of this identifier is the second-level domain.

Domain names have become so widely accepted that they are now featured on billboards, advertisements in magazines, and on business cards.

While businesses that do not compete against each other can share variations of a similar name, only one entity can register a specific domain name. For instance, the name "eagles" may refer to a football team, rock group, investigative service, wildlife refuge, or the Boy Scouts. However, only one of these entities may be assigned the domain name **www.eagles.com.**

Therefore, trademark disputes involving domain names have been the source of a great deal of litigation.

Domain names are assigned on a first-come, first-served basis without any type of investigation by the registering company of whether the name violates a prior trademark.

This absence of a monitoring system has encouraged a number of entrepreneurs to register the domain names of well-known companies or individuals in the hope of exacting a financial reward when the trademark owner or famous person wishes to use the name as an internet address. Others purposely register misspellings or variations of a name, anticipating that the site will be frequented by people who incorrectly type the address or who are unaware of how to properly spell the domain name. Since the enterprise is paid by advertisers for each visit or "hit" to the site, this practice can be financially rewarding. This "bad faith" intent to profit from the reputation of another person's name is called "cyberpiracy" or "cybersquatting."

B. Anticybersquatting Consumer Protection Act

In order to protect businesses and consumers against the improper registration of domain names and to promote the growth of electronic commerce, Congress enacted the **Anticybersquatting Consumer Protection Act.** This legislation makes it difficult for entrepreneurs to lay claim to a domain name that is similar to a well-known person, company, or product line for the purpose of receiving a windfall profit.

Testimony was presented during the Congressional hearings on this piece of legislation to illustrate some of the many abuses that have surfaced involving domain names. For instance, when Mobile and Exxon went public with their proposed merger, an individual registered every possible variation of a resulting domain name, including **"mobil-exxon.com,"** **"exxon-mobil.com,"** and **"mobilexxon.com."** Similarly, a representative of Warner Brothers reported that the company was asked to pay $350,000 for the rights to the domain names of **"warner-bros-records.com"** and **"warnerpictures.com."**

The **Anticybersquatting Consumer Protection Act** prohibits the registration or use of a domain name that is identical to, confusingly similar with, or dilutive of a trademark or name of another with the bad faith intent to profit from the goodwill of that mark. Not only may the cyberpirate lose the ownership of the domain name, but the entrepreneur may be required to pay actual damages to the aggrieved party, such as lost profits, or statutory damages in an amount no less than $1,000 and not exceeding $100,000 per domain name. These damages can increase quickly and to surprisingly high amounts.

One of the major ways in which cybersquatters can profit from domain names is through online advertisements, which is a thriving business. Advertisers pay between 10 and 25 cents each time an internet user clicks on one of their ads posted on a website, and according to the Interactive Advertising Bureau Internet, advertising revenues in the U.S. during the first six months of 2010 were $12.1 billion. This figure included banner ads, rich media, digital video and sponsorships.[31] **Electronics Boutique Holding Corp. v. Zuccarini, 54 U.S.P.Q. 2d 1705 (E.D. Pa., 2000)** involved a cypersquatter, who improperly registered the domain name "Electronics Boutique" in a variety of misspelling in order to generate advertising revenue from each site visit. Statutory damages in the amount of $500,000 were awarded to the plaintiff in this case, along with legal costs, because of this improper registration.

Mr. Zuccarini was sued a second time by a different domain name owner who objected to the defendant's tactics in registering names that were similar to his website address. In 2001, a Federal Court of Appeals in **Shields v. Zuccarini** found in favor of a graphic artist who marketed cartoons under the name joecartoon.com. Zuccarini registered five variations of the plaintiff's website address: joescartoon.com; joecarton.com; joescartons.com; joescartoons.com; and cartoonjoe.com. Visitors to a Zuccarini website were greeted by advertisements for other sites and for credit card companies. People were also "mouse-trapped," meaning that they were unable to exit the site without clicking through a succession of advertisements. The court found the work of the graphic artist to be famous and entitled to protection under the Anti-Cybersquatting Consumer Protection Act. The defendant was found to have purposely registered a series of names that were confusingly similar to that of the plaintiff for the sole purpose of diverting customers for profit. The magnitude of the problem was revealed by the testimony of Zuccarini himself, who admitted that he owned more than three thousand web sites and earned between $800,000 and $1,000,000 a year from their use.

The Anticybersquatting Consumer Protection Act should send a clear signal to those entrepreneurs who improperly register a domain name by letting them know that they will be held accountable for their actions.

C. Icann

The **Internet Corporation for Assigned Names and Numbers (ICANN),** a non-profit corporation, is recognized by the United States government as the business which coordinates the management of the Internet's domain-name system and IP address numbers. It was created in 1998 by a broad coalition of Internet's business, academic, technical and user communities. Its core mission includes ensuring a secure and stable global internet. All those who register a domain name with this corporation are required to submit disputes to an approved dispute resolution service, or they must file a lawsuit against the domain-name holder in a court of proper jurisdiction. If the parties proceed to arbitration, either side may litigate an adverse determination in court. ICANN is located at **www.icann.com.**

D. WIPO

The **World Intellectual Property Organization (WIPO)** is the leading dispute resolution service for disagreements arising out of the registration and use of internet domain names. This international organization has rendered hundreds of decisions involving domain names disputes dealing with a number of Fortune 500 companies and celebrity personalities. This organization's influence and the magnitude of the problem involving the use of domain names is demonstrated by the number of arbitration claims filed. In 1999, only one case was in dispute, but WIPO has currently processed over 39,000 cases. For instance, Julia Roberts brought a claim against Russell Boyd over his registration of the domain name **"juliaroberts.com,"** and she was successful in obtaining a transfer of the Internet address. The Arbitration Panel found that Boyd had improperly registered not only the domain name of Ms. Roberts, but that of several other famous movie and sport stars as well. **Julia Fiona Roberts v. Russell Boyd, WIPO Case No. D2000 - 0210.** Pizza Hut successfully retrieved the name **"pizzahut.org"** from an entrepreneur who registered the name in bad faith. **Pizza Hut v. R. J. Inc., WIPO Case No. D2000 - 0939.** The World Wrestling Federation was awarded the names of **"www.wwf.com"** and **"www.stonecold.com,"** even though these domain names had been previously registered to Matthew Bessette. The Arbitrators found that the domain names were confusingly similar to the marks **"WWF.com"** and **"stonecold.com." World Wrestling Enterprises, Inc. v. Matthew Bessette, WIPO Case No. D2000 - 0256.**

Yet, all domain name disputes are not this easy to resolve. In order to obtain a disputed domain name, the complainant must prove three elements:

1. That the disputed domain name is identical or confusingly similar to the trademark or service mark to which it has rights;

2. That the respondent has no rights or legitimate interests with respect to the domain name; and

3. That the disputed domain name has been registered and is being used in bad faith.

One way to ensure that an entity does not choose an improper domain name is to hire a professional service to determine if the contemplated name creates a conflict with an existing business. For example, an article published by Harvard Law School recommends the commissioning of a domain search organization, such as Thompson and Thompson. This business can locate domain names that are similar to the name selected. I-Watch is a useful service that alerts users to when a new name is registered that may interfere with an existing domain name or trademark.

The Attorney General's Office of the United States has also become involved in domain name disputes and will seize control of a website's name that violates the law.

Surprisingly, domain name disputes still arise. For example, "The Beach Boys" are a famous pop band that is known for their harmonies. They have sold millions of records over more than five decades. This Hall of Fame band still tours and Brother Records, Inc., owns the intellectual property rights to The Beach Boys music.

It is not surprising that multiple tribute bands have formed to perform the songs of this famous group around the world. While the name, "The Beach Boys" is trademark protected, one tribute band registered the Doman name "beachboys.org." This prompted a claim by Brother Records, Inc. to stop the use of the name and to obtain ownership of the website. That is the subject of the next case.

WIPO Arbitration and Mediation Center
Brother Records, Inc. v. Good Vibrations
Case No. D2017-2287

1. The Parties

The Complainant is Brother Records, Inc. The Respondent is Good Vibrations of Great Britain.

2. The Domain Name and Registrar

The disputed domain name is "beachboys.org."

3. Factual Background

Brother Records, Inc. is a recording company which owns intellectual property rights to the famous rock band "The Beach Boys".

According to the Complaint, The Beach Boys is one of the most famous bands in the world. The band has been performing and recording music for over 50 years. Through the Complainant's successful marketing and promotion of The Beach Boys, the band is one of the most commercially successful and influential bands of all time and fans have come to associate The Beach Boys with Brother Records, Inc. The Complainant estimates that The Beach Boys' record sales have reached between 100 and 350 million records worldwide.

The Complainant owns a number of registered trademarks for The Beach Boys, the earliest of which appears to have been registered on January 3, 1978.

The Respondent is Good Vibrations, a Beach Boys tribute band based in the United

Kingdom. The Respondent registered the Disputed Domain Name of "beachboys.org" on May 14, 2002.

4. Parties' Contentions

It is alleged that the Disputed Domain Name "beachboys.org." is identical or confusingly similar to the Trade Mark, "The Beach Boys". The Disputed Domain Name fully incorporates the Trade Mark "The Beach Boys," but without the prefix "the."

The Respondent is using the Disputed Domain Name to intentionally attract, for commercial gain, Internet users to its website by creating a likelihood of confusion with the Trade Mark. This is evidence of bad faith under our Domain Name Policy.

The Respondent registered the Disputed Domain Name with prior knowledge of Brother Records, Inc. and the Trade Mark, "The Beach Boys". This is clear from the fact that the Respondent is a tribute band to The Beach Boys.

Brother Records, Inc claims that the Respondent is intentionally using the Disputed Domain Name to divert Internet users seeking the Complainant with the hope of increasing Internet traffic to the Respondent's website and increasing the value of the Disputed Domain Name. The Respondent clearly intends to make a commercial gain by diverting customers of the Complainant and fans of The Beach Boys to its own website.

5. Discussion and Findings

To succeed, the Complainant must demonstrate that the elements enumerated in paragraph 4(a) of the Domain Name Policy have been satisfied, namely:

(i) The Disputed Domain Name is identical or confusingly similar to a trade mark or service mark in which the Complainant has rights; and

(ii) The Respondent has no rights or legitimate interests in respect of the Disputed Domain Name; and

(iii) The Disputed Domain Name has been registered and is being used in bad faith.

A. Identical or Confusingly Similar

Paragraph 4(a)(i) of the Policy provides that the Complainant must establish that the Disputed Domain Name is identical or confusingly similar to the Trade Mark. The Disputed Domain Name in this case incorporates the Trade Mark with the prefix "the" omitted. The Panel finds that the Disputed Domain Name is confusingly similar to the Trade Mark. The Complainant succeeds on the first element of the Policy.

B. Rights or Legitimate Interests

Paragraph 4(a)(ii) of the Policy provides that the Complainant must establish that the Respondent has no rights or legitimate interests in respect of the Disputed Domain Name.

The Panel finds that the Complainant has made out a *prima facie* case. The Respondent has not used the Disputed Domain Name in connection with a *bona fide* offering of goods and services. While the Panel does no doubt that the Respondent is a legitimate tribute band, the Respondent's use of the Disputed Domain Name in connection with those services is not *bona fide*. The Respondent's use of the Disputed Domain Name is likely an attempt by the Respondent to divert Internet users seeking a website relating to The Beach Boys to the Respondent's website. As the Respondent's use of the Trade Mark in the Disputed Domain Name is unauthorized, such use cannot be considered *bona fide*.

The website at the Disputed Domain Name cannot be likened to a fan site, the operation of which may confer rights or legitimate interests. Instead, the website at the Disputed Domain Name promotes a tribute band which is operating for commercial gain. In such circumstances, the use of the Trade Mark in the Disputed Domain Name is not legitimate. The Respondent could have selected another term which would not have carried the same implied affiliation, and which made the Respondent's position as a tribute band more clearly from the outset.

Based on the above, the Panel considers that the Respondent has no rights or legitimate interests in the Disputed Domain Name. The Complainant succeeds on the second element of the Policy.

C. Registered and Used in Bad Faith

Paragraph 4(a)(iii) of the Policy provides that the Complainant must establish that the Respondent has registered and is using the Disputed Domain Name in bad faith.

The Respondent is a tribute band for The Beach Boys. The Respondent's likely intention was to attract Internet users who are fans of The Beach Boys to the Respondent's website at the Disputed Domain Name.

The Panel considers that, by registering and using the Disputed Domain Name, the Respondent is intentionally attempting to attract, for commercial gain, Internet users to its website by creating a likelihood of confusion as to the source, sponsorship or affiliation that website or its services.

6. Decision

For the foregoing reasons, the Panel orders that the Disputed Domain Name "beachboys. org" be transferred to the Complainant.

SECTION 12.9
E-DEFAMATION

E-mail has clearly established itself as an effective method of communicating with other parties. People around the world have created e-mail addresses in order to receive and send messages. The transmission of the communication, however, can only be accomplished by the use of an online service, such as America Online, Inc., Comcast, Verizon, or Prodigy.

Defamatory messages transmitted through the Internet occur with some frequency, likely as the result of the impersonal and less formal nature of Internet communications. Users often do not practice the same discretion and caution in sending instant messages or e-mails as when composing and mailing letters, and because e-mail messages lack voice contact, they are often less personal than telephone conversations. Web identities and e-mail addresses also provide Internet users with a sense of anonymity in message-writing and web chats, which increases the likelihood that inappropriate statements will be made, and because of the ease with which duplicate copies of messages can be sent to others, more people are being exposed to false or inappropriate statements than would normally occur with the mailing of a letter.

A. Requirements

A lawsuit for a defamatory e-mail transmission is still based upon established tort principles. The sender of the communication will be responsible if: **(1)** the transmission is false **(2)** it harms the reputation of another and **(3)** it is communicated to a third person. Therefore, the liability of the author of the defamatory Internet transmission will be no different than if that communication was sent through the mail, posted on a billboard, or written in a newspaper. A more difficult issue concerns the liability of the e-mail service which is used to transmit the defamatory note. Publication of a false statement is a necessary element of a claim for defamation, and only the party or parties who publish the message can be subject to liability. In this way, a newspaper who prints a defamatory story written by a freelance reporter is liable for the false comment just as though it had authored the story itself. An Internet service is also considered a publisher, since they took part in the distribution of the message. **Zeran v. America Online, Inc., 129 3ʳᵈ 327 (4ᵗʰ Cir., 1997).** But should an Internet service be held responsible for a false message because its server is used to transmit the defamatory communication? Unlike a newspaper or telegraph company whose publication of the false material can only occur through the direct participation of a representative of the company, an e-mail provider is similar to a telephone company that exercises no editorial control over the transmission. While newspapers can be responsible as the publisher of a defamatory comment, a telephone company is not liable. The responsibility of an internet service provider for defamation is the issue in **Lunney v. Prodigy Services Company.** In finding that an Internet service provider has no responsibility for the transmission of a defamatory message, the court concluded that the Internet company had not participated in the preparation of the message, exercised any discretion or control over its content, or in any way assumed editorial responsibility.

LUNNEY V. PRODIGY SERVICES COMPANY
1996 U.S. DIST. LEXIS 17090 (N.D. CALIF., 1996)

Usurping the name of Alexander Lunney, an imposter opened a number of accounts with Prodigy Services Company (Prodigy). The imposter posted two vulgar messages in Lunney's name on a Prodigy bulletin board and sent a threatening, profane electronic mail message in Lunney's name to a third person. Lunney has sued Prodigy, asserting that he has been stigmatized by being falsely cast as the author of these messages. The issue is whether Prodigy may be held liable for defamation.

For the reasons that follow, we hold that the complaint against Prodigy was properly dismissed.

After opening several membership accounts with Prodigy under slightly different variants of the name Alex or Alexander Lunney, the imposter transmitted an e-mail message, under Lunney's name, to a local scoutmaster. The subject line of the message read **"How I'm Gonna' Kill U;"** the body was vulgar in the extreme. After receiving the e-mail, the scoutmaster alerted the police and they readily accepted Lunney's innocence in this episode.

Lunney sued Prodigy, claiming that Prodigy was derelict in allowing the accounts to be opened in his name, and was responsible for his having been stigmatized and defamed.

Lunney's defamation action is grounded in established tort principles. Although they were fashioned long before the advent of e-mail, these settled doctrines accommodate the technology comfortably.

As distinguished from e-mail communication, there are more complicated legal questions associated with electronic bulletin board messages, owing to the generally greater level of cognizance that their operators can have over them. In some instances, an electronic bulletin board could be made to resemble a newspaper's editorial page; in others it may function more like a "chat room." In many respects, an ISP bulletin board may serve much the same purpose as its ancestral version, but uses electronics in place of plywood and thumbtacks.

Lunney argues that because Prodigy, in its membership agreements, reserves for itself broad editorial discretion to screen its bulletin board messages, it should be liable as a publisher of such messages. Prodigy argues that while it reserves the right to screen its bulletin board messages, it is not required to do so, does not normally do so and, therefore, cannot be a publisher of electronic bulletin board messages posted on its system by third parties.

Even if Prodigy "exercised the power to exclude certain vulgarities from the text of certain bulletin board messages," this would not alter its passive character in "the millions of other messages in whose transmission it did not participate," nor would this compel it to guarantee the content of those myriad messages. In this case, Prodigy was not a publisher of the electronic bulletin board messages.

Lunney appealed this adverse determination to the United States Supreme Court, but the Justices refused to hear the appeal. This action by our top judiciary allows the New York appellate court decision to remain in place as valid law.

B. Communications Decency Act

The **Communications Decency Act** was enacted by Congress in 1996 because of its desire to protect interactive computer services from the growing number of lawsuits being filed against Internet providers as the result of the improper conduct of its customers. The legislature found that a growing number of Americans rely on this interactive media for an array of educational, political, cultural, and entertainment services. To promote the continued development of the internet, Congress concluded that immunity from suit was needed. As the court noted in **Zeran v. America Online, 129 F. 3rd 327 (4th Cir., 1997):**

"Congress' purpose in providing immunity was evident. The amount of information communicated via interactive computer services is staggering. The specter of tort liability in an area of such prolific speech would have an obvious chilling effect. It would be impossible for service providers to screen each of their millions of postings for possible problems. Faced with potential liability for each message republished by their services, interactive computer service providers might choose to severely restrict the number and type of messages posted. Congress considered the weight of the speech interests implicated and chose to immunize service providers to avoid any such restrictive effect."

Section 230 of the Communications Decency Act indicates that "no provider or user of an interactive computer service shall be treated as the publisher or speaker of any information provided by another information content provider." In other words, a computer service has no responsibility to an injured party for the transmission of a defamatory message simply because its network is used to transmit the false message.

The protection afforded by this statute is so broad that America Online was found to have no liability for defamatory comments contained in the *Drudge Report*, even though AOL paid Matt Drudge to include his investigative report on its service. The report provides the exclusive writings of this Internet journalist with links to many online news sources. America Online was not a passive party to the defamatory transmission. Rather, it actively advertised the Report by issuing a press release which made "clear the kind of material Drudge would provide to AOL subscribers –gossip and rumor –and urged potential subscribers to sign onto AOL in order to obtain the benefits of the Drudge Report." **Blumenthal v. Drudge 992 F. Supp. 44 (D. D.C., 1998.)**

The Federal Court of Appeals in 2003 reaffirmed the grant of immunity to internet providers in **Carafano v. Metrosplash.com.** Star Trek fans may remember Ms. Carafono as the actress, Chase Masterson, who played Leeta on *Deep Space Nine*. In an identity theft case, an unknown person created a dating profile for the actress on Matchmaker.com that was sexually suggestive, threatening, and contained Carafano's home address and telephone number. Carafano sued the dating service for the disclosure of her personal information.

Matchmaker.com countered by asserting immunity under the Communications Decency Act as a provider of an interactive computer service. The appellate court dismissed the lawsuit and noted that Congress made a clear policy choice by refusing to impose tort liability on companies that serve as intermediaries for the injurious messages posted by others.

In 1997, the Supreme Court limited the application of the Act by striking down that part of the law that prohibited the transmission of indecent or patently offensive materials over the internet. The continued immunity for internet providers, however, was unaffected by this ruling.

A second clause in the Communications Decency Act provides that no civil liability will attach if the internet service makes a good faith effort to actively police access to obscene, violent, harassing, or otherwise objectionable material on its site. In other words, this provision will protect an Internet service provider that wishes to affirmatively oversee or edit information posted on its bulletin board or website service.

During a street protest in Dallas on July 7, 2016, Micah Johnson ambushed and killed five police officers and injured nine others. Apparently, he was angry over police shootings of black men and avowed that he "wanted to kill white people, especially white officers."

A subsequent investigation revealed that the shooter liked the Facebook page of the African American Defense League, whose head advocated the killing of police officers across the U.S. Johnson's profile photo on Facebook showed him raising his arm in a Black Power salute, along with a Black Power symbol and a flag connected to the Pan-Africanism movement. These symbols represent nonviolent black empowerment, "but have also been co-opted by extremist groups with racist views."[32]

The families of the victims filed suit against Twitter, Facebook, and Google claiming that they should be responsible for the incident, since they gave a platform to Hamas and its affiliates for radicalizing Micah Johnson by allowing the terrorist organization to post messages that influenced Johnson to shoot the police officers. Does the Communications Decency Act provide immunity for such a claim? This is the issue in **Pennie v. Twitter, Inc.**

PENNIE V. TWITTER, INC.
2017 WL 5992143 (N.D. CAL. 2017)

The general premise of Plaintiffs' Complaint is that Defendants have provided material support to Hamas by allowing Hamas and its affiliates to use Defendants' social media platforms, despite Hamas's designation as a terrorist group under United States law. According to Plaintiffs, "Hamas's use of Defendants' sites" was responsible "in part" for "radicalizing" Micah Johnson, who killed five police officers and wounded several other people when he "ambushed and fired upon a group of police officers in Dallas, Texas."

Hamas, founded during the First Intifada in 1987 as an offshoot of the Muslim Brotherhood, is a militant Palestinian organization that has "carried out thousands of terrorist attacks in Israel, the West Bank, and Gaza, murdering hundreds of Israeli and U.S. citizens...and wounding thousands more." The United States has designated Hamas as a Foreign Terrorist Organization.

Plaintiffs allege that "without Defendants Twitter, Facebook, and Google (YouTube), Hamas' ability to radicalize and influence individuals to conduct terrorist operations outside the Middle East would not have been possible." Hamas operates an official English-language Twitter account with more than 37,000 followers, and an Arabic-language account with 281,000 followers, among other accounts, and "has used Google (YouTube) and Facebook in a similar manner." All Defendants place advertisements on and thus derive revenue from Hamas postings. Plaintiffs assert liability on the grounds that Defendants provide "infrastructure" to Hamas, profit from Hamas's use of their service and "create unique content" by placing ads on Hamas's posts, and, in the case of Google, share advertising revenue with Hamas.

The crux of Plaintiffs' complaint is that Hamas is connected to various purported "black separatist hate groups" that in turn influenced Johnson to shoot police officers. To connect Hamas to such "groups," Plaintiffs identify a scattershot of statements from social media users whom Plaintiffs characterize as "Hamas sympathizers and members" expressing solidarity with what Plaintiffs characterize as "the uprising in Ferguson."

Twitter moved to dismiss based on the Communications Decency Act (the "CDA"), which provides in relevant part that "no provider or user of an interactive computer service shall be treated as the publisher or speaker of any information provided by another information content provider." **47 U.S.C. § 230(c)(1).**

Plaintiffs do not meaningfully allege that Hamas itself carried out the attack, or even that it intended for such an attack to occur. Instead, they allege that other Palestinians and Palestinian organizations expressed general support for groups protesting police violence against African Americans, including some such groups that have staged protests or rallies where speakers or demonstrators called for killing police officers, and that "Micah Johnson was radicalized, in part, by these organizations calling for the murders of police officers."

The CDA immunizes Defendants from Plaintiffs' claims because Plaintiffs' theory of liability rests largely on the premise that Defendants should be held responsible for content created and posted by users (here, Hamas and its affiliates) of Defendants' interactive computer services. The CDA states in relevant part that "no provider or user of an interactive computer service shall be treated as the publisher or speaker of any information provided by another information content provider." **47 U.S.C. § 230(c)(1).** This section immunizes providers of interactive computer services against liability arising from content created by third parties, so long as "the interactive computer service provider is not also an 'information content provider,' which is defined as someone who is 'responsible, in whole or in part, for the creation or development of the offending content. Separated into its elements, section **230(c)(1)** protects from liability only a provider or user of an interactive computer service, that the plaintiff seeks to treat as a publisher or speaker of information provided by another information content provider. As far as this Court is aware, every court that has considered the issue has held that the CDA bars claims similar to those presented here, even where the user posting objectionable content to an interactive service.

Plaintiffs argue that the CDA does not apply because they do not seek to hold Defendants liable as publishers or speakers of other people's content. Plaintiffs contend that their claims "do not depend upon the content that Hamas or its operatives post," but instead on Defendants allowing Hamas to use their services, arguing that since Defendants are prohibited by federal criminal law from providing support to Hamas, they have no discretion to permit the use of their resources by Hamas, and need not exercise any editorial discretion to comply with the laws barring material support to terrorist organizations.

First, this characterization of Plaintiffs' claims is false. Plaintiffs explicitly base their claims on the content that Hamas allegedly posts, because absent offending content, there would be no basis for even the frivolous causal connection that Plaintiffs have alleged between Defendants' services and the Dallas attack. Second, as other judges of this Court have noted, Defendants could only determine which accounts are affiliated with Hamas by reviewing the content published by those accounts—the substantive posts and media that users share, as well as the names and profile pictures that users post.

Next, Plaintiffs contend that Defendants can be held liable as creators of content, rather than merely interactive service providers, because Defendants select advertisements to pair with content on their services—allegedly including content posted by Hamas—"based on what is known about the viewer and what the viewer is looking at." An "entity that is responsible for the creation or development of information" is not immune under the CDA for liability related to the publication of that information. The Ninth Circuit has interpreted the term "development," however, "as referring not merely to augmenting the content generally, but to materially contributing to its alleged unlawfulness." In other words, a website helps to develop unlawful content, and thus falls within the exception to Section 230, if it contributes materially to the alleged illegality of the conduct.

Plaintiffs do not allege that Defendants "materially contributed" in any way to the actual content of Hamas social media posts. They do not claim that Defendants' ads, which are themselves third-party content, are objectionable, or that the ads played any role in making Hamas's content unlawful.

Plaintiffs do not plausibly allege a connection between Hamas and the Dallas shooting, and thus fail to establish that Defendants' alleged support of Hamas was a proximate cause of Plaintiffs' injuries. Plaintiffs' claims are also barred by the CDA. Defendants' motion is therefore granted, and the action is dismissed with prejudice.

**SECTION 12.10
THE EMBARRASSING
INTERNET
PHOTOGRAPHS**

PROBLEM TWELVE—B

**PARK, BROWN & SMITH, P.C.
ATTORNEYS AT LAW
MEMORANDUM**

TO: All Law Clerks

FROM: Peter Smith, Esquire

RE: Embarrassing Photographs

Tony Roberts contacted the firm about an incident that occurred in the locker room following the Stallions clinching of a playoff spot. With five seconds remaining on the clock, the team lined up to kick a 54-yard field goal. When the ball was snapped, the quarterback faked the kick and threw a pass to an open receiver, who walked into the end-zone. The Stallions erupted in wild jubilation. The players continued their celebration in the locker room as they dressed and talked to the reporters.

This crazy scene was witnessed by a ten-year-old fan who had won a drawing to be the team's mascot for the day. Little Aaron Berman was in awe as he snapped picture after picture with his dad's digital camera. The next day, Aaron wrote an essay about his experience and sent the message in an e-mail to his friends along with the photographs of the players. Unfortunately, the pictures showed some of the players in various stages of undress. Things got out of hand when Aaron's uncensored shots were e-mailed around the country. Tony learned of this delicate problem and called, hoping that we could stop the distribution of the pictures on the Internet. I immediately contacted the Internet service providers, who either ignored my calls or claimed that there was nothing they could do. This response is unacceptable. I am sure Internet service providers have the technology to trace the path of the photographs from Aaron's computer and to put a stop to the distribution of these pictures. They could also send a message to its subscribers to honor the privacy of the players by deleting the unauthorized images.

I would like to file a lawsuit against the Internet service providers whose sites were used to transmit the pictures. Read **Joe Doe v. Franco Productions** and let me know the answer to the following questions:

1. What arguments may we make on behalf of the Stallions against the Internet service providers?

2. What defenses will the Internet service providers raise to our lawsuit?

3. Who should succeed in the case? Please explain your answer, so that I will know whether the case is worth pursuing. If helpful, you may include materials from this chapter on "Defamation and the Internet."

DOE v. FRANCO PRODUCTIONS
2000 WL 816779 (N.D. ILL., 2000)

The Plaintiffs were intercollegiate athletes who, without their knowledge or consent, were videotaped in various states of undress by hidden cameras in restrooms, locker rooms, or showers. The resulting videotapes were sold by various means, including websites hosted by Genuity. net and TIAC.net that included still images of the Plaintiffs taken from the videotapes. They instituted this action to obtain monetary damages and injunctive relief for intrusion into the Plaintiffs' seclusion against the alleged producers and distributors of the videotapes, and against Defendants GTE Corporation and GTE Internet (together "GTE"), the respective successors to

Genuity.net and TIAC.net. The Court dismissed Plaintiffs' previous complaint, finding that GTE was a service provider and therefore immune from suit under the **Communications Decency Act, 47 U.S.C. §230 ("CDA").** After the Court granted leave to amend, Plaintiffs filed their amended complaint. They re-alleged their previous claims, this time making their allegations against GTE in their capacity as website host. Presently, GTE moves this court to dismiss the amended complaint against them.

Plaintiffs assert that they are seeking to hold GTE liable for their "own conduct" in "knowingly failing to restrict content" under *§230 (c)(2). Section 230(c) (2)* provides immunity to those who restrict or enable restriction to objectionable material. Thus, Plaintiffs reason because GTE did not restrict or enable restriction to objectionable material, they are not entitled to immunity under this section. However, what Plaintiffs ignore is that by seeking to hold GTE liable for their decision not to restrict certain content, it is seeking to hold them liable in a publisher's capacity.

The **CDA** creates federal immunity against any cause of action that would hold computer service providers liable for information originating from a third party. Immunity under the **CDA** is not limited to service providers who contain their activity to editorial exercises or those who do not engage in web hosting, but rather, "Congress . . . provided immunity even where the interactive services provider has an active, even aggressive role in making available content prepared by others." **Blumenthal v. Drudge, 992 F. Supp. 44, 52 (D.D.C., 1998).**

By offering web hosting services which enable someone to create a web page, GTE is not magically rendered the creator of those web pages. *See 47 U.S.C. (C)(1).*

For the reasons set forth above, the Court grants Defendant GTE's motion to dismiss.

Name   **Please Print Clearly**

1. What arguments may we make on behalf of the Stallions in order to
   assert a cause of action against the Internet service providers?

_____

_____

_____

_____

_____

_____

_____

_____

2. What defense will the Internet service providers raise to our lawsuit?

_____

_____

_____

_____

_____

_____

_____

_____

_____

3. Who should succeed in winning the case? Please explain your answer so I may know whether the case is worth pursuing. If helpful, you may include materials from the subsection of the book on "Defamation and the Internet."

SECTION 12.11
E-PRIVACY

The Internet has opened new avenues of communication for millions of people. From e-mail transmissions to researching the purchase of a product, this electronic information super highway has something for everyone. The technology, however, comes with a price–an intrusion into the user's privacy. A personal message sent to another can be duplicated with little effort and sent to hundreds of people. The online ordering of a product may result in the disclosure to a third person of personal information, such as a telephone, credit card, or social security number. Visits to the World Wide Web leave a digital trail which can be retrieved by a merchant or marketing service. Even a person's e-mail account at work may be monitored by an employer.

A. Common Law

Whether the offending conduct is actionable will frequently depend on whether the intrusion is substantial and highly offensive to a reasonable person or if legislation is in place to prohibit the conduct in question.

People have the right to be left alone and to enjoy their privacy. This principle has its foundation in the Bill of Rights and has long been recognized as a common law tort. For instance, **the Restatement (Second) of Torts** defines **invasion of privacy** as:

> One who intentionally intrudes, physically or otherwise, upon the solitude or seclusion of another or his private affairs or concerns, is subject to liability for invasion of his privacy, if the intrusion would be highly offensive to a reasonable person.

Placing a small video camera in the ceiling of the bathroom at work would be a substantial and highly offensive intrusion into a person's privacy. Likewise, repeated and unwarranted telephone calls at all hours of the day and night to a former spouse would be actionable.

This tort will have equal application in the world of electronic commerce when a cause of action arises in one of the following contexts:

1. Misappropriation of a person's name or likeness for another's financial gain;

2. Disclosure of a private embarrassing fact;

3. Publicity that places a person in a false light; and

4. An unreasonable intrusion upon a person's privacy.

A case that received international attention involving invasion of privacy issues occurred in 2010 when the Lower Merion School District had to pay $610,000 to settle litigation involving pictures taken of a student in his bedroom from a school-issued laptop. The School District admitted that it had activated the cameras on the computers to obtain webcam photographs and screen shots from unsuspecting student laptops in an effort to find missing computers. These images were obtained through remote tracking technology activated by school employees to spy on students inside their homes. The surveillance became known after a vice principal cited a laptop photo in support of an accusation that a student was engaged in improper behavior.[33]

B. Electronic Communications Privacy Act

The **Electronic Communications Privacy Act** was enacted in 1986 to expand the scope of the federal wiretap laws by making the hacking into a computer a crime. The Act provides the primary statutory protection against the interception of electronic communications, including e-mail transmissions. Penalties can be either criminal or civil, and the legislation applies to the improper conduct of both the government and private sectors. Generally, the legislation prohibits **(1)** the intentional interception, use, or disclosure of electronic communications obtained during transmission; and **(2)** the improper accessing of stored electronic communications on a system used by the public. These protections are broad enough to cover hackers as well as disclosures of e-mail messages by a public internet service provider, such as Comcast and Net Zero to a third party.

Even though a person deletes an e-mail message from the hard drive or relies upon an Internet service to automatically delete messages after a certain number of days, a copy of that communication still exists. Internet service providers routinely create a back-up file of all communications.

This type of stored electronic data can be lawfully reviewed by an Internet service provider for such things as marketing or quality assurances purposes. The stored messages, however, may not be disclosed to a third party without a sheriff's sale or search warrant.

The protections afforded by the **Electronic Communications Privacy Act** were found to have been violated when AOL voluntarily disclosed to the Navy, the name of a sailor who listed his marital status as "gay" in his screen profile. In issuing an injunction to block the sailor's involuntary discharge, the court noted that the Navy's inquiry directed to an AOL service representative, in order to learn the sailor's identity, was "likely illegal" under the Act. **Timothy McVeigh v. Cohen, 983 F. Supp. 215 (D.D.C., 1998).** As the court stated:

> The **ECPA,** enacted by Congress to address privacy concerns on the Internet, allows the government to obtain information from an online service provider– as the Navy did in this instance from AOL–but only if **(1)** it obtains a warrant or **(2)** it gives prior notice

to the online subscriber and then issues a subpoena or receives a court order authorizing disclosure of the information in question.

It must be noted, however, that immediately following 9/11, then President Bush signed into law the **USA Patriot Act,** which allows a service provider that reasonably believes a third party is in imminent danger of bodily harm to disclose that information to a law enforcement agent.

The Electronic Communications Privacy Act also provides no protection against the disclosure of an electronic message by the recipient of the communication. This type of disclosure must be covered by other principles of law, such as the breach of a confidential relationship or invasion of privacy.

C. Employer Issues And The Internet

Consider the following work-place issue: Michael Smyth figured he was safe and could talk with impunity while using his employer's e-mail. After all, his employer repeatedly assured the Pillsbury workers that all e-mail messages on the company's electronic communications system could not be intercepted or used against an employee as grounds for termination. In response to e-mail messages from his supervisor which Smyth opened on his home computer, Smyth decided to provide his supervisor with some "editorial input" concerning the sales management team. He threatened to "kill the backstabbing bastards" and referred to the planned holiday party as the "Jim Jones Koolaid Affair." These creative efforts of expression were not well received by Pillsbury after they intercepted Smyth's private e-mail messages. The company exercised its own creative efforts of expression when Pillsbury terminated the worker's employment, despite the company's prior assurances of message confidentiality. **Michael Smyth v. Pillsbury Company, 914 Supp. 97 (E.D. Pa., 1996).**

This case clearly raises the question as to whether an employer can monitor the e-mail accounts of employees without violating invasion of privacy principles. Employers have legitimate reasons for wanting to monitor the electronic communication accounts provided to their employees. Good business practice dictates that the e-mail accounts of workers be reviewed for such things as illegal activity, sexual harassment in the work place, disclosure of trade secrets, productivity and quality control. Employers can even use programs which automatically scan their e-mail systems for violations of company policy, such as the viewing of pornographic materials, online betting, or playing the stock market while on company time.

Generally, it is not considered an invasion of privacy for an employer to monitor its e-mail system. The employer's need to regulate its e-mail takes precedent over privacy interests of the worker. The Electronic Communications Privacy Act also allows monitoring of employee communications, if the electronic communication service is used in the ordinary course of business, or if the monitoring takes place with the employee's consent. For instance, businesses routinely implement privacy statements informing its employees that the employer reserves the right to review company-supplied e-mail accounts for quality assurance purposes.

What ever happened to Mr. Smyth's suit against Pillsbury in view of the company's repeated assurances of e-mail confidentiality? The court was still unimpressed with the former employee's claim and found that the actions of Pillsbury did not invade the plaintiff's privacy. The court noted:

> We do not find a reasonable expectation of privacy in e-mail communications voluntarily made by an employee to his supervisor over the company's e-mail system notwithstanding any assurances that such communications would not be intercepted by management. Once Plaintiff communicated the alleged unprofessional comments to his supervisor over an e-mail system which was apparently utilized by the entire company, any reasonable expectation of privacy was lost.

> Even if an employee had a reasonable expectation of privacy in the contents of his e-mail communications over the company e-mail system, we do not find that a reasonable person would consider the defendant's interception of these communications to be a substantial and highly offensive invasion of his privacy. The company's interest in preventing inappropriate and unprofessional comments or even illegal activity over its e-mail system outweighs any privacy interest the employee may have in those comments.

The Supreme Court of New Jersey in **Blakey v. Continental Airlines, Inc.,** has now placed employers on notice that business owners may incur financial liability if they fail to monitor a company-sponsored electronic communication system once the employer knows or has reason to know that the system is being used to transmit inappropriate comments.

Subsequently, the court in **Dyer v. Northwest Airlines Corp.** clarified the scope of the Electronic Communications Privacy Act by dismissing a lawsuit against Northwest Airlines for disclosing the names, addresses, credit card numbers, and travel itineraries of its passengers to the government. The court determined that the airline was not a provider of electronic communication services within the terms of the Act and was not subject to the disclosure restrictions of the law.

The Twenty-First Century has seen the amazing growth of social media. It is so popular because the Internet connects millions of people with each other, to gather and share information and experiences, and to create friendships or professional alliances.[34]

Facebook has more than 175 million users who have distinctive user names and passwords to access their accounts, as well as the profiles of friends. Users may transmit messages to each other through the Facebook website, either by e-mail or by postings made on a user's wall.[35]

What happens when an employer receives copies of a person's private Facebook transmissions from a co-worker and uses that as a basis to discipline the worker? Is that a violation of the law?

EHLING V. MONMOUTH-OCEAN HOSP. SERVICE CORP.
2013 WL 4436539 (D. N. J., 2013)

Deborah Ehling is a nurse at Monmouth-Ocean Hosp. Service Corp. (MONOC). Plaintiff's claims arise out of an incident involving Plaintiff's Facebook account.

Facebook is a widely-used social-networking website. Every Facebook user must create a Profile Page, which is a webpage that is intended to convey information about the user. However, Facebook has customizable privacy settings that allow users to restrict access to their Facebook content. Plaintiff maintained a Facebook account and selected privacy settings for her account that limited access to her Facebook wall to only her Facebook friends. Plaintiff added many of her MONOC coworkers as friends, including Tim Ronco. Unbeknownst to Plaintiff, Ronco was taking screenshots of Plaintiff's Facebook wall and emailing them to a MONOC manager.

On June 8, 2009, Plaintiff posted the following statement to her Facebook wall:

"An 88 yr old sociopath white supremacist opened fire in the Wash D.C. Holocaust Museum this morning and killed an innocent guard. Other guards opened fire. The 88 yr old was shot. He survived. I blame the DC paramedics. I want to say 2 things to the DC medics. 1. WHAT WERE YOU THINKING? and 2. This was your opportunity to really make a difference! And to the other guards. . . . go to target practice."

After MONOC management was alerted to the post, Plaintiff was suspended *with* pay. Plaintiff argues that Defendants violated the Federal Stored Communications Act ("SCA"). Plaintiff argues that her Facebook wall posts are covered by the SCA because she selected privacy settings limiting access to her Facebook page to her Facebook friends.

The issue is whether the SCA applies to Facebook wall posts. Congress passed the Electronic Communications Privacy Act, which was intended to afford privacy protection to electronic communications. Title II contains the SCA, which was designed to "address access to stored wire and electronic communications and transactional records."

The SCA covers: (1) electronic communications, (2) that were transmitted via an electronic communication service, (3) that are in electronic storage, and (4) that are not public. Facebook wall posts that are configured to be private meet all four criteria.

First, Facebook wall posts are electronic communications. To create Facebook wall posts, Facebook users transmit writing, images, or other data via the Internet from their computers or mobile devices to Facebook's servers.

Second, Facebook wall posts are transmitted via an electronic communication service. Facebook provides its users with the ability to send and receive electronic communications, including private messages and Facebook wall posts.

Third, Facebook wall posts are in electronic storage. When Facebook users post information, the information is immediately saved to a Facebook server.

Fourth, Facebook wall posts that are configured to be private are not accessible to the general public. The touchstone of the Electronic Communications Privacy Act is that it protects private information.

Because Plaintiff chose privacy settings that limited access to her Facebook wall to only her Facebook friends, the Court finds that Plaintiff's Facebook wall posts are covered by the SCA.

Having concluded that the SCA applies, the Court next evaluates whether a SCA's statutory exception applies. The authorized user exception applies where (1) access to the communication was "authorized," (2) "by a user of that service," (3) "with respect to a communication . . . intended for that user." In this case, all three elements of the authorized user exception are present.

First, access to Plaintiff's Facebook wall post was "authorized." Ronco voluntarily provided Plaintiff's Facebook posts to MONOC management without any coercion or pressure.

Second, access to Plaintiff's Facebook wall post was authorized "by a user of that service." It is undisputed that Ronco was a Facebook user: Plaintiff acknowledged that she added Ronco as a Facebook friend.

Third, Plaintiff's Facebook wall post was "intended for that user." Plaintiff's wall posts were visible to Plaintiff's Facebook friends. When Plaintiff posted the comment about the museum shooting, Ronco was one of Plaintiff's Facebook friends. Thus, the post was intended for Ronco.

In conclusion, access to Plaintiff's Facebook wall post was authorized by a Facebook user with respect to a communication intended for that user. Therefore, the authorized user exception applies and Defendants are not liable under the SCA.

D. Social Password Protection Laws

Some employers have recently started asking workers to divulge their user names or passwords for their personal accounts. It is maintained that access to personal accounts is needed to safeguard proprietary information or trade secrets, to comply with federal financial regulations, or to prevent the employer from being exposed to legal liabilities. Employees question whether mandating access to personal accounts is an invasion of employee privacy.[36]

Known as anti-snooping laws, lawmakers started introducing laws in the beginning of 2012 to prohibit employers from requesting passwords to personal Internet accounts as a condition of employment. A number of states, including New Jersey, have passed laws prohibiting these types of requests, and many other jurisdictions are considering this type of legislation.[37] While the laws vary, there is one uniform prohibition: all prohibit employers from requesting or requiring that applicants or employees reveal their user name, password, or other information needed to access a personal social media account.[38] Some states have comparable legislation to protect students in public colleges and universities from having to provide access to their social networking accounts.[39]

<table>
<tr><td>

SECTION 12.12
KATHY'S SOCIAL
MEDIA ACCOUNT

PROBLEM TWELVE—C

</td><td>

PARK, BROWN & SMITH, P.C.
ATTORNEYS AT LAW
MEMORANDUM

</td></tr>
</table>

To: All Law Clerks

FROM: Peter Smith, Esquire

RE: Kathy's Social Media Account

Since you are leaning about the law pertaining to an employer asking for a worker's passwords to his or her social media account, I thought that you could help me with a problem involving Kathy that is somewhat related.

Kathy's brushes with the law continue. Six months ago, she was arrested and charged with possession of drugs with the intent to distribute. This is a serious charge, but I have been able to work out a plea deal where Kathy will only receive two years probation with no jail time. During the discussions with the judge, the prosecutor surprised me by asking the judge to impose as a condition of parole, a requirement that Kathy provide her probation officer with all passwords to her social media accounts. The government claimed this was the only way that the probation officer could monitor Kathy's progress and make sure that she is not in contact with any drug dealers or engaged in any drug related activities.

I have never heard of such a thing. There are laws that prohibit employers from asking for the passwords of their employees' accounts and I would like to think that the same rationale would apply to defendants in criminal cases. The only case I could find that is even remotely similar is **People v. Ebertowski.** Please read that opinion and let me know if you think we can successfully challenge this condition of probation as being unreasonable.

PEOPLE v. EBERTOWSKI
228 CAL. APP.4TH 1170 (CAL. 2014)

The police made contact with Defendant while investigating a brandishing of a gun offense. Defendant was highly intoxicated, provided a false name and birth date to the officer, and physically resisted the officer. The officer determined that a felony warrant was out for Defendant's arrest. Defendant repeatedly threatened the officer and the officer's family and stated that he would sexually assault the officer, the officer's wife, and the officer's daughter. He repeatedly identified himself as a member of the "Seven Trees Norteno" gang, and told the officer that he was "screwing with the wrong gangster." During the booking process, Defendant was uncooperative, made gang signs, and urinated on the floor several times.

After Defendant entered his no contest pleas, the prosecutor asked the court to impose two probation conditions: (1) The Defendant shall provide all passwords to any electronic devices, including cellular phones, computers or notepads, within his or her custody or control and shall submit said devices to search at any time without a warrant by any peace officer. (2) The Defendant shall provide all passwords to any social media sites, including Facebook, Instagram and Mocospace, and shall submit said sites to search at any time without a warrant by any peace officer. The prosecutor told the court that the two requested conditions "should be imposed because the Defendant has used social media sites historically to promote the Seven Trees Norteno criminal street gang."

Defendant claims that the password conditions were unconstitutionally overbroad because they were not narrowly tailored to their purpose so as to limit their impact on his constitutional rights to privacy, speech, and association.

A probation condition that imposes limitations on a person's constitutional rights must closely tailor those limitations to the purpose of the condition to avoid being invalidated as unconstitutionally overbroad. Under this doctrine, a governmental purpose to control or prevent activities constitutionally may not be achieved by means which sweep unnecessarily broadly and thereby invade the area of protected freedoms. A law's over breadth represents the failure of draftsmen to focus narrowly on tangible harms sought to be avoided, with the result that in some applications the law burdens activity which does not raise a sufficiently high probability of harm to governmental interests to justify the interference.

Defendant is a criminal street gang member who promotes his gang on social media, makes violent threats in person to armed police officers, and physically resists armed police officers. The evident purpose of the password conditions was to permit the probation officer to implement the search, association, and gang insignia conditions that were designed to monitor and suppress defendant's gang activity. Without passwords for Defendant's devices and social media accounts, the probation officer would not be able to search them under the unchallenged search condition in order to assess Defendant's compliance with the unchallenged association and gang insignia conditions. Access to all of Defendant's devices and social media accounts is the only way to see if Defendant is ridding himself of his gang associations and activities, as required by the terms of his probation, or is continuing those associations and activities, in violation of his probation.

Defendant's constitutional privacy rights are not improperly abridged by the password conditions any more than they are by the search condition. Even where there is (1) a legally protected privacy interest; (2) a reasonable expectation of privacy under the circumstances; and (3) conduct constituting a serious invasion of the privacy interest, the constitutional right to privacy is not violated if the invasion of the privacy interest is justified because it substantially furthers one or more legitimate competing or countervailing privacy or non-privacy interests.

Here, the competing interest is the state's interest in preventing Defendant from continuing his violent gang associations and activities. Defendant's involvement with his gang has produced a man willing to threaten and physically resist armed police officers. Such a person poses an extreme danger to public safety. The minimal invasion of his privacy that is involved in the probation officer monitoring Defendant's use of his devices and his social media accounts while Defendant is on probation is outweighed by the state's interest in protecting the public from a dangerous criminal who has been granted the privilege of probation.

Defendant asserts that the trial court abused its discretion in imposing the password conditions because these conditions were not reasonable under the circumstances. Trial courts have broad discretion to impose such reasonable probation conditions as it may determine are fitting and proper to the end that justice may be done and generally and specifically for the reformation and rehabilitation of the probationer. A condition of probation will not be held invalid unless it (1) has no relationship to the crime of which the offender was convicted, (2) relates to conduct which is not in itself criminal, and (3) requires or forbids conduct which is not reasonably related to future criminality.

Defendant's current offenses were threatening and resisting a police officer for the benefit of his gang. The password conditions were related to these crimes, which were plainly gang related, because they were designed to allow the probation officer to monitor Defendant's gang associations and activities. Defendant's association with his gang was also necessarily related to his future criminality. His association with his gang gave him the bravado to threaten and resist armed police officers. The only way that Defendant could be allowed to remain in the community on probation without posing an extreme risk to public safety was to closely monitor his gang associations and activities. The password conditions permitted the probation officer to do so. Consequently, the password conditions were reasonable under the circumstances, and the trial court did not abuse its discretion in imposing them.

PROBLEM TWELVE—C
ANSWER SHEET   **Name**   **Please Print Clearly**

1. What did the court say about the constitutional privacy rights of a defendant and how far may the government go without violating those rights?

_____

_____

_____

_____

_____

_____

_____

2. What are the proper circumstances for the conditions of parole as noted by the court?

_____

_____

_____

_____

_____

_____

_____

3. Do you think it is a proper condition of parole that Kathy must disclose her social media passwords so that the probation officer can monitor her activities? Please explain the rationale for your answer.

_____

_____

_____

_____

_____

_____

_____

_____

_____

_____

_____

_____

_____

_____

_____

_____

_____

SECTION 12.13
E-CONTRACTS

The Internet has forced businesses to ponder how they can form legally binding contracts in e-commerce transactions but the answer is simple. Electronic contracts and electronic signatures are just as enforceable as traditional paper contracts, and general principles of contract law have equal application.[40] In online contracts, however, security safeguards were missing in the past. In other words, it is easy to be a victim of fraud when doing business online.[41]

A. Electronic Signatures in Global and International Commerce Act

The technology industry realized early on the built-in problems associated with online communications and created systems and procedures for fulfilling the legal requirements of authenticity, writing and signature, and confidentiality.[42] This was primarily done though Federal legislation passed in 2000, the **Electronic Signatures in Global and International Commerce Act (ESGICA),** which ensured the validity of contracts entered into electronically.[43]

An **electronic contract** is simply an agreement fashioned and "signed" in an electronic form—without paper. For instance, Tyler's Sports Bar and Grill sends an email to a beer distributor to buy 100 cases of imported beer. The vendor accepts and sends back a confirming email with an electronic signature. Since an ink signature isn't possible on an electronic contract, entities use different formats to demonstrate their signature, such as typing the signer's name, pasting in a scanned version of the signer's signature, clicking an "I accept" button, or using cryptographic "scrambling" technology.[44]

B. Click-Wrap Agreements, Browsewrap Agreements and Shrinkwrap Licenses

New terms have been introduced with electronic contract and the purchase of computer software: click-wrap agreements and shrinkwrap licenses.

Computer software may be obtained by downloading the program from the Internet or by installing the software from a CD. In each case, the software is accompanied with a license that limits the buyer's remedies in the event that the software does not work properly.

A **clickwrap license** will accompany the installation of a program from the web. The user is required to click through a series of screens before the program can be successfully installed. These screens contain non-negotiable terms and conditions imposed by the seller. Most people do not read these materials and merely click "I accept" to the questions, since it is the only way to advance the installation.

A **shrinkwrap license** receives its name from the fact that computer software bought in a store is packaged in a cellophane shrinkwrap. When the box is opened, the CD is contained in an envelope that includes a printed license. By opening the envelope or by using the software, the buyer agrees to be bound by the terms of the license.

A **browsewrap agreement** is a variation of a clickwrap agreement where a website's terms and conditions are posted on the website usually as a hyperlink at the bottom of the screen.

These licenses are generally enforced by the courts, even though they favor the software company, limit the buyer's rights in the event of a software problem, and are seen by the user for the first time after the software has been purchased.

FTEJA V. FACEBOOK, INC.
841 F. SUPP.2d 829 (S.D. N.Y., 2012)

Mustafa Fteja, a resident of New York, "was an active user of facebook.com." But on September 24, 2010, Facebook allegedly disabled Fteja's account "without warning" and "without reason." Fteja "has numerous times tried all channels to resolve this matter by procedures outlined on" the Facebook "website." However, Fteja alleges that these attempts "have been ignored." Fteja therefore surmises that Facebook "discriminated" against him, specifically that he is a Muslim.

Fteja filed this action in New York. Facebook moved to transfer this action to the United States District Court for the Northern District of California.

The Northern District of California would be a proper venue for this action. Venue is proper in "a judicial district in which a substantial part of the events or omissions giving rise to the claim occurred . . . ." The Northern District of California would be such a district because the nub of Fteja's claim is that Facebook wrongfully disabled his account and the employees responsible for disabling accounts work at Facebook's headquarters in California which is in the Northern District of California.

The parties devote substantial attention to the forum selection clause contained in the terms and conditions that govern Facebook users' accounts. That clause provides as follows:

> You will resolve any claim, cause of action or dispute you have with us . . . exclusively in a state or federal court located in Santa Clara County California . . .

The Facebook sign-up process works as follows. A user is asked to fill out several fields containing personal and contact information. The user is then asked to click a button that reads "Sign Up." After clicking this initial "Sign Up" button, the user proceeds to a page entitled "Security Check" that requires a user to reenter a series of letters and numbers displayed on the page. Below the box where the user enters that letter-number combination, the page displays a second "Sign Up" button similar to the button the user clicked on the initial page. The following sentence appears immediately below that button: "By clicking Sign Up, you are indicating that you have read and agree to the Terms of Service."

The Terms of Use appear to be a kind of so-called "browsewrap" agreement where website terms and conditions of use are posted on the website typically as a hyperlink at the bottom of the screen. In other words, a browsewrap agreement usually involves a disclaimer that by visiting the website—something that the user has already done—the user agrees to the Terms of Use not listed on the site itself but available only by clicking a hyperlink. Here, by contrast, the second Sign–Up page indicated that additional action beyond merely visiting that page, namely, clicking "Sign–Up," would manifest agreement to the Terms of Use.

Facebook's Terms of Use have something in common with so-called "clickwrap" licenses, "in which an online user clicks 'I agree' to standard form terms . . . ." A clickwrap agreement presents the the end-user with a message on his or her computer screen, requiring that the user manifest his or her assent to the terms of the license agreement by clicking on an icon. Because the user has signed the contract by clicking

'I agree,' even commentators who have called for limits on browsewrap agreements find "nothing inherently troubling about enforcing clickwrap licenses." There is no reason why that outcome should be different because Facebook's Terms of Use appear on another screen rather than another sheet of paper. It is not too much to expect that an internet user whose social networking was so prolific that losing Facebook access allegedly caused him mental anguish would understand that the hyperlinked phrase "Terms of Use" is really a sign that says "Click Here for Terms of Use."

For the reasons discussed above, the Court concludes that Fteja assented to the Terms of Use and therefore to the forum selection clause therein. Fteja agreed to litigate all disputes regarding his Facebook account "exclusively in a state or federal court located in Santa Clara County," California.

SECTION 12.14
STATUTE OF FRAUDS

Most agreements do not have to be in writing to be enforced by the courts, and oral agreements can be just as valid as formal written contracts. The **Statute of Frauds**, however, requires that certain types of agreements be in writing and be signed by the parties to the contract. This includes contracts for the sale of land, the sale of goods worth more than $500 dollars, and contracts which cannot be performed in less than one year.

When you purchase an item online from a retailer, your order is quickly confirmed by the vendor in an e-mail with a confirmation number and tracking number, but these return messages are not sent as a courtesy. Rather, they represent the seller's attempt to create a written record as evidence of compliance with the Statute of Frauds and to insure the validity of the order.

Because of the importance of electronic commerce, a number of states have passed legislation to validate electronic contracts and signatures. For example, New York tackled the problem by enacting the **Electronic Signature and Records Act** that provides that an electronic signature may be used in place of a signature affixed by hand. The law further provides that the "use of an electronic signature shall have the same validity and effect as the use of a signature affixed by hand." These statutes, however, are not uniform in approach and create uncertainty in the business world.

Congress remedied the situation in 2000 by enacting the **Electronic Signatures in Global and National Commerce Act,** which is also known as **E-SIGN**. This compliance with the Statute of Frauds is achieved by providing that a signature, contract, or other record relating to a digital transaction may not be denied legal effect solely because it is electronic in nature. Examples of electronic signatures include a personal identification number used to access a person's on-line account with a business, such as amazon.com or e-bay, a typed or automatic signature that is affixed at the end of an e-mail, or something that is encrypted. Therefore, businesses may now proceed with their online contracts secure in the knowledge that their agreements will be enforced by the courts across the land.

It is important to note that while the Electronic Signatures in Global and National Commerce Act eliminates the barriers to transacting business electronically, consumers still enjoy the full protection of the law available to them with paper contracts. Also, no person can be forced to enter into an electronic contract, and they may continue to do business in the traditional fashion.

The United States is not the only country to consider electronic signatures and internet contracts. The law firm of Baker and McKenzie maintains a website that summarizes how the nations of the world have responded to this issue.

For example, Japan has enacted the **Electronic Signatures and Certification Services** that is designed "to promote the diffusion of information using electromagnetic electronic methods and information processing through securing the smooth utilization of electronic signatures . . . by the presumption of the genuine . . . authenticity of electromagnetic records . . . and the prescription of other necessary matters concerning electronic signatures."

SECTION 12.15 REVIEW CASES

1. Jcom, Inc. operated a website that catered to the sale of adult entertainment services. The company used the trademark "Barbie's Playhouse" on their website, along with a doll-like figure that resembled the form of a Barbie doll. The address of the website was **"www.jcomlive.com/barbie.htm."** Mattel brought suit against JCom., Inc., under the *Lanham Act* for the defendant's violation of the Barbie trademark and under the Federal Trademark Dilution Act. Will Mattel be successful? **Mattel, Inc. v. JCom, Inc. 1998 U.S. Dist. LEXIS 16195 (S.D. N.Y., 1998).**

2. America Online publishes updated stock quotations on a continual basis. This data is supplied by independent third parties who monitor the various stock exchanges. On several occasions, AOL posted

incorrect information concerning the stock price and share value of Ben Ezra, Weinstein & Co., Inc. This prompted a lawsuit by the firm against AOL for defamation and negligence. Is the Internet service liable for the posting of the misinformation about the value of the firm's stock, or are they protected by the Communications Decency Act? **Ben Ezra, Weinstein & Co., Inc. v. America Online, Inc., No. 99-2068 (10ᵗʰ Cir., 2000).**

3. An entrepreneur operated a website under the domain name **"www. Painewebber.com."** Visitors to the site would automatically be linked to a pornographic website. Painwebber, Inc., filed an injunction against the website operator to enjoin them from using the internet domain name. Did the website operator violate the Anticybersquatting Consumer Protection Act? **Paine Webber, Inc. v. www.painwebber. com, 1999 U.S. Dist. LEXIS 6551 (E.D. Va., 1999).**

4. Comedy III Productions has the exclusive right to the exploitation of the trademarks and images of the Three Stooges. But prior to Comedy III's exclusive rights, companies that were affiliated with Robert Walsh possessed a license to sell Three Stooges merchandise. That prior agreement explicitly warned the licensees that they had no right to continue selling Three Stooges products after the expiration of the agreement. Yet following the expiration of that license, a Robert Walsh-controlled company made available for sale on the Internet a "Golf With Your Friends Embroidered Golf Shirt," which incorporated the images of the Three Stooges. Does the website's advertising of the Three Stooges products by a Walsh-affiliated company violate any rights possessed by Comedy III Productions? Will Comedy III Productions be successful under the Lanham Act for a trademark infringement? **Comedy III Productions, Inc. v. Robert C. Walsh, Jr., et al., 1996 U.S. Dist. LEXIS 5710 (S.D. N.Y., 1996).**

5. AOL offers a wide variety of "chatrooms," where its users can converse through messaging. One such chatroom was used by a subscriber to display and sell photographs of an 11-year-old boy who had engaged in certain sexual acts with the subscriber. While the adult pled guilty to criminal charges, the parents of the minor sought to hold AOL liable for the transmission of the photographs, because their internet chatroom was used. Is AOL responsible for the transmission of the photographs over their system, or are they protected by the Communications Decency Act? **Jane Doe v. America Online, Inc., Case No. 97-25-87 (Fla. Dist. Ct. App., 1999).**

6. Microsoft Network is an online computer service that utilizes a clickwrap license that prospective members must agree to if they wish to use the MSN internet site. The membership agreement appears on

the computer screen in a scrollable window next to two blocks that provide the choices, "I agree" or "I don't agree." The agreement, among other things, requires any user who wishes to bring suit against Microsoft Network to file the claim in the State of Washington. Caspi brought a class-action lawsuit against the Internet service provider in New Jersey because of an increase in the membership fees attributable to a change in the service plan. Will Microsoft be successful in having the case dismissed from the New Jersey court because Caspi's choice of jurisdiction violates the clickwrap agreement? **Caspi v. Microsoft Network a/k/a MSN, L.L.C., 732 A.2d 528 (N.J. Super., 1999).**

SECTION 12.16
INTERNET REFERENCES

For more information on Internet law, see the following sites:

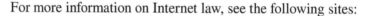

- **www.phillipsnizer.com** *or* **www.perkinscoie.com**
  Both Internet sites provide summaries of court decisions on Cyberlaw. Cases are arranged by issue and the sites are maintained by law firms that specialize in intellectual property.

- **www.gigalaw.com**
  This site provides articles on various Internet law issues.

- **http://legal.web.aol.com**
  AOL provides legal information and court opinions on Cyber-law issues.

Footnotes:

1. William Gindlesperger, Why Intellectual Property Is Protected By The U.S. Constitution, http://www.manufacturing.net/articles/2011/06/why-intellectual-property-is-protected-by-the-us-constitution (last visited October 2, 2013)

2. Intellectual Property, Legal Information Institute, Cornell University School of Law, http://www.law.cornell.edu/wex/intellectual_property (last visited October 2, 2013)

3. *Id.*

4. *Id.*

5. Understanding the Different Kinds of Intellectual Property, For Dummies, http://www.dummies.com/how-to/content/understanding-the-different-kinds-of-intellectual-.html (last visited October 2, 2013)

6. *Id.*

7. What is a Copyright?, The Copyright Society of the USA, http://www.copyrightkids.org/ (last visited October 2, 2013)

8. *What Is a Copyright*, Findlaw, http://smallbusiness.findlaw.com/intellectual-property/what-is-copyright.html (last visited February 5, 2018.)

9. "Fair Use," United States Copyright Office, http://www.google.com/search?q=fair+use&btnG=Search&h1=en&sa=2 (Last visited October 30, 2010).

10. *Id.*

11. *Id.*

12. Trademark Basics, The United States Patent and Trademark Office, http://www.uspto.gov/trademarks/basics/ (last visited October 2, 2013).

13. Trademark, Legal Information Institute, Cornell University School of Law, http://www.law.cornell.edu/wex/trademark (last visited October 2, 2013).

14. *Trademark Examples: Everything You Need to Know*, Upcounsel, https://www.upcounsel.com/trademark-examples (last visited February 5, 2018.)

15. Trademark, Legal Information Institute, *supra.*

16. What is a Patent?, The Copyright Society of the USA, http://www.uspto.gov/patents/ (last visited October 2, 2013).

17. Lee Grayson, *Examples of Patents*, Legalzoom, http://info.legalzoom.com/examples-patents-21353.html (last visited February 6, 2018.)

18. Patent Requirements, Welcome to Bitlaw, http://www.bitlaw.com/patent/requirements.html (last visited October 2, 2013).

19. *Id.*

20. *Id.*

21. Patents, The United States Patent and Trademark Office, http://www.uspto.gov/inventors/patents.jsp (last visited October 2, 2013).

22. Melanie Radzicki McManus, Trade Secrets We Wish We Knew, How Stuff Works, http://money.howstuffworks.com/10-trade-secrets.htm (last visited October 2, 2013).

23. **Coca-Cola Bottling Co. of Shreveport, Inc. v. Coca-Cola Co., 107 F.R.D. 288 (D.C. Del., 1985).**

24. Melanie Radzicki McManus, Trade Secrets We Wish We Knew, How Stuff Works, *supra.*

25. Closely Guarded Trade Secrets, Daily Finance, http://www.dailyfinance.com/photos/closely-guarded-trade-secrets/?photo=2#!fullscreen&slide=987664 (last visited October 2, 2013).

26. What is a Trade Secrets, World Intellectual Property Organization, http://www.wipo.int/sme/en/ip_business/trade_secrets/trade_secrets.htm (last visited October 2, 2013).

27. *Id.*

28. See http://www.louisvuitton.com/info/fake/index.html (Last visited October 30, 2010).

29. *Retail E-Commerce Sales in the United States from 2016 to 2022 (in million U.S. dollars)*, Statista, https://www.statista.com/statistics/272391/us-retail-e-commerce-sales-forecast/(last visited February 6, 2018.)

30. *Domain Name*, Wikipedia, https://en.wikipedia.org/wiki/Domain_name (last visited February 6, 2018.)

31. "Internet Ad Revenues Break Records, Climb to More Than $12 Billion for First Half of 10," IAB, http://www.iab.net/about_the_iab/recent_press_releases/press_release_archive/ press_release/pr-101210. (Last visited November 12, 2010.)

32. *2016 Shooting of Dallas Police Officers Wikipedia*, https://en.wikipedia.org/wiki/2016_shooting_of_Dallas_police_officers (last visited February 6, 2018.)

33. Lower Merion School District Settles Webcam Spying Lawsuits for $610,000, Huff Post, December 11, 2010, http://www.huffingtonpost.com/2010/10/11/lower-merion-school-distr_n_758882.html (last visited October 2, 2013).

34. What is Social Networking?, Social Networking, http://www.whatissocialnetworking.com (last visited November 14, 2010).

35. **Facebook, Inc. v. Wallace, 2009 WL 3617789.**

36. Employer Access to Social Media Usernames and Passwords 2013, National Conference of States Legislatures, http://www.ncsl.org/issues-research/telecom/employer-access-to-social-media-passwords-2013.aspx (last visited October 4, 2013).

37. *Id.*

38. Philip L. Gordon and Joon Hwang, United States: Patchwork of State Social Media Password Protection Laws Creates Challenges For Employers, July 15 2013, http://www.mondaq.com/unitedstates/x/250566/employee+rights+labour+relations/Patchwork+Of+State+Social+Media+Password+Protection+Laws+Creates+Challenges+For+Employers (last visited October 4, 2013).

39. *Id.*

40. Electronic Signatures and Online Contracts, Nola.com, http://www.nolo.com/legal-encyclopedia/electronic-signatures-online-contracts-29495.html (last visited October 4, 2013).

41. John S. Foster, Liability and Legal Issues, Electronic Contracts and Digital Signatures, Corbin Ball Associates, http://www.corbinball.com/articles_legal/index.cfm?fuseaction=cor_av&artID=506 (last visited October 4, 2013).

42. *Id.*

43. Electronic Signatures and Online Contracts, Nola.com, *supra*.

44. *Id.*

Anticybersquatting Consumer
    Protection Act
Browsewrap Agreement
Clickwrap Agreement
Communications Decency Act
Copyright
Copyright Act
Copyright Clause
Descriptive Mark
Domain Name
e-Contracts
e-Defamation
e-Privacy
e-SIGN
Electronic Communications
    Privacy Act (ECPA)
Electronic Signature and
    Records Act
Electronic Signatures and
    Certification Services
Electronic Signatures in Global and
    International Commerce Act
Electronic Signatures in Global
    and National Commerce Act
    (ESGICA)

Fair Use
Fanciful Mark
Federal Registration
Federal Trademark Dilution Act
Form of material expression
Generic Mark
Infringement
Intellectual Property
Internet
Internet Corporation for
    Assigned Names &
    Numbers (ICANN)
Invasion of Privacy
Lanham Act
Patent
Shrinkwrap License
Statute of Frauds
Suggestive Mark
Trade Secrets
Trademark
Trademark Dilution
Trademark Infringement
USA Patriot Act
World Intellectual Property
    Organization (WIPO)

CHAPTER 13

LAW AND PUBLIC POLICY
BY: KEVIN J. FANDL, J.D., PH.D.

Governments will always play a huge part in solving big problems. They set public policy and are uniquely able to provide the resources to make sure solutions reach everyone who needs them. They also fund basic research, which is a crucial component of the innovation that improves life for everyone.

—**Bill Gates**

SECTION 13.1
INTRODUCTION

Public policy is the broad set of rules and principles that a government establishes through legislative, executive and judicial actions. The study of public policy is the examination of how those rules and principles are formed and ultimately implemented in practice. Public policy analysis deciphers the rule that a particular decision of an appellate court may have on certain individuals or businesses by assessing the policy principles that underlie that decision; how federal rules and regulations promulgated by the executive branch affect our rights and responsibilities; how a piece of legislation emerges after months of debate and compromise; and many other relationships between principles and actions.

The government plays a significant role in the lives of individuals and businesses. A single court decision can change how an entity, such as a corporation, may influence elections; a federal agency regulation can increase the cost of doing business by adding new safety requirements for goods or services; and Congress can pass a law that mandates the provision of health insurance or other benefits for employees, for instance. These are three very basic, but very real examples of how governmental decisions affect our lives.

Compliance is a growing field that focuses on requirements under state and federal regulatory law that mandate certain actions by firms. Regulations in all fields, from health care to environment to labor, create certain obligations for businesses that must be followed. Failure to do so often results in monetary penalties and sometimes more severe penalties, such as loss of certain licenses or even incarceration of the agents of the business. Because public policy forms the creations of these rules, we focus in this chapter on both public policy and compliance.

The goal of this Chapter is to help the reader better understand how public policy emerged as the central element of effective governance and how these policies have shaped firm and individual behavior over time.

**SECTION 13.2
A BRIEF HISTORY OF
PUBLIC POLICY**

The evolution of public policy has its roots in government administration far back in this country's history.[1] **Public administration** refers to "public leadership of public affairs directly responsible for executive action."[2] In other words, it refers to the actions taken by the government to implement policy.

President Woodrow Wilson is said to be the "father of public administration." Before becoming President in 1913, Wilson published an article entitled, "The Study of Administration" in which he said: "it is the object of administrative study to discover, first, what government can properly and successfully do, and, secondly, how it can do these proper things with the utmost possible efficiency and at the least possible cost either of money or of energy."[3] Wilson's approach focused on four key tenets:

- Separation of politics and administration,

- Comparative analysis of political and private organizations,

- Improving efficiency with business-like practices and attitudes toward daily operations, and

- Improving the effectiveness of public service through management and by training civil servants, merit-based assessment

Wilson's approach aimed to create a cadre of professionals who would manage essential government functions apart from the politics that drove decisions in the past. He wanted to eliminate the spoils system that rewarded political and financial support with key positions in the administration. Instead, the future President wanted to establish a system that rewarded merit and experience.

Throughout the early 20th century, Wilson's model of public administration succeeded in creating a more effective government led by professionals. During this period, the United States asserted itself as a world power and led the country to be seen as a model for effective government institutions. However, this positive view changed with the decision to enter the war in Vietnam in 1965. The extended conflict and the significant loss of American lives, coupled with doubts about the wisdom of being involved militarily, led to uncertainty over the effectiveness of the U.S. government. Add to this conflict the Watergate scandal in 1974 and trust in government dropped precipitously. "The picture that has emerged, correct or not, was that of government against the people."[4]

However, there was also change on the horizon during this time. Starting as early as the 1940s and accelerating into the 1960s and 70s, scholars began to study public policy and administration as a separate discipline. As the government expanded and everyday lives and business activities were more regularly impacted by government products and services, more interest was generated in facilitating a professional, expert-based public sector.

SECTION 13.3 THE EXECUTIVE BRANCH AND THE PRIVATE SECTOR

Following the events of the 1970s, incoming presidential administrations campaigned on promises of protecting people from the federal government and of reducing its role in their lives. Both the administrations of Presidents Reagan and George H.W. Bush took steps to curtail the power of federal government in some contexts. For instance, President Reagan appointed a controversial head of the newly-empowered Office of Personnel Management (OPM), who made it his mission to reduce the ranks of public servants. The Office of Management and Budget was given new powers to control the promulgation of agency rules and regulations. Also, more leadership positions in federal agencies were filled with political appointments rather than professional career civil servants. This became known as the **Era of Deregulation.**

This shift in public administration was accompanied by budget cuts and a push to move federal government positions to private contractors. Yet at the same time as civil service agencies were shrinking, the Department of Defense saw substantial increases in their staff and funding. "[S]everal Department of Defense units found themselves in trouble because they could not efficiently meet the need for dramatically expanded contract development and administration."[5]

The incoming Clinton Administration in 1993 continued the approach of the Reagan and Bush administrations in downsizing federal government. In their seminal book at the time, *Reinventing Government,* David Osborne and Ted Gaebler provided a different approach to minimizing the problems of a large federal government. They suggested adopting efficiencies found in the private sector, such as broad use of contractors and consultants for single tasks, market-oriented strategies in lieu of regulation, and negotiated strategies rather than legal action where possible. This model became known as **New Public Management (NPM).**

The Clinton Administration adopted NPM and attempted to move toward a more efficient public sector that treated recipients of government services as clients and U.S. citizen taxpayers as shareholders. However, this approach has been criticized on several grounds. One of the most significant critiques has been that government is quite distinct from the private sector and should not be so closely aligned with its approach. For instance, the private sector is subject to market forces while government is subject to appropriations from Congress; the private sector is relatively free of political influence while the government is directed by political actors; and, the objectives and incentives behind private sector action are usually profit-driven, whereas the government functions to provide certain services regardless of their profitability.

Despite these concerns, the incoming George W. Bush Administration continued these reform efforts. His administration highlighted agency performance standards and also human resource management. Bush adopted the **Program Assessment Rating Tool** (PART) in 2004 in an effort to increase accountability for federal programs. As a result of this initiative, over 150 programs have seen budget cuts or have been eliminated completely.[6]

Another significant focus of the Bush Administration was on human capital management. Seeking to create a more corporate-like culture in government, Bush established the **Strategic Human Capital Management Initiative,** which instituted scorecards that each agency would complete to rate the performance of their managers.

It is worth noting the language of the Government Accountability Office Report on human capital in 2003, which drove much of the strategic development of the Bush program:

> "Nevertheless, despite building momentum for comprehensive and systematic reforms, it remains clear that today's federal human capital strategies are not yet appropriately constituted to meet current and emerging challenges or to drive the needed transformation across the federal government. The basic problem, which continues today, has been the long-standing lack of a consistent strategic approach to marshaling, managing, and maintaining the human capital needed to maximize government performance and assure its accountability. Importantly, although strategic human capital management remains high risk government wide, federal employees are not the problem. Rather, the problem is a set of policies that are viewed by many as outdated, overregulated, and not strategic. Human capital weaknesses in the federal government did not emerge overnight and will not be quickly or easily addressed. Committed, sustained, and inspired leadership and persistent attention on behalf of all interested parties will continue to be essential to build on the progress that has been and is being made, if lasting reforms are to be successfully implemented."[7]

The Bush Administration further strengthened this push for more effective human capital management by establishing **Chief Human Capital Officers** in all executive branch agencies through the **Homeland Security Act** of 2002.[8]

Several scandals interrupted the process of further deregulation and began to poke holes in the NPM approach. As you will see from the brief summaries below, privatizing government had several negative consequences, which led to a reversal of the approach of the previous several administrations. Among these negative consequences were a series of corporate and financial scandals throughout the 1990s and 2000s that might have been prevented or mitigated but for deregulation. The following are a few examples.

A. The WorldCom Case

Worldcom was the second largest telecommunications company in the United States after AT&T. Under the leadership of Bernie Ebbers, the company purchased smaller telecom companies, including the $37 billion acquisition of MCI Communications in 1997 (the largest corporate merger ever). However, as the telecommunications market became more competitive in the 1990s, and following a Department of Justice decision to block Worldcom's proposed merger with Sprint in 2000, Worldcom's stock value began to decline. Ebbers took out a personal loan of $400 million from Worldcom to cover his investments in other industries, which Worldcom agreed to in order to prevent Ebbers from selling off his Worldcom stock. In 2002, a group of internal auditors at Worldcom worked in secret to uncover an $11 billion accounting fraud used to hide the decreasing Worldcom assets. This report was presented to the Worldcom board of directors, which dismissed the executives involved in the fraud. Worldcom eventually declared bankruptcy in 2002.

B. The Enron Case

Enron was an energy company based in Houston, Texas, that built and operated power plants and natural gas pipelines in the United States and, to a lesser extent, abroad. Enron reported revenues of $101 billion in 2000 and was considered one of the best companies to work for due to its generous employee pensions. In 2001, an investigation of Enron's accounting practices revealed that it had taken active steps to hide its losses and boost its perceived value to investors. When this scandal was made public, Enron's stock price fell from $90 in the summer of 2001 to near $0 by the end of that year. In December of that year, Enron filed for bankruptcy. Several Enron executives were prosecuted for fraud, including CEOs Ken Lay and Jeff Skilling, as well as CFO Andrew Fastow. The Enron collapse inspired to a great extent the **Sarbanes-Oxley Act.**

C. The Subprime Mortgage Case

During the early part of the 2000s, low interest rates and incentives (such as 100% financing) encouraged investment in the U.S. housing market. Many of the loans made to consumers during this time were **subprime loans**—loans to consumers with less stable credit histories and income than traditional borrowers. These subprime mortgages were then packaged together and sold to investment banks as mortgage backed securities. **Investment banks** make-up part of the shadow banking system, which is not subject to the same rules and regulations as depository banks are. The investment banks sold those securities widely to domestic and foreign investors. Beginning around 2006, interest rates on many subprime loans began to adjust upward, making it harder for borrowers to make their monthly payments. Many defaulted, leading to foreclosure on the mortgages, thereby devaluing the mortgage-backed securities held by investors. As investors stopped buying into these securities, the shadow banking system could no longer lend money to other banks, driving the economy into a crisis by 2008. This ultimately led to the passage of the **Dodd-Frank Act** in 2010.

As a result of these scandals, the Presidential campaign in 2008 focused significantly on corporate and financial reform. The key issue was whether more government oversight was the right approach to bringing corporations and the financial sector into check or whether the private sector should be left to self-regulate while government continued to shrink. Ultimately, President Obama's approach of more government oversight won popular support. But this was only one facet of the broad public sector reform that began in 2009.

D. Recent Updates in the Regulatory Agenda

The Obama Administration came into office after campaigning not for further deregulation or privatization of government, but rather for broad policy reform. As noted in the National Affairs magazine shortly after Obama's first election, "To address these challenges [the economy, the environment, terrorism, etc.], Obama insists, we must come up with comprehensive policies that account for the entire sweep of interconnected social and economic factors contributing to the problem, and whose coordination will contribute to its solution."[9] This was a major shift in thinking and a retreat from the efforts to limit the role of the federal government in the lives of American citizens.

The Obama Administration used broad policy mandates to set in motion a reconsideration of a number of issues, from the decriminalization of marijuana to recognition of gays in the military to bans on assault weapons. Yet, likely the most memorable policy aspect of his Administration will be the **Patient Protection and Affordable Care Act** of 2010.[10] This Act, passed by a democratic Congress, withstood challenge at the U.S. Supreme Court and repeal efforts by a newly Republican-controlled House of Representatives. The highly controversial Act expanded the role of the federal government in regulating health insurance coverage for many Americans by requiring individuals to have health insurance or be subject to a federal tax, preventing sub-standard insurance policies, creating state-run insurance exchanges for those without private insurance, and expanding Medicaid eligibility for the poor, among other things. This exemplified a shift toward a broader role for government than in previous administrations.

The pendulum of regulatory action swung yet again with the 2016 election of Donald Trump. President Trump campaigned on a promise of extensive deregulation, similar to the Regan Era. In its first year, the Trump Administration touted deregulation at the rate of 22 deregulatory actions for every regulatory action taken in 2017. This includes the withdrawal or delay of 1,500 regulatory actions. President Trump stated, "We will get rid of the redundancy and duplication that wastes your time and your money." The deregulatory process was proceeding so rapidly that it became difficult to track the changes, leading the Brookings Institute to establish an online tool to track deregulatory actions.

SECTION 13.4 CORPORATE GOVERNANCE

A. Firm Regulation over Time

Corporations have historically operated with little government oversight or regulation. Corporations have been afforded the same legal rights and responsibilities (with a few exceptions) as individuals since at least 1844 in the United States.[11] This meant that they could own property, make investments, buy goods and services, and so forth. Yet there was little clarification in the law in the 19th century about how to hold corporations liable for their actions that affected shareholders and other citizens. For instance, in the mid-1800s, farmers in the Western United States contended that major railroad corporations were abusing their power by discriminating between similarly situated consumers in their price structures. They raised their concerns with Congress and ultimately prevailed in facilitating the passage of the **Interstate Commerce Act** of 1887. This Act established one of the first major regulatory agencies, the **Interstate Commerce Commission (ICC).**

The ICC was unique in its power to regulate railroads and, later, the trucking industry, by issuing rules to prevent discrimination and to encourage fair practices. Corporations successfully challenged the ICC's power to set rates, among other things, in the late 1800s, limiting their enforcement powers.[12] However, after the turn of the century, the ICC began to acquire more powers through a series of Congressional acts seeking to expand the regulation of the railroad and subsequently other transportation industries. By the 1950s, the ICC had broad regulatory power over ferries, railroads, trucks, bridges, and related transport elements.

The ICC was abolished in 1995, but the agency's regulatory role set the stage for a number of powerful regulatory agencies, including the Federal Trade Commission in 1914, the Federal Communications Commission in 1934, and the Securities and Exchange Commission in 1934, among others. Today, a host of regulatory agencies have a role to play in the operations of the private sector. A list of examples follows:

- Federal Trade Commission—www.ftc.gov

- Federal Communications Commission—www.fcc.gov

- U.S. Securities and Exchange Commission—www.sec.gov

- National Labor Relations Board—www.nlrb.gov

- Federal Aviation Administration—www.faa.gov

- Consumer Product Safety Commission—www.cpsc.gov

- Environmental Protection Agency—www.epa.gov

- Occupational Safety and Health Administration—www.osha.gov

- Transportation Security Administration—www.tsa.gov

- Consumer Financial Protection Bureau—www.consumerfinance.gov

Today, businesses as well as consumers face a wide array of regulations that carry the force of law. Most business-oriented regulations are meant to promote fairness and protect consumers; however, complex and often conflicting rules add transactional costs for many businesses that fall within the regulatory scope of one or more agencies. However, it is important to note that these agencies, while they possess rulemaking power, do not establish the laws that affect businesses. This power is Constitutionally reserved for the legislative branch. Below are two examples of recent legislation that further extended the ability of the government to regulate the private sector, largely as a reaction to the corporate and financial crises of the 1990s and 2000s.

B. The Sarbanes-Oxley Act of 2002

The accounting scandals of the 1990s and early 2000s that led to the downfall of Enron and Worldcom shook the financial world at its core. Investors began to lose confidence in corporate boards that seemed to operate above the law, as well as in auditing firms that were supposedly keeping corporations in check in their accounting practices. Accordingly, both entities came under fire in a series of congressional hearings that ultimately led to the passage of the **Sarbanes-Oxley Act** (SOX) in 2002.[13]

SOX addressed the two main culprits responsible for the recent financial scandals—corporate executives and outside accounting firms. First, it established standards ensuring that financial auditors are completely independent from the corporation itself so as to avoid any conflicts of interest. This means that an audit firm may not consult on non-audit matters with the same corporation that it is auditing.

To address corporate executive behavior, SOX requires corporate executives to take individual responsibility for the financial reports submitted by the corporation. This means that corporate officers must personally certify the accuracy of quarterly financial reports and they will face forfeiture of benefits and civil penalties for noncompliance. In a nutshell, this provision closed a loophole whereby corporate executives could disclaim knowledge of what was in their company's financial statements. They are now on the hook whether they read the statements or not.

Other important elements of SOX include the establishment of criminal penalties for the manipulation, alteration or destruction of financial records, enhanced requirements for financial disclosures and additional internal controls, and a strengthening of penalties for corporate fraud. Overall, SOX has been well-received, though critics contend that it makes doing business in the United States more difficult due to the enhanced reporting and internal controls required.

C. The Dodd-Frank Act (2010)

The **Dodd-Frank Wall Street Reform and Consumer Protection Act** of 2010 was passed as a response to the housing and ultimate financial crisis of the mid-2000s that led to the "Great Recession." The target of Dodd-Frank was the banking and investment industries, which were seen as the major culprits in the financial crisis. The goal of the Act was to improve financial stability by increasing transparency and accountability in the financial sector.

The Act is extensive and goes a long way in changing the way that banks do business. It creates a host of new regulatory agencies set-up to monitor the banking and financial sectors in order to identify and reduce risks and protect consumers. These agencies must report regularly to Congress about perceived risks and measures taken to reduce them.

One of the major targets of the Act is the non-bank investment industry, such as hedge funds, which were discussed earlier as a significant factor leading to the financial crash in the mid-2000s. Previously, small hedge fund managers were not required to register with the SEC. However, Dodd-Frank eliminated that exception and placed new registration and reporting requirements on these managers as well as others in the investment industry.

Another significant creation of Dodd-Frank is the **Consumer Financial Protection Bureau (CFPB),** which began operating in 2011. This federal agency has oversight over credit card companies, payday lenders, mortgage servicing companies, and other non-bank financial operations. Their role is to protect the interests of consumers in the use of financial products and services. The agency has a centralized structure, giving the director significant investigative and regulatory powers over the financial services industry. Republicans in Congress objected to this structure and blocked President Obama's first nominee to head the agency, Elizabeth Warren. The second nominee, Richard Cordray, was also opposed but was ultimately appointed while Congress was in recess. His appointment was subsequently approved by the Senate.

To better understand the relationship between the laws that affect businesses and the regulations that enforce those laws, we turn to the rulemaking process and the Administrative Procedure Act.

A. Administrative Law and the APA

During President Franklin Delano Roosevelt's administration in the early 20th century, a number of federal agencies were established to promote employment and economic recovery following the Great Depression. Roosevelt ran on a platform of reform and recovery. During his campaign in 1932, he argued, "Throughout the nation men and women, forgotten in the political philosophy of the Government, look to us here for guidance and for more equitable opportunity to share in the distribution of national wealth... I pledge myself to a new deal for the American people. This is more than a political campaign. It is a call to arms."[14]

Roosevelt used his first 100 days in office to pass a tremendous amount of legislation through Congress and to issue Executive Orders through his own administration that were collectively called the New Deal. This included the creation of agencies such as the Securities and Exchange Commission (1933), the Social Security Act (1935), the Tennessee Valley Authority (1933), and numerous others.

These acts significantly expanded the role of the Executive branch in society. Congress began to worry that too much power was being wielded by these rapidly expanding federal agencies and that individuals and businesses were more at risk of diminishing the value of the separation of powers. Accordingly, Congress enacted the **Administrative Procedure Act (APA),** as a way to justify "the nation's decision to permit extensive government, but to avoid dictatorship and central planning."[15]

"The basic purposes of the APA are (1) to require agencies to keep the public informed of their organization, procedures and rules; (2) to provide for public participation in the rulemaking process; (3) to establish uniform standards for the conduct of formal rulemaking and adjudication; and (4) to define the scope of judicial review."[16] To better understand the role of judicial review in the process of both law and rule-making, one must go back to the foundations of the United States.

In 1800, outgoing Federalist President John Adams took steps to ensure the continued application of his policies. After Thomas Jefferson had been elected, the next President but before he took office (during a "lame duck session"), Adams pushed the Judiciary Act of 1801 through the Federalist-controlled Congress. That Act added ten District Courts, doubled the number of Circuit Courts to six, and gave the President the power to appoint Federal judges and justices of the peace. Just prior to leaving office, Adams appointed a group of "midnight judges," including 16 federal circuit judges and 42 justices of the peace. Congress approved these in one fell swoop. However, by law, for the commissions to be effective, the individual selected had to receive the commission physically before it expired. Most commissions were delivered before Jefferson took office, but those remaining were blocked by Jefferson upon taking office. William Marbury was one of the intended justices of the peace that did not receive his commission in time. When the secretary of state, for Madison, refused to deliver the commissions, Marbury brought suit directly to the U.S. Supreme Court.

The substantive question presented to the Court was whether Jefferson's administration should be forced to deliver the commission to the outstanding justices of the peace. However, more importantly, the Court was also asked to determine whether Congress has the power to pass statutes that conflict with the Constitution and, if not, which body is responsible for finding such acts unconstitutional.

In **Marbury v. Madison,** the Court unanimously decided that it had jurisdiction to hear cases challenging the constitutionality of a statute. However, it further decided that the Judiciary Act of 1789, which granted the Supreme Court the power to grant writs of mandamus forcing someone to take a particular action, was an invalid extension of its Article III powers and accordingly it was unconstitutional. In sum, the Court confirmed that it had the power to review Acts of Congress; however, in this case, by finding the 1789 Act invalid, it did not force Jefferson to give Marbury his commission.

This case is important in the area of administrative law and public policy because it confirms the U.S. Supreme Court's power to hear challenges to Acts of Congress and to find them invalid when they conflict with the Constitution. It enshrined the principle so commonly accepted today that the Supreme Court is the ultimate protector of the Constitution. Chief Justice Marshall, in his opinion, said, "It is emphatically the province and duty of the Judicial Department to say what the law is. Those who apply the rule to particular cases must, of necessity, expound and interpret that rule. If two laws conflict with each other, the Courts must decide on the operation of each."

At the time, this decision was particularly controversial. President Jefferson said of the decision, "You seem to consider the judges as the ultimate arbiters of all constitutional questions; a very dangerous doctrine indeed, and one which would place us under the despotism of an oligarchy. Our judges are as honest as other men, and not more so." Yet the decision prevailed and became a central aspect of our constitutional democracy.

The **Marbury** decision set the tone for many Supreme Court cases in the subsequent years and it set the tone for the relationship between the judicial branch and the legislature. However, what it did not address was the relationship between the legislature and the executive. Given that Congress can pass laws so long as they do not conflict with the Constitution, what should happen when they pass a law granting powers to an executive agency? Can that agency interpret that law to meet their needs? How much room do they have to adapt the law to their own understanding of it? These questions led to the famous **Chevron** case.

The Clean Air Act, passed in 1963 to research and eventually enforce air quality standards, was amended in 1977 under the Carter Administration to encourage compliance by states that were failing to meet clean air standards established under the Act. The amendment required states to establish a permit program regulating "new or modified major stationary sources of air pollution." The Environmental Protection Agency (EPA), an executive branch agency created in 1970 by President Richard Nixon, interpreted this statute to mean that any new or modified device in a plant had to meet these standards. However, during the Reagan Administration in 1981, the newly-administered EPA reinterpreted the Act to allow new or modified sources of pollution so long as the overall plant was operating within the limits of the statute. An environmental protection group challenged this interpretation.

The key issue in **Chevron** was not about the substance of the law but rather about whether the courts had the ability to interpret the meaning of the statute that the agency was interpreting. The Supreme Court established a two-part test to answer this question. First, the court must look at the statute to assess whether the statute unambiguously addresses the issue that the agency has attempted to interpret. If so, the court defers to the Congress and lets their interpretation stand. If not, or if the statute is ambiguous, the court considers whether the agency's interpretation of the statute is reasonable. If so, the court will let the agency decision stand. In the **Chevron** case, the Supreme Court defined to the interpretation of the agency.

The significance of this decision in administrative law is clear. The court excluded itself from the interpretations of statutes by federal agencies, giving broad power to those agencies in their interpretation of statutes. Thus, while **Marbury** solidified the Court's power to declare Acts of Congress unconstitutional, **Chevron** confirmed that valid statutes can be interpreted relatively freely by federal agencies.

B. The Regulatory Process

Federal agencies are guided by their **enabling statutes,** which are enacted by Congress to define the scope of agency power. But they are also guided by subsequent statutes and appropriations that enhance or change their function and, often, their budget. So while each federal agency is vested with a number of inherent powers, it is often the case that these powers expand and even infringe upon the powers of other agencies over time.

The statutes that guide agency actions leave a great deal of leeway for interpretation. When an agency interprets the meaning of a statute by issuing public guidance, we say that they are engaged in rulemaking. **Rulemaking** is the "agency process for formulating, amending, or repealing a rule."[17] In other words, this is the process of publicizing the agency interpretation of a statute that will affect individuals and businesses for the foreseeable future.

The rulemaking process is generally public and open to feedback from interested parties. Traditionally, agencies followed the formal rulemaking process when they intended to issue a new rule (interpretation of a statutory provision or authority). This process involved publishing the proposed rule in the **Federal Register** and soliciting comments from interested parties who read about the rule. Those comments would be reviewed and responded to and, if necessary and reasonable, the rule would be adjusted in accordance with the comments. Then, unless the rule was highly unpopular and withdrawn, a final rule would be published in the Federal Register. This process often led to judicial challenges to the agency action, questioning the agency's interpretation and challenging its authority.

More recently, two new forms of rulemaking have been utilized by some agencies. The most common is **Hybrid Rulemaking.** This involves a more thorough preliminary process founded on the rulemaking record. Because courts often lack the expertise to properly assess highly technical rules, the rulemaking record provides relevant background research and review conducted by the agency, showing that it took appropriate measures to understand the issue, solicit feedback from experts, consider the policy implications, and so forth, before publishing the rule. This has helped to strengthen the agency's case when a published rule is challenged in court.

The last form of rulemaking is known as **Negotiated Rulemaking.** This process is less widely utilized and tends to be reserved for rules that are controversial or would likely lead to a judicial challenge. In this form of rulemaking, the agency begins by publishing a call to establish a committee to review the proposed rule before it is published in the first place. The committee consists of representatives from interested communities and industries that would lend valuable feedback to the agency before the rule becomes public. Once the committee completes its review process, the agency then begins the formal rulemaking process by publishing the proposed rule with the hope that it will be less likely to be challenged in court.

Footnotes:

1. Phillip J. Cooper, "Public Law and Public Administration" (2006) at 86, citing *Rooke's Case,* 5. Co. Rep. 996, 77 Eng. Rep. 209) (describing an action by the Commissioner of Sewers to levy a fee on the repair of a seawall and how this led to a case brought by the property owner against whom the fee was levied).

2. Appleby, Paul 1947. "Toward Better Public Administration," *Public Administration Review* Vol. 7, No. 2 pp. 93-99.

3. Wilson, Woodrow, "The Study of Administration", *Political Science Quarterly* 2, June 1887.

4. Cooper, *supra,* at 107.

5. *Id* at 113.

6. http://georgewbush-whitehouse.archives.gov/omb/expectmore/part.html.

7. GAO-03-120 Strategic Human Capital Management.

8. HS Act Sec. 1311.

9. http://www.nationalaffairs.com/publications/detail/obama-and-the-policy-approach.

10. Pub. L. 111-148 (2010).

11. Louisville, C. & C.R. Co. v. Letson, 2 How. 497, 558, 11 L.Ed. 353 (1844).

12. **See, e.g., Interstate Commerce Commission v. Cincinnati, New Orleans and Texas Pacific Railway Co., 167 U.S. 479 (1897).**

13. Pub. L. 107-204, 116 Stat. 745 (2002).

14. "The Roosevelt Week", *Time,* New York, July 11, 1932.

15. Shepard, George. *Fierce Compromise: The Administrative Procedure Act Emerges from New Deal Politics.* 90 N.W. U. L. Rev. 1557 (1996).

16. http://www.law.fsu.edu/library/admin/1947cover.html *Attorney General's Manual on the Administrative Procedure Act* (1947).

17. 5 U.S.C. 551(5).

KEY TERMS

Administrative Procedure Act
(APA)
Chief Human Capital Officers
Compliance
Consumer Financial Protection
Bureau (CFPB)
Era of Deregulation
Dodd-Frank Act
Federal Agencies
Federal Register
Hybrid Rulemaking
Homeland Security Act
Interstate Commerce Act
Interstate Commerce

Commission (ICC)
Investment banks
Negotiated Rulemaking
New Public Management (NPM)
Patient Protection and Affordable
Care Act
Program Assessment Rating Tool
Public Administration
Public Policy
Rulemaking
Sarbanes-Oxley Act
Strategic Human Capital
Management Initiative
Subprime Loans

Abandon Property — that property which has been discarded and the owner has no intention of reclaiming.

Acceptance — the unconditional promise by a party to be bound by the terms of an offer.

Activist — a judge who views his/her role as bringing about social change.

Administrative Agency — a governmental body charged with administering and implementing particular legislation; administrative agencies have legislative, executive, and judicial powers.

Adverse Possession — a means of acquiring title by possessing and using property for a required statutory period of time in a way that is adverse, actual, open, and exclusive.

Affirm — when a decision is affirmed, the appellate court determines that the lower court reached the correct decision.

Agreement of Sale — a document entered into between a buyer and seller to reflect the future transfer of an asset such as land.

Agreement on Trade Related Aspects of Intellectual Property Rights — requires all signatory nations to enforce the Paris and Berne Conventions to create minimum standards of protection for intellectual property.

Alimony — the obligation of a person to provide periodic payments of support to a spouse or former spouse.

Alter-ego Theory — piercing of the corporate veil in order to impose personal liability upon corporate officers, directors and stockholders.

Alternative Dispute Resolution — an alternative way of resolving a legal dispute without going through the court system.

Annulment — occurs when there is a legal impediment to a marriage so that the union is null and void from its inception.

Anti-cybersquatting Consumer Protection Act — Federal Legislation which protects businesses and consumers against the improper registration of a domain name.

Apparent Authority — involves those situations where the master's conduct or words would lead another to conclude that the agent is clothed with the authority to act on the master's behalf.

Appellant — person who appeals the lower court's decision.

Appellee — party against whom the appeal is filed.

Arbitration — a form of alternate disputed resolution often used in a commercial setting where both parties agree to have a third party or arbitrator resolve a controversy.

Arraignment — that process in which a defendant is charged with a crime, given the bills of indictment and a date is set for the trial.

Articles of Incorporation — the formal application for a corporate charter which articles must contain the proposed name of the business, the term, purpose, number of shares, and information about the initial corporate officials.

Association of Southeast Asian Nations — an organization of nations that stimulates economic growth, cultural development and social progress in Southeast Asia.

Assumption of the Risk — a defense to a negligence action asserting that when the plaintiff knows of the danger but voluntarily exposes himself to the harm, the plaintiff will be barred from recovery.

Attractive Nuisance — that doctrine which affords protection to young children who trespass upon the land of another whose land contains an inviting, but dangerous condition.

At-Will Employee — refers to an employment situation in which the employee is not under contract to work for a definite period of time and can be discharged at anytime.

Auction With Reserve — an auction that is merely inviting people to make an offer and no contract is formed until the gavel is struck.

Auction Without Reserve — the highest bidder will obtain the item regardless of the bid.

Bailee — the person in possession of personal property in a bailment.

Bailee's Lien — a bailee may retain possession of an item until a bailor pays the bailee's compensation.

Bailment — the delivery of personal property by the owner to another person usually for a particular purpose.

Bailor — the owner of personal property in a bailment.

Bankruptcy — those protections given to a debtor by offering a fresh start or the ability to repay the obligations over a period of time.

Bankruptcy Fraud — a scheme to defraud a creditor through the filing of a bankruptcy petition or the making of a fraudulent representation concerning a bankruptcy.

Bench Trial — a trial with no jury where the judge decides both factual and legal questions.

Berne Convention for the Protection of Literary and Artistic Works — deals with the protection of authorship.

Bilateral Contract — the exchange of mutual promises that give rise to a contract.

Bill — the form used for the introduction of proposed legislation.

Bill of Lading — a document evidencing the receipt of goods for shipment issued by an entity engaged in the business of transporting or forwarding goods.

Bribery — offering something of value to another with the intent of influencing that person's opinion or to have something done in return by that entity.

Burglary — the entering of a building or occupied structure not open to the public at the time with the intent to commit a crime.

Business Judgment Rule — requires that directors of a business use their best judgment in making decisions for the corporation.

Business Visitor — one who enters the premises for a business purpose.

Buy and Sell Agreement — provides for manner of compensation for the interests of the deceased or withdrawing owner.

Buyer in the Ordinary Course of Business — a person that buys goods in good faith, without knowledge that the sale violates the rights of another person in the goods, from a person in the business of selling goods of that kind.

Capacity — a requirement of a valid contract in which the party is of proper age or sound mind.

Caption — that part of a case that identifies the parties to the lawsuit.

Carriage of Goods by Sea Act — provides protection to ocean carriers against claims made by the owners of cargo arising from loss or damage to their goods.

Certificate of Incorporation — a document issued by a state once a corporation has been formed.

Chain Style Business Operation — a franchisee operates the business under the name of the frachisor and must follow standard methods of operations.

Chapter 11 Bankruptcy — a reorganization that allows the debtor to regain solvency by seeking an adjustment of its obligations, either by reducing the debt or by extending the time for repayment.

Chapter 13 Bankruptcy — a wage earner's plan that allows an individual with regular income to develop a plan to repay all or part of the debts over time.

Chapter 7 Bankruptcy — a straight bankruptcy that extinguishes the debts and allows the person to start over.

Chattel — all forms of personal property: animate (living), inanimate, tangible (physical) or intangible.

Child Support — that sum of money awarded to the custodial parent or caregiver for the support of a child for such things as food, shelter and medical expenses.

Circuit Court of Appeals — the intermediate appellate court in the federal court system.

Classical Theory — this ethical theory refers to the liability imposed on corporate insiders who trade on the basis of confidential information obtained by reason of their position within the business.

Clickwrap License — an agreement that is provided by the distributor or manufacturer of software which is contained in the packaging of the product and contains non-negotiable terms and conditions imposed by the seller.

Closely Held Organization — a business owned by only a few people.

Comity — the principle that allows for the recognition of the rules and laws of a foreign jurisdiction in this country.

Commerce Clause — that part of the Constitution that gives Congress the power to regulate commerce and trade between states.

Common Law Marriage — a marriage in which the parties have the capacity to marry, agree to be married, and hold themselves out to the world as being married. This concept is no longer recognized in Pennsylvania.

Communication Decency Act — legislation to protect interactive computer services from the growing number of lawsuits being filed against internet providers as a result of the improper conduct of its customers.

Comparative Negligence — a defense to a negligence action which holds that as long as the plaintiff's negligence is not greater than the defendant's, the plaintiff may recover damages, but the verdict will be reduced by the percentage of the plaintiff's negligence.

Compensatory Damages — a sum of money that will return an aggrieved party to the status quo as though nothing ever happened.

Concurrent Ownership — a term used when ownership to property is shared and title is held by two or more people (see also "joint ownership").

Concurring Opinion — an opinion written by a judge who agrees with the outcome of the case but wants to note a difference in logic for reaching the decision.

Conditional Fee — a form of ownership which conveys all the rights of ownership so long as the owner complies with a certain condition (see also "fee simple defeasible" or "qualified fee").

Condominium — a multi-unit structure where a resident owns the unit together with an interest in the common areas.

Conflicts of Law — rules to determine whose laws should apply to a transaction when there are multiple jurisdictions involved.

Consolidate Budget Reconciliation Act — requires employers with twenty (20) or more employees to permit departing employees the right to retain group health coverage at their own expense for up to eighteen (18) months as long as they are not terminated for gross misconduct.

Conspiracy — an agreement between two or more people to commit an unlawful act or to do a lawful act in an unlawful manner.

Constitutional Relativity — the concept that the constitution was intentionally written in broad and vague terms to ensure that the constitution could adapt to changing times.

Consumer — refers to an individual who enters into a transaction primarily for personal, family, or household purposes.

Contract Implied-in-Law — a contract that arises by implication to prevent unjust enrichment.

Contract — the exchange of promises voluntarily made by those whose agreement is enforceable in court; the five essential elements of a contract are: offer, acceptance, consideration, capacity, and legality.

Contributory Negligence — the failure of the plaintiff to act as a reasonable person under the circumstance. This is a complete bar to recovery.

Convention — an agreement negotiated by members of an international organization in which the resulting document is open to adoption by member states and other nations.

Convention on the International Sale of Goods — provides that many international contracts dealing with the sale of goods will be enforceable even if not reduced to a writing because the Statute of Frauds is not widely followed outside of the United States.

Conveyancing — the processing and transferring of title between the owner of real estate and the buyer.

Copyright — the granting of property rights, including the exclusive ability to reproduce and distribute copyrighted materials, to display the work publicly or to create a derivative product, such as the development of a screen play from a novel.

Copyright Infringement — the unauthorized distribution of a copyrighted work.

Corporation — an artificial entity created under the authority of a state's law whose ownership is not necessarily tied with the management of the corporate organization.

Counter-Offer — a change in the terms of the offer by the offeree that revokes the original offer.

Court of Common Pleas — the trial court in the state court system.

Crime — a violation of those duties which an individual owes to the community and for breach of which the law requires that the offender make satisfaction to the public; an offense against society or the state that violates a penal law and carries a possible punishment of imprisonment.

Criminal Complaint — a statement of facts about a crime which later becomes the basis for formal charges against the accused.

Criminal Trespass — the unlawful entry into real estate without permission or the legal right to be there.

Damages — money awarded to an injured person as the result of the wrongful or improper conduct of another or by a breach of contract.

Defamation — a statement that is false and tends to harm the reputation of another or to lower her in the estimation of the community.

Defendant — the party who is being sued.

Defined Benefit — refers to a pension sponsored by a company that provides specified monthly payments upon retirement.

Defined Contribution Plan — refers to a plan in which the employer will match a contribution made by an employee and that sum will be placed into the employee's investment plan.

Derivative Suit — litigation brought by a minority shareholder on behalf of the corporation to contest the illegal or improper acts of the majority.

Descriptive Mark — a mark that cannot identify the source of goods. Rather, it describes some feature or characteristic of the product.

Destination Contract — the seller is required to deliver the goods to a specific destination and the risk of loss does not pass until the items have been properly delivered to that destination.

Directors — individuals who set the objectives or goals of the corporation, and appoint the officers.

Dissenting Opinion — a judge writes a dissent when he or she disagrees with the result reached by the majority; the dissent has no value as precedent.

Dissolution — a change in the ownership of an organization that changes the legal existence of that organization.

Distributorship — a manufacturing concern that licenses a dealer to sell its products such as an automobile dealership.

Divorce — the legal dissolution of a marriage.

Documents of Title — documents used to prove ownership, e.g. a title to a car, a deed to a house, or a bill of sale for merchandise.

Domestic Partnership — a relationship in which an unwed couple, including those of the same sex, can acquire legal rights and protections by contract to the other's assets.

Double Jeopardy — the protection afforded by the Fifth Amendment which provides that no person shall be tried twice for the same crime.

Drug Free Work Place Act — applies to employers who have contracts of a $100,000.00 or more with the federal government or receive aid from the federal government. These employers are required to develop an anti-drug policy for their employees.

Duty of Care — establishes the type of behavior a person must exhibit in a given situation; the basic rule is that a person must conform to the standard of care of a "reasonable person under the circumstances."

Easement — the granting of the right by the owner to use a part of the land by another entity.

e-Contract — a voluntary exchange of promises between two or more people that constitutes a legal obligation which contract is created through an Internet transmission.

e-Defamation — a defamatory message transmitted through the Internet.

Eighth Amendment — the Constitutional protection that prohibits cruel and unusual punishment.

Electronic Communications Privacy Act — provides the primary statutory protection against the interception of electronic communications, including e-mail transmissions.

Electronic Fencing — the use of the Internet to sell property gained through unlawful means.

Electronic Signatures in Global and National Commerce Act — legislation that will make online transactions the equivalent of a signed paper contract.

Embezzlement — occurs when someone takes ownership to property that has been entrusted to him/her with a fraudulent intent to deprive the owner of that property.

Eminent Domain — the power of the government to take private property for public use.

Employee Hazard Communication Standard — the rules adopted by the Occupational Safety and Health Act (OSHA) to protect employees from the dangers associated with chemicals and other toxins in the work place.

Employee Retirement Income Security Act (ERISA) — is a federal law in which the government regulates pension funds to help insure the long term financial security of those funds by reducing fraud and mismanagement.

Encumbrance — any right or interest that someone has in another's property.

Entrustment — the giving of possession of goods to a merchant who deals in goods of that kind.

Equal Employment Opportunity Commission (EEOC) — an agency of the United States Government that enforces the federal employment discrimination laws which state that discrimination is prohibited on the basis of age, race, sex or creed.

Equity — the power of the court to fashion an equitable remedy when a remedy at law is not available.

Escheat — the doctrine under which property will revert to the state if there are no legal heirs.

Estate — refers to a person's interest or rights to land.

Estate at Sufferance — the lowest interest in land and refers to a person who retains possession of the land with no title.

European Community — an organization comprised of European countries whose purpose is to achieve economic unity and whose objectives include the free movement of goods, services, labor, transportation and capital among member states.

European Contract Law — created by the European Union, this law provides for a uniform law on contracts.

European Court of Justice — is the supreme judicial authority of the European Union which retains jurisdiction over European Union legal matters that cover not just the relationship among member states but also regulates non-member business enterprises that operate within the European Union.

European Union — a membership of countries in Europe to foster economic growth.

Express Authority — occurs when an agent has received written or spoken words that signify the principal has delegated authority to the agent and the agent has accepted the grant of power to act of behalf of the master.

Express Contract — the parties spell out the specifics of the agreement in direct terms.

Expropriation — the taking of property by a foreign government without adequate compensation.

Fair Labor Standards Act — refers to legislation that establishes a minimum wage, a ceiling on the number of hours an employee can work weekly, child labor protection and equal pay for equal work regardless of gender.

Fair Use — an exception to the Copyright Act which permits the utilization of copyrighted work for the restricted purpose of criticism, comment, news reporting, teaching, scholarship or research.

Family Court — the court that decides juvenile cases and matters involving the family unit.

Family Law — those rights, duties and obligations involving marriage, the family, a civil union, domestic partnership, divorce and other family related issues.

Family Limited Liability Partnership — is a business entity in which the partners are related to each other and it is used as an estate planning tool.

Fanciful Mark — consists of made up words which serve as a product's brand name.

Family Medical Leave Act — requires an employer to provide up to twelve (12) weeks of unpaid leave in any twelve (12) month period for family needs, such as the birth or adoption of a child, caring for a child or parent, or for the employee's own serious illness.

Federal Register — is the official publication of the United States Government and provides access to Presidential Orders and federal laws.

Federal Trademark Dilution Act — legislation to protect the owner of a famous mark from dilution regardless of the likelihood of confusion between the products.

Fee Simple Absolute — the most complete form of ownership in real property and includes the right to possess, use and exclude others in the property.

Fee Simple Absolute Estate — the most complete form of ownership of real property which includes the right to possess, use, exclude others, encumber and alienate the property.

Fee Simple Defeasible Estate — a form of ownership which conveys all the rights of ownership so long as the owner complies with a certain condition (see also "conditional fee" or "qualified fee").

Foreign Corruption Practices Act — this law makes it illegal for United States companies and their agents to bribe foreign officials.

Foreign Sovereign Immunities Act — the law that deals with the immunity of foreign governments in the United States. Those entities, or officials however, are not immune when conducting commercial activities.

Foreign Trade Anti-Trust Improvements Act — makes it illegal when anti-competitive conduct outside of the United States has a direct, substantial, reasonable and foreseeable impact on commerce within the United States.

Forum non-conveniens — means that the place of the trial is inconvenient for the parties or the witnesses involved in the trial.

Fourth Amendment — the Constitutional provision that prohibits an unlawful search and seizure by the police.

Franchise — is an agreement in which the owner of a trademark, trade name or copyright allows another to offer its products for sale or use in a geographic area.

Franchisee — the owner of the store offering the item to the public.

Franchisor — refers to the owner of the business idea.

General Agreement on Tariffs and Trade — an international treaty that requires member countries to abide by certain rules of trade, prohibits discrimination in national regulations covering imports and prevents the establishment of import quotas. Its abbreviation is GATT. This organization has been replaced by the World Trade Organization.

Generic Mark — merely describes a type of product regardless of its source.

Gift — a transfer of title to property without payment or compensation.

Gift Causa Mortis — the transfer of personal property made in contemplation of one's approaching death.

Globalization — the process of global businesses supported by governments to deregulate and liberalize world markets and redefine the legal rules that govern commercial relationships.

Good — personal property that is both tangible and movable.

Good Samaritan Statute — a law which provides immunity to certain classes of health care providers in the event that he/she renders emergency help to a person in danger.

Grand Jury Indictment — that process in which 23 people determine whether probable cause exists to warrant a person standing trial for a crime.

Hague Rules — limits the liability of carriers when loss or damage occurs. Liability is based upon the cause and amount of the loss.

Harter Act — sets forth the liability of ocean carriers for cargo loss.

Health Insurance Portability and Accountability Act (HIPAA) — legislation that forbids discrimination based on health or medical conditions. It also protects the records of a patient from disclosure.

Hostile Environment — a type of sexual harassment that does not involve specific consequences like economic loss, but under which a victim suffers a down-graded work atmosphere, pervaded with unpleasantness.

Housing Code — the rules established by a township, city or state to establish minimum standards for an apartment.

Housing Cooperative — a form of entity that owns the real estate but allows a person to use the premises.

Identity Theft — the use of a victim's personal information to obtain a financial advantage, such as the misappropriation of a credit card or money from a bank account.

Identity Theft and Assumption Deterrence Act — a Federal law that makes it a crime to misuse the identifying information of another.

Illusory Promise — the act or performance of a contract that is left solely to the discretion of one party.

Implied Warranty of Habitability — the right of a residential tenant to insist that the premises are fit for human habitation.

Imputed Negligence — the concept that because of a special relationship that exists between the parties, one person can be held liable for the negligence of the other; also called vicarious liability.

Incorporators — individuals who apply for a charter to start a corporation.

Independent Contractor — one who undertakes to perform the act requested on his own and is not subject to the control of an employer.

Infliction of Emotional Distress — this tort arises when a person uses extreme or outrageous conduct causing severe emotional distress to another.

Injunction — an equitable order issued by a court that directs a person to do something (mandatory injunction) or not to do something (prohibitory injunction).

Insider Trading — occurs when corporate insiders, such as officers, directors and employees, buy or sell stock in their own company based upon information that has not yet been released to the public.

Intangible Property — property that is not a physical object, e.g. a patent or trademark.

Intentional Tort — when a wrongdoer purposely sets out to harm another.

Inter Vivos — a gift made while the donor is alive.

Interference with a Contract — occurs when a party wrongfully interferes with an existing contract or a future business opportunity.

International Chamber of Commerce — sets forth trade term definitions that have been generally accepted in the global business market place.

International Court of Justice — the judicial branch of the United Nations which consists of fifteen judges representing all of the world's major legal systems.

International Emergency Economics Powers Act — a law that grants authority to the President to place restrictions on trade and international financial transactions.

International Monetary Fund — encourages international trade by maintaining stable foreign exchange rates and works closely with commercial banks to promote orderly exchange policies with members.

Internet Corporation for Assigned Names and Numbers — a non-profit corporation recognized by the United States Government as the business which coordinates the management of the internet domain name system and IP address numbers.

Intoxication — this act is not a defense to a crime unless it negates a specific mental state.

Invasion of Privacy — the international tort consisting of an unwarranted intrusion upon a person's right to be left alone.

Joint Ownership — a term used when ownership to property is shared and title is held by two or more people (see also "concurrent ownership").

Joint Tenancy with the Right of Survivorship — a form of concurrent or joint ownership in which the co-owners have essentially equal rights to the property; if one co-owner dies, her share will pass to the surviving co-owner.

Judge — the person who presides over the trial and decides questions of law.

Judicial Remedies — refers to the remedies that the court can fashion to compensate an aggrieved party who has been injured by the conduct of another or to grant equitable remedies such as an injunction or declaratory judgment.

Judicial Restraint Oriented — a judge who believes his/her role is merely to make sure a rule is constitutional. The term generally refers to a judge that is conservative.

Jurisdiction — refers to the power of a court to determine the merits of a dispute and to grant an aggrieved party relief.

Jurisdiction Over the Person — the power of the court to hear a dispute involving the parties of a case.

Lanham Act — federal legislation that regulates trademark law.

Larceny — the taking and carrying away of property of another without consent and with the intention of depriving the other of the goods permanently. It is now called theft.

Lease — an encumbrance upon property where a landlord holds property as a fee simple absolute but has given a tenant the rights to possess and use the property exclusively.

Legal Capacity — the capacity of the organization to sue and be sued in its own name.

Legality — the requirement of a valid contract in which the purpose and subject matter of the agreement must be legal.

Lessee — a tenant who is given the rights to possess and use the property exclusively by a landlord who holds property as a fee simple absolute.

Lessor — a landlord who holds property as a fee simple absolute but has given a tenant the rights to possess and use the property exclusively.

Lex Mercatoria — refers to the international norms that are created by commercial entities.

Libel — the publication of defamatory matter by written or printed words.

Licensee — a person who comes on the property of another with the owner's consent or with a legal right to be on the land. It generally refers to a social guest.

Life Estate — an ownership interest which is limited to the life of the person holding it.

Limited Liability Company (LLC) — a business entity that offers limited liability to its owners who are also known as members. It is less formal then a corporation in that the business does not have to maintain minutes and hold formal meetings of its owners.

Limited Liability Partnership (LLP) — this is a hybrid between a partnership and corporation in which the limited liability partners manage the business on a routine basis.

Limited Partnership — a hybrid between a general partnership and a corporation which has the attributes of a partnership except that the limited partners are not permitted to be involved in the control or operation of the business.

Liquidated Damages — a sum of money agreed upon by contracting parties in advance that will be paid in the event of a default or breach of contract.

Long Arm Statute — provides the court with jurisdiction over non-resident defendants who commit a tort within a state, own property within a state or do business within a state.

Lost Property — this is property in which the owner has involuntarily and accidently parted with the asset and does not know where to find it.

Majority Opinion — a decision reached by more than half of the judges of an appellate court panel; a decision rendered by the majority of the court which is the law.

Making a False Statement to a Bank — this crime occurs when someone knowingly makes a false statement of a material fact or overvalues property for the purposes of inducing a bank to take action.

Manufacturing Plant Franchise — the frachisor provides the franchisee with the essential ingredients or formula to make a particular product such as between Coca-Cola and a Coca-Cola Bottling plant.

Marriage — this is a contract to marry for life.

Mediation — a form of alternate dispute resolution used primarily in disputes between labor and management; mediation is advisory in nature.

Mens Rea — the necessary state of mind that a perpetrator must have to be found guilty of committing a particular crime; criminal intent.

Merchant — a person that deals in goods of a particular kind or otherwise holds itself out by occupation as having knowledge or skills peculiar to the practices or goods involved in the transaction.

Minimum Contact — the court can hear a case when a defendant has taken actions that are purposely directed towards the forum state.

Mini-trial — a form or alternate dispute resolution where the parties submit their case to a panel of experts or neutral advisor who suggest the likely outcome if the case were to go to court.

Miranda Warnings — those rights guaranteed by the Fifth Amendment. These warnings are designed to notify the person that he/she does not have to speak to the police.

Misappropriation Theory — imposes liability on outsiders who trade on the basis of confidential information obtained by reason of their relationship with a person possessing insider information.

Mislaid Property — that property which has been voluntarily and intentionally placed somewhere by the owner but forgotten.

Mistake — allows a contract to be rescinded if the enforcement of the agreement would be unconscionable or if the other party had reason to know of the mistake or he/she caused the mistake.

Money Laundering — a crime involving the concealment of the real source of illegally obtained money by having a third party claim ownership to the currency.

Montreal Convention — expanded the liability of airlines to one hundred and fifty thousand dollars a person without the need to show fault and by giving more protection to air travelers for such things as lost baggage.

Moral Obligation — this type of promise does not constitute a valid contract since it lacks the necessary elements to form an enforceable agreement.

Mortgage — a lien that a bank or lender may record against real property to secure that person's interest in the asset until the loan has been repaid.

Municipal Court — the lowest court in the state court system, which handles such matters as small claims cases, landlord/tenant problems and minor criminal offenses.

Negligence — the failure to do what a reasonable person would do under the circumstances; the three elements of negligence are 1) a duty, 2) breach of duty, 3) the negligence must be the proximate cause of the harm, and 4) the person sustains damages.

Negligence in Hiring an Employee — refers to the potential liability of an employer for the actions of an employee. Typically, the employer is liable on negligence grounds for the hiring and retaining of an employee whom the employer knew or should have known to be dangerous, incompetent, dishonest or the like.

Neighborhood Justice Centers — programs where local cases, usually neighborhood or family disputes, are decided by a panel of local residents.

No Duty to Rescue Rule — the rule under which the law does not force a person to help a stranger in an emergency unless that person has somehow caused the problem or has a special relationship to the party.

Nominal Damages — provide a remedy where a technical wrong has been committed but no actual harm has resulted.

Non-binding Trial — see "mini-trial."

Non-Conforming Use — the use of property that is inconsistent with the current zoning code but which allows the user to maintain the current use.

North American Free Trade Zone (NAFTA) — provides for the reduction and elimination of almost all trade tariffs and goods moving among United States, Canada and Mexico.

Occupational Safety and Health Act (OSHA) — imposes a general duty on most employers to provide a work place free of recognized hazards, causing or likely to cause, death or serious harm to employees.

Offer — a proposal by one party to the other showing a willingness to enter into a valid contract.

Officers — individuals who manage the daily operations of the corporation.

Original Jurisdiction — refers to the trial court.

Orphans Court — the court that hears matters involving estates such as will contests.

Ownership — those rights that a person has with respect to property that he/she may exercise to prevent others from using that property.

Pain and Suffering — an amount of money to compensate an individual for the anguish and discomfort he/she has endured because of the carelessness of another.

Palimony — is the support and provisions given to assets of non-married parties assets based upon a contract entered into by the parties before separation to share their assets.

Partnership — an agreement between two or more people to share a common interest in a commercial enterprise and to share profits and losses.

Past Consideration — an agreement to base future performance on a prior obligation.

Patents Convention for the Protection of Industrial Property — provides basic rights of protection in trademarks.

Patriot Act — grants authority to the United States government to freeze foreign assets held in the United States.

Pension Benefit Guarantee Corporation — this law insures that defined benefit plans will protect retirees in the event that their employer's pension fund fails.

Permanent Injunction — a final resolution of a dispute issued after a full hearing of all relevant factors.

Personal Property — consists of all property that is not land or attached to land; the two kinds of personal property are tangible and intangible; includes such things as a car, book, clothes, and furniture as well as bank accounts, stocks, bonds, patents and copyrights.

Piercing the Corporate Veil — when the corporation is being misused so that the shareholders are treated like partners and have unlimited liability for the organization's debts.

Plaintiff — the party who initiates the case.

Possession — a means of acquiring personal property.

Postal Reorganization Act — a federal law that makes it an unfair trade practice to send unsolicited products to a consumer in the mail.

Precedent — the process whereby judges apply the decision and rules or prior cases to the present case over which they are presiding; see also "stare decisis."

Preliminary Arraignment — a court proceeding that occurs within hours of a person's arrest at which time the person is informed of the charges, bail is set and the date for the preliminary hearing is scheduled.

Preliminary Hearing — the first hearing at which a victim or witness is called to testify in order to establish that there is a basic case to hold the defendant for trial.

Preliminary Injunction — an order granted as an emergency measure before a full hearing on the merits can be held.

Pre-Nuptial Agreement — a contract entered into before a marriage or civil union that spells out the financial consequences in the event the union fails.

Principles of International Commercial Contract — those principles that do not carry the weight of law but may be referenced by a foreign court or arbitration panel to interpret ambiguous contract provisions when the contract rules do not provide adequate guidance.

Private International Law — exams relationships created by commercial transactions and utilizes treaties, agreements, and the individual laws of nations to resolve business disputes.

Private Judging — a form of alternate dispute resolution used when parties are constrained by time and can afford to hire a private judge; private judging proceeds as a normal trial would be conducted.

Private Law — involves matters between individuals; most common forms are contract, tort, marriage, and property law.

Private Securities Litigation Reform Act of 1995 — provides a safe harbor or lack of accountability by a company who issues statements that are considered financial forecasts of the business.

Procedural Law — the way that substantive law is made, enforced, and administered.

Production — refers to the process of when a person takes scraps of material and creates another item through his/her labor.

Products Liability — the concept of holding sellers of defective products liable for harm caused to the user, consumer, or his property even though the seller has exercised all possible care in the preparation and sale of the product; also called strict liability. The law is contained in Section 402A of the Restatement (Second) of Torts.

Property — everything that may be owned, either as real property or personal property.

Property Law — deals with the rights and duties that arise out of the ownership or possession of real or personal property; defines and enforces the rights and responsibilities that accompany ownership.

Protocol — an agreement on a matter considered to be of a less significant impact than the subject of a convention.

Proximate Cause — requires that there be a reasonable connection between the negligence of the defendant and the harm suffered by the plaintiff.

Proxy — an agent appointed by a shareholder for the purposes of voting the shares.

Public International Law — exams the relationships between nations and uses rules that are binding on all countries in the international community.

Public Law — involves the rights of society as a whole, and those interests are usually handle by a government agency; most common forms are criminal, constitutional, and administrative law.

Publicly Held Organization — a business owned by many people and includes those whose stock is traded on a public exchange.

Punitive Damages — a sum of money awarded to punish the tort-feasor for his or her misconduct so that the type of incident in question will never occur again.

Purchase — the transfer of title from one owner to another for payment or compensation.

Qualified Fee — a form of ownership which conveys all the rights of ownership so long as the owner complies with a certain condition (see also "fee simple defeasible" or "conditional fee").

Quid Pro Quo — a type of sexual harassment where an employee is expected to give in to sexual demands or suffer the loss of some specific job or benefit.

Quiet Title Action — with respect to real property, a suit in which the court is asked to determine who among several contenders has ownership rights to a given piece of property.

Real Property — land and everything attached to the land.

Receiving Stolen Property — intentionally obtaining property of another that has been stolen, or believed to be stolen.

Reformation — a remedy that allows modification of a contract that does not reflect the true intention of the parties.

Registration Statement — this is a document filed with the SEC by a corporation to let the governmental agency know that the business is going to sell its stock to the public.

Remainder — a future interest in real property.

Remand — the appellate court remands—or sends back—a case to the trial court when the appellate court finds that the trial judge committed an error in deciding the case or additional evidence must be obtained.

Res Judicata — "the thing has been decided."

Rescission — the voiding of a contract for some reason such as misrepresentation, fraud, duress, undue influence or impossibility, under which each party must return the property they received from the other.

Respondeat Superior — refers to the agent or employee of a company who has the authority to bind the business when he/she acts within the scope of the authority.

Restitution — a remedy to prevent one party from unfairly benefiting at the expense of another.

Retail Theft — a crime involving the theft of property that occurs at a commercial establishment open to the public.

Reverse — the appellate court reverses a decision when it finds that the lower court's decision was incorrect.

Reversionary Interest — when property reverts back to the original owner or the owner's legal heirs if that person is no longer living.

Rights Theory — the ethical theory that focuses on the reasons for actions.

Risk of Law — determines which party bears the responsibility if the goods are lost or damaged.

Robbery — larceny plus the additional requirement that the taking be accomplished by force or threat of force.

Sale — is the passing of title from the seller to the buyer for a price.

Sarbanes-Oxley Act — this federal law only applies to publicly traded companies and seeks to increase corporate accountability, enhance financial disclosures and combat corporate and accounting fraud.

Sealed Bid — used in construction, municipal and service contracts in which a party requests bids that only constitute an invitation to negotiate.

Search Warrant — a court order allowing the police to search a person or premise.

Securities and Exchange Commission (SEC) — an agency created following the stock market crash of 1929 to enforce the provisions of the Securities Exchange Act. Its primary mission is to protect investors, maintain fair and efficient markets and to facilitate capital formation.

Security — refers to an investment such as a note, stock, bond and evidence of indebtedness, certificate of interest or participation in any profit sharing agreement.

Security Council — is a branch of the United Nations; consists of fifteen countries, has the power to authorize military action and to sever diplomatic relations with other nations.

Security Exchange Act of 1933 — allows the SEC to regulate the trading of securities, investigate securities fraud, regulate securities dealers, supervise mutual funds and recommend administrative sanctions for violation of the security laws.

Security Exchange Act of 1934 — regulates the subsequent sale of securities and requires the registration of security exchanges, brokers and dealers of markets in which securities are traded.

Seller — a person that sells or contracts to sell goods.

Shipment Contract — occurs when the seller is required to ship the goods and the risk of loss passes to the buyer when conforming goods are delivered to the carrier.

Short Swing Profits — refers to a rule in which company insiders, who buy and sell their firm security within a six (6) month period, must return any profits made from those transactions to the business.

Slander — a defamatory statement that is verbal or oral in nature.

Social Host Liability — liability imposed upon a person who furnishes alcohol beverages to a guest. The term does not include bars and other establishments who serve liquor on a commercial basis.

Sole Ownership — when only one person enjoys the bundle of rights and liabilities of a property.

Sole Proprietorship — a business owned by only one person.

Sovereign Immunity — the concept that prohibits suits against any level of the government unless the sovereign gives its expressed consent to the litigation.

Special Damages — those losses in a breach of contract that are foreseeable, reasonably certain and unavoidable.

Specific Performance — an equitable remedy for breach of contract that is used when money damages are inadequate to make the aggrieved party whole.

Standing — the concept that a plaintiff in a lawsuit must have a direct and substantial interest in the outcome of the case that he or she intends to bring.

Stare Decisis — the process whereby judges apply the decision and rules of prior cases to the present case over which they are presiding; (see also "precedent").

Statute of Frauds — the requirement that certain agreements be in writing in order to be enforceable by the court.

Statute of Limitations — the time period within which an aggrieved party must institute suit or the claim will be forever barred.

Strict Liability — see "products liability."

Subchapter S Corporation — has all the characteristics of a corporation except that its shareholders must report profit and losses on their individual tax returns.

Subject Matter Jurisdiction — the type of case a court can hear.

Substantive Due Process — the requirement that the law be fundamentally fair; legislation must be capable of serving a legitimate public interest, and the law cannot be vague.

Substantive Evidence — the standard used in administrative hearings. The term merely requires that a finding by a referee be supported by relevant evidence that a reasonable mind would accept as adequate to support a conclusion.

Substantive Law — this is the "actual law" which defines the duties and rights of members of society.

Suggestive Mark — requires imagination in order to figure out the nature of the product which the mark represents.

Supreme Court — the highest court in the state or country.

Tangible Property — a physical object.

Temporary Restraining Order (TRO) — an injunction granted without notice to the other side.

Tenancy by the Entirety — a special form of co-ownership for married couples which carries the right of survivorship; however, neither spouse can convey his or her interest in the property since each spouse owns a 100 percent interest in the property.

Tenancy in Common — a form of concurrent or joint ownership in which the co-owners have essentially equal rights to the property; if one co-owner dies, his share will pass to his heirs.

Testamentary Gift — property given by will.

Tipper/Tippee Theory — this deals with someone who acquires insider information as a result of a corporate insider's breach of that person's fiduciary duty to the corporation.

Tipping — the supplying of insider information to another who does the trading of the stock of a company from which the confidential information has been learned.

Title — the right of ownership.

Tort — a private civil wrong against an individual or business for which the court will award money damages; torts are classified into the categories of negligence or intentional torts.

Tort Damages — a sum of money that should place the injured party in as substantially a good position as she had occupied before the injury.

Trademark — is a word, name, symbol or slogan which identifies the origins of a product or services from those of a competitor.

Trademark Infringement — occurs when there is a likelihood of confusion as to the source, origin, or sponsorship of a product in a commercial environment.

Trading with the Enemy Act — this law was passed by Congress to restrict trade with nations at war with the United States.

Treasure Trove — property that has been hidden or concealed for so long as to indicate that the owner is probably dead or unknown.

Treaty — an agreement between two or more countries.

Trespasser — one who comes upon the premises of another without consent and with no legal right to be on the property.

TRO — (temporary restraining order) an injunction granted without notice to the defendant.

U.S. — Canada Free Trade Agreement — a pact to phase out all tariffs and quotas between the two countries and guarantees equal treatment for those that invest across the border.

Unenforceable Contract — the agreement has the technical requirements of a contract but won't be enforced by the court.

Uniform Commercial Code — a uniform act that regulates the sale of goods and certain other commercial transactions.

Unilateral Contract — a promise for an act that gives rise to a contract.

United Nations — its primary goal is to "save succeeding generations from the scourge of war" and authorizes "collective measures for the prevention and removal of threats to peace, and for the suppression of acts of aggression or other breaches of the peace."

United Nations Commission on International Trade Law — develops standardized commercial practices and agreements.

United States Constitution — the legal document which establishes the fundamental rights of United States citizens and protects them from unlawful governmental interference.

United States District Court — is the trial court in the federal court system.

Utilitarian Theory — the theory of ethics that focuses on the consequences of actions.

Valid Contract — a contract that satisfies all of the requirements of a binding agreement.

Variance — permits a use of property that is not designated in the zoning code for the property.

Venue — the place where a case should be heard.

Vicarious Liability — see "imputed negligence."

Void Contract — refers to an agreement that lacks one or more of the essential elements of a valid contract.

Voir Dire — process for selecting a jury by which members of the jury are questioned by the judge or attorneys to ascertain whether they are suitable to serve at trial; issue of prejudice, conflicts of interest, and philosophies of life are explored.

Warranty of Habitability — the obligations imposed upon the landlord to maintain a leased premise in a condition fit for human habitation.

Warsaw Convention — limits compensatory damages in a personal injury action against an airline in international travel.

Whistleblower — a person who feels compelled to get certain information into the hands of people who can act to correct a problem when it seems that the problem cannot be corrected otherwise.

White Collar Crime — those illegal acts perpetrated in a business setting.

Winding Up — that process in which partners move to terminate a partnership by collecting the business assets, paying the debts and providing the partners with the remaining value of the business.

Worker Adjustment and Retraining Notification Act — requires firms with one hundred (100) or more employees to provide sixty (60) days notice if they lay off one-third or more of their workers at any location employing at least one hundred and fifty workers, drop five hundred employees at any location, or close a plant employing at least fifty workers.

Worker's Compensation — refers to the liability of an employer for the injuries sustained by an employee during the course of the employment.

World Bank — promotes economic development in poor countries by making loans to finance necessary development projects and programs.

World Intellectual Property Organization — the leading dispute resolution service for disagreements arising out of the registration or use of internet domain names.

World Trade Organization (WTO) — was designed to reduce trade barriers and cover the international sale of goods among its members.

Writ of Certiorari — an appeal to the United States Supreme Court.

Zoning — rules created by local governments to regulate the development and use of property.

CPSIA information can be obtained
at www.ICGtesting.com
Printed in the USA
BVHW090726080120
568902BV00006B/29/P